★ ★ ★   **LOOK AWAY!**

NEW AMERICANISTS ★ *A Series Edited by Donald E. Pease*

★ ★ ★ # LOOK AWAY!

THE U.S. SOUTH IN NEW WORLD STUDIES

Edited with an Introduction by Jon Smith and Deborah Cohn

DUKE UNIVERSITY PRESS ★ DURHAM AND LONDON 2004

© **2004 DUKE UNIVERSITY PRESS.** All rights reserved.
Printed in the United States of America on acid-free paper ∞
Designed by Rebecca M. Giménez. Typeset in Adobe Minion by
Keystone Typesetting, Inc. ★ Library of Congress Cataloging-in-
Publication data appear on the last printed page of this book.

FOR GAIL, PETER, AND NOAH

★ ★ ★ CONTENTS

ACKNOWLEDGMENTS

We, the editors, met at a panel that Debbie put together for the 1998 MLA conference, had a "you got chocolate in my peanut butter" scholarly moment, and a few weeks later, on Martin Luther King Day, found ourselves agreeing to coedit this volume—via e-mail, of course. In fact, while most books are measured in pages, we prefer to measure this one in e-mails: over the course of five years, five thousand of them, chiefly between the editors. Rarer face-to-face talks have ranged from Oxford (Mississippi) to Nashville, from San Francisco to New York, and from Montreal to Puerto Vallarta. If the book is long, the conversation has become our own New World epic. We are grateful to the editors of *El Escribano '95* for permission to reprint Jane Landers's "Slave Resistance on the Spanish Frontier: Fugitives, Maroons, and Banditti in the Age of Revolutions," *El Escribano '95* 32: 12–24. Thanks also to Princeton University Press for permission to reprint substantial portions of Kirsten Silva Gruesz's contribution from her book *Ambassadors of Culture: The Transamerican Origins of Latino Writing* (2001). Portions of Lois Parkinson Zamora's essay originally appeared in the *American Jour-*

nal of Semiotics 3.1 (1984): 50–67. Ilan Stavans's essay first appeared in slightly different form in the *Michigan Quarterly Review* 40.4 (fall 2001): 628–39. We wish to thank the Albert H. Small Special Collections Library at the University of Virginia for permission to publish materials from the William Faulkner Foundation Papers Concerning the Ibero-American Novel Project in Helen Oakley's essay. We wish to thank David Vinson for compiling the index and the Office for the Dean of Arts and Sciences at the University of Montevallo for generously funding his work. We are indebted to Jennifer Smith at Indiana University for her careful contributions to the final phase of manuscript preparation. We extend particular gratitude to our contributors for their patience and support. Jon thanks Debbie, Debbie thanks Jon. Most of all, we wish to thank our family members Peter Sauer, Noah Sauer, and Gail Smith, not least for putting up with five thousand e-mails.

JON SMITH AND DEBORAH COHN

Introduction: Uncanny Hybridities

Long before American studies began to abandon monolithic formulations of Americanness, white U.S. southerners were justly questioning such narratives of U.S. identity as fictions imposed by a rich, imperial, white Northeast. As Allen Tate famously put it in his 1945 essay "The New Provincialism," "not even literary nationalism could abort a genuine national literature when it is ready to appear; when, in fact, we become a nation" (536). C. Vann Woodward would argue fifteen years later in *The Burden of Southern History* that "the South had undergone an experience that it could share with no other part of America—though it is shared by nearly all the peoples of Europe and Asia—the experience of military defeat, occupation, and reconstruction" (190). Yet these and other dominant, oppositional constructions of southern identity offered by white male southerners, from the Confederate flag to (until the past decade or so) the canon of southern literature, themselves constitute exclusionary and exceptionalist myths: imagining unique ligatures between the South and the Old World, they figure (white) southern culture and history as a corrective to the provincial hubris of the imperial United States.

What happens, however, if we look away from the North in constructing narratives of southern identity? If we define "America" hemispherically, for example, the experience of defeat, occupation, and reconstruction—particularly if this historical trauma is broadened to include the African American experience of defeat under slavery—is something the South shares with *every* other part of America. Like others building critically on Woodward's foundations, we do not define southern "defeat" simply as southern white men's surrender at Appomattox. As Edward Ayers points out, "Americans have grown far too comfortable with the Civil War, lulled into assuming its inevitability and its outcome, granting it a moral purpose it assumed only gradually and against the will of many who fought for the Union. . . . It is too simple a story, both for the North and for the South" ("What We Talk About" 78). Fred Hobson, expanding a different aspect of Woodward's legacy, notes that "Woodward was attributing these qualities to white southerners, but poverty, frustration, failure, and a *felt* knowledge of history also apply, even more strongly if for quite different reasons, to black southerners" (2).

Those reasons may in fact not be all that different, for such qualities, among both white and black southerners, derive from a different and more globally recognizable kind of defeat: the South's continuing experience of New World plantation colonialism, a system that, both before and after the war, most benefited white men in distant metropoles (something often complained of in white southern discourse) and most burdened black southerners (something almost never complained of in white southern discourse). Immanuel Wallerstein traces "the creation of a new peripheral region . . . the extended Caribbean, stretching from northeast Brazil to Maryland," during the emergence of the modern capitalist world-system (166–67), and as the frame narratives in Charles Chesnutt's conjure tales make abundantly clear, Emancipation in the U.S. South no more marked the end of black southerners' involuntary participation in such a colonial economy than did, say, Cuban emancipation twenty-one years later. George Handley notes in *Postslavery Literatures in the Americas* that

> despite its domestic attempt to move beyond the legacies of slavery
> after the Civil War, the United States manifested the symptoms of the
> plantation discourse by exploiting land and slave labor beyond U.S.
> boundaries while attempting to keep at bay the Africanized Creole
> cultures that it had helped to forge. The South essentially was the first
> colony of U.S. imperial expansion.[1] The Union's attempt to integrate
> the New South after the Civil War fortified on an international scale

the very plantation structures the North had decried, structures it had depended on for its economic growth. (20)

Following Malcolm X, Houston Baker in *Turning South Again* has quite specifically argued that plantation technologies for restricting the social and physical mobility of African Americans, carceral technologies first modeled at Parchman Farm and Tuskegee Plantation, have persisted throughout the United States, eventuating "a privatized, corporate gulag of United States incarceration in the [twenty-first] century" (94).

Patricia Nelson Limerick's replacement of the influential division by Frederick Jackson Turner of Western history into pre- and post-closing of the frontier with her own vision of that history as *The Legacy of Conquest: The Unbroken Past of the American West* thus suggests a useful model for deep-southern history as well. Despite white southern fetishization of the Lost Cause, comparatist work can envision a history at once broader and more precise, one that might bear the title *The Legacy of Colonialism: The Unbroken Past of Plantation America*. From such a perspective, the U.S. Civil War, crucially in parallel with the War of 1898, represents not a decisive break in southern (or U.S. or New World) history but merely one more step in wresting control of this global-southern region's land, (largely black) labor, and capital from local elite white (or *creole*, in Mary Louise Pratt's useful adaptation of the term) men by other elite white men in distant, global-northern metropolises.[2]

The very factors that allegedly make the South exceptional within the context of the United States thus make it acutely familiar within broader categories of Americanness and postcoloniality. Once placed within this matrix, however, Allen Tate's assumption that the South *is* a nation—for, as Michael O'Brien, Michael Kreyling, and Richard Gray have variously argued, Tate and the other Agrarians meant by *region* what Benedict Anderson means by *nation* or *imagined community*—also breaks down, for in a hemispheric or global context Virginia and Louisiana might well be said to have less in common than, say, Cuba and the Dominican Republic—or, for that matter, Cuba and Louisiana, Havana and New Orleans.

Indeed, till recently both white and black constructions of a "South" (like white constructions of "America") have tended to elide geographical, demographic, and economic differences within the region's borders and similarities across them. Thadious Davis's landmark 1987 essay "Expanding the Limits," for example, cites Hugh Holman's famous call for "no more monoliths" but also speaks quite monolithically of the South as "a region that, though fraught with pain and difficulty, provides a major grounding for identity" for African Americans (Davis 6) and of "the ritual of hundreds of black family reunions and homecomings held annually from Virginia to Texas" (11). Such references, along with Davis's astute points about "gestures of bonding with the region," "the choice of a regional identity along with a racial one," and "a complex but felt truth about the necessary intersection of race and region" (11), suggest that, appealing as the concept may be, black southernness needs to be treated as skeptically as any other nativist attempt to imagine community. Unsurprisingly, such skepticism itself has come most forcefully from African American cultural critics, from Malcolm X and John O. Killens to Houston Baker. Interestingly, while postcolonial theory has had no difficulty engaging with Paul Gilroy's early work on black British identity, the discipline's failure to acknowledge this rich, nuanced, and problematic body of thought on "U.S. Southern Black" as an identitarian category impoverished that field—prior to the work of Riché Richardson—every bit as much as a similar failure has impoverished both African American and (U.S.) southern studies, as Davis argues.

Precisely *because* African Americans "rank among the principal creators of the culture of the New World" (Joyner 31), New World, U.S., and southern cultures cannot be accurately delineated without reference to the similar influences of African American cultures across the borders of the southern United States, as well as the differences within those cultures. Stanley Engerman notes that "the British West Indies were, after the first decade of settlement, about 90 percent black slave, only ten percent white. The U.S. was only 10–15 percent slave, and even the South was only about 40 percent black slave" (47). Edward Ayers breaks these figures down further: "Black Southerners made up over two-thirds of the people in the Black Belt but accounted for only about a tenth of those in the mountains and on the Western Prairies" (*Promise* 6). The South, in such a view, becomes a space where the African diaspora's northern areas overlap the southern reaches of the English conquest of North America— in degrees so varying that it becomes difficult, once again, to speak of the region as unified at all except, paradoxically, in its difference from (and similarity to) the greater whiteness further north, the greater blackness further south.[3]

In retrospect, then, both Tate and Davis face much the same problem Dipesh Chakrabarty notes in writing about postcolonial historiography of India: "the project of provincializing 'Europe' cannot be a nationalist, nativist, or atavistic project. . . . [O]ne cannot but problematize India at the same time as one dismantles 'Europe'" (21). The advantage black southern critics like Davis have over Tate, at least, is their understanding that what Rey Chow argues of Hong Kong in *Ethics after Idealism* is equally true of the U.S. South: it "presents a problem that is crucial but rarely discussed in postcolonial debates, namely, the struggle between the dominant and subdominant within the 'native' culture itself" (153).

Twenty years of critical work by Davis, Trudier Harris, Jerry Ward, Fred Hobson, Minrose Gwin, Peggy Whitman Prenshaw, Michael O'Brien, and others has articulated that struggle, and not just regarding dominant and subdominant "races." By the late 1990s, anthologies such as Anne Goodwyn Jones and Susan Donaldson's *Haunted Bodies* (1997) and John Howard's *Carryin' On in the Lesbian and Gay South* (1997) were usefully complicating what had once been rather straitjacketed ideas about southern gender roles. Michael Kreyling in *Inventing Southern Literature* (1998) argued that racism and sexism "present inventors and reinventors [of southern tradition] with problems that render the continuity of the South—and its literary practices—all but impossible" (182). In *The Narrative Forms of Southern Community* (1999), Scott Romine dispatched Cleanth Brooks's fetishization of "true community," pointing out that "insofar as it is cohesive, a community will tend to be coercive" (2). Patricia Yaeger in *Dirt and Desire* (2000) examined "the ways the South has helped encode American ways of racial knowing: of both overconceptualizing and refusing to conceptualize an obscene racial blindness" (xii). Houston Baker, who had already deconstructed the white-southern fetishization of place in *Workings of the Spirit* (1991), designated the (male) black-southern experience a sort of passport to understanding "the dynamics of an unfolding world of postcolonial colored people" (*Critical Memory* 9). And Suzanne Jones and Sharon Monteith's collection *South to a New Place* (2002) and Tara McPherson's *Reconstructing Dixie* (2003) re-placed the region within complex networks of economic lineages and urban spaces.

Indeed, mainstream southern studies has so recently moved away from nativist assertions of community, place, the presence of the past, and so on that, even given the emerging centrality of black southernness to the discipline, to characterize even a genuinely biracial (and increasingly multiracial) U.S. South as a postcolonial space oppressed by what Joel Williamson calls "the imperial North" (78) might be considered a regression to southern apologetics. It is not, if only because, as the quotations from Chakrabarty and Chow above attest, postcolonial studies has finally begun to move beyond the romance of otherness, that is, the simplistic moral dichotomy between "bad" colonizer and "good" colonized that fails to differentiate among and within colonized cultures. Critics such as Chow (149–67) and, in the Caribbean context, J. Michael

Dash (x–xi) see in this romance a fundamental flaw of much earlier postcolonial theory. Bizarrely enough, the Agrarians themselves partook of it when they compared the plight of white southern culture (highly pastoralized and sanitized) to that of equally romanticized Native American civilizations: peaceful, art-loving cultures wiped out by Yankee materialism.[4] It is a mistake contemporary critics would do well not to repeat.

How then might we conceptualize U.S. southern culture in a way that acknowledges its postcolonial status without ignoring the region's signal histories of oppression, its cultural specificity, *and* its cultural diversity? We might begin by concentrating on the Deep South not as a unified or imagined community but as a scene of the cultural conflicts that white imaginings of community seek to forget, as a locus of literally disciplined bodies in a (largely) postplantation realm still dealing with the legacy of race slavery. Baker's recent work offers one route. In *Turning South Again* he argues that, via Tuskegee Plantation and Parchman Farm, the southern plantation became the model for the national penal system, and the penal system became the central technology—both literally and figuratively—for controlling black mobility in the United States. In *Critical Memory,* he breaks down a different border, arguing, for example, that Richard Wright's "astute awareness of interconnections among race, power, economics, urbanity, and technology in the United States (an understanding conditioned precisely by his southern *racial* memory and his own brand of Marxist analysis) enabled him to join a global company of thinkers intent on achieving black, global, empowering modernity" (8). The plantation—more than anything else—ties the South both to the rest of the United States and to the rest of the New World.

Baker is concerned with the effects of embodied racial violence more as they establish or fail to establish the preconditions for black modernist enunciation than as they affect literary form per se. However, such a formal focus appears not only in Yaeger's thesis but also in Antonio Benítez-Rojo's argument about Caribbean literature in "The Repeating Island." Embodiment is problematic in Benítez-Rojo's essay—in a familiar pattern, the nurturing landscape is feminized, the seed-implanting author/intellectual masculinized—but if one substitutes *southern* for *Caribbean* in the passage below, Benítez-Rojo nevertheless closely foreshadows Yaeger's attention to exploding bodies, repetition, and "literature obsessed with its own limitations" (Yaeger, *Diet and Desire* 12–13).

This *mestizaje* is a concentration of conflicts, an exacerbation brought about by the closeness and density of the Caribbean situation. Then, at a given moment, the binary syncretism Europe-Africa explodes and scatters its entrails all around: here is Caribbean literature. This literature should not be seen as anything but a system of texts in intense conflict with themselves. The Caribbean poem, story, and novel are projects conceived to shore up not the effects of an explosion or crisis in universal values, but rather of their own explosion, their own void, their own *black hole,* which "repeats" endlessly through Caribbean space. (Benítez-Rojo 105)

Both Yaeger and Benítez-Rojo reject—or defer—dialectical models of cultural interaction that would posit southern or Caribbean culture as simply the product of a European thesis and African antithesis (or, more interestingly, the reverse). Dialectic is, at bottom, a familial metaphor of generation(s), and it follows that at points these critics explicitly reject "mulatto" models of the cultures they study. Even when Yaeger describes "transgressively hybrid" characters, she specifically points out she is "not speaking about mulatto figures here" (*Dirt and Desire* 31). Benítez-Rojo argues that to call Caribbean literature mestizo is "a positivist and logo-centric argument, an argument that sees the biological, economic, social, and cultural 'whitening' of the Caribbean black as a series of steps toward 'progress,' thus legitimating conquest, slavery, colonization, and dependence" (105). It should not surprise us that each of the ten "innumerable conflicts" Benítez-Rojo claims are found in Caribbean literature also forms the central conflict of at least one major work of U.S. southern literature by such writers as G. W. Cable, Charles Chesnutt, William Faulkner, and Alice Walker.[5] Likewise, it should not surprise us that many of Yaeger's concerns—gargantuas, monstrosities, throwaway or disappeared bodies, repressed trauma, landscapes of melancholy, even literal dirt-eating—appear in major texts by male and female Caribbean and Spanish-American writers such as Isabel Allende, Edwidge Danticat, Gabriel García Márquez, Jamaica Kincaid, Cristina Peri Rossi, and Marta Traba.

It would be erroneous, however, simply to assimilate the U.S. South into the Caribbean, as García Márquez has most famously done, apparently with Bill Clinton's assent. In 1999 the Colombian author claimed that a discussion with Carlos Fuentes, William Styron, and President Clinton about how the Caribbean is a vast "historical and cultural space extending from the north of Brazil to the Mississippi delta"—a recapitulation of an argument García Márquez has been making for three decades—led Clinton to "happily proclaim his own Caribbean affiliation" (2). Such facile assimilation would replicate the pernicious either/or habit common in the formation of imagined communities and particularly in the formation of southernness against which we've been argu-ing: either you're southern (or Caribbean or American—or, for that mat-ter, black or feminine or heterosexual) or you're not. Better to deploy Fuentes's formulation when, addressing a U.S. audience, he observed that while Sinclair Lewis is "yours," "William Faulkner is both yours and ours, and as such, essential to us" (119).

To get a better sense of what it might be to be *both* "American" and Latin American or Caribbean—to talk about region without talking about essential identities or "heritage"—one can consider Benítez-Rojo's depiction, also in "The Repeating Island," of Dr. Martin Luther King Jr.:

> This man was a North American without ceasing to be a Carib-bean, or the other way around. His African ancestry, the texture of his humanism, the ancient wisdom in his words, his improvisatory na-ture, his cordially high tone, his ability to seduce and be seduced, and above all, his vehement status as a "dreamer" (*I have a dream...*) and performer, all make up the Caribbean element of a man who is un-questionably idiosyncratic in North America. Martin Luther King oc-cupies and fills the space in which Caribbean thought (L'Ouverture, Bolívar, Martí, Garvey) meets North American black discourse; that space can also be filled by the blues. (103)

This is a fascinating passage for those interested in the U.S. South, for King's persona, like the blues, is hardly idiosyncratic in that space, a space in which are imbricated both a "Yankee" sensibility often erroneously taken as the United States' norm and a post-plantation sensibility recog-nizable in varying degrees and kinds in every state that borders the Carib-bean Sea, the Gulf of Mexico, or the western verges of the black Atlantic from Brazil to Virginia. King's performance of a heteronormative south-ern masculinity (for gender and sexuality shape Benítez-Rojo's character-ization at least as much as region) actually exemplifies a variety discussed most recently by Richard Yarborough in *Haunted Bodies.* Almost all Benítez-Rojo's criteria can, in fact, be applied to such Protestant, straight, white, quintessentially "southern" men (each of whom has been widely discussed as black) as Elvis Presley and Bill Clinton.

Rather, what generates the South's peculiar cultural tension is its posi-tion as a space of degrees of overlap *between*, its simultaneous embodi-ment of, the Yankee and the plantation. This overlap appears, for example, in King's profound Protestantism; it appears in Fuentes's description of Faulkner, another Southern hybrid; and it appears in *Faulkner, Mississippi* when Edouard Glissant describes Faulkner "coldly yet passionately ap-proach[ing] the limits of his query" (31). Implicit in Glissant's diction is the famous 1785 letter from Thomas Jefferson to the Marquis de Chastellux laying out the differences between North and South (qtd. in O'Brien 3).

In the North they are	In the South they are
– cool	– fiery
– sober	– voluptuary
– laborious	– indolent
– independent	– unsteady
– jealous of their own liberties, and just to those of others	– zealous for their own liberties, but trampling on those of others
– interested	– generous
– chicaning	– candid
– superstitious and hypocritical in their religion	– without attachment or pretensions to any religion but that of the heart

As Michael O'Brien points out, "this observation was not, strictly speaking, sectional, for Jefferson saw a waxing and waning of these qualities in proportion as one moved from North to South. Pennsylvania was a happy medium" (3).

If we are to avoid modernity's fetishization of the nation-state and the imagined community, we need to return to a provisional version of Jefferson's literally prenational vision of North and South. In such a modified reading, the U.S. South comes to occupy a space unique within modernity: a space simultaneously (or alternately) center and margin, victor and defeated, empire and colony, essentialist and hybrid, northern and southern (both in the global sense). While the U.S. South is no "happy medium," it is a zone where the familiar dichotomies of postcolonial theory—unstable enough since the early 1990s—are rendered particularly precarious. If there is such a thing as U.S. southern identity, white or black, it consists neither in those traits that have historically been identified as "southern" and oppressed by an imperial North, nor in those traits that make it clearly part of the hegemonic United States, an oppressor of those further south.[6]

Rather, the potential for southern distinctiveness consists in what might be called the South's literally uncanny (*unheimlich*) hybridity. To critics who imagine themselves, more or less unproblematically, as either Third World or First World, the U.S. South has appeared compellingly as both familiar and exotic, both Self and Other. Such uncanniness enables and governs not only the formulations of Fuentes, García Márquez,

Benítez-Rojo, and Glissant but also the bizarre English preoccupation with the U.S. South recently chronicled by Helen Taylor in *Circling Dixie* and the Yankee dialectic of rejecting and embracing the South character-ized by Susan-Mary Grant in *North over South* and McPherson in *Re-constructing Dixie*. As the uncanny double of both the First and Third Worlds, the U.S. South of course calls attention to (and enables displace-ment of) the First World traits of putatively Third World writers and the Third World traits of the putatively First World. If, as Ella Shohat has argued, "the term 'post-colonial' would be more precise . . . if articulated as 'post-First/Third Worlds theory' or 'post anti-colonial critique,' as a movement beyond a relatively binaristic, fixed and stable mapping of power relations between 'colonizer/colonized' and 'center/periphery' " (134), then the U.S. South represents an ideal field for such study.

Indeed, U.S. southern experiences sometimes seem to represent a co-vert *source* of postcolonial discourse. What southernist fails to cock an eyebrow when Iain Chambers writes, "post-colonialism is perhaps the sign of an increasing awareness that it is not feasible to subtract a culture, a history, a language, an identity, from the wider, transforming currents of the metropolitan world. It is impossible to 'go home' again" (74), or when such critics as R. Radhakrishnan (37), Paul Gilroy (1), and Homi Bhabha (Seshadri-Crooks 370) describe postcoloniality or hybridity as "double consciousness"? Perhaps U.S. southern cultures and literatures seem so apt for postcolonial study precisely because the central-ized terms of their experiences of exile and problematic identity are always already embedded in its disciplining discourse.

Postcolonial theory is not, of course, the only recent movement to deal with problematic identity; queer theory has also grown useful in re-thinking regional and national identities. In "Queering the South: Con-structions of Southern/Queer Identity," Donna Jo Smith wryly notes that to some, "the term *southern queer* is redundant: Since the South is already an aberration, what is a southern queer but deviance multiplied? In other words, did Truman Capote really need to tell the world that he was a pervert? After all, he was from south Alabama" (370). Smith's conclusion may be usefully applied to southern identities at large: "To best illuminate southern queer experiences, we must leave open questions of identity, both queer and southern, and explore how our subjects have negotiated their same-sex desire within this region and how that experience has been mediated by complex, intersecting identities" (382).

Despite the similar phrasing, Smith is well beyond Davis's model here. In Judith Butler's familiar schema—on which Smith bases her own—identity is performative and situational. What one has, at best, is a set of individual, situated, often conflicting phenomenological approaches to regional, as to gender, identity. Joseph Urgo (ix–xvi) and Charles Reagan Wilson (153–66) emphasize this welter of contingencies in their recent accounts of William Faulkner's subject position vis-à-vis "America"; Richard King does the same for Richard Wright in this volume. Poet James Applewhite emphasizes the performativity of his own regional identity in the four lines of "Southern Voices" that close V. S. Naipaul's *A Turn in the South.*

> This colorless tone, like flour,
> Patted onto the cheeks, is poor-white powder
> To disguise the minstrel syllables lower
> In our register, from a brownface river. (qtd. in Naipaul 307)

Applewhite presents his flat, white, North Carolina dialect as racial and regional performance, as a negotiation of Smith's "complex, intersecting identities," and most specifically as a means of denying what his poetry affirms—the African roots of U.S. southern culture.

Naipaul, however, wants to read Applewhite as articulating an essential South, a south of "*defeat*," a South that shares in the global-southern "decline narrative" that King has elsewhere identified in Faulkner's work and that Ayers rather lampoons.[7] "It was that sense of a special past, the past as a wound," writes Naipaul, "that I missed almost as soon as I went north to Virginia, to Charlottesville. There was history there in quantity—Jefferson, Monticello, the University of Virginia. But that was history as celebration, the history of the resort, the history that was causing the subdivisions (or housing developments) to multiply in Virginia, and was even threatening the fox hunt. . . . [It was not] a more desperate kind of New World history, [not] a poorer land reflecting this history" (306–7). Though it represents a step beyond traditional southern nativism, Naipaul's is precisely the vision we wish this volume to *avoid*. Somewhere around Lynchburg, Naipaul has drawn and crossed a border out of an essentialized South. Virginians themselves do this, of course, though they tend to draw the line a little further north, around Warrenton. South of that line, including Charlottesville, is "the South"; north of it are simply the deregionalized suburbs of the nation's capital. Mississippians, by contrast, tend to draw their line between South and North somewhere across the Carolinas, thereby demonstrating something of the arbitrariness of the whole enterprise. As Yaeger puts it in her introduction to *The Geography of Identity*, "social geography's insistence on the interstitial, hybrid nature of place—its refusal to conceptualize location as either ethnically or ideologically bounded—also offers an important antidote to some of the dead-end binarisms within cultural studies" (15). Indeed, writes Yaeger, "the turn to geography . . . can also represent an act of progressive political intervention. . . . [T]his invention also challenges any symptomatic nostalgia for a world of lost objects and alterities" (17)—here, the nostalgia for a fetishized past-as-wound.

In short, Charlottesville—to Naipaul and to any others who would define the (national, hemispheric, or global) South unproblematically by its "experience of defeat," even its defeat under colonialism—is queer, hybrid, progressive, threatening, an aberration, and for that very reason we wish to stress its southernness. Barbara Ladd has examined nineteenth-century northern U.S. concerns about the formerly French and Spanish South's connotations of blackness, connotations that threatened to make it less "American" than the North: "if the white southerner's insistence that 'Creoles' are 'white'—and only 'creoles' (lowercase) are mixed—is intended to protect the southerner from being aligned too closely with former slaves or with colonialism in the New World, the creole metaphor also marks the southerner as a dangerous border figure, someone who might look like an American and claim to be so (with greater fervor than other Americans at times) but who carries within him- or herself traces of the displaced and who might at some point act traitorously to undermine the progressive nation" (xv–xvi).

In Ladd's reading the South came to be constructed by the North as "dangerous territory—a kind of national 'id' (to state the case too strongly)" (xii–xiii). With its libidinal connotations of commerce, blackness, the body—commerce in black bodies—the South must be repressed to achieve the "coherence" (Miller viii) of a disembodied, spiritual, New England Puritan theology, the stable ego of the Americas. But if the Deep South must be repressed to define a pure America (see also Baker and Nelson 235), so too must Charlottesville—dangerous in a different way— be repressed to define a defeated South. With its world-class university, its old and new money driving up real-estate prices throughout Albemarle County, its liberal politics and active gay community, its low tolerance for fundamentalisms, its increasingly technology-based economy, and even its proximity to a national park offering bits of that rarity in the South, the sublime, Charlottesville represents the sort of prosperous, progressive South (never a "new South") that must be repressed to continue narrating the region in terms of colonized global-southern decline. There are aspects of such a Charlottesville in nearly every southern city Naipaul visits and names a chapter after—Atlanta, Charleston, Tallahassee, Jackson, Nashville, Chapel Hill, though perhaps not Tuskegee—

but such hybrid urbanity endangers "symptomatic nostalgia for a world of lost objects and alterities," and Naipaul for the most part elides it.

The title of this volume, *Look Away!*, therefore resolutely opposes nostalgic and decline narratives. First and foremost, the title insists that we redirect the critical gaze of southern studies outward, away from the nativist navel-gazing that has kept mainstream southern studies methodologically so far behind American studies. Indeed, by taking, with deep irony, our title from "Dixie"—a song that, after all, may have been written by black Ohioans (Sacks), thus displaying precisely the kind of border-crossing, interracial hybridity that white southern nativism has sought to repress—we wish to refute for good the fetishization of community, hierarchy, place, and so on of another "Dixie"-titled anthology: the paradigm of white southern nativism, *I'll Take My Stand*.[8] Yet if the title makes a postsouthernist gesture, it makes an equally post-Americanist one, a response to Amy Kaplan's warning:

> The new pluralistic model of diversity [in American studies] runs the risk of being bound by the old paradigm of unity if it concentrates its gaze only narrowly on the internal lineaments of American culture and leaves national borders intact instead of interrogating their formation. That is, American nationality can still be taken for granted as a monolithic and self-contained whole, no matter how diverse and conflicted, if it remains implicitly defined by its internal social relations, and not in political struggles for power with other cultures and nations, struggles which make America's conceptual and geographical borders fluid, contested, and historically changing. (15)

We have in this volume attempted to move beyond traditional (and even progressive) "Americanist" perspectives, preferring for the most part to see what results from a direct conversation between progressive southernists and critics who have historically focused on other zones of U.S. hegemony. We hope thereby to avoid the reinscription of the Americanist hegemony that bothered Tate and that continues to concern so many comparatist scholars—and that George Handley so trenchantly warns against in this volume. We hope, indeed, to have envisioned a liminal south, one that troubles essentialist narratives *both* of global-southern decline *and* of unproblematic global-northern national or regional unity, of American or southern exceptionalism. Perhaps, when all is said and done, we will have begun to push the center of American studies some few hundred kilometers closer to that realm of "colonial subjects who interrupt the monologue of nationalist"—and southernist—

"literary history" (12) that Srinivas Aravamudan has called the "trop-icopolitan." Perhaps we will have begun to push postcolonial and sub-altern studies a few hundred kilometers northward, too.

That vision is, almost by definition, the result of collaboration—and collective endeavors tend to generate manifestoes. However, while the past decade has seen myriad manifestoes about decentering, recentering, rethinking, rearranging or re-envisioning American studies, and while our own claims should be clear—not least from the previous paragraph—we hope this book may ultimately be more about praxis. That is, we hope the diversity of critical methodologies employed in the essays that follow offer multiple ways of actually *doing* New World studies, and we wish still more that the following twenty-one ways of looking at the New World blackbird might offer, when combined, something more than the sum of the following parts. Part 1 of this volume examines Caribbean—particularly Cuban, Martinican, and Trinidadian—negotiations with the southern reaches of the imperial northern neighbor. Part 2 rethinks the U.S. South largely through the lens of postcolonial theory and post-modern geography. Part 3 examines William Faulkner's role in the con-struction of an imagined global-southern community resistant to par-ticular goals of a global-northern economy that global southerners know full well does not operate in their own best interests. Part 4 examines the relationship between Greater Mexico and the U.S. South. Finally, in the Posdata (postscript), Ilan Stavans offers a posthistoricist vision of trans-lation and the individual talent. Stavans grounds Borges's translations of Faulkner not in shared experiences of colonialism but in a shared appreciation—and "mastery"—of literary artifice.

As with any collection, these groupings are somewhat arbitrary, and we would encourage readers to consider, for example, Robert Brink-meyer Jr. and Debra Rae Cohen's essay on California in light of the Greater Mexico section, or Stavans's Posdata in light of the essays by Steven Hunsaker, say, or Wendy B. Faris. Even with *that* said, however, there remains much, much more to be done. What of Katherine Anne Porter's and Cormac McCarthy's treatments of the complex intersections between the South, Texas, and Mexico?[9] Where is discussion of Zora Neale Hurston, whose *Tell My Horse* offered an early argument for simi-larities between Haitian and U.S. black cultures? Where are the studies of the U.S. South's *northern* "border," the problematic zone that might include the office-park-smothered northern Virginia Civil War battle-fields, southern Indiana, and the Ohio River—a fluid border that for Harriet Beecher Stowe, at least, is most porous when frozen solid? What of the "experience of defeat" of Cherokee and Creek, Chippewa and Choctaw and Seminole? What role does Appalachia play in this model, besides sharing in colonial exploitation, even if more through company-town mining than through plantation agriculture? Speaking of Greater Mexico and the U.S. South, what questions of identity and hybridity are raised by the performances of El Vez, the "Mexican Elvis," who sings a Spanglish version of "That's All Right, Mama" called "Está Bien Mama-cita" and a version of "Never Been to Spain" that condemns Columbus and continues, "My native land is called Mexico / I'm not Hispanic from across the Atlantic / Soy de Mexico [*sic*]"? If the wars of 1861–1865 and 1898 are as similar as this introduction claims, where are the comparatist studies of U.S. southern and Puerto Rican writers—particularly, say, during the Cold War, when separatist rhetoric in both conquered territories notably diminished? One could go on—but regardless of the editors' best efforts, every book omits. If southernist scholars stop speaking of "the South" as though its borders were clear; if Americanist scholars start thinking of the southern plantation as the New World paradigm rather than the exception within American exceptionalism; if postcolonialist scholars begin to address the questions the U.S. South raises regarding the First World/Third World binarism; and if, perhaps, we cease to speak of "southern identities" except as contingent and performative, this volume, incomplete as it necessarily is, will have done its work.

NOTES

1. See, however, Clement Eaton's argument that "the Mexican War was an adventure in imperialism of the South in partnership with the restless inhabitants of the West. It was provoked by a Southern President and fought largely by Southern generals and Southern volunteers" (cited in Limón 13).

2. The terms *creole* and *Creole* are tellingly unstable in New World studies. Pratt translates the Spanish *criollo* literally to designate "persons born in America and claiming [pure] European (or white) ancestry" (112–13). Handley refers to "Afri-canized Creole" cultures, and Ladd notes Louisianans' distinction between Creole (white) and creole (mixed) cultures.

3. This notion of overlap appears to have been first advanced by James Crisp in a graduate history course at North Carolina State University (see Crisp; Peacock).

4. See Gray on Andrew Lytle (135–41) and Brinkmeyer on John Crowe Ransom (8–10).

5. "And so Caribbean literature is the expression of innumerable conflicts: of the black who studied in Paris; of the white who believes in the Yoruba *orichas* or the voodoo *loas*; of the black who wants to return to Africa after so many centuries; of the mulatto who wants to be white; of the white man who does not want his child to marry a black;

of the white man who loves a mulatto woman; of the black woman who loves a white man; of the black man who despises the mulatto; of the rich black and the poor white; of the white who claims that race does not exist—but why go on?" (Benítez-Rojo 105)

6. Though Carl Degler argues that white southern support for U.S. military activities abroad has tended to exceed national levels (15–17), Louisville native Muhammad Ali's characteristically pithy "No Viet Cong ever called me nigger" expresses many southern African Americans' sense of common cause with others oppressed by these enterprises.

7. "From its very beginning," writes Ayers, "people have believed that the South, defined against an earlier South that was somehow more authentic, more real, more unified and distinct, was not only disappearing but also declining. Jefferson's South declined into the delusion of Calhoun's South, which declined into the incompetency of Jefferson Davis's South, which declined into the corruption of the carpetbaggers' South, which declined into the poverty and inbreeding of Faulkner's South, which declined into the race baiting of George Wallace's South, which declined into the scandals of Jim Bakker and Jimmy Swaggart" ("What We Talk About" 69).

8. In this context, the use of "New World Studies" in the subtitle and throughout the volume is not meant to suggest a creole "ascension narrative" of "the Americas" as (simply?) a new or empty space of European redemption. As with "Third World," "global south," and so on, *every* term for "the Western Hemisphere" derives from European and Eurocentric cartographic imaginations, and, troubling as the phrase may be to some, we find "New World Studies" preferable to the alternatives. It places its biases up front, making them easier to neutralize than various covert tributes to Amerigo Vespucci. At the same time, it nods to the difficulty of applying "European" languages to "American" phenomena, a difficulty that—troped as wordless wonder or marvel—is central not only to several of these essays but also to much of the history of New World critical practice, especially in the Caribbean. Finally and not inconsequentially, it's relatively pithy. However, in part precisely *because* "New World Studies" has often referred to work dealing with parts of the Caribbean where Native American genocide was early and total, the phrase could (if unremarked) tend to privilege the perspectives of those of European and African descent in the hemisphere. So could the fact that beyond Jane Landers's essay we were unable to secure work on Native "Americans" in the South for this volume. Postcolonialist works in progress on southern Indians by Melanie Benson and Annette Trefzer, no doubt among others, will help rectify this difficulty.

9. José Limón addresses both these treatments, among others, in *American Encounters*; see also Deborah Cohn's chapter on Porter and Juan Rulfo in *History and Memory in the Two Souths*.

WORKS CITED

Anderson, Benedict R. *Imagined Communities: Reflections on the Origin and Spread of Nationalism*. London: Verso, 1991.

Aravamudan, Srinivas. *Tropicopolitans: Colonialism and Agency, 1688–1804.* Durham, N.C.: Duke UP, 1999.

Ayers, Edward L. *The Promise of the New South: Life after Reconstruction.* New York: Oxford UP, 1992.

——. "What We Talk about When We Talk about the South." *All Over the Map: Rethinking American Regions.* Ed. Edward L. Ayers, Patricia Nelson Limerick, Stephen Nissenbaum, and Peter S. Onuf. Baltimore, Md.: Johns Hopkins UP, 1996. 62–82.

Baker, Houston A., Jr. *Critical Memory: Public Spheres, African American Writing, and Black Fathers and Sons in America.* Athens: UP of Georgia, 2001.

——. *Turning South Again: Re-Thinking Modernism/Re-Reading Booker T.* Durham, N.C.: Duke UP, 2001.

——. *Workings of the Spirit: The Poetics of Afro-American Women's Writing.* Chicago: U of Chicago P, 1991.

Baker, Houston A., Jr., and Dana D. Nelson. "Preface: Violence, the Body, and 'the South.'" *American Literature* 73.2 (June 2001): 231–44.

Benítez-Rojo, Antonio. "The Repeating Island." *Do the Americas Have a Common Literature?* Ed. Gustavo Pérez-Firmat. Durham, N.C.: Duke UP, 1990. 85–106.

Brinkmeyer, Robert H., Jr. *Remapping Southern Literature: Contemporary Southern Writers and the West.* Athens: U of Georgia P, 2000.

Brooks, Cleanth. "William Faulkner." *The History of Southern Literature.* Ed. Louis D. Rubin Jr. et al. Baton Rouge: Louisiana State UP, 1985. 333–42.

Chakrabarty, Dipesh. "Postcoloniality and the Artifice of History: Who Speaks for 'Indian' Pasts?" *Representations* 37 (winter 1992): 1–26.

Chambers, Iain. *Migrancy, Culture, Identity.* London: Routledge, 1994.

Chesnutt, Charles. *The Conjure Woman and Other Conjure Tales.* Ed. Richard H. Brodhead. Durham, N.C.: Duke UP, 1995.

Chow, Rey. *Ethics after Idealism: Theory-Culture-Ethnicity-Reading.* Bloomington: Indiana UP, 1998.

Cohn, Deborah. *History and Memory in the Two Souths: Recent Southern and Spanish American Fiction.* Nashville, Tenn.: Vanderbilt UP, 1999.

Crisp, James E. "The Demographic Background of Slavery and the Sectional Conflict." Unpublished History 243 syllabus, North Carolina State University, 1985.

Dash, J. Michael. *The Other America: Caribbean Literature in a New World Context.* Charlottesville: UP of Virginia, 1998.

Davis, Thadious. "Expanding the Limits: The Intersection of Race and Region." *Southern Literary Journal* 20.1 (spring 1988): 3–11.

Engermann, Stanley. "Response to Charles Joyner." *The South and the Caribbean.* Ed. Douglass Sullivan-González and Charles Reagan Wilson. Jackson: UP of Mississippi, 2001. 43–48.

Fuentes, Carlos. "Central and Eccentric Writing." *Lives on the Line: The Testimony of Contemporary Latin American Authors.* Ed. Doris Meyer. Berkeley: U of California P, 1988. 111–25.

García Márquez, Gabriel. "En primera persona." *El País* [Spain] 24 Jan. 1999: 2.

Gilroy, Paul. *The Black Atlantic: Modernity and Double Consciousness*. Cambridge, Mass.: Harvard UP, 1993.

Glissant, Edouard. *Faulkner, Mississippi*. Trans. Barbara Lewis and Thomas C. Spear. New York: Farrar, 1999.

Grant, Susan-Mary. *North over South: Northern Nationalism and American Identity in the Antebellum Era*. Lawrence: UP of Kansas, 2000.

Gray, Richard. *Southern Aberrations: Writers of the American South and the Problems of Regionalism*. Baton Rouge: Louisiana State UP, 2000.

Handley, George. *Family Portraits in Black and White: Postslavery Literatures in the Americas*. Charlottesville: UP of Virginia, 2000.

Hobson, Fred. "Introduction." *South to the Future: An American Region in the Twenty-First Century*. Ed. Fred Hobson. Athens: U of Georgia P, 2002. 1–12.

Holman, C. Hugh. "No More Monoliths, Please: Continuities in the Multi-Souths." *Southern Literature in Transition: Heritage and Promise*. Ed. Philip Castille and William Osborne. Memphis, Tenn.: Memphis State UP, 1983.

Jones, Suzanne, and Sharon Monteith, eds. *South to a New Place*. Baton Rouge: Louisiana State UP, 2002.

Joyner, Charles. "Comparative Slavery: African Culture in the South and the Caribbean." *The South and the Caribbean*. Ed. Douglass Sullivan-González and Charles Reagan Wilson. Jackson: UP of Mississippi, 2001. 21–43.

Kaplan, Amy. " 'Left Alone with America': The Absence of Empire in the Study of American Culture." *Cultures of United States Imperialism*. Ed. Amy Kaplan and Donald E. Pease. Durham, N.C.: Duke UP, 1993. 3–21.

Kreyling, Michael. *Inventing Southern Literature*. Jackson: UP of Mississippi, 1998.

Ladd, Barbara. *Nationalism and the Color Line in George W. Cable, Mark Twain, and William Faulkner*. Baton Rouge: Louisiana State UP, 1996.

Limerick, Patricia Nelson. *The Legacy of Conquest: The Unbroken Past of the American West*. New York: Norton, 1987.

Limón, José E. *American Encounters: Greater Mexico, the United States, and the Erotics of Culture*. New York: Beacon, 1998.

McPherson, Tara. *Reconstructing Dixie: Race, Gender, and Nostalgia in the Imagined South*. Durham, N.C.: Duke UP, 2003.

Miller, Perry. *Errand into the Wilderness*. Cambridge, Mass.: Harvard UP, 1956.

Naipaul, V. S. *A Turn in the South*. New York: Knopf, 1989.

Nairn, Tom. *The Break-Up of Britain*. London: New Left, 1977.

O'Brien, Michael. *The Idea of the American South, 1920–1941*. Baltimore, Md.: Johns Hopkins UP, 1979.

Peacock, James. "The South in a Global World." *Virginia Quarterly Review* 78.4 (autumn 2002): 581–94.

Pérez Firmat, Gustavo. "Introduction: Cheek to Cheek." *Do the Americas Have a Common Literature?* Ed. Gustavo Pérez Firmat. Durham, N.C.: Duke UP, 1990. 1–5.

Pratt, Mary Louise. *Imperial Eyes: Travel Writing and Transculturation*. London: Routledge, 1992.

Radhakrishnan, R. "Postmodernism and the Rest of the World." *The Pre-Occupation of Postcolonial Studies.* Ed. Fawzia Afzal-Khan and Kalpana Seshadri-Crooks. Durham, N.C.: Duke UP, 2000. 37–70.

Romine, Scott. *The Narrative Forms of Southern Community.* Baton Rouge: Louisiana State UP, 1999.

Sacks, Howard L., with Judith Rose Sacks. *Way Up North in Dixie: A Black Family's Claim to the Confederate Anthem.* Washington, D.C.: Smithsonian Institute, 1995.

Seshadri-Crooks, Kalpana. "Surviving Theory: A Conversation with Homi Bhabha." *The Pre-Occupation of Postcolonial Studies.* Ed. Fawzia Afzal-Khan and Kalpana Seshadri-Crooks. Durham, N.C.: Duke UP, 2000. 369–79.

Shohat, Ella. "Notes on the 'Post-Colonial.'" *The Pre-Occupation of Postcolonial Studies.* Ed. Fawzia Afzal-Khan and Kalpana Seshadri-Crooks. Durham, N.C.: Duke UP, 2000. 126–39.

Smith, Donna Jo. "Queering the South: Constructions of Southern/Queer Identity." *Carryin' On in the Lesbian and Gay South.* Ed. John Howard. Albany: New York UP, 1997. 362–84.

Tate, Allen. "The New Provincialism." *Essays of Four Decades.* Chicago: Swallow, 1968. 535–55.

Taylor, Helen. *Circling Dixie: Trans-Atlantic Perspectives on U.S. Southern Culture.* Newark, N.J.: Rutgers UP, 2000.

Urgo, Joseph R. "Introduction." *Faulkner in America.* Ed. Joseph R. Urgo and Ann J. Abadie. Jackson: UP of Mississippi, 2001. ix–xxvii.

Wallerstein, Immanuel. *The Modern World System.* 3 vols. New York: Academic, 1980.

Williamson, Joel. *New People: Miscegenation and Mulattoes in the United States.* New York: Free Press, 1980.

Wilson, Charles Reagan. "Our Land, Our Country: Faulkner, the South, and the American Way of Life." *Faulkner in America.* Ed. Joseph R. Urgo and Ann J. Abadie. Jackson: UP of Mississippi, 2001. 153–66.

Woodward, C. Vann. *The Burden of Southern History.* 3d ed. Baton Rouge: Louisiana State UP, 1993.

Yaeger, Patricia. *Dirt and Desire: Reconstructing Southern Women's Writing, 1930–1960.* Chicago: U of Chicago P, 2000.

——. "Introduction: Narrating Space." *The Geography of Identity.* Ed. Patricia Yaeger. Ann Arbor: U of Michigan P, 1996. 1–38.

Yarborough, Richard. "Race, Violence, and Manhood: The Masculine Ideal in Frederick Douglass's 'The Heroic Slave.'" *Haunted Bodies.* Charlottesville: UP of Virginia, 1997. 159–84.

Zamora, Lois Parkinson. *The Usable Past: The Imagination of History in Recent Fiction of the Americas.* Cambridge: Cambridge UP, 1997.

——. *Writing the Apocalypse: Historical Vision in Contemporary U.S. and Latin American Fiction.* Cambridge: Cambridge UP, 1989.

PART ONE

THE U.S. SOUTH AND THE CARIBBEAN

Through their explorations of the relationship between the South and the Caribbean, the essays in this first section of *Look Away!* set the agenda for the transgression of boundaries laid by region(alism) and nation(alism) that is the hallmark of the essays in this collection. Edward Ayers has recently observed that, when the South is viewed from outside the U.S., its differences from the North collapse, and it seems to be just as "American" as its northern counterpart (72). Thus he urges scholars to explore the "connections between local and state, local and national, local and international" in order to assess the differences and similarities that separate and join South and North, as well as the South and other regions (80). Fred Hobson concurs with this imperative, observing that the South is a region that "is no longer even *perceived* as standing alone [but, rather] must be seen in the larger picture" (2). Hence the evolution of the region's designation from "the South" into "the American South" and, ultimately, "the U.S. South" (1): this transformation reflects the increasing awareness of the region's positionality, the fact that "south"—not to mention "American"—is a relative term whose meaning is contingent on a geopolitical context fraught with power imbalances both inter- and intranationally.

The geographic units bridged by the essays in this section are united in part by language: English, of course, is shared by William Faulkner and V. S. Naipaul, but French and Spanish, too, are reminders of the colonial histories that at one time joined Louisiana and Martinique—and, at another time, Louisiana, Cuba, and the rest of Spanish America. These geographic units are also joined to one another by their roles in the slave trade and as part of the plantation system that pervaded the Americas. Within this system, as Ralph Lee Woodward Jr. notes, "the Caribbean . . . came to be the classic region . . . , the area to which Europeans came first to plant colonial enterprises, and from which they left last" (127). These essays thus reconfigure the U.S. South's traditional borders by treating the region as part of a geographic area that encompasses the Caribbean nations and coasts—"the Black Atlantic" in Paul Gilroy's formulation, "Plantation America" for others—as well as the Gulf of Mexico. They follow Edouard Glissant's lead in tracing how Yoknapatawpha County—and the South as a whole—"is linked with its immediate surroundings, the Caribbean and Latin America, by the damnation and miscegenation born of the rape of slavery—that is, by what the country creates and represses at the same time" (88). George B. Handley explores cultural, literary, and historiographic commonalities shared by the South and the rest of Plantation America. In particular, he studies the broader region's development as a "societal area" determined and marked not just by the presence of the plantation but also by the collective synchronic and diachronic effects of African slavery and by the difficulty of finding adequate forms of literary representation for this experience. For Kirsten Silva Gruesz, in turn, New Orleans is both a "prototypically 'Southern' city" and "a Caribbean city" in the antebellum years, a hybrid space in which the presence of black, French, and Spanish communities problematized the city's relationship with national codes and politics: while Cuban separatists (who were opposed to the abolition of slavery in Cuba) aligned themselves with the South's slaveholding aristocracy, the French and Spanish generally opposed Anglo-American dominance; Hispanophone newspapers, in turn, decried U.S. intervention in Mexico during the U.S.-Mexican War as neocolonial expansionism and urged political opposition.

Jane Landers examines the geopolitics of the southeastern frontier in the age of revolutions, focusing not on the European contenders but on the black actors whose roles in the same dramas have been less well studied. Many factors contributed to the endemic violence in the region.

The St. Mary's River formed an international border between a weak Spanish government in Florida and successive Anglo governments to the north—first that of the British and, after the American Revolution, that of the new and ambitious United States. The political instability resulting from the war and from the subsequent French and Haitian revolutions weakened social control and enabled slaves to engage in the events or escape, depending on their perceived self-interests, and the almost impenetrable swamps and forests of Florida and Georgia provided some refuge for those who chose the latter course. Landers's work draws on a wide variety of Spanish archival materials as well as English-language sources. J. Michael Dash examines how Edouard Glissant in his later works looks to Faulkner, in whom he finds a post-identitarian poetics that he yearns to see in the Caribbean. He also turns his gaze more generally toward the South, where he finds material to support his challenge to the Caribbean's exclusionary identity politics. He sees in the Mississippi River in particular a geographic analogy to the region's cultural heterogeneity, defined by Peruvian critic Antonio Cornejo Polar as not hybridized, not synthesized, and discontinuous.

Whereas the preceding essays break down regional and national conceptualizations of Caribbean and "southern" literatures, the following essays further join the South to the Caribbean by actual, physical journeys: the "turns in the South," as it were, of V. S. Naipaul, Gustavo Pérez Firmat, and Loreta Janeta Velazquez offer new reflections on the South and reveal the travelers' relationships to their own homelands (and their attendant experience of place, time, and race) to be both transformed and mediated by their journeys. Through his analysis of Velazquez's experiences as a cross-dressing Confederate soldier, Jesse Alemán blurs the geopolitical borders separating Cuba and the Old South—which shared a history of slavery, a belief in an aristocratic "old order," and positioning against the political interventions of a North—and collapses other binary categories on which the identities of the South and the United States as a whole are predicated. Steven Hunsaker explores the contradictions of exile identity and the attendant questions of patriotism and national affiliation in Cuban-American literary critic Pérez Firmat, who is torn between his loyalties to Cuba, where he was born, and to the South, where he spent many years as an adult and which, he feels, mediates his transition to U.S. citizenship. And Leigh Anne Duck argues that, in investigating southerners' narratives of cultural identity, Naipaul manifests a transference that enables him to reconsider his hostility toward such narratives and to discover their importance in his early process of identification. He deflects the conflicts that emerge in this process, however, by creating an uncompromising and phantasmatic account of "redneck" identity.

WORKS CITED

Ayers, Edward, et al. *All Over the Map: Rethinking American Regions*. Baltimore, Md.: Johns Hopkins UP, 1996.

Glissant, Edouard. *Faulkner, Mississippi*. Trans. Barbara Lewis and Thomas C. Spear. N.Y.: Farrar, 1999.

Hobson, Fred, ed. *South to the Future: An American Region in the Twenty-First Century*. Athens: U of Georgia P, 2002.

Woodward, Ralph Lee, Jr. "The Political Economy of the Caribbean." *The South and the Caribbean*. Ed. Douglass Sullivan-González and Charles Reagan Wilson. Jackson: UP of Mississippi, 2001. 127–45.

Por el camino de la mar	By the way of the sea
Hay que aprender a recordar	You've got to learn to remember
lo que las nubes no pueden olvidar. . . .	what the clouds cannot forget. . . .
¿Cómo vais a olvidar	How are you going to forget
lo que las nubes aún pueden recordar?	what the clouds still remember?
¡Duro recuerdo recordar	Relentless memory to remember
lo que las nubes no pueden olvidar	what the clouds cannot forget
por el camino de la mar!	by the way of the sea!

—NICOLÁS GUILLÉN, "Elegía"

GEORGE B. HANDLEY

A New World Poetics of Oblivion

The historical patterns that characterize the U.S. South also connect it to a larger region of the Americas.[1] These patterns, most notably European colonization, Amerindian genocide and displacement, and African slavery, have served to create a region of perplexing but compelling commonality among Caribbean nations, the Caribbean coasts of Central and South America and Brazil, and the U.S. South (which in this broader context, of course, would then be a "north"), an area known as Plantation America.[2] These historical parallels, however, should not become justification for assuming that one can find facile homogeneity in the Americas; social, racial, and cultural similarities in the New World cannot be ignored any more than they can be definitively identified. Without careful comparative consideration of both what emerges and what may have been lost in the at times brutal and violent interaction of cultures in the New World, the leap from the local to the hemispheric will effectively result in an elision of important regional differences. To do so would be to imagine that the commonalities that bring New World cultures together were never subject to original violence or historical trauma; it is to ignore and perpetuate the untraceable facts of New World oblivion.

Defining the contours of our American parallels is challenging not only because the contemporary cultures of the Americas are so divergent but also because the historical events that they presumably share, although central to the formation of New World communities, often defy our capacity to recuperate them as representable, sayable stories. A complete understanding of events such as the murder and displacement of millions of Amerindians or the Middle Passage of African slavery and its subsequent legacies of untold suffering for millions of Africans and their descendents is often beyond representation because the lived realities were either initially understated or erased in historical documentation in an attempt to conceal accountability. And, of course, dead victims cannot speak; those who did survive had little or no access to written expression, and their testimonies often held feeble legal force. This is to say nothing of the daunting task of simply finding adequate forms of representation with which to sum up such atrocities.

Sympathetic discourses that have tried to recover a more accurate sense of the nature of this violence and its lasting effects have done so most often as rhetorical witnesses of a past no longer accessible. Such discourses, however, often omit careful consideration of the dizzying authorial challenge of giving representative force to such cataclysms. Very little of New World literature and its critical reception has succeeded in awakening from a fundamental numbness toward these primal hemispheric scenes. New World writers who do overcome this numbness paradoxically do so by beginning with a recognition not of the realities of the events per se but of the existence of a saturated, collective amnesia about them. In these cases, readers are typically taken through two levels in the suspension of disbelief, first on the level of historical experience ("Could this really have happened?") and then again in working through the trauma of what they have been asked to *imagine* as real ("What difference does it make that it did happen?"). This double suspension of disbelief does not create further numbness precisely because it points with greater honesty and humility to the enormity of the challenge of representation that New World history presents. It also acknowledges that the evidence that remains of historical parallels in the New World is, due to the violent and traumatic nature of its history, fragmented, partial, and while undeniable, ultimately unknowable.

Because New World history has blocked historiographic access to much of its evidence, historical reconstruction would benefit from a poetics that acknowledges that whatever the contours of a total history might look like, the past can only be known in its remnant parts.[3] It is perhaps ironic that despite the important lead of comparative historical studies on slavery and the genocide of Native Americans, literature and imagination are perhaps even more necessary. While historiography has emerged with valuable (if always tentative) New World death statistics, a poetics that recognizes oblivion—that is, not what is remembered but what is forgotten and therefore unsayable—offers a potentially more ethical way to give representative shape to these elusive historical patterns that link the U.S. South to other regions of slavery. While history yearns for the knowable story of the hemisphere, a contextualization of the American South within the literary imagination of greater Plantation America allows one to assess a broader range of representational choices about similar places and histories and thereby to at least begin to appreciate what is forgotten in the forging of imagined communities. As Jean-François Lyotard has written, literature that effectively responds to historical loss "does not say the unsayable, but says that it cannot say it" (47). For that reason, literature, if it is worthy of the task of addressing the problem of oblivion, refuses monumentalization or the seduction of a permanent recuperation of the past, because it mourns what it cannot say every time it tries to say it. Literature serves as further oblivion, then, but only in the sense that it offers pardon or amnesty, as the word *oblivion* also implies, to the past's refusal to enter completely into representation. The question of forgiveness of the perpetrators is laid aside since that implies using the logic of historical causation that would still privilege and monumentalize the crimes; only the past's elusiveness is forgiven. I do not pretend that this poetics of oblivion is unique to our hemisphere and not highly relevant to, say, Old World problems of historical memory. However, precisely because of the particular hemispheric reach of the events that shook modern American cultures at their foundations, it seems imperative that one recognize that oblivion has played an integral role in the formation of the national cultures of the Americas. On the basis of examining partial and local fragments, one can only begin to outline the extent of what has been erased from New World memory. This, in turn, presents an ethical obligation to learn to read cross-culturally throughout those regions affected by the historical patterns of Plantation America and to commemorate that which was lost in their mutually shared histories. Only by transgressing the borders of nationalism and regionalism (and thereby situating the literature of the U.S. South in a field of New World literature, for example) can a poetics of oblivion realize its capacity to participate in a perpetually necessary compensation for history's absence.

To speak of oblivion, of course, is risky business. Assessing the devastation suffered by indigenous populations risks failing to recognize the ways in which native cultures have survived, adapted, and transformed themselves in the wake of Columbus's arrival. A poetics of oblivion potentially becomes a kind of negative sublime that expresses a neocolonial wish to erase a still-thriving and vital indigenous presence in the Americas.[4] To invoke oblivion in relation to the Middle Passage risks a further dismissal of the lifeways and rhythms of African culture that have found new roots in American soil. It can be argued, in fact, that the Middle Passage has signified a new transformation and flourishing of African memory in the Americas, as evidenced by an increased interest in the history of slave experience in much recent fiction from the United States and the Caribbean.[5] In either case, to speak of oblivion might overstate the power of European colonization of the New World to control or obliterate contestatory cultural and political memories.

Failing to recognize the fact of oblivion (that something has been lost and is no longer accessible) runs parallel risks, however, chief among which is the risk of perceiving existing memories of conquest, enslavement, and colonization as naturally born from history itself, not as selected recollections that have emerged in the context of a struggle among competing powers of representation. Even though one's sympathies are clearly with the victims of such historical events, one risks identifying traces and transformations of ancestral cultures as significations of their original form. To do so is to render the historical agency behind colonialism and slavery invisible and to imagine anachronistically that current expressions of devotion to Africa or to Native America, or imaginative acts of historical recovery signify a pre-Columbian primordiality. This is an oedipal risk since one elides one's own imaginative desire by mythologizing origins and presenting them to oneself not as manifestations of one's own desire but as objectively given historical realities.

Literature can only suggest, point to, or imagine a larger context of which there are only fragmentary tales or cultural echoes. For this reason, two Nobel laureates, well acquainted with the ironies of New World history, explain that language of necessity fails but that this is not a cause for lamentation but rather an opportunity to pay homage to those histories that can never be summed up. Toni Morrison, in her Nobel acceptance speech of 1993, insisted that "language can never live up to life once and for all. Nor should it. Language can never 'pin down' slavery, genocide, war. Nor should it yearn for the arrogance to be able to do so. Its force, its felicity, is in its reach toward the ineffable" ("Nobel" 321). In his 1992 Nobel speech, St. Lucian poet Derek Walcott stated, "Break a vase, and the love that reassembles the fragments is stronger than the love which took its symmetry for granted when it was whole" (*What the Twilight Says* 69). Poetic language is an expression of this love; it is an expression of a self-conscious desire for wholeness, not a pretension to mimeticism.

Both writers imply that the limits of representation are both a symptom of historical events that have rendered language weak *and* a limitation inherent in language itself. It seems that if one doesn't at least admit both possibilities, either the specific historical quality of New World experience becomes insignificant and easily transferable to any other context *or* history becomes almost enshrined in its ubiquitous power to limit language and is granted a permanent primordial position always in demand of linguistic obeisance. That is to say, a poetics of oblivion might certainly become necessary in other historical contexts both because the historical events themselves create similar crises of language and because all languages presumably suffer similar limitations. However, one must be careful not to assume that all problems of oblivion are equal; to do so means that either all languages transcend history altogether or that one doesn't really need to pay attention to the particulars of any one region's history. The poetics articulated by Walcott and Morrison sees language as symptomatic representation of a primary historical oblivion but also as autonomous performative mourning for what has been forgotten. While it is likely true, as William Handley argues, that "the history of slavery . . . suggests that the structure of allegory and mourning is neither universal nor inevitable as a human and linguistic predicament" (685), Walcott and Morrison insist that the historical preconditioning of language nevertheless should not burden the language user with the anxieties of historical primordiality nor imbue the traumatic historical event with a kind of sacred mysticism.

A New World poetics is a kind of pendular swing between language's correspondence to its own rootedness in historical events and to its own self-referentiality. It is transferable to other historical situations but not without due modifications since the value of language's limitations can only be determined by the specific ways language is used in relation to specific events.[6] The user of language, when speaking of oblivion, must both recognize the contours of that history that language inadequately summons and the potential for self-referential limitations inherent in linguistic representation, limitations that, to some degree, are not entirely dependent on that history and are therefore potentially transhistorical.

These limitations are, in this sense, both historically grounded but also always *potentially* ontological. This pendular swing is important for ethical reasons since each pole presents a dilemma. If language is the source of the limitation, its user must ask if the chosen form of linguistic representation does not therefore become complicit in perpetuating the original oblivion that lies at the root of the New World story. On the other hand, if oblivion is always attributable to the event itself and to historical agents in the past, then representation is always innocent and never takes any historical risks since it would appear that it stands outside of history altogether. A New World poetic language moves between these risks, now self-questioning, now interrogating history.

One sees this pendular swing in both Morrison and Walcott when they in turn insist that the limitations of poetic language, although presumably an ontological problem, signify something grounded and specific that lies beyond words. Their poetic language reconstructs a conscious fiction of historical rootedness, and in its self-consciousness it betrays its own failure. This is because, ultimately, what is more important than language is what it cannot say. As Walcott stated in 1974, "We may not even need literature, not that we are beyond it, but in the archipelago particularly, nature, the elements if you want, are so new, so overpowering in their presence that awe is deeper than articulation of awe" ("The Caribbean" 12). A poetics of oblivion declares that what is said, what is remembered, is always less than that which it reaches for; language always defers to what it tries to express, but not because the past, or the present, is a sublime muse but because ultimately what matters more than language is what it tries to represent. Or as Walcott phrases it in his recent collection of poems, *The Bounty*, "memory is less than the place which it cherishes" (27).

What Morrison and Walcott describe is an ethics of reading New World history. J. Hillis Miller insists that an ethics of reading begins with a recognition that every text responds to some "thing" that "demands it be respected by being put in words" (105). That thing can never be finally summed up in language because to try to do so is to simply repeat the problem by displacing that thing once more. Every text, then, "only gives itself. It hides its matter or thing as much as it reveals it. . . . It is unfaithful to the thing, by being what it is, just these words on the page" (121). This explains the compelling need itself to write, to try and put it into words again and again. If that thing in Miller's paradigm were some historical event or truth that demanded to be spoken or represented, as soon as something textual appears, history is merely displaced once again. History, then, does not obtain the power of the sublime simply because history and language are always codependent.

Because identity in the New World—and the language used to define it—is always "fragmentary, based on a gleam of racial memory," Walcott concludes that "history is irrelevant, not because it is not being created, or because it was sordid; but because it has never mattered, what has mattered is the loss of history, the amnesia of the races, what has become necessary is imagination, imagination as necessity, as invention" ("The Caribbean" 7, 6). In summary, Walcott insists that "amnesia is the true history of the New World" (*What the Twilight Says* 39). A poetics of oblivion acknowledges historical erasure in the history of the New World and thereby avoids the "malaria of nostalgia and the delirium of revenge," which would likely follow any transparent conception of historical episte-mology (54). For this reason, Edouard Glissant has repeatedly stressed the opacity of the past while at the same time emphasizing the need to *imagine* the totality of that history, *as if* we were capable of making it transparent to our perception (*Poetics* 55).[7] He suggests that the represen-tative figure of this kind of poetic knowing is the one who is errant, not the discoverer or the conqueror, but one who, like a post-disillusionment Quixote, "conceives of totality but willingly renounces any claims to sum it up or to possess it" (21).

This poetics implicitly argues with Hegel's dialectic that determined that the future belonged to "America," by which Hegel meant those areas of the United States that he could identify in his time as embodying and furthering the development of Western civilization because of their rejec-tion of racial amalgamation (81). Hegel declares, "America is . . . the land of the future, where, in the ages that lie before us, the burden of the World's History shall reveal itself—perhaps in a contest between North and South America" (86). Hegel's claim is rendered ironic by the poetics of oblivion precisely because it is the Other America of the plantation and/or racial amalgamation that is the site not of historical memory, but of oblivion, of that which the advancement of the Western dialectic left behind and unaccounted for. This is not a new site of radical and essen-tialized alterity or difference (since that would simply fall into the dy-namics of the dialectic by way of the antithesis) but one that acknowl-edges that oblivion and historical erasure are undeniable even if they cannot be known. The Hegelian dialectic doesn't account for historical events for which there is no record or for the inevitability that in many cases there will never be a sufficient account; therefore it ignores the possibility that some events will inevitably fall outside the bounds of the dialectic that is supposed to perpetually produce historical meaning. Historical meaning, of course, will not always be recoverable by a poetics of oblivion. Amnesia cannot simply overturn the Hegelian dialectic or be essentialized, because it signifies what is essentially unknowable. To be ethical, any poetics of oblivion would always have to retrace its steps to acknowledge its failures, even if that means forsaking a thirst for historical meaning.

A New World poetics of oblivion suggests that Hegel's mapping of world history is perhaps upside down, since it will be the spaces of oblivion that will inevitably resist and fundamentally change the direction of, and perhaps render unpredictable, the historical outcomes of the dialectic. If the United States has become the bearer of the burdens of Western history as Hegel prophesied, it is time to acknowledge that those burdens are weighed by historical amnesia about the Other America Hegel dismissed, not by the extent to which the United States has perpetuated Western legacies. This poetics involves unreading representations of the past in order to invoke what lies underneath what has been said and remembered. It recognizes the fact of amnesia in New World history and that therefore, as the Martinican *Créolité* manifesto declares, "our chronicle is behind the dates, behind the known facts: *we are words behind writing.*" For this reason, "only poetic knowledge, fictional knowledge, literary knowledge . . . can discover us, understand us and bring us, evanescent, back to the resuscitation of consciousness" (Bernabé et al. 896). The recourse to fictional language, a language of the imagination, is crucial to this transformation of oblivion in filling in the "space between memory and history, . . . the space left by historical omission" (Pedersen 51) because it attempts to stand only rhetorically in the stead of an absent history.

THE AHISTORICAL SEARCH FOR ROOTEDNESS IN LITERARY REGIONALISM

If Walcott and Morrison are right about New World history, then one must imagine that both what one writes and what one reads can never bring oblivion into full representation. One cost of ignoring this problem is that one's readings tend to reduce literature to its mere content, and one reads merely for thematic confirmation of a politics of historical recovery in order to hastily establish a regional rootedness.[8] This, in turn, leads to a narrowly nationalistic assessment of literatures that treat subjects, such as slavery or injustices against Native Americans, that are really of hemispheric relevance.

The regionalist use of indigenous and African themes throughout the Americas in the development of national literatures is a case in point. From James Fenimore Cooper of the United States to Brazil's José de Alencar, the indigenous presence has enabled typically Euro-American writers the advantage of identifying a New World difference in their literature that helped to justify and found a new national and cultural independence from European models. The same has been true of writers of slavery and its history such as Cuba's Cirilo Villaverde, Brazil's Bernardo Guimarães, or George Washington Cable and Harriet Beecher Stowe from the United States. The exoticism of Afro-American cultural practices and dialects allows a literary demarcation of racial difference that simultaneously identifies new roots in American soil and controls, if not expels, new racial difference within the nation. This is because, as Scott Romine argues with regard to definitions of a U.S. southern community, "the autochthonous ideal . . . is predicated on the presence of a self-evident world, [but] . . . the rhetoric of community thus tends to defer the threat to a position beyond the communal boundary" (15). That is, "community is enabled by practices of avoidance, deferral, and evasion; in a certain sense, as [Allen] Tate implies, community relies not on what is there so much as what is, by tacit agreement, not there" (3). Because of this deferral, thematic sympathy toward the victims of New World history clearly does not guarantee a successful discursive reversal of past evils.

Regionalism, and its accompanying celebration of a fixed notion of place as background, is essentially a narrative of national progress, as Allen Tate once argued.[9] Even after the emergence of literature by Afro Americans—beginning with slave narratives in the United States and the Caribbean primarily and followed by poetry, novels, and essays—critics typically valued its apparent contributions to national ends. In the United States the reaction against the containments of nationalism since the 1960s inspired the study of ethnicity apart from national literary histories. However, this increase in literary specialization has, perhaps unintentionally, helped to rigidify a separate discussion about "race" outside of the national dialogue, thus abdicating any national responsibility for an accounting of race and racial difference. Toni Morrison and others have helped to argue why black and white literatures in the United States, at least, need to be brought back into the scope of a rigorous comparative scholarly eye, but as long as such comparative work remains trapped within national and regional boundaries and focuses on a thematics, and not a poetics, of identity, the binary oppositions that have infected our reading of race will remain largely intact.[10]

Transnational comparative investigations into literatures in the Americas could help to uncover myriad parallels of experience throughout the hemisphere, but such criticism is a rarity because readings of New World literatures remain trapped within the myopia of nationalism. This is not merely a function of the linguistic obstacles presented by other "American" languages. If it were, the availability of much New World literature in translation would have single-handedly created a new literary sensibility. The refusal to establish transnational links related to the history of European immigration, the conquest of indigenous peoples, and the enslavement of Africans has more to do with a refusal to acknowledge the truly cataclysmic power of New World history. Nationalism relies on establishing cultural and historical roots in a local place, which has typically involved representations of racial and environmental differences that respond rhetorically to the nation's colonial challengers and yet signify its secure, fixed, and almost sacred rootedness in a particular place. Such rhetoric, as Glissant's critique of the idea of the root suggests, is anything but historical since it displaces historical rootedness with an ahistorical conception of racial identities, despite the historical reality of diaspora that lies at the very foundation of New World nationalities (*Poetics* 11–22). Racial myths of national origins simply ignore the devastation suffered at the hands of European settlers and ignore the oblivion, erasure, and fragmentation of New World resettlement. Glissant explains that the construction of New World identities, particularly those of the U.S. South and the rest of Plantation America, occurs "by proceeding not from preserved folklores . . . but from these *traces*, and by combining them with countless other elements, from China or India or the Middle East, and so on, with so many conflicts to resolve" ("Creolization" 273). The New World subject faces the rather paradoxical "obligation to remake oneself every time on the basis of a series of forgettings" (273), since every step forward in forging a new identity and sense of place from the fragments created by New World experience means forsaking nostalgia for some forgotten whole.

Typically, however, a search for national rootedness often neglects to consider its own "forgettings" and sinks into the realm of a kind of touristic regionalism, or what Glissant calls the "folkloric" (*Caribbean* 101). This is usually because the nationalistic impulse too hastily jumps from the particular to the general because of a thirst for transcendence, and thus the specific qualities of oral language and of the historical qualities of the landscape are glossed over. As a result, literary nationalism, rather than emphasizing the plasticity and historical nature of its own expression, becomes teleological in its search for fixed origins. It disguises its performance of desire for rootedness as rootedness per se. And landscape merely becomes a site "of relative permanence within time and change" (Ladd 16).

All forms of nationalism, as Ernest Renan once suggested, of course rely on "forgetting, . . . even . . . historical error" for their justification (11), but in the context of the New World, one has to weigh the specific costs of what Toni Morrison has called "national amnesia" (qtd. in Bröck 34), which has not fully accounted for the losses of African slavery and violence against countless Amerindian peoples. In a situation that calls for imaginative literature to compensate for that which historiography cannot or will not document, literary nationalism has instead believed rather unapologetically in the muse of history, in the idea that historical origins are fully knowable and are the ultimate inspiration for the writer. What is brought into representation is offered and read as a sign of historical and regional origins in the New World, and in the creation of a southern community that which is not or cannot be represented fades into insignificance, as Romine notes.

Just as race can be emptied of history, so too can the local landscape; literature of place attempts to articulate reconciliation with the historical fact of displacement but in so doing becomes potentially complicit in the story of violent transplantation. There is little question that an interest in the specificities of place, in the physical qualities of one's environment, and in "the cultural and political ramifications of geography" character-izes much postslavery and postcolonial fiction, a connection not lost on recent nature writers in the United States, for example (Barnes 150).[11] Writers keen on redressing the wrongs of the past have frequently ques-tioned the abandonment of history and of respect for place that seems to characterize so much New World experience.[12] Regaining a sense of his-torical belonging to place helps to resist colonial discourse because it involves a radical resituation of the marginalized, a speaking from and to those circumstances that have been passed over. The risk is that in the name of establishing autonomy from the past, the local environment will merely become an eternal sign, emptied of history.[13]

Whether race or place stands in for absent history, the tendency in much regionalist literature and among its readership has been to cele-brate a new point of origin, divorced from that chaotic and cataclysmic past declared no longer relevant to the concerns of a national legitimacy. Ironically, recourse to place or to race is typically an attempt to *recover* history. Regional qualities are typically read diachronically and, for that matter, anachronistically as representing a national past that nurtures current identity as a nation. But the literature that most honestly confronts the challenges of historical oblivion in Plantation America is paradoxically the most true to history, since it acknowledges the insufficiency of regionalisms and their insufficient memory.

Ultimately regionalism cannot escape the conditions, the historical ironies, of its emergence. According to Carlos Alonso, early-twentieth-century literary regionalism developed in Latin America in response to a crisis initiated by the encroachment of the United States, which the literature attempted to cure, and yet the works of regionalism tended to "re-enact that crisis in their own rhetorical structure" (7). Alonso explains: "the attempt to produce a text of autochthony places the writer in an eccentric perspective with respect to his or her own cultural circumstance" (6). This means that "affirmations of cultural autochthony exhibit simultaneously two irreconcilable attributes: an essentialist, ahistorical conception of cultural identity, and an explicitly historical agenda for facilitating the imminent manifestation of that essence" (11). By virtue of their recourse to this ahistorical identity, regionalist writers are placed outside the native essence they depict, despite their intention to speak from within that essence; their work is therefore expressive of and conditioned by their alienation. Eudora Welty made a distinction, for this reason, between "place," a term to refer to the insider's emotional experience with location, and "regionalism," which "is essentially an outsider's term" (132). Regionalism mythologizes a new origin in a New World place in order to establish rootedness and therefore further contributes to New World amnesia.

THE RETURN OF AN UNTRACEABLE HISTORY

Regionalism is a literary manifestation of what the Guianese writer Wilson Harris contends are the oedipal risks of nationalism: "the reaction to dread" often leads to "the withdrawal into cells of ideological or racial or cultural purity" or what he calls "political incest" ("Oedipus" 10). Regionalism, in its retreat from the historical horrors of colonialism and imperialism, often resorts to these dehistoricized racial and cultural ideologies and thus disguises its own imitation of the father culture in the very name of a nationalist rebellion against him. The trap of regionalism is that it cannot cure the degradation it depicts because it *needs* a disease or colonial trauma in order to establish its anti-imperialist authority.[14] Such writing is, then, a kind of paternalism itself, to follow Alonso's argument, since it relies on the eccentric and ahistorical position of the writer who, by virtue of his own disguised position outside history, can offer cures with no account of his own historical genesis. The paternalism of literary regionalism has the potential to be perpetually recycled by an eternal recourse to a diseased past for which it continually offers itself as a cure.

What contributes to this erasure of human historical accountability in the land, according to William Faulkner, is land ownership. Ownership inherently contradicts the facts of New World history because it is fundamentally tied to the anxiety about genealogical legitimacy, an anxiety initiated by the violence of New World history. Ownership serves to invent identity because it will always keep history at bay, at least any history that is inclusive of a heterogeneous past.[15] As Faulkner expresses in "The Bear,"

> On the instant when [the Native American] discovered, realized, that he could sell [land] for money, on that instant it ceased ever to have been his forever, father to father to father, and the man who bought it bought nothing. . . . Because He told in the Book how He . . . made the earth first and peopled it with dumb creatures, and then He created man to be His overseer on the earth and to hold suzerainty over the earth . . . not to hold for himself and his descendants inviolable title forever, generation after generation, to the oblongs and squares of the earth, but to hold the earth mutual and intact in the communal anonymity of brotherhood, and all the fee He asked was pity and humility and sufferance and endurance and the sweat of his face for bread. (255)

The arrogance of ownership is that it parcels off, sets apart, and fails to recognize kinship with what lies beyond the boundaries ownership creates; it is a pretension to purity and inviolable difference regarding that which lies within those boundaries, and it defers, as Romine has argued, a confrontation with the difference expelled in order to expedite that purity. And this, of course, is also the inherent thrust of nationalistic views of regionalism wherein the local color of place is appropriated as a pure expression of national origins and identity. Nationalism, in this sense, simply serves as a centralized form of cultural ownership, whereby regions are kept within boundaries and apart from any "foreign" claims.

Faulkner suggests that a New World sense of place is established by an awareness of the historical presence of various peoples in the landscape, and the only way to assure that a sense of place does not simultaneously displace others is to abdicate ownership and accept mutual responsibility for that history through action and labor. "The Bear" describes New World history as "that dark corrupt and bloody time while three separate people had tried to adjust not only to one another but to the new land which they had created and inherited too and must live in for the reason that those who had lost it were no less free to quit it than those who had gained it were" (283). Faulkner argues for an open-ended relationship with the land that recognizes the folly of a belief in genealogical inviolability and embraces the ironies as well as the possibilities of a *collective* history. As Lois Parkinson Zamora contends, this historical imagination of New World writers involves "the countenancing of multiple, coexisting, conflictual, *unfinished* histories" (196, emphasis added). Faulkner's sense of place concerns itself with synchronic, cross-cultural relationships across the landscape rather than with diachronic singular claims to its history. This is a kind of regionalism that expresses a yearning for belonging simultaneously with a fear of a possible irrevocable demarcation from others and from the past.

A sense of place that neither ignores an absent history nor pretends to replace it demonstrates that identities and landscapes alike are haunted by the appearance of metonymical fragments of a larger range of possibilities. Jean Rhys's *Wide Sargasso Sea*, the classic postcolonial revision of *Jane Eyre*, depicts Rochester trying to find his own transplanted place in a post-slavery context. Rochester has come into ownership of a former plantation, but its history is inaccessible to him because of both his cultural distance and nature's inexorable indifference to human history. On a walk he discovers illegible evidence of the plantation's history: "The path was overgrown but it was impossible to follow it. . . . How can one discover the truth I thought and that thought led me nowhere. No one would tell me the truth. Not my father, nor Richard Mason, certainly not the girl I had married. . . . There had been a paved road through this forest. The track led to a large clear space. Here were the ruins of a stone house and round the ruins rose trees that had grown to an incredible height . . . Under the orange tree I noticed little bunches of flowers tied with grass" (104).

Rochester conflates here the mysteries of Afro-Caribbean culture (signified by the bound bunches of flowers), the truths of the history of slavery, and the potency of nature. Nature, then, is simply a signifier of the lies that have buried historical truth. When he asks Baptiste, one of the black servants, about the meaning of the road and ruins and about the existence of ghosts or zombies in the location, the answer is repeatedly and tersely, " 'No road' " (106). When confronted with the mysteries of the past and the competitive claims his Afro-Caribbean subjects have on that past, Rochester's attitude is to try and take possession of what he cannot know. And this leads him to play the role of the neocolonial despoiler. His sense of place flees rather than embraces the ironies of history and becomes reduced to the arrogance of ownership.

Rhys implies that the remedy for this arrogance means not simply *including* multiple histories in some kind of facile multiculturalism but also somehow acknowledging those histories that cannot be included precisely because New World history has made them unavailable. In Walcott's recent collection of poems, *The Bounty*, he provides a poetics of place that counters Rochester's example of a maniacal need to dominate place and history.

> . . . your devotion
> to pursue those bleached tracks that disappear into bush, in the
>   rain—
> something of weight in the long indigo afternoon,
> the yam vines trying to hide the sugar wheel's ruin;
> of something unconnected, oblique as if, after the motion
> of history, every object we named was not the correct noun. (48)

The "motion of history" renders language always displaced, or at least always "as if" displaced, since to be certain of the precise nature of the displacement is to believe in the capacity to define history's motions exactly. Language, in its recovery of the past, or perhaps in its recovery *from* the loss of the past, resorts to "as if" constructions, to similes, metaphors. History's traces arise in Walcott's poetry, as they do in Rhys's novel, as not entirely traceable because they are mere metonyms that language cannot dominate. In fact, one will always have to suspect that language will have misnamed.

The absent histories that inform Walcott's poetics are, of course, those of the untold suffering that resulted from the genocide of countless unknown Amerindians, a destruction that went hand-in-hand with the introduction of African slaves and the sufferings of countless others under slavery, signified above by the trace of "the sugar wheel's ruin." Two particularly poignant examples of his poetics of oblivion are "The Sea Is History" (1979) and "Air" (1969). In the former, he claims that the sea holds within its vaults submarine monuments of death and silence.

> Where are your monuments, your battles, martyrs?
> Where is your tribal memory? Sirs
> in that grey vault. The sea. The sea
> has locked them up. The Sea is History. (*Collected Poems* 364)

"Air" describes the verdant power of the rain forest to renew itself perpetually and also laments nature's capacity to devour traces of Amerindian genocide and the Middle Passage with indifference. The poem concludes with a melancholy mourning for a history that nature will not allow him to recover: "there is too much nothing here" (*Collected Poems* 114). His poetry implies, as does my epigraph from Cuban poet Nicolás

Guillén, that historical reconstruction through a poetic language means doing the impossible: imagining a history that only nature has witnessed.

A poetics of oblivion involves commemoration but with little or no recourse to monumentalization or institutionalization of the past. It represents a past that is not outside of time but ever subject to its reformation in the present. Even as the past is remembered, attention is drawn to the present that gives representative shape to that past. Michel de Certeau argues that when representations of the past are "historicized" in this manner, one discovers that "time is precisely the impossibility of an identity fixed by a place" (147). Conceptions of rootedness in a place that disguise time are merely "dogmatic" (151). A poetics of oblivion seeks a history that is alive precisely because it cannot be reified, embodied, or immured. The past must be perpetually recalled through the imagination, but because it is only recovered as an untraceable ruin, it signifies the insufficiency of a sense of place and belonging. For this reason, Lawrence Buell has insisted that a "new world aesthetics of the not-there" has helped New World writing to make the transition from a neocolonial pastoral language of environmental appropriation to one that delineates the contours of a genuinely new sense of place (73). "Place-consciousness in literature," he writes, is "an incompletion undertaken in awareness that place is something we are always in the process of finding, and always perforce creating in some degree as we find it" (260). Historicity emerges as the chief symptom of historical oblivion, since the absence of a recoverable past is always haunting our places of enunciation, like 124 Bluestone Road in Toni Morrison's *Beloved*. A poetics of oblivion perpetually recreates a sense of place, generates the need for more stories, and will always highlight, self-consciously, one's own desire for rootedness. It leads to the paradox of having to declare perpetually, as does Morrison, that "this is not a story to pass on" (*Beloved* 275). One recognizes the kind of belonging one's cultural expressions make possible to be a function of a present awareness of incompletion and need for rootedness. As Glissant means when he talks of a need "to renew the visions and aesthetics of relating to the earth," rootedness is not a myth of origins, detached from one's own representational choices, but becomes a process by which one sees oneself working through one's historical ironies (*Poetics* 148).

CROSS-CULTURAL IMPLICATIONS

A poetics of oblivion begins with a passionate search for history but ultimately, according to Glissant, it "renounc[es] the notion, the beginning of history. These kinds of failure matter. Failure leaves a trail that permits others to go forward. The literary work, so transcending myth, today initiates a cross-cultural poetics. . . . In its impenetrable nature history feeds our desire" (*Caribbean* 82). His point is that if history is a muse, it is because it fails to be recovered and hence produces a desire to return, not to a diachronic past per se, but to those synchronic parallels of historical experience that lie across a multinational and multicultural landscape. Diachronic history fails to inspire because, within one nation's borders, what it reveals is merely a part of a greater range of possibilities, the contours of which one can only imagine cross-culturally.

A powerful example of how this failure becomes meaningful is in a little-known essay by Wilson Harris from 1973, entitled "A Talk on the Subjective Imagination." In this essay, Harris argues, "Clearly there is a signal lack of imaginative daring to probe the nature of roots of community beyond fixed or static boundaries. Also there is a signal lack of imaginative daring to probe the function of roots as a criterion of creativity and capacity to digest and liberate contrasting spaces" (37). As an example of the kind of imaginative daring he refers to, he describes an episode on the Potaro River, a tributary of the Essequebo that runs out of Brazil into the Atlantic, where he had been working on a project to gauge the river for its potential hydroelectric power. At one point, the boat began to take water, and it became necessary for the crew to cut the rope attached to one of two anchors. When they returned to continue work three years later, the identical problem occurred, but instead of cutting the rope they yanked on it until the anchor moved and the boat righted itself. On pulling the anchor into the boat, they discovered that it had hooked into the very same anchor they had lost three years before. The appearance of these two anchors provided Harris an epiphany: "It is almost impossible to describe the kind of energy that rushed out of that constellation of images. I felt as if a canvas around my head was crowded with phantoms and figures. I had forgotten some of my own antecedents—the Amerindian/Arawak ones—but now their faces were on the canvas. One could see them in the long march into the twentieth century out of the pre-Columbian mists of time. One could see the lost expeditions, the people who had gone down in these South American rivers. One could sense a whole range of things, all sorts of faces—angelic, terrifying, daemonic—all sorts of contrasting faces, all sorts of figures" (40–41).

Harris's own subjective imagination allows him to situate his experience in the context of a heterogenous community's experience with the same place. The anchor represents a relic, a ruin from a previous attempt to root in a place ever shifting in a flowing current of time. Precisely because the repetition of his attempt to gain a tenuous hold on place is so uncanny, so against the odds created by a violently changing place, he doesn't conclude that the signification of language can correspond to its signified in a place. Rather he learns that repeated attempts to name place reveal hints and phantoms of multiple and now faded human histories, which haunt his own attempt at anchoring himself there. He contends that "the mystery of the subjective imagination lies, I believe, in an intuitive, indeed revolutionary, grasp of a play of values as the flux of authentic change through and beyond what is given to us and what we accept, without further thought, as objective appearances. It is not a question of rootlessness but of the miracle of roots, the miracle of a dialogue with eclipsed selves which appearances may deny us or into which they may lead us" (47).

Harris describes an imagination that refuses to accept one's place as given, as naturally beyond the contingencies of human history. Harris's poetic imagination works through and past objective appearances to arrive at the violent and changing flux of human history and values. This proscribes ownership since language fails to remove place from the history that is embedded in it. And it reveals that the miracle of roots does not lie in the possibility of finding oneself uniquely rooted and belonging to physical space but in the inevitability of failure in doing so. Rather than lamenting this as a kind of doomed rootlessness, however, Harris insists that precisely because of this failure, one is in a greater position to realize the potentials of a "heterogenous community beyond static cultural imperatives" (45).

Ironically, the New World's history of exploitation is precisely that which makes this kind of community possible, since it brought together seemingly incompatible peoples within the same landscapes. According to Harris, those discourses that would subject the "fantastic density of place" to the mere "poetry of science" and reduce it to "banalities" can only be overcome by linguistic humility, the kind advocated by Morrison and Walcott (38, 41). Harris explains further that "one was aware of one's incapacity to describe it, as though the tools of language one possessed were inadequate. It was pointless describing the river as running dark, the trees as green, or the rocks as grey. All this seemed less to do with the medium of place and more to do with the immediate tool of the word as representing or signifying 'place' " (38–39). Only by discovering the "relative faces of the dynamic mystery of language," as he later describes in the anchor episode, does he feel he has made "a groping but authentic step into the reality of place" (39).

Glissant also contends that the tragedy of our response to New World history is to ignore the evidence of the "subterranean convergence of *our histories*" (*Caribbean* 66, emphasis added). A simple process of digging into the history of a people in a local place leads to the inevitable discovery, like that of a "deep map," that one people alone do not possess a place or have a solitary history in it; only comparative New World readings expose what Glissant calls the "subterranean convergence of our histories," the "concealed parallels in history" that haunt New World places (66, 60). Landscape, then, "is not saturated with a single History but effervescent with intermingled histories, spread around, rushing to fuse without destroying or reducing each other" (154). This means that a contextualization of the U.S. South within the larger geography of Plantation America exposes a broader range of representational choices by which to understand the particular acts of deferral that have facilitated conceptions of southern community. The way ideology erases competing histories within a place is thereby more effectively exposed. The bodies of those thrown overboard in the Middle Passage, as Glissant expresses for example, "*sowed in the depths the seeds of an invisible presence. And so transversality, and not the universal transcendence of the sublime, has come to light. It took us a long time to learn this. We are the roots of a cross-cultural relationship. Submarine roots: that is floating free, not fixed in one position in some primordial spot, but extending in all directions in our world through its network of branches*" (67).

If underneath New World land- and seascapes lie concealed parallels, one returns to the question of how such parallels will find their way into representation so as to be recognizable. Harris suggests, as does Miller in his account of the ethics of reading, that those parallels can only be hinted at through repeated attempts to name them. Miller contends that only through this process of trying to say again what failed the first time to sum up does one begin to understand that there is some "thing" to which multiple texts respond. Through comparative readings of, say, experience related to the Middle Passage and slavery, one doesn't recover that history in its entirety but does begin to catch a glimpse of that "thing," that ethical obligation necessitated by historical omission, that has motivated the written text and to which it repeatedly responds. And the fact that different stories respond to the same ethical obligation liberates "the real thing latent in both" (123). Miller explains, "Only if there is difference and deviation is it possible to distinguish between a knowledge simply of what the text says, which is relatively without value, and a knowledge of what the text represents or allegorizes, the 'thing' . . . that gives the text whatever authenticity, value, and interest it may have" (117). So comparative readings of literatures across the Americas will not help one to understand the histories that are lost per se, since they will always be lost, but the nature and scope of New World desire to respond to historical oblivion.

It is precisely this ethical injunction, introduced by New World history, that is frequently ignored in literary criticism. Criticism is the process by which one grants, at least officially and institutionally, what literature signifies, and if all that one reads in the literatures concerning the historical paradigms of New World history and of Plantation America is that which signifies either a small-scale regionalism or a national exceptionalism, then one helps to institutionalize a long pattern of imperialist compartmentalization of the region. Janice Radway's recent address to the American Studies Association tried to move the academic disciplines of the field away from the tradition of exceptionalism in the United States in order to begin to outline the borders of a new field that extends beyond the limitations of the nation as defined strictly by its geopolitical borders. She insisted that the move away from conceptions of identity as a "naturalized essence of property" does not "diminish the importance of place or geography in the effort to understand societies and culture. Rather it demands a reconceptualization of both as socially produced through relations of dependence and mutual implication, through relationships established socially and hierarchically between the near and far, the local and the distant" (14).

While this philosophy is not altogether incompatible with the poetics I argue for, Radway (along with American studies scholars) leaves unstated why she believes a U.S.-based discipline, without aggressive comparative work, will achieve the desired revision of "America" in a broader hemispheric context.[16] This rethinking is generated and understood primarily within the confines of the field of American studies (and more likely, within English departments, except perhaps at the few privileged institutions that enjoy interdisciplinary luxuries not afforded most U.S. or Latin American universities). Radway rightly insists that U.S. national and linguistic origins lie in a diversity of languages and geographies, but she implies, dangerously, that such diversity is not really necessary to know or to understand except in the theoretically abstract. Without any clear delineation of a comparative regional dialogue, one is left to wonder: what will guarantee that the shift from the specific dynamics of U.S. culture to the broader hemispheric context will not simply expand U.S. cultural discourses onto a "pan-American" map?

While the recent rethinking of American studies seems to take lightly the responsibility to account for different histories and places in the Americas, the opposite tendency crops up in recent thinking about creolization in the Martinican *Créolité* manifesto, "In Praise of Creoleness," by

Jean Bernabé, Patrick Chamoiseau, and Raphael Confiant. In this latter case, the particulars of place and history (and gender as well) are seen as overriding factors in the shaping of a cross-cultural understanding of the Americas. Hence, rather than passing over alternative American sites because their differences are not deemed important, the *créolistes* ignore those differences precisely because they are not shaped by the same conditions that have given birth to their particular conception of *créolité*. They explain that "Creoleness is the *interactional or transactional aggregate* of Caribbean, European, African, Asian and Levantine cultural elements, united on the same soil by the yoke of history" (891). Specifically, it is a cultural mix that results from "the brutal interaction, on either insular or landlocked territories . . . of culturally different populations. . . . Generally resting upon a plantation economy, *these populations are called to invent the new cultural designs allowing for a relative cohabitation between them*" (893). Creoleness is, therefore, an attractive conception of cultural heterogeneity that stresses two important ingredients missing in most Americanist attempts to redefine "American" culture. First, they insist on the comparative *interaction* of cultures. That is, they do not lose sight of the mutual agency of contestatory cultures, and secondly they focus on the brutal and at times violent nature of this interaction.

The problem, however, is that their almost fetishized notion of creoleness turns out to be more exclusive of other comparable New World experiences than their rhetoric might suggest. Even though they are careful to distinguish Creoleness from the general hemispheric phenomenon of Americanization, which they understand to involve more generic challenges of adaptation experienced by myriad immigrant groups in the Americas, they nevertheless offer creoleness as a kind of telos for New World history. While Glissant and others have stressed the chaotic aspects of creolization in the Americas, this manifesto sacralizes almost messianically this interaction of culture, to the point that it seems to be the predictable telos of globalization. They express faith that creolization is likely the future of world cultures as long as globalization continues to bring diverse cultures into closer proximity. This is never clearly explained in light of the fact that at the present only plantation economies of the U.S. South and some metropolitan areas—such as Miami, New York, Los Angeles, or New Orleans—have seen similar conditions for creolization, as they themselves admit. So how that grand fusion will occur on a global scale seems rather vague.

In other words, the interaction of cultures is believed to *always* generate newness, which signifies an impatience to jump from the local to a broader region without recognizing the differences or the forgotten features that were left behind and never entered into the Creole mix. Clearly this notion of creolization fails to recognize the inevitability of forgetting and of oblivion, as does Glissant when he argues that creolization results from a "series of forgettings" ("Creolization" 273). If creolization is a model for New World intercultural understanding, it is insightful not just because it helps one to embrace what is new in the New World but simultaneously points to what has been lost in the process and can never be recovered; it recognizes the inevitability that something will be left out in the creation of new possibilities. Without this recognition, all one has is another version of a dialectic of history, not a poetics of oblivion.

This mistake is evident in the *Créolité* manifesto, since its writers have clearly denounced the contributions of other Creole writers, either because they are not Creole enough or presumably because they are women (Arnold, "*Créolité*" 37). James Arnold explains, "The male *créolistes* at present appear to be driven by an ideological overdetermination to conform to the same teleological project: a certain locale is required, whereas others are no longer legitimate; a certain use of Creole is mandated, whereas the creolization of the text by writers who do not belong to their orthodoxy is explained away as insignificant; and finally a certain gendering of characters, narrators, and even the symbolic geography of their fiction is rigorously imposed—and then theorized—in such a way that those who envisage their creative project differently can be dismissed as somehow not truly serious" ("Erotics" 19). That is, the fusion will be a false one since unwanted elements are simply ignored.

One is faced, then, with the same dilemma raised by Walcott and Morrison. Either one chooses to believe that the gaps and violence of history and place shape language or that language is ontologically limited by its inherent brokenness. Faced with this dichotomy, one must either choose a cross-cultural model that imposes one region's experience onto all others or a cross-cultural model that imposes the shape of one New World language onto all regions. But a poetics of oblivion rejects this dichotomy as false, insisting that the simultaneity of the gaps in New World history and in language itself makes unlikely the possibility of knowing which one obstructs more our access to the past and to place. It is in accepting this uncertainty that one can begin to appreciate the truth that oblivion lies at the root of both our New World language practices and our historical experiences. One should embrace the need for comparative understanding of the U.S. South not because one anticipates facile parallels with other American experiences but because one recognizes that parallels cannot be ignored any more than they can be definitively identified. That scholars have only recently recognized the need to study "American" culture in a broader New World context is perhaps symptomatic of the fact that U.S. culture is beginning to take account of its history of amnesia. But unless literary critics take seriously the obligation to look elsewhere in the Americas to understand concretely the different ways in which different literatures have responded to New World history, there is little chance that such desire will result in anything more than democratic fantasies facilitated by imagined ahistorical otherness. At the same time, however, without recognition of what is unknown and what cannot be known about the inter-American past or contemporary parallels, it will little matter what one does pretend to know, since one will have fantasized a hemispheric community that was always immune to violence, trauma, or loss.

NOTES

The author wishes to acknowledge the able editorial guidance of Jon Smith and Deborah Cohn without whose help and encouragement this essay would not have been written.

1. Guillén epigraph: translation mine.

2. Such is the paradigm offered by Rex Nettleford in his *Caribbean Cultural Identity* and explored in greater depth in the book he co-edited with Vera Lawrence Hyatt, *Race, Discourse, and the Origin of the Americas.*

3. Edouard Glissant states that "not knowing this totality [of history] is not a weakness. Not wanting to know it certainly is. Consequently we imagine it through a poetics; this imaginary realm provides the full-sense of all these always decisive differentiations" (*Poetics* 154).

4. I borrow the term "negative sublime" from Dominick LaCapra, who has critiqued the emergence of the negative sublime in literature and criticism about the Holocaust (*History and Memory*).

5. Carl Pederson claims that a simple look at recent fiction about slavery is enough to conclude that "The Middle Passage emerges as more of a bridge than a breach, a space-in-between where memory entails reconstructing the horrors of the voyage westward and retracing the journey of Africans to the Americas" (43). My book, *Postslavery Literatures in the Americas*, argues that the impact of slavery's history has generated an extraordinary outpouring of parallel literary expression throughout the Americas.

6. It is for this same reason that there is some tension in my own terminology of a "New World" poetics, as opposed to perhaps a more specifically postslavery poetics. One might argue that the term pays homage to the European perspective of the apparent "newness" during the "discovery" of the Americas. I use the term to argue for the irrevocable changes that the European arrival initiated, for better or for worse, among a diversity of peoples and that have shaped modernity in the hemisphere. Although I invoke the broader context of all of the Americas, I wish to consistently bring the term into correspondence to the specificities of Plantation America that link

the U.S. South to areas southward. I do so because I suspect that tentative applications beyond the strictly geographic boundary of slavery may also be insightful.

7. Glissant explains that it is impossible for historical knowledge not to become infected by the oblivion it tries to vanquish in its activity: "the stubborn determination of analytical thought makes it possible to continue infinitely this perspective of deferral. Really, however, it is only the human imaginary that cannot be contaminated by its objects. Because it alone diversifies them infinitely yet brings them back, nonetheless, to a full burst of unity. The highest point of knowledge is always a poetics" (*Poetics* 139).

8. For example, Wolfgang Binder's explanation for the paucity of direct references to the Middle Passage in African American literature is that "the need seems to be felt to fully claim one's American territory, to assert one's birthright on that side of the ocean" (554–55). He underestimates the centrality of the Middle Passage in the literature he examines (not to mention various literatures outside the United States that might have more completely informed his discussion) and misreads the signs of its absent history that haunts the entire narrative of Toni Morrison's *Beloved*. He mistakenly concludes that the novel focuses "on African American history during Reconstruction and after, with slavery time as a base determining to a considerable degree the (historical) present. [The novel does not give] the middle passage particular emphasis" (554). Binder fails to see Morrison's point in *Beloved* that the Middle Passage and other legacies of the unspeakable lie at the very heart of African American experience. Precisely because the Middle Passage is unspeakable, incapable of being represented, it can only be indirectly referenced and felt. This kind of thematic focus thus undermines its own intentions to find the Middle Passage in literature, because it looks at poetic language as merely a language of information, rather than a language of allegory (see Morrison's "Unspeakable Things").

9. See Tate's "New Provincialism." Barbara Ladd has also written that "nationalism sought to stabilize place as background for a drama of national progress" (56).

10. For examples of this recent emphasis on the interdependency of black and white literatures in the United States, see Morrison's *Playing in the Dark*, Eric Sundquist's *To Wake the Nations*, and Henry Wonham's edited collection *Criticism and the Color Line*.

11. Barry Lopez, a nature writer from the United States, senses this connection between recovering a sense of place and the impulses of postcolonialism: "the real topic of nature writing, I think, is not nature but the evolving structure of communities from which nature has been removed, often as a consequence of modern economic development. It is writing concerned, further, with the biological and spiritual fate of those communities. It also assumes that the fate of humanity and nature are inseparable. Nature writing in the United States merges here, I believe, with other sorts of postcolonial writing, particularly in Commonwealth countries" (8).

12. Wendell Berry, for example, writes that for the typical American citizen, "geography is artificial; he could be anywhere, and he usually is" (53). Berry traces this crisis of contempt for place to the very beginnings of New World colonial history: "at the same time that they 'discovered' America, these men invented the modern condition of being away from home. . . . [T]hey arrived contemptuous of whatever existed before

their own coming, disdainful beyond contempt of native creatures or values or orders" (54–55).

13. I have discussed in greater detail the ironies of a sense of place in relation to nature writing in the United States and in Derek Walcott's work in my essay "A Postcolonial Sense of Place and the Work of Derek Walcott."

14. I am indebted to Juan Gelpí's argument about the perpetuation of paternalism in Puerto Rican literature. He writes, "If one of the foundational myths with which our literary history has armed itself is trauma—the wound, the fissure of colonialism—our critical discourse, then, is going to dedicate itself to sealing or healing this fissure; it will try to cure it" (8). James Cox similarly argues that regionalism, such as in the South, depends paradoxically on the fact that "regions are always ending. That is the fate of their imaginative space before the ever-encroaching Union" (783).

15. Michael Kreyling has argued that the invention of identity means "keeping history at bay" (xii). He provides a keen account of the ways in which literature and literary criticism in the South served to "invent" southern identity much in the way Benedict Anderson argues national identities are "imagined communities." Kreyling's argument leaves one wondering, however, how the "forgetting" that has enabled the invention of the South can be effectively identified or recalled without presuming the same epistemological power to make the South, its history and identity, transparent, even if it is now only an "imagined" entity. I would suggest that the power of his argument would be enhanced by a cross-cultural approach to the invention of the South against the background of hints of other "souths" *to the south*, accounts of which were deferred or repressed in that invention.

16. See, for example, Carolyn Porter, Hortense Spillers, and Kaplan and Pease.

WORKS CITED

Alonso, Carlos J. *The Spanish American Regional Novel: Modernity and Autochthony*. New York: Cambridge UP, 1990.

Arnold, A. James. "*Créolité*: Cultural Nation-Building or Cultural Dependence?" *(Un)Writing Empire*. Ed. and introd. Theo D'haen. Amsterdam, Netherlands: Rodopi, 1998. 37–48.

———. "The Erotics of Colonialism in Contemporary French West Indian Literary Culture." *New West Indian Guide* 68.1 and 2 (1994): 5–22.

Barnes, Fiona R. "Dismantling the Master's Houses: Jean Rhys and West Indian Identity." *International Women's Writing: New Landscapes of Identity*. Ed. Anne E. Brown and Marjanne E. Goozé. Westport, Conn.: Greenwood, 1995. 150–61.

Bernabé, Jean, Patrick Chamoiseau, and Raphael Confiant. "In Praise of Creoleness." Trans. M. B. Taleb-Khyar. *Callaloo* 13.4 (autumn 1990): 886–909.

Berry, Wendell. *The Unsettling of America: Culture and Agriculture*. San Francisco: Sierra Club, 1996.

Binder, Wolfgang. "Uses of Memory: The Middle Passage in African American Literature." *Slavery in the Americas*. Ed. Wolfgang Binder. Würzburg: Königshausen und Neumann, 1993. 539–64.

Bröck, Sabine. "Postmodern Mediations and *Beloved*'s Testimony: Memory Is Not Innocent." *Amerikastudien* 43.1 (1998): 33–49.

Buell, Lawrence. *The Environmental Imagination: Thoreau, Nature Writing, and the Formation of American Culture.* Cambridge, Mass.: Belknap P of Harvard UP, 1995.

Cox, James. "Regionalism: A Diminished Thing." *Columbia Literary History of the United States.* Gen. ed. Emory Elliott. New York: Columbia UP, 1988. 761–84.

De Certeau, Michel. "History: Ethics, Science, and Fiction." *Social Science as Moral Inquiry.* Ed. Norma Haan, Robert Bellah, Paul Rabinow, and William Sullivan. New York: Columbia UP, 1983. 125–52.

Faulkner, William. "The Bear." *The Portable Faulkner.* Ed. Malcolm Cowley. New York: Penguin, 1977. 197–320.

Gelpí, Juan. *Literatura y paternalismo en Puerto Rico.* Río Piedras: Editorial de la Universidad de Puerto Rico, 1993.

Glissant, Edouard. *Caribbean Discourse: Selected Essays.* Charlottesville: UP of Virginia, 1989.

———. "Creolization in the Making of the Americas." *Race, Discourse, and the Origin of the Americas: A New World View.* Ed. Vera Lawrence Hyatt and Rex Nettleford. Washington: Smithsonian Institution P, 1995. 268–75.

———. *Poetics of Relation.* Trans. Betsy Wing. Ann Arbor: U of Michigan P, 1997.

Guillén, Nicolás. *Obra poética. 1922–1958.* Ed. Angel Augier. La Habana: Editorial Letras Cubanas, 1985.

Handley, George B. "A Postcolonial Sense of Place and the Work of Derek Walcott." *ISLE* 7.2 (summer 2000): 1–23.

———. *Postslavery Literatures in the Americas: Family Portraits in Black and White.* Charlottesville: UP of Virginia, 2000.

Handley, William. "The House a Ghost Built: *Nommo*, Allegory, and the Ethics of Reading in Toni Morrison's *Beloved*." *Contemporary Literature* 36.4 (1995): 676–701.

Harris, Wilson. "Oedipus and the Middle Passage." *Crisis and Creativity in the New Literatures in English.* Ed. Geoffrey V. Davis and Hena Maes-Jelinek. Atlanta, Ga.: Rodopi, 1990. 9–21.

———. "A Talk on the Subjective Imagination." *New Letters* 40 (1973): 36–48.

Hegel, Georg Wilhelm Friedrich. *The Philosophy of History.* Trans. J. Sibree. New York: Colonial, 1900.

Hyatt, Vera Lawrence, and Rex Nettleford, eds. *Race, Discourse, and the Origins of the Americas: A New World View.* Washington: Smithsonian Institution P, 1995.

Kaplan, Amy, and Donald E. Pease, eds. *Cultures of United States Imperialism.* Durham, N.C.: Duke UP, 1993.

Kreyling, Michael. *Inventing Southern Literature.* UP of Mississippi, 1998.

LaCapra, Dominick. *History and Memory after Auschwitz.* Ithaca, N.Y.: Cornell UP, 1998.

Ladd, Barbara. "Dismantling the Monolith: Southern Places—Past, Present, and Future." *South to a New Place.* Ed. Suzanne W. Jones and Sharon Monteith. Baton Rouge: Louisiana State UP, 2002. 44–57.

Lopez, Barry. "We Are Shaped by the Sound of Wind, the Slant of Sunlight." *High Country News* 30.17 (14 Sept. 1998): 1, 10–11.

Lyotard, Jean-François. *Heidegger and "the Jews."* Trans. Andreas Michel and Mark S. Roberts. Minneapolis: U of Minnesota P, 1990.

Miller, J. Hillis. *The Ethics of Reading: Kant, de Man, Eliot, Trollope, James, and Benjamin.* New York: Columbia UP, 1987.

Morrison, Toni. *Beloved.* New York: Plume, 1988.

——. "Nobel Lecture." *Georgia Review* 49.1 (spring 1995): 314–30.

——. *Playing in the Dark: Whiteness and the Literary Imagination.* New York: Vintage, 1992.

——. "Unspeakable Things Unspoken: The Afro-American Presence in American Literature." *Criticism and the Color Line: Desegregating American Literary Studies.* Ed. Henry B. Wonham. New Brunswick, N.J.: Rutgers UP, 1996.

Nettleford, Rex. *Caribbean Cultural Identity.* Los Angeles: Center for Afro-American Studies and UCLA Latin American Center, 1978.

Pedersen, Carl. "Sea Change: The Middle Passage and the Transatlantic Imagination." *The Black Columbiad: Defining Moments in African American Literature and Culture.* Ed. Werner Sollors and Maria Diedrich. Cambridge, Mass.: Harvard UP, 1994. 42–51.

Porter, Carolyn. "What We Know that We Don't Know: Remapping American Literary Studies." *American Literary History* 6.3 (fall 1994): 467–526.

Radway, Janice. "What's in a Name? Presidential Address to the American Studies Association, 20 November, 1998." *American Quarterly* 51.1 (1999): 1–32.

Renan, Ernest. "What Is a Nation?" *Nation and Narration.* Ed. Homi Bhabha. New York: Routledge, 1990.

Rhys, Jean. *Wide Sargasso Sea.* New York: Norton, 1975.

Romine, Scott. *The Narrative Forms of Southern Community.* Baton Rouge: Louisiana State UP, 1999.

Spillers, Hortense, ed. *Comparative American Identities: Race, Sex, and Nationality in the Modern Text.* New York: Routledge, 1991. 1–25.

Sundquist, Eric J. *To Wake the Nations: Race in the Making of American Literature.* Cambridge, Mass.: Belknap P of Harvard UP, 1993.

Tate, Allen. "The New Provincialism." *Essays of Four Decades.* Chicago: Swallow Press, 1968. 535–46.

Walcott, Derek. *The Bounty.* New York: Farrar, 1997.

——. "The Caribbean: Culture or Mimicry?" *Journal of Interamerican Studies and World Affairs* 16.1 (February 1974): 3–13.

——. *Collected Poems 1948–1984.* New York: Farrar, 1992.

——. *What the Twilight Says: Essays.* New York: Farrar, 1998.

Welty, Eudora. "Place in Fiction." *The Eye of the Story: Selected Essays and Reviews.* New York: Random, 1990. 116–33.

Wonham, Henry B., ed. *Criticism and the Color Line: Desegregating American Literary Studies.* New Brunswick, N.J.: Rutgers UP, 1996.

Zamora, Lois Parkinson. *The Usable Past: The Imagination of History in Recent Fiction of the Americas.* New York: Cambridge UP, 1997.

KIRSTEN SILVA GRUESZ

Delta *Desterrados:* Antebellum
New Orleans and New World Print Culture

When contemporary New Orleanians press a comparison between their city and Paris, it is to magnify that French influence, which continues—nearly two centuries after Napoleon sold off the land of King Louis—to be its most marketable commodity. Touting New Orleans as the most exotic place to which one can travel without crossing an ocean or a border, the city's tourism industry buys and sells good times (*laissez les bon temps rouler*), old times (*le Vieux Carré*), and a temporary escape from Time (one official nickname is the City that Care Forgot). But my reference to Walter Benjamin's famous essay intends, rather, to invoke a different simulacrum of Paris: *el París hispano*, the distant center of much of Latin America's intellectual life well into the twentieth century. To a lesser degree, antebellum New Orleans also served as a significant locus of Spanish-language cultural activity in the Americas. Since the nineteenth century, New Orleans has appeared to most of its Latin American visitors and immigrants as a resonantly *familiar* space, less alien—by virtue of its climate, religion, and ethnolinguistic diversity—than the rest of the *yanqui* North. The city's very geographical liminality, its strategic position in the midst of what Joseph Roach calls "the circum-Caribbean," suggests it as a particularly fruitful place from which to reexamine the ideological process of "southering" that has shaped both northern views of the U.S. South and U.S. views of Central and South America in general.

NEW ORLEANS, CAPITAL OF THE
(OTHER) NINETEENTH CENTURY

Particularly since the city's occupation during the Civil War but beginning well before then, New Orleanians have perceived themselves as the targets of northern anxieties about southern difference, particularly but not exclusively about racial difference. As has been amply documented, nineteenth-century New Orleans epitomized the most vilified forms of southern racial violence: first as the endpoint of that feared movement "downriver," the infamous New Orleans slave market; then as the site of the worst manifestations of Reconstruction-era resistance to northern sovereignty. Placed in a position of hierarchical dependency on northern and midwestern manufacturing by the end of the century, New Orleans became increasingly associated in the national imaginary with the contagion (and potential containment) of a suspect developmental backwardness, a hovering chaos, presumed to be endemic to *all* southern space. New Orleans thus defies a fixed location in the geographical imaginary: it evades the frames of U.S. nationalism, as well as their affiliated divisions into regional characteristics, more powerfully than perhaps any other major city. Instead, it serves instead as a kind of conduit point—not only between Gulf and River, North and South, East and West, but also between polarized characterizations of Self and Other: it can be made to figure both as the epitome of southern difference and as an exceptional case within it.

At the same time, New Orleans suggests a reconfiguration of hemispheric imaginaries as well. The notion of New Orleans as the point of overlap between two Souths, situated between different but not entirely incommensurate worlds, became a civic marketing tool during the 1940s and 1950s, when trade with Central and South America was given new priority and the slogan "New Orleans: Gateway to the Americas" greeted visitors at the airport. (In a sign of the new vogue for globalization, the slogan was recently updated to "New Orleans: Linking the Americas to the Globe.") But the city's positioning between Anglo and Latino political entities, languages, and knowledge structures cannot ultimately be reduced to the celebratory emblem of a bridge or gate. For Latin Americans and Latinos writing from or about New Orleans, the city also symbolizes the instantiation of political positions associated, rightly or wrongly, with the U.S. nation-state: expansionism, military interventionism, economic and cultural imperialism. Jefferson Davis's 1848 comment to the U.S. Senate that "the Gulf of Mexico is a basin of water belonging to the United States" expressed not only the potency of southern expansionism during the antebellum years but also New Orleans's inevitable role as a nexus of U.S. desires to wield power within the circum-Caribbean (Brown 29). Rather than a "bridge" between the Americas, then, New Orleans may be better understood as a contested borderland, a "*trans-frontera* contact zone" of different vectors of cultural, political, and economic activity, to borrow José David Saldívar's contemporary formulation (12). A detailed reading of the Spanish-language newspaper *La Patria*—published in New Orleans at a pivotal moment in hemispheric relations, that is, the U.S.-Mexican War and the enthusiasm it spawned for further territorial adventurism in the Yucatán, Central America, and Cuba through the early 1850s—reveals that the Hispanophone print community in this prototypically southern city shaped an early pan-Latino subjectivity, whose discursive and political possibilities were in turn foreclosed by Anglo-American expansionism.[1]

Opening its mouth to the major inland shipping route of the North American continent, the Mississippi, New Orleans swiftly became the most significant point of transit between the northeastern states and the western territories after its incorporation into the United States by the Louisiana Purchase of 1803. It had the fourth largest population among U.S. cities and was the nation's second busiest port: a prototypical location for the sort of diverse and unruly community that Mary Ryan identifies in her revisionist study of nineteenth-century public spheres (22–23). With its once substantial population of *gens libres de couleur* and its vital French culture disrupting dominant codes of national affiliation to create hybrid cultural spaces and alternative aesthetic possibilities, New Orleans was always one of the most linguistically and racially diverse cities in the United States. The tremendous influx of Anglo-Americans from the North during the 1830s, as well as a flood of immigrants from Ireland and Germany in the late 1840s and 1850s, altered the balance of power of the once dominant Creole class without really displacing them. The population self-identifying as "Creole" had incorporated a good number of Spanish speakers during the thirty years of Spain's rule, and afterward Louisiana became one of the destinations of choice of refugees from Cuba and Saint-Domingue fleeing the chaos of the Haitian revolution.[2] Like Havana, to which it bears a more than superficial resemblance, the port of New Orleans was a nexus of trade in goods and slaves, smuggling, piracy, capital ventures, immigration and emigration, troop movements, filibustering adventurers, and travel between the eastern U.S. states and points southward.

Midcentury New Orleans was thus, fundamentally, a *Caribbean* city, strategically positioned within the transportation and communications system of the Gulf of Mexico's half-moon, linked to Cuba, Puerto Rico, Santo Domingo, and Mexico's Gulf Coast and Yucatán. Joseph Roach nicely describes it as "a circum-Caribbean cosmopolis with old family fortunes and colonial architecture already in various stages of decay (more like Venice, say, than Dodge City), through which the commerce of the nation's regions and the world's nations passed" (179). Roach's *Cities of the Dead* illumines the city as a space in which African ritual practices, distilled through their peregrinations across the Atlantic, were absorbed by the sponge of a dominant Anglo-American culture through a process he labels "surrogation": a process of domestication, whitening, and concealment. Such instances of transculturation occurred in tandem with patterns of commercial exchange—most notoriously, traffic in the emblematic commodities of sugar and slaves, although one could add cotton, tobacco, salt pork, and coffee with perhaps less symbolic richness.[3] While Roach focuses on performances of music and movement that preserve African communal memory through surrogation, I am interested in the city's role in directing traffic in *information* and in the way Hispanophone print culture impressed itself into subsequent polemics—as well as into poetics in the greater Latin Caribbean.

Expatriates and émigrés from around the Caribbean and Spanish America would have found New Orleans the least alienating city in the nation. It had a substantial population of Spanish speakers, and many among these groups knew French and thus could get by without speaking a word of English. Accordingly, in the years following Mexican independence, many of the liberal enemies of Iturbide and then Santa Anna went into exile there, including José Antonio Mejía and Valentín Gómez Farías (from 1834–1835 and again in 1840–1845). From New Orleans, they raised funds and volunteers to aid the Texan revolt against Santa Anna's centrist regime, although both later participated in various Mexican governments; Gómez Farías reluctantly served as Santa Anna's vice-president during the years of the U.S. invasion. Later, the exiled ex-governor of Oaxaca, Benito Juárez, lived in the city for nearly two years, where he made a living rolling cigars (or, by other reports, selling fish in the French Market) while plotting the 1854 Plan de Ayutla with Melchor Ocampo and other key figures of the Reforma (Hamnett 51–53). Equally significant were the constant comings and goings of Cubans—loyalist tradesmen with a strong allegiance to the mother country; separatist agitators such as Cirilo Villaverde, author of the classic antislavery novel *Cecilia Valdés*; and a group of poets who would likewise use literature to foment sentimental outrage when they published the pathbreaking anthology *El laúd del desterrado* (The Exile's Lute) in 1858: Pedro Santacilia, Leopoldo Turla, Miguel Teurbe Tolón, and especially José Agustín Quintero, who eventually settled permanently in the city as an editor for the *New Orleans Daily Picayune* and authored its famous dueling code (Montes-Huidobro 129–72).

Like the Francophone Creoles, with whom they shared a neighborhood in the French (as opposed to "American") Quarter of the city, these exiled writers or *desterrados* identified nostalgically with a homeland that for them froze in time at the moment in which they left it. The French and Spanish together forged a community oppositional to Anglo-American dominance, but at the same time, as the sectional conflict over slavery intensified, other alliances developed between the Cuban separatists—most of whom were doubtful that slavery could or should be abolished on the island—and the southern slaveholding aristocracy. The movement toward Cuban annexation attained its greatest strength among both U.S. and Cuban constituencies with the New Orleans-based Narciso López filibusters of 1850–1851, which were in turn strongly affected by the outcome of the Mexican invasion. New Orleans was favored as a launching point for southern-led filibustering: while William Walker may be most famous for this, Pierre Soulé, one of the city's most prominent citizens, masterminded several filibustering expeditions while his political rival, John Slidell, was responsible for the disastrous 1845 attempt to purchase California cheaply from the Mexican government. Central America—particularly the northerly zone extending through Nicaragua, El Salvador, and Honduras—and southern Mexico, between the Yucatán Peninsula and Chiapas, were sites of intense interest to investors with stakes in building a transisthmian canal and/or railroad that would be nearer to the port of New Orleans than the Darien Straits. Later in the century, the New Orleans-based Louisiana Tehuantepec Company enlisted the region's weightiest political figures—successive rival senators Soulé, Slidell, and Judah P. Benjamin—in an almost successful bid to carve a canal through Mexican territory. Thus the city fostered initiatives that would contribute to Latin America's subjugation as well as those that sought its independence.

Each of these events was thirstily covered by the vibrant and multilingual print culture of New Orleans, which reached global as well as local and national audiences. The first Spanish-language newspaper in the United States, *El Misisipí*, was founded there in 1806, and prior to the Civil War at least twenty-three periodicals in Spanish were published in the city, making it the undisputed capital of Hispanophone print production.[4] (New York, the nearest contender, had only thirteen.) Most of these papers, like their English counterparts, came and went, leaving few traces, but among those that survive one can trace the shifts already witnessed in Spanish-American attitudes toward the rising Anglo-American world order. *El Telégrafo*, in 1825, praised the freedom of speech that could be found in the new republic, in contrast to the autocracy and chaos of Europe. The longer-lived *L'Abeille* (*The Bee*) and its ideological opponent, *L'Avenir du Peuple*, both printed Spanish-language sections throughout the 1830s; by 1840 nearly half the contents of the latter were in Spanish. The democratic *Abeja* strongly defended both Creole and cosmopolitan interests, claiming to be "batallando contra estas gentes" ["battling those people"] who, in their view, wanted to exclude from the city and country "el que no habla y piensa como ellos" ["whoever does not speak or think like them"]. Some Hispanophone papers were even international in scope: for at least the first six months of 1844, for example, the venerable liberal weekly *Diario del gobierno de la República Mexicana* was published in New Orleans—a case of an institution, rather than an individual, in exile. Villaverde founded a paper called *El Independiente* in New Orleans in 1853, of which no copies survive; it probably looked much like *La Verdad*, a separatist organ based in New York from 1848 to 1852, which evolved into *La Revolución* as its editors moved away from their earlier support of annexation (Carbonell 151). But the printed artifact that left the most textual traces was *La Patria*, which was published consistently, albeit with two name changes, from 1845 to 1851. Within its pages, competing visions of *cubanidad* and *mejicanidad* were imagined and fiercely defended against and through each other, interpellated through transactions with a yanqui culture whose imperial designs were becoming increasingly readable during that decade and a half.

Of course, due to its geographical advantages, New Orleans was pivotal in U.S. print culture as well. Since the city was a logical transfer point for settlers, supplies, and arms moving westward into Texas, New Orleans journalists served as primary filters of news of the Lone Star Republic from the 1830s onward. The war with Mexico was the first war to be covered by modern journalistic techniques in both Americas, and the highly competitive New Orleans dailies thrived on their proximity to the center of action and officer's gossip; they developed an impressive communications infrastructure of express couriers via horse, steamboat, and railway, as well as the rudimentary but fast-spreading technology of the telegraph. The Whig *Picayune* also put its own reporters on the field, foremost among them its founder, George Wilkins Kendall, who would later write a popular illustrated history of the war (Reilly, "War Press").[5] The press competed to see who could get dispatches from the front to the Northeast most quickly, which earned them considerable respect among even the chauvinistic New York papers, which often reprinted the stories verbatim. The hawkish views of the *Picayune* and the *Delta* reflected those of most Anglo-American citizens of New Orleans, who—with their economy bolstered by the large-scale movement of men and matériel passing through the city—became the most enthusiastic backers of the war in the nation. However, it was *La Patria*, with its reporters inside and outside Mexico and with access to other Spanish-language sources, that frequently scooped the other New Orleans papers, and its updates were widely disseminated; however, the editors' distinctly anti-expansionist perspective on the war was not (Reilly, "War Press" 82; Reilly, "Voice of Dissent" 91).[6]

Founded as *El Hablador* (The Gossip, or The Talker, or The Tattler) by Victoriano Alemán and the Louisiana-born Eusebio Juan Gómez in 1845, *La Patria* was the most ambitious and ultimately significant Spanish-language publication in the U.S. during the period, read apparently even by President Polk (Reilly, "Voice of Dissent" 333). First published as a triweekly, then briefly as a daily, and finally as a biweekly, *La Patria* was listed as one of the five largest-circulation papers in the 1850 city business directory.[7] Although circulation figures are as difficult to estimate as the number of Spanish speakers in antebellum New Orleans, the paper at its height claimed a subscriber's list of 800 and aimed to expand to reach a Spanish-speaking audience in the United States that it estimated at 30,000 (327). At the outset Gómez and Alemán were openly optimistic and idealistic about the influence they hoped the journal would have. The tone of those early issues of *El Hablador* is self-consciously literary, indeed verging on the precious, as in this excerpt begging for subscribers: "Nuestro principal objeto es el de poner al *Hablador* tan cuco, que no haya hombre, mujer, joven ni vieja, niño ni anciano, blanco ni negro, grande ni chico, que no se enamore hasta los tuétanos de él" ["Our primary object is to make the *Hablador* so adorable that there won't be a man or woman, youth or elder, child or old man, white or black, big or small, who won't fall in love with it right down to the marrow"] (1 Jan. 1846).

When the paper was retooled as *La Patria* in January 1846, it had a new subtitle, *Organo de la población española de los Estados Unidos*, and a more solemn editorial voice.[8] This would seem to suggest that the paper was directed at Spaniards, yet a self-advertisement reprinted in every issue that spring implies that the adjective describes *language*, not nationality. The editors repeatedly stressed, "La población española de Nueva Orleans es indudablemente la más variada de cuántas existen no sólo en esta ciudad sino en toda la Unión" ["the Spanish population of New Orleans is undoubtedly one of the most diverse not only in this city but in the whole of the Union"]; this diversity, they felt, would extend the paper's cultural reach. In the next paragraph, they speak of the necessity of having a paper to represent the interests of "las poblaciones Hispano-Americanas," by which they seem to mean those who intended to live for the long term among *los americanos*—"hoy, que vemos ante nosotros un brillante porvenir" ["today, we see before us a brilliant future"] (*La Patria*, 4 July 1848). At some point during 1847, the front-page masthead became visually more provocative, featuring an image of a seated man before an inkwell (an emblematic *letrado*), flanked on his left by a U.S. flag with the banner of Spain behind it and on his right by the flags of the United States and Mexico. Accordingly, news items from west of New Orleans (Mexico and Texas) and from its east (Spain and its Caribbean empire) vie for importance with news from the northeastern United States. Only by turning toward *each* of these cardinal points could *La Patria* fulfill its stated mandate to report "todo aquello que concierna a nuestra nación" ["everything that concerns our nation"] (*La Patria*, 4 July 1848), for—as the three flags suggest—that patria is a no-man's land, a nonspecific site of affiliation and identification.

If the newspaper's title refuses any final affiliation with one particular country, its implicit definition of the homeland becomes more and more oriented toward linguistic rather than statist connotations: "No es menos para todas las Américas donde se conserva aún, y donde se conservará siempre el hermoso idioma castellano" ["It's intended as well for *all* the Americas where the beautiful Castilian language is preserved, and always will be"] (*La Patria*, 4 July 1848). By mid-1846, this print community was already well shaped. *La Patria* advertised that it had seven sales agents in bookstores and publishing offices in New Orleans; one each in Terre aux Boeufs, Baton Rouge, Mobile, and St. Augustine; two each in Havana and Matanzas; one each in Trinidad, Puerto Príncipe (now Camagüey), and Santiago de Cuba; and throughout México and the Yucatán, including in Veracruz, Mexico City, Jalapa, Orizaba, Puebla, Tampico, Mérida, and Campeche. Later issues listed sales offices in San Antonio, Matamoros, Corpus Christi, and New York (*La Patria*, 9 Apr. 1846). Both the imagined and the material realms circumscribed by *La Patria*, then, encouraged a dual identification with the transnational space of Spain and Latin America *as well as* with fellow Spanish-speakers repatriated to—or at least established in—the United States; it opened up the possibility of a Latino vision of common interest among communities spread very widely across North America on the basis of their shared language and culture.

READING *LA PATRIA*: HISPANOPHONE PRINT CULTURE AND MEXICAN EXPANSIONISM

Gómez in particular seems to have occupied a relatively mobile position with respect to the Spanish and English spheres of influence. In 1846 he was nominated as General Winfield Scott's field interpreter and quickly commissioned as a lieutenant colonel in the U.S. army. Almost immediately, however, there were allegations that he had leaked to the Mexicans secret plans divulged in a meeting with Scott, and his appointment was suddenly rescinded on the grounds that he, the Louisiana-born editor of *La Patria*, was un-American; he was, ironically, a man without a patria (Reilly, "Voice of Dissent" 332–36). According to Reilly, as Alemán and Gómez maintained an antiwar stance, relations between this "órgano de la población española" and the sphere of Anglophone journalism grew increasingly strained, even to the point where their mail deliveries of international newspapers were apparently stolen.

From the beginning, well before Taylor's troops had begun their march to Texas, Gómez and Alemán expressed outright suspicion of U.S. designs on the rest of the hemisphere and particularly on northern Mexico: "La extraordinaria facilidad con que se ha concluido y celebrado la anexión de Tejas; la poca o ninguna resistencia que ha hallado el pueblo Norte-Americano en esta agregación, ha hecho que el Gobierno como los demás individuos que componen esta grande Unión, hayan llegado a figurarse que todo lo pueden" ["The astonishing ease with which the annexation of Texas was brought about and celebrated, and the little or no resistance to this annexation that the North Americans have encountered, has brought it to pass that the Government, like the rest of the individuals who compose this great Union, has come to believe that it can do anything it wishes"] (*La Patria*, 10 Dec. 1846). *La Patria*'s coverage of the war can be only incompletely represented since a crucial year, 1847, is missing, but a representative sampling of editorials during 1846 and 1848 shows that Gómez and Alemán maintained a consistent rhetoric about the newspaper's aims and probable political consequences, pointing to the contradiction between the *theory* of U.S. republicanism and the *prac-*

tice of interventionism. On 4 June 1846, shortly after the declaration of war, they wrote that, following a relatively long period of postrevolutionary peace, "se ve la mitad del Nuevo Mundo envuelta en una guerra lastimosa y poco provechosa" ["we now witness half the New World involved in a shameful and less-than-advantageous war"]. They argue that the invasion of Mexico is a violation of the nation's founding principles: "Entonces rechazaban a los invasores y resistían al tirano opresor que trataba de dominarlos cruelmente: pero hoy se nos presenta el reverso de la medalla, y esta gran nación que tachaba siempre la injusticia de los usurpadores, sigue las huellas y los malos ejemplos de otras naciones dominadas por la tiranía y la injusticia" ["At that time, the United States repelled the invaders and resisted the tyrannical oppressor who tried to dominate them cruelly: but today we see the reverse side of the coin, and this great nation, which has always criticized the injustices of usurpers, is now following the steps and the bad examples of other nations dominated by tyranny and injustice"]. As great admirers of republican principles, they argued, "no podemos ver con indiferencia que despojándose de su sinceridad y sanos principios, adopte el pueblo de los Estados Unidos doctrinas tan contrarias a las de su institución. . . . La guerra con Méjico . . . se llevará a cabo de la manera más sangrienta, es una guerra injusta y peligrosa a la Unión Norte-Americana" ["we cannot look on with indifference as the people of the United States, robbing themselves of their sincerity and their healthy principles, adopt doctrines so contrary to their founding. . . . The war with Mexico . . . will be brought about in the bloodiest possible manner; it is an unjust war and dangerous to the North American Union"].

Although *La Patria* was not alone in the New Orleans print community in opposing the war, it was, ironically, in the company of northern abolitionists—strange bedfellows given the fact that *La Patria* supported the plantation system that was the economic motor of the Deep South and of Cuba, although it did not fabricate fearful scenarios of racial violence or amalgamation in the way that some other southern periodicals did. Although self-identified as a Whig paper, *La Patria* preferred relentless analysis to partisan politics, acknowledging the political instability in Mexico and spewing abundant criticism of Santa Anna. Very early on, in a particularly trenchant psychological observation, it suggested that the average citizen's enthusiasm for the invasion of Mexico emerged more from a sense of restless, romanticized adventurism than from the more obvious economic and territorial gains. " 'Marchemos a la ciudad de Méjico,' dicen los americanos, creyendo que tan fácil es el hacer como el decir. . . . Bien se sabe que la mayor parte de los que se empeñan en llevar a cabo la guerra lo hacen guiados por la necia esperanza de que han de hallar innumerables riquezas en las minas, y ricas alhajas en los templos, que tratan de loquear en el momento que lleguen a ellos. ¡¡Qué ilusión!! ¡Qué moralidad!" ["Let's march all the way to the City of Mexico! the Americans say, believing it's as easily said as done. . . . It is well known that the majority of those who insist on prosecuting this war are guided by the ridiculous hope that they are going to find untold riches in the mines, and rich jewels in the temples, talking this nonsense as soon as they get there. What a fantasy! What morality!"] (4 June 1846).[9]

Even after the end of the war, Gómez and Alemán continued to reiterate their interpretation of the founding fathers' interdiction against launching wars to "conquistar territorios, o quitar a otras naciones los que las pertenecen" ["conquer territories or take from other nations the territories that belong to them"]. Yet on the same page, they endorse the Whig presidential ticket, which featured the popular U.S.-Mexican War hero Zachary Taylor, which must have stuck in their collective craw. But the alternative—a Democratic Party splintered along sectional lines, with the offshoot Free-Soil Party's strong connections to northern abolitionists—was too interested in pursuing "la anexión de la Isla de Cuba, el Canadá y lo que ha quedado a los mejicanos de las Californias" ["the annexation of the Isle of Cuba, Canada, and what remains to the Mexicans of the Californias"]. A graphic box on top of the editorial read, in various decorative typefaces, "Cass, Cuba, California, Canada" to scare off readers from voting for the Democratic candidate, Lewis Cass (14 Nov. 1848).

La Patria encouraged its readers to see events in the hemisphere not as national issues but as part of the global distribution of postcolonial power, pointing out similarities between what had happened in Mexico—a territorial "purchase" forced on a weakened, divided, impoverished nation in order to further U.S. expansionist ends—and what might occur in Cuba, which had been the object of purchase offers for three decades. Thus, though they joined other papers in condemning as "barbarous" the Mayan Indians who rebelled against the Yucatecan elites when the Guerra de Castas broke out, they supported central Mexican governance of the fractious state rather than encouraging U.S. intervention—a tactic enthusiastically backed by some in Congress. Although expansionists such as John O'Sullivan had been spreading the gospel of continentalism and a "Caribbean empire" for some time, *La Patria* pointed out this commonality to mobilize a defensive sensibility in its readership, broadening the geographical imaginary of individuals toward a more unified political agenda based on opposition to U.S. incursion into Spanish America.

If Gómez and Alemán, like all newspaper editors during this highly partisan era, envisioned their mission as a form of political activity, they never lost sight of its broader aim of cultural ambassadorship, particularly of the need to react against the harsh stereotyping of their "race" that the war had encouraged by convincing Anglo-Americans that Spanish speakers were as lettered, diverse, and intelligible as they—if not more so. "Antes que se publicara *La Patria*, la opinión general que se tenía en los Estados Unidos de los Españoles . . . era en extremo desfavorable según lo probaban los escritos que casi diariamente aparecían en los periódicos del idioma nativo. Y aun nosotros mismos hemos tenido la ocasión de afirmar esa opinión durante nuestros viajes en esa época por los Estados del Sur, Este, y Norte, y desde 1845 hemos estado combatiendo las más denigrantes ideas que se veían manifestadas en los periódicos de la Unión" ["Before *La Patria* began publishing, the general opinion in the United States regarding Spaniards . . . was extremely unfavorable, according to the writings that appeared almost daily in the journals in the Spanish periodicals of that time. And we ourselves have had the opportunity to verify this judgment during our travels through the states of the South, East, and North, and since 1845 we have been fighting against the most denigrating ideas that one sees manifested in the newspapers of the Union"] (*La Patria*, 18 May 1849).

In addition to this resistant and *corrective* activism, Gómez and Alemán for a brief period in 1848 struck out in a novel direction: they enlisted a Dr. Matthewson, former editor of the Veracruz paper *El Genio de la Libertad*, to edit a new English-language section for *La Patria*—a trajectory, perhaps the first in the history of Latino journalism, that reversed the trend of Spanish papers evolving out of sections in established English ones. The prospectus for the newly bilingual paper published on 14 April classifies English as a necessary language because of its practicality, with Spanish identified as the language of reason and aesthetics.

In presenting to the public this miniature specimen number of *La Patria* in the English and Spanish language, we shall state, in as brief a manner as possible, the prominent imperatives that induce us to make the change, and the principal advantages that are likely to result from it. There have been causes in operation for some time past, are in operation now, and will continue in operation hereafter, which will in the future materially affect our relation, not only with Mexico, but in all probability with the people of Spanish America. The intercourse between the English and Spanish inhabitants or races of the Western Hemisphere is, in a political and commercial, as well as in a social and moral point of view, becoming every day more intensely interesting, and hence it is of the utmost importance for them to study and understand each other's language in order to live in peace and harmony as occupants of the same Continent, and members of Great Republics. This useful and desirable object can be attained, to a certain extent, through the medium of our paper; for the leading articles will appear in each number both in English and Spanish, and the translations will be rendered as literal as the spirit of the language will admit. Our English subscribers will, therefore, have the opportunity of becoming familiar with the Spanish language in all its native beauty, simplicity, and uniformity; and our Spanish subscribers will have a like opportunity of becoming familiar with the English language, which, though Lord Byron calls it the

> —Harsh northern, whistling, grunting guttural
> Which we're obliged to hiss, and spit, and sputter all,

yet, is unsurpassed, if not unequaled, in its practical application to useful purposes.

This bilingual experiment envisions facing-page translations as an instrument of painless assimilation, yet in this case the assimilation is to be mutual. The target is not simply the subject population but *both* the "English and Spanish inhabitants or races of the Western Hemisphere." Moreover, its plea for mutual comprehension takes place within the dominating context of the paper's tradition of imposing an unrepentantly Latin American perspective on local events.

Here, English is the alien language, an imported British "grunting guttural" that one is obliged to maintain as a commercial lingua franca. This English prospectus (which only *seems* like an awkward translation; it does not appear in Spanish) insisted that the paper would continue to be "independent and impartial," "neutral but not passive" in politics. That month, the English page praised the appointment of Stephen Kearney, who had marched across the southwest to occupy New Mexico, as the new governor of Veracruz; yet it also describes the war as "the North American *invasion*," in keeping with *La Patria*'s traditional usage. The experiment with the dual-language edition—which was noted by the Anglophone papers—lasted only a few months, for reasons that seem self-evident, given their rivals' avid support of adventurism in the hemisphere.[10]

The paper's defense of *hispanidad* clearly brought them at times into adversarial relations with other local papers: the *Delta*, the *Picayune*, and later the *Crescent*, which included Walt Whitman as an editorial staff member. One pointed editorial castigates periodistas que pasan en sociedad por hombres sensatos, y que se cree están en su sano juicio porque redactan un periódico *en inglés,* que bien visto, es la simpleza más grande del mundo, cuando se hace por los medios ordinarios o *de costumbre* en los Estados Unidos, los cuales consisten en recortar trozos de aquí y allá y llenar así columnas enteras. Naturalmente unos hombres que no saben hacer otra cosa que redactar un papel con *tijeras* y *almidón,* en el momento que se ven obligados a salir de su esfera y tomar la pluma para tratar de un asunto de gravedad, desbarran como locos, y dicen más disparates que palabras; ¡y cuidado que los señores ingleses necesitan bastantes palabras para decir pocas cosas!

journalists who pass in society as sensible men, and who believe that they have great judgment because they edit a newspaper *in English*— which, seen properly, is the simplest thing in the world when it's done the ordinary or *customary* way in the United States, which consists of cutting up pieces from here and there and filling entire columns this way. Naturally, some men who don't know how to do anything else besides edit a paper with *scissors and starch* start talking nonsense like crazy men as soon as they have to leave their little sphere and take up a pen to deal with a serious matter, or they fire more shots than words— and watch out, because Englishmen need plenty of words to say very little! (*La Patria,* 13 Oct. 1848)

The English language is here associated with imitation (cut and paste) and excess (taking too many words to say too few things). At least as practiced by journalists, English tends toward mere linguistic accumulation rather than quality; it even encourages militarism ("más disparates que palabras"). Gómez and Alemán's critique of a particular linguistic prejudice—the reflexive tendency of those who possess the dominant language to assume that theirs is the only language of persuasion and art—does not undo their complicity in upholding racialized chattel slavery, but it does indicate a powerful awareness of the workings of less obvious forms of domination and subordination.

CENSORSHIP AND THE HISPANOPHONE CULTURE OF THE BOOK

In an ironic but highly suggestive twist of fate, when Whitman—one of those scissors-and-paste journalists (and, for that matter, scissors-and-paste *poets*)—left the *Crescent* and Crescent City late in May 1848 to return to New York, his successor at the paper was William Walker—the same William Walker who would go on, in the following decade, to invade Baja California and Sonora with a group of filibusters, then arrange his own election as president of Nicaragua before being executed by a Honduran firing squad. Sometime that year, Victoriano Alemán, co-founder of *La Patria*, argued with Walker in the street over some political difference, and the two came to blows. Walker, according to witnesses, came out ahead, leaving Alemán bruised and battered (Reilly, "Voice of Dissent" 337). Presumably this was the end of whatever "friendship" had existed between *La Patria* and the *Crescent*, and the effort at ambassadorship through Matthewson's bilingual edition failed around the same time. But it was far from the end of *La Patria*'s efforts to consolidate a transamerican print community based in New Orleans in the language that that bilingual prospectus had praised for its "native beauty, simplicity, and uniformity." To the contrary, Gómez and Alemán moved the paper out of J. Sollée's multilingual print offices at 137 Chartres Street and set up their own quarters in Exchange Alley with the intention of branching out into book and magazine publishing and retailing. The Imprenta de la Patria announced its first local production in 1848: a nicely made engraved literary and satirical magazine, *La Risa: Enciclopedia de Estravagancias*, which shared some materials with a publication of the same name in Madrid. The editors wrote separate introductions to the first issue of the "Edición Americana." Gómez's begins with a humorous meditation on the proverb "He who runs with the wolves learns to howl" and concludes that living among the "yankis," fondly referred to as "two-legged wolves," has taught him eccentricity.

> ¿En qué de las cuatro partes del globo se encuentra una nación más extravagante que la gran confederación de treinta Estados con distintas leyes para cada uno, y de costumbres, usos, y abusos tan diametralmente opuestos? ¿en qué rincón del mundo pudieran hallarse reunidas más extravagancias que las que se ven amontonadas en esta ciudad de la *media-luna*? Muchos creerán tal vez que la mitad de sus habitantes son lunáticos, o que todos sean semi-lunáticos, por la simple razón de apellidarse (a causa de la curva que forma el río a su frente) la ciudad de la *media-luna*. Y quizás no falte quien se imagine que ésta es tierra de Moros . . . y si tal pensaren no van por cierto muy errados.

> In which of the four parts of the globe can one find a nation more extravagant than the great confederation of thirty States, each one with different laws and with customs, uses, and abuses so diametrically opposed? In what corner of the world could one discover more

eccentricities in one place than those that pile up in this city of the *crescent moon*? Many people might believe that half of its inhabitants are lunatics, or that all are half-lunatics, for the simple reason of its being called (due to the curve that the river forms at its head) the *Crescent City.* And perhaps there will be others who imagine that this is a land of Moors . . . and if they think so, they're not so far wrong. (Gómez 4)

From this perspective, the heterogeneity of the various states in North America is not (as Whitman felt) a source of strength but rather a bewildering chaos capable of inducing madness. Jokes about the "wolves" who howl under the Louisiana moon provide great fodder for Gómez, the more lively writer of the two editors; his introduction skewers the strange and "wild" customs of the Crescent City. To him, all *Luisianeses* are Yankees, an appellation that the city's Creoles, Anglo-Southerners, and polyglot European immigrants might reasonably have protested. In this riff on the city's nickname Gómez is punning, of course, on the etymology of *lunatic*, the association of wolves with the moon, and the crescent shape of the scimitar by which Spain and Europe symbolized Islamic Moors in their historic confrontations. But who are the Moors here? In one sense, they are the boorish, aggressive, Anglo-Americans wielding scissors or swords; but in another sense, this would seem to be an archly racist reference to the city's substantial black and mixed-race population. The jesting, dismissive categories of "moros" and "yanquis" allow Gómez to position this literary experiment within the interstices of an already marginal place: he puns on the claim that the enterprise was inspired by the *espíritu yanki* (Yankee spirit); the spirit of speculation and risk-taking, as well as the "espíritu embotellado, *alias* whisky." Alemán's own introduction follows this up with a direct swipe at "periodistas 'a lo Yanky' es decir, periodistas de tijera y engrudo, de *corta* y *pega*" ["journalists in the Yankee style, which is to say, journalists of scissors and paste, of *cut and paste*"]. This contrast between original composition and news-gathering on the one hand and imitation or "thievery" on the other was a recurring theme in *La Patria*'s depiction of Anglophone print culture.

In addition to publishing a few issues of *La Risa*, Gómez and Alemán tried to make their office a center of Hispanophone culture. Issues of *La Patria* advertise meetings of a *Sociedad Literaria Española* at an address next door in Exchange Alley, and an announcement asking readers to identify themselves for a planned *Directorio de los españoles residentes en los Estados Unidos* headquartered at the paper's offices appears in the 14 June 1849 issue. While I have found no trace of this directory, the advertisement is intriguing because it again takes "un español" to mean a Spanish *speaker* rather than a Spanish national, since it also asks contributors to state their native country. They occasionally published lists of letters waiting at the post office with Spanish, Italian, or Portuguese names, so apparently their outreach extended to those communities as well; in one typical issue there are sixty such names. They sold books at the Librería La Patria as well, although ads also appear for another Librería Española at 141 Chartres Street. By 1849, *La Patria* had apparently established a particularly close relationship with a New York weekly, *El Correo de los Dos Mundos*, of which no copies survive. As the 2 May issue states, subscribers to one could get a discount on the other, as well as a special price on "todas las publicaciones literarias que se hagan en una u otra oficina" ["all the literary publications that are produced in either office"]. The ad goes on to announce that the New York paper's publishing arm had just issued Spanish translations of Lamartine's *Confidences* and *Rafael*.

The publications issuing from the Imprenta La Patria itself were eclectic: they include a translation, done locally, of a biography of "General" Tom Thumb, whose tour through New Orleans they had covered enthusiastically. Also heavily advertised in every issue of *La Unión* in 1851 (that is, after the paper's second renaming) was their translation of the labor agitator and Catholic convert Orestes Brownson's *Opiniones de un Anglo-Americano acerca de la expedición Cubana y los anexionistas*, published as a twenty-page pamphlet, which was apparently later distributed in Havana and New York. Translated from an article in *Brownson's Quarterly Review*, it takes direct aim at the "partidarios de las expediciones piráticas contra Cuba" ["supporters of the piratical expedition against Cuba"], the so-called *Lopecistas*. If advertisements in the paper are a fair indication, the books they sold at the office were mainly novels and scientific and educational tomes from Madrid and Paris, shipped through Havana, and they were fairly expensive.

Perhaps out of frustration with the limitations Spain imposed on the free spread of print culture, perhaps out of a deeper ideological disagreement, Gómez and Alemán openly flouted the colonial censorship policy in Cuba. Early issues of *El Hablador*, for instance, had featured a serial novelette, *Los misterios del Cerro en la temporada de 1844: Historia que parece cuento* (The Mysteries of Cerro in the Year 1844: A True Story that Seems Fictional), a roman à clef styled after Eugène Sue's outrageously popular *Mystères de Paris* and set in a neighborhood on the outskirts of Havana. Particularly revealing, in light of the rift that would later develop between the paper's editors and the Cuban separatists, is that (as a footnote explains) the story was written by an *habanero* but was not publishable in the Caribbean colonies; thus, *El Hablador* thumbed its nose at the censor by presenting the tale unexpurgated and declared its hope that the story would make it to the islands (1 Jan. 1846; Fornet). Given the fact that packets from Veracruz, Mérida, and other independent cities in Spanish America frequently called in New Orleans, it is likely that some books proscribed in Cuba were sold either at Librería La Patria or elsewhere in the city, perhaps at one of the other multilingual Vieux Carré print offices like Levy or Sollée that distributed the paper.

As vehemently protective of Spanish culture and of Spanish-American territorial integrity as the paper's editorials were, on an early occasion the editors published a poem expressing strong anti-Spanish sentiments, the anonymously authored "La Patria," which appeared on 2 April 1846. That "homeland" is neither Spain nor Mexico, the possible patrias alluded to by the flags flanking the Stars and Stripes on the cover illustration, but *Cuba.* As if to encourage a connection to the title of the newspaper, the word *patria* appears repeatedly in majuscules or italics throughout the poem—as are words describing specifically Cuban fauna, like *tojosa* (a kind of Cuban dove), *sinsonte* (mockingbird), *colibrí* (a hummingbird), *palma* (understood to be the royal palm José María Heredia had already enshrined as the national symbol), and *cocuyo* (lightning bug). Some of these terms had entered Spanish from Taíno and thus signaled a move toward an indigenously Cuban literary language. "La Patria" is a classic Cuban exile poem in that it identifies the homeland with birth and motherhood, and all their sacred sentimental associations; it starkly contrasts the cold northern weather to the paradisical climate of the Caribbean; and it closes with a plea to maintain "el sublime fuego / de patria y de libertad" ["the sublime fire of homeland and liberty"].[11]

¿Qué importa que, esclava imbécil,
te aduermas libre de penas
al ruido de las cadenas
de tu bárbara opresión? . . .
¿Qué importa que gimas ora
si sabes, patria querida,
que ha de llegar una aurora
de celeste resplandor?
Y entonces, aunque el tirano
truene de rabia y de ira,
será el mundo americano
del viejo mundo Señor.

What does it matter, dumb slave,
that you fall asleep, carefree,
to the sound of the chains
of your barbarous oppression? . . .
What does it matter that today you cry out
as long as you know, beloved country,
that someday a day will dawn
with celestial brilliance?
Then, although the tyrant
should thunder in anger and ire,
the American world will become
lord of the Old World.

The old revolutionary analogy of republics in chains—the idea of colonial subjection of the *mundo americano* by the *Viejo Mundo*—sets up the prophetic conclusion of the poem. But to utter this analogy in the context of New Orleans only deepens the inherent paradox of its inability to acknowledge racialized chattel slavery as the foundation of the very plantation economy its imagery romanticizes (see Poyo 1–19; Foner 11–29).[12]

Throughout the paper's history, Cuba maintained a significant presence in both the literary and editorial sections—not surprising, given that country's proximity to New Orleans. But the paper's early critiques of the Cuban censor were heavily modulated over the years. "La literatura cubana," an unsigned article that appeared on 13 October 1848, laments the fact that it will not be circulated on the island despite the fact that "ni una sola idea tiene, como se verá, que respire conspiración, libertad, ni ninguno de esos fantasmas que son la pesadilla de los gobernantes de la Isla" ["it doesn't have a single idea, as you will see, that breathes conspiracy, liberty, or any of the ghosts that are the nightmares of the island's governors"]. The fact that Cuban writing "ocupa ya un lugar distinguido en la república de letras" ["already occupies a distinguished place in the republic of letters"] ought to grant it the same autonomy and access to public speech that other such "republics" have: "A pesar del sistema de censura que se empeña en apagar el desarrollo de las luces—sistema conocido en todo el mundo, y sobre el que no queremos hacer ninguna reflexión por ser una materia demasiado importante y cuyo tratado no tendrá fin—brilla el talento de sus hijos" ["Despite the system of censorship that persists in snuffing out the progress of enlightened thought—a system known throughout the world, which we don't want to reflect on further because it is too important a matter and dealing with it here would go on forever—the talent of her sons shines brilliantly"]. A condemnation of censorship emerges from this sentence, only to be locked between dashes that refuse to argue the point, thus effectively repressing the issue with the same force as the censor. A full-blown critique of colonial policy or outright support of Cuban independence, however, would have alienated the Spanish mercantile interests (who presumably formed the base of their readership) in the city and beyond.

Although most of the poetry published in *La Patria* is less overtly political than "La Patria," the fact that the paper reprinted José de Espronceda's "El 2 de mayo," a poem that protests the "dissolute court of the monarchs," suggests its broader allegiance to the liberal spirit of European reform. *La Patria* regularly republished items from a cosmopolitan array of journals and magazines with which they had an exchange relationship (despite Alemán's insistence on the originality of their journalism, the exigencies of filling four folio pages two or three times per week made that a necessity). Some of the selections in their "Poesías" corner were attributed to newspapers in Madrid, Havana, or Mexico. One of the most regular sources was *El Siglo XIX* of Mexico City, the most important liberal organ of the time; it was edited at one point by Guillermo Prieto, whose strongly anti-Yankee and pro-Enlightenment views are in keeping with Gómez's and Alemán's. Gómez and Alemán seemed to make up for their implicit support of—or rather, failure to protest fully—the regime of colonial censorship in Cuba by vigorously circulating controversial print matter from elsewhere. With regard to Mexico, the paper was as scornful of Iturbide's failed empire as of Santa Anna's militaristic populism. One issue reprints a scabrous satirical poem entitled "Contra-Danza de Santa Anna," attributed to the St. Augustine-based *Florida Herald* (*La Patria* 15 Sept. 1848). During the war months they printed a poem allegedly written by a Spaniard in the album of a well-known actress, Doña Isabel García Luna de Santa María, lamenting her decision to leave Madrid for a position at the Teatro Nacional in Mexico.

> Isabel, ¿qué beneficio
> esperas de un edificio
> que se ha quedado sin *Tejas?*
> ¡Tanto va (y a sus oídos
> cuando a aquella playa abordes,
> lo dirán hondos gemidos)
> de los Estados discordes
> a los *Estados Unidos!*

> Isabel, what good
> can you expect from a building

that finds itself with no roof?
So much (and when you board
for that distant shore,
you'll hear heartfelt sobs)
goes from those discordant states
to the *United States*! (*La Patria*, 5 July 1848)

The "building" which finds itself with no *tejas*, the traditional roof tiles, is a reference to the loss of Texas, the uppermost "roof" of a once far-reaching territory, the Estados Unidos de México, that seemed to be caving in on its center. The author's teasing remark that the actress, too, might be "annexed" to the United States seems only half in jest.

THE LÓPEZ FILIBUSTERS AND THE QUESTION OF CUBAN ANNEXATION

The Hispanophone sphere of print culture summoned into being by Gómez and Alemán thus freely mingled works from and about Mexico, Spain, and the Spanish Caribbean. Yet the political undercurrent to this imagined print community—the utopian ideal of a pan-Latino subjectivity united by its opposition to U.S. expansionism—was undone by the question of Cuba. Gómez and Alemán walked a tightrope with their stated aim of tolerating differences within the Spanish-speaking community, particularly over the question of Cuba; they insisted that their paper upheld general opinions, not individual ones. However, there seemed to be no consensus on what those opinions were. It is ironic, given *La Patria*'s vigorous attempts to build a sense of solidarity with the broader imagined community of Spanish speakers and to forge connections to the Anglophone sphere of print, that the paper was eventually undone by differences over Cuba within its community, fomented by a very different kind of Hispano-Anglo alliance: the movement to annex Cuba. Prior to the 1860s, many Cuban patriots concluded that between two evils—incorporation within the U.S. or a fragile independence subjected to constant threats from foreign powers—the former was preferable. Gómez and Alemán at first seemed incredulous that, after the lamentable example of Mexico, any among their constituency could be in favor of the annexation of Cuba: "*Sabemos positivamente* [que] hay en esta ciudad (y creemos que hay otras de la Unión) cierto *club* que se reúne en cuando para tratar de la extensión de la República, y que en ese *club* se ha hablado de la 'conveniencia' de poseer la Isla de Cuba; pero si no estamos mal informados, el tal club se compone exclusivamente de AMERICANOS, y no creemos haya entre ellos un solo cubano o español: pero si todos los que proyectan la *Independencia* o la *Anexión* de la Isla de Cuba son semejantes a los de Nueva Orleans, creemos que hay poco que temer" ["We know for sure that there is in this city (and believe there are others in the Union) a certain *club* that meets occasionally to discuss the extension of the Republic, and that in this *club* they have spoken of the "convenience" of owning the isle of Cuba; but if we are not misinformed, this club is composed exclusively of AMERICANS, and we don't believe that there is among them a single Cuban or Spaniard—but if all those who are plotting the *Independence* or *Annexation* of that island are like the fellows in New Orleans, the patria is safe"] (*La Patria*, 18 Oct. 1846). In a flight of fancy, the editorial then gleefully imagined that if the United States were to attempt to gobble up the island of Cuba, Uncle Sam would suffer terrible indigestion (a prophecy that has proven true again and again). However, by dismissing annexation as a Yankee scheme and refusing to leave open a space of principled opposition to Spanish rule in Cuba (a stance their own choice of literary materials would seem to support), the editors effectively excluded from participation in their public sphere many of those who should have been among the paper's greatest supporters: a group of young romantic revolutionaries who wrote patriotic poetry in the model of Espronceda, Lamartine, and Larra. Many of these writer-activists joined forces in New Orleans with the Narciso López filibusters, memorializing his "martyrdom" in *El laúd del desterrado*.

Although López, a Cuban property-owner born in Venezuela, has the distinction of having been the first to plant the current national flag on Cuban soil, his legacy is the subject of considerable historical controversy. (That flag, incidentally, was designed in New Orleans by an exiled poet and first flown in that city; a neglected memorial on Poydras Street bears witness to this forgotten fact.) López spoke of his two "liberatory" expeditions as an execution of the will of the Cuban people, but his troops in fact found few supporters on the island; and for most post-1959 Cuban historians, López's "revolution" is hopelessly tainted by its association with U.S. slaveholding interests. Through the late 1840s and in various attempts to raise funds and men, López's political beliefs shifted with the winds: originally an abolitionist, for instance, he came to support the maintenance of slavery on the island in order to win over southern planters.[13] The two López filibusters in 1850 and 1851 became less about Cuban autonomy than they were about adventurism (many of his "freedom-fighters" were bored mercenary veterans of the U.S.-Mexican War) and about economic speculation; many investors expected the U.S. Treasury to pay off the Cuban bonds López sold at the same high rate as it had paid to Texas bondholders. Strongly backed by John O'Sullivan, who coined the phrase "Manifest Destiny," López and his allies were familiar figures in the Anglophone press, both North and South: for a brief moment López's *filibusteros* were the vortex to which national debates over the sectional slavery conflict were drawn. Both expeditions were launched from New Orleans, and the *Crescent*—like the *Picayune* and the *Delta*—endorsed them with the same giddy enthusiasm it had brought to military interventions in Mexico and the Yucatán.

This forced *La Patria* into an increasingly extreme defense of the very colonial regime it was formerly willing to critique; the vitriol against "certain *clubs*" increased in intensity when the editors became aware that there were *cambiacasacas* (turncoats), as they called them, among the *raza española*. It is probable that *La Verdad*, the New York newspaper once edited by Villaverde and underwritten by O'Sullivan and Moses Beach, editor of the *New York Sun*, was widely distributed in New Orleans and acted as a competing Spanish-language voice to *La Patria* there.[14] Yet the paper's relations with the Anglophone newspapers were still cordial enough that Alemán's marriage to María Dolores García in the city cathedral was mentioned in all the major newspapers; the *Delta* even thanked Alemán for sending some wedding cake and champagne along with his announcement and wished the couple a "long life and happy union" (30 April 1850).

However, later that summer, López successfully guided his first expeditionary force, some 500 men, to Cuba by way of the Yucatán (an earlier group had been prevented from leaving the country by U.S. port authorities). The first incursion ended within a day, and on his return to the United States López was arrested for violating the Neutrality Act; his trial occupied the front pages of all the New Orleans newspapers. A master of self-promotion, López bartered this arrest into public outrage and managed to raise a stronger, richer army for a second assault in 1851. His troops held a position at Las Pozas for nearly three weeks before Spanish troops captured and executed López and one of his officers, Lieutenant John Crittenden, the nephew of a U.S. senator, in August. *La Patria* changed its name to *La Unión* in 1851, perhaps to clarify its ideological commitment to federalism, and added a new coeditor, but held firmly to its anti-interventionist stance. When word of the executions of López and Crittenden arrived and *La Unión* declared that the filibusteros had gotten the punishment they deserved, an angry mob burned down the offices and bookstore, nearly killing Alemán and destroying six Spanish-owned cafés, two tobacco shops, and the office of the Spanish consulate (Reilly, "Voice of Dissent" 325–26).[15] The loss of *La Patria* effectively foreclosed for decades the possibility of an oppositional Latino print organ positioned within the United States that could serve as the emblem and the material apparatus of an imagined community of Spanish speakers located both within the national sphere and across the hemisphere at large.

At stake in reimagining the diversity of nineteenth-century New Orleans and its "Latin" character to account for these Spanish-speaking and Latin American axes is not only the development of a Latino sensibility by way of print communities. To consider New Orleans as a center of Hispanophone cultural activity is to call into question the traditional geography of American studies, including its most recent turn toward revisionist regionalism and the critique of southering that impels the present collection of essays. Just as that critique requires one to interrogate the ways in which the South has served as the screen for various projections of *national* anxieties and desires—from romantic-exotic tropes of racial and cultural difference to extremes of violence to symbolic expulsion from the national body—so too does it involve an interrogation of "southern" space within *transnational* discursive contexts. As the example of *La Patria* suggests, New Orleans does not unilaterally epitomize some imagined South: to Central and South Americans, it stands in as *the North*, despite a familiarly "Latin" character to the city on which they all remark. This slippery ambivalence, this historically situational oscillation between imagined locators like South and North, center and periphery, promises to reveal much about the way in which the Ameri*cas* have been systematically repressed as the abjected Other of America in its singular usage as synonym for the U.S. nation-state.

NOTES

1. This essay is excerpted in part from chapter 4 of my book *Ambassadors of Culture: The Transamerican Origins of Latino Writing,* in which I argue that the U.S. national imaginary was *itself* constructed in the nineteenth century through repressed reference to, and rejection of, an Other America coded as dark, Catholic, backward, and linguistically alien. A crucial counterdiscourse emerged among the developing Spanish-language print communities that were regionally centered in largely rural border zones like Texas, California, and New Mexico, as well as in cosmopolitan exile hubs like New Orleans and New York. Notions of the public sphere as a source of nascent political identification and of the role of print culture in fostering such communities are theorized in the book's introductory chapter.

2. On race in antebellum Creole society, see Domínguez as well as Hirsch and Logsdon. Bell describes the impact of refugees from Santo Domingo on the Creole population and their intermarriage with *gens libres de couleur*; Bell also details the participation of those free persons of color in the Mexican wars of independence (49–63).

3. For other extended meditations on trans-Caribbean slavery and its links to New Orleans, see Gilroy, Curtin, and Paquette.

4. MacCurdy claims that there were a dozen Spanish periodicals in the city between 1840 and 1851, the period of greatest Spanish immigration and of filibustering activity (20). In the course of this investigation I found references to other periodicals not included in MacCurdy's definitive bibliography: in *La Patria* (18 Mar. 1849) there is a lengthy review of Spanish papers in the city preceding that publication. According to this article, there was a short-lived 1828 newspaper titled *El Español*; another called *El Misisipí*, published by Ramón Soler for several months between 1834 and 1835; a *Fénix* that published a few issues in 1843; and one "señor Cocco" gathered subscribers to a publication called *La Avispa* and invested in a press, but subscribers never received copies. "Vingut" (perhaps the Cuban Javier Vingut, who taught languages in New York and published there) produced *La Indiana* for a few months, and "el señor Quintana Warnes" published *El Padilla* for more than six months in 1845.

5. The democratic *Delta*, the middle-of-the-road *Crescent* (for which Walt Whitman wrote), and the *Commercial Times* were also, whatever their other editorial positions, so strongly hawkish that they were collectively called "The War Press of New Orleans." Kendall's history of the war was illustrated with the lithographs by the German Karl Nebel (who had last been to Mexico a decade before). There is a recurring advertisement in *La Unión* throughout 1851 for a "Historia Ilustrada de la Guerra entre los EEUU y Méjico" for sale at the Librería La Patria, but I cannot determine whether this was an actual translation of Kendall's text, an original history written in Spanish, or simply a Spanish ad for the English book.

6. In "Voice of Dissent" especially, Reilly has done a remarkable job of retracing the responses of English-language newspapers to the existence of *La Patria*. While this work is invaluable, it is based on only a few stray copies of the newspaper itself. Apparently he did not have access to the holdings of the Historic New Orleans Collection, which has on microfilm *El Hablador* for 1846; the entire runs of *La Patria* for 1846 and 1848; and the whole of *La Unión* from 3 January 1851 to 20 August 1851, just before the editorial offices were attacked and burned by a mob. While the crucial years 1847 and 1850 are still missing (there are stray copies from 1847 at the American Antiquarian Society, which I have not seen, and one at the Louisiana State Museum and Archives, which I have), it remains for a historian of journalism to return to this greater archive of primary sources and make another effort to write a more complete history than Reilly's or than I am able to do here.

7. See Cohen. Only three of the others were English; the French bilingual paper *L'Abeille* was an important presence up to the Civil War.

8. The article on 18 March 1849 giving an overview of the history of Spanish papers in New Orleans (see note 4) ends with the overriding moral "*de la importancia de sostener en esta ciudad un periódico español . . . sostener con decoro y energía los intereses de aquellos que se ven aislados,–puede decirse–en un país extraño*" ["*the importance of maintaining a Spanish newspaper in this city. . . . to uphold, with dignity and energy, the interests of those who find themselves isolated, one might say, in a strange country*"] (emphasis in original).

9. Johannsen and Merk, notably, interpret the broad psychological underpinnings of the U.S.-Mexican War from within the framework of romantic adventurism.

10. For instance, the *New Orleans Crescent*, which frequently announced its indebtedness to "our friends at *La Patria*" for news of the hemisphere, published this notice on the editorial page on 10 April: "LA PATRIA—(our country.) By an advertisement which will be found in another column, it will be seen that D. Juan Gomez has associated with him in the editorship of the Patria, Dr. Matthewson, formerly known as editor of the Vera Cruz 'Genius of Liberty.' The Patria will be enlarged to the medium size of the daily paper, and will be published in the future in Spanish and English. We wish that success to the enterprise which we have no doubt will attend it. We will again refer to the subject, when our columns are less crowded." But the *Crescent*'s identification of *La Patria* as a "friend" must have been vexed, given that Gómez and Alemán opposed annexation and adventurism, while M'Clure and Hayes, the *Crescent*'s editors took just the opposite stance, as of course did Walt Whitman, who was a staff member on that paper. Their editorials called Mexico a place of "anarchy and semibarbarism" populated by "animals" and denounced the crafters of the Treaty of Guadalupe Hidalgo for having "abandon[ed] three-quarters of our conquests" rather than having taken possession of all the territories south to the Sierra Madre as well as Mexico's lucrative Gulf ports (*Crescent* 11 March 1848, 1).

11. I have not yet been able to identify this poem as the work of any known Cuban writer; although it bears a strong resemblance to the works of the later *Laúd del desterrado* group, it cannot be found among their works. José María Heredia also had a poem titled "La Patria," on which this may be partially modeled, although its language is less pointedly "cubanized." Gómez de Avellaneda's "¡Al Partir!," which begins "¡Perla del mar! . . . ¡Hermosa Cuba!," is also a classic of the genre.

12. A similar logic of compromise informed liberal sentiment about slavery. Most found the institution distasteful but felt that abolition would bring civil chaos or a Haiti-like race war. On the contradictions of Cuban liberalism, see in general Martínez.

13. Chaffin reviews the historiograpy on 1–10. Foner labels López unsympathetically as a tool of southern slaveholding interests (41–66). Chaffin presents him, perhaps more interestingly, as a charismatic opportunist who possessed a genuine desire for Cuban self-rule but lacked the ability to perceive the severe ideological rifts within his own coalition.

14. Merk presents *La Verdad* as a sham mouthpiece for O'Sullivan and Beach, excluding the Cuban contribution almost entirely. Rodrigo Lazo, in "The Cuban Newspapers of New York" (unpublished ms.), powerfully contradicts that assertion.

15. The next Spanish paper in New Orleans, *El Pelayo*, appeared in September 1851 under the editorship of E. San Just. On a smaller scale than *La Patria* and *La Unión* and without their literary ambitions, surviving issues of *El Pelayo* contain ads for the remainder of the inventory of the Librería La Patria and list Gómez as a sales agent for various books and subscriptions. An anti-López poem titled "Invasión de la Vuelta-Abajo" appears in issue 1.29. The last extant issue was published in December 1851.

WORKS CITED

Bell, Caryn Cossé. *Revolution, Romanticism, and the Afro-Creole Protest Tradition in Louisiana, 1718–1868*. Baton Rouge: Louisiana State UP, 1997.

Brown, Charles Henry. *Agents of Manifest Destiny: The Lives and Times of the Filibusters*. Chapel Hill: U of North Carolina P, 1980.

Carbonell, José. "Evolución de la cultura cubana." *La poesía revolucionaria en Cuba*. Vol. 6. La Habana: Siglo XX, 1928.

Chaffin, Tom. *Fatal Glory: Narciso López and the First Clandestine U.S. War against Cuba*. Charlottesville: UP of Virginia, 1996.

Cohen, H. *Cohen's New Orleans Directory, including Jefferson City, Carrollton, Gretna, Algiers, and McDonough, for 1850*. Microform ed. New Orleans: Office of the Picayune, 1850.

Curtin, Philip D. *The Rise and Fall of the Plantation Complex: Essays in Atlantic History*. Cambridge: Cambridge UP, 1990.

Dabney, Thomas Ewing. *100 Great Years: The Story of the Times-Picayune*. Baton Rouge: Louisiana State UP, 1944.

Domínguez, Virginia R. *White by Definition: Social Classification in Creole Louisiana*. New Brunswick, N.J.: Rutgers UP, 1986.

Fornet, Alfonso. *El libro en Cuba: Siglos XVIII y XIX*. La Habana: Editora Letras Cubanas, 1994.

Gilroy, Paul. *The Black Atlantic: Modernity and Double Consciousness*. Cambridge, Mass.: Harvard UP, 1993.

Gómez, Eusebio Juan. "Introduction." *La Risa* 1.1 (1848): 3–6.

Gruesz, Kirsten Silva. *Ambassadors of Culture: The Transamerican Origins of Latino Writing*. Princeton, N.J.: Princeton UP, 2002.

Hamnett, Brian R. *Juárez*. London: Longman, 1994.

Hirsch, Arnold R., and Joseph Logsdon. *Creole New Orleans: Race and Americanization*. Baton Rouge: Louisiana State UP, 1992.

Johannsen, Robert Walter. *To the Halls of the Montezumas: The Mexican War in the American Imagination*. New York: Oxford UP, 1985.

Jumonville, Florence M. *Bibliography of New Orleans Imprints, 1764–1864*. 1st ed. New Orleans: Historic New Orleans Collection, 1989.

Kanellos, Nicolás. "A Socio-Historic Study of Hispanic Newspapers in the United States." *Recovering the U.S. Hispanic Literary Heritage*. Ed. Ramón Gutiérrez and Genaro Padilla. Houston: Arte Público, 1993. 107–28.

Kanellos, Nicolás, and Helvetia Martell. *Hispanic Periodicals in the United States, Origins to 1960: A Brief History and Comprehensive Bibliography*. Houston: Arte Público, 2000.

Kendall, John Smith. "Some Distinguished Hispano-Orleanians." *Louisiana Historical Quarterly* 18 (1935): 40–55.

MacCurdy, Raymond R. *A History and Bibliography of Spanish-Language Newspapers and Magazines in Louisiana, 1808–1949*. Albuquerque: U of New Mexico P, 1951.

Martínez, Urbano. *Domingo del monte y su tiempo.* La Habana: Unión de Escritores y Artistas de Cuba, 1997.

May, Robert E. "Young American Males and Filibustering in an Age of Manifest Destiny: The United States Army as a Cultural Mirror." *Journal of American History* 78.3 (1991): 857–86.

Merk, Frederick. *The Monroe Doctrine and American Expansionism, 1843–1849.* New York: Knopf, 1966.

Montes-Huidobro, Matías. *El laúd del desterrado.* Houston: Arte Público, 1995.

Paquette, Robert L. *Sugar Is Made with Blood: The Conspiracy of La Escalera and the Conflict between Empires over Slavery in Cuba.* 1st ed. Middletown, Conn.: Wesleyan UP, 1988.

Poyo, Gerald E. *"With All, and for the Good of All": The Emergence of Popular Nationalism in the Cuban Communities of the United States, 1848–1898.* Durham, N.C.: Duke UP, 1989.

Reilly, Tom. "A Spanish-Language Voice of Dissent in Antebellum New Orleans." *Louisiana History* 23.4 (1982): 325–39.

——. "The War Press of New Orleans." *Journalism History* 13.3–4 (1986): 86–95.

Reinders, Robert C. *End of an Era: New Orleans, 1850–1860.* New Orleans, La.: Pelican, 1964.

Roach, Joseph R. *Cities of the Dead: Circum-Atlantic Performance.* New York: Columbia UP, 1996.

Robin, Joseph Jay. "Creoles, Cotton, Calabooses." *The Historic Whitman.* University Park: Pennsylania State UP, 1973. 181–205.

Ryan, Mary P. *Civic Wars: Democracy and Public Life in the American City during the Nineteenth Century.* Berkeley: U of California P, 1997.

Saldívar, José David. *Border Matters: Remapping American Cultural Studies.* Berkeley: U of California P, 1997.

——. *The Dialectics of Our America: Genealogy, Cultural Critique, and Literary History.* Durham, N.C.: Duke UP, 1991.

JANE LANDERS

Slave Resistance on the Southeastern
Frontier: Fugitives, Maroons, and Banditti
in the Age of Revolution

Historians have long commented on the violent nature of the southeastern frontier in the eighteenth and nineteenth centuries. This was an era of revolutions and international intrigue, and from a European perspective the critical issue was territorial sovereignty. Many of the earlier historical treatments of the period adopt that focus and thus tend to underplay the role of nonwhite actors in the dramas.[1] However, these contests for empire also had important consequences for the region's slaves. All the Europeans employed their bondsmen, in one fashion or another, to advance their military goals, and in some cases these black soldiers were critical to the balance of power. Military service was one route out of slavery, but there were others. Slaves became adept at interpreting political events and manipulated them, when possible, to achieve freedom. The initiative and action of the slaves—their acts of resistance, flight, *cimarronaje* (creating fugitive communities in remote areas), and social banditry—also shaped the course of international, as well as local responses.

Although many slaves who remained on plantations did at times resist bondage, those who fled challenged the slave systems around them in more autonomous ways. Several viable options were open to a fugitive slave on the southeastern frontier. Taking advantage of a royal offer of religious sanctuary first offered in 1693, hundreds of runaways from South Carolina and Georgia made their way to St. Augustine before the end of the first Spanish regime in 1763. There they were given lands to homestead and arms to bear in defense of the Spanish Crown. The Spaniards even granted the fugitives a town of their own, Gracia Real de Santa Teresa de Mose, established in 1738. When English masters came seeking the return of their chattel, the Spaniards refused to return them, and this information clearly inspired more slaves to attempt escape. The most serious of the slave uprisings in the eighteenth century, the Stono Rebellion of 1739, occurred only one year after Mose's founding. Carolina slaves killed more than twenty whites, destroyed plantation properties, and gathered recruits along the road to St. Augustine, their stated destination. The English denounced Spain's provocative sanctuary policy, but neither diplomatic negotiations nor military action staunched the flow of runaways. In fact, it was not a one-way flow, for the Spaniards encouraged the freedmen to return and raid English plantations. The former slaves also formed an effective guerrilla force that the Spanish Crown regularly deployed against English and Native American expeditions from Carolina and Georgia (see Landers, "Gracia Real").[2] The battle at Mose, in which black and Native American allies helped rout invading forces from Georgia and Carolina, is generally acknowledged to have been the decisive factor in Oglethorpe's failure to take Florida in 1740 (Spalding 112, 114; TePaske 143). When the Spaniards evacuated to Cuba in 1763, their free black allies left with them rather than be returned to chattel slavery by their former masters (Landers, "Gracia Real" 29; Landers, *Black Society*).

During the twenty years the English ruled Florida (1763–1784), they established flourishing plantations manned by slaves imported from other southern plantations and from Africa. Blacks outnumbered whites in Florida two-to-one for most of the English period. Then, in the last years of the American Revolution, when first Charleston and then Savannah were captured by the Patriots, Loyalist planters flocked to East Florida. They brought with them an estimated 8,000–9,000 slaves, further skewing the racial makeup of Florida. The English eventually sought security in a slave code, but acts of resistance continued and unknown numbers of slaves still escaped English control to live in Native American or maroon communities.[3]

Early in the course of the Revolution, Virginia's royal governor, Lord

Dunmore, borrowed the tactic that had been so successful for the Spaniards, offering arms, freedom, and land to slaves who would enlist in the service of George III. Many took advantage of the offer and were freed, although most died of smallpox aboard Dunmore's ships. In other cases the British armies simply stole slaves. Thomas Jefferson estimated Virginia lost 30,000 slaves during Cornwallis's raid; David Ramsey estimated a loss of 25,000 in South Carolina; and Georgia was said to have lost seven-eighths of its total slave population (Ogg 276).[4] Black soldiers fought for the English in Virginia, South Carolina, Georgia, and finally in East Florida's provincial militia and Rangers. Lord Dunmore hoped to use his "Ethiopian" troops to seize Spanish possessions in West Florida and Louisiana—including critical ports such as Pensacola, Mobile, Natchez, and New Orleans—but these plans went unrealized. The Loyalists were defeated, and remnants of Dunmore's black forces, calling themselves soldiers of the King of England, took refuge in the woods and swamps along the Savannah River, much to the consternation of local planters.[5]

By the Treaty of Paris, the Spanish returned to Florida in 1784, and hundreds of slaves introduced by the English availed themselves of Spanish law to claim religious sanctuary in St. Augustine. As in the earlier Spanish period, these freedmen proved a valuable source of skilled labor and military reserves for the Spanish community. Once again Florida became a haven for runaways, and there were constant complaints from Anglo planters who claimed their very livelihood was threatened by the continued loss of slaves.

The frontier was even more unsettled by a group of men "without God or king" who had from the announcement of the cession, taken to raiding East Florida's riverine plantations for slaves and other "moveable property." The outgoing English government had declared these men outlaws, and even the new Spanish regime's offer of clemency did little to end the raids. Eventually Governor Juan Manuel de Zéspedes was forced to arrest or deport those bandits who did not leave of their own accord, but in the interim many slaves and probably some free persons of color were taken from Florida. The Georgians charged, and they were probably correct, that even more of their legally owned slaves were harbored by the Spanish.[6]

In 1790 the Spanish government finally yielded to the strong persuasions of Thomas Jefferson, the secretary of state for the new government of the United States, and abrogated the sanctuary policy.[7] Despite the diplomatic agreements ending sanctuary, tangled disputes over slave property continued for many years because the United States sought the return of all escaped slaves who entered Florida after 1783, while the Spanish Crown offered up only those who entered after the notice ending sanctuary had been posted in 1790. The U.S. government appointed James Seagrove to solicit the return of American slaves, or their comparable value, from the Spaniards, and Georgia's governor appointed his own representative, Thomas King, to assist in that effort.

Each side prepared lists of missing slaves, and while the English lists offer little more than the names and owners of the missing slaves, the Spanish lists offer interesting insights into the make-up of the slave community in East Florida. Most of the descriptions remark on the slaves' "country marks," such as scars on the cheeks and missing top front teeth, and on their supposed age, physical build, height, and skin color. Although some were specifically described as being natives of Angola and Guinea, even they were still said to be able to speak a variety of languages, and most spoke English. One woman, Gega, born in Georgia, spoke "regular Spanish" and very good English and "Mexican." The slaves included field hands and servants, as well as skilled craftsmen such as sawyers and carpenters, and none was valued at under 300 pesos. No value was given for Don Felipe Fatio's missing slave, Nero, because Fatio did not want money for him; Nero's parents had a large family on Fatio's plantation, and Fatio sought to reunite them.[8]

The abortive 1795 invasion of Florida by backwoodsmen recruited by the French revolutionary, Citizen Genet, created new strains on Florida-Georgia relations. It also led to even more disruption and dislocation on the Florida-Georgia border, and many more slaves were lost by both sides. The Spanish government embargoed slaves known to belong to rebels associated with the plot and temporarily halted the reciprocal return of slaves, but by 1797 the Spanish governor had returned thirty-seven of the forty-three missing slaves claimed by Georgian owners. These were apparently all that the Spanish had in custody, for Thomas King informed the Spanish governor he was pleased that the negotiations were settled so amicably.[9]

Not all runaways, however, were in the custody of the Spaniards, and because these maroons sought refuge in remote areas, they escaped repatriation. Although many historians have alleged that there was less slave resistance in the United States than in other slave societies, Herbert Aptheker's early work clearly documented the existence of at least fifty maroon communities in the South, dating from the late seventeenth century up to the Civil War. Because Aptheker's important study relied solely on English-language sources, even this number seriously undercounts the phenomenon.

Many maroon communities were located near water, which allowed access to riverine resources as well as escape by canoes and pirogues. In Georgia the maroons concentrated their communities along the Savannah River, where Lord Dunmore's "Ethiopians" also settled (Aptheker). In 1787 a joint force of South Carolina and Georgia militias, accompanied by Catawba Indian allies, spent some time searching for a sizeable settlement near Patton's Swamp, which they had determined to destroy. By chance they encountered some of the blacks in canoes, and exchanged fire. They gleefully and erroneously reported having killed the band's leader, Sharper, who later reappeared, as if from the dead. Eventually the militias stumbled on the blacks' hideout, killed the lookout, and proceeded with their attack on the stockaded settlement. Six of the unlucky maroons were killed outright, and more were presumed injured, by the "blankets . . . clotted with blood" they left behind. The attackers destroyed some twenty-one houses and took seven "boats" before heading home with the women and children they had taken prisoner. The next day, they encountered Sharper and eighteen members of his community, headed for the Indian nation, and another fight ensued. Once again, Sharper and some of the others were able to escape, although nine women and children were captured (*Independent Journal*). It is interesting to note that in 1787, a fugitive named Sharper and his wife, Nancy, were among those petitioning for sanctuary in St. Augustine.[10]

Although Sharper's community was broken up, other maroon settlements arose, and the problem of maroon banditry continued to unsettle the frontier. In 1797 United States Commissioner James Seagrove wrote the Spanish governor from Point Petre, "The notorious fellow, Titus, with some negroes from Florida, made their way along the seacoast until they got into the Savannah River and among the rice plantations where he was well acquainted. There Titus formed a party with some other outlying negroes who became very troublesome to the people by plunder and as a receptacle for runaways." Once again, an armed force was sent in after the maroons, with orders to kill those who did not surrender. Although they discovered and fired on Titus's band, most of the maroons escaped, "it being a very thick swamp." Some were captured and taken to the Savannah prison, but none were found dead, although the correspondent reported "a quantity of blood found on the ground." He added, "Parties are constantly after them and there is little doubt they will be taken or killed."[11]

Although Titus's followers were described as "negroes," in the tri-racial Southeast white colonists had always been equally, if not more, concerned about alliances among fugitive blacks and Native Americans, and it was standard practice among Europeans to try to prevent it (see Gallay). Black/Native American uprisings against the Spaniards date to 1525 when Lucas Vázquez de Ayllón attempted Spain's first settlement in North America at San Miguel de Gualdape, located somewhere between modern-day South Carolina and Georgia. That community, which included the first known contingent of African slaves in the present-day United States, was weakened by disease, starvation, death, and mutiny. The joint uprising of Native Americans and black slaves in 1526 sounded its death knell. The surviving Europeans straggled back to Santo Domingo, but at least some of the African slaves from that settlement stayed behind to live among their Native American allies. Similar black and Native American uprisings took place in other European colonies. Over the next three hundred years, the Spaniards, as well as the English and French, tried to regulate the separation of blacks and Native Americans. They also employed blacks as soldiers against hostile tribes to encourage enmity between them and paid Native Americans to capture or kill runaway slaves. Nevertheless, some nations, such as the Creek, regularly harbored the fugitives, and miscegenation further strengthened the bonds between these groups. When blacks and Native Americans defied Europeans and lived in villages together, they came under attack, and during periods of European conflict the danger was exacerbated (Landers, "Africans"; Wood 3–5; Willis).[12] Given the chaos arising from these circumstances, as well as the major population shifts that occurred as a result of the American Revolution and the consequent rise in abduction of blacks, it is not surprising that increasing numbers of blacks and Native Americans found themselves "outlaws" and formed maroon settlements together. Some of the amalgamated communities even included whites.

The supporters of William Augustus Bowles are a case in point. For almost twenty years this former Loyalist turned director general of the "State of Muscogee" maneuvered to achieve an independent Native American nation in the Southeast and to this end negotiated with government officials in the Bahamas, Quebec, London, Spain, Sierra Leone, and the United States. The quixotic Bowles is often dismissed for his grandiose schemes, which at one time included plans for the invasion and liberation of Mexico and Peru, and later involved a declaration of war against Spain; however, he attracted quite a following. Not only did he gather support from the Creek, Cherokee, and Seminole nations but from whites and blacks as well. Many of his contemporary observers, and indeed many later-day historians, saw Bowles as a self-interested scoundrel, but he maintained support among his black and Native American allies for close to two decades and must have spoken to their dreams or represented their perceived best hope for a free life in the face of Anglo domination of the Southeast.[13]

Inspired by audacious leadership and English support, in 1800 Bowles's followers began a series of raids on southeastern plantations, in a declared "war" on Spain. From Point Petre, U.S. Commissioner James Seagrove wrote the prominent East Florida planter and magistrate John McQueen, "There are several dreadful vagabonds with parties of Indian and Negroes now [following] Bowles for plunder and if opposed no doubt murder. Robert Allen, that noted young villain with three of the free Negroes from Lotchoway made their appearance near Colerain on Saturday last. Allen and two of his Negroes were taken and [were] under the care of the federal officials from that place, but from [thence] Allen made his escape into Florida where is his party of from twenty-five to thirty Indians, Negroes and infamous whites all of them direct from Bowles headquarters . . . with orders to plunder and break up all the settlements in Florida."[14]

Although he could spare no regular troops for the northern frontier, Governor Enrique White ordered John McQueen to arm his slaves and attempt to capture Bowles. The governor also employed his free black militia, augmented by black soldiers from Spanish Santo Domingo, on regular patrols to check the depredations, but still the raids continued. Major planters such as Francis Fatio, Josiah DuPont, and John McQueen himself were among those who lost slaves and property to Bowles's guer-rillas. Finally, after three years of war, Bowles was taken prisoner at a Native American congress and shipped in chains to Havana, where he died.[15]

The death of one man, however, did not signal the end of slave re-sistance in the region nor of the paranoia of the Anglo planters. When Georgian "Patriots," led by George Mathews and encouraged, not very covertly, by the U.S. government, seized Amelia Island in 1812 and de-clared the "Republic of Florida," one of their principal complaints was that the Spanish lured away slaves and then had the gall to arm and use them against their former masters. They made direct allusions to the ferocious slave revolt in Santo Domingo and promised no quarter to any blacks taken under arms. Governor David Mitchell warned, "They have armed every able-bodied negro within their power. . . . [O]ur southern country will soon be in a state of insurrection." The Patriot leader, John McIntosh, echoed these sentiments when he wrote Secretary of State James Monroe, "Our slaves are excited to rebel, and we have an army of negroes raked up in this country, and brought from Cuba to be con-tended with . . . the whole province [Florida] will be the refuge of fugitive slaves; and from thence emissaries . . . will be detached to bring about the revolt of the slave population of the United States."[16]

The poorly supplied and supported governors of Florida tried frantically to pursue a diplomatic resolution to this new threat, but in the meantime they again employed their black and Native American allies as guerrillas on the frontier. The Seminole nation was already wary of the land-hungry Georgians, and the Spanish governors sent black emissaries to fan their distrust. Many runaway slaves from Georgia had found refuge among the Seminoles led by Chief Payne and his successors. They lived in a sort of feudal arrangement with the Seminoles, residing in their own villages, and providing their "masters" with annual tribute and military service. They intermarried with the Seminoles and became their trusted interpreters and advisors in war councils. These "village Negroes," as they were called in English-language sources, recognized that Georgian rule would return them to slavery, and so they became among the fiercest enemies of the Patriot forces. The Spaniards stood to lose their colony, the blacks their freedom, and the Seminoles their rich lands and cattle herds.

The Spaniards astutely capitalized on this convergence of interests. While the governor maintained Spanish neutrality by remaining in St. Augustine, blacks and Native Americans successfully harried the Patriots. They raided their camps, burned and sacked their plantations, stole away and armed their slaves. They also waged psychological warfare, engaging in scalpings and mutilations, which horrified the invaders. In one important incident Lieutenant Prince Whitten, an escaped slave from Georgia, led a group of about fifty to seventy blacks and a handful of Native Americans in a well-executed ambush of a Patriot supply convoy that was escorted by twenty U.S. Marines. Prince's force attacked the supply convoy at night, taking down Marine Captain John Williams, his sergeant, and the wagon horses in the first volley. The next morning they transported their wounded and the sorely needed supplies to St. Augustine. The demoralized Patriot forces began to pull back. When later that month a force led by Colonel Daniel Newnan failed to break up the Native American towns near Lotchoway and was mauled by King Payne's polyglot warriors, the invasion was spent.[17]

Despite the failure of the Florida Republic, it was not long before the United States perpetrated other violations of Spanish sovereignty, and it followed an interventionist foreign policy for the remainder of the decade. These actions were motivated, in part, by territorial ambitions, but another driving force was the fear that Britain would displace the weakened Spanish regimes in the Southeast. During the War of 1812 the British had encouraged slaves to desert plantations and enlist in British service, just as they had during the American Revolution. In 1815 they employed some of these black troops in an attack on the village of St. Mary's in Georgia (Abernethy 108–9). Although the war officially ended shortly thereafter, peace did not immediately follow.

In 1814 Colonel Edward Nicholls had established a large number of fugitive slaves from Georgia, Mobile, Pensacola, and St. Augustine, and Native Americans allied to the British at a small fort at Prospect Bluff on the Apalachicola River, about twenty-five miles north of the Gulf of Mexico. An estimated force of 1,100 warriors, including several hundred blacks, garrisoned the fort. Their village was behind the fort, and they had planted extensive corn fields that were said to stretch along the river for more than forty-five miles (Covington; Millington).

Nearby, the Georgians were also establishing settlements, and General Andrew Jackson demanded the "immediate and prompt interference of the Spanish authority to destroy or remove from our frontier this banditti" (Millington 11). Although the Spanish governor answered that he would need specific orders from Spain, he sent Captain Vicente Sebastian Pintado to investigate and attempt to retrieve the slaves belonging to Spanish owners in East and West Florida. Pintado first went to Havana and met with British Vice Admiral Alexander Cochrane, who promised assistance. Pintado took with him lists of the missing slaves and the names of their owners. One hundred thirty-six slaves were claimed from Pensacola, including seventy-eight men, twenty-three women, eight boys, four girls, and twenty-three whose sex was not given. The black man identified as the commander at the fort, Garson, appears on the list as the slave of Don Antonio Montero, who had also lost four other men and three women. Pintado's reports offer other evidence about these people, including their age, color (black or mulatto), their family status, in some cases the circumstances by which they arrived at Prospect Bluff, their occupations, and their stated value. Ambrosio, a former slave of Forbes and Company, was a shoemaker valued at 900 pesos. Harry, belonging to the same company, was a caulker and navigator who knew how to read and write and was valued at 2,000 pesos. Others were sailors, master carpenters, bakers, servants, laundresses, cooks, sawyers, masons, cartwrights, and field hands. If this group is representative, and there is no reason that it should not be, the blacks who lived at this settlement were certainly equipped to be self-sufficient. While they may not have been "black Robin Hoods," as Aptheker called them, neither were they the parasitical "villains" described by the Americans.[18] When Pintado finally arrived at Prospect Bluff, Colonel Nicholls would not allow the slaves to be forcibly returned. In Pintado's presence Nicholls disarmed the men, paid them for their service, and gave each a discharge from service. He told the blacks that new orders precluded him from transporting them to British possessions as had earlier been promised by Admiral Cochrane, and he warned that when the English departed, the maroons would be preyed on by the Americans as well as their Native American allies. Only twenty-eight of the 128 fugitive slaves interviewed agreed to return with Pintado, and overnight several of those ran away or changed their minds. The Spanish were able to convince only ten interviewees to return voluntarily, and all of those were women.[19]

Meanwhile General Jackson had already ordered General Edmund Pendleton Gaines to destroy the fort, which was "stealing and enticing away our negroes" and which had "been established by some villain for the purpose of murder, rapine, and plunder." Gaines charged Lieutenant Colonel Duncan L. Clinch with the job, and Clinch was reinforced by the Coweta Creeks, led by William McIntosh. Garson and a Choctaw chief commanded jointly and had at their disposal ten cannons, several thousand muskets and sidearms, ammunition, and military stores. Garson informed a Creek delegation sent by the Americans that "he had been left in command of the fort by the British government and that he would sink any American vessels that should attempt to pass it." He also stated (as it turns out, prophetically) that he would blow up the fort rather than surrender. When the battle actually began on 27 July 1816, the blacks in the fort hurled insults as well as cannon shots at the Americans and made it clear they would fight to the death. Indeed, that was their fate, for the first American shot hit their powder magazine and blew up the fort. There were only forty survivors of the explosion and few of those lived long. Garson and the Choctaw chief were handed over to the Creeks and murdered (Milligan 10–17).

Another devastating blow came in 1818 when a force of Tennessee volunteers, led by General Jackson, invaded Florida and in a three-week campaign burned almost 400 black and Seminole homes near the Suwannee, destroyed most of the group's food supplies, and spirited away herds of their cattle and horses. Blacks and Seminoles put up a brave fight, but their northern settlements were ruined and their populations dispersed to the west and south of Florida (Brown, *Peace River* 9–10). Despite this disaster, slave resistance did not cease in the Southeast. Numbers of blacks and Native Americans had anticipated the attacks at Prospect Bluff and at the Suwannee and had returned to the peninsula to live among the Seminoles at their resettled villages at Tampa Bay and elsewhere. While it is beyond the scope of this essay to treat the First and Second Seminole Wars, it is well known that blacks played important roles in those protracted conflicts, eventually accompanying the Seminoles in their exile to Oklahoma.[20]

From this survey of only some of the more well-known examples, it should be clear that slave resistance was a constant in the Southeast and that the region's history can make important contributions to the historiographical debates on this theme. The tri-racial nature of the southern frontier and the varieties of available evidence present exciting possibilities for historical research. The voluminous English-language documents need to be reworked from different perspectives, and the Spanish documents are only beginning to be mined. Archaeologists are starting to investigate more black and Native American sites, and their work will shed new light on important questions of material culture. Oral history offers yet another important methodology for exploring this past. It has accurately been noted that those who write history, shape it, and thus scholars have an obligation to do a better job of incorporating the lives of the many non-Europeans who formed the majority population as they reshape the history of the Southeast.

NOTES

1. Examples of a more traditional treatment include those of Herbert E. Bolton and Mary Ross and of Robert L. Gold. Other works such as John J. TePaske's *The Governorship of Spanish Florida, 1700–1763* and J. Leitch Wright's *Florida in the American Revolution* devote more attention to non-Europeans in eighteenth-century Florida. Sylvia Frey's *Water from the Rock* discusses Florida only briefly. For better coverage of the Spanish "borderlands" see Weber.

2. On the history of Carolina see Wood and Crane.

3. Wright, *Florida* and "Blacks." Two important studies of the British plantation period in Florida by Daniel L. Schafer are, "'Yellow Silk Ferret'" and "'A Swamp of an Investment'?" On Oswald's efforts in British Florida also see Hancock.

4. These estimates probably included those slaves "stolen" away by the armies and those who "stole themselves" by running away.

5. See Quarles, Wright ("Loyalist Asylum"), and Aptheker.

6. For examples of the complaints and countercharges see Lockey's *East Florida, 1783–1785*. For more on the disorder see Parker's "Men without God or King." On the fugitive slaves who won freedom see Landers, "Spanish Sanctuary" and *Black Society*.

7. Royal decree in letter from Luís de las Casas to Governor Zéspedes, 21 July 1790, Letters from the Captain General, 1784–1821, reel 1, East Florida Papers, Library of Congress, available on microfilm at the P. K. Yonge Library of Florida History, University of Florida, Gainesville (hereafter cited as EFP). Also see Wright (*Florida*) and Landers ("Spanish Sanctuary").

8. Relations of Missing Slaves, May 1797, To and From the United States, reel 41, EFP. For more on Fatio see Parker, "Success."

9. Thomas King to Governor Enrique White, 10 October 1797, reel 41, EFP.

10. Census Returns, 1784–1814, reel 148, EFP.

11. James Seagrove to Governor Enrique White, 4 July 1797, reel 42, EFP.

12. The definitive work on the Ayllón colony is Paul E. Hoffman's *A New Andalucia*.

13. See McAlister; Wright, *William Augustus Bowles*. For more recent studies of Native American diplomacy in the Southeast, see Dowd's *A Spirited Resistance*, Saunt's *A New Order*, and Gallay's *Indian Slave Trade*.

14. James Seagrove to John McQueen, 24 June 1800, reel 42, EFP.

15. Enrique White to Juan McQueen, 12 September, 1801, reel 55, EFP; Orders for General Biassou, 1801, reel 55, EFP; Report of Fernando de la Puente, 19 August 1809, reel 68, EFP; Review Lists of the Free Black Militia of St. Augustine, 1802, Papeles Procedentes de Cuba, 357, Archivo General de Indias, Seville, Spain (hereafter cited as AGI); Rogers.

16. Patrick, "Letters"; Davis, "United States Troops"; Porter.

17. See Patrick, *Florida Fiasco*; Porter 186–94; J. H. Alexander; Davis, "Troops" (July 1930 and Apr. 1931).

18. List of the blacks belonging to owners in Pensacola, 4 May 1815, Santo Domingo 2580 (hereafter cited as SD), AGI.

19. Vicente Sebastian Pintado to José de Soto, 29 April 1815, SD 2580, AGI; Vicente Sebastian Pintado to José de Soto, 6 May 1815, SD 2580, AGI; Vicente Sebastian Pintado to José de Soto, Owner's Declarations, 8 May 1815, SD 2580, AGI.

20. See Wright, "A Note"; Mahon, *History*; Porter; Klos; Brown, *Peace River*; Brown, "Sarrazota."

WORKS CITED

Abernethy, Thomas P. "Florida and the Spanish Frontier, 1811–1819." *The Americanization of the Gulf Coast, 1803–1850*. Ed. Lucius F. Ellsworth. Pensacola, Fla.: Historic Pensacola Preservation Board, 1972. 88–120.

Alexander, J. H. "East Florida Invasion." *Florida Historical Quarterly* 56 (July 1977): 280–96.

Aptheker, Herbert. "Maroons within the Present Limits of the United States." *Journal of Negro History* 24 (Apr. 1939): 167–84.

Bolton, Herbert E., and Mary Ross. *The Debatable Land: A Sketch of the Anglo-Spanish Contest for the Georgia Country*. Berkeley: U of California P, 1925.

Brown, Canter, Jr. *Florida's Peace River Frontier*. Gainesville: UP of Florida, 1991.

——. "The 'Sarrazota or Runaway Negro Plantations': Tampa Bay's First Black Community, 1812–1821." *Tampa Bay History* 12 (fall–winter 1990): 5–19.

Covington, James W. "The Negro Fort." *Gulf Coast Historical Review* 5 (spring 1990): 72–91.

Crane, Verner W. *The Southern Frontier, 1670–1732*. New York: Norton, 1981.

Davis, T. Frederick, ed. "United States Troops in Spanish East Florida, 1812–13." *Florida Historical Quarterly* 9 (July 1930): 3–23.

——. "United States Troops in Spanish East Florida, 1812–13." *Florida Historical Quarterly* 9 (Apr. 1931): 259–78.

——. "United States Troops in Spanish East Florida, 1812–13." *Florida Historical Quarterly* 9 (Jan. 1931): 135–55.

Dowd, Gregory Evans. *A Spirited Resistance: The North American Indian Struggle for Unity, 1745–1815.* Baltimore, Md.: Johns Hopkins UP, 1992.

Frey, Sylvia. *Water from the Rock: Black Resistance in a Revolutionary Age.* Princeton, N.J.: Princeton UP, 1991.

Gallay, Alan. *The Indian Slave Trade: The Rise of the English Empire in the American South, 1670–1717.* New Haven, Conn.: Yale UP, 2002.

Gold, Robert L. *Borderland Empires in Transition: The Triple Nation Transfer of Florida.* Carbondale: Southern Illinois UP, 1969.

Hancock, David. *Citizens of the World: London Merchants and the Integration of the British Atlantic Community, 1735–1785.* Cambridge: Cambridge UP, 1995.

Hoffman, Paul E. *A New Andalucia and a Way to the Orient: The American Southeast during the Sixteenth Century.* Baton Rouge: Louisiana State UP, 1990.

The Independent Journal or the General Advertiser (New York) 20 June 1787.

Klos, George. "Blacks and the Seminole Removal Debate, 1821–1835." *The African American Heritage of Florida.* Ed. David R. Colburn and Jane L. Landers. Gainesville: UP of Florida, 1995. 128–56.

Landers, Jane L. "Africans in the Land of Ayllón: The Exploration and Settlement of the Southeast." *Columbus and the Land of Ayllón: The Exploration and Settlement of the Southeast.* Ed. Jeannine Cook. Darien, Ga.: Lower Altamaha Historical Society, 1992. 105–33.

——. *Black Society in Spanish Florida.* Urbana: U of Illinois P, 1999.

——. "Gracia Real de Santa Teresa de Mose: A Free Black Town in Spanish Colonial Florida." *American Historical Review* 95 (Feb. 1990): 9–30.

——. "Spanish Sanctuary: Fugitives in Florida, 1687–1790." *Florida Historical Quarterly* 62 (Sept. 1984): 296–313.

Lockey, Joseph Byrne. *East Florida, 1783–1785: A File of Documents Assembled and Many of Them Translated.* Berkeley: U of California P, 1949.

Mahon, John K. *History of the Second Seminole War, 1835–1842.* Gainesville: U of Florida P, 1967.

McAlister, Lyle N. "William Augustus Bowles and the State of Muskogee." *Florida Historical Quarterly* 40 (Apr. 1962): 317–28.

Milligan, John D. "Slave Rebelliousness and the Florida Maroon." *Journal of the National Archives* 6 (spring 1974): 5–18.

Ogg, Frederick Austin. "Jay's Treaty and the Slavery Interests of the United States." *American Historical Association Annual Report,* 1901. 2 vols. Washington, D.C.: American Historical Association, 1902. 1:275–98.

Parker, Susan R. "Men without God or King: Rural Settlers of East Florida, 1784–1790." *Florida Historical Quarterly* 64 (Oct. 1990): 135–55.

——. "Success through Diversification: Francis Philip Fatio's New Switzerland Plantation." *Colonial Plantations and Economy in Florida*. Ed. Jane G. Landers. Gainesville: UP of Florida, 2000. 69–82.

Patrick, Rembert W., ed. *Florida Fiasco: Rampant Rebels on the Georgia-Florida Frontier, 1810–1815*. Athens: U of Georgia P, 1954.

——. "Letters of the Invaders of East Florida, 1812." *Florida Historical Quarterly* 28 (July 1949): 53–60.

Porter, Kenneth Wiggins. *The Negro on the American Frontier*. New York: Arno, 1971.

Quarles, Benjamin. "Lord Dunmore as Liberator." *William and Mary Quarterly* 15 (1958): 494–507.

Rogers, Harlan C. "A Military History of Florida During the Governorship of Enrique White, 1796–1811." Master's thesis, Florida State University, 1971.

Saunt, Claudio. *A New Order of Things: Property, Power, and the Transformation of the Creek Indians, 1733–1816*. Cambridge: Cambridge UP, 1999.

Schafer, Daniel L. " 'A Swamp of an Investment'? Richard Oswald's British East Florida Plantation Experiment." *Colonial Plantations and Economy in Florida*. Ed. Jane G. Landers. Gainesville: UP of Florida, 2000. 11–38.

——. " 'Yellow Silk Ferret Tied Round Their Wrists': African Americans in British East Florida 1763–1784." *The African American Heritage of Florida*. Ed. David R. Colburn and Jane L. Landers. Gainesville: UP of Florida, 1995. 71–103.

Spalding, Phinizy. *Oglethorpe in America*. Athens: U of Georgia P, 1984.

TePaske, John J. *The Governorship of Spanish Florida, 1700–1763*. Durham, N.C.: Duke UP, 1964.

Weber, David J. *The Spanish Frontier in North America*. New Haven, Conn.: Yale UP, 1992.

Willis, William S. "Divide and Rule: Red, White, and Black in the Southeast." *Journal of Negro History* 48 (July 1963): 157–76.

Wood, Peter H. *Black Majority: Negroes in South Carolina from 1690 through the Stono Rebellion*. New York: Norton, 1974.

Wright, J. Leitch. "Blacks in British East Florida." *Florida Historical Quarterly* 54 (July 1975–Apr. 1976): 425–42.

——. *Florida in the American Revolution*. Gainesville: UP of Florida, 1975.

——. "Lord Dunmore's Loyalist Asylum in the Floridas." *Florida Historical Quarterly* 46 (Apr. 1971): 370–79.

——. "A Note on the First Seminole War as Seen by the Indians, Negroes, and Their British Advisors." *Journal of Southern History* 34 (Nov. 1968): 565–75.

——. *William Augustus Bowles, Director General of the Creek Nation*. Athens: U of Georgia P, 1967.

For what one senses as ideas or what one
exposes in words becomes so foreign to what
one accumulates in oneself as rocks.

—EDOUARD GLISSANT, *Le case du commandeur*

J. MICHAEL DASH

Martinique/Mississippi: Edouard
Glissant and Relational Insularity

douard Glissant's enormous importance to francophone literature as a whole and to Caribbean thought in particular is related to his retrieval of the concept of location and ground from a reductive colonialist discourse without resorting to the nativist essentialism that dominated cultural politics in earlier Caribbean theories.[1] His conception of island space that resists both erosion and comprehension yet that could only be stabilized within a larger, totalizing plane of intelligibility is the hallmark of a Glissantian poetics. Writing in the sixties in the shadow of Césairean negritude and Fanonian nationalism, which both attempted to fix postcolonial space in terms of ideological planes of intelligibility, he developed the idea of relational space that would allow both for the palpable materiality of ground as well as a global "prise de conscience." More specifically, he broke with the anticolonial thrust of an Atlantic-oriented contestation of the colonizing metropole or a nostalgia for a pure, redemptive origin to develop the idea of Caribbean island space within a New World archipelago. As he himself so tellingly put it, "place grows and widens out from its irreducible center as much as from its incalculable borders" (*Tout-Monde* 29).

It was precisely the inability to restore historical continuities and authentic rootedness that represented for Glissant the Caribbean's potential to establish new connections and envision repeated crossings. The absence of a stabilizing center, of a pure origin meant that new and unpredictable relations could be established using unconscious and obscure pathways or traces. In this regard, Glissant was less interested in the emergence of an Antillean self-consciousness or establishing ethnic difference in the face of metropolitan France. His focus turned to the Americas and the extent to which the meaning of Martinique and the Caribbean could be revealed through the "ailleurs" of the New World. Therefore, his literary project is in part the creation of a collective, hemispheric consciousness in the Caribbean through a crucial detour via the Americas. Similarly, the Caribbean becomes "the Other America," that is, the incalculable, archipelagic edge of the Americas that is necessary for its own hemispheric self-definition.

Increasingly, he seems to suggest that only in this way can that island space be freed from the preoccupation with creating a grounding center and opened out to new possibilities of representation. Indeed island space then becomes a metaphor for rethinking place in a wider sense; all places must be opened out to their archipelagic dimensions. As he put it in his *Traité du Tout-Monde* (*Treatise of the Tout-Monde*), "Archipelagic thought is well suited to the ways of our worlds. It draws on their ambiguous, fragile and drifting nature. It is in accord with the practice of diversion which is not the same as flight or rejection. . . . Archipelagic thought, in its multiplicity, opens up these seas to us. . . . The lands I inhabit become starbursts of archipelagoes" (31, 43).

Consequently, Glissant's meditations on Caribbean space are characterized by a process of detour, delay, and substitution, a moving outward in time and space in order to understand better the point of departure. This process of relational play allows for creolizing secular forces to destabilize endlessly the temptation to grounded difference. Historical detours or what Glissant called a prophetic vision of the past can be found in his studies of Louis Delgrès and Toussaint L'Ouverture. Literary departures take him to the work of St John Perse, Alejo Carpentier, Victor Segalen, and William Faulkner, and geographical detours take him to the Tout-Monde in general and the Americas in particular.

Glissant's interest in the South as "an incalculable border" of Caribbean island consciousness goes back to articles published on William Faulkner and the 1964 publication of his *Le quatrième siècle* (*The Fourth Century*). In this novel, with its recognizably Faulknerian overtones, he raises the question of a new world anxiety about origins and genesis, which pushes the characters to seek an originary truth. Glissant credits Faulkner with a creative perversion of the need for a genealogical quest and in particular *Absalom, Absalom!* with "a heretical destruction of the sacred notion of filiation" (*Poétique* 71). It is this novel that is most valued by Glissant for its treatment of fratricidal conflict, family entanglements, and an infringed moral code, features characteristic of what Glissant categorized as the narrative of the Americas. "Linearity gets lost. The longed-for history and its nonfulfillment are knotted up in an inextricable tangle of relationships, alliances and progeny, whose principle is one of bewildering repetition.... [H]ere man has lost the way and keeps turning in his tracks" (*Discours* 148).

Yet, Glissant's work is not merely a blind extension of Faulkner's, as he sees the latter's insightful treatment of the New World plantation as ultimately lacking in relationality. "Faulkner who shares with those who belong to the New World an obsession with the past, totally ignores the rest of the American continent.... This is a weakness. Fixed in his isolation, the Faulknerian hero (witness and victim) is cut off from the world" (*Intention* 182). Glissant sets out, therefore, to open the atavistic insularity of Faulkner's world to the plantation past of Martinique—an enterprise markedly different from rewriting Shakespeare's *Tempest*, Conrad's *Heart of Darkness*, or Defoe's *Robinson Crusoe*, which had marked a previous generation's oppositional practice of writing back to or reformulating the metropolitan canon.

Le quatrième siècle is Glissant's narrative of the Americas and is filled with a restrained skepticism that allows him both to question whether the historical truth is ever attainable and to sympathize with the need for such a longing. In the novel, which is a sustained dialogue between two narrator-protagonists—an old healer named Longoué and a young researcher, Mathieu, who is anxious to establish the chronology of a lost history—Glissant repeatedly enacts the gap between lived experience fitfully remembered and the narrative of history that is destined to supplant yet be destabilized by lived memory. There may be here echoes of the novel *Go Down, Moses*, in which Sam Fathers reactivates the ghosts of a past that makes the young Isaac McCaslin doubt his legitimacy. Glissant's old storyteller can in fact be read as a play on a Moses who is the unwitting origin of a textual genealogy as well as the incarnation of a relational orality. He is not the incarnation of the people's memory but the ambiguous point of a shared anxiety to know the past, which is not completely available to those who witness it nor to those who wish to systematize it nor even to those who wish to narrate it. Longoué's presence in the novel points both to the presentness of the past as well as its capacity to exceed one's ability to narrate it.

It is this implicit critique of modernity in concentrating on the limits of the knowable that makes this novel and Glissant's relational poetics so very American. The opening up of the plantation past and the inbred plantation household to the anxieties of the postslavery present allows Glissant to suggest that American identity is marked by this negotiation between past and present, between a specifically Martinican past and the possibility of reading it through a hemispheric narrative. Both Glissant and Faulkner are calling into question, in the Caribbean and the South respectively, a nostalgia for pure origins or sacred filiation and suggesting that the obsessive quest for such origins can lead only to unstable narratives that ultimately make identitarian insularity impossible. It is this reading of Faulkner that prompts Glissant to call the latter's work "one of those pulsating moments of a modern poetics of relationality" (*Poétique* 34).

What is important in this dialogic or rhizomatic practice of New World relationality is the destabilizing of the inherent meaning of island ground, whether the Plantation South or the Martinican hillside, in favor of an idea of archipelagic space activated by horizontal relations and indirect detours. In *Absalom, Absalom!* Haiti can be read as the South's Other, which makes the quest for filiation absurd. The other island on the outside, like a trace of repressed memory, which cannot function as the site of lost origin but a zone of opacity that makes any possibility of any genealogy impossible, is central to Glissant's archipelagic poetics and may well have its roots in the surrealist emancipation of the meaning of the object and its openness to the play of detour and deferral. Note, for instance, André Breton's 1941 visit to the Caribbean, and to Martinique in particular, when his own reading of Martinique as tropical paradise was disrupted by both his internment at the hands of the Vichy regime and the corrupt world of the French colony. In a remarkable dialogue with his fellow exile André Masson, as recorded in *Martinique, charmeuse de serpents*, the magus of surrealism turned wandering refugee observed, "Don't you find it at the same time extraordinary and necessary that the rock of the island that leads to the open sea should indeed be Diamond Rock?" (32).

Diamond Rock can be construed as an instance of the surrealist procedure of "le hasard objectif" or objective chance, which unexpectedly makes connections between disparate objects, between the island space of Martinique and the liberating openness of the sea of multiple meanings. In placing their emphasis on the irreducibly mysterious object of Diamond Rock and not on the island space of Martinique, Breton and Masson do project the island as native land but stress the openness of "ground" to a play of detour, ruse, and ambiguity. Consequently, the dark monolith of Diamond Rock, both volcanic and marine, scintillating yet opaque, is imaginatively configured as the object that liberates the colonized island space from predetermined meanings and, in particular, Martinique from its metropolitan ties.

In so privileging Diamond Rock, an uninhabited "îlet" projected outside of the island into the Caribbean Sea, Breton and Masson are suggesting a liberating opacity for island space, thereby freeing it from colonial stereotypes and a reifying exoticism. Martinique may be seen in terms of Rousseau's "Snake Charmer" but no such aesthetic or psychological recuperation is possible for Diamond Rock. This emphasis on a mysterious and destabilizing island specificity appealed to Glissant two decades later because of its clear anti-assimilationist and anti-universalist thrust as much as its resistance to the myth of stable foundational space. This was particularly important in an island where departmentalization was in 1946 the strategy of Aimé Césaire and Martinique's radical left and where assimilationist ideas were diffused throughout the local population; it raised the possibility of promoting a non-assimilationist specificity, which had generally been absent from local radical political thought. In the same way that revolutionary Haiti destabilized Faulkner's South, so Diamond Rock opened Martinique, the ultimate French colony, to a complex New World relationality.

Glissant's surrealist-derived poetics construe Martinique neither in terms of a journey into the perilous interior nor in terms of visions of lost innocence. Island space is captive neither to imposed stereotypes of organicist nostalgia nor to a salutary derangement of the senses, the usual tropes of travel writing, but is, rather, outside and unknown, littoral and opaque. The coast, with its conventional associations of subjugation and vulnerability, has all the mystery of an interior, of a space whose circumference remains ungauged and whose borders are incalculable. Such a presentation of island space can even be interpreted as Glissant's mapping of psychic space, with the water's edge representing the line that divides waking consciousness from the constant return of repressed memory, transparency continuously disrupted by opacity. Often Glissant suggests that the Caribbean Sea, "the blue savannas of memory or imagination" (*Poétique* 19), functions as a disruptive force within a Caribbean and New World unconscious. This welcome estrangement makes island space not homely but relational.

The historically contested space of Diamond Rock, emblematic of New World space, reemerges as a blankness that resists writing but invites multiple readings at the same time. Simultaneously somber and fabulous, bleakly impenetrable but suggestive of shattered facets of light, Diamond Rock is an uncanny echo of the Bakhtinian image of the dialogic play between word and world; the word's intention is directed like a ray of light toward the object, which produces "a spectral dispersion in an atmosphere filled with alien words, value judgments and accents . . . the atmosphere that surrounds the object makes the facets of the image sparkle" (Bakhtin 277). Edouard Glissant's unswerving exploration of an explosive relatedness and an inclusive horizontality since the fifties marks an important rupture with anticolonial writing, which conceived of space in terms of concealment, of strategic interiority and anteriority, claiming the right to otherness and difference in terms of the values of an imagined aboriginal heartland or a prelapsarian past. The anticolonial paradigm of home as redemptive ground is not replaced by empty nomadism but by the destabilizing space of the littoral, where "irreducible" centers open out to the archipelagic Caribbean Sea and the play of hemispheric relationality.

WRITING ROCKS

The object is the rock and the beach, and when we think we have reached the heart of the rock, the horizon of the beach defiantly stretches out to infinity. Never identical with itself, the object invites us to discover one by one the pieces with their symbolic function of the puzzle of our identity.

—ANNIE LE BRUN, *A Distance*

Make this rock explode. Collect the pieces and spread them across the expanding surface.

Our identities relay each other, and in so doing collapse in all their empty pretension, those hierarchies hidden or forced through subterfuge to persist in glorification. Do not give in to these maneuvers of the identical.

Open to the world the field of your identity.

—EDOUARD GLISSANT, *Traité du Tout-Monde*

In both these epigraphs the same deconstructive appeal is apparent. Le Brun's rock with its limitless horizons and Glissant's exploded rock both suggest a rupture with a poetics of containment and fixed, exclusive identities. In both instances the expedition leads outward not inward through the contemplation of the irreducible opacity of the rock. In both instances a new kind of traveling is suggested. It is this phenomenon that Glissant calls errancy, a journeying beyond foundational certitudes, over exploded ground. As he claims in *Poétique de la Relation*, "Errancy comes with the negation of all poles and all metropoles, whether they are linked or not by the voyager's act of conquest" (31). Glissant from his earliest work is fascinated by the relation of consciousness to location and the knowledge gained from the new way of seeing that errancy implies. As he says in his first book of essays, *Soleil de la conscience*, he is undertaking a new kind of ethnography from this post-identitarian journeying beyond fixed notions of space and identity; he already senses from the opening lines that "there will no longer be culture without all cultures, no longer a civilization which can be the metropole for others" (11).[2]

Soleil de la conscience is sited in Paris, surprisingly, given the usual associations of sun and the tropics. The title does, however, suggest the symbolic manipulation of space and objects that is characteristic of this peculiar travel book, which suggests a reversibility between pole and metropole. In the same way that Masson and Breton focus on Diamond Rock in their Martinican journey, Glissant focuses on what he calls "l'île de Paris" (the island of Paris). Evident in both instances is the use of the "hasard objectif" to render the familiar strange and Glissant's provocative association of Paris with "le rocher du Diamant." Paris is projected outside of Europe—a site of explosive relationality. "Thus Paris, in the heart of our time, receives, uproots, obscures and then clarifies and reassures. I suddenly know its secret: Paris is an island, which pulls in from all sides and immediately diffracts" (*Soleil* 11).

The idea of the metropolitan world hardening into an island with a consciousness-raising openness, at the same time the object of desire and beyond one's grasp, haunts Glissant's imagination. If one takes his early epic poem *Les Indes* as an example, it is clear that each island named the Indies holds an enormous power of seduction, as it remains opaque and mysterious to the discoverer, who exhausts himself trying to master the space. The idea of a seductive luminosity is also associated with the island of Lambrianne—possibly created from *lames brillantes* (shimmering waves)—in Glissant's first novel, *La Lézarde*. The characters in this work travel through a world of splendor and shadow where an ambiguous light continuously prevails. The entire movement of this first novel takes us from "the flame" to "the explosion," a constant movement back and forth between shadow and light, interior and exterior. The light of this novel does not provide a definitive illumination but leads to an explosive force that drives some characters further outward, and it draws others back to the shadows.

Another interesting point of similarity between *Soleil de la conscience* and *La Lézarde* can be seen in the manipulation of snow in the former and the sand bar in the latter. In *Soleil de la conscience* the snow represents an opening, the crystallization of the world of l'île de Paris. It is visualized as foam. . . . "The first time that my eyes beheld its foam, it was like a rainfall. I already knew it. Better yet, it broke the gray to finally give to winter the unique shimmer of its language. So advances the real image of the cold season, its essence prefigured; it brings an end to waiting and opposes luminously, it is almost hot. . . . With it I leave behind indecision to be borne up to the extreme opposite of my order" (*Soleil* 11).

The liberating poetic charge of the objective object world, which takes the narrator/traveler on a journey of salutary disorientation, is equally evoked in *La Lézarde* in terms of a sand bar, a scintillating point in the dark sea that invites the characters to open themselves to the outside world, thereby creating new material conditions for their released subjectivity. "Valerie, still not moving, tried to enter the bar or let the bar enter her heart, her breast, with its concentrated violence. And as darkness descended on the sea, she saw more and more clearly the outline of foam, like an exposed root, but one whose call reached out through space towards her" (*Ripening* 159). Valerie is sensitive to the invasive presence of the sand bar in the tropical dusk, just as the foaming snow in winter was an earlier revelation. Glissant's manipulation of these two images of sand and snow demonstrates the way in which encounter with the objective world becomes the first, sensuous moment of knowing. Foaming snow and scintillating sand bar suggest the crystallization of the opaque reality from which they emanate. The bar almost foreshadows Diamond Rock as it is the tortured creation of the river, a submarine fermentation, and roots itself in the sea.

The narrative of Glissant's early novel is marked by the interaction between displaced characters and ambiguous matter. One of the characters, the political activist Mycea, attempts to reduce the opaque multiplicity of the sand bar. The bar serves as an intermediary that allows her to consider her relations with the members of the group as well as the disturbing moral issue as to who was responsible for the assassination of the government agent Garin in the novel. "Mycea was afraid; Mathieu seemed very tired. She did not know exactly what she was up against. . . . She looked at the bar, screwing up her eyes to reduce to a thin line what she knew to be the turbulence of the open sea. . . . As she looked out at the bar, Mycea asked herself a question with serious moral implications: Did Thael have sole responsibility for Garin's death?" (154). The struggle for moral or ideological manipulation of the object is seen in the act of squinting, but the bar is not a simple object in itself. Its sensuous immediacy does not allow for passive control. "She thought that Mathieu would never cross the bar, but in a way she was proud that it was so. He had overcome his frail body, he was the weakest one, but he would not shrink from his commitment. . . . Mycea felt he was also quite ill and that she would have difficulty in restoring his health. Her eyes filled with sparkling tears, through which the sun broke into fragments and the sand bar began to look like a burst of frightened stars" (155). She is overcome by emotion, and the bar explodes to life in a spectral dispersion of ambiguities.

The character of Mycea, haunted by the resistance of concrete things to abstract manipulation, is central to Glissant's literary enterprise and the unstable vision of his new relational order. The enigmatic, scintillating rock and the prismatic vertigo it unleashes reappear in various characters who are wedded to a material space they can never understand or exhaust. Mycea, in the novel most devoted to her, *Le case du commandeur* (*The Overseer's Cabin*), explicitly articulates Glissant's archipelagic vision. "Marie Celat would run to those places on the sea shore where when it was clear you could recognize Dominica to the north, with its rugged accompaniment of steep sloping sides, or St. Lucia to the south, which seemed to rise from the quiet sand and the spreading green water; she would hail the islands" (*Commandeur* 215). Mycea, who exemplifies a "littoral" psyche, is always prey to the invasive flow of the "blue savannas" of repressed memory. Consequently she is the only one so dislocated and open in the novel to the exploding island rocks, diffracted across the Caribbean Sea. Her delirium allows her to move beyond insular identity to relational identity, beyond territorial symmetries and imperial binaries to a healing vision of a postnational New World homelessness, an imagined collectivity of dislocated Creole cultures.

AU SUD DE CE SUD

The frontier is like sand that is always shifting but that, far from swallowing up the contradictions that it has thrown up or happened on in the vicinity, enlarges them, exposes them, explodes them to the infinite reaches of its disruptiveness. . . . Faulkner's writing, winding along the length of this current, riding these waves, making this threshold visible, truly establishes his work in turn as a frontier.

—EDOUARD GLISSANT, *Faulkner, Mississippi*

The real is a body of meanderings and life knocks against each of its twists and turns. Real and lived constitute an infolding. Considering them together comes down to constructing a rhetoric, through a slow process of unfolding that aims at illuminating rather than convincing, at persuading oneself rather than confusing the reader, tacitly self-assured, under an excess of explanation.

—EDOUARD GLISSANT, *Traité de Tout-Monde*

Increasingly Glissant's works have become travel books or are sited away from the deferred space of the île/rocher of Martinique/Diamant.[3] It is as if the challenge of Diamond Rock's slippery referentiality invites greater and greater exploration of frontier zones of rock, sand, and sea. In the disruption of colonial and anticolonial relations evident in the doubling of "île de France" and "île du diamant" in *Soleil de la conscience* is the beginning of a series of errancies that disrupt and decenter the rules of discourse that bind metropole and colony, center and margin. In his later fictionalized or documentary errancies, Glissant is less preoccupied with the discursive colonial attachments that have bound the Caribbean and France and prefers to concentrate on trajectories that take him through the Americas, in particular what he calls the South and its south. The Americas represent for him a postcolonial space, not of a benign creolization or happy hybridity but an explosively baroque ground that is neither foundational nor originary. As in the past, Diamond Rock remains emblematic of this postoriginary world of nonreductive opacities and deferred identities. Glissant makes the connections explicit in the chapter appropriately entitled "The Real–The Deferred" in *Faulkner, Mississippi*. "The landscapes of the Americas invite this spreading out. Even when cultivated, they lose nothing of their excess, which is however not related to their actual surface. . . . [T]he most diamantine islet set as if on the edge of some imminent eruption . . . opens out, calls out to the far distance, stirs up winds and hurricanes. Knotted concentration spreads out like the contagious sap of liquid lava" (215).

Faulkner, Mississippi—which could have been equally entitled Glissant/Faulkner, Martinique/Mississippi, Glissant/Mississippi, or arguably Lézarde/Mississippi since it is the river that becomes emblematic in both works—is an obvious example of this later phase of "frontier" travel writing in the Americas. Glissant's archipelagic poetics is indebted to Faulkner's interrogation of the pure ethnicity. From the outset, Glissant sees Faulkner as obsessed with racial and cultural entanglements in the South that cannot be unraveled. Consequently, the haunting desire for linear history and pure origins that preoccupies writers in the Americas is made ironic by the intrusive and hybridizing force of history. Glissant is predictably drawn to a novel like *Absalom, Absalom!* in which the trace of Caribbean connections with the South, and by extension the Americas, is represented through the country of Haiti as a disruptive site of New World relationality. For Faulkner as for Glissant, the past is neither redemptive nor transparent but seems perpetually lost in opaque island rocks.

To this extent, Faulkner and the South are important stops in Glissant's journey outward beyond certain binarisms in colonial thought. Faulkner's narratives are used to launch his early assault on exclusionary identity politics in Caribbean literature. If the absence of origins is the only foundation of New World identities, then, as Glissant declares in *L'intention poétique*, the narrator is condemned to revealing that which cannot be revealed: "there is nothing unveiled here. No absolute explanation. Unveiling would have led to a solution for this vertigo. . . . The novel unveils a veiled secret that never becomes purely unveiled but manifests itself in the very mechanism of unveiling" (171). No secret truth can be brought to light in this journey into the past, which Glissant characterizes as the exemplary opacity of Faulkner's narrative technique. He would later, in *Poétique de la relation*, return to this element in Faulkner's evocation of the anguish over the lost past in the American imagination. Faulkner's insights provide Glissant with an early modern example of post-identitarian poetics in the Americas, one that he regrets has not spread to the south of Faulkner's South. "The embattled origin, the sacred but henceforth inexpressible enigma of rootedness, make of this universe that is Faulkner's one of the pulsating moments of a modern poetics of relationality. I once regretted that such a universe had not spread further into the surrounding area: the Caribbean, Latin America" (34).

The various references to Faulkner and the South that can be found throughout Glissant's major essays come to a culmination in *Faulkner, Mississippi* as Glissant prepares for a third phase of errancy beyond Martinique/France, Caribbean/Americas to Diamant/Tout-Monde. The nonfoundational aspect of Faulkner's narrative, its inability to unveil, returns with oracular force as a central theme in *Faulkner, Mississippi*. Glissant now calls this type of narration "une écriture en différé" (a deferred writing) and describes it as "the incomparable suspension of writing which denies the story's foundational capacity, but which by this very denial founds another dimension, a poetics, not of narration, but of the relation between the narrated and the unsayable which underpins it. When Faulkner says that he is a failed poet, we should understand that he is aware of having already explored that other dimension in which writing, hesitant and crashing in on itself, gives rise in turn to the impossible encounters of poetry" (192).

The story's loss of its authorial center, its "foundational capacity," as space loses its foundational origin, produces in Glissant's view of Faulkner's South an interzone of indeterminacy in which signs, objects, space itself seem constantly out of focus. Glissant calls it a "lieu dédoublé" or space that doubles back on itself. It is a world of the banal and the quotidian shadowed by a monstrously destabilizing darker side, like the diamantine concentration of the rock facing the sea's eruption. In this narrative borderland, claims of territory and legitimacy are tragically absurd. Glissant tackles the question of foundational illegitimacy in the South when he concludes in *Faulkner, Mississippi* that this space symbolically breaks with all claims to legitimacy: "The South is the kingdom of Denmark" and "*The Hamlet* is really and truly *the only* Hamlet" (208). The doubling of space is also tracked in terms of the mingling of smells that hang over the plantation, both in the Caribbean and the South. Magnolia mixes with the smell of the distillery in Glissant's mind, the perfume of the great houses with fermenting sugarcane, both replacing the dank smell of the primordial woods. In this space there is no single legitimate smell but a profusion of smells that proliferate in the unpredictably fertile space of the plantation. Jasmine and verbena are only some of the illegitimate fragrances that thrive in this quintessentially New World space where flowers are but the external blossoming of hidden, internal truths. "In the drawing rooms, which duplicate in their jumble sumptuous European tastes, or in the torpid shade of the verandah, the smell of verbena allays curses and prolongs melancholy. Outside, 'in the heat of the night,' magnolias (or jasmines) burn themselves out in secret" (204).

For Glissant, the symbol of the South is the Mississippi River. "A land that is a river, a river lived like a country" (208). The river's twisting, meandering trace responds to Glissant's ideal of chaotic relationality, which undoes power relations and territorial impulses. The Mississippi, a littoral trace, represents the path of New World heterogeneity with its infolding and unfolding that never produces equilibrium or synthesis. The peculiar logic of the river dominates Faulkner's world as the Lézarde River dominated the universe of Martinique in Glissant's first novel. Like the Lézarde River the Mississippi is a serpentine coil of loops and fissures. "The river is not governed by linearity, you can put your foot twice into the same water. . . . [T]he Mississippi forms a frontier. That is it piles up the real, from both sides of an unnamed crevasse, and hurls it into the unknown. A paradox, which triggers all around the disturbed experience of a time in chaos. . . . [T]he moving force seems to cross, cut deep into something, lands, hills, lands again, which, because they are tugged along by it, seem uncertain of their destiny, always ready to tumble into the improbable or the unknown. Yes, a frontier river" (209–10). For Glissant, this frontier river is the true protagonist of Faulkner's world, all the more important because it was never directly described. Its gravitational pull is everywhere and nowhere. *Faulkner, Mississippi* is ultimately about post-colonial renegotiations of the frontier zones of the Tout-Monde.

The diffracting and concentrating cadences that were earlier associated with inscrutable Diamond Rock now become a more generalized poetics of interaction between rock and sand, lava and sap, imagination and reality. In this regard, a kinship is established between writers as disparate as William Faulkner and Michel Leiris in Glissant's later writing. Leiris descending the staircase of life's gravitational pull and Faulkner's imagination seized by the torrent of the Mississippi River become exemplary sites in Glissant's disengagement from a colonizing identitarian politics. In his revisioning of the southern writer, Faulkner is as much a surrealist as Leiris, and the Mississippi borderland could well be *Afrique fantôme*. Glissant presents Faulkner's South as an unsettled, dynamic border in which the novelist refuses to name and shrink his plantation world but "sows the seeds for a poetics of becoming, a nexus for diverse cultures" (263).

> Faulkner's world is a frontier. Not only because the Mississippi River is its invigorating torrent, in which the Yoknapatawpha and Tallatchie rivers appear, more so than tributaries or branches, as its mythic daughters, not only because the whole South, and by extension the state of Mississippi and consequently its projection, Yoknapatawpha County, are actually frontier-sites, but also and especially because the writing and the technique Faulkner used to re-create these places—this Place—has also literally stirred up something: movement, hesitation, transition, from fixed identities and settled truths to the spell of the possible and the impossible all mixed together. (310–11)

In this way Glissant speculates about the importance of the particularity of place, of locational opacity in the poetics of frontier worlds. This becomes the model for a new cycle of novels, "les romans des batutos," which is first explained in the inaugural text in this series, *Tout-Monde*, which celebrates the whirlwind of relationality. In the epigraph to this novel, Glissant archly writes, "So Mathieu began to formulate for himself another way of frequenting the world, a burning adventure of the imagination, a real transformation of the mind and sensibility, what another would soon call relational contact, yes, whose meaning he accumulated in himself, in an imperceptible but continuous piling up. A journey without organization, a rupture of horizons, of which he would later understand how to make sense" (48).

In proclaiming this new ideal of a voyage that effaces the conventional project of journeying from center to periphery, Glissant is literally and imaginatively breaking free from the colonial bond that holds Martinique and France together in a repetitive process of "retour" and "detour." His contemplation of the South and Faulkner results in a poetics of the littoral, of frontier zones that ultimately produce the ideal negation of metropoles, well beyond the transatlantic France-Martinique entanglement in *Soleil de la conscience*. This new daring in Glissant's oeuvre problematizes profoundly conventional ways of categorizing Caribbean or American literature—in national or regional terms—since his new novels locate a poetics of place in opaque zones of resistance and acquiescence. Glissant is describing here an extreme case of the poetics of relationality, which connects disparate spaces such as opaque rocks and global frontiers. The writer as wanderer is destined to cultivate gardens of opacity on the sands of contact between lived and real, as Glissant suggests in his epigraph to *Traité du Tout-Monde*.

What Glissant most appreciated about two writers whose lives and works haunted him as much as Faulkner's and Leiris's—St John Perse and Victor Segalen—is the problematizing of the journey by these two writers. In his meditation on departure and arrival in these poets he roams far from the classic notion of the journey from familiar to unknown. The traveler never escapes to the horizon but takes his point of departure with him. The horizon may well be not external at all but internal. Glissant observes in Segalen's work the relation between travel and self-knowledge and the extent to which the encounter with the other does not lead to a facile exoticism but rather represents a plunge into the unknown, the opaque that activates the imagination. What is important in Segalen's case is the tension between internal and external reality and the subject's capacity to savor diversity (the right to difference) without yielding to the temptation of fixing or appropriating the other. A similar tension is the point of departure of Perse's quest. Here he seems to find the equivalent of the Diamant-Martinique relationship in Perse's home on the "Îlet-les-Feuilles" in the port of Pointe-à-Pitre: "No doubt a small island sheltered within a port is the most secure repository of the urge to wander. Îlet-les-Feuilles in the port of Pointe-à-Pitre. A small island in the anchorage of a larger island, bordered, not by sandy beaches twisted with mangrove, but by the scrawl of tall ships that keep tugging at it. . . . Îlet-les-Feuilles. Sea and Forest. This natural world that engenders and dictates his style" (*Traité du Tout-Monde* 31). L'îlet-les-Feuilles, anchored between island space and open sea, deconstructs the idea of home as refuge and imposes on Perse the poetics of this space of destabilizing errancy.

Glissant's recent formulations of "la pensée archipelique" and "le Tout-Monde" are attempts to establish abstract categories for the new, almost postmodern intensity given to the idea of errancy. In such a model the idea of the West is destabilized to become the Tout-Monde, and the concept of home becomes irredeemably relational. Archipelagic thought encompasses detour in its fullest sense and the impossibility of "retour" in a Césairean sense. In his work, as is evident in the epigraphs referring to Faulkner and Leiris, Glissant increasingly attempts to conceptualize space in terms of frontier zones that become patterns of archipelagos, ever-expanding detours like that frontier river, the Mississippi, between rock and sea. "The volcano's water carved a watercourse through the tormented topography of the ocean's depths, between the islands, and perhaps joined the Guyanas to Yucatan, across these craters scattered among the islands, on this trembling summit where the earth questions the earth" (*Tout-Monde* 224).[4]

One is reminded of Mycea's delirium, which allows her to envision the liberating poetics of rock and sea, self and Other in terms of a poetics of opacity.[5] In opposition to a territorializing impulse to saturate objects and spaces with meaning by projecting psychic needs onto them, Glissant increasingly insists on a poetic vagabondage through a world of disrupted localities where Faulknerian traces of the puzzlingly concrete collide with horizons of another "South" in a renewed poetics of detour and opacity.

NOTES

1. Glissant, *Commandeur*, 189.
2. As developed in "The Secret Life of Things," Bill Brown's notion of "rehabilitative reification," which seems close to the surrealist ideal of objectification, seems relevant to Glissant's use of the material world and nonreductive opacity in the constructing of the subject. See also Brown, "Thing Theory."
3. Epigraph translations are mine.
4. Of related interest is Peter Hallward's extensive close reading of Glissant in his recent *Absolutely Postcolonial*. Despite his many insights into Glissant's theory, Hallward overstates Glissant's complicity in postcolonial theory's post-territorial agenda and overlooks his continued insistence on the importance of individual opacities.

5. Michael Taussig in *Mimesis and Alterity* may well be describing this process when he identifies a new phase of anthropology "where 'us' and 'them' lose their polarity and swim in and out of focus. This dissolution reconstellates the play of nature in mythic pasts of contractual truths. Stable identity formations auto-destruct into silence" (246).

WORKS CITED

Bakhtin, M. *The Dialogic Imagination*. Austin: U of Texas P, 1981.

Breton, André. *Martinique, charmeuse de serpents*. 2d. edition. Paris: Pauvert, 1972.

Brown, Bill. "The Secret Life of Things." *Critical Inquiry* 24.4 (1998): 935–64.

——. "Thing Theory." *Critical Inquiry* 28.1 (autumn 2001): 1–16.

Glissant, Edouard. *La case du commandeur*. Paris: Seuil, 1981.

——. *Le discours antillais*. Paris: Seuil, 1981.

——. *Faulkner, Mississippi*. Paris: Stock, 1996.

——. *L'intention poétique*. Paris: Seuil, 1969.

——. *La Lézarde*. Paris: Seuil, 1958.

——. *Poétique de la relation*. Paris: Gallimard, 1990.

——. *Le quatrièmè siècle*. Paris: Seuil, 1964.

——. *The Ripening*. London: Heinemann, 1995.

——. *Soleil de la conscience*. Paris: Seuil, 1956.

——. *Tout-Monde*. Paris: Gallimard, 1993.

——. *Traité du Tout-Monde*. Paris: Gallimard, 1997.

Hallward, Peter. *Absolutely Postcolonial*. Manchester, England: Manchester UP, 2001.

Le Brun, Annie. *A Distance*. Paris: Carrère, 1985.

Taussig, Michael. *Mimesis and Alterity*. New York: Routledge, 1993.

JESSE ALEMÁN

Crossing the Mason-Dixon Line in Drag: The Narrative of Loreta Janeta Velazquez, Cuban Woman and Confederate Soldier

"**M**adame Velasquez [*sic*] is not of Spanish birth or origin, but is an American and probably from the North," former Confederate General Jubal Early indignantly wrote to Tennessee Congressman William H. Slemons on 22 May 1878.[1] Early had come across a copy of Loreta Janeta Velazquez's sensational 1876 Civil War narrative, *The Woman in Battle*, and was so outraged by its historical inaccuracies, glaring omissions, and above all its impossible autobiographical account of a cross-dressed Cuban Confederate soldier that he wrote Slemons to declare Velazquez and her book fakes. After all, Early had allegedly met and exchanged letters with Velazquez, which raised the general's skepticism. "The solecisms in grammar contained in her letter," Early complained, "do not result from the broken English of a foreigner, but are the blunders of an American whose education is imperfect. Her appearance and voice are those of an American woman, and has no resemblance to those of a cultivated Spanish lady. If she is really Spanish in origin, then her associations with camp life have thoroughly Americanized her" (Early to Slemons). As the lore of the Civil War has it, women who "associated with camp life" were prostitutes, but even as Early slanders Velazquez, his argument turns back on itself, for to associate Velazquez with camp life places her on the Confederate lines.[2] More important, Early's indignation betrays his anxiety, however unconscious, about how *The Woman in Battle* threatens normative gender categories, clear national identities, and their tenuous relationship between fact and fiction.

Along with pointing out inaccurate details in the narrative, Early rests his argument against *The Woman in Battle* and the identity of its author on his contention that Velazquez neither writes like nor resembles a "Spanish lady." Certainly, she is no "true type of a Southern woman" either, those "pure and devoted" ladies of the Confederacy (Early to Slemons). Only a Yankee hack, Early implies, would have the audacity to imagine a Cuban woman who dons men's clothes, takes up arms for the South, enjoys several clandestine romances with men and women, and then writes about her exploits for money. It should come as no surprise, then, that even though Early claims to have met Velazquez, he dismisses her as a "pretender" (Early to Slemons). And he would not be the last to do so. Despite the estimated four hundred women who joined the Civil War in men's clothes (Livermore 119–20), most historians still echo Early's skepticism and question the veracity of the Velazquez narrative.[3] Francis Simkins, for instance, rejects the authenticity of the text and concludes that "the stories of her adventures have an air of the tawdry and the unreal" (81). Sylvia Hoffert comes to a more emphatic conclusion: "If we assume that all of her claims must be confirmed by other evidence in order to be judged true, then we must conclude that much of her story is untrue simply because there is not enough evidence available to substantiate it" (31). And Mary Massey considers the dubious autobiography a "composite picture of several women's experiences published or rumored at the time and later enlivened by the author's vivid imagination" (82). In other words, either Velazquez is an outrageous counterfeit or she is an outrageous liar, leaving Simkins, Hoffert, and Massey uncertain whether "Loreta Janeta Velazquez" is a nom de plume for an anonymous author having fun at the expense of the South or an actual historical figure who tried to write an autobiography but produced pulp fiction instead.[4]

While not necessarily motivated by the issue of determining Velazquez's veracity, several literary critics nevertheless read the text qua narrative. Richard Hall finds convincing circumstantial evidence in the account that supports its historical "truth"; more important, he considers it an "honest account" because Velazquez constructs a flawed persona who recounts her successes as well as her failures (207–11). Similarly, Jane

Schultz, who draws a distinction between fiction and autobiography, takes a rhetorical approach to the book, arguing that as a narrator Velazquez creates an "ideal audience, one that will be more charmed than offended when it infers her meaning. . . . Her matter-of-fact approach to her masculine demeanor is calculated not to shock but to inform" (33). As Kathleen De Grave has it, however, Velazquez's rhetoric betrays her status as a "confidence woman" who relies on a series of tropes and performances of identity to deceive others (116), and Elizabeth Young reads *The Woman in Battle* as a picaresque novel that uses cross-dressing as a means of collapsing the difference between masculinity, femininity, and the historical (re)construction of the nation. The life of Velazquez speaks to the construction of gender identity, Young contends, while the narrative challenges the formation of the nation's identity in general ("Confederate" 185).

As Young's argument makes clear, cross-dressing is at the center of the narrative's ontological and epistemological identity crisis, but if gender identity, as the text often demonstrates, is a performed process without a stable referent, then historical veracity and even authorship are troubled markers of *The Woman in Battle*'s authenticity as well. The narrative's gender transgressions have not gone unnoticed by critics who view Velazquez's cross-dressing as an act that destabilizes the South's normative gender categories, but as Jubal Early's letter indicates, *The Woman in Battle* also collapses racial and national identities, a point often lost on historians who doubt the truth of Velazquez's cross-dressing scenes but either trust or ignore Velazquez's claim to be a Cuban woman with a Spanish colonial heritage. While most historians indefatigably track down references to Lieutenant Harry T. Buford—Velazquez's nom de guerre—in Civil War records, none have traced the existence of a Loreta Janeta Velazquez in Cuban or U.S. records, and Elizabeth Young's otherwise smart analysis of Velazquez's text unproblematically treats her as a "Southern white woman" rather than as a Cuban woman passing as, among other things, a Southern white man (*Disarming* 161). To recall Early's letter again: the question is not only whether the Velazquez text is true but also whether Velazquez herself is truly "a Spanish lady" or simply an American, "probably from the North" (Early to Slemons).[5]

In this sense, Velazquez's ethnonational identity must be considered in the same light as her floating gender categories; her purported Cuban identity is a historically performed construct that, on the one hand, challenges the idea of essential ethnic identity and, on the other, imagines an ideologically authentic connection between Cuba and the Confederacy during the nineteenth century. Stuck somewhere in between Juan

Francisco Manzano's 1839 *Autobiography of a Slave*, the only published slave narrative written before the official abolition of slavery in Cuba, and José Martí's abolitionist and anticolonial writings, which have become dernier cri in new American studies, *The Woman in Battle* uses cross-dressing as a socially symbolic act that reveals a transnational cultural relationship between gender, race, and national identity in the Americas. While the text certainly critiques Yankee imperialism, it does so from the standpoint of a Cuban woman passing as a white Southern man writing a narrative mediated by a Yankee editor. So, just as cross-dressing collapses normative gender categories and confuses the readability of sexuality, it also works to blur the ethnonational differences between Cuba and the South to enact a literary and historical merger between two geopolitical regions connected by a common history of slavery, a shared fiction of Old World white gentility, and a mutual enemy in Yankee economic and territorial expansion. By imagining a Cuban woman who passes as a Confederate soldier and Yankee spy, *The Woman in Battle* collapses the literal and symbolic binary categories represented by the embattled Mason-Dixon line and generates instead a civil war of positionality that reconstructs gender, race, and national identity markers across the colonial terrain of the Americas.

The cross-dressed production of *The Woman in Battle*—ostensibly authored by Velazquez but edited by C. J. Worthington, a former Yankee naval officer—immediately indicates the overdetermined uncertainty of identity that characterizes the events in the narrative. Beginning with Velazquez's 1842 birth in Cuba, where she claims a colonial heritage that reaches as far back as Don Diego Velazquez, Cuba's conqueror and first governor, the narrative recounts Velazquez's move to New Orleans in the 1850s, where she attends an all-girls Catholic school. Much to the chagrin of her father, who fought in the U.S.-Mexican War and never lost his animosity for Americans, Velazquez elopes with an American southerner on the eve of the Civil War. As it shifts her national status from Cuban to Cuban-American, Velazquez's marriage to a southerner marks a moment of Americanization that places her within a traditional heterosexual matrix of southern womanhood, but the start of the Civil War sets off a gendered civil war within Velazquez. As she puts it, "I have no hesitation in saying that I wish I had been created as a man instead of a woman" (130).[6]

Velazquez's husband objects to her cross-dressing, but he dies conveniently early in the narrative, leaving Velazquez free to enact an alternative gender identity. She becomes a southern man, dons the name Harry T.

Buford, and participates in the battles of Bull Run, Balls Bluff, and Shiloh before turning to espionage.[7] She poses as a northern woman, infiltrates the ranks of the Yankee secret service, and works as a double agent to support the Confederate cause from the other side of the Mason-Dixon line. Eventually, the Yankee secret service even hires her to find herself, the "woman who is traveling and figuring as a Confederate agent" (516).

As Judith Butler explains, "Gender does not denote a substantive being, but a relative point of convergence among culturally and historically specific sets of relations" (*Gender Trouble* 15). With every shift in identity, Velazquez enters a new "set of relations" that determine her gendered performances, but her cross-dressing also exposes the cultural and historical contingencies that prescribe the gendered identities she assumes. While drag is not necessarily subversive, Butler argues, it can "serve a subversive function to the extent that it reflects the mundane impersonations by which heterosexually ideal genders are performed and naturalized and undermines their power by virtue of effecting that exposure" (*Bodies* 231). Gender performances are also socially symbolic acts that take place on a historical stage, though, and Velazquez's cross-dressing makes clear that the Civil War, like most wars, brought normative gender categories to a crisis. Consider Velazquez's disguise, for instance. A tailor makes her "half a dozen fine wire net shields," which she wears "next to [her] skin" around her chest (58). As she explains, "They proved very satisfactory in concealing my true form, and in giving me something of a man, while they were by no means uncomfortable" (58). Over the wire shield, she wears a silk shirt, an undershirt with a shoulder brace, and a heavy belt around the waist "to make the waistbands of [her] pantaloons stand out to the proper number of inches" (58). "With such underwear as I used," Velazquez concludes, "any woman who can disguise her features can readily pass for a man" (58).

Velazquez's transformation highlights the sartorial performativity of gender, as Butler suggests, but it also signals a historically specific ideological crisis in southern gender categories. Velazquez in effect wears an inverted hoopskirt, a faddish dress at the outbreak of the Civil War that, as Drew Gilpin Faust notes, "generally coincided with the emergence of Victorian ideals of domesticity and with the triumph of the ideology of a separate woman's sphere" (223). The hoopskirt consisted of steel hoops covered in cloth and cinched at the waist. It enclosed upper-class Victorian women, Faust explains, within their own private space, concealing the female body and making it seemingly impenetrable. But as the war continued, dress materials became scarce, and for upper-class southern women, fashion was no longer a commodity they could afford. The marker of southern womanhood, and all of the cultural categories the hoopskirt maintained, became a casualty of war. "The distinctions separating upper-class women from women of the lower orders became less sharp," Faust concludes, "and ladies gained a freedom of movement often required by their new wartime responsibilities" (225). They left the feminized confines signified by the hoopskirt and entered the public sphere to work, to nurse soldiers, and when bread got too expensive, to riot in the streets. As she turns hoopskirt into hoopshirt, then, Velazquez symbolically indicates a greater crisis in gender created by the Civil War, one that perhaps culminates with Jefferson Davis's rumored attempt to elude Yankee forces at the end of the war by donning his wife's hoops.[8]

So while Velazquez's transvestism enacts the performativity of gender, it also reveals the historical fissures that create the occasion for transvestism to denaturalize normative heterosexual gender roles in the first place. Indeed, contrary to Butler's claim that cross-dressing usually reaffirms heterosexual gender categories—and Butler is mainly considering male-to-female drag—Velazquez's transvestism creates a sexual civil war that enters the drawing rooms, theaters, and houses of the Confederacy to trouble the myth of white southern womanhood as Velazquez/Buford flirts with women, plays on their affections, and then rebuffs their advances. As Velazquez explains, "I had some curiosity to know how love-making went from the masculine standpoint, and thought that the present would be a good opportunity to gain some valuable experience in that line" (75). So Velazquez/Buford carries on a flirtation with Miss Sadie Giles, "a fair flower of the Arkansas forest" (75), enjoys the courtship of "a pretty widow" in Pensacola (87), and finds some "amusement, too, to carry on a bit of a flirtation with a nice girl" named Miss E. in Leesburg (111) to name only a few of Buford's "conquests" (91). Of course, not all drag performances are necessarily homosexual, but Velazquez's gender transgressions as Buford foreshadow her later protolesbian moments in the narrative. She seduces a chambermaid, for instance, to gain access to the hotel quarters of northern officers (450), and while touring the West, she passes the night in bed with a woman characterized by her penchant for cussing, drinking, and the "formidable-looking knife and six shooter" around her waist (579). Velazquez relishes her same-sex adventures while she is disguised as Buford, often chastising southern women who too quickly cast their affections on dashing young soldiers, but she remains more reticent about her protolesbian scenes with the chambermaid and frontier woman, perhaps suggesting that her role as Buford allows Velazquez to enact her queer desire within seemingly heterosexual norms of Victorian culture.

While the protolesbian scenes in which Buford acts as a "lady's man" challenge the myth of southern womanhood (90), Velazquez's four marriages, which ostensibly affirm her heterosexuality, bring southern masculinity to a homoerotic crisis as well. Her first husband introduces Velazquez to cross-dressing and takes her out on the town for a night with the guys, albeit reluctantly. Her second husband welcomes Velazquez's role-playing. Disguised as Buford, Velazquez reveals to Captain Thomas C. DeCaulp that his female lover and fellow solider are one and the same; DeCaulp gladly marries Velazquez anyway but asks her to wear a dress instead of a soldier's uniform to the wedding. Highlighting the performativity of normative gender roles, the wedding dress reverses the specter of Velazquez's protolesbianism as her confession and marriage to DeCaulp affirm her heterosexuality. However, the confession scene also outs DeCaulp's own homoerotic desire. " 'Well, captain, don't you think your lady-love looks the least bit like your friend Harry Buford,' " Velazquez/Buford asks, kneeling in uniform next to DeCaulp's hospital bed. After a moment of confusion, DeCaulp indeed recognizes his fiancée disguised as a man and exclaims, " 'I love you ten times more than ever for this, Loreta!' " (332). Ironically, in a moment of compulsory heterosexuality, Velazquez's cross-dressing creates a fissure in the construction of southern masculinity and femininity, with Velazquez wearing the soldier's uniform and DeCaulp helplessly feminized in a hospital bed. "In this description," Elizabeth Young explains in *Disarming the Nation*, "the normalizing ritual of heterosexual marriage coexists with the possibility, as much exciting 'sensation' as unsavory threat, of two men marrying each other" (170).

Indeed, sensationalism informs Velazquez's disguised same-sex seductions, be they seductions of men or women. Yet the narrative remains dubiously silent about Velazquez's sexual encounters with women, such as the chambermaid or the rugged frontierswoman, when Velazquez is figuring as a woman, suggesting that while her transvestism generates sexual sensation, it also opens a narrative space for the enactment of protolesbian desire. It was not uncommon, for instance, for women, especially officers' wives or lovers, to follow men to the front lines, and sometimes these camp followers donned men's uniforms to prolong their stay on the front. Under these circumstances transvestism facilitates rather than challenges heterosexual conventions, but while Velazquez does follow her first husband to battle, she maintains her disguise as Buford long after her husband's death. All four of Velazquez's husbands die quickly in the narrative, and aside from her second engagement, Velazquez rarely recounts her heterosexual courtships. Instead, such scenes receive perfunctory treatment in contrast to the considerable attention Velazquez gives to describing her seduction of women as Buford. Velazquez's cross-dressing takes a queer turn as her role as Buford allows her to seduce women under a heterosexual masquerade, which in turn naturalizes her same-sex encounters when she is passing as a woman. The chambermaid and frontierswoman seemingly become part of Velazquez's adventures, yet the absence of sensationalism surrounding their narration marks them as different—that is, queer—from the rest of the text's sexual exploits.

Velazquez's gender ambivalence also embodies the competing power codes that narrate the South's changing status during the war. With the start of the war, when the South was heady with secession, Velazquez symbolized the South's masculinity by donning a Confederate uniform, and Buford's string of successes with the ladies immediately follows the South's victory at Bull Run. "In the context of exaggerated masculinity on the battlefield," Young explains, "Velazquez's military success authorizes her after-hours romances" (*Disarming* 171). As the South wanes, Velazquez's disguise becomes increasingly dilapidated until she sheds her uniform and more often passes as a woman. This process of (re)feminization, Young continues, unintentionally undermines the South's attempt to reconstruct its masculinity after the war. With the North seizing on Jefferson Davis's escape attempt in drag as an apt symbol for the feminized defeat of the South, southerners generated a counterdiscourse through lost-cause iconography that valorized the heroics of southern manhood and reconceptualized southern women back into the private realm of white purity. "Symbolically speaking, Southerners used the memory of the Civil War not only to make a man out of the boyish South, but to prove that the region was a boy and not a girl in the first place" (181). However, underneath the uniform, shoulder braces, and wire hoops, "Velazquez *is* a girl," Young concludes (181), and thus she legitimates the feminization of the South her narrative works against.

But if the South is not masculine after all, it may not be southern either, for Velazquez is not quite a white southern woman, as Young has it; rather, she claims to be a Cuban woman passing as a white southern man, which suggests that her transvestism works transnationally to consolidate the ethnonational differences between two slaveholding regions on the decline. Velazquez opens her narrative by invoking a Spanish colonial heritage, claiming roots in history as well as in art. She writes, "Both in Spain and in the Spanish dominions on this side of the Atlantic, is the name of Velazquez well known and highly honored. Don Diego Velazquez, the conqueror and the first governor of Cuba, under whose superintendence the expedition which discovered Mexico was sent out, was one of my ancestors, and Don Diego Rodriguez Velazquez, the greatest artist that Spain ever produced, was a member of my family" (39). As if her family's sugar plantation in Puerto de Palmas were not enough to link Velazquez to the South's slave economy, Velazquez dons a Spanish colonial legacy, quite similar to the South's slave culture, as a way of positioning herself within the Confederacy. Her Spanish heritage thus becomes the narrative's historical unconscious, a symbol of Cuba and its colonial history that generates a geocultural connection between Cuba and the Confederate South when both regions are embattled in civil strife over anticolonial independence and slavery. As Velazquez puts it, "I am a Cuban, and am a true Southern sympathizer" (502).

As early as the 1830s, black slavery in Cuba was unpopular with Cuban intellectuals, but as Ada Ferrer notes, by midcentury "enslaved and free people of color together constituted a majority of the [Cuban] population, outnumbering those identified as white. That white population, educated in the fear of black and slave rebellion, looked to Haiti and clung to Spain in fear" (2). Following Cuba's anticolonial and abolitionist insurgency, which culminated with the start of the Ten Years' War against Spain in 1868, Velazquez must find an alternative yet equivalent colonial slave system to legitimate her sense of white privilege and social status, which her family enjoyed in Cuba's slave economy. At first, Velazquez turns to compulsory heterosexuality to create a symbolic union between Cuba's criollo class and the Confederacy. Despite her father's hatred of Americans and her arranged betrothal to a Cuban, Velazquez breaks with Cuba's Old World traditions and elopes with an American southerner (48). She even converts from Catholicism to Protestantism, becoming a member of the Methodist church in an act of cultural assimilation, gender rebellion, and independence that symbolically annexes her into the Confederacy. Her first marriage is a transnational merger that positions Velazquez in a space of white privilege that she and the criollo class in general enjoyed in Cuba before its abolotionist insurgency movements.

The Civil War dissolves her first marriage, however, just as it threatens to dissolve the potential for Cuban annexation into the South, so Velazquez takes on her disguise as Buford to show that even a Cuban woman can be a "genuine Southerner" (503). While her homoerotic marriage to DeCaulp generates a gender crisis, then, it also enacts a criollo desire to merge Cuban independence with southern secession. Indeed, as early as 1850, Narciso López, a criollo Cubano, led a failed filibuster invasion of

Cuba with the hope of U.S. annexation, and many, though not all, of his recruits were southerners. Meanwhile, in Cuba, the Club de la Habana, an organization of Cuban criollos, actively pursued Cuban annexation into the United States. As Tom Chaffin explains, "The United States seemed the best alternative to royalist Spain: an option that promised relative autonomy, a likely end to the slave trade, but immediate protection of Cuban slavery—and all without massive social upheaval" (12). In contrast to the many Cubans who espoused anticolonial and abolitionist independence, though, Velazquez as Buford enacts a neocolonial fantasy that imagines an independent Cuba consolidated with an independent South to create a new southern slavocracy. Velazquez even buys a slave named Bob, who not only functions as part of Buford's performed southern masculinity but also indicates Velazquez's distance from the emerging revolutionary discourses in Cuba. "Cuban rebels spoke of a raceless nation," Ferrer notes, "in the period that represented the nadir in American racial politics. Thus, the escalation of racial violence, the spread of spatial segregation by race, and the dismantling of political gains made during Reconstruction in the South occurred in the United States precisely as black and mulatto leaders gained increasing popularity and power in Cuba" (4).

Velazquez's cross-dressing thus must be read as reactionary rather than revolutionary. Faced with a "colorless" Cuba, Velazquez becomes Buford to fight for the slave economies that undergird the color hierarchies in Cuba and the Confederacy. The clothes determine Velazquez's identity, and as she turns from Cuban woman into southern man, so too do Cuba and the South become interchangeable regions consolidated through an ideology of whiteness propped up by black slave labor. The collusion between national identities is telling, for it suggests that Cuba is a southern cause just as much as the South is a Cuban cause, certainly adding new meaning to what José Martí would call "Our America" nearly two decades later.[9] In fact, at the height of the Civil War, Velazquez considered herself an American, and as if to prove her American patriotism, she vowed to fight for Cuban independence in much the same way that her Cuban nationalism led her to fight for the South.

> I begrudged that this fair island should be the dependency of a foreign power; for I was, despite my Spanish ancestry, an American, heart and soul, and if there was anything that could have induced me to abandon the cause of the Southern Confederacy, it would have been an attempt on the part of the Cubans to have liberated themselves from the Spanish yoke. . . . [I] more than half resolved that should the

Cubans strike a blow for independence, I would join my fortunes to theirs, and serve their cause with the same assiduity that I was now serving that of the Confederacy. (248)

For Velazquez, Cuba and the Confederacy are involved in related anti-colonial conflicts—while the South fends off Yankee imperialism, Cuba struggles to free itself from Spanish dominion. Unlike Martí, however, Velazquez is not advocating Cuba's abolitionist insurgency. Rather, as Buford, she mouths a southern desire for Cuba's independence so that it may be annexed as part of the South's slavocracy. A Cuban in southern uniform, Velazquez "ideologically incorporates" (Epstein and Straub 4) a new anticolonial Confederacy that looks away from Spain and the North to reconstruct an independent, transnational South that maintains a colonial fantasy of white privilege.

The defeat of the South, though, brings an end to Velazquez's cross-dressed colonial fantasy. On the level of gender, her return to female at-tire symbolically feminizes the defeated South, but on the ethnonational front, her return from Buford to Velazquez puts Cuba back on the mar-gins of the United States. Indeed, Velazquez begins to call herself Cuban immediately following General Lee's surrender. At first, she claims her Cuban identity to find domestic work in a friendly Copperhead house in the North (502). After Lincoln's assassination, however, Velazquez claims to be Cuban as a way of distancing herself from the war and Lincoln's death. When an acquaintance asks her, " 'What do your people think of the war?' " she responds laconically, " 'O, they think it is very bad; but it is to be hoped that it is about over now' " (513). Finally, as she lights out of the country for Europe, she befriends two Spaniards, claims to be of "Spanish descent," and even speaks to them in Spanish (520). It may be no coincidence that she assumes her Cuban identity again after Colo-nel Baker, head of the North's secret services, hires Velazquez—whom he believes to be a Northern spy—to find herself (516). Her return to a Cuban identity, moreover, signals her increasing marginality in the United States. She goes from being a domestic worker to being an exile on the domestic front, heading off to Europe with her Cuban brother be-cause Reconstruction has no place for Cuban Confederates.

When she returns to the United States, she finds the South "in the hands of ignorant negroes" and "white 'carpet-baggers' " (535). As with many defeated southerners, Velazquez can no longer imagine an eth-nonational identity for herself in the American South. Thus, she pro-poses a colonization trip to Venezuela in the hopes of discovering a new South, one that will reconstruct Cuban whiteness and southern slavery as an alternative to Yankee America. But the group of southern exiles she heads encounters free blacks in Venezuela, too. As Velazquez puts it, "It would have been just as well to have remained at home and fought the battle for supremacy with the free Negroes and carpet-baggers on familiar ground" (543). She finds it no better in Georgetown, Guyana, where they "were beset by negroes" (553), and Velazquez is dubious of the black woman who runs the town's main hotel (554). Port Spain, off of Trinidad, proves equally displeasing to Velazquez: "It was a very dingy-looking settlement, with a very ragged and dirty native population. There were a few Englishmen, but the majority of the people were negroes or half-breeds, whose habitations were disgustingly dirty and squalid" (558). And finally, when the ship stops at Puerto Rico, Velazquez refuses to go ashore, "not liking the looks of the place" (565).

Ironically, the colonization expedition ends where Velazquez began— Cuba. She calls on military friends with the "Spanish forces," realigns herself with Spain's domination of Cuba, and even dresses in a soldier's uniform to pass as "a young Spanish officer who had been educated in England" (566). However, in the same way that Velazquez considers her cross-dressing a process of "unsexing," as she calls it, her transvestism also enacts a process of ethnic erasure that has her performing her own Cuban identity poorly. As she explains, "my Spanish accent was none of the best, my long non-use of the language having caused me to lose the faculty of speaking it in such a manner as to do entire credit to my ancestry" (567). While the defeat of the South puts an end to her performance as Buford, her transvestism in general puts an end to her Cuban identity. At best, she finds herself in the dislocated identity status of a Cuban-American, a hyphenated subject with no clear place in the Americas. Failing to find a new South in Latin America, she travels the U.S. frontier, traversing Utah, Nevada, California, Arizona, and New Mexico, and the narrative ends with Velazquez on the road back to the South via Texas. It is a homecoming of sorts, since her father once owned land in Texas, but there is no home to which Velazquez can return. Her father had lost his land grant with Texas's 1845 annexation.

In the end, the link between the U.S.-Mexican War and the Civil War suggests that Velazquez was always already a dislocated subject in the Americas, which may explain the fluidity of her gender, racial, and national identities. With the conquest of Cuba, Don Diego Velazquez initiated a Spanish colonial diaspora throughout the Americas, which Loreta Janeta Velazquez inherits. She has no home in Cuba, no land in Mexico, and no place in the United States. She has no nation and no identity either, for she enacts so many identities—Buford, an Anglo woman from the North, a Canadian, a French Creole, an English woman, and, of course, a Spanish lady—that the essential self she proudly traced to Spanish colonialism winds up being nothing more than a simulacrum. Velazquez's performativity turns her into her own worst enemy: "I had a not ill-founded distrust of these people," she writes of Copperheads, "who are neither one thing nor the other" (431). Her cross-dressing performances thus highlight how ethnonational identity, like gender identity, passes through and for multiple categories, bringing them all into a crisis of representation that reveals identity to be more of a fiction than a fact.

It is has not been my intention to authenticate the Velazquez narrative and its authorship but to suggest just the opposite—cross-dressing in *The Woman in Battle* speaks to the impossibility of authenticity altogether. Gender, race, and nation are sartorial performances that dislodge stable identity markers, wreaking havoc, as they did for Jubal Early, on ideologies, national institutions, and literary histories that demand readable signs of subjectivity. What Karen Christian says of contemporary U.S. Latina/o literature indeed holds true for *The Woman in Battle:* "Latina/o fiction suggest[s] that cultural identity is not static or naturalized but involves a certain degree of cross-dressing, of drag, in a metaphoric sense. . . . [B]oth cultural identity and gender identity resemble drag shows that parody the notion of essentialized identity categories" (16). As a southern narrative, *The Woman in Battle* inadvertently disrobes Confederate manhood and nationalism to reveal a Cuban woman; Velazquez's transvestism, though, troubles the notion of an essential or authentic Cuban identity and suggests instead that ethnonational categories, as with gender identities, are historically performed constructions based on strategic distinctions and alliances. Thus, *The Woman in Battle* offers a proslavery, anticolonial America that radically complicates the significance often bestowed on José Martí and the impact of 1898 for Cuba and the Americas.

In fact, *The Woman in Battle* troubles recent transnational arguments for the Americas as an oppositional site to U.S. imperialism. In his forward to Roberto Fernández Retamar's *Caliban and Other Essays*, for example, Fredric Jameson writes, "We, therefore, need a new literary and cultural internationalism which involves risks and dangers, which calls us into question fully as much as it acknowledges the Other, thereby also serving as a more adequate and chastening form of self-knowledge" (xii). For Jameson, Fernández Retamar's decolonial writings initiate a process of internationalism that checks the colonial hegemony of American and European literary and cultural production, and for Fernández Retamar,

Martí's anticolonial works insist on an internationalism that understands America as a transnational, mestiza nation rather than as a provincial Yankee one. This genealogy of Cuban anticolonialist discourse is not lost on José David Saldívar, who argues that the common literature of the Americas is a dialectical one that pits Yankee America against the mestiza Americas. Martí's "Nuestra América," Saldívar explains, "can provide us with the central oppositional codes upon which to base a dialectical view not only of the American continent but of the many literatures of the Americas" (67). And the contributors to *José Martí's "Our America"* take up Saldívar's point. As the editors explain, "The collective objective of the collection is . . . to explore the tension in Martí's work between national and transnational perspectives, a tension that makes his analysis of the Western Hemisphere's different national formations and their intrahemispheric relations extremely significant for reconfiguring the way we think about 'America' " (Belnap and Fernández 3–4).

What happens to this anti-Yankee "Nuestra America," however, if one considers it through Velazquez's Cuban-Confederate consolidation? Certainly, her pro-Confederate stance places her in opposition to the "giant in seven league boots," as Martí called the North. On one of her espionage missions across the Mason-Dixon line, for instance, Velazquez discovers the wealth of the North and contrasts it with the paucity of the South's economic resources. Not lost on her is the economic boom the war provides for northerners at the expense of the South. While the war keeps southern men away from home and blockades cut off international trade to the South, domestic work and international commerce thrive in the North. The war "actually appeared to be making the North rich," Velazquez exclaims (384), and the war industry inevitably finds its way onto the battlefields. After the southern defeat at Fort Donelson, Velazquez realizes that "we [the South] were contending with a resolute and powerful enemy, whose resources were enormously superior to ours, and who was evidently bent upon crushing us to the earth, and compelling us to submit to his dictation" (184).

While the problem of slavery distinguishes Martí from Velazquez, the Cuban-Confederate anticolonialism she enacts nevertheless challenges the patriarchal genealogy of colonial critique that New Americanists, in their revision of the Americas, trace back to Martí. Velazquez envisions an "Our America" too, one that is quite different from Martí's mestiza nationhood but similar in its opposition to Yankee America. She imagines an America where the hacienda converges with the big house, where Spanish *criollismo* becomes southern whiteness, and where Cuba finds its masculinity in southern manhood. Redrawing the georacial cartography of the Americas to place Cuba at the center of a complex relationship with U.S. slavery and Reconstruction, Velazquez troubles the discourses of anti-imperialism, racial colonialism, and exile that inform the works of Martí and Retamar. Equally important, her text raises the very "risks and dangers" Jameson advocates in constructing an internationalism that "calls us into question fully as much as it acknowledges the Other" (xii). With Velazquez, the dialectic of Our America risks becoming dialogic as the South passes for Cuba and Cuba passes for the South, each complicit with slavery and equally determined to secure independence from imperialism. One might even say that transvestism in *The Woman in Battle* brings the Americas into a transnational crisis of identity as it blurs the line between Cuba and the Confederacy, self and Other, America and América.

The Spanish colonial legacy that Velazquez invokes at the start of her narrative perhaps even enables the possibility of *The Woman in Battle*—its authorship, authenticity, and imaginary Americas—enacting a historical erasure of its own ethnonational subject. Velazquez's namesake not only connects her to the conqueror of Cuba but also to Don Diego Rodriguez Velazquez, "the greatest artist Spain ever produced" (39). His masterpiece, of course, is *Las Meninas* (1656), a piece that ostensibly represents handmaidens waiting on Spain's royal infanta Margarita but in effect calls the entire process of representation into question. To the left, the painter represents himself standing before a large canvas; the infanta and her maids appear in the foreground; a duenna and male escort occupy the middle ground; and a gentleman framed by a lit doorway stands in the background. Two paintings hang on the far wall, and between them a mirror faintly reflects the king and queen, though they do not appear in the canvas space. "But though Velázquez intends an optical report of the event," Helen Gardner explains, "authentic in every detail, he seems also to intend a pictorial summary of the various kinds of images in their different levels and degrees of 'reality'—the 'reality' of canvas image, of mirror image, of optical image, and of the two imaged paintings" (601). Indeed, the viewer sees only the back of the painter's canvas, so that it remains uncertain whether the painter, who looks out at the viewer, is painting a portrait of the king and queen, the infanta, the entire family scene, the very painting itself, or perhaps even its viewer.

The painting's subtle mirrorings, Michel Foucault notes, generate a series of "feints" that render the object of representation invisible (3). The painter's gaze points to the spectator, but the spectator is not represented in the painting. Presumably, the king and queen stand in the spectator's space, so they too are outside of the canvas space, impossibly reflected in a mirror that "cuts through the whole field of the representation," Foucault explains, "ignoring all it might apprehend within that field, and restores visibility to that which resides outside all view" (8). While the painting itself seemingly captures what the mirror misses, moreover, it also reproduces the mirror's erasure. From left to right: the painter with palette standing before his canvas; a mirror in the background between two completed but obscure paintings; light flooding the room from a side window; human subjects; and finally, the back of the painter's canvas. The painting, Foucault continues, "presents us with the entire cycle of representation: the gaze, the palette and brush, the canvas innocent of signs . . . , the paintings, the reflections, the real man . . . ; then the representation dissolves again: we can see only the frames, and the light that is flooding the pictures from outside" (11). Representation has come and gone, yet the object of the painter's painting remains invisible, leaving Foucault to conclude that the self-conscious representation of representation captures its "pure form": "And, indeed, representation undertakes to represent itself here in all its elements, with its images, the eyes to which it is offered, the faces it makes visible, the gestures that call it into being. But there, in the midst of this dispersion which it is simultaneously grouping together and spreading out before us, indicated compellingly from every side, is an essential void: the necessary disappearance of that which is its foundation—of the person it resembles and the person in whose eyes it is only a resemblance" (16).

An Italian viewer noticing how the thin paint strokes of *Las Meninas* dissolve into each other exclaimed, " 'It is made of nothing, yet there it is!' " (Gardner 603). The same might also be said of *The Woman in Battle* and its authorship: the text exists, but its authenticity and authorship dissolve in cross-dressed sartorial signs of identity that reveal as much as they conceal about Cuba, the South, and the complex relationship they share with U.S. colonialism. Velazquez passes as Buford, but in his role as Yankee editor, C. J. Worthington passes as Velazquez. North, South, and Cuba converge to blur the distinctions between masculine and feminine, the United States and Cuba, and the history and fictions of the Mason-Dixon line. Each mirror each other and in the process generate their own erasure, making authenticity and authorship floating signifiers that inhabit the Velazquez text but never quite make their presence known. As the text's transvestism suggests, gendered, racial, and national identities involve a process of representation without a stable referent. *The Woman in Battle* thus inherits from *Las Meninas* its ontological and epistemological crisis: it represents the process of representation and inevitably renders its own subject invisible. It may not be an irony of history after all that a cloud of doubt lingers over Loreta Janeta Velazquez and her authorship of *The Woman in Battle*. Rather, it may be that representation itself has erased its own subject and with it, the imaginary lines that divide the Americas.

NOTES

I owe thanks to the panelists and audience who heard a version of this essay at the 2000 American Studies Association Conference. My revisions of the essay also enjoyed the benefit of a lively discussion at the 2000 Recovering the U.S. Hispanic Literary Heritage Conference, with especially helpful comments from Nicolás Kanellos, Genaro Padilla, Erlinda Gonzales-Berry, John-Michael Rivera, and Andrea Tinnemeyer. Joseph Gonzales, Juan Buriel, and Amberley Pyles indefatigably assisted me with research on Velazquez, which was generously underwritten by the University of New Mexico's Center for Regional Studies. Finally, Minrose Gwin and William L. Andrews encouraged and guided my scholarship on Velazquez, the Civil War, gender studies, and issues of autobiographical authenticity. Needless to say, whatever shortcomings remain in the essay reveal my own myopia.

1. Jubal Early to W. F. Slemons, 22 May 1878 [hereafter Early to Slemons], Tucker Family Papers no. 2605, Southern Historical Collection, Wilson Library, University of North Carolina, Chapel Hill. Quotations from the Tucker Papers used by permission.

2. Mary and Molly Bell had been passing for two years among Confederate troops as Tom Parker and Bob Martin before a captain accused them of "demoralizing his men." In 1864 the case was brought before Early, who sent the Bell sisters to prison in Richmond—they were still wearing their Confederate uniforms (Hall 103).

3. While the exact number of women who cross-dressed as men during the war may be elusive, Civil War scholars DeAnne Blanton and Lauren M. Cook have thoroughly documented the frequency with which women dressed as men during the war, noting that reasons ranging from romance to patriotism inspired women on both sides of the Mason-Dixon line to take up arms.

4. Leonard and Kaufman offer compelling arguments on Velazquez's identity while Blanton and Cook have established the historical veracity of most of the events in the narrative. I handle the debate on Velazquez's authorship and authenticity more thoroughly in "Authenticity, Autobiography, and Identity: *The Woman in Battle* as a Civil War Narrative," the introduction to my forthcoming reprint of *The Woman in Battle*.

5. I will take up this issue further in my closing comments, but let me suggest now that I am less concerned with finding a historical Velazquez than I am with exploring how *The Woman in Battle* generates an ontological and epistemological crisis in gender identity that not only calls into question the distinction between Confederate and Cuban nationalities but also challenges the process of authenticating the text's authorship and, in the greater picture, the existence of Velazquez. To this end, I consider Velazquez as a character both in *The Woman in Battle* and in the embattled history surrounding the question of her identity.

6. Faust documents a long list of similar expressions found in the diaries of southern

women. "Nearly every female Confederate diarist at some point expressed the desire to be a man," Faust explains (231).

7. I should mention that Sarah Seelye, also known as Franklin Tompson, fought for the North in drag at the Battle of Bull Run (Wiley 337), and Amy Clarke donned a Confederate uniform to fight at the Battle of Shiloh (Faust 202–3).

8. On 15 May 1865 the *New York Times* ran the following dispatch of Davis's capture: "The captors report that [Jefferson Davis] hastily put on one of Mrs. Davis' dresses and started for the woods, closely pursued by our men, who at first thought him a woman, but seeing his boots while running suspected his sex at once. The race was a short one, and the rebel President was soon brought to bay. . . . He expressed great indignation at the energy with which he was pursued, saying that he had believed our Government more magnanimous than to hunt down woman and children" (qtd. in Silber 29). Nina Silber, Gaines M. Foster, and Elizabeth Young aptly analyze the cultural significance of Davis's escape attempt in drag as a symbolic event that feminized the South and generated discourses of masculine conquest in the North.

9. As Jeffrey Belnap argues, Martí and Velazquez share an interest in the sartorial performativity of national identities. European bracelets and nail polish mark the Europeanized intellectual, Belnap notes, while Martí calls for a "cross-identification" between European education and Native American civilization as symbolized by headbands and sandals (194).

WORKS CITED

Alemán, Jesse. "Introduction: Authenticity, Autobiography, and Identity: *The Woman in Battle* as a Civil War Narrative." *The Woman in Battle.* By Loreta Janeta Velazquez. Rpt. ed. Madison: U of Wisconsin P, 2003.

Belnap, Jeffrey. "Headbands, Hemp Sandals, and Headdresses: The Dialectics of Dress and Self-Conception in Martí's 'Our America.'" *José Martí's "Our America": From National to Hemispheric Cultural Studies.* Ed. Jeffrey Belnap and Raúl Fernández. Durham, N.C.: Duke UP, 1998. 191–209.

Belnap, Jeffrey, and Raúl Fernández. "Introduction: The Architectonics of José Martí's 'Our Americanism.'" *José Martí's "Our America": From National to Hemispheric Cultural Studies.* Ed. Jeffrey Belnap and Raúl Fernández. Durham, N.C.: Duke UP, 1998.

Blanton, DeAnne, and Lauren M. Cook. *They Fought Like Demons: Women Soldiers in the American Civil War.* Baton Rouge: Louisiana State UP, 2002.

Butler, Judith. *Bodies that Matter: On the Discursive Limits of "Sex."* New York: Routledge, 1993.

——. *Gender Trouble: Feminism and the Subversion of Identity.* New York: Routledge, 1990.

Chaffin, Tom. *Fatal Glory: Narciso López and the First Clandestine U.S. War against Cuba.* Charlottesville: UP of Virginia, 1996.

Christian, Karen. *Show and Tell: Identity as Performance in U.S. Latina/o Fiction.* Albuquerque: U of New Mexico P, 1997.

De Grave, Kathleen. *Swindler, Spy, Rebel: The Confidence Woman in Nineteenth-Century America.* Columbia: U of Missouri P, 1995.

Epstein, Julia, and Kristina Straub. "Introduction: The Guarded Body." *Body Guards: The Cultural Politics of Gender Ambiguity.* Ed. Julia Epstein and Kristina Straub. New York: Routledge, 1991. 1–28.

Faust, Drew Gilpin. *Mothers of Invention: Women of the Slaveholding South in the American Civil War.* Chapel Hill: U of North Carolina P, 1996.

Ferrer, Ada. *Insurgent Cuba: Race, Nation, and Revolution, 1868–1898.* Chapel Hill: U of North Carolina P, 1999.

Foster, Gaines M. *Ghosts of the Confederacy: Defeat, the Lost Cause, and the Emergence of the New South, 1865 to 1913.* New York: Oxford UP, 1987.

Foucault, Michel. *The Order of Things: An Archaeology of the Human Sciences.* New York: Vintage, 1994.

Gardner, Helen. *Art Through the Ages.* 6th ed. New York: Harcourt Brace Jovanovich, 1975.

Hall, Richard. *Patriots in Disguise: Women Warriors of the Civil War.* New York: Paragon, 1993.

Hoffert, Sylvia D. "Madame Loretta [*sic*] Velazquez: Heroine or Hoax?" *Civil War Times Illustrated* 17.3 (1978): 24–31.

Jameson, Fredric. Foreword. *Caliban and Other Essays.* By Roberto Fernández Retamar. Trans. Edward Baker. Minneapolis: U of Minnesota P, 1989. vii–xii.

Kaufman, Janet E. "'Under the Petticoat Flag': Women Soldiers in the Confederate Army." *Southern Studies* 23 (1984): 363–75.

Leonard, Elizabeth D. *All the Daring of a Soldier: Women of the Civil War Armies.* New York: Norton, 1999.

Livermore, Mary. *My Story of the War.* Hartford, Conn.: A. D. Worthington, 1888.

Martí, José. "Our America." *Our America: Writings on Latin America and the Struggle for Cuban Independence.* Ed. Philip S. Foner. Trans. Elinor Randall et al. New York: Monthly Review P, 1977. 84–94.

Massey, Mary Elizabeth. *Women in the Civil War.* Rpt. ed. Lincoln: U of Nebraska P, 1994.

Retamar, Roberto Fernández. *Caliban and Other Essays.* Trans. Edward Baker. Minneapolis: U of Minnesota P, 1989.

Saldívar, José David. "The Dialectics of Our America." *Do the Americas Have a Common Literature?* Ed. Gustavo Pérez Firmat. Durham, N.C.: Duke UP, 1990. 62–84.

Schultz, Jane Ellen. "Women at the Front: Gender and Genre in Literature of the American Civil War." Diss. U of Michigan, 1988.

Silber, Nina. *The Romance of Reunion: Northerners and the South, 1865–1900.* Chapel Hill: U of North Carolina P, 1993.

Simkins, Francis Butler, and James Welch Patton. *The Women of the Confederacy.* Richmond, Va.: Garrett and Massie, 1936.

Velazquez, Loreta Janeta. *The Woman in Battle.* Ed. C. J. Worthington. Richmond, Va.: Dustin, Gilman, 1876.

Wiley, Bell Irvin. *The Life of Billy Yank: The Common Soldier of the Union.* New York: Doubleday, 1971.

Young, Elizabeth. "Confederate Counterfeit: The Case of the Cross-Dressed Civil War Soldier." *Passing and the Fictions of Identity.* Ed. Elaine K. Ginsberg. Durham, N.C.: Duke UP, 1996. 181–217.

——. *Disarming the Nation: Women's Writing and the American Civil War.* Chicago: U of Chicago P, 1999.

STEVEN HUNSAKER

Citizenship and Identity in the Exile

Autobiographies of Gustavo Pérez Firmat

"**S**oy un ajiaco de contradicciones, / un puré de impurezas" ["I am a stew of contradictions, / a purée of impurities"] (*Bilingual Blues* 28). With these lines from "Bilingual Blues," the Cuban-American poet and critic Gustavo Pérez Firmat gives voice to the troubled sense of self that defines his exile. That sense of unresolved contradiction also colors his autobiography, *Next Year in Cuba* (1995), a narrative in which Pérez Firmat juxtaposes the disruption and loss of exile against the new possibilities and identities that life in the U.S. South makes possible. In other words, Pérez Firmat describes his life after leaving Cuba in terms of both pain and promise, loss and new life. The unsettled quality of exile identity in *Next Year in Cuba* manifests most concretely in the fact that shortly after its publication, Pérez Firmat translated and republished it in Spanish as *El año que viene estamos en Cuba* (1997). The two texts and languages are evidence of two generally complementary, if often competing, exile identities. The forced combinations of English and Spanish, Cuban identities and southern sensibilities produce anything but a stable compound, and tensions about everything from national identity to romantic love, marriage to citizenship unsettle Pérez Firmat's sense of place and self throughout *Next Year in Cuba*.

However troubled, Pérez Firmat's conclusions are ultimately hopeful. Firmly rooted in an American present rather than a Cuban past, Pérez Firmat writes with an optimism that separates him sharply from another Cuban-American exile autobiographer, Pablo Medina. Oriented almost exclusively toward his Cuban childhood, rather than toward his American manhood, Medina presents the trauma of exile in somber terms that run counter to Pérez Firmat's bright optimism. Medina notes, "I thought that changing nationalities was as easy as changing clothes, speech patterns, books to read. Twenty years . . . of wanderings taught me that nationality is in the soul, if it is anywhere, and to change that requires much more than window dressing of one's body or tongue or mind. The Americanization I sought for so long required the annihilation of memory, that tireless lady who is forever weaving and unweaving her multicolored tapestries. I don't believe anyone can do that by natural means" (x). Tellingly, Medina subtitles his book "A Cuban Childhood," and he dedicates it to his parents; Pérez Firmat, on the other hand, subtitles his autobiography "A *Cubano*'s Coming of Age in America," and he dedicates the book to his American-born children.

Because they promote his acculturation by forcing the issues of time and change, Pérez Firmat's children are in large measure responsible for the hopeful quality of his narrative. Bryan S. Turner defines cultural citizenship as "those social practices which enable a competent citizen to participate fully in the national culture" (159), and it is precisely his ability to participate in a new culture without fully surrendering the old that inspires Pérez Firmat's hopeful take on exile. Since his American-born children link him to a new national culture and to the English language without forcing the surrender of his affective ties to Cuban culture and to the Spanish language, he can describe himself as more than just an exile. In a characteristic passage from his book of cultural criticism, *Life on the Hyphen*, Pérez Firmat says, "Once an exile, always an exile; but it doesn't follow that once an exile, always *only* an exile" (11). In that spirit, Pérez Firmat confronts the rift between the self and the place of origin, presenting his new life in the United States in terms of losses *and* gains, Cuban *and* Cuban-American languages, Cuban *and* U.S. citizenship.

Pérez Firmat's optimism distinguishes him from others in similar circumstances, but the psychological and political trauma of dispossession necessarily links him to exiles who view the loss of the homeland and life in the adopted land primarily in terms of violation and loss. Edward

Said describes exile as "the unhealable rift forced between a human being and a native place, between the self and its true home" ("Mind" 49). Said, a Palestinian exile, continues, "The essential sadness of the break can never be surmounted. . . . The achievements of any exile are permanently undermined by his or her sense of loss" (49). Pablo Medina strikes a similar note even as he points toward resolution. Speaking of the cold New York winter that his family encountered on arrival from Cuba, he writes, "Suddenly I was surrounded by ice, and I jumped into the white mounds with all the enthusiasm I could muster. I renounced allegiance to the country of my birth when I became an American citizen, yet the blood still pulled and memory called. Thus it was that I became two persons, one a creature of warmth, the other the snow swimmer. The first would be forever a child dancing to the beat of the waves; the second was the adult, striving to emerge from the river of cold—invigorated, wise, at peace with life" (113).

Said, in contrast, reaffirms his abiding sense of loss and displacement against the backdrop of a life-threatening illness in his memoir, *Out of Place*. He states, "To this day I still feel that I am away from home, ludicrous as that may sound, and though I believe I have no illusions about the 'better' life I might have had, had I remained in the Arab world, or lived and studied in Europe, there is still some measure of regret. This memoir is on some level a reenactment of the experience of departure and separation as I feel the pressure of time hastening and running out. The fact that I live in New York City with a sense of provisionality despite thirty-seven years of residence here accentuates the disorientation that has accrued to me, rather than the advantages" (222).

Although the pain, loss, and dislocation of exile are central for all three writers, Pérez Firmat reaches very different conclusions regarding exile's meaning and effects. In Said's terms, one might say that Pérez Firmat accentuates advantages rather than disorientation, while Medina suggests a kind of middle ground. This is due in part to the fact that, unlike Said and despite his very real yearning for a place that he can call his own, Pérez Firmat does not posit a natural link between self and place. Said suffers a perpetual sense of being "out of place" in exile, but Pérez Firmat insists that he has achieved the status he calls "after-exile." It is after-exile because Pérez Firmat has abandoned the idea of return to Cuba and with it, the notion that he must live in a state of suspended animation while waiting to return. As he says in the prologue to *Next Year in Cuba*, "The exile is someone for whom this marriage [between person and place] has broken up; the 'after-exile' is someone who has sought out a new relation between person and place, someone who's found, or founded, another home" (13). Because he sees the tie between the self and the home in provisional rather than in natural terms, Pérez Firmat can step back and view the spectacle of a "Carolina Cuban" slowly coming to resemble his southern neighbors with melancholy, self-deprecating humor rather than with bitterness. Given that slow metamorphosis from Cuban to Carolina Cuban, it comes as no surprise that Pérez Firmat claims compounded rather than wounded identities.

Acting as catalysts of their father's cultural change, Pérez Firmat's children introduce much of the hope of *Next Year in Cuba* through their less self-conscious blending of Cuban and American cultures. As Isabel Alvarez Borland observes, "Both his children and his American wife, Mary Anne, become viable bridges that might enable him to effect solutions and adjustments to life in North America" (72). Although he is tormented by the implications of legal citizenship, Pérez Firmat focuses his narrative on the ways that exile opens doors to cultural citizenship through the agency of his children and his second, American wife. He gives his children credit for bringing about this transformation when he writes, "I gave Cuba to my kids, and they have reciprocated by giving me America. Partly by design and partly by accident, we have reached a middle ground between assimilation and exile. As they grew up, so did I. I didn't grow away from Cuba, for I'm as Cuban now as I ever was. I'd rather say that I grew out of Cuba, that *I learned to treat exile as something other than a disability*" (*Next Year* 255; emphasis added).

This acculturation takes place in a distinctly if stereotypically southern setting. The South that Pérez Firmat presents in *Next Year in Cuba* is painted in broad strokes, serving primarily as an exotic but benign background for the exile's passage toward citizenship. Pérez Firmat offers a lighthearted caricature of the South, with references to rednecks, bare feet, country music, toothless old men, and rebel yells, but it is not the particular human or physical geography of the South that interests him. It is, rather, the sense that the South offers the exile a space in which to be Cuban and to become a Carolina Cuban with very little interference.

For all his interest in the peculiarities of southern life, Pérez Firmat emphasizes the fact that his neighbors in North Carolina consider him exotic. For example, he notes, "If you say *qué hubo* [what's up] the guy next to you thinks you're muttering in Chinese" (253). Nonetheless, despite the exotic quality attributed to someone who speaks Spanish in Chapel Hill, any conflicts occasioned by the arrival of Cuban exiles in Florida and North Carolina are, at least for Pérez Firmat, almost exclusively internal conflicts produced by the exile's sense of displacement in the new land. Pérez Firmat does not experience or is perhaps simply not interested in narrating open ethnic or racial conflict. He notes of his high school years in Florida, "I search my memory now and I cannot come up with one single example of feeling ostracized or discriminated against because I was Cuban" (70). Much as the South itself functions as background in *Next Year in Cuba*, the only overt instance of racial conflict is literally unheard and out of sight. Writing of his move from an apartment to the home in Chapel Hill that becomes a kind of miniature Little Havana, the author remembers, "The last thing I did before clearing out of the apartment where we had lived for the past several years was remove my name tag from the front door. When I did so, I found the following sentence scribbled on the back of the name tag: 'Go Home Spic' " (247–48).

Elsewhere, the generally benign background of the South paradox-ically becomes foreground as Pérez Firmat describes himself and his children beginning to talk, look, and act like their Carolina neighbors. For example, in "Limen," Pérez Firmat ponders the passage from exile in Miami to exile from Miami in North Carolina, presenting that change of place and cultural context in terms of the loss of intimate language and by stressing the imposing presence of new sounds, words, and names.

> We took David back up just when
> he was beginning to learn to speak,
> to say agua and mamá and galletica.
> (Miami es mar y calor y comida.)
> Just when he was on the threshold,
> at the limen,
> perinatal to his past, to me,
> we delivered him to y'alls and drawls,
> to some place I've never lived in all these years
> I've been living there.
> (My words are also agua and mamá and galletica
> and a few improper names like El Farito,
> Chirino, and Dadeland, which is not English
> now, though it used to be.)
> Just as David was beginning to say
> the language I breathe in,
> we moved him up and inland away
> from warmth and water,
> knotting his tongue—my tongue—with distance. (*Bilingual Blues* 7)

The Cuban exile in Miami takes his child into an uncertain second exile in North Carolina, an exile marked not by political conflict but by gener-ational shifts and by cultural and linguistic separation from the warmth and familiarity of Spanish in Miami. The controlling idea of this poem is the difference between the child and his new surroundings, but its emotive power lies in the fact that childhood in English-speaking North Carolina means that the child will necessarily experience the world in a different register and through a different language and culture than does the father.

Pérez Firmat presents these generational difficulties as if they were specific to the exile experience, and he uses them to support the claim he makes throughout *Next Year in Cuba* that he is an exile rather than an immigrant. This separation contradicts the way critics of the autobiographical writings of immigrants and exiles traditionally combine the two groups. For example, *immigration* is used generally to encompass migrations of all kinds and motivations, just as the autobiographies of those who present themselves primarily in terms of entering a new country (immigrants), those who portray themselves in relation to the birth country rather than in relation to the country of adoption (emigrants), and those who are compelled to leave their homelands (exiles) are grouped together as immigrant autobiography. The failure to acknowledge the varieties of the migrant experience obscures both the diverse motives for migration and differences in the way the new land and one's place in it are understood and presented. Consequently, an emphasis on immigration to the exclusion of emigration or exile gives undue importance to assimilation into the host culture. The tendency to assume that the United States is the destination when one speaks of immigrants and autobiography is evidence of the need for more careful distinctions.

Contrary to the assumption that the United States is the default immigrant destination and source of immigrant autobiographical writing, many immigrants, emigrants, and exiles from countries such as Russia, Austria, Italy, Spain, Japan, Lebanon, India, and Greece have made their new homes throughout Spanish America and Brazil and then produced autobiographies about their experiences. Interestingly, although the years of most intense immigration into Latin America were early in the twentieth century, most autobiographies written by these immigrants have appeared only during the past few decades. Despite differences in period, tone, and audience, these autobiographers share an interest in establishing cultural citizenship in their adopted homes, an interest that is complicated by a profound ambivalence. What makes their narratives compelling is the fact that while some of them claim the right to contribute to the social heritage of the nation, others defer or are prevented from making such a contribution.

In her 1997 presidential address to the Organization of American Historians, Linda K. Kerber spoke on "The Meanings of Citizenship." Taking up the question of the ambivalent or unrooted immigrant, she said,

> A taxi driver from Zaire recently explained to me that although he was grateful for many opportunities, he had not become a citizen, unable to overcome his deep resentment against the United States for complicity in the destabilizations that accompanied the assassination of Patrice Lumumba in 1961, which had forced his family to flee. A woman from Guatemala told a National Public Radio (NPR) reporter last year that taking the oath of citizenship meant for her simultaneously a commitment to the United States, where she had lived for decades, and the wistful abandonment of a dream that someday she would run for office in a democratic and stable Guatemala. These people look on the Statue of Liberty with a decidedly bifocal gaze. (852)

Immigrant autobiographers writing in Latin America do not look on the Statue of Liberty, but they do turn a critical eye toward similar symbols of their respective national homes. As is the case with the United States in Kerber's examples, these immigrant autobiographers seem to regard their new nations with equal parts desire and suspicion. In terms reminiscent of Bryan S. Turner's definition, Elizabeth Faue defines cultural citizenship as "a sense of both belonging to and owning a culture" (312); an eagerness for just that kind of belonging and an ambivalence toward such ownership are evident in, to take just three examples, Emelia de Zanders's *Memorias de una inmigrante* (Venezuela, 1988), Julio Szapu's *El camino de un inmigrante* (Argentina, 1985), and Matsuko Kawai's *Sob dois horizontes* (Brazil, 1988).

Even in years of heaviest immigration, the number of migrants arriving in Latin America is admittedly much lower than for corresponding years in the United States. Thomas H. Holloway notes, "Between 1870 and 1930, 10 million immigrants arrived at South American ports along the coast from Rio de Janeiro to Buenos Aires, resulting in a net population inflow of perhaps 7 million" (242). In contrast, nearly 9 million immigrants entered the United States between 1901 and 1910 alone, with reduced but still very large figures for subsequent decades (U.S. Census Bureau 10). Despite the reduced numbers, the lower overall population of the Latin American countries that received those 7 million immigrants makes the impact of immigration arguably greater in Latin America than in the United States. For example, Holloway cites statistics showing that 44 percent of the population of the Buenos Aires province of Argentina was foreign born in 1914 and that fully half of the population of Montevideo, Uruguay, was foreign born by 1900 (241). Holloway further notes that by 1895 "about one-quarter of the Argentine population was foreign born, a proportion that rose to 30 percent by 1914" (241). In the United States, on the other hand, the percentage of foreign-born residents reached a high point of 14.7 in 1910 (Kennedy 58).

Although rates of immigration vary widely, the many countries from which migrants arrive, the range of countries into which they immigrate, and the subsequent choice of a destination in the Americas indicate that immigration is an authentically hemispheric issue. Its importance as an inter-American issue goes far beyond current interest in the U.S.-Mexican border region to include such issues as assimilation, ethnic identity, class identity, comparative immigration policy, and the meanings of and access to citizenship—all in a broad hemispheric context. In the immigrant autobiographies of Pérez Firmat, Medina, and Said, as in those of Zanders, Szapu, and Kawai, citizenship is always a central issue, but given the reservations and misgivings of these immigrant writers regarding their new homes, they tend, like Kerber's taxi driver, to view those homes with a "bifocal gaze."

Of the few scholars writing on immigrant autobiography in the United States, none has had more to say about its cultural implications than William Boelhower. Boelhower stresses assimilation in his reading of immigrant autobiographies, and he assumes an assimilationist bent in his analysis of immigrant culture generally. For example, he calls immigrant autobiography a "schooling genre" (305), emphasizing the immigrant's need and desire to adopt the cultural norms of the host country if he or she is to become a citizen. He notes that the immigrant must "assume the culturally central *figura* of student. He must go to school, must learn the ABC's of the host culture" (298). He later concludes, "Even more than those who are born American, the immigrant autobiographer has to work at internalizing the code of citizenship if he or she hopes to understand the American Way" (314).

Leaving aside the question of the immigrant's desires regarding citizenship and assimilation, it is clear that Boelhower's model presupposes a one-way process in which immigrants are transformed because the host country transforms them. Gordon Hutner explains the prevalence of this kind of narrative by describing the immigrant's desire to please two distinct groups of readers. First, recognizing the desire of a portion of the

American reading public to see the immigrant cast off ethnicity in order to assimilate, certain immigrants write specifically to fulfill that expectation. Second, aware that additional immigrants will follow, others write to give evidence of the possibility of Americanization. Hutner argues, "Out of the crucible of the New World experience came a story of newly achieved selfhood, a tale of transformation that immigrant readers might use for a model for encountering their own fantasies, anxieties, even terrors. At the same time, the gratification for an audience of American citizens also lay in the authenticizing pleasure of observing the proof of others' assimilation. To this end, immigrant autobiography is closely tied to stories about the striving for legitimation, the up-by-the-bootstraps chronicle that brings together values of personal fulfillment with possibilities of cultural facilitation, stories that eventually signify the American dream" (xii–xiii). Boelhower, for his part, believes so strongly in the immigrant's desire for citizenship and assimilation that he proposes a separate category, "ethnic autobiography," for immigrant narratives that do not follow an assimilationist trajectory. He writes, "Ethnic autobiography is what immigrant autobiography becomes when it puts local ties . . . above the global code of citizenship" (310).

In distinguishing immigrant from ethnic autobiography, Boelhower uses the term *immigrant* literally, referring specifically to those who are coming into the United States rather than to those who might more properly be identified as leaving the home country—emigrants or exiles. Since he concentrates on those narratives oriented strongly toward the country of adoption rather than toward the country of origin, it is no surprise that assimilation figures prominently in his theory. In fairness to Boelhower, it must be acknowledged that many, perhaps most, immigrant autobiographies fit the pattern he describes, but as Pérez Firmat makes clear, there are other patterns. Recalling his mother's insistence that they were a family of exiles rather than a family of immigrants, Pérez Firmat writes, "The exile and the immigrant go through life at different speeds. The immigrant is in a rush about everything—in a rush to get a job, learn the language, set down roots, become a citizen. He lives in the fast lane, and if he arrives as an adult, he squeezes a second lifetime into the first, and if he arrives as a child, he grows up in a hurry. Not so with the exile, whose life creeps forward an inch at a time. If the immigrant rushes, the exile waits. He waits to embark on a new career, to learn the language, to give up his homeland. He waits, perhaps indefinitely, to start a new life. If immigration is an accelerated birth, exile is a state of suspended animation that looks every bit like a slow death" (121–22). Although Pérez Firmat exaggerates the immigrant's single-minded pursuit of citizenship to the point of caricature, the contrast he establishes between immigrants and exiles is key. The immigrant's focus on citizenship in the new home may be the most common mode of migrant autobiography, but Pérez Firmat makes it clear that it is certainly not the only mode.

Pérez Firmat opens his discussion of these issues with two very different scenes of exile. Despite his repeated insistence that he is not an immigrant, the second episode reads like a celebration of becoming more immigrant than exile. The first episode, on the other hand, is a collective assertion of exile identity. It takes place during a 1991 Willy Chirino concert in Miami that Pérez Firmat attends with his American wife. Chirino, also a Cuban exile, brings the crowd to near frenzy when he begins a song that "confidently forecasts an end to Castro's thirty-year dictatorship" (*Next Year* 4). As Chirino calls out the names of liberated communist-bloc countries, the audience responds by shouting "¡¡Libre!!" [Free!!]. Anticipating the fall of Castro, the song reaches its climax as Chirino finally calls out "¡¡Cuba!!" In its thunderous response, the audience joins Chirino in a kind of prayer for an end to exile, a prayer charged with the hope and expectation that Cuba will soon join the list of liberated countries. Recalling the concert, Pérez Firmat writes, "Thirty years of waiting, thirty years of hopes and frustrations, thirty years of broken promises and abortive plans, are jammed into the two syllables of the Spanish word for freedom" (4–5).

For all the emotional intensity of the concert and the equally intense feelings of allegiance and belonging that it inspires, Pérez Firmat recalls this experience only to conclude that *regreso*—return to Cuba—is not likely and perhaps not even desirable. As is true of his autobiography generally, whatever nostalgia there is in this scene is offset by an insistence that life goes on, that time in exile does not have to be lost time, and that ultimately "we must begin to define ourselves not by our place of birth, but by our destination" (9). He wonders, "Could I, who have lived in the United States much longer than I lived in Cuba, actually go back to the Havana of my childhood? Could my father make good on his promise to return? Would my mother make good on her threat not to? Could we get our home and our business back? Could we resume lives that had been interrupted for half a lifetime? *Caught up in the mood of the moment*, I imagine that all these things are not only possible but likely. I believe that I'm about to find my place, about to recover the life I lost as a child. Yes, I can go home again" (5; emphasis added). Pérez Firmat ironically undercuts his affirmation of belonging because he feels, as is evident in the second episode, as much at home among southerners at a Durham Bulls baseball game in North Carolina as among fellow exiles at a Willy Chirino concert in Miami. More to the point, in the second episode Pérez Firmat again presents his sense of belonging and his emotional ties to place, people, and home through a public gesture, but this time in Durham, North Carolina, rather than in Little Havana. He asserts the ties that establish his group identity in the United States by portraying himself singing the national anthem with compatriots who neither notice his presence nor object to his participation. "Looking at the American flag fluttering above the center-field fence," he says, "I put my hand over my heart and belt the song out, like everyone around me. . . . It moves me to be singing in unison with my children, who know no other nation's anthem" (7).

Pérez Firmat describes this ballpark in loving detail, lingering over the "skimpily clad, good-looking *americanas*" (6) and savoring the smell of the omnipresent tobacco to root himself in a specific place and time, self-consciously presenting himself as a Cuban who is no longer passing as southerner and citizen but as a Carolina Cuban who recognizes that he has become in fact both southerner and citizen. He describes his feelings for North Carolina in terms of rootedness instead of exilic displacement when he says, "Although I don't feel about North Carolina the way I do about Miami, this place is also home. My children and stepchildren were born here; the only houses I have ever owned are located here; this is where I have spent all of my professional life. In fact, I have lived in Chapel Hill longer than in any other place, including Havana and Miami. If all these years in North Carolina haven't quite made me a good ole boy, a *cubanazo* redneck, spick and hick in equal parts, they certainly have colored my tastes and values. By now, American sights and sounds are so embedded within me that I know I would find it difficult to spend the rest of my life only among Cubans" (5–6). With a confidence that will later fail him, Pérez Firmat insists that immersion in the sights, sounds, and smells of the South does not imply the loss of his Cuban self. Stressing the role of his children in learning to put exile aside, Pérez Firmat writes,

> Sitting with my children in the cheap seats of the Bulls stadium, clad in Duckheads and sneakers and sipping warm beer, I feel like I've just stepped out of an Alabama CD. Surrounded by soft drawls and rebel yells, I forget that I haven't heard or uttered a word of Spanish in several hours. This evening my history as a Cuban exile no longer seems so central to my life; more important than where I come from is the fact that I'm here with my children, who are not exiles, and who have made it possible for me to look upon North Carolina as my

home. I emerge from the stadium heartened, even exhilarated, by the experience of belonging to a community of people who live in the country of their birth. Walking back to the car holding hands with David and Miriam, I feel rooted, in my place. (7–8)

If it is a contradiction to be both *cubanazo* and redneck, if it is a contradiction to be moved one moment by powerful feelings of patriotism for one's homeland and by similar feelings for one's adopted home the next, the conflict does not invalidate either sentiment for Pérez Firmat. Though he refuses as a schoolboy to pledge allegiance to the flag of the United States (56), and though he cannot bring himself to vote as an adult (273), Pérez Firmat insists that he belongs in North Carolina and, by extension, in the United States. That belonging is built on contradictions and uncomfortable juxtapositions that strain his careful distinctions between exiles and immigrants, but he nonetheless claims cultural citizenship in the United States. He does this most explicitly by comparing his love for his *patria* (homeland) and his *país* (country) to the bond he feels to his parents and the love he feels for his wife. "Cuba is my *patria*, the United States is my *país*. Cuba is where I come from, the United States is where I have become who I am. When I pledge allegiance, I have to do it to two flags at once" (271). He continues, "I love Cuba with the involuntary, unshakable love that one feels for a parent. I love the United States with the no-less-intense but elective affection one feels toward a spouse. I cannot choose not to love Cuba; perhaps I could choose not to love the United States, as I could choose not to love Mary Anne, but I don't want to. Even if originally a marriage of convenience, a relation of such long standing creates ties that aren't easily broken. Although my marriage to the United States hasn't always been peaceful, it has given me many of the richest and happiest moments of my life" (271–72).

Because he feels intense ties to both the United States and to Cuba, Pérez Firmat's refusal to surrender his claim to exile status is a way of keeping, at least symbolically, a foot in both worlds. Furthermore, that exile status gives Pérez Firmat an edgy, cosmopolitan cachet unavailable to the refugee or immigrant. "Exile is in fashion," states Ian Buruma, going on to describe the contemporary image of the exile in ways that may illuminate some of Pérez Firmat's motives.

> Once it was consumption—pale, sunken cheeks, spatters of blood on a white linen handkerchief, and so on—that suggested an artistic sensibility and a poetic soul. Now it is exile that evokes the sensitive intellectual, the critical spirit operating alone on the margins of society, a traveler, rootless and yet at home in every metropolis, a tire-

less wanderer from academic conference to academic conference, a thinker in several languages, an eloquent advocate for ethnic and sexual minorities—in short, a romantic outsider living on the edge of the bourgeois world.

This may sound frivolous. For exile is surely no fun. There is nothing glamorous about the poor, shivering Tamil, sleeping on a cold plastic bench at the Frankfurt railway station, or the Iraqi, fleeing from Saddam's butchers, afraid of walking the streets of Dover, lest he be attacked by skinheads; or the young woman from Eritrea, standing along a minor road to Milan, picking up truck drivers so that she can feed her baby. These are not fashionable figures, they are genuine outcasts, and they have nothing in common with the multicultural intellectuals whom we honor as the poets of postcolonial discourse. (33)

The shivering Tamil, the fearful Iraqi, and the desperate Eritrean woman call to mind the tremendous gulf between the exile experience of writers and intellectuals like Pérez Firmat, Medina, and Said and that of exiles who might more accurately be called refugees. These vignettes also point to the variety within the Cuban exile population. As Isabel Alvarez Borland notes,

Since 1959, more than 700,000 Cubans have settled in the United States. The first migration, from January 1959 to October 1962, was composed of about 250,000 men and women as well as their children. Between December 1965 and April 1973, another 400,000 Cubans emigrated. In 1980, the Mariel boatlift produced a third wave—nearly 120,000 people. The Mariel migration was different from the previous waves in the way it was perceived by the larger society. Unlike the Cuban who immigrated between 1959 and 1973, the Cubans of Mariel were not considered legitimate refugees. . . . In Miami, the Marielitos faced many obstacles. Jobs were scarce because the country was in an economic recession. Also, since many of the Mariel immigrants were black, they faced racial discrimination in addition to political discrimination from their fellow Cubans. Because of these factors, the Marielitos have had much more difficulty in adapting than the immigrants of the first two waves. The *balseros* or raft people comprised the largest and fourth wave of immigrants, a wave that reached its peak in August 1994. (5)

The cachet and cosmopolitan chic available through an exile identity may say as much about Pérez Firmat's desire to separate himself from lower income refugees like the Marielitos as about affective ties to a lost homeland. Exile allows him to maintain a sense of distance from other social groups and a detachment from the United States, and he is loath to surrender that distance. He states at one point, "As an exile, my experience is different from that of immigrants in that I came to this country fully intending to return to my homeland as soon as possible" (*Next Year* 10). Here and elsewhere Pérez Firmat reminds his reader of the important distinctions between immigrants and exiles, but his ambivalence about regreso and his affinity for the life and the self that he finds in the United States blurs the very distinction that he wants to emphasize.

The torn ambivalence of an autobiographer like Pérez Firmat underscores the error of focusing too narrowly on assimilationist autobiographies like those favored by Boelhower. Such texts present a misleading image of the immigrant experience because, as Gordon Hutner observed, they leave out "how the country is changed . . . by . . . what the masses of 'undistinguished' Americans have conferred upon the country's collective identity" (xv). That question of the exile's contribution to the host country is a constant if understated theme throughout *Next Year in Cuba*. It appears, for example, in Pérez Firmat's descriptions of how Cuban exiles transform Miami, in his discussion of the growing and diverse Hispanic presence in the United States, and, on a smaller scale, in his attempt to transfer the *ambiente* or hominess of Miami to North Carolina. This is not to suggest that Pérez Firmat ignores American customs, ways, and values. On the contrary, Pérez Firmat takes great delight in his description of the new possibilities presented by American schools, American English, American rules, and American girls. However, Pérez Firmat is as concerned with the ways in which Miami becomes Cuban as he becomes American as he is with internalizing an "American Way." In the following passage, for example, Pérez Firmat celebrates the tangled languages and cultures of his years at La Salle High School, remembering that

> Even as we absorbed American culture, we tended to "Cubanize" things we came in touch with. In football a tackle was *un palo* (the same word was used to denote a drink, a home run, and sexual intercourse); in basketball a blocked shot was *un tapón*. A nerd was *un mechero*, a drunk *un curda*, and a good-looking American girl was a *yegua* (but Cuban ones were *jebitas*). The school's signature cheer was one I had learned in Cuba: "*Bon-bon-chié-chié-chié. / Bon-bon-chié-chié-chiá. /Lah-Sah-Yeh, Lah-Sah-Yeh, / rrah-rrah-rrah!*" The emotional high points of each basketball game came when the cheer-

leaders, who were American, started into a *bon-bon-chié*. (Although many girls in our sister school, Immaculata, were also Cuban, they considered it vaguely slutty to parade in front of a crowd in a tight sweater and short skirt.) It was wonderful to see perky Catholic girls like Marti and Nancy lead a throng of rowdy Cuban teenagers in a *bon-bon-chié*. Here we were, Cuban exiles in a foreign country, playing a sport like football or basketball and screaming in Cuban, being led by American cheerleaders in the same cheers we would have chanted in Havana. (69)

The relationship described here between host, exile, culture, and language suggests that Boelhower's assertion of a citizenship that depends on the immigrant's ability to internalize American culture is insufficiently broad, since there seems to be neither a way to determine who is internalizing whom nor any possibility of identifying a stable American Way to internalize.

The emotional distance between Pérez Firmat's take on the exile condition and that of the Marielitos or balseros is so great that one might conclude that they describe entirely different conditions. Furthermore, given the various political motives for claiming exile status and for insisting on a deep and continuing attachment to a lost homeland, the mere fact that writers like Said, Medina, and Pérez Firmat call themselves exiles reveals little about their respective autobiographies. Curiously, and in ways that underscore his difference from Said and Medina, Pérez Firmat feels his exile from Miami more keenly than his exile from Cuba. As Alvarez Borland notes, the fact that Pérez Firmat grew up in Miami "presents an idea of exile and displacement of a different sort, for here the displacement is not from the country of origin . . . but from Miami as the ethnic enclave" (73). When he yearns for the community and the wholeness that adulthood and professional life have taken from him, Pérez Firmat longs for the ambiente of Miami. Even so, nostalgia for community and family does not lead to a return to the comforts of home. This is true for many reasons, but perhaps primarily because Pérez Firmat is enough of an immigrant to find return unappealing. Much as the growing distance between father and son makes Pérez Firmat uncomfortable when his father asks if he would return to Cuba, so the growing emotional distance between Miami and North Carolina, between Cuban-American and Cuban exile identities makes permanent return to a less troubled, less complex, and less productive identity unthinkable. Pérez Firmat observes, "Exile can be a dead end or it can be an access ramp, but I doubt that it's ever a road that circles back to its beginning" (*Next Year* 271).

For all the struggles with exile and identity that make his experience unique, Pérez Firmat's autobiographical presentation of self in English and then in Spanish is not unique. Esmeralda Santiago, a Boston-based writer and producer, and Ariel Dorfman, a novelist, dramatist, and professor of Spanish at Duke University, have also published English autobiographies that were later translated into Spanish: Santiago first published *When I Was Puerto Rican* (1994) and then her own translation, *Cuando era puertorriqueña* (1994); Dorfman followed up *Heading South, Looking North* (1998) with his *Rumbo al sur, deseando el norte* (1998). The translation from English to Spanish raises for all three writers complex questions of audience and identity. In his translation, for example, Pérez Firmat ironically uses Spanish to "afirmar mi pertenencia . . . a la sociedad norteamericana" ["affirm my belonging . . . in U.S. culture"] (*Año que viene* 1), but there is much more at play in the relationship between these texts than a simple affirmation of belonging. Translation is in some ways a figurative stretching of what it means to claim U.S. citizenship, but given the repeated clashes in Pérez Firmat's two texts between Cuban and U.S. family traditions, forms of manhood, and political ideals, it is clear that the stretching is anything but an innocently inclusive solution. Duality comes at the price of loosened ties to one's homeland and to one's native tongue, and the possibility of gaining one seems always to imply the nagging possibility of losing the other. Pérez Firmat is anxious to show his reader that he can present himself both in English and in Spanish just as he can be both *Cubano* and *Americano* simultaneously, but he seems haunted by the thought that his dual identities might just as easily cancel each other out as add to one another. It is, ultimately, a lived contradiction rather than a comfortable blend of identities.

Given that uneasiness, Pérez Firmat holds his separate identities in tense but productive balance. Like those separate but linked identities, and despite Pérez Firmat's argument for the unity of the two books, *Next Year in Cuba* and *El año que viene estamos en Cuba* are not two versions of one book but two separate autobiographies with two distinct audiences and underlying sensibilities. Near the conclusion of *El año que viene estamos en Cuba*, in a passage that does not appear in *Next Year in Cuba*, Pérez Firmat writes,

> Después de escribir el mismo libro dos veces, la primera en inglés y ahora en español, todavía no sé dónde anclarme. Al redactar la versión en inglés, quise convertirme en americano. Al traducirlo al español, me siento más cubano que nunca, y sospecho que si lo hubiera escrito primero en español, el libro hubiera salido muy distinto.

After writing the same book two times, the first time in English and now in Spanish, I still don't know where to cast anchor. When I was writing the version in English, I wanted to make myself an American. Now, translating it into Spanish, I feel more Cuban than ever, and I suspect that if I had written it in Spanish first the book would have turned out very differently. (197–98)

Who Pérez Firmat is, in other words, depends in great measure on who his reader is. This, in turn, clearly depends on the language in which he writes. The issue of language choice alone suggests that it is disingenuous to present the link between *Next Year in Cuba* and *El año que viene estamos en Cuba* as a simple matter of translation. The material omitted from the Spanish text and the material supplied in Spanish but absent in English, meanwhile, provide definitive evidence of a much more complex relationship.

The changes in the Spanish text range from the elaboration of short paragraphs on adolescent "crushes" to the wholesale deletion of extensive passages that figure prominently in the English version. Oddly, long passages that detail the history and cultural significance of dominoes and canasta appear in both books, although one might expect a Spanish-speaking reader to bring much more familiarity with these table games to the book than an English-speaking reader. Meanwhile, the long and sala-cious story of Pérez Firmat's passion for the American woman who be-comes his second wife vanishes in the Spanish narrative. When he de-scribes his family's reaction to his affair with this American woman, Pérez Firmat returns to his contrast between exiles and immigrants in ways that suggest reasons for his deletion of the story from the Spanish text. "I don't think their problem was simply my impending divorce, but the fact that my relationship with Mary Anne threatened our integrity as an exile family. By leaving a Cuban woman for an American one, I was not only changing spouses, I was putting our family on a different track. In effect, I was behaving like an immigrant, not an exile" (*Next Year* 215).

Although *El año que viene estamos en Cuba* is ultimately more timid and less brazen in tone than the breezy, devil-may-care *Next Year in Cuba*, what is significant is not the specific differences between the texts but the fact that the differences exist, that there are things that Pérez Firmat is not comfortable saying to a Spanish-reading audience; that he is, in fact, a different person in Spanish. He writes, "Rather than merging Cuba and America, I oscillate endlessly, sometimes wildly, between the two. My life is less a synthesis than a seesaw" (274). At the American extreme of one of those wild oscillations, Pérez Firmat panics and refuses to accompany his American wife to cast his ballot on election day. Even after formal naturalization and a great deal of careful preparation, Pérez Firmat cannot bring himself to vote. He explains, "I just couldn't do it. First I got angry, and then I began to cry. I heard myself saying, 'I can't do this to my father. I'm not American, I'm Cuban.' I heard myself saying, 'What does Chapel Hill have to do with me? This isn't my country and it will never be my country.' Incredibly, I heard myself saying, 'I want to go back to Cuba'" (273). If there is a frontier between Pérez Firmat's Cuban and Cuban-American identities that keeps them forever separate yet forever linked, that frontier is citizenship.

In "Home" Pérez Firmat describes the pain inherent in a liminal position between the desire for unencumbered citizenship and the longing for origins, pleading for the authenticity and the security of untroubled belonging.

> Give a guy a break.
> Take him back, let him step
> on soil that's his or feels his,
> let him have a tongue,
> a story, a geography.
> Let him not trip back and forth between
> bilingualisms,
> hyphens,
> explanations.
> As it is he's a walking-talking bicameral page.
> Two hemispheres and neither one likes the other.
> Ambidextrous.
> Omnipossibilist.
> Multivocal.
> Let him stop having to translate himself
> to himself
> endlessly.
> Give the guy a break:
> crease him, slip him into an envelope,
> address it, and let him go.
> Home. (*Bilingual Blues* 22)

Boelhower suggests that the desire for formalized assimilation and citizenship motivates immigrant autobiographers. Pérez Firmat and the aforementioned immigrant autobiographers from Latin America do indeed seek citizenship, but in ways that are more complex and troubled than Boelhower seems to anticipate. It is one thing to assert cultural citizenship, and quite another to formally separate oneself from the homeland. Citizenship is, in short, a prize whose perceived rewards and costs vary widely from case to case. Citizenship is, moreover, a stance used to stage a public identity as well as an indication of what the immigrant has become. The conflicted desires for and rejection of citizenship in Pérez Firmat's Spanish and English autobiographies demonstrate that immigrant and exile autobiographical identities are as much a matter of for whom and in what language one writes as they are a matter of who writes.

WORKS CITED

Alvarez Borland, Isabel. *Cuban-American Literature of Exile: From Person to Persona.* Charlottesville: UP of Virginia, 1998.

Boelhower, William. "The Necessary Ruse: Immigrant Autobiography and the Sovereign American Self." *Amerikastudien* 35 (1990): 297–319.

Buruma, Ian. "The Romance of Exile." *New Republic* 12 Feb. 2001: 33–38.

Dorfman, Ariel. *Heading South, Looking North: A Bilingual Journey.* New York: Penguin, 1998.

——. *Rumbo al sur, deseando el norte: Un romance en dos lenguas.* Buenos Aires: Planeta, 1998.

Faue, Elizabeth. "Class and Cultural Citizenship." *Labor History* 39 (1998): 311–14.

Holloway, Thomas H. "Immigration." *Encyclopedia of Latin American History and Culture.* Ed. Barbara A. Tenenbaum. New York: Scribner's, 1996. 239–42.

Hutner, Gordon. *Immigrant Voices: Twenty-Four Narratives on Becoming an American.* New York: Signet Classic, 1999.

Kawai, Mitsuko. *Sob dois horizontes.* São Paulo: Editora do escritor, 1988.

Kennedy, David M. "Can We Still Afford to Be a Nation of Immigrants?" *Atlantic Monthly* Nov. 1996: 52–68.

Kerber, Linda K. "The Meanings of Citizenship." *Journal of American History* 84 (1997): 833–54.

Medina, Pablo. *Exiled Memories: A Cuban Childhood.* Austin: U of Texas P, 1990.

Pérez Firmat, Gustavo. *El año que viene estamos en Cuba.* Houston: Arte Público, 1997.

——. *Bilingual Blues: Poems, 1981–1994.* Tempe, Ariz.: Bilingual Press/Editorial Bilingüe, 1995.

——. *Life on the Hyphen: The Cuban-American Way.* Austin: U of Texas P, 1994.

——. *Next Year in Cuba: A Cubano's Coming of Age in America.* New York: Anchor, 1995.

Said, Edward W. *Out of Place: A Memoir.* New York: Knopf, 1999.

——. "The Mind of Winter: Reflections on Life in Exile." *Harper's* Sept. 1984: 49–55.

Santiago, Esmeralda. *Cuando era puertorriqueña.* New York: Vintage, 1994.

——. *When I Was Puerto Rican.* New York: Vintage, 1994.

Szapu, Julio. *El camino de un inmigrante.* Buenos Aires: Grupo Editor Latinoamericano, 1985.

Turner, Bryan S. "Postmodern Culture/Modern Citizens." *The Condition of Citizenship*. Ed. Bart van Steenbergen. London: Sage, 1994. 153–68.

U.S. Census Bureau. *Statistical Abstract of the United States: 1999*. 119th ed. Washington, D.C.: Government Printing Office, 1999.

Zanders, Emilia de. *Memorias de una inmigrante: Altibajos de una familia europea en Venezuela*. Caracas: Ediciones del Congreso de la República, 1988.

LEIGH ANNE DUCK

Travel and Transference:

V. S. Naipaul and the Plantation Past

A notoriously critical travel writer, V. S. Naipaul strikes a more tolerant tone in his 1989 *A Turn in the South*. Though this work is not devoid of the racism and elitism seen in his earlier writings, these problems are somewhat mitigated by his recognition of commonality with his interviewees. He is especially interested in their descriptions of a sense of "home," a feeling of connection to a particular space that derives its hold on individuals from their own memories, which are linked to the history of that space. Naipaul claims to find U.S. southerners "so congenial" because their descriptions of this bond suggest that it is complicated, not idyllically empowering or nurturing. Viewing the United States as "the world motor of change," he is pleased to find some of its residents "coming to terms with a more desperate kind of New World history, and a poorer land reflecting this history" (307). His observations of the South allow Naipaul to reconsider his relationship to Trinidad—the home of his youth, and a nation he has denigrated—because these spaces and societies share a history of slavery. But his attraction to his interlocutors' sense of "the past as a wound" does not alleviate the tension between the diverse senses of loss he encounters in their descriptions of that past (306), particularly between the white southerners who memorialize "the Cause" and the black southerners who negotiate a history of violence, slavery, and apartheid. Though Naipaul asserts, at the beginning of his work, that this distinction—the "race issue"—"would quickly work itself out" as his travels progress (25), it is actually displaced in his narrative by his fascination with the figure of the "redneck," who is purported to have a relationship to local space that is not compromised by history or change.

This travelogue, which Naipaul erroneously presented as his "last travel book" (25), marked a welcome turning point in his career, the development of a more reflective and dialogic approach to the study of culture. Similarly, this collection marks a changing approach to studies of the U.S. South, one that challenges the field's tradition of monolithic identity narratives not only by looking at internal diversity but also by looking at external continuities. In this context, Naipaul's work serves as both a positive and a negative example. Both volumes—his and ours— "look away"; both could be said to stage responses to crises of identification; both contemplate, at some level, modes of cultural analysis. In such processes, Immanuel Wallerstein suggests, looking away can productively challenge definitions of culture that rely on "a bundle of traits" or "tradition," approaches that drive "one's vision inward" (204). A more encompassing view, as exemplified by Naipaul and by the essays gathered herein, can more readily subject old narratives to critical investigation.

But Naipaul demonstrates that even this mode of inquiry can be impeded by transference, psychological responses shaped by precisely the "old narratives" one seeks to critique, including those provided by scholarly disciplines. These fields of study, through their own repressions, teach what discussions are taboo and what questions should be feared. As Carl Gutiérrez-Jones points out, "Problems embedded in objects of study may come to replicate themselves in unselfconscious ways during [scholarly] analysis" (81). Perhaps no discipline is more vulnerable to such transference than U.S. southern studies, a tradition long dominated by writers who insisted on the "collective basis of unity" and by critics who belied the "community['s]" practices of "coercion" (Romine 22, 2). White southerners, particularly after Reconstruction, successfully used narratives of cultural identity to restrict both participation in and consideration of regional culture, proclaiming that their "folkways" irrevocably fixed the south in the social patterns of the slaveholding era (Sumner 77–78; Woodward, *Strange Career* 103–4). Thus this field provides extraordinary evidence of the dangers that can emerge from extensive and uncritical interest in cultural identity, and little demonstration of how one might conduct a more modulated and analytic investigation of the topic.

Still, as Naipaul provides a case study for this collection, the U.S. South may prove useful as a case study for cultural studies. Given that appeals to "history" and "tradition" so often produce exclusivist and essentialist accounts of identity, it may seem that identity should instead be theorized in rigorously presentist terms (Michaels 675–85). Naipaul's meditation on the postplantation Americas attests, however, to the fact that even in a relentlessly modernizing world, individuals often understand their own lives through reference to history, narrating their connections to the past in ways that vitally influence their beliefs and actions in the present. Such understandings may prove sustaining and beneficial, particularly when they are flexible and open to interrogation, that is, when they do not serve to disavow painful contradictions in one's sense of self or to support a punitive approach to others. When such identity narratives do serve to reinforce a repression—to bolster an individual's sense of attachment to an unfeasible ego-ideal, for example—denying their importance may only intensify their holders' melancholic attachments to the imagined past. Accordingly, it seems vital that practitioners of cultural studies model ways of questioning such relationships to the past while working through our own transferences. Naipaul's travelogue demonstrates that, caught between the wish to escape the past and the desire to fulfill its perceived demands, a writer is granted what may be a tempting dispensation—the opportunity to relegate one's contemporaries to history.

"THE PAST LIVING ON"

In a 1990 essay Stuart Hall considers the difficulties of representing and understanding cultural identity through the example of those who live or have lived in the Caribbean islands. Multinational and multiracial, these persons share a relationship to a past of discontinuity that comprises slavery, colonization, and indentured labor. But this history of displacement, in Hall's argument, provides a unifying relation to a heterogeneous past, a sense of similarity within difference. He notes that configurations of cultural identity often rely on the sense of a coherent past, which can be beneficial in postcolonial contexts, providing "stable, unchanging and continuous frames of reference and meaning . . . to set against the broken rubric of our past" (223, 225). This relationship to the past, however, provides its "resources" through the imagination—the "*production*" of cultural and historical continuity, and the active "*posi-*

tioning" of individuals in meaningful relationships to the past (224, 226). Based in part on the recognition of rupture—a sense that the space with which one feels connected is also a space historically linked to pain and unfreedom—such narratives of identity allow for restorative imagery, an understanding of the past as a literal site of "plenitude" (236). Thus the image of the Caribbean islands provides a visual representation through which one can contemplate affective connections to the past: "Who can ever forget, when once seen rising up out of that blue-green Caribbean, those islands of enchantment? Who has not known, at this moment, the surge of overwhelming nostalgia for lost origins, for 'times past'?" (236).

Years before the publication of Hall's essay, it seemed one could find the answer to this rhetorical question in the person of V. S. Naipaul. Notorious for his acerbic *The Middle Passage*, the 1962 work describing his travels in the Caribbean, he is also famous for his cosmopolitanism. Described as a "colonial without a country" (Ramadevi 12), he has disavowed any sense of affiliation with Trinidad, the country of his birth, and with India, the country from which his grandparents migrated; he identifies himself only ambivalently with England, the country in which he chiefly resides (Atlas). He levies most of his criticism against postcolonial persons or communities that express devotion to local or diasporic "heritage." Naipaul's early writings, as they assert his own lack of any lasting and intimate connection to a particular place or tradition, also castigate those who express such attachments.

Naipaul tends not to even define "culture" as Hall does—as diverse, but not discrete, sets of systems in which all persons participate. Rather, his early writings treat *culture* as an evaluative term, a construct best achieved by imperial England, which serves as the standard against which he compares other societies (Said). In Edward Said's words, these travel narratives, relentlessly asserting Naipaul's own critical opinions, allow for "no dialogue" (22). Accordingly, his insistent detachment from any local culture has been said to produce not greater objectivity in his travel writing but rather a forced refusal of identification between the author and his interlocutors; in these works, he seems unable to tolerate others' belief that their lives derive meaning from a relationship to the past, as if this belief threatened his own self-understanding (Weiss 14).

Among Naipaul's travelogues, however, *A Turn in the South* marks a shift in both narrative style and authorial self-presentation. Where his previous travel writings were dominated by the author's often scathing assessments of his interviewees, this book consists largely of dialogue; here he seeks, as he explains in the later *Beyond Belief*, to be "in the background, trusting to his instinct, a discoverer of people, a finder-out of stories" (xii). This dispersal of narrative authority between a newly speculative Naipaul and his interlocutors is uneven and incomplete, varying largely according to his racial identification of his interviewees (Rampersad). But this aspect of Naipaul's writing is less extreme here than previously, as he interrogates his racist assumptions and often seeks to overcome them. The unmistakable effect of his stylistic shift is to suggest attempts at empathy, efforts apparently fueled by his interest in his interviewees' understandings of their relationships to their local space and its history. Having often represented himself as detached from any cultural space and scornful of any fascination with the past, he here suggests that his chief mode of relating to others is to compare their relationships to a localized past with his own.

Naipaul begins this work by distancing himself from such understandings, arguing that he has no sense of home, unlike Howard, an acquaintance from the U.S. South who is said to have "a patch of earth he thought of as home, absolutely his" (*Turn* 3). Though Howard has described this "home" in terms of its association with his mother, Naipaul describes it as a physical space, "a landscape of small ruins," that is imbued with a time, "a richer and more complicated past than I had imagined" (10, 11). In doing so, he both constructs the town of Howard's youth as a space drenched in a past and emphasizes his difference from his interlocutors, suggesting that here he must learn to understand a kind of relationship that is unfamiliar to him. He makes this difficulty explicit by explaining that he sometimes has difficulty understanding Howard's attempts to talk about "the unmentionable past" because he, Naipaul, is a "stranger" (18).

This representation of himself as a person alienated from any such ambivalent attachment is compromised, however, by the degree to which he *does* comprehend the experience of Howard and his family. Even in speaking of his difficulties in communication, he suggests that he errs by overemphasizing his difference from Howard. Recording Howard's complaint about the " 'continuity' " of the town in which he grew up, Naipaul writes that he has assumed Howard meant "the past living on," but then retracts that interpretation, explaining that he "had this trouble with Howard's words sometimes; I was too ready to find in them meanings he didn't intend" (3). His initial interpretation is, however, palpably correct: though the family members claim a distance from the past (11), having "had too much" of it (8), they present him with a tour of it, taking him to cemeteries and familial landmarks. This passage emerges as a study in disavowal: though Naipaul finally realizes that he has comprehended exactly what Howard meant to say, he reemphasizes his "strange[ness]" in the very paragraph in which he concedes that understanding.

Though he repeatedly stages his anxiety that his different background might render his attempts to understand these southerners futile, Naipaul often reveals, in doing so, the degree to which his Caribbean past facilitates his interpretation of their experience. Shortly after beginning the book "with the home that Howard had," Naipaul explains that this "idea of traveling in the American South" occurred to him during the Republican convention in Dallas in 1984 (23), when he realized that the "old slave states" would have more in common with the countries of the Caribbean than would the rest of the United States (24). This sense of a similar history fuels not only his understanding of southern social structures and interactions but also his interpretation of the landscape. He notes, for example, that South Carolinian oaks look much like Trinidadian saman trees, imported as shade trees from Central America. This visual resemblance again reminds Naipaul that all of these were plantation societies, shaped by similar experiences of heat, forced labor, and colonial management (80–81).

His own relation to that past helps him to understand "the historical darkness" he senses in conversation with Howard's mother, Hetty, who seems uncomfortable talking about her extended familial history, in large part because she lacks access to knowledge about it (11). Recognizing that the multiple dislocations imposed on African Americans during slavery produced ruptures in the sense of family continuity, Naipaul compares that loss to his own family's experience of indentured servitude: for "the grandson of immigrants from India to Trinidad, ancestors as close as grandparents are mysterious" (86). Much of his narrative is suffused by such comparisons: observing the way historical understandings and experiences shape U.S. southerners' senses of home, Naipaul also reexamines his own relationship to history and to Trinidad.

Naipaul takes pleasure in visual aspects of this investigation, becoming practically addicted to decaying images of the past. After spending some time in a Tennessee Nissan plant, much later in the narrative and in his journey, he finds it "a relief to get outside and to see, in the distance, a relic of the old world: a corrugated-iron barn, against trees" (261). Though he identifies such images with hard and unrewarded labor, Naipaul's tone in describing them is unmistakably elegiac, as they remind him of scenes from his childhood. Associated with "the hard crop, originally the slave crop," these barns suggest some linkage to "the small country town where I lived, at the very edge of the sugarcane fields, acres upon acres, scene of bitter labor" (270–71). He explicitly represents such memories as personal restorations, emerging "from some unplaceable time in my childhood" and "like snapshots from very far back" (268, 271).

Naipaul tells us that his first thoughts of writing about the U.S. South corresponded with an epiphany—his sudden realization that "Trinidad . . . would have had more in common with the old slave states of the Southeast than with New England or the newer European-immigrant states of the North" (24). He suggests that his failure to realize this cultural similarity earlier results from a repression: the reports of southern racial violence that he heard in his childhood had been "too shocking . . . and had made me close my mind to the South." But as his narrative progresses, it appears that this journey unseats other disavowals as well, for as he opens his mind to the U.S. South, he acknowledges his identification with the postplantation landscapes of his youth.

"CONSOLING UNION . . .
THE UNEXPECTED, MOVING IDEA"

Freud argued not only that the repressed returns but also that it returns in transference: "whole series of psychological experiences" may be "revived, not as belonging to the past, but as applying to . . . the present moment" (*Fragment* 234). Psychoanalysis explores transference as it emerges in patients' relationships with an analyst trained in helping them to work through their compulsions to repeat past dynamics and behaviors. But Freud held that transference surfaces in other relationships as well and may even become conscious through the process of sublimation. Certainly, Naipaul's shifts of tone and approach suggest extended and critical thought; Rob Nixon argues that Naipaul's autobiographical reflection while writing *Finding the Center* (1984) and *The Enigma of Arrival* (1987) marked a transitional point in his professional life (Nixon 102). If, as Dominick LaCapra and Carl Gutiérrez-Jones have argued, transference can appear in relationships between scholars and their objects of study, it seems all the more likely to surface as Naipaul traverses reminiscent landscapes and converses with others about their processes of identity formation (LaCapra 9; Gutiérrez-Jones 81).

But while transference can be associated with a pleasurable sense of familiarity and intimacy, it also recalls experiences that were once overwhelming, problems that once seemed unsolvable. Here, Naipaul contemplates not only the images but also the experiences of his childhood and the "half-buried" ways in which they might influence his adult behavior and his contemporary sense of self (*Turn* 33). Most immediately, he is confronted with the fact that, though he has repeatedly attacked others' attachments to cultural, racial, or religious identities, such a concept played a significant role in his own psychological development.

Responding to a white woman who insists that one articulates a sense of self in part through one's affiliation with a locale, a community, and their history, Naipaul parenthetically reconsiders his initial resistance: "(And yet, at another level, and with another, half-buried part of myself, I understood. Perhaps in a society of many groups or races everyone, unless he is absolutely secure, lives with a special kind of stress. Growing up in multiracial Trinidad as a member of the Indian community, people brought over in the late nineteenth and early twentieth centuries to work the land, I always knew how important it was not to fall into nonentity)" (33). As a result of this memory, he begins to believe that such notions of identity serve to sustain those who believe their social and economic status may be threatened and to help them maintain some sense of empowerment in a difficult and changing world. Recognizing his own experience with this dynamic, he restrains his usual critique of its logic. Though he has often argued that one must let go of anxieties and loyalties associated with the past if they do not suit one's contemporary world, he now argues that people must reckon with the difficulties of "how to know the truth and hold on to one's soul at a time of great change" (285).

While Naipaul's newfound ability to contemplate the influence of cultural identities in individual lives lends greater richness and flexibility to both his narrative and his conversations with others, it is significant that it emerges first in his conversations with white southerners (Nixon 108). This focus on white identities not only circumvents the problem of his antiblack racism but also facilitates his association of the painful southern past with contemporary capitalist development, which, as he notes, disproportionately benefits white southerners. Naipaul explains that, from childhood, he idealized England and the United States in part for their commodities, claiming he would have been "delighted . . . to be told as a child that Trinidad had once been known for its tobacco. To me tobacco was glamorous, remote, from England (in absurdly luxurious airtight tins), or American (in soft, aromatic, cellophane-wrapped packets), something from an advertisement in *Life*" (279). Recognizing Trinidad as a colonial producer of goods, he romanticized the nations where these products were prepared for the market, and this association seems to fuel his attraction, as well as his transferential relationship, to the postplantation United States.

Though the southern United States was considered, during the 1930s, the victim of intranational colonial exploitation (Tindall 477), Naipaul notes that by the time of his travels, much of the region is thoroughly imbricated in the national economy. In Charleston, for example, there are "rich suburbs . . . the naval station . . . a large and pretty middle-class area, acquired and consolidated during a time of white panic . . . [and] black housing projects, bald brick buildings going baldly down to scuffed earth" (*Turn* 78). Describing a racially delimited distribution of wealth, he notes also its effect on manifestations of the city's past: whereas "the tourist trade . . . keeps historical Charleston in working order," such that "money has begun to come back to some of the old families," "there are no tourists" in the old African American sections of town, and "the blacks seem like squatters" (78). For Naipaul, though, this understanding of Charleston's economy seems to increase his attraction to its cultural past. Configuring contemporary Charleston as a site for white manipulation of capital, and Central and South American postplantation societies as sites of exploited black labor (89), he associates white southerners more with economic imperialism than with economic exploitation. Perhaps for this reason, he is able to indulge their fixations on a cultural past.

Here, Naipaul tolerates even the most historically violent and restrictive formulation of white southern cultural identity—the idealization of Confederate heritage. Developing the impression that some white southerners' devotion to the antebellum past is "like religion" (101), he explains this attachment as "grief and the conviction of a just cause; defeat going against every idea of morality, every idea of the good story . . . the helpless grief and rage (such as the Shias know) about an injustice that cannot be rehearsed too often" (100). Though Naipaul tells one interviewee that his cultural agenda consists of "emotion without a program" (106), he extends this person a remarkable degree of empathy in light of the fact that, in writing about Islam in his 1981 *Among the Believers*, he vilifies the association of religious faith with ideas of heritage.

In Naipaul's description of the ways in which history has "made" him, however, such disjunctures seem inevitable; he makes little attempt in this work to conceal that his perceptions are shaped by racial prejudices. Rather, remembering his childhood as he compares it to those of his interlocutors, he unapologetically revisits his early fixations on racial difference. During his youth, he explains, he could recognize neither the mental and emotional nor the domestic lives of black Trinidadians. Though he insists that he respected black professionals without acknowledging their "racial attributes," he explains that, once in "an out-of-school relationship with them," he became focused on the likelihood that their home lives did not include the same "rituals and attitudes" that shaped his own: "I became aware of the physical quality of Negroes, and of the difference and even, to me, the unreality of their domestic life" (58). Though this account of Naipaul's inability to recognize black personhood may come as no surprise to those who have read *The Middle Passage* (Dayan 159–61), it is represented as something of a revelation to him.

This acknowledgment does not preclude the reemergence of his prejudices, which are apparent in several of his interviews with black southerners, but it does require him to question his initial judgments. He represents this epiphany as the result of both his "unsatisfactory" meeting with Marvin Arrington, an African American politician, and his experience, immediately following, of "going down into the street" and viewing the "Caribbean . . . aspect" of downtown Atlanta (57). Naipaul suggests that he is "assailed by a very old feeling of constriction and gloom" because of his mere presence among black people in a "semi-derelict" urban environment (57). Though, as Joan Dayan notes (163), his explanation for that gloom reveals his racism, his historicization of that racism enables him, in this text, to reinterpret his experiences. He recognizes, for example, what he calls Arrington's "spikiness" not as an unpleasant characteristic but as a response to a systemic problem: "Just as civil-rights legislation gave rights without money or acceptance, so perhaps city politics gave position without strength" (58). Furthermore, it enables him to recognize his own role in creating "the old barrier" that he perceives between himself and his African American interviewees. (It is unclear whether he recognizes the degree to which this tension could emerge from his interlocutors' familiarity with his earlier writing. Maurice Crockett, for example, initially says to him, "and it was like a prepared statement, 'Most people from outside see us as ethnically deprived, semiliterate'" [128]. Naipaul, having written all that and worse about black people in other countries, seems hurt but somehow indicates that he "had come to listen," after which the interview appears to proceed well.)

As several critics have noted, Naipaul becomes more astute about race in *A Turn in the South* than he has been in previous works (Dayan 162; Nixon; Rampersad). He continues to dismiss Caribbean and African racial politics as tribalism (31) and is at first prepared to dismiss Atlanta's Hosea Williams as a "performer" (63). But as he listens to Williams describe both his civil-rights activism and his entrepreneurship, Naipaul realizes that his initial assessment was incorrect and is impressed both with the movement's achievements and by its continuing challenges. He begins to understand why Maurice Crockett, living in a racist environment, would find sustenance in "rediscovering, reasserting, his blackness"

(129). Naipaul speaks of this as a "truce with irrationality"—a response to the region's past and ongoing racism that enables black southerners to lead productive and fulfilling lives. From this perspective, he is able to understand that narratives and experiences of coherent cultural identity can be valuable to southern African Americans and argues that it is "the final cruelty of slavery: that now, at what should have been a time of possibility, a significant portion of black people should find themselves without the supports of faith and community evolved during the last hundred years or so" (135). It appears that, after attending to white southerners' narratives of cultural identity and reconsidering his own experiences of cultural identity, he has become more amenable to contemplating similar aspects of black southerners' lives.

"THE PAST AS A WOUND"

Despite Naipaul's expanded interest in configurations of cultural identity, he consistently evades the fact that though southerners may be "made by the same history" (306), they remember and memorialize different aspects of that history. As he explores the effects of the regional past, Naipaul seems driven to suggest that, though it "wounded" people differently, it might have shaped them similarly, providing a "common language and common religion" (41). Immediately impressed by the sense of "consoling union" and the "idea of community" he perceives at an African American church during his preliminary visit to North Carolina (15), he hears of the importance of such communal relationships from a great majority of his interviewees, both black and white. He concludes that the link between religion and identity is "almost universal" in the southern United States and that this connection provides sustenance in the face of a divisive and still influential past (33). But he seems unable to reconcile this desire for unity among the members of these churches and communities with his recognition that the institutions are segregated and that they emerged in response to diverse needs and desires, as well as diverse relationships to historical events.

Of course, Naipaul acknowledges that, while "nearly all" of his African American interviewees are alienated from the antebellum past (125), several of his white interlocutors have an exaggerated sense of attachment to it. Naipaul repeatedly asks those who describe their affection for the Confederacy how such a cause could be defended, and they consistently seek to separate the history of slavery from that of antebellum southern life, to speak of the two as distinct phenomena, only coincidentally related. Naipaul finds "a torment in this way of reasoning": "that very special Southern past, and cause, could be made pure only if it was removed from the squalor of the race issue" (103, 106). As he reveals this irrationality, he also seeks to historicize the southern past in more detail than is suggested by those who evoke the Civil War as a single and monolithic rupture. Accordingly, he understands the regional past to exist "layer upon layer" (35), and includes in his discussion the histories of Native American removal, the lynching and disenfranchisement of African Americans, and global immigration.

But the effect of this method, in this text, is to erase distinctions between the diverse groups, with their differing—and also internally diverse—relations to power, that have experienced these changes: "the Indians, disappearing after centuries; the poor whites; the blacks; the war and all that had come after; and now the need everyone felt, black and white, poor and not so poor, everyone in his own way, to save his soul" (35). Naipaul treats white grief over the Confederate "cause," biracial evangelical Christianity, and African American civil-rights activism as congruent examples of southern community and continuity. This attempt to diminish the significance of differences in and abuses of power is crystallized in his conclusion, with regard to both the southeastern United States and Caribbean nations, that "long after any group can be held responsible, succeeding generations live on as victims or inheritors of old history" (225). This formulation acknowledges past harm but disavows the sources of that harm; for Naipaul to acknowledge the effects of history, he must paradoxically refuse to historicize their causes.

This displacement is so marked as to suggest that Naipaul's transferential "travel on a theme" evokes potent resistance, a refusal or even inability to recognize how his analysis has been truncated (25). His topic, as he frames it, is not "the race issue," which "quickly worked itself out," but the existence and usefulness of cultural identity, "that other South—of order and faith, and music and melancholy" (29). Apparently unable to recognize that in a postslavery and postapartheid society still shaped by racial injustice "the race issue" cannot be severed from consideration of cultural identity, he reveals the limits beyond which he refuses to explore this transference. His personal reflections suggest that his resistance corresponds to a lifelong conviction that cultural identifications, when recognized as such, should be concealed, secluded from heterogeneous social spaces that might necessitate negotiation of conflicting identifications.

As he compares his interlocutors' experiences and understandings of identity with his own, Naipaul repeatedly refers to his belief that people find security in affiliating themselves with communities they believe to be homogeneous. Though he has often censured this move, and continues to do so in his discussions of "black political adulation" in Caribbean and African nations (31, 227), he seems to detect this predilection so readily because it is an intimately familiar response. As he attempts to understand his interviewees' interest in identity, he suggests that affiliation with perceived similarity and distancing from perceived difference have performed a vital function in maintaining his own sense of self: "I remember my shock, my feeling of taint and spiritual annihilation, when I saw some of the Indians of Martinique, and began to understand that they had been swamped by Martinique, that I had no means of sharing the world view of these people whose history at some stage had been like mine, but who now, racially and in other ways, had become something other" (33). Observing another Caribbean society, one he expects to maintain the barrier between persons of African and Indian ancestry that he felt as a child, he experiences not merely surprise when he perceives that he is mistaken, but a dissolution of self, a "feeling of the void" (33).

This moment constitutes not a new challenge to his sense of identity but the culmination of a long-held fear—the realization of the "special kind of stress" he claims to be inherent in multiracial societies. He repeatedly suggests that he has long believed that to negotiate social space one must produce and mobilize not one flexible identity but rather two sharply differentiated ones—one intimate and familial Indian self, and one public self that belies Indian cultural identifications: "One of my earliest ideas . . . was that there were two worlds: the world within, the world without. To go out of that gate was to be in a world quite different from the one in the house; to go back through that gate at the end of the school day was to shed the ideas of the world outside. Everyone lives with ideas like these; everyone has different sets of behavior. But in a racially mixed society, especially one where race is a big issue, the different worlds have racial attributes or overtones. Distinctions and differences can have the force of taboos—things sensed rather than consciously worked out" (158). Naipaul's description suggests more a negatively charged negotiation of identity than a dexterous switching of codes, or a potentially critical process of reformulating identifications (Mirón 79–82). In his representation, he risked not only confusion or even loss of social status but utter desubjectification—a "fall into nonentity" (33). Because his professional life suggests a profound attachment to a cosmopolitan ego ideal, he could seem to have exchanged a colonial identification for an imperial one (the "unmarked" self of liberalism), but his identification with his "Indian family" is, as described in this text, equally profound (58).

Rather, he seems to have maintained two identifications that he understood to be mutually exclusive. Given that these "rituals and attitudes" are so sharply demarcated, and that Naipaul represents transgression of these delimitations as tantamount to "taboo," he seems almost to have formed conflicting ego-ideals—an idealized identification that necessitates, even in less discordant circumstances, powerful repression (Lacan 134). Certainly, Naipaul describes images of entire selves—analogous to clothing ensembles, which may be "shed and reassumed, as one went to school and returned home"—each with its own behaviors and beliefs (58). In their apparent completeness but equally apparent insufficiency—competent and certain in their own spheres but limited to those spaces—each imago stages both the fantasy of inhabiting a secure ego and the impossibility of such. Naipaul's identifications with these imagos, both "Indian" and "non-Indian," are repeatedly lost and reattached, but never fully, as each waits to undergo the process again on the journeys to and from school. Because the "objects" that are continually "lost" already belong to the ego (introjected images of parents, teachers, or other persons to whom the young Naipaul was attached), these identifications would probably be melancholic, in which frustrated love for the object is expressed as reproach or even hatred, directed toward the self, for the incorporated object's deficiencies (Freud, "Mourning"; Cheng 177–79).

Such a structure of identification would help to explain the venom Naipaul has long directed toward persons openly invested in ethnic, racial, and religious identities. Such persons claim the right to enact and embrace their cultural traditions and identifications "out of that gate," "outside the family house," breaking the rules Naipaul so rigorously applied to himself (158, 58). This association of traditions with restricted spaces illuminates his claim that attachments to cultural and racial identity produce "prisons of the spirit" (154); he believes such identifications are unable to negotiate heterogeneous social spaces, the institutions and interpersonal relationships of societies shaped by conflict. Crucially, Naipaul does not suggest that he has experimented with such negotiation; in his representation, the "gate," from his earliest experience, served to demarcate not only social space but also the ego. This bifurcation would help to explain the sense of "stress" Naipaul attributes to multiracial societies. In his understanding, attempts to dismantle this separation between local-cultural identifications and cosmopolitan-"unmarked" ones suggest disrupting the very structure of identity, risking "nonentity." From this perspective, persons who enact cultural identifications in social space threaten to stage precisely such dissolution. Thus, the contempt Naipaul has unleashed against identitarian narratives may reflect reproaches once turned against an identification of his own.

Whereas Naipaul has often projected his frustrations with cultural identification onto others, here he responds with a more sublimated transference, recognizing that his interlocutors' explorations of identity elicit emotional and psychological dynamics from his personal past. Though this impressively expands both his technique and his understanding of these interviews and quite likely allows for increased self-understanding, it does not enable him to subject his early beliefs about identification to critical analysis. This narrative is marked less by resentment than, explicitly, by "melancholy" (154); rather than articulating his concerns about the ways in which conflicting cultural identifications interact in southern social space, he either denies that conflict or absorbs his concern in barely articulated affective discomfort.

Midway through the narrative—corresponding with Naipaul's arrival in Mississippi, a state with a reputation "even in Alabama . . . for poverty and racial hardness" (155)—Naipaul's melancholy becomes palpable. Early in the narrative, he claims that in the U.S. South "there were two world views almost, two ways of seeing and feeling that could not be reconciled. And this was depressing" (58). In this section of the text, that depression is muted, expressed as physical enervation, vulnerability to asthma, and dependence on air-conditioning. Seeking a different interpretation of "the racial issue" (160), Naipaul determines in Mississippi "to consider things from the white point of view, as far as that was possible" (160, 189), but he displaces much of what he hears. Listening to an interviewee's remembrances of violence and of interracial injustice, he concludes with an assessment of interracial commonality: "In no other part of the world had I found people so driven by the idea of good behavior and the good religious life. And that was true for black and white" (164). Given that his transferential travel has led, by this point, to both personal discomfort and deep-seated resistance, it is not surprising that Naipaul should here produce, through dialogue and fantasy, a figure who denies the possibility of transference.

"JUST AN OLD REDNECK"

The transferential aspects of Naipaul's narrative may be most observable at the stage where they seem to be foresworn, that is, as he constructs his version of a "native," an aestheticized approximation of an ideal type of early-twentieth-century ethnography (Clifford 21, 24). Represented as having cultural traits entirely different from those of the traveler, living in isolation from the traveler's world, such figures may be narrated vividly, mythically; this is their immediate appeal for Naipaul. Speaking with Campbell, "the new kind of young conservative," Naipaul becomes bored as he hears of "family and values and authority . . . all quite predict-ably," and asks about the meaning of the term *redneck* (*Turn* 204). Campbell answers in "concrete, lyrical terms," describing rednecks as a "population" with a clearly delimited territory, specifiable physical attributes, and consistent material practices—habitat, diet, apparel, leisure practices, and wages. He states that rednecks live "out in Rankin County," fish in "Pearl River," and eat at Shoney's, where "you'll get the gravy all over it" (204, 206–7). Campbell holds that rednecks "have to project" an "image," and are uninterested in eliciting empathy from viewers: "They don't give a damn. They want people to know: 'I'm a redneck and proud of it'" (208). From Campbell's viewpoint, rednecks encourage "the denial of transference through total objectification of the other and the constitution of the self . . . as a transcendental spectator of a scene fixed in amber" (LaCapra 34).

Naipaul's delight at this moment of the text is palpable, and his melancholy is replaced by enthusiasm over his new find: "I hurried out to see them, as I might have hurried to see an unusual bird or a deer. And there, indeed, they were, bare-backed, but with the wonderful baseball hats, in a boat among the reeds, on a weekday afternoon" (*Turn* 213). But while his dehumanizing rhetoric, reminiscent of such colonial explorers as William Byrd, indicates Naipaul's lack of transference with rednecks themselves, his configuration of the redneck seems precisely calibrated to respond to the anxieties and desires expressed in his more obviously transferential narrative.

As configured by Naipaul, rednecks are untroubled by the relationship between their personal or cultural relationship to the past and those exemplified by others in their social space, because instead of memorializing or negotiating the past, they inhabit it. In Campbell's words, "They're not adapting, and they're being left behind" (211). It is this perception that fuels Naipaul's representation of himself as a discoverer: he has found an anachronism and must explain how he came upon this "threatened species" (*Turn* 213). He understands rednecks as the descendants of pioneers, replicating the practices of their ancestors and struggling valiantly to preserve their culture (222). Believing that they experience no generational change—"He's been raised that way. His father was just like him" (206)—Naipaul speaks of the redneck both as "the unlikely descendent of the frontiersman" and as "the frontiersman" (213).

Because they are, in Naipaul's representation, temporally separated from contemporary social space, shaped by an unmediated attachment to the past, they are also immune to contemporary conflict and negotiation. It is for this reason, in part, that Naipaul can represent himself as a defender of rednecks. Expressing appreciation for them, as he understands them, he cannot imagine that they would care to challenge his interpretation, for he has heard that they are "too little educated to understand human behavior, or to understand people who were not like themselves" (212). (It is worth noting that Naipaul's objectification of the "redneck" is not exceptional. Some initial reviewers appreciated his attention to a figure typically insulted and dismissed in American sociopolitical commentary [Woodward, "Rednecks" 7; Genovese 33], while others felt he was insufficiently derogatory [Brown 402; Shattuck 3].) Though Naipaul recites the claim that rednecks are distinguished by racial hatred, he deemphasizes this aspect of the accounts he hears, which would require him to consider their role in contemporary conflicts. He focuses instead on challenges that emerge from modernization, which is reducing redneck "hunting grounds" (218) and requires a compartmentalization of religion (244), such that subsequent generations might cease to replicate the lives of their parents.

Finally, this construction of the redneck exemplifies for Naipaul the familiar sense of deep division between the "world within" the gate and the "world without." Naipaul believes that negotiation of social space produces anxiety for rednecks. Observing a man in a hotel lobby "walking delicately" in his cowboy boots, Campbell explains the discrepancy: "He's as lost as a goose. He's never been on a tiled floor in his life" (212). Naipaul goes further, theorizing that rednecks eat excessively in order to emulate the revered figure of Elvis, but also, more importantly, to produce "fatness" as a protective measure against modernity, one that allows, through the manipulation of flesh and the blocking of corridors, "a simple form of self-assertion" (*Turn* 226). Distanced from modernity, this image of the redneck community is also remarkable for its internal homogeneity—a quality Naipaul has valued, but never quite found, throughout the text. Where other southerners fear separation from community or being "cut out of the herd" (47)—Naipaul's "nonentity"—such need for individuation would be unlikely among this group, which is said to be undifferentiated in preference, practice, and even genetic material (207).

Naipaul's explication of this theory varies between roguish, often ruthless absurdity and apparent sincerity. He seems fascinated by the idea that he has discovered "people with a certain past, living out a certain code" (213), but he suggests that this code is manifested in the eating of fast food, such that french fries and Twinkies represent "a real-life version of manna" (226). Arguing that he has uncovered a culture rooted in traditions that provide an "idea of a complete, created world and a complete, divinely sanctioned code" (233), he finds the manifestations of this lasting pioneerism in cowboy boots, Graceland, and contemporary country music. Even the colossal classism and sexism of his account are exceeded by its ludicrousness: one simply cannot argue that such commodities, spectacles, and media productions separate people from modernity.

But Naipaul's fascination with the redneck serves a psychological purpose, enabling him to disavow the contradictions that emerged in his earlier investigations of southern cultural identities in two related ways. First, it allows him to ignore the southern history of oppression and division; though he acknowledges that the poor of both races suffered during slavery and in its aftermath, he is concerned here only with those aspects of the past that the redneck is said still to inhabit. Imagining life in an ungoverned and unstructured frontier, existing before the development of plantations, he is able to forget "that difficulty about the cause" that emerged in previous discussions with white southerners, as well as the differences in feeling and in interpretation that prevented the past from serving as a unifying principle in southern identity. Consequently, the rednecks' purported relationship to the past serves a second purpose for Naipaul: it enables him to contemplate the sort of "religion of the past" that he found so attractive early in the text, but here seemingly freed of its political and intellectual contradictions.

Through this process, he confirms that such an investment in the past cannot be maintained. Even Naipaul's figure of the redneck, said to hold a relationship to the past marked by neither rupture nor any kind of change, will be forced, he concedes, to acknowledge modernity. Accordingly, he hears the lyrics of country music as elegies not only "for the South" but also for his earlier ideal of a homogeneous community bound by "old history and myth, old community, old faith" (248). After exulting in his idea that the redneck maintains an unbroken relationship with a past way of life and an unchanging space, he mourns the inevitable extinction of such an identity formation.

Astonishingly, after this performance, Naipaul represents an articulation of identity that dispenses with absolutes—the insistence that everyone in a community must share a common relationship to the past, the idea that racial division is inevitable, and his old belief that attachments to a localized space and history are inherently damaging. He begins to consider the idea that one can hold a relationship with place and society that is flexible and discontinuous. His new acquaintance, Jim Applewhite, describes his feelings toward the region of his birth as ambivalent, claiming both "a sensation of being so utterly at home in, and a part of, a place, that one feels somehow coextensive with the place," and "a sense of separateness in being in part of myself an observing stranger in my own native land" (303). It is as if Naipaul is able to comprehend such statements—which, as he acknowledges, perfectly describe his experience—for the first time, though he remembers hearing them from Howard before he even got on the plane heading southward.

Realizing that this sense of self-division and ambivalence toward the place of one's childhood is not a property of himself alone and is contingent neither on certain racial or national affiliations nor on specific individual experiences, Naipaul reconsiders the experience of cultural identity, recognizing that such identity is both influenced by the past and endlessly shifting, both traceable and ineffable. Naipaul, who seemed melancholic over his inability to resolve such contradictions when he first reached Mississippi, now seems simply content. In the final paragraphs of the text, he speaks of the coexistence of commonality and difference as if he had always been able to do so.

This ability seems to have developed through the transference manifested in his journey—his attempts to understand his own identity, as well as those of various groups through their relationships to history, and to repress the implications of that history. But that repression, crucially, remains intact. Naipaul's questions about the significance of race and of history are never answered in this book but are redirected through the production of, and brief indulgence in, an identity narrative that admits no complication whatsoever. When Campbell, for example, who finally admits that he is "probably a redneck myself," attempts to understand how that aspect of his identity might coexist with the other identity narrative to which he is devoted—one of self-sufficiency and hard work—Naipaul will have none of it, assuring his readers, "I got him back to the subject of redneck sex" (209).

EPILOGUE

The models of identity offered by Naipaul, in both his account of his childhood and in his production of the redneck, are stark: either a secure cultural identification fixated on a past time and restricted space, incapable of negotiating changing social spaces, or an identity that represses its affiliations with traditions or communities. His narrative evasions of this quandary—denial of conflict over cultural beliefs and narratives, or individuated melancholia—are unacceptable. But his investigative method, though truncated, may hold some promise. Through contemplating commonalities between his background and those of his interlocutors, he is at least able to acknowledge the fears and desires that shape his evasions and, through such admissions, to attend more rigorously to narratives he might previously have dismissed. What remains is to subject those fears and desires themselves to critique, to consider whether identity as he has come to understand it is in fact identity as it must be.

Edouard Glissant, another Caribbean traveler in the U.S. South, has concluded that this is a central question in a world changing so quickly that "we find ourselves confined inside this deathly pale multitude even before we can witness the collective putrefactions of the dead bodies that we already are" (220). Taking a transferential Faulkner as his guide through fictional and factual southern landscapes, he concludes that, though contemporary "struggle" feels confining, a more closed and tradi- tional form of association, in such a world, amounts to "the exclusionary lives of those who assemble in groups only to be able to separate them- selves from others" (220). Expressing a desire "to enter into a new emo- tion and an unprecedented feeling of the world collectivity, where we neither lose nor dilute ourselves," he concludes, "This is difficult" (220). And yet, as he argues, this is a world that requires multiple kinds of sustenance, both cultural exchange and tradition, both "wandering" and "roots" (223). Naipaul may have faltered, in part, because the very tra- dition that enabled his transference—the romanticization of the Con- federacy—is one hostile to other traditions, one that sought not only isolation from but absolute suppression of coexisting cultural forms. Where Naipaul backs away, suggesting that cultural identifications must be either shared or secluded, Glissant insists on negotiation, "the difficult Relation."

WORKS CITED

Atlas, James. "V. S. vs. The Rest." *Vanity Fair* Mar. 1987: 64–8.

Brown, Rosellen. "Dazzled by the Light." *Dissent* 36.3 (summer 1989): 401–3.

Cheng, Anne Anlin. *The Melancholy of Race.* New York: Oxford UP, 2000.

Clifford, James. *Routes: Travel and Translation in the Late Twentieth Century.* Cam- bridge, Mass.: Harvard UP, 1997.

Dayan, Joan. "Gothic Naipaul." *Transition* 59 (1993): 158–70.

Freud, Sigmund. *Fragment of an Analysis of a Case of Hysteria ("Dora").* Abr. *The Freud Reader.* Ed. Peter Gay. New York: Norton, 1995. 172–239.

——. "Mourning and Melancholia." *The Freud Reader.* Ed. Peter Gay. New York: Norton, 1995. 584–89.

Genovese, Eugene. "They'll Take Their Stand." *New Republic* 13 Feb. 1989: 30–34.

Glissant, Edouard. *Faulkner, Mississippi.* Trans. Barbara Lewis and Thomas C. Spear. New York: Farrar, 1999.

Gutiérrez-Jones, Carl. *Critical Race Narratives: A Study of Race, Rhetoric, and Injury.* New York: New York UP, 2001.

Hall, Stuart. "Cultural Identity and Diaspora." *Identity: Community, Culture, Difference.* Ed. Jonathan Rutherford. London: Lawrence and Wishart, 1990.

LaCapra, Dominick. *Representing the Holocaust: History, Theory, Trauma.* Ithaca, N.Y.: Cornell UP, 1994.

Lacan, Jacques. *The Seminar of Jacques Lacan, Book I: Freud's Papers on Technique, 1953–1954.* Ed. Jacques-Alain Miller. Trans. John Forrester. New York: Norton, 1988.

Michaels, Walter Benn. "Race into Culture." *Critical Inquiry* 18.4 (summer 1992): 655–85.

Mirón, Louis F. "Postmodernism and the Politics of Racialized Identities." *Race, Identity, and Citizenship: A Reader.* Ed. Rodolfo D. Torres, Louis F. Mirón, and Jonathan Xavier Inda. New York: Blackwell, 1999. 79–100.

Naipaul, V. S. *Beyond Belief: Islamic Excursions among the Converted Peoples.* New York: Random House, 1998.

——. *A Turn in the South.* 1989. New York: Vintage, 1990.

Nixon, Rob. "V. S. Naipaul, Postcolonial Mandarin." *Transition* 52 (1991): 100–113.

Ramadevi, N. *The Novels of V. S. Naipaul: Quest for Order and Identity.* New Delhi: Prestige, 1996.

Rampersad, Arnold. "V. S. Naipaul: Turning in the South." *Raritan* 10.1 (summer 1990): 24–47.

Romine, Scott. *The Narrative Forms of Southern Community.* Baton Rouge: Louisiana State UP, 1999.

Said, Edward. "Expectations of Inferiority." *New Statesman* 16 Oct. 1981: 21–22.

Shattuck, Roger. "The Reddening of America." *New York Review of Books* 30 Mar. 1989: 3–5.

Sumner, William Graham. *Folkways: A Study of the Sociological Importance of Usages, Manners, Customs, Mores, and Morals.* Boston: Ginn, 1906.

Tindall, George. "The 'Colonial Economy' and the Growth Psychology: The South in the 1930's." *South Atlantic Quarterly* 64.4 (autumn 1965): 465–77.

Wallerstein, Immanuel. "What Can One Mean by Southern Culture?" 1988. *Geopolitics and Geoculture: Essays on the Changing World-System.* Cambridge: Cambridge UP, 1991.

Weiss, Timothy F. *On the Margins: The Art of Exile in V. S. Naipaul.* Amherst: U of Massachusetts P, 1992.

Woodward, C. Vann. "Rednecks, Millionaires, and Catfish Farms." *New York Times Book Review* 5 Feb. 1989: 7.

——. *The Strange Career of Jim Crow.* 3d ed. New York: Oxford UP, 1974.

★ ★ ★ **PART TWO**

RETHINKING RACE AND REGION

The second part of this book, "Rethinking Race and Region," endeavors to remap imagined communities of the South by focusing on similarities across traditional borders, as well as by exploring differences within the putatively "solid South." The essays in this section compare formulations of the South's identity to those of other regions in the United States and to U.S. nationalism as a whole; at the same time, they examine constructions of African American identity that encompass the South and the developing world.

Historians have long noted a colonial relationship between the U.S. South and the Northeast, but critics have been slow to apply recent advances in postcolonial theory to the cultures that arose from that relationship. Scott Romine argues that the identitarian debates within white southern nationalism after Reconstruction reflected the conflicted status of nationalism as it typically emerges from a colonial state. Although writers such as Frantz Fanon have sanctioned postcolonial nationalism as a necessary form of resistance, many commentators—notably Edward Said in *Culture and Imperialism*—have been critical of its regressive nativist tendencies, valorizing in its place a necessary and vital cosmopolitan hybridity. Southern nationalism was enunciated and attacked in almost precisely these terms. From Henry Grady to the Nashville Agrarians, the progressive and conservative strands of southern nationalism have proceeded in an uneasy relation to one another that duplicates in salient ways the condition of postcoloniality. At the same time, both discourses attempt to appropriate a precolonial ideal along the lines Tom Nairn suggests in observing that nationalism encourages societies to "propel themselves forward to a certain sort of goal (industrialism, prosperity, equality with other peoples, etc.) by a certain sort of regression by looking inwards, drawing more deeply upon their indigenous resources, resurrecting past folk-heroes and myths about themselves and so on." Romine focuses his analysis on the novels of Thomas Nelson Page and Thomas Dixon Jr., two writers also paired by the likes of C. Vann Woodward and Walter Benn Michaels, because the novels—*Red Rock* and *Gordon Keith* by Page, the Reconstruction trilogy by Dixon—offer two contrasting nationalist narratives of how, during Reconstruction, things fell apart and were ultimately restored to a "proper equilibrium."

In this part, as well, John T. Matthews explores racial questions and practices in several of Faulkner's earlier novels. In *Light in August* (1932) in particular, Faulkner is interested in some of the social and cultural practices by which southern communities maintained the ideology of intraracial purity in the face of its obvious contradiction by the growing phenomenon of interracial mixture. Additionally, he moves to examine mental technologies like the fetish of skin and racial stereotype in order to imagine how the South defended itself more consciously from the certainty of change. Drawing from the work of Homi Bhabha, Matthews considers the U.S. South from Reconstruction through the 1930s, when modernization finally prevailed, as a complex post- and neocolonial society. As white landowners attempted to recolonize emancipated blacks, they sought simultaneously to free themselves from northern control. The terrain of contested ex-colonial wills thus can be seen to host a set of social relations governed by the exercise of common colonial relations and habits of representation. The South's racial hybridity must be both confronted and ignored by whites seeking segregation's repeated legitimation, a task furthered by the logic of the fetish, which permits privileged objects to substitute for the knowledge of loss and difference embedded in identity formation. Likewise, stereotype expresses both the need to subjugate the dominated Other and the powerful desire to repossess what has been abjected. Faulkner describes the failing authority of such practices and indicates the sites from which a recognition of the South's historical hybridity might be admitted and imagined.

In his essay on Richard Wright, Richard King explores what Wright called his "double vision" of the modern world. Where W. E. B. DuBois's original articulation of "double consciousness" in *The Souls of Black Folk* (1903) talked of an external and internal split between being a "Negro" and being an "American," Wright's doubleness extended that division to an explicitly global setting marked by two historically crucial processes: the Cold War and the decolonization of the former European colonies. King examines what Wright meant by the terms *modern* and *modernization* in three late, nonfiction works: *Black Power* (1954), *The Color Curtain* (1956), and *White Man, Listen!* (1957). In these texts, Wright restages the conflict he had identified in America between African American folk culture and the forces of modernization as embodied in the divided consciousness of northern black ghettoes. At the global level, this conflict emerged as one between indigenous traditional cultures and the forces of modernization led by the West. Ultimately, Wright was faced with a tragic choice in a world confronted with irreconcilable forces. At times the conflict was between two "rights": the coherence of traditional cultures of meaning and western progress via rationality. At other times, the collision involved two "wrongs": western capitalist imperialism with otiose and dysfunctional local cultures. In addition to exploring Wright's intellectual, moral, and political dilemmas, King establishes the continuity of his commitment to modernity in his work from the mid-1940s until his death in the 1960s, and between his exploration of the plight of African Americans and his analysis of the situation of third-world societies.

Robert Brinkmeyer and Debra Rae Cohen explore how a number of white southern writers represent California—both the reality and the myth—and Los Angeles in particular, in order to negotiate aspects of postmodernism and regional identity. In looking at this rather dramatic turn west in the southern literary imagination (even though it is a commonplace, it is nevertheless true that literature by white southerners has for the most part been grounded firmly in Dixie and along a north-south geocultural axis), the authors come to an understanding of the nature of place, space, and community in postmodern southern literature. The authors begin with a brief discussion of the West and its place in the twentieth-century southern literary imagination (drawing from Brinkmeyer's *Remapping Southern Literature: Southern Writers and the West*), setting the context for the postmodern turn and discussing authors such as Ann Patchett, Frederick Barthelme, Dorothy Allison, Tim Gautreaux, and Darcey Steinke.

Lois Parkinson Zamora's essay in this collection offers a comparative analysis of the role of film in Walker Percy's *The Moviegoer* (1960) and

Manuel Puig's *Betrayed by Rita Hayworth* (1968), as well as discussing how this medium functions in different areas of the Americas. Michael Wood, English critic and reviewer, has commented that "movies matter a lot to contemporary Latin American writers," citing the actual involvement in filmmaking or film criticism and/or the fictive uses of cinematic material of numerous Latin American writers. For these authors, continues Wood, the movies "combine the fan's pleasure with the technician's interest, and suggest an ideal apprenticeship in fantasy—or more precisely in the art of connecting fantasy to the world. Hollywood, and the French and German film industries, were dream factories for Latin America" (Wood 44). Such an assertion remains as relevant now as it was when it was made in 1980. Nonetheless, the comparatist may hesitate for a moment to wonder whether the movies have mattered any less to U.S. writers and, more specifically, whether Hollywood has fueled the fantasies of writers of the South. Zamora approaches this question in the first section of her essay by comparing the intertextual use of movies in *The Moviegoer* and in *Betrayed by Rita Hayworth*. Despite the great differences between the provincial Argentina of the 1930s portrayed by Puig and the New Orleans of the 1950s created by Percy, the problem of correlating incompatible cultural media is the principal thematic and structural concern of both novels. Next, Zamora proposes several comparative generalizations about the social function of films in the U.S. South and in Latin America. In her third section, she draws on the work of James Baldwin and Ralph Ellison to expand the definition of southern literature from a geographical category to a conceptual one, asserting that the South is a state of mind and that writers who write insightfully *about* the South belong to this region as surely as writers who write from *within* it. Finally, she further breaches geographical parameters by asking why movies have mattered (to use Wood's term once more) in *many* regions of the world where communities are engaged in defining themselves culturally, politically, and socially. Ultimately, Zamora explores the *function* assigned by postcolonial communities to their various art forms, particularly literature and film.

WORKS CITED

Wood, Michael. "The Claims of Mischief." *New York Review of Books* 24 Jan. 1980: 43–44.

"Can't you see that your so-called States are now
conquered provinces? That North Carolina and other
waste territories of the United States are unfit to
associate with civilized communities?"

—Austin Stoneman to Abraham Lincoln,
  in THOMAS DIXON JR., *The Clansman*

SCOTT ROMINE

Things Falling Apart: The Postcolonial

Condition of *Red Rock* and *The Leopard's Spots*

Walker Percy's famous quip that a truly
new South would be one in which no
one spoke of a New South anymore sug-
gests the fundamentally discontinuous character of southern identity.
But the division of Souths into old and new has itself a point of historical
origin. Of the year 1865, Thomas Dixon Jr. claims, "Henceforth all events
would be reckoned from this; 'before the Surrender,' or 'after the Surrender'" (4). Conservatives have tended to overlay a cultural defeat on
the military one, marking surrender as a moment in which an essential
South is compromised, perhaps beyond repair. For Richard Weaver, Appomattox represented not merely a military surrender but a "surrender
of initiative" that would put the southern tradition forever at bay, while
Allen Tate, commenting that "no nation is ever simply and unequivocally
beaten in war," laments the South's inferiority to the Irish in preserving
tradition, "though much less than the Irish have we ever been beaten in
war" (168–69). This essay argues that "southern tradition" as Weaver and
Tate conceive it was not so much destroyed as enabled by the experience
of defeat, and further, it was enabled in a recognizable way as a selective,

fetishized set of icons and memories culled from the messiness of history and consigned forever to a past irretrievable except through representation. If the southern tradition is *by definition* at bay—that estrangement from tradition is not a limitation but a condition of white southern identity as it emerged in the postbellum era—then Dixon's ruptured history follows patterns of cultural trauma found worldwide.

In *The Location of Culture*, Homi Bhabha writes that, for imperialized peoples, "Remembering is never a quiet act of introspection or retrospection. It is a painful re-membering, a putting together of the dismembered past to make sense of the trauma of the present" (63). It is precisely such a dismembering and re-membering, a collective attempt to make sense of a fractured past and a traumatic present, that in part characterizes two novels of Reconstruction, Dixon's *The Leopard's Spots: A Romance of the White Man's Burden, 1865–1900* (1902) and Thomas Nelson Page's *Red Rock: A Chronicle of Reconstruction* (1898). To approach these works from a postcolonial perspective necessitates at the outset an awareness that Reconstruction can, only in a conditional and provisional way, be considered a colonial or imperial encounter. In addition to obvious political, historical, and economic differences, one must confront the radical difference in racist discourse as it functioned in the postbellum South and in imperialist encounters as they are generally understood. Given that white racism served as an antidote to and not a justification for "imperialism" as it was practiced by the victorious North, the hazards of comparing the white South and the native peoples of Asia or Africa are clear enough. As Rey Chow observes, the metanarrative of "resistance" thrives in an age skeptical of metanarratives and carries with it an "implicit . . . dichotomy between the pernicious power on top and the innocent, suffering masses at the bottom" (113). And while Chow's nuanced complication of that metanarrative is hardly necessary here, my use of postcolonial theory limits itself to an examination of how cultural identity emerges from the traumatic experience of military, political, and economic domination. And here the similarities between the U.S. South and other dominated cultures are not insignificant. As Edward Said writes, "We must not minimize the shattering importance of that initial insight—peoples being conscious of themselves as prisoners in their own land—for it returns again and again in the literature of the imperialized world. The history of empire . . . seems incoherent unless one recognizes that sense of beleaguered imprisonment infused with a passion for community that grounds anti-imperial resistance in cultural effort" (214).

To speak of southern identity as originating from the kind of trauma

Bhabha and Said describe is to revise a traditional understanding of the South's tragic ordeal. If having a "tragic sense" has served to distinguish the South as the grown-up cousin of an adolescent America, having a traumatic sense connects it with cultures around the world.[1] Tragedy is an aestheticized form of trauma and a rather self-congratulatory one: who wouldn't prefer being tragic to being traumatized? But what Chidi Okonkwo says of Africa applies to the white South as well: "The psychological carnage inflicted on the colonized by the colonizer is real, its effects long-lasting, not just in the people's relationship with Europe but also in the colonized people's own concept of self-worth" (114–15). Originating in psychological carnage and not bracing, ennobling experience, the formation of modern white southern identity captured by Page and Dixon registers the irrevocable alteration produced by the Reconstruction encounter. To be sure, the cultural effort recorded in—and, in some respects, constituted by—their novels deploys two tropes pervasive among imperialized peoples: first, of a homogeneous people assaulted by a hostile power; second, of a past, a kind of Golden Age, dispossessed by imperialist force. But as Chow observes, both "past" and "people" as they figure in narratives of resistance are always selective and therefore "impure" (114–15, 151–58). While Page and Dixon strategically attempt to preserve the purity and, to some extent, the homogeneity of the people, neither attempts to recover the past—the Old South—that they imagine. In history's nightmare, things fall apart, and awaking to a new day requires the Old South be consigned to an archive irretrievable except through strategic representation.

Organized around themes of resistance, the cultural identities that emerge from *Red Rock* and *The Leopard's Spots* are inherently hybridized, interstitial, and reactionary, and it is here that postcolonial studies provides its most valuable insights into the modern formation of white southern identity. As Bhabha observes, "It is in the emergence of the interstices—the overlap and displacement of domains of difference—that the intersubjective and collective experience of nationness, community interest, or cultural value are negotiated" (2). Writing of the antebellum era, Jefferson Humphries suggests how telling about the South is, invariably, to tell against the North, and while the limitations of southern essentialism are becoming increasingly clear, this essay addresses not merely cultural dialogics but the particular form of dialogism that takes place within, as Said puts it, "an unequal relationship between unequal interlocutors" (191). What happens, in other words, when military and political domination enters the domain of cultural dialogics? For Page this encounter replaces localized tradition with a decentered, hybridized conception of culture, while Dixon's emergent culture is at once more nativist and more progressive. In an ironic turn for an anti-imperial novel, *The Leopard's Spots* offers an atavistic commitment to white supremacy articulated in the messianic language of empire.

In his 1892 essay "The Want of a History of the Southern People," Page calls for southern control of historical representation, sounding a note frequently heard among imperialized peoples. "There is no true history of the South," he writes. "In a few years there will be no South to demand a history" (*Old South* 346). Offering *Red Rock* as a corrective to northern versions of Reconstruction, Page exposes what he considered an attempt, "under the euphemism of reconstruction," to "destroy the South," leaving it "dismembered, disfranchised, denationalized" (4).[2] At the same time, *Red Rock* is anything but antinorthern: for most of *Red Rock*'s northerners, Reconstruction is a principled assault on economic disorder, racial tyranny, and cultural backwardness. Page's counterdiscourse, then, must decode the distortions enabling this view. The novel's villain, the aptly named Jonadab Leech, maintains an elaborate propaganda network through which he advances his personal interests in the name of national imperatives. Able to manipulate the press and to "pos[e] as patriots and advocates of law and order" in the nation's capital, Leech and his scalawag minion Hiram Still mobilize the power of "most potent men in the councils of the nation" (240). Through his letters, Leech commands a network of power, both political and moral. "Leech wrote to the authorities that he and his party must have power to preserve the union; he wrote to Mrs. Welch that they must have it to preserve the poor freedmen. The authorities promised it, and kept the promise. It was insanity" (199). Adept at cultural iconography, Leech undertakes an imaginary defense of the union and the freedman.

In exposing what the missives miss, Page exploits the distinctively imperialist distance that enables Leech to mislead his correspondents. In considering the ramifications of imperial distance, Bhabha reflects on T. H. Macaulay's observations on the dispatches from the Directors of the East India Company. Macaulay views these texts as "dispatches of hypocrisy," claiming that "the just and humane sentiments" articulated in England "being interpreted [in India], mean simply, 'Be the father and oppressor of the people; be just and unjust, moderate and rapacious'" (qtd. in Bhabha 95). In contrast, Bhabha calls attention to the inherently "multiple and contradictory belief that emerges as an effect of the ambivalent, deferred address of colonialist governance" (95). "Such a split in enunciation," Bhabha continues, "can no longer be contained with the 'unisonance' of civil discourse. . . . For it reveals an agonistic uncertainty contained in the incompatibility of empire and nation; it puts on trial the very discourse of civility within which representative government claims its liberty and empire its ethics" (95–96). As Walter Benn Michaels observes, American anti-imperialists at the turn of the century attacked specifically the incompatibility of nation and empire, and it is precisely the split enunciation Bhabha observes that Page foregrounds as an enabling condition of Reconstruction imperialism. It is not merely that Leech uses propaganda to advance his interests but that good intentions in the North pave a particular road to hell in Dixie. Brilliantly exploiting the anxieties surrounding the question of whether the postbellum South constituted states or "conquered provinces," as Dixon's villain puts it, Page affirms civil discourse while exposing how Leech's distortions preclude it.

Civil discourse is reaffirmed only when the Welch family crosses the boundary between North and South. Prior to her departure to the Red Rock region, Mrs. Welch is committed to her philanthropic society and fully duped by Leech's letters, published pseudonymously in the aptly named *Censor*. When Reely Thurston, a Union officer who has served time in the Red Rock region, correctly identifies the author of the letters, pronounces him a bald-faced liar, and provides a counternarrative of white benevolence and black consent, Mrs. Welch is outraged. Her prejudice remains in evidence when she arrives in the Red Rock region, where she pronounces the disorderly landscape and poor roads to be clear evidence of shiftlessness. Her driver, however, begins to provide a counternarrative, explaining that "some says it's the Yankee carpet-baggers steals all the money" (326). When Mrs. Welch provides a glowing account of the "shipshape" North, the driver responds "more dryly than before," "Maybe, that's where they puts the money they steals down here" (326). If as Zora Neale Hurston famously said you have to "go there to know there," Mrs. Welch is beginning to surmount the deficits of distance learning. Indeed, she has already learned an important lesson when, immediately on her arrival, she overhears a speech given by a freedman politician named Nicholas Ash. That lesson is this: when interpreted in the South, her just and humane sentiments mean simply, as Ash puts it, "We've got 'em down, and we mean to keep 'em down, too, by——!" (321). It is not long until her letters home suggest to her philanthropic society that she "was already succumbing to the very influence she repudiated" (333). The wife of an unscrupulous financier declares, "I never knew anyone go down there who did not at once abandon all principles and fall a victim to the influence of those people" (333).[3]

Defeat in the Civil War settled the question of the South's separate political existence.[4] Albert Taylor Bledsoe's *Is Davis a Traitor?* (1866) was anomalous even in its own time as a belated theoretical defense of states' rights; it would be well into the next century before states' rights would emerge as part of a new, vital discourse. What regional identity was possible for the South, then, could be articulated only in the language of culture. It is in this context that Walter Benn Michaels's assertion that *Red Rock* rigidly separates culture and state seems eminently reasonable (17–18). The novel, however, reveals the historical contingency of this separation. Ultimately, the presence of an invading force necessitates a revision of culture in which insular localism gives way before the dispossessing forces of history. *Red Rock* begins with an elegy to antebellum oligarchy and provincialism—in fact, the reader is addressed as the "real provincial" in comparison with the mistress of "old time courtesy and high breeding" (x)—but ends with "the old Country" (vii) situated within an amorphous, hybridized form of nationalism. When northern visitors arrive before the war, they are strangers and guests; when political differences arise, social propriety demands that the conversation be ended (30–31). "We interfere with nobody," the southern spokesman intones. "All we demand is that they shall not interfere with us" (30). This insularity is precisely what the war renders impossible, and with it a conception of culture as a set of norms and practices impervious to the outside.

Of the colonial encounter in China, Rey Chow writes, "'The Chinese'—people/culture/value—is what makes China China—that is, what no one can change or take away; at the same time, 'the Chinese' is what 'the West' can endanger—that is, what someone can change and take away" (116). I want to argue that *Red Rock* traces a shift from the former understanding of cultural identity to the latter; finally, the essence of the Old Country proves susceptible to the contingencies of history and domination. This shift is most clearly elaborated in the figure of Dr. Cary, the local Unionist, who, Cassandra-like, predicts ruin and is best able to deal with it when it arrives. For Dr. Cary, honor renders identity impervious to history's vicissitudes. This is why, when his old college friend, Senator Rockfield, offers him financial assistance, he declines despite the economic devastation that has visited his family and region. "War," he intones, "cannot plunder Virtue" (246). Speaking in the stoic tones that would become a distinctive part of a certain southern repertoire,

Dr. Cary epitomizes the gentleman too principled to succeed under the new dispensation: his material failure proves his virtue. Given such attitudes, one would expect an ideological consonance between Dr. Cary and Jacquelin Gray, the dispossessed heir of Red Rock plantation, when the latter returns from a long trip abroad. "It seemed to him that, in his travels, his horizons had widened. On the high seas or in a foreign land, it had been the flag of the nation that he wanted to see. He had begun to realize the idea of a great nation that should be known and respected wherever a ship could sail or a traveler could penetrate; of a re-united country in the people of both sides, retaining all that the best of both sides, should vie with each other in building up the nation, and should equally receive all its benefits" (257).

When Jacquelin presents to Dr. Cary, "the person who had first suggested the idea to his mind" (258), his idea of "complete acceptance of the new situation" (257), the erstwhile Unionist responds that Reconstruction has rendered Jacquelin's vision "Utopian." "It is now *vae victis*," Dr. Cary says, "and the only hope is in resistance. . . . The miscreants who rule us know no restraint but fear" (258). Previously impervious to assault, cultural identity now appears vulnerable to the degradations of Reconstruction. Even Dr. Cary suspends his stoicism to go momentarily nativist, describing resistance as the necessary action of culture.

But while resistance occasionally exists as a cultural imperative, Page's dominant strategy is one of compromise and hybridization. If, as Michaels suggests, no government in Red Rock "can quite be legitimate" (17), it is equally (and paradoxically) true that no government can quite be illegitimate. Despite its anti-imperialism, Red Rock never fully sanctions resistance outside the law. This is why Jacquelin threatens Hiram Still, the former overseer of Red Rock who currently owns it illegally, that should Still disturb the family graveyard "*without a decision of court authorizing him to do so,* he would kill him, even if he had the whole Government of the United States around him" (262; emphasis added). That miscreants like Still and Leech control the courts points up the paradox of Jacquelin's speech: it is precisely because Still does have the "whole Government" around him that Jacquelin's qualification negates his threat. A similar paradox informs Dr. Cary's speech later in the novel when he unsuccessfully urges a group of men planning a jailbreak to remedy the "wrongs we are suffering . . . by law, and not by violence" (428). Even though the situation demands illegal action, Steve Allen, the leader of the men who free the prisoner, later admits that he merely "tided over that crisis" (533).[5] Only when government is aligned precisely with Leech does illegal action obtain even a provisional sanction, and then only as a deferral of a more permanent resolution. This moment comes when Leech imprisons virtually the entire male population of the community, including Dr. Cary, for treason and rebellion. Despite Leech's pretense to be "but the humble instrument of the law" (485), "suddenly the two had become one. Leech was the Government, and the Government was Leech: no longer merely the State—the Carpet-bag Government—but the Government. . . . For the first time he was not only hated, but feared" (488). The shift is significant: Leech is no longer an outside force, a temporary source of injustice, but a symbol of systematic and efficacious oppression. This is why a yeoman veteran affirms that he "never would have surrendered, if I'd thought it ud 'a come to this" (482). Culture is no longer impervious to the state Leech represents.

The ramifications of this shift are profound: most notably, the hostile state provides a set of conditions in which culture must be articulated if it is to survive. In offering a more permanent elaboration of Dr. Cary's measured strategy, Page turns to the courts and two instances of frustrated injustice. The first trial, a civil case between Still and Jacquelin over the ownership of Red Rock plantation, does the double service of clarifying the technology of state oppression while envisioning possible forms of cultural hybridity. The significance of the trial is not lost on its participants, who "recognized on both sides that it was not now a mere property question, but a fight for supremacy. The old citizens were making a stand against the new powers" (473). As a townsman recognizes, "it was a civilization on trial" (456). Throughout the trial, the judge leaves little question as to his blatant bias, and despite clear evidence of Still's fraud, he instructs the jury to bring in a verdict clearing Still and his co-defendant Mr. Welch, who has in good faith purchased from Still a portion of the estate. At this point, however, Mr. Welch rises and publicly renounces his claim to the land, asserting that he is "not willing to hold another man's property which he lost by fraud" (467). Bound by a code of personal honor, Mr. Welch enunciates cultural similarity in the arena of political difference. The similarity is noted by the townsfolk, who opine variously that he is not a Yankee, that he is "more like our people than like Yankees," or that he proves that some Yankees are "better than them we know about" (469). "Civilization" thereby survives the trial (itself deferred) by identifying cultural norms that can be marked neither "ours" nor "theirs."

Personal honor figures prominently in the second trial as well. But if the antebellum rule was "honor defended is honor retained," Steve Allen's trial for Ku Klux terrorism shows how the rules have changed under the new regime. Steve's involvement in the Ku Klux is minimal, and after the initial disarming of Leech's black militia, he actively opposes the "cowardly body of cut-throats, who rode about the country under cover of darkness, perpetrating all sorts of outrages and villainies for purposes of private vengeance" (528). But the nation is obsessed with recent Ku Klux outrages, and Leech, "pos[ing] as a public-spirited man," casts Steve as an arch-terrorist, again deploying the national press to portray his trial as "the signal of a complete collapse of the opposition to the Government" (533). The discursive imbalance of power is again in evidence, as the local press "raved in impotent rage, and declared that open war would be better than the oppression to which they were subjected" (535). The primary evidence against Steve is his admission to Ruth Welch of his involvement in early Ku Klux activities, which she inadvertently divulges. The marriage plot that solves this particular crisis—Ruth marries Steve and therefore cannot testify against him—had, by the time Page wrote *Red Rock*, long served as a trope of sectional reconciliation, and the necessity of this particular form of hybridity is perhaps self-evident. As the townsfolk recognize, "There was no Mason and Dixon line in love" (561).[6]

But if the solution is obvious, the precise nature of the problem is more intriguing. Even if "open war" is impossible, it is difficult to see why Steve should not remain a culture hero irrespective of the trial's outcome. But, on the contrary, imprisonment even in these circumstances means permanent dishonor for Steve, who recognizes that "deserved or not, a conviction and sentence to the penitentiary placed a stigma on him never to be erased. All his high hopes would be blighted, his future ruined; he would have brought disgrace on his family; he could never more face men as he had done heretofore; he would not be fit to speak to a lady" (562). Paradoxically, it is Steve's commitment to honor—he cannot kill Leech the night before the trial, despite having the opportunity to do so—that makes his shame inevitable. The excessive loading of meaning onto Steve's trial extends Dr. Cary's early revision of identity; no longer is it necessary merely to defend honor, but to defend it successfully. If war cannot plunder virtue, the courts, it seems, can. Again, Page insists on culture as something peculiarly fragile, something uniquely subject to Leech's regime. This is why "civilization" can be put, as Page writes, "on trial," why Steve's trial threatens to become "the final struggle between the old residents and the new invaders . . . the beginning of the total subjugation of the people" (559).

Reading *Red Rock* this way foregrounds the historicity of a specific understanding of culture and the potential for loss that it carries. In the end, Page's representation of an insular culture compelled to defend itself shifts subtly but irrevocably toward a conception of culture constituted by defense and counterdiscourse, a culture essentially reactive (if not precisely reactionary) in nature and for this reason unable to imagine itself as fully continuous with its past. As Bhabha observes, "The 'right' to signify from the periphery of authorized power and privilege does not depend upon the persistence of tradition; it is resourced by the power of tradition to be reinscribed through the conditions of contingency and contradictoriness that attend upon the lives of those who are 'in the minority' " (2). It is here, in the interstices between an essentialized "tradition" and historical contingency, that the postcolonial condition of *Red Rock* emerges most forcefully. But if the interstitial location of culture is clear, its content is decidedly ambiguous. What Bhabha calls the estrangement of "originary identity or 'received' tradition" (2) is especially felt by Jacquelin, for whom the death of Dr. Cary, the "best and most enduring type" of the old life, suggests that "the foundations were falling out—as though the old life had passed away with him" (557). But the "old life" that passes with him—and this ambiguous phrase is typical of Page's references to the "old ways"—is never precisely articulated, nor are the values that Jacquelin must preserve, as Dr. Cary's cultural heir, under the new dispensation. While Dr. Cary has the luxury of performing martyrdom, Jacquelin must endure, his identity conditioned by the trauma of Reconstruction.[7] *Red Rock*'s ambiguous ending, in which Jacquelin figures prominently, conspicuously fails to produce a moment of restoration in which the old ways are regained in any absolute sense. Although the carpetbagger "harpies" are finally "put to flight" (580), Jacquelin never fully repossesses the family plantation: against the wishes of the older generation, he compromises with the dollar-grubbing Still, who retains half the property. Although it is tempting to read this ambiguous resolution as a kind of allegory between the forces of modern rapacity and those of cultural inheritance (conceived broadly), the more fundamental reference is to the ongoing negotiation that will make compromise the ground of culture.[8]

Compromise is made less onerous in that Page's enunciation of political difference is framed by an enunciation of cultural similarity: Mr. Welch proves, for example, that "gentlemen are the same the world over." But if "northern" values can be reconciled with the old ways in some version of cultural hybridity, it is clear that imperial practices cannot. One of the recurring traumatic loci of the encounter between the old residents and the new invaders involves a rupture in paternalistic racial hierarchies. Although Page deploys a stock set of faithful retainers and degraded opportunists, the defining characteristic of his freedman is his utter lack of identity. Freedmen provide, for Page, the perfect mob, infinitely malleable—for better or for worse—to the will of their white leaders, and it is here that Leech's influence is felt most insidiously. He is, literally, the agent of black discontent, as Steve explains during a parade of the black militia. "Mr. Leech," Steve says, "You are the controlling spirit of these negroes. They await but your word. So do we. . . . We have stood all we propose to stand. You are standing on a powder magazine" (234–35). Midway through the novel, the imperial threat is explicitly racialized, and whiteness itself is subject to assault. Nevertheless, the contingent nature of racialized culture is revealed when the Ku Klux, in its only sanctioned act of the entire novel, easily and bloodlessly disarms the Negro militia.[9] From this point on, Page's novel quickly retreats from the nativist prospectus provided in the preface: "They were subjected to the greatest humiliation of modern times: their slaves were put over them—they reconquered their section and preserved the civilization of the Anglo-Saxon" (viii). Even if Negro "insolence" continues to manifest itself intermittently—indeed, "by some curious law, whenever a step was taken against the whites the negroes became excited" (488)—never again does whiteness constitute a particular object of assault. To put the matter another way, culture is threatened long after whiteness is.

In strategically severing race and culture, Page attempts to reconcile southern paternalism with northern philanthropy as embodied by Mrs. Welch: local practices must be reconciled with national norms. This is why the community saves Mrs. Welch's colored school when it is attacked by the Ku Klux, despite the fact that it is "conducted on foreign principles" (398) and threatens the existing colored school, which is "regarded in part as representative of the old system" (398). For Page, cultural identity in no way terminates in a verbalized commitment to white supremacy, nor does it finally acquire any explicit terminus. The infinite deferrals that constitute culture necessitate its continued enunciation: culture, finally, can never be said because it must be said against; the discourse of southernness becomes, inevitably, a counterdiscourse. It is in this respect that Red Rock typifies a pervasive way of talking about the South in which deferred, unfixed notions of culture masquerade as essentialist concepts, or, alternatively, essentialist concepts like "the civilization of the Anglo-Saxon" are lost in a series of deferrals. As practices to be integrated with or wielded against whatever happens along the current of history, the "old ways" constitute an endlessly flexible and ambiguous category. As a project of regaining the essence of tradition, southernness can never be won because defense constitutes what "essence" it has.

As much as any other postbellum text, *Red Rock* traces the process by which Reconstruction dislocated the South's cultural identity. Throughout his career, Page enshrouded a particular version of the Old South with elegiac mists and conceptual fog and in so doing initiated a persistent and repetitive act of cultural memory. But the haziness of Page's South—Old and New—does not necessarily subvert the coherence of the identity emerging from it. The durability of resistance culture is to some degree dependent on its flexibility, its ability to diminish the importance of divisive or historically obsolete practices, norms, and sites of cultural meaning. Others will always come along to ground identity in new projects, new practices. The Nashville Agrarians, for example, hardly agreed about which Old South they meant to preserve—indeed, they claimed that southern agrarianism "does not stand in particular need of definition" (xlvi)—but their common antagonist, an "American or prevailing way" committed to industrialism (xxxvii), permitted a coherent campaign of cultural warfare.[10] In "Reconstructed but Unregenerate," his contribution to *I'll Take My Stand,* John Crowe Ransom situates the Agrarian project in the aftermath of Reconstruction, whose "persecution made the South more solid and more Southern in the year 1875, or thereabouts, than ever before" (17). The history of empire and of the U.S. South bears witness to this fact. And where *Red Rock* maximizes ambiguity and hybridity, the imperialist dimension of Reconstruction also initiated more focused projects of culture resistance. Where Page hedged, Thomas Dixon would speak with excruciating clarity.

In *Culture and Imperialism*, Said writes that for the imperial subject to accept nativism is "to accept the consequences of imperialism, the racial, religious and political divisions imposed by imperialism itself. To leave the historical world for the metaphysics of essences like negritude, Irishness, Islam or Catholicism is to abandon history for essentialisations that have the power to turn human beings against each other" (276). Said's cautionary move is situated amid a pervasive discourse in postcolonial studies regarding the validity of nativist nationalism as a response to imperialism. But while commentators from Frantz Fanon to Benita Parry have argued eloquently for the necessity of nativism as a means of overturning oppression and establishing a coherent cultural identity, Said typifies a trend toward foregrounding the limitations of nativist projects.[11] Though Dixon's *The Leopard's Spots* can serve as a case study in the pathology of nativism, this does not imply moral equivalence. However, even if Dixon's program of white supremacy is indefensible in a way that, for example, Aimé Césaire's Négritude is not, it follows recognizable patterns in establishing a vision of a radically unified nativist culture. Dixon permits one to add, provisionally, whiteness to Said's list, not in its usual role as a rationale for imperialist conquest but as an essentialist reaction against it. (That whiteness cannot both justify and suffer imperialism is central to Dixon's project.) Whereas *Red Rock*'s chronological and geographical deferrals—into the past as a resource, against the North as a discursive condition—blunt the emergence of a vital and energizing nativism, *The Leopard's Spots* deploys nativism in an explicitly and exclusively racialized form: what is "native" to the South is Anglo-Saxon civilization in its uncorrupted form. There is no North to take into consideration and only a negligible Old South to throw into relief the hybridity of the New South. Race, culture, and state cohere seamlessly—at least the seams are hidden. Reconstruction is cast as a simple moral contest for cultural supremacy: under the influence of carpetbaggers like Simon Legree, the South gathers "into two hostile armies . . . with race marks as uniforms—the Black against the White" (84).

There is, in short, no middle ground, no space for compromise. This crucial difference between *Red Rock* and *The Leopard's Spots* can be seen in the novels' respective approaches to speech. In *Red Rock* it is mostly the carpetbaggers and their black subalterns who give speeches; serious sentiment is reserved for conversations. In *The Leopard's Spots* there is nothing to discuss, and speeches produce the aural imagery of the white nation. The novel's ideological hero, the Reverend John Durham, speaks with a special authority. As a minister, he "never stooped to controversy. He simply announced the Truth. The wise received it. The fools rejected it and were damned. That was all there was to it" (40). To illustrate his point, Dixon has Durham announce the Truth to an especial fool, Miss Susan Walker of Boston, who, as a structural analog of Mrs. Welch in Page's novel, has come south with philanthropic notions of aiding the freedmen. "Your work," Durham informs her, "is to sow the dragon's teeth of an impossible social order that will bring forth its harvest of blood for our children. . . . [T]he most effective service I could render [your cause] would be to box you up in a glass cage, such as are used for rattlesnakes, and ship you back to Boston" (46–47). But like the older generation of Page's novel, Durham plays only a minimal role in the novel's action. The plot trajectory of the protagonist, Charlie Gaston, must therefore consist of a purification of speech as the young representative of the postwar generation learns to speak Durham's untainted dialect of white supremacy. There are obstacles to overcome, notably Gaston's sentimental commitment to the Negro. When, for example, his childhood companion Dick is found to have raped a white woman,

Gaston tries unsuccessfully to prevent the white mob from lynching him. Finally, however, he gives "A Speech That Made History" in which he echoes the rhetorical question Durham poses repeatedly (97, 198, 242, 333) as the central issue facing the South and the nation: "Shall the future North Carolinian be an Anglo-Saxon or Mulatto?" (438).

But whence the necessity of white supremacy? Why must Anglo-Saxons and not, say, southerners constitute the culture of resistance? Why must whiteness serve as the organizing theme of cultural identity? Herein lies a paradox at the core of Dixon's novel. Although his usual explanation for the necessity of white supremacy recurs to an especially virulent brand of racial essentialism, he simultaneously portrays race and race relations as products of historical forces. The Reconstruction encounter, for example, results in "the complete alienation of the white and black races as compared with the old familiar trust of domestic life": "When Legree finished his work as the master artificer of the Reconstruction Policy, he had dug a gulf between the races as deep as hell. It had never been bridged. The deed was done and it had crystallized into the solid rock that lies at the basis of society. It was done at a formative period, and it could no more be undone now than you could roll the universe back in its course" (200). However offensive Dixon's deployment of this insight, there is no denying its historical accuracy. Moreover, the process of interracial "alienation" crystallizes not only the structure of race relations but the conceptualization of race itself. The narrative logic of Dixon's novel must therefore progressively eliminate exemplars of the "old familiar trust" such as Nelse, who remains committed to whites despite the opprobrium he receives from his racial cohort. But if Dixon partially "solves" the historical content of blackness by progressively foregrounding characters whose loathsome nature derives from their "Africanness" (that is, their "innate" barbarism), it is not a logic to which he is especially committed. As Durham observes, "If you train the Negroes to be scientific farmers they will become a race of aristocrats, and when five generations removed from the memory of slavery, a war of races will be inevitable, unless the Anglo-Saxon grant this trained and wealthy African equal social rights. The Anglo-Saxon can not do this without suicide" (335). In a similar vein, Gaston later realizes that a race war will result when "culture and wealth would give the African the courage of conscious strength" (382). The contradictory logic here dictates that while Anglo-Saxon civilization must protect itself from an intrinsically barbaric "African" influence, the African must be kept from advancing so that he will not threaten Anglo-Saxon civilization. In effect, the freedman does not become "African" until he becomes powerful; the leopard's spots do not appear until the leopard becomes dangerous. This conceptual impasse manifests itself conspicuously in the career of George Harris, the black protégé of the Radical Republican Everett Lowell. Although George is his equal in education and "culture" (391), Lowell prevents his allowing George to court his daughter Helen because of "racial instinct."

It is finally the threat posed by the freedman that proves more troubling than his barbarism. The essentially contingent nature of race for Dixon thus supersedes his contingent essentialism—that is, his notion that the "true" nature of the African merely happens to manifest itself in a time of political crisis. A similar tension appears in Dixon's conception of the Anglo-Saxon. Dixon repeats a key semé in white postbellum discourse in which cultural trauma is displaced from losing the war to the Reconstruction crisis. As Durham explains, Lee would never have surrendered had he dreamed of the attempt to "destroy the Anglo-Saxon civilization of the South" and to "ram" down Anglo-Saxon "throats" projects of "Negro domination, or Negro deification, of Negro equality and amalgamation" (136). Where southerners were honorably defeated by military might, Anglo-Saxons were intentionally humiliated by Radicals bent on revenge; cultural identity is at stake only in the latter instance.[12] By situating whiteness as the traumatized subject of the Reconstruction encounter, Dixon simultaneously equates whiteness and civilization while registering the gap between whiteness and the civilization it "ought" to entail. Standing at once for civilization and for the imperative to restore it, whiteness shifts from essence to contingency as a project of regaining power. By replacing southerner with Anglo-Saxon, Dixon enables a narrative of restoration. Anglo-Saxons might win a war of the races where southerners had lost on the battlefield, and their victory might prove broader in scope than a secessionist project limited by its very provincialism.

Dixon's Reconstruction trilogy was suggested to him by the historical trilogy of Henryk Sienkiewicz, whose account of Polish heroism and suffering at the hands of invading Cossacks, Turks, and Swedes provided a model for Dixon's understanding of Reconstruction. Like *The Clansman* (1905) and *The Traitor* (1907), *The Leopard's Spots* is highly derivative; indeed, in its derivativeness lies its most striking formal feature: its reprisal of Simon Legree, George Harris, and several minor characters from Harriet Beecher Stowe's *Uncle Tom's Cabin*. It is difficult to overstate the influence of Stowe's novel in the South.[13] Certainly it was not lost on Dixon, who uses Stowe as an example of the power of individual action: "A little Yankee woman wrote a crude book. The single act of that woman's will caused the war, killed a million men, desolated and ruined the

South, and changed the history of the world" (*Leopard's Spots* 262). Although numerous denunciations of Stowe and "anti-Tom" novels had appeared before the war, Stowe's shadow lingered as late as the turn of the century. Page frequently referred to Stowe in his essays, and Mrs. Welch in Red Rock is an explicit reworking of the character of Miss Ophelia, down to her physical revulsion to African Americans.[14] But in a novel he intended to call *The Rise of Simon Legree*, Dixon's use of Stowe's characters is especially notable as a technique frequently employed by colonial and postcolonial writers. As Said says, revisions of European narratives of exploration and empire—of Shakespeare's *The Tempest* by Caribbean and Latin American writers such as Aimé Césaire, José Enrique Rodó, and Roberto Fernández Retamar; of *Heart of Darkness* by African writers such as Tayeb Salih and James Ngugi—embody attempts to "recover forms already established or at least influenced or infiltrated by the culture of empire" (210). In *The Leopard's Spots* Simon Legree functions explicitly as what Said calls the "same trope carried over from the imperial into the new culture and adopted, reused, relived" as a means of "speak[ing] and act[ing] on territory reclaimed as part of a general movement of resistance" (211, 212). But whereas Bertha Rochester, whose re-vision by Jean Rhys in *Wide Sargasso Sea* enacts, according to Gayatri Spivak, "an allegory of the general epistemic violence of imperialism" (258), Legree is not so much revised as resuscitated: rumors of his demise, the novel reports, proved "a mistake" (84). After dressing as a German immigrant woman for two years to avoid being drafted, Legree becomes a Union man and carpetbagger bent on the utter prostration of the South, an effort in which he is joined by "Dave Haley, the ex-slave trader from Kentucky," and Tim Shelby, who "had belonged to the Shelbys of Kentucky" (86, 87). Eventually, the epitome of the abuses of chattel slavery becomes a perpetrator of white slavery; after he is expelled by the Klan, he moves North and selects his female victims from among his vast empire of factories and from among the daughters of men he has ruined financially (399–400). Legree is not so much contested as elaborated: Stowe's picture, Dixon implies, is essentially accurate, although a man enabled by slavery to indulge his sadistic desires is equally enabled by Reconstruction imperialism and, later, by the industrial nightmare of wage slavery.

Other borrowings from Stowe are more explicitly adversarial. Dixon's version of Miss Ophelia is sent packing, ideologically speaking. Likewise, as Sandra Gunning observes (36), Dick is cast as an irredeemable Topsy, complete with exaggerated dialect, unkempt appearance, dubious parentage ("Haint got [no father]. My mudder say she was tricked, en I'se de trick" [98]), and dogged commitment to his white companion. But Gaston is no little Eva, and where Topsy's "mighty wicked" nature (212) is mitigated by compassion and Christian redemption, Dick is just mighty wicked. But whether overtly or covertly adversarial, Dixon's revision of *Uncle Tom's Cabin* attempts to subvert the moral hegemony extended by Stowe's novel, understood by Dixon as a grotesquely sentimental commitment to the Negro as the "ward of the nation." The banishment of the Negro from this role requires that nationhood be revised as a collective identity organized around the object-cathexis of whiteness. Ultimately, Dixon incarnates his vision, and "when the Anglo-Saxon race was united into one homogeneous mass . . . the Negro ceased that moment to be a ward of the nation" (409).

As Michaels brilliantly shows, Dixon's fetishistic attitude toward whiteness parallels a similar fetishism of the state (17–23), which likewise acquires a contingent meaning. As Gaston says, it is "on account of the enfranchisement of the Negro" that "the people of the South had to go into politics" (280). Where Page allows Leech to become the state, Dixon maintains a strict boundary between the state and the carpetbaggers so as not to taint the former; here, the courts frustrate Radical oppression rather than enabling it.[15] Even more than in Red Rock, the emerging culture must authenticate itself within the framework of state power. "Government is the organized virtue of the community," Gaston says, and "politics is religion in action" (281). Legree's regime, as Dixon calls it, is banished by the Klan barely a third of the way into *The Leopard's Spots*, and in the space of a few pages; and while Dixon lacks Page's ambivalence toward the Klan, its lack of access to official state structures necessitates that the Klan be discarded as soon as its provisional function is served. The remainder of the novel confronts that dissonant sense of unfinished business—of the cultural identity that will emerge from the condition of bondage—pervasive in the history of empire. As Albert Memmi observes, "When the day of oppression ceases, the new man is supposed to emerge before our eyes immediately . . . but . . . this is not the way it happens" (88). The ensuing agon, explicitly political in nature, concludes some two decades later only when the emerging state's racial purity is assured.

In order to become the new man of the Anglo-Saxon nation, Gaston must reject a Faustian bargain common in novels of colonialism: the opportunity to collaborate. When Allan McLeod, the Dixie quisling of the novel, extends to Gaston the opportunity to join the Republican Party, personal gain and alignment with a less provincial, more cosmopolitan worldview prove attractive temptations. The opportunity is all the more tempting since, at the level of policy, Gaston is "in accord with the modern Republican utterances at almost every issue" (197), while he disagrees with a Democratic party dominated by "old moss-backs" (193). Nevertheless, even as McLeod suggests that Gaston's commitment to race politics is belatedly reactionary, Gaston resists "The Voice of the Tempter" (as the chapter is titled) by elaborating the intersection of racial purity, imperialism, and historical progress: "The name Republican will stink in the South for a century, not because they beat us in war, but because two years after the war, in profound peace, they inaugurated a second war on the unarmed people of the South, butchering the starving, the wounded, the women and children. . . . Their attempt to establish with a bayonet an African barbarism on the ruins of Southern society was a conspiracy against human progress" (194).

Again, history frames and defines essence: to be a Republican is to forfeit whiteness. Politics, for Dixon, has nothing to do with interests and everything to do with identity, but the Democratic party can capture the essence of white identity only in reaction to the Republicans' "second war on the unarmed people of the South." More important, as Dixon situates the South as the pure victim of northern conquest, he borrows the progressive racist vision of international imperialism. In an instance of what Stephen Arata calls "reverse colonization"—in which "what has been represented as the 'civilized' world is on the point of being overrun by 'primitive' forces" (108)—Yankee imperialism stands exposed as a "conspiracy against human progress" only in relation to "normative" imperialism and "natural" racial hierarchies.

Dixon's progressivism necessitates a profound ambivalence toward the Old South. Although he undertakes a weak defense of the antebellum slave order, he is mostly critical of the Old South's political backwardness, parochialism, and resistance to modernity. The South's emergence on the world historical stage is necessitated, even enabled, by its defeat in the war, itself minimized in importance. As Durham observes, "We fought for the rights we held under the old constitution, made by a slave-holding aristocracy. But we collided with the resistless movement of humanity from the idea of local sovereignty toward nationalism, centralization, solidarity" (332). This is why Dixon's localism—selectively celebrated by Richard Weaver—can exist only as a staging ground, a white enclave from which to launch the project of the Anglo-Saxon nation.[16] In his climactic "Speech That Made History," Gaston admits to a certain narrowness and provincialism and publicly detests "shallow cosmopolitanism" and the "dish water of modern world-citizenship" (441). "I love the South," he says, "the stolid silent South, that for a generation has sneered at paper-made policies, and scorned public opinion. The South, old-fashioned, mediaeval, provincial, worshipping the dead, and raising men rather than making money, family loving, home building, tradition ridden" (441). And yet, like Durham, he is openly critical of the South's resistance to modernity: "The Old South fought against the stars in their courses—the resistless tide of the rising consciousness of Nationality and World-Mission. The young South greets the new era and glories in its manhood. He joins his voice in the cheers of triumph which are ushering in this all-conquering Saxon. Our old men dreamed of local supremacy. We dream of the conquest of the globe. Threads of steel have knit state to state. Steam and electricity have silently transformed the face of the earth, annihilated time and space, and swept the ocean barriers from the path of man. The black steam shuttles of commerce have woven continent to continent" (435). For Dixon, the antidote to the nightmarish industrialism practiced by Legree is not to restore localism but to reconceive modern economy as a tool of empire, a means of asserting the South's presence on the world's stage. As a repository of pure Anglo-Saxon culture, a "trust for civilization" raised up by God "as he ordained Israel of old" (435), the South must reject "local supremacy" and embrace "World-Mission." To Michaels's assertion that *The Leopard's Spots* is an anti-imperialist novel, one must add the crucial qualification that Dixon sanctions "normative" imperialism, in contrast to the reverse colonization of Reconstruction, as a cultural imperative.[17] As Gaston says in reference to the Spanish-American war, "Our flag has been raised over ten millions of semi-barbaric black men in the foulest slave pen of the Orient. Shall we repeat the farce of '67, reverse the order of nature, and make these black people our rulers?" (435). In rendering a vision of the invisible empire made visible, Dixon opposes imperialism by returning to it as a world historical force.

If Dixon's South borrows the modern nation-state from its conqueror, it borrows little else.[18] Dixon insists on, as Benita Parry puts it, an "implacable enmity between native and invader," a "construction of a politically-conscious, unified revolutionary Self, standing in unmitigated opposition to the oppressor" ("Problems" 32, 30). And yet in turning the provincial southern Saxon into one of the "all-conquering" variety—and here one may view the histrionics as an index of cultural trauma—Dixon is forced to expand the boundaries of "Saxon." Where Page preserves class boundaries, Dixon represents them only as barriers to be overcome as the various fires of crisis—Reconstruction, the Spanish-American war, the political turmoil from which Gaston emerges triumphant—work to unite in "one homogeneous mass" (409) the various white classes and ethnicities that populate the South and the nation. What is striking about Gaston's speech is not so much its mixture of atavistic and progressive sentiments—a common feature of nationalist discourses—but that both atavism and progressivism combine to invert, as part of an evangelical effort, the power relation of the Reconstruction encounter.[19] Beginning with the product of trauma (homogeneous whiteness conceived as object-cathexis), Dixon moves outward in concentric spheres—region, nation, empire—with missionary zeal.

Imperialism provided Dixon with a way not only of understanding and structuring the trauma of Reconstruction, but of overcoming it. And while Gaston's projected "conquest of the globe" remained on the drawing board, Dixon's vision of a new nation founded on whiteness found a receptive American audience. Fully elaborated by the 1920s, according to Michaels, Dixon's brand of nativism helped make "Americanness into a racial inheritance and culture into a set of beliefs and practices dependent on race—without race, culture could be nothing more than one's actual practices and therefore could never be lost or recovered, defended or betrayed—but not reducible to race—if it were nothing but race, it could also not be lost or recovered, it could only be a fact, never a project" (185). Although Michaels does not consider the extent to which American nativism derives from the white South's experience of Reconstruction, it is interesting to speculate as to whether white America came to think of culture as something that could be lost or recovered, defended or betrayed, because the South had understood its cultural identity in precisely this way. That is, does the equation Michaels observes between race and culture originate in the crucible of Reconstruction and the white South's complex negotiation of race and practice, culture and history, essence and contingency? Does the genealogy of threatened whiteness, so central to modern American identity, derive from America's own internal imperialism?

These are, perhaps, related to the kinds of hypothetical scenarios that white southerners have always relished in reference to the Civil War. As Gavin Stevens observes in *Intruder in the Dust*, every "southern boy fourteen years old" can imagine ("not once, but whenever he wants it") Pickett's Charge and "think This time. Maybe this time" (125, 26). "Because we lost the war" was how Walker Percy explained the South's distinctiveness, and it may be that a certain strain of white southern identity turns on the question, what if we hadn't? What if cultural identity could be expressed as national identity? But the white South lost the war, and its sense of dislocation, of that ever-receding, pristine, purely hypothetical world preceding the experience of loss, devastation, and domination makes it virtually generic among the world's cultures.[20] In another respect, however, the South's postimperial experience differs dramatically from the norm: the white South's grand narrative of Reconstruction quite literally captivated its conqueror. As Grace Elizabeth Hale shows in *Making Whiteness*, the white South successfully marketed a version of race and reconstruction that terminated in "whiteness [as] the homogenizing ground of the American mass market" (168). "Few episodes of recorded history more urgently invite thorough analysis and extended reflection than the struggle through which the southern whites, subjugated by adversaries of their own race, thwarted the scheme which threatened permanent subjection to another race" (xv).

Less than two decades after Page fretted over the want of a southern history, the northern historian William Archibald Dunning replicated Dixon's narrative of Reconstruction to preface his landmark 1907 study of the subject. Dixon's vision helped make white supremacy the South's leading export as the century turned, and despite the efforts of W. E. B. Du Bois and others to contest the Dunning school and to affirm America's biracial culture, it was Dixon's version that won the day.[21] If the trauma of Reconstruction links the white South with cultures around the world, its transformation of trauma into an exportable commodity—a means of recolonizing white America, as it were—renders it a tragic anomaly.

NOTES

1. For a psychoanalytic examination of the traumatic, narcissistic construction of white southern identity, see Smith. Drawing on Holocaust historians and theorists, Smith argues that the Lost Cause myth, along with the "senses" of place, community, and history long perceived to be determinants of southern identity, represent crippling fetishistic tendencies among white southerners unable or unwilling to confront cultural trauma.

2. Although the action of the novel takes place in a distinctive locale, Page intended a broad statement on Reconstruction. In a 1900 letter to Henry Simms Hartzog, he writes, "I intended 'Red Rock' for a 'composite picture,' as you phrase it, or rather, I intended it for a picture that would stand for the south generally under the conditions that prevailed in reconstruction times, rather than only for Virginia" (qtd. in Gross 160).

3. As Mrs. Welch begins to master the gap between the sentimental narrative of sectional rehabilitation and its literal reference, her daughter Ruth falls victim to a different influence. Perceiving the South as a "land of chivalry" in which she can drink "at the springs of pure romance" (346), Ruth's commitment to romantic notions of the South comes to fruition in her marriage to the dashing Steve Allen. In *Red Rock* as in

his popular early fiction, especially *In Ole Virginia* (1887), Page brilliantly exploits exotic, romantic—one might say "orientalist"—images of the South.

4. Although serious questions of political theory did not play a large part in the postbellum discourse of the Old South, the culture of politics did, usually in the context of bemoaning contemporary trends. Howard Melancthon Hamill, for example, writes that "the service of the paid political manager, the conciliation of the party 'boss,' the subsidizing of the party 'healers,' the utilization of the party press in flaming, self-laudatory columns and even pages of paid advertising matter, ad nauseam and ad infinitum, as in recent Southern political contests—all these latter-day importations and inventions of 'peanut' politics would have merited and received the unmeasured contempt of the politicians of the Old South" (61).

5. The jailbreak is itself remarkably law-abiding. When a ruffian demands that the crowd "hang every d——-d nigger and dog in the place" (427), he is immediately called out and sent home by Allen. This man later testifies against the jailbreakers (484). In another instance of a pattern found throughout the novel, McRaffle, one of the most reckless Ku Klux participants early on, eventually shifts his loyalty to Leech. Page's logic is to dissociate virulent racism from southern culture by associating it with opportunists lacking a core commitment to "the cause." Dixon's use of Simon Legree follows a similar pattern.

6. See Nina Silber's *The Romance of Reunion* for a broad examination of sectional reconciliation; for the role marriage played in this process, see especially 110–23. See also Keely and Censer for discussions of marriage as a trope of sectional reconciliation between North and South. For an examination of marriage in the negotiation of Latin American nationalisms see Sommer. Interestingly, it is Steve—whose southern chauvinism is more pronounced than Jacquelin's—who marries a northerner, while the more cosmopolitan Jacquelin marries the epitome of southern womanhood, Blair Cary.

7. One of the conventions of the southern reconstruction chronicle is that the protagonist is too young to have served in the war and therefore reaches maturity during Reconstruction. In addition to Jacquelin Gray and Charlie Gaston, the titular heroes of Joel Chandler Harris's *Gabriel Tolliver* and George Washington Cable's *John March, Southerner* meet this criterion. The association of youth and nationalism—whether postcolonial or not—is typical. The Hitlerjungen in Nazi Germany, for example, referred to older people as *Friedhofsgem sei* (cemetery vegetables), while novels of decolonization often center on a young person (usually a young man) coming of age as the colonized people acquires political autonomy.

8. This theme would inform Page's next major novel, *Gordon Keith* (1903), whose titular hero moves from province to metropolis and learns to negotiate honor in the world of modern business. As Fred Hobson notes, Page's progressivism was similar to that of Henry Grady, whose deployment of the Old South likewise existed in harmony with a vision of economic progress (139). For Page, slavery's primary limitation was that it prevented the South's development. In "The Old South," for example, he writes "slavery was banishing from [the South] all the elements of that life which was keeping stride with progress without" ("Old South" 30). In his prewar visit to Red Rock, Mr.

Welch makes a similar argument, suggesting that "Slavery is doomed as much as the Stage-coach, and the Sailing vessel" (30).

9. Following a pattern widely practiced in the southern press, Page presents the Ku Klux raid as a benign jest. The terrified freedmen, for example, report that the Klansmen "had drunk bucketfuls of water, which the negroes could hear 'sizzling' as it ran down their throats" (239). The comedy of black terror is repeated in Joel Chandler Harris's *Gabriel Tolliver*, where the Knights of the White Camellia terrify a black church with a bizarre procession. They single out a freedman politician, who later maintains, after an encounter with a "fire-breathing" horse, "that the back of his head would have been burned off if 'de fier had been our kind er fier' " (254).

10. See Reed for an interesting examination of how *I'll Take My Stand* replicates key themes of nationalist movements elsewhere.

11. In *The Wretched of the Earth* Fanon's commitment to holistic nationalism as a pragmatic remedy to the psychological divisions imposed by colonialism is less than absolute, although his skepticism tends to focus on the desirability of such projects in the postcolonial state. Calling attention to the Western pedigree of antinationalism, Parry writes, "It is surely necessary to refrain from a sanctimonious reproof of modes of writing resistance which do not conform to contemporary theoretical rules about discursive radicalism" ("Resistance" 179). Said and Bhabha thus stand accused of privileging theory over praxis.

12. Compare Page (482; cited above); unlike Dixon, Page's threatened culture is not explicitly racialized. Both novels represent a brief interlude of economic devastation but cultural coherence immediately after the war. In *Red Rock* this moment includes a scene of racial restoration and optimism in which Dr. Cary's freed slaves willingly take up subservient roles on his estate (58–62); this interracial harmony is shattered by the arrival of Leech. Dixon's novel begins with a "scene of peaceful rehabilitation" dominated by the South's "good faith" commitment to "Mr. Lincoln's dream" of peaceful reconstruction; this is destroyed by "the Apostles of Revenge" and their schemes of "revengeful ambition" (17–18).

13. "George Harris, Jr." in *The Leopard's Spots* is the son of Eliza and George Harris in Stowe's novel, although he is only designated as "Harry" in that work.

14. See Page, *Red Rock* 344; Stowe 143.

15. Specifically, the Fourteenth Amendment and the writ of habeas corpus are cited by a judge to support the legal rights of accused Klansmen (*The Leopard's Spots* 81–82). For a northern view of how Klan terrorism was enabled by constitutional rights see Albion Tourgée's *A Fool's Errand*, a novel in which "the judicial philosophers of our American bench" are described as having "reconciled themselves to neutrality in the more recent conflict for liberty" (336).

16. In a striking instance of citing out of context, Weaver uses the quotations cited immediately below to argue for Dixon's commitment to the "doctrine of particularism," which "teaches that internationalism and cosmopolitanism are but disguises for those who have no true character" (305). Predictably, there is no reference to Dixon's celebration of the "resistless movement of humanity from the idea of local sovereignty toward nationalism, centralization, solidarity."

17. Jack Raffetto points out that, as a minister in New York's Church of the People, Dixon explicitly defended America's "new imperial democracy" (and in particular the Spanish-American War) from the pulpit, although his justification of American imperialism often involved its differentiation from European imperialism in that the empire of democracy would "conquer no territory and hold it subject," but rather "proclaim that . . . all men are born free and equal" (Dixon, *Sermons* 29). Needless to say, Dixon departs from this egalitarianism in his novels.

18. According to Benedict Anderson's contested model, this pattern is pervasive among subjects of imperialism. Nationalism, Anderson argues, is a European product "pirated" (67) by other cultures and often used against European "imperial official nationalism" (118) in the form of nativist revolutions. As Anderson writes, "The 'nation' proved an invention on which it was impossible to secure a patent" (67). It is important to note that the kind of nationalism Dixon valorizes did not exist even in the Confederate States of America, whose constitution, following a states' rights political philosophy, placed strict limits on the powers of the central government.

19. Tom Nairn, for example, observes that nationalism encourages societies to "propel themselves forward to a certain sort of goal (industrialism, prosperity, equality with other peoples, etc.) by a certain sort of regression—by looking inwards, drawing more deeply upon their indigenous resources, resurrecting past folk-heroes and myths about themselves and so on" (348).

20. Faulkner speculated that Walter Scott's popularity in the South derived from a "kinship perhaps between the life of Scott's Highland and the life the Southerner led after Reconstruction. They too were in the aftermath of a land which had been conquered and devastated by people speaking its own language, which hasn't happened too many times" (*University* 135).

21. Page essentially rewrote *Red Rock* in his last novel, the posthumously published *The Red Riders* (1924), and it is striking how the submerged racial theme of the earlier novel becomes the focus of the later one. Whereas Page portrays mainly the misdeeds of the illegitimate Ku Klux in *Red Rock*, he defends the Red Riders (based on the Klan) as having "saved the civilization of a part of the United States which had helped to create them. It was revolutionary. It was only justifiable as any revolution is justifiable" (318). *The Red Riders* has much more in common with Dixon's *The Clansman* than it does with *Red Rock*.

WORKS CITED

Achebe, Chinua. *Things Fall Apart.* 1958. New York: Knopf, 1992.

Anderson, Benedict. *Imagined Communities: Reflections on the Origin and Spread of Nationalism.* Rev. ed. London: Verso, 1991.

Arata, Stephen. *Fictions of Loss in the Victorian Fin de Siècle.* Cambridge: Cambridge UP, 1996.

Ashcroft, Bill, Gareth Griffiths, and Helen Tiffin. *The Empire Writes Back: Theory and Practice in Post-Colonial Literatures.* London: Routledge, 1989.

Bhabha, Homi K. *The Location of Culture.* London: Routledge, 1994.

Bledsoe, Albert Taylor. *Is Davis a Traitor?* 1866. North Charleston, Va.: Fletcher, 1995.

Cable, George Washington. *John March, Southerner.* New York: Grosset, 1894.

Censer, Jane Turner. "Reimagining the North-South Reunion: Southern Women Novelists and the Intersectional Romance, 1876–1900." *Southern Cultures* 5.2 (1999): 64–91.

Chow, Rey. *Ethics after Idealism: Theory-Culture-Ethnicity-Reading.* Bloomington: Indiana UP, 1998.

Dixon, Thomas, Jr. *The Clansman.* New York: Doubleday, 1905.

——. *Dixon's Sermons.* New York: F. L. Bussey, 1899.

——. *The Leopard's Spots: A Romance of the White Man's Burden, 1865–1900.* New York: Doubleday, 1902.

Dunning, William Archibald. *Reconstruction: Political and Economic, 1865–1877.* New York: Harper, 1907.

Fanon, Frantz. *The Wretched of the Earth.* Trans. Constance Farrington. New York: Grove, 1966.

Faulkner, William. *Faulkner in the University: Class Conferences at the University of Virginia 1957–1958.* Ed. Frederick L. Gwynn and Joseph L. Blotner. 1959. New York: Vintage, 1965.

——. *Intruder in the Dust.* New York: Random, 1948.

Fitzhugh, George. *Cannibals All! Or, Slaves without Masters.* Ed. C. Vann Woodward. Cambridge, Mass.: Belknap, 1960.

Gross, Theodore L. *Thomas Nelson Page.* New York: Twayne, 1967.

Gunning, Sandra. *Race, Rape, and Lynching: The Red Record of American Literature, 1890–1912.* New York: Oxford UP, 1996.

Hale, Grace Elizabeth. *Making Whiteness: The Culture of Segregation in the South, 1890–1940.* New York: Pantheon, 1998.

Hamill, Howard Melancthon. *The Old South: A Monograph.* Dallas: Smith and Lamar, n.d.

Harris, Joel Chandler. *Gabriel Tolliver: A Story of Reconstruction.* New York: McClure, 1902.

Hobson, Fred. *Tell about the South: The Southern Rage to Explain.* Baton Rouge: Louisiana State UP, 1983.

Humphries, Jefferson. "The Discourse of Southernness: Or How We Can Know There Will Still Be Such a Thing as the South and Southern Literary Culture in the Twenty-First Century." *The Future of Southern Letters.* Ed. Jefferson Humphries and John Lowe. New York: Oxford UP, 1996. 119–33.

Keely, Karen A. "Marriage Plots and National Reunion: The Trope of Romantic Reconciliation in Postbellum Literature." *Mississippi Quarterly* 51.4 (1998): 621–48.

Memmi, Albert. *The Colonizer and the Colonized.* Trans. Howard Greenfield. New York: Orion, 1965.

Michaels, Walter Benn. *Our America: Nativism, Modernism, and Pluralism.* Durham, N.C.: Duke UP, 1995.

Nairn, Tom. *The Break-Up of Britain.* London: New Left, 1977.

Okonkwo, Chidi. *Decolonization Agonistics in Postcolonial Fiction.* Houndsmills, England: Macmillan, 1999.

Page, Thomas Nelson. *Gordon Keith.* New York: Scribner's, 1903.

———. *The Old South: Essays Social and Political.* 1892. New York: Scribner's, 1906.

———. *In Ole Virginia: Or, Marse Chan and Other Stories.* 1887. Chapel Hill: U of North Carolina P, 1969.

———. *The Red Riders.* New York: Scribner's, 1924.

———. *Red Rock: A Chronicle of Reconstruction.* New York: Scribner's, 1898.

Parry, Benita. "Problems in Current Theories of Colonial Discourse." *Oxford Literary Review* 9.1–2 (1987): 27–58.

———. "Resistance Theory/Theorising Resistance: Or Two Cheers for Nativism." *Colonial Discourse/Postcolonial Theory.* Ed. Francis Barker et al. Manchester, England: Manchester UP, 1994. 172–96.

Raffetto, Jack. "Dixon and the Spanish American War." Paper delivered at Thomas Dixon and the Making of Modern America Symposium, Winston-Salem, North Carolina, April 2003.

Ransom, John Crowe. "Reconstructed but Unregenerate." *I'll Take My Stand: The South and the Agrarian Tradition.* By Twelve Southerners. 1930. Baton Rouge: Louisiana State UP, 1977. 1–27.

Reed, John Shelton. "For Dixieland: The Sectionalism of *I'll Take My Stand.*" *A Band of Prophets: The Vanderbilt Agrarians after Fifty Years.* Ed. William C. Havard and Walter Sullivan. Baton Rouge: Louisiana State UP, 1982. 41–64.

Said, Edward. *Culture and Imperialism.* New York: Vintage, 1993.

Silber, Nina. *The Romance of Reunion: Northerners and the South, 1865–1900.* Chapel Hill: U of North Carolina P, 1993.

Smith, Jon. "Southern Culture on the Skids: Punk, Retro, Narcissism, and the Burden of Southern History." *South to a New Place: Region, Literature, Culture.* Ed. Suzanne W. Jones and Sharon Monteith. Baton Rouge: Louisiana State UP, 2002. 76–95.

Sommer, Doris. *Foundational Fictions: The National Romances of Latin America.* Berkeley: U of California P, 1991.

Spivak, Gayatri. "Three Women's Texts and a Critique of Imperialism." *Critical Inquiry* 12.1 (1985): 243–61.

Stowe, Harriet Beecher. *Uncle Tom's Cabin: Or, Life among the Lowly.* 1852. New York: Norton, 1994.

Tate, Allen. "Remarks on the Southern Religion." *I'll Take My Stand: The South and the Agrarian Tradition.* By Twelve Southerners. 1930. Baton Rouge: Louisiana State UP, 1977. 155–75.

Tourgée, Albion W. *A Fool's Errand.* 1879. Cambridge, Mass.: Belknap, 1961.

Twelve Southerners. *I'll Take My Stand: The South and the Agrarian Tradition.* 1930. Baton Rouge: Louisiana State UP, 1977.

Weaver, Richard M. *The Southern Tradition at Bay: A History of Postbellum Thought.* Ed. George Core and M. E. Bradford. New Rochelle, N.Y.: Arlington House, 1968.

Say dont didn't.
Didn't dont who.
Want dat yaller gal's
Pudden dont hide.

—WILLIAM FAULKNER,
   Light in August

JOHN T. MATTHEWS

This Race Which Is Not One:

The "More Inextricable Compositeness"

of William Faulkner's South

When Joe Christmas, the protagonist of Faulkner's *Light in August* (1932), first learns a significant difference between men and women by being told about menstruation, he reflexively pictures female bodies as damaged: "In the notseeing and the hardknowing as though in a cave he seemed to see a diminishing row of suavely shaped urns in moonlight, blanched. And not one was perfect. Each one was cracked and from each crack there issued something liquid, death-colored, and foul. He touched a tree, leaning his propped arms against it, seeing the ranked and moonlit urns. He vomited" (189).

The association of a woman's sex with an opening, with a crack that breaches integrity, recalls Freud's hypothesis about how males negotiate the anxious supposition that the basis of sexual differentiation is female "castration." Whether because of the literal shock of first glimpsing the female genitalia, as Freud proposes, or because of the infant's even earlier experience of non-self-sufficiency, as Lacan more complexly elaborates it, the threat to integrity calls for imaginative resolution. Freud suggests that under certain conditions, the "sexual aberration" of fetishism arises in response to an abnormal fear of sexual difference.[1] Fetish objects accommodate the contradictory demands of the anxiety: they represent the knowledge of "feminine lack" (by typically evoking female sexual anatomy); at the same time, they furnish compensatory objects of sexual pleasure, things to fill the lack. Working in two directions, the fetish permits a kind of knowing not-knowing.[2]

Faulkner suggests how fetish-effects help Christmas manage the knowledge of difference. The novel's language tightens and knots around a process described above as "seem[ing] to see" through "notseeing." The image of the urn represents the menace of difference to Christmas while it seeks to protect him against knowing what he has seen into. It is as if insight must also be regurgitated. Joe takes in the knowledge of female difference so "hard" that it becomes forgettable as part of the very process by which it becomes known: "Then it was three or four years ago and he had forgotten it, in the sense that a fact is forgotten when it once succumbs to the mind's insistence that it be neither true nor false" (186).

In Faulkner's South, descending from centuries of race-based chattel slavery, the shock of sexual difference always registers on a racialized terrain. As the male figures the female body as a matter of lack, so the white man understands black as being a corrupted whiteness. Winthrop Jordan points out that it did not occur to colonists to identify themselves racially as "white" until the late seventeenth century (95). Until then, New World settlers distinguished themselves as English among Negroes and Indians, as Christians among heathen or savages. The condensation toward a single scale of difference—"white over black," in Jordan's phrase—was precipitated by pressures to regulate the assimilation of nonwhite immigrants and to establish a clear basis for American slavery (95–96). As that system began to gain legal standing in the American colonies during the 1660s, a standard of visible difference between master and slave proved optimal. Legal safeguards for racial "purity" emerged in sanctions against miscegenation. Jordan concludes that "white persons of both sexes in *all* the English colonies were affected in a more general way by the tensions involved in miscegenation" (149). White heterosexual identities were defined under multiple racial constraints: wives and mothers of planters were to avoid sexual congress with the slave class; the mixed offspring of white masters and black slaves were to be regarded as nonentities; and projections of black sexual prowess would haunt white partners of both genders.[3] In the period after Emancipation and Reconstruction, relations between the sexes became even more intensely imbricated with race.[4] As so much southern writing testifies—perhaps none more eloquently than Faulkner's in its long look back across his region's past—it was impossible to learn gender without learning race.

That the white male southerner's encounter with the sight/site of sexual difference involved the entanglement of racial difference may be illustrated in an earlier chapter of Joe Christmas's life, when as a fourteen-year-old he fails his initiation into sexual manhood. Thrust by a group of friends into a shed where a black girl waits to be made use of, Joe recoils at his sudden engulfment by "womanshenegro" (156). As before, he experiences the female as a lack: "something, prone, abject," but this time the blackness of "she" fuses "woman" to "negro": "Leaning, he seemed to look down into a black well and at the bottom saw two glints like reflections of dead stars" (156). A vacancy that reflects death, sexual difference doubles racial difference. The looker sees the absence that marks Negro and woman as lack but cannot see through his own seeing; he sees glints but does not recognize them as his own eyes reflected in the gaze of an Other. Joe, who understands himself to be white at this point, will repeatedly startle at the threat posed by a race, like a sex, which is not one.[5]

Faulkner's preoccupation with the encoiling of sex and race has always been obvious, though his development as a novelist has most often been described as a progressive excavation of buried historical knowledge and emotional acknowledgment.[6] According to this general account, Faulkner's first major novel, *The Sound and the Fury* (1929), elaborates the nostalgic defensiveness of the declined ex-slaveholding gentry, represented by the Compson family, as they enter modernity. The tortured path to a knowledge of historical responsibility, guilt, and shame condemns the young Quentin Compson to self-destruction on the eve of adulthood, a gesture that coincides with the modernizing South's turn toward critical self-reflection on its past. Faulkner's subsequent novels through *Intruder in the Dust* (1948) are broadly held to dramatize a struggle toward the conscious knowledge, confessional remorse, and accepted end of racial exploitation. The sixteen-year-old Ike McCaslin takes the moment of initiation to its ultimate conclusion by discovering in his first reading of his family's plantation ledgers the cryptic but irrefutable evidence of his ancestors' brutalities against man and nature, slave and wilderness. No worse knowledge awaits any Faulkner protagonist than Ike's final admission that incest and miscegenation, twin evils from which the ideals of family and gentility would seem to require defense, already serve as their cracked foundations.[7]

What has been less remarked on in Faulkner's account of ruling southern mentalities, however, is the strategic usefulness of the sort of knowledge that functions in the open, not as the secretion of repressed information but as an enabling enchantment of obvious but unacceptable truth. With *Light in August* Faulkner concludes an imaginative program that, over the course of several novels, undoes the masquerade of sexual and racial fetish in the Jim Crow South. The knowledge that primary personal and social differences were based on fictions of purity and self-sufficiency constituted the open secret of the South's closed society. Modern southern majorities held to imaginative and social forms that accommodated knowledge of the injuries of mastery by permitting disavowal of that knowledge. Such a seeing not-seeing corresponds to the structure of fetish, a form of knowledge that allows one to say: *I know this to be true, and yet I believe otherwise.*

An important element of Faulkner's writing about his world involves challenging the power of fetishistic thinking. The special power of fetish depends on the visibility of its operation. Like Poe's purloined letter, the fetish goes into open hiding. The power of southern fetishes like skin color, blood, and racial stereotype derives from their ability to admit their fictionality while exercising their effects. It is not so much unconscious or buried, repressed or suppressed truth that worries Faulkner, but highly developed social and psychological technologies like fetish that enable the white South to perpetuate beliefs, and hence protect advantages, in the face of their evident falsehood.

In the U.S. South, as in other colonial-style regimes, certain customs of representation sought to uphold racial distinction. In the 1920s Jim Crow South of *Light in August* stereotype played a foremost role in maintaining racial difference. Joel Williamson describes the emergence in the late 1880s of the image of the Negro male as a "black beast rapist" (82), a stereotype that reflected white fears about new black social and economic freedoms. This construct licensed accusations of sexual assault and punishment for it; between 1889 and 1899 there were nearly 200 lynchings a year, with two out of three victims African Americans (85). The stereotype of the bestial Negro meant to deny the humanness of blacks, although its phantasmal nature reflected as much white men's fear of what white women might want as their fear of what black men might want to do. One of Faulkner's purposes in *Light in August* involves exposing the function of the stereotype in the white imagination.

In his study of colonial habits of thought and social practices, Homi Bhabha explores the stereotype as a fetish that addresses the contradiction of racial difference.[8] On the one hand, the stereotype insists that racial difference is absolute, natural, and visible; on the other, it carries the suspicion that all humans share common skin, race, and culture: "For fetishism is always a 'play' or vacillation between the archaic affirmation of wholeness/similarity—in Freud's terms: 'All men have penises'; in ours: 'All men have the same skin/race/culture'—and the anxiety associated with lack and difference—again, for Freud 'Some do not have penises'; for us 'Some do not have the same skin/race/culture' " (74).

For Bhabha, the stereotype is "the primary point of subjectification in colonial discourse, for both colonizer and colonized" (75), because it specifies the racial content of the formation of social identities. Drawing on Lacan's model of the mirror phase, in which the child organizes an ego through an identification of himself or herself as reflected in another person or object, Bhabha outlines how race complicates the process by which subjects are formed in racial societies. For Lacan, the act of self-identification reprises the child's earlier negotiation of dependence on the mother (or maternal figure). This sense of an original lack of self-sufficiency structures mature identity as well; in the mirror stage, the child condenses her or his amorphous somatic experience into an image of the self, internalized as the ego ideal.[9] Lacan holds that the fear of castration associated with the glimpse of the mother's sex, enforced by oedipal prohibition, actually derives as a back-formation from the more fundamental sense of non-self-sufficiency.[10]

In Bhabha's delineation of the mirror stage under colonial circumstances, stereotype figures in the subject's effort to identify him- or herself as not the other. As the fiction of female castration negotiates the contradiction of self-sufficiency (maleness without difference) and its lack (femaleness as difference), so racial stereotype constitutes an " 'impossible' object" (81) that mediates racial difference. Stereotype affirms the natural visible purity of whiteness by fixing the subhumanity of blackness. At the same time, as fetish it bears the "taint" (81) of its origin as fantasy, as an imaginary solution: stereotype binds "fantasy and defense—the desire for an originality which is again threatened by the differences of race, colour and culture" (75). Racial stereotype stimulates fantasies of desire, Bhabha observes, because it functions as fetish in an economy of pleasure. The fetish cannot mediate the fear of difference without providing a compensatory sexual pleasure. Consequently, in racial societies stereotypes invariably mix phobia and sexual desire. They express ambivalence, and function dynamically. Bhabha contributes a theoretical vantage on the complex deployment of stereotypes in *Light in August* by suggesting how they are not fixed points of identification but rather anxiously repeated formulas of sex and race, desire and domination, pleasure and power (67).

Joe Christmas's racial identity serves as a useful point of departure for an analysis of racial fetish, because it has so regularly been misrepresented. Joe is not a person of mixed race who is struggling to find his true identity as black or white; he is not a black person seeking to pass for white, nor a white person who has discovered he is black; nor finally is he a person of unknown race seeking proof of his "true" racial identity. Rather, he "is" a white person, whose only known surviving relatives are white, who lives as a white man at every moment pictured in the novel, but who comes to suspect that his whiteness is not pure or original: "I think I got some nigger blood in me. . . . I don't know" (196–97). The anxiety that besets Joe reflects the foundational uncertainty of majority identity in a racial society.[11] Over the course of the novel, Joe falls victim to the South's refusal to admit the open secret of racial hybridity. His career traces an exemplary arc, through which a white man, presumably even one like Faulkner (who once wrote an article for *Ebony* entitled "If I Were a Negro"), must confront the fetish-fictions of southern life. In doing so, Faulkner suggests the failure of such fantasies to sustain indefinitely the ways of racial discrimination.[12]

The image of "blanched" vases leaking "deathcolored" fluid indexes the two key fictions of racial discrimination in the South: skin and blood.[13] Joe encounters problematic exercises of these racial fetishes. Not only do such markers pervade Faulkner's version of southern racial discourse, but they operate specifically as fetish objects—that is, as declarers of the unacknowledged truth of their own falseness. When Christmas's partner in moonshine asserts to the Jefferson marshal that Christmas is actually a "nigger" who's been living with a white woman "in plain sight" of the whole town for three years, he proclaims his confidence in the natural visibility of racial difference: "soon as I watched him three days I knew he wasn't no more a foreigner than I am. I knew before he even told me himself" (98). Having learned this "truth," the marshal now sees it always to have been true: " 'A nigger,' the marshal said. 'I always thought there was something funny about that fellow' " (99). Such a statement sees through the falseness of detectable racial difference at the same time it refuses to admit that knowledge: I know I could not see, and yet still I saw.

The many moments in *Light in August* like the marshal's, in which a gap closes between what one realizes now and what one always knew, points to a distinctive quality of time that one might characterize as the *temporality of fetish*. The marshal *now* learns what he has *always* known. The formulation sidesteps the discrediting of racial purity that Joe's mistaken identity as a white man imports. Present knowledge is fissured by a previous deception that must be denied, while the earlier certainty of racial purity has been delegitimized. Exactly as the fetish uses a secondary form of knowledge (the equivocation of the fetish object) to neutralize the earlier more traumatic one of seeing difference, the narrator of *Light in August* staunches past doubt with present certainty. Byron faults himself for being "too stupid to read" (83) that the column of smoke "right yonder in plain sight" was warning him to keep Lena Grove away from trouble. The narrator asserts that Christmas's name is an "augur of what he will do, if other men can only read the meaning in time" (33). Yet such signs can never be more than the retrospective fixing of meaning. They model the folded temporality of fetish, which binds original anxiety over heterogeneity to its resolution as unattended insight. The most notorious sentence in *Light in August* may offer a reading of this temporality: "Memory believes before knowing remembers" (119). What one *must* see as the trace memory of original in-self-sufficiency determines what one *does* see as conscious knowledge of the past.[14]

The ability of stereotype to guard the "natural" visible fixity of race depends on the untroubled exercise of what Fanon calls the epidermal schema (112).[15] In *Light in August* Faulkner exhibits the failure of skin to execute the fetish of stereotype. Joe's skin poses the problem of hybridity to the U.S. South's epidermal binarism. In the following description of Joe's face under McEachern's inspection, one may glimpse an anxious determination to enforce visible racial identity. The narrator notices that under the forcible imposition of authority, Joe's "face was now quite white despite the smooth rich pallor of his skin" (150). *Pallor* is the wrong word, of course, since *despite* anticipates a word contrary to rather than synonymous with *white*. *Luster* would do, but it might admit a blackness within Joe's whiteness. Instead, the semitautology measures the ferocious will to subdue any contrary darkness to a shade of white.

When Joe reveals his suspicions about being Negro to his white mistress, he points to what he takes to be obvious evidence: "You noticed my skin, my hair" (196). But no one, starting with himself, can confirm Joe's race by his skin, and Bobbie responds that his appearance has suggested to her only that he might be "a foreigner." She simply refuses to believe "it"—"You're lying," she says—and Joe lets the matter drop—"All right," he replies (197). However, after Joe murders his adoptive father at a country dance, Bobbie rages that she'll have nothing more to do with him: "Me f . ing for nothing a nigger son of a bitch" (218). Once Joe kills, he has "always" been black: "Getting me into a jam, that always treated you like you were a white man" (217). Joe's truthful lie about white skin/black blood now is seen through, but only to affirm more hysterically the lying truth of racial essence.

Joe's skin invariably prompts a kind of forgetful reading. As he makes his way north, Joe sleeps with numerous prostitutes, all of whom he avoids paying by telling them afterward that he is a Negro. Sometimes they curse him, sometimes they beat him, but their outrage always prevents them from acknowledging him as a paying customer. In the North, though, Joe encounters a white woman who doesn't care whether he's black or "just another wop" (225); she just wants his money, the same as that of any of her black patrons. The episode sickens Joe because "he did not know until then that there were white women who would take a man with a black skin" (225). In at least two ways this cannot be true. Bobbie has already had sex with Joe as a Negro, at least according to her parting insult, so he does know there are such white women; and though Joe does have sex with such women, he does not possess black skin, so he's not one of those men. The logic of fetish riddles the assertion that Joe "did not know until then," since what he learns is an open fiction installed as a truth.

Faulkner suggests in *Light in August* that Joe Christmas always experiences identity as a function of fetishized color. When he is five years old and living in an orphanage for white children, Joe begins sneaking into a young female dietitian's room. Joe makes a habit of eating a helping of the woman's toothpaste each time he visits, so in this respect the child finds an object of gratification that addresses maternal lack (his mother having died giving birth to him): "The dietitian was nothing to him yet, save a mechanical adjunct to eating, food, the diningroom, the ceremony of eating" (120). As one might predict, though, this effort to negotiate anxious dependence on unreliable mother figures gets conflated with the confrontation of sexual and racial difference.

The narrator goes on to point out that the woman has a further impact on Joe "as something . . . pleasing in herself to look at—young, a little fullbodied, smooth, pink-and-white, making his mind think of the diningroom, making his mouth think of something sweet and sticky to eat, and also pinkcolored and surreptitious" (120). The other children have already begun calling Christmas "Nigger," so Joe's spying on the dietitian involves looking at the mysteries of both sex and race, or perhaps the mystery of sex as race. The young woman's body is indivisibly female and white, "pink-and-white," and Joe must mediate the double difference of colonial subjectivity: am I the same/am I different? The toothpaste functions as the fetish-object, which attaches sexual pleasure to the traumatic fear of difference. The toothpaste possesses status as an imaginary object, exactly the thing to make a "mouth think." To eat in such a way is to derive sexual pleasure from something not normally a sexual object, the toothpaste that is both the female sex ("sticky," "pinkcolored") as well as the fictional penis attributed to the mother as castrated male ("the cool invisible worm as it coiled onto his finger" [121]). Again, insight into sexuality is processed as regurgitation; Joe vomits when he is once trapped into staying longer, and eating more, than he plans. The dietitian catches him as a result, concluding that the child has been spying on her furtive lovemaking with a staff doctor. She articulates precisely the position from which the anxiously uncertain white male looks at difference: "Spying on me! You little nigger bastard!" (122). Not only is he called "nigger," but he must endure the humiliation of being found "pinkfoamed," hiding in "the pinkwomansmelling obscurity behind the curtain" (122). Feminized and racialized in a single stroke, Joe loses the alibi of fetish.[16]

The other prop for southern segregation was what Bhabha refers to in another context as "the analytics of blood" (75). That this novel of racial ambiguity ultimately discredits the authority of the metaphor of racial blood few doubt.[17] But Faulkner's demystification of it requires thinking about how the idea of blood governs concepts of race even (perhaps especially) when no one believes in it. Joe makes the obligatory references to his "black blood," as do others, but without much conviction that it means anything. When Joe has been beaten off by Bobbie's protectors, they offer to draw blood to find out if Joe is telling the truth about being a Negro, since he "*dont look like one*" (219). They don't intend this seriously, however, joking, as they strike him again, that they need "*a little more blood to tell for sure*" (219). No one expects to see black blood, though everyone speaks as though it exists.

The absurd climax of the novel's analytics of blood occurs when Jefferson's resident intellectual, the Harvard-trained lawyer Gavin Stevens, explains to his college classmate the nightmarish events that have convulsed the town: Joanna Burden's murder, Joe Christmas's arrest, and the criminal's slaying when he tries to escape. Stevens summarizes Joe's life as a battle of warring bloods: "all those successions of thirty years before that which had put that stain either on his white blood or his black blood, whichever you will, and which killed him" (448). Seen this way, Christmas becomes the pawn of a metaphor:

> But his blood would not be quiet, let him save it. It would not be either one or the other and let his body save itself. Because the black blood drove him first to the negro cabin. And then the white blood drove him out of there, as it was the black blood which snatched up the pistol and the white blood which would not let him fire it. And it was the white blood which sent him to the minister. (449)

Faulkner derides the myth of blood here, anticipating the later analogy he draws between Grimm's deadly hunting of Christmas and the playing of a game. The blood plot ultimately explains nothing of motive or behavior, but it does reinforce racial stereotype and hence racial power. Black blood is sly and ruthless, white restrained and hopeful. "And then the black blood failed him again, as it must have in crises all his life" (449). Stevens speaks for the fetish of blood, a fantasy that makes the behavior of the black man explicable to the white, even as it guards the inscrutable difference between them.[18]

Faulkner traces the agency of the fetish to its source and makes the reader witness the repugnant scene of its origin. After he corners the fleeing Christmas in Reverend Hightower's kitchen, Percy Grimm empties his automatic into him and then, in a final act of racial torture, castrates the dying Negro. The narrator describes Joe's body as seeming "to collapse, to fall in upon itself, and from out the slashed garments about his hips and loins the pent black blood seemed to rush like a released breath" (465). Blood *becomes* black at the site of sexual difference. Anxiety about white male self-sufficiency constitutes the function of fetish in the segregated South. Grimm exclaims to Christmas, "Now you'll let white women alone, even in hell" (464), a remark spoken through Grimm by stereotype. "Woman" and "Negro" are made "she" in the same violent stroke. Joe here becomes one of the blanched vases himself, leaking death at the rupture that marks lack. The fetish of black blood undergirds Grimm's identity as both white and male. Joe's mutilated body constitutes the impossible object of racial fetish: the Negro as "castrated" white.[19]

Correspondingly, the novel represents the black penis precisely as it would the "female penis": as a fiction to be known without being seen. Once when Joe shows himself to white passengers in a passing automobile, the novel leaves the exposure unnarrated, so that Joe's member both appears and remains hidden: "Then he could hear the car. He did not move. He stood with his hands on his hips, naked, thighdeep in the dusty weeds, while the car came over the hill and approached, the lights full upon him. He watched his body grow white out of the darkness like a kodak print emerging from the liquid. He looked straight into the headlights as it shot past. From it a woman's shrill voice flew back, shrieking. 'White bastards!' he shouted. 'That's not the first of your bitches that ever saw. . . . . . .' But the car was gone" (108; ellipses in original). The language of the novel fails to see what it is looking at. "Castrated" by narrative circumlocution and his own elliptical reference, Christmas occupies the position of a white man looking at his black penis, which is not there. The moment hysterically pictures the Negro as castrated white man *and* the black phallus as the white man's empowering fetish object.

Joe's execution by stereotype also underscores how the fetish of "black blood" solves anxiety by combining the denied knowledge of racial sameness with sexualized pleasure. Grimm's admiration for Christmas's technique as an escapee—"Good man," he murmurs—draws them together in a nearly erotic intimacy. As he pursues Joe, Percy wears an "expression of fulfillment, of grave and reckless joy" (461). That ecstasy points to the aberrant pleasure Freud attributes to the fetish, which displaces the "normal" object of sexual pleasure with an associated substitute. In Faulkner's probe into race and desire in the segregated South, stereotype intrudes at the outset as that which produces pleasure rather than that which prohibits it. When the white Joanna Burden and her black vassal Joe Christmas violate the South's primary taboo, neither does so to fulfill sexual desire for the other. Instead, they derive gratification from racial stereotype itself.

Joe enters the Burden house as if entering a plot. He picks up the whiff of the "rich odor of the dark and fecund earth"—the odor he associates with Negroes—and steals like a "cat" to the porch, where he climbs through a window (229–30). Feeling like "a thief, a robber," Joe takes Joanna nightly, entering "by stealth to despoil her virginity each time anew" (234). Joanna encourages this ritual of stereotype, crying out "Negro, Negro, Negro" and pretending that "she resisted to the very last" (235). For both of them, sexual pleasure is found in the very fetish that would keep them apart. It is not Joe Christmas but Negro ravishment from which Joanna takes pleasure, and it is not the still-young single woman Joe meets but the manless plantation mistress who calls forth his lust. Faulkner brilliantly demonstrates how mental constructs gain their power from the way they become sources of erotic pleasure in themselves.[20]

In Bhabha's scheme the ambivalence of phobia and desire in stereotype owes to the double instability of identity in racial societies. The "stereotype" is "a form of knowledge and identification that vacillates between what is always 'in place,' already known, and something that must be anxiously repeated . . . as if [for example] the bestial sexual license of the African that needs no proof, can never really, in discourse, be proved" (66). Stereotype defends against the instability inherent in racial identification, for both the majority and minority members of a society. By enunciating identity according to the discourse of racial difference, the subject's integrity rests on a racialized version of Lacanian splitting. The consequence, according to Bhabha, is an "ambivalence in the structure of identification that occurs precisely in the elliptical *in-between*, where the shadow of the other falls upon the self" (60). Anxiety arises not just from doubt about whether the Other *can* be fixed as entirely separate, inferior, visible, and knowable; it arises more deeply from the sense of loss generated by the repudiation of the not-self. The racial stereotype stages the awful binding of desire for the abjected Other and that desire's prohibition.

Joanna takes on the features of her ravisher, as if acknowledging desire for the shadow of herself that the black man represents. It is she who hides "waiting, panting, her eyes in the dark glowing like the eyes of cats" (259). Such lust lays bare the terrible hunger for all that has been given up to form majority identity. Joe notices that Joanna's ambivalence takes nearly material form during their intimacies. The "two creatures that struggled in the one body" (260), Joanna's, occupy the narcissistic plat-form upon which the white subject plays out the drama of white identity. The majority self internalizes blackness both as abject Other (not I) and as the trace of splitting or alienation that constitutes the ego (I as other). This double movement Bhabha has described as a combination of narcis-sism and aggressivity—narcissism in the recognition of self-sameness and ego-formation, and aggressivity toward the reminder of lack or non-self-sufficiency represented by the self as discrete image (77).

Joe's rage inscribes the lack of original wholeness and sufficiency that shadows identity in general but that fills with particular sexual and racial content in societies like the South's. His wrathful rejection of food pre-pared for him by Mrs. McEachern and later by Joanna Burden expresses the aggressivity involved in subject-formation. McEachern's authoritari-anism abnormally extends Joe's childish dependence, and the boy cannot stand to see his own weakness mirrored in Mrs. McEachern's subjugation to her husband. Joe dumps the dishes of food she prepares for him—in spite at her "helplessness" to "neither alter" nor "ignore" her plight (167). Then, like the helpless dependent he is, Joe furtively eats the "outraged food . . . like a savage, like a dog" (155). When Joanna prepares meals for Joe, he treats them with similar ambivalence, first eating them, then destroying them for signifying his racial subjection: "*Set out for the nig-ger. For the nigger*" (238). He names this "woman's muck" with "the preoccupied and oblivious tone of a child playing alone" (238). Food bears the character of fetish, associated as it is with maternal satisfac-tion of the child's need. It is not surprising that it should function with the repetitive forgetfulness of fetish, too. Years after Joe first ruins Mrs. McEachern's dishes, he has to reinvent the solution for Joanna's: "*This is fun. Why didn't I think of this before?*" (238).

The premise of *Light in August* involves putting a white man through the process of establishing his identity and hence exposing the fiction of pure racial difference. Faulkner creates scenes of white subject-formation that must be read doubly as palimpsests of black subjugation. Perhaps the most telling instance occurs during Simon McEachern's education of his adopted son. Whether the lesson addresses Calvinism or capitalism, McEachern treats the boy like a slave in need of civilizing. His new father will Christianize Joe, teaching him to "fear God and abhor idleness and vanity despite his origin" (143). The small planter points "with a mittened fist which clutched the whip" toward the unfamiliar place Joe will learn to call "Home" (143). The moment of arrival coincides with Joe's renaming by his new master, who rejects the "heathenish" "Christmas" and exercises his "legal right" to change it (144): " 'He will eat my bread and he will observe my religion,' the stranger said. 'Why should he not bear my name?' " (145). McEachern's violent efforts to gain Joe's submission, however, stimulate only adamantine resistance. Like a beaten slave, Joe throttles his resentment until it blows altogether. Tracked down after an escape one night, Joe lashes out when his father confronts him; he crushes McEachern's skull with a chair and boasts, "I said I would kill him some day!" (206).

Joe's uprising resembles nothing so much as the scene of physical defiance that typically springs free the protagonists of ex-slave narratives. Frederick Douglass, for example, recounts how one day he abruptly attacks his current master: "I seized Covey hard by the throat; and as I did so I rose. He held on to me, and I to him. My resistance was so entirely unexpected, that Covey seemed taken all aback. . . . I watched my chance, and gave him a heavy kick close under the ribs" (103). To be white is to enact a binding to/freeing from the reviled other. The formation of Joe as a white subject in the South cannot be separated from the process of racial subjection. Positioned historically as the Jim Crow afterthoughts of the antebellum plantation, McEachern and Christmas replay one of the South's most familiar stories. It is a story practiced so unthinkingly and repetitively by Faulkner's plantocratic families—the Sartorises, DeSpains, Sutpens, McCaslins, Compsons—that the compromising of white identity by black never occurs to the founders. Faulkner delineates the workings of such a mechanism by putting it in plain sight and daring us to read it despite its obviousness.

Barbara Ladd has shown that *Light in August* transpires in a modernizing South that undergoes the loosening of racial and sexual boundaries.[21] As Joe Christmas evokes the growing phenomenon of racial passing, which calls into question any confidence in visible racial difference,

Lena Grove represents the threat of reproductive vagrancy, which augurs a dangerous mix of freedoms for "womanshenegro." Ladd takes the double plot of *Light in August* as evidence for the intersection of these two social narratives, in which the increasing indetectability of race encounters the lowered value of female chastity. Working-class white women like Lena, Ladd notes, were thought especially likely to disregard racial and marital protocols in their sexual behavior. When he meets the obviously pregnant, obviously unmarried, and surprisingly unembarrassed Lena on the road to Jefferson, Armstid understands that she represents a modern version of female independence: "You just let one of them get married or get into trouble without being married, and right then and there is where she secedes from the woman race and species and spends the balance of her life trying to get joined up with the man race. That's why they dip snuff and smoke and want to vote" (14–15).

The composite nature of southern identity and social forms becomes more visible during this moment of stressful change in the 1920s, but the mixture of majority and minority subjectivity is, after all, a truism characterizing the South's psychology, economics, and social relations through its long history as a colonial-style society. Toward the end of *Light in August*, the Reverend Gail Hightower succumbs to a vision of a South in which—puzzlingly to him—sameness obscures difference. Hightower sees what was always there to see, that is, the "inextricable compositeness" (491) of all those whose identities have been fatally segregated by the South's revered fathers: "his wife's; townspeople['s], members of that congregation which denied him . . . ; Byron Bunch's; the woman with the child; and that of the man called Christmas" (491). Hightower finds that "his own is among them" and that "they all look a little alike, composite of all the faces which he has ever seen" (491). Hightower observes in amazement that even the two faces whose violent difference has most plagued his South—the faces of racial supremacy and subjugation, of white Percy Grimm and black Joe Christmas—are themselves twinned and entwined: the two faces "strive . . . in turn to free themselves one from the other, then fade and blend again" (492). Hightower's epiphany induces the apprehension that majority identity is inextricably bound to minority identity.

Hightower sees more, however, than black and white's inextricable oneness. He glimpses a "blend" of "compositeness" that points beyond the deadly binarism of Jim Crow. Everywhere one looks, really looks, in Faulkner's South, faces reflect incalculable mixtures. Sam Fathers, whose father is a Chickasaw chief and his mother at least part-black, is neither white nor simply Negro: "his skin wasn't quite the color of a light nigger and his nose and his mouth and chin were not nigger nose and mouth and chin" (*Collected Stories* 344). Lucas Beauchamp, descended from a master and his Negro slave, nonetheless represents another kind of not-quiteness: "the face the color of a used saddle, the features Syriac, not in a racial sense but as the heir to ten centuries of desert horsemen . . . the composite tintype face of ten thousand undefeated Confederate soldiers almost indistinguishably caricatured" (*Go Down, Moses* 104–5). This description of Lucas strains to exceed "racial sense" by casting about for markers somehow derived from cultural history or social mimicry. The fetishizing of visible identifiers in a binary grid obscures the knowledge of a shared continuum rather than absolute difference. The fetish of black skin, blood, and bestiality displays itself as a real fantasy while preventing a seeing through to a different sort of difference. This would be "that possibility of difference and circulation which would liberate the signifier of *skin/culture* from the fixations of racial typology, the analytics of blood, ideologies of racial and cultural dominance or degeneration" (Bhabha 75).[22]

In *Light in August* the Burden family's whiteness reveals itself as emphatically complex and derivative. The original New Englander Calvin Burden marries a dark woman "of French Huguenot stock" (241). After their son Nathaniel marries a Mexican named Juana, Calvin startles upon meeting her as if he has seen his departed wife's "ghost" (246). The inextricable compositeness of the Burdens forms a sedimentary past for Joanna herself, who is named for her father's foreign first wife and who descends from bloodlines openly confused by what her grandfather calls one "black Burden" after another. Joanna extends the force of amalgamation professionally, Byron Burch observing, with suggestive if unintentional ambiguity, that "she is still mixed up with niggers" (53). The Burdens prove to be a white family ghosted by Mexicans and French Huguenots, as well as Negroes. Outsiders who remain marginal to their adopted community, the Burden family occupies just the position that lets it serve as a reminder of the hybridity that Jefferson's native whites prefer not to notice.

Joe's ambiguous paternity intimates the actual sociological heterogeneity of Faulkner's South. The only evidence for his father's being a Negro comes from Joe's grandparents. Doc Hines, his grandfather, assumes instantaneously that the seducer of his daughter must be black, although the young circus worker identifies himself as Mexican to Milly. Mrs. Hines reports that the circus owner subsequently confirms this conclusion: he "said how the man really was a part nigger instead of Mexican, like Eupheus said all the time he was" (377). But to be part

Negro does not rule out being Mexican, of course, and the effect of the sentence is to expose "nigger" as a kind of anti-euphemism for "foreign." The segregated South sought to overstate race as exclusively a matter of twoness rather than not-oneness. Faulkner wants his readers to see that that mixture produces purity rather than befalls it.

In the face of the plain refutation of racial purity and binarism, the agency of fetish begins finally to fade toward the vestigial in Faulkner's South. Lena Grove practices a form of self-deception that mimes the logic of fetish but has none of its power to dehumanize and damage. As she sets out after the lover who abandons her, Lena pursues an openly false lead. Although the townspeople warn her that the man she expects to find at the Jefferson sawmill is not her Burch but actually a Bunch, she simply assumes that the difference does not matter: "I thought they had just got the name wrong and so it wouldn't make any difference. Even when they told me the man they meant wasn't dark complected" (51). Lena presses on by sleight-of-ear and -eye. She constructs a scenario that contradicts plain evidence, hoping that "Bunch" might be "Burch" as implausibly as a dark man might be taken for light. Throughout the South's history, the fantasm of essential difference in skin color was as fundamental as confidence in the natural referentiality of language. They made all the difference. How startling to find someone to whom they no longer make any difference.

The South's increasing compositeness does get Lena all "mixed up." At one point she even signals that the lover who deserts her may be a Negro. The man Lena seeks by the name of Lucas Burch has changed his name to Joe Brown by the time he arrives in Jefferson. We know that his complexion is darker than Christmas's, and before Byron finally contrives their reunion, he refers to Joanna's murder by "a nigger." Lena's response is curious, suggesting that she may know all too well who that Negro is: "And I could feel her watching me the same as I can you now, and she said 'What was the nigger's name?' " (304). By the end of the novel she's not even sure of the identity of her unnamed child. Listening to Mrs. Hines confuse the baby with her infant grandson of long ago, Lena worries that "she might get me mixed up, like they say how you might cross your eyes and then you cant uncross" (410). The crossed "I" of mixed race, like the "X" or cross that turns "Christmas" into "X-mas" on Hightower's signboard, suspends pronouncements of identity across the uncertainty of heterogeneity and anonymous origin. The X is neither black nor white, nor both. It is the mark of numerous races, colors, fathers—a composite that awaits a name.[23]

Being all mixed up, as Mrs. Hines's confusion makes Lena, proves one powerful indication that southern codes might be revisable. Lena Grove introduces mayhem into familiar assertions of identity. When she sees that Bunch is not the Burch she seeks, Byron catches the confusion: "I don't reckon I am. Who is it I aint?" (50), Byron says. "I dont recall none named Burch except me, and my name is Bunch" (51). By the end of the novel, Byron glimpses how new discursive formations would produce a new social order. He climbs a hill and thinks to himself how such a vista looks "like the edge of nothing. Where trees would look like and be called by something else except trees, and men would look like and be called by something else except folks. And Byron Bunch he wouldn't even have to be or not be Byron Bunch" (424). Significantly, this insight takes place as he finally reaches a view of the burned-out past, the Burden "plantation . . . broken now by random negro cabins," with oak trees demarcating the voided center where the house once stood. Later, when Byron imagines returning to Lena and taking up an indefinite fate, he muses, "*And then I will stand there and I will. . . . . . .* He tries it again: *Then I will stand there and I will. . . . . . .* But he can get no further than that" (441; italics and ellipses in original). Byron edges elliptically toward an unpredicated future.

When Joe Christmas finds his way to Jefferson, he asks a young black boy about the Burden mansion and who might live there. After telling him a little about Miz Burden, the boy turns away, singing "tuneless[ly]" to himself.

> *Say dont didn't.*
> *Didn't dont who.*
> *Want dat yaller gal's*
> *Pudden dont hide.* (228)

The lyrics may be cryptic, but they are decipherable. What's "want[ed]" is the "yaller gal's [p]udden," slang for female genital organs—"pudding," "pudendum."[24] One aspect of this desire that would rattle southern whites involves the boy's longing for "yaller" pudden, the yellowness at once a future objective and historical trace of miscegenation. Even more shockingly, the boy is moved to sing by thinking of Joanna Burden; one wonders whether the girl's yellow color might not also signify Joanna's hybridity and new premises for sexual desire in racial heterogeneity. In the first two lines the boy plays with the constraints on black speech and identity (say/don't/didn't/who), but the negatives are released in the last two lines as black desire says what it wants. To undo the effect of the fetishes that support the self-sufficiency of white masculinity, the fictional site of racial and sexual differentiation must be called out of hiding.

The place of female difference need not be miscalled male castration any more than blackness need be understood as deficient whiteness. The pudden don't hide any longer, then, and in fact it makes its appearance by appropriating the very thing that would conceal it—the phallus—for a less familiar connotation of "pudden" is the *male* sex organ.[25] Here the work of fetish vacates its expected place, and sex and race seem to break free of the either/or lock.

The open secret of *Light in August*, like the open secret of southern racism, is not indeterminacy but hybridity. The problem of Joe Christmas's racial identity, if formulated as the question of his not knowing whether he is black or white, begs the question of the question. The fetish addresses the peculiar requirements of the binary scopic organization of racial majority in the South. The confidence in visible race needs a subterfuge by which mixture can be rendered obvious yet unnoticed, by which it can be admitted but not avowed. The fetish of stereotype powerfully binds such contradictory energies. As *Light in August* begins to see, and *Absalom, Absalom!* and *Go Down, Moses* go on to say, hybridity in 1931 is the white South's unacknowledged history, not just its dreaded future. The stereotype as fetish prolongs the white South's determination to enchant the modernizing scene into apparent conformity with colonizer fantasies. But Faulkner understood that the "menace" looming before an unseeing South actually stood behind it, having already destroyed the pretense of blood purity. Somewhere in the lull between what memory already believed and knowing hoped not to remember, the colonial South thought it could live on. That South looked directly at a fate that was already its past and present, but could not see it. Or, as a townsman jokes horribly about Joanna Burden's corpse, whose nearly severed head has twisted grotesquely to face backward: "if she could just have done that when she was alive, she might not have been doing it now" (92).

NOTES

I wish to thank Richard Godden, Anita Patterson, Eliza Richards, Philip Weinstein, and the anonymous readers for Duke University Press for their unusually detailed and helpful comments on earlier versions of this essay.

1. Freud discusses fetishism as a perversion in "Aberrations" (19–21).

2. In her recent revisionist account of southern women's writing, Yaeger makes a powerful case for associating forms of open but disavowed knowledge primarily with domestic experience. In their daily lives, she argues, southern women were more likely to encounter the obsessive repetition of unthinkable social tensions. In the matter of race, Yaeger focuses on "ideas that are present but unacknowledged—on thought itself

as an act of refusal" (94). "But what is most missing from Faulkner's fiction and most present in southern women writers such as [Alice] Walker and [Eudora] Welty is a sense of the ways in which racial knowledge functions in the everyday" (97). Yaeger's interest in free-floating unorganized knowledge leads her toward an analysis of the life of objects in southern writing, precisely the sort "that seem to be hiding in plain sight" (99). Yaeger's distinction of southern women's writing from the sort of oedipalized repression of knowledge that is generally understood to characterize Faulkner's fiction makes an enormously valuable correction in southern literary studies. However, the effects Yaeger describes may also be appreciated against the background of earlier imaginative efforts to accommodate the contradictions of chattel slavery. Knowledge about race that is both admitted and disavowed has a long history in southern letters. Such knowledge appears emphatically in Jefferson and Poe, for example, for whom the suspicion of racial relativity threatens confidence in white superiority. Forms of denied knowledge about racial inequity and suffering circulate through much antebellum literature and are renovated in post-Reconstruction contexts. I hope in this essay to demonstrate Faulkner's interest in fetish as knowledge, though I believe Yaeger's claims about his differences from the writers she discusses remain valid. In contrast to Yaeger's, my argument relies on a model of fetish that has explicit conceptual roots in psychoanalytic usage and that is developed as an analytical tool in postcolonial studies.

In *Killers of the Dream* Lillian Smith comments pertinently on the way southern whites learned to cherish skin color as a "Badge of Innocence" and superiority in the face of national contempt for their region: "But we clung to the belief, as an unhappy child treasures a beloved toy, that our white skin made us 'better' than all other people. And this belief comforted us, for we felt worthless and weak when confronted by Authorities who had cheapened nearly all that we held dear, except our skin color. There, in the Land of Epidermis, every one of us was a little king" (90).

3. Baptist has recently argued that sexual fetishism was practiced with, or even as, a form of commodity fetishism by slave-traders in the antebellum U.S. South. Examining the correspondence of the Franklin, Armfield, and Ballard slave-trading firm, one of the largest suppliers of slaves to the frontier plantations of Louisiana, Mississippi, and Arkansas during the 1830s, Baptist discovers evidence of thoroughgoing sexual exploitation of female slaves as standard behavior. Not only did these white traders describe their own sexual use of their human merchandise, they also revealed how they specialized in providing "fancy maids"—that is, light-skinned young females—for sexual service to plantation masters. Baptist proposes that a kind of commodity fetishism must have enabled slave traders to half-forget that they were dealing in humans; according to Marx, the commodity erases the value of human labor and use once the value of the good has been set by the market. In the instance of slaves, the slave's commodification screened out the function of the traders' and planters' sexual use of the "product." In the sexual fetishization of the mixed-race slave women, the pleasure and power derived from their abuse in effect helped eroticize commodification more generally, furthering the ends of nineteenth-century market capitalism. Baptist summarizes his richly suggestive speculation: "the traders insist in accidental testimony that sexual fetishes and commodity fetishism intertwined with such intimacy that

coerced sex was the secret meaning of the commerce in human beings, while com-modification swelled its actors with the power of rape" (1621).

4. Williamson specifies a "particular conjunction of sex and race that seized the South in 1889" during a period of economic recession and emergent populism that decisively threatened prerogatives of the white male planter still held from antebellum times (83).

5. Irigaray criticizes Freudian accounts of ego formation for making masculine phallic heterosexuality the ruling model of identity. The inescapable consequence is that the female's "lot is that of 'lack,' 'atrophy' (of the sexual organ), and 'penis envy,' the penis being the only sexual organ of recognized value" (23). Instead, Irigaray argues for an understanding of female sexuality as multiple: "Her sexuality, always at least double, goes even further: it is *plural*" (28). In referring to Irigaray's idea of plurality, I wish to signal that feminist critiques of the Freudian model generally end up faulting it for its underestimation of the social and historical overdetermination of what it considers universal schemes. One incentive for continuing appropriation of certain psycho-analytic tools is that the masculinist and (as postcolonial reflection suggests) racialist assumptions of the methods of inquiry correspond so tellingly with the social and cultural forms to be examined. Ultimately, Irigaray's call for a recognition of the inadequacies of feminine lack to account for female sexuality and subject-formation parallels postcolonial attempts to dismantle the colonial binarisms of racial mastery and subject formation in such societies. Psychoanalytic concepts such as the fetish, for example, have proven exceptionally useful to feminist projects precisely as they have been applied to specific forms of cultural expression dominated by a masculinist imaginary, such as Hollywood cinema. Mulvey's *Fetishism and Curiosity* is a primary example. Gamman and Makinen explore the possibilities in sexual fetish practices for further female emancipation. Krips tests the limits of psychoanalytic versions of fetish when they are applied to social practices. Krips observes that Freud distinguishes between forms of behavior that when performed by individuals must be considered perverse but when enacted in communities are considered normal. Krips seeks the intersection between psychological and social instruments of analysis and proposes fetish as the most promising of all such analytic concepts. Moreover, he argues that fetish—as a form of conscious knowledge condensed in concrete objects and pieces of behavior—may function progressively, and not simply as a guarantor of an ignored status quo.

Stokes corroborates the importance of fetish in performing the cultural work of openly hiding the interrelations of heterosexuality and whiteness. Stokes draws on Monique Wittig's description of heterosexuality as "a non-existent object, a fetish, an ideological form which cannot be grasped in reality, except through its effects" (40–41; qtd. in Stokes 14). As something "imaginary and real," heterosexuality functions like whiteness, Stokes contends, and in fact whiteness in the post–Civil War South estab-lished itself most effectively by attaching itself to other abstractions of "normalcy" like heterosexuality. Stokes's chapter on Griffith's *Birth of a Nation*, a film that appeared twenty years before *Light in August*, suggests how images of black menace must be both seen and disregarded. One example: the film's focus on a bare black foot during a scene in a Reconstruction legislature functions as a fetish object of the black penis

(Stokes 167), registered as the ultimate menace to white supremacy and yet invisible as such.

6. Bleikasten examines the mutual reinforcement of Southern "ideology" by codes of race and gender. Wittenberg, in her study of the power of language to shape identity in the novel, affirms that Joe is "as confused about his sexual identity as about his racial identity, [and] he conflates the two during intimate moments with Joanna Burden" (158). Though he treats them ultimately as separate, if nonetheless related and equally important, Weinstein's discussion of race and gender in *Light in August* and in Toni Morrison's *Beloved* focuses on the function of ideology to structure identity: "This text written during one of the most virulently racist periods of the South explores the nightmare of a figure immersed in a culture that would fetishize all boundary definitions so as to keep them immaculately preserved. White is so opposed to black that one drop can denature you. Male is so opposed to female that homosexual fantasies circulate as a sort of cultural unconscious" (*What Else* 171). Weinstein does not employ *fetish* in a technical sense. Also see Fowler, "Joe Christmas"; and Clarke.

7. Three of the most original and influential books on Faulkner share this widespread premise. Irwin reads the Faulknerian text as a vast elaboration of oedipal repression— of mortality, incestuous sexual desire, revenge. Sundquist interprets Faulkner's career as a reluctant and deferred rendezvous with the problem of race; the novels preceding *Light in August* conduct experiments in form, preparing for but also evading a confrontation with the historical realities of slavery and segregation. These realities Sundquist considers functionally repressed in the mind of the white South, and the sequence from *Light in August* to *Absalom, Absalom!* (1936) and *Go Down, Moses* (1942) represent various attempts to undo that repression. Godden develops a method of reading Faulkner that looks to detect the "secretions" of the "unthinkable" social "trauma" associated with the "material conditions of labor" (7). His approach requires a view that knowledge must be found other than where it appears. All these works, and others that share their understanding of textuality as a form of repression (I include my own Derridean reading of Faulkner), assume a depth-model for Faulkner's depiction of social epistemology.

8. Bhabha designs the terms of his analysis for postcolonial regimes of the British Empire. In important respects, however, the U.S. South resembles such racial regimes, and Bhabha's own use of southern examples reinforces this view. With some qualifications, southern historiography endorses an understanding of even the New South as shaped by colonial logic. By the 1890s, New Southern economics and racial mores required containment of the fact and history of racial mixture. Hybridity had to be confined to the system's blind spot. The demand for cheap labor helped erect Jim Crow to push black workers back toward a fixed hierarchy of racial identities. Southern employers were determined to "re-colonize" an indigenous black population that had begun to experience race nationhood during Reconstruction. At the same time, white southerners also were seeking to "de-colonize" themselves from "foreign" federal government and military force, though they contradictorily had to retain their dependence on northern capital to build a New South. Wright describes the economy that persisted from slaveholding to the modern South as essentially colonial. While

Wright distinguishes the southern situation from strict colonialism, he argues that "it was a country that lacked a strong indigenous technological community with the capacity to adapt techniques to the region's distinctive labor, resources, and markets" after the Civil War (14). One might think of some white New Southerner as occupying a complex colonial double-bind, one in which as ex-colonial subject he partially resisted the North, while as neocolonial master he sought to subdue ex-freedmen. Faulkner seems aware of the awkwardness: he refers to the house of the Yankee abolitionist Burdens as "a colonial plantation" (36), a designation that superimposes internal and external colonization (the plantation master/the Yankee invader), and he compares a city pimp and his sidekick carpetbagging in Yoknapatawpha to "two white men" in "an African village" (214).

9. Lacan summarizes: "The *mirror stage* is a drama whose internal thrust is precipitated from insufficiency to anticipation—and which manufactures for the subject, caught up in the lure of spatial identification, the succession of phantasies that extends from a fragmented body-image to a form of its totality that I shall call orthopaedic—and, lastly, to the assumption of the armour of an alienating identity, which will mark with its rigid structure the subject's entire mental development" (4).

10. See Krips 31 on this point.

11. I agree with Sundquist that "Christmas seems nearly a perverse caricature of white racial hysteria" (75), though I see Joe as an embodiment of the fundamental instability of majority identity under racism and his confusion as a necessary byproduct of the mechanism of white subject formation.

12. In addition to the conceit of imagining himself a Negro for the *Ebony* piece, Faulkner also comically plays with racial confusion in his description of an emergent author in his second novel, *Mosquitoes.*

> "I got to talking to a funny man. A little kind of black man—"
> "A nigger?"
> "No. He was a white man, except he was awful sunburned and kind of shabby dressed. . . ."
> "What was his name? Did he tell you?" . . .
> ". . . . Oh yes: I remember—Faulkner, that was it." (144–45)

13. See Bhabha 75. Considerations of race in *Light in August* predictably occupy center stage in criticism of the novel. There is Sundquist's chapter on Faulkner's sense of southern tragedy as the fatal inextricability of white and black lives, and the distortions imposed on both as a result. Davis thoroughly examines the powerful disfiguration of black lives by the imposition of racial stereotype during Jim Crow. Snead analyzes the force of Joe Christmas to transgress the binary "semiotic codes" of the segregated South; he also makes provocative remarks on what Jefferson's townspeople know but cannot afford to admit and on the process of misrecognition (see especially 85–88). In *What Else But Love?* Weinstein considers the effect of interpellation on Joe Christmas as a racial subject. Doyle explores how the sense of the body in pursuit of its own self-apprehension opens up a moment of time that allows for the entry of social signs of difference—white over black, male over female. Her phenomenological account of this

"gap" is consonant with the effects of fetish I explore, although Doyle relies primarily on a model of ideological interpellation drawn from Althusser to explain the consequences of this "existential lag" (342).

14. A grotesque example of the fictional time of fetish occurs in Faulkner's short story "Dry September." Rumor has spread through town that a black man has insulted a white woman, and the boys in the barbershop meditate action. The fact that there is no evidence that anything at all happened does not trouble the ringleader: "Happen? What the hell difference does it make? Are you going to let the black sons [of bitches] get away with it until one really does it?" (*Collected Stories* 172).

15. Also see Bhabha 78.

16. See Weinstein's *What Else But Love?* for a reading of this scene as Joe's interpellation as male and black (167–72). Weinstein's discussion treats race and gender as independent but aligned categories of identity. Following Althusser, Weinstein emphasizes the power of ideology to call (or "hail") individuals according to recognized subject positions. In her study of arrested oedipalism in the novel, Fowler concentrates on the function of this scene as Joe's witnessing the primal scene of parental copulation (see especially *Return* 77–79). Fowler describes Joe's responses to traumatic scenes like this one in terms of repression.

17. Watson demonstrates how Faulkner exposes the purely metaphorical status of the idea of "blood": "By repeatedly bringing blood to the surface of the human body, cutting in *Light in August* mobilizes the power of literal meaning and the natural world as a rejoinder to the discursive system that puts 'blood' in service of racial exploitation and violence" (69).

18. Romine discusses how the discourse of blood is one of the social narratives that determine the events of *Light in August* (149–95).

19. In speaking of Joe's sensation that he and Joanna exchange gender roles during their ferocious lovemaking, Davis remarks, "The Negro has been castrated by his subservient role in southern life. Unable to express his manhood, he has assumed external behavioral patterns which the dominant culture associates with the female" (139).

20. Krips explains the fetish as a special instance of an object that substitutes for the implacable and unanswerable demand for self-sufficiency (for recovery of the somatic indistinguishability of self and mother, for example): "desire is what happens to need when its object is traded for something more accessible but less satisfying" (22). Lacan names these substitutes "*objets a.*" Krips points out that the objet a is always haunted by reminder of the originary lack that it seeks to fill (21).

21. See Hale for a comprehensive treatment of the way a national sense of (unconsciously white) identity has been established through identifying *race* with *blackness*.

22. Glissant explores the denial of racial mixture in Yoknapatawpha. He describes Faulkner's South as a "composite culture that suffers from wanting to become an atavistic one [one that venerates racial and cultural purity] and suffers in not being able to achieve that goal" (115). Glissant makes provocative remarks about creolization and hybridity as denied realities in the South Faulkner represents, ones that demand the full disclosure that the fiction characteristically defers.

23. In so many casual ways, the unseen seen begins adjusting to a new tolerance for

realities that scandalize the old beliefs. Armstid, for example, cannot accommodate the idea of an unaccompanied pregnant girl on the open road, and so "apparently Armstid has never once looked full at her. Yet he has already seen that she wears no wedding ring. He does not look at her now" (12). Nonetheless he already identifies Lena as the sort of unprecedented young woman who, if she will travel openly pregnant and unmarried, could well "dip snuff and smoke and want to vote" (15). The incomprehensible relation between the white supremacist Hineses and the Negro community that listens to Doc's sermons and feeds the couple meals produces a similar sort of looking askance: "the public ignoring of the fact of that charity which they received from negro hands, since it is a happy faculty of the mind to slough that which conscience refuses to assimilate" (341).

24. See Ruppersburg 131 for commentary on the song.

25. According to the on-line *Slang Dictionary*, "to pull one's pud" means to masturbate. *Pud* evidently is used to refer to the penis only in this expression.

WORKS CITED

Baptist, Edward E. " 'Cuffy,' 'Fancy Maids,' and 'One-Eyed Men': Rape, Commodification, and the Domestic Slave Trade in the United States." *American Historical Review* 106.5 (Dec. 2001): 1619–50.

Bhabha, Homi. *The Location of Culture.* New York: Routledge, 1994.

Bleikasten, André. "The Closed Society and Its Subjects." *New Essays on* Light in August. Ed. Michael Millgate. New York: Cambridge UP, 1987. 81–102.

Clarke, Deborah. "Gender, Race, and Language in *Light in August.*" *American Literature* 61 (1989): 398–413.

Davis, Thadious. *Faulkner's "Negro": Art and the Southern Context.* Baton Rouge: Louisiana State UP, 1983.

Douglass, Frederick. *Narrative of the Life of Frederick Douglass, An American Slave.* Ed. Benjamin Quarles. Cambridge, Mass.: Harvard UP, 1960.

Doyle, Laura. "The Body against Itself in Faulkner's Phenomenology of Race." *American Literature* 73.2 (2000): 339–64.

Fanon, Frantz. *Black Skin/White Masks.* 1952. Trans. Charles Lam Markmann. New York: Grove, 1967.

Faulkner, William. *Collected Stories.* New York: Random, 1950.

——. *Go Down, Moses.* 1942. New York: Vintage International, 1991.

——. "If I Were a Negro." *Ebony* Sept. 1956: 70–73.

——. *Light in August: The Corrected Text.* New York: Vintage, 1990.

——. *Mosquitoes.* New York: Liveright, 1925.

Fowler, Doreen. *Faulkner: The Return of the Repressed.* Charlottesville: UP of Virginia, 1997.

——. "Joe Christmas and 'Womanshenegro.' " *Faulkner and Women.* Ed. Doreen Fowler and Ann Abadie. Jackson: UP of Mississippi, 1986. 141–61.

Freud, Sigmund. "The Sexual Aberrations." *Three Essays on Sexuality.* Trans. James Strachey. New York: Basic Books, 2000. 1–38.

Gamman, Lorraine, and Merja Makinen. *Female Fetishism*. New York: New York UP, 1994.

Glissant, Edouard. *Faulkner, Mississippi*. Trans. Barbara Lewis and Thomas C. Spear. New York: Farrar, 1999.

Godden, Richard. *The Fiction of Labor: William Faulkner and the South's Long Revolution*. New York: Cambridge UP, 1997.

Hale, Grace Elizabeth. *Making Whiteness: The Culture of Segregation in the South, 1890–1940*. New York: Random, 1998.

Irigaray, Luce. "This Sex which Is Not One." *This Sex Which Is Not One*. Trans. Catherine Porter, with Carolyn Burke. Ithaca, N.Y.: Cornell UP, 1985.

Irwin, John T. *Doubling and Incest/Repetition and Revenge*. Baltimore, Md.: Johns Hopkins UP, 1975.

Jordan, Winthrop. *White over Black: American Attitudes toward the Negro, 1550–1812*. 1968. New York: Norton, 1977.

Krips, Henry. *Fetish: An Erotics of Culture*. Ithaca, N.Y.: Cornell UP, 1999.

Lacan, Jacques. "The Mirror Stage as Formative of the Function of the I as Revealed in Psychoanalytic Experience." *Écrits: A Selection*. Trans. Alan Sheridan. New York: Norton, 1977. 1–7.

Ladd, Barbara. *Nationalism and the Color Line in George Washington Cable, Mark Twain, and William Faulkner*. Baton Rouge: Louisiana State UP, 1996.

Matthews, John T. *The Play of Faulkner's Language*. Ithaca, N.Y.: Cornell UP, 1982.

Mulvey, Laura. *Fetishism and Curiosity*. Bloomington: Indiana UP, 1996.

Romine, Scott. *The Narrative Forms of Southern Community*. Baton Rouge: Louisiana State UP, 1999.

Ruppersburg, Hugh M. *Reading Faulkner: Light in August*. Jackson: UP of Mississippi, 1994.

Slang Dictionary. http://members.tripod.com/~jaguarpage/slang.htm.

Smith, Lillian. *Killers of the Dream*. 1949. New York: Norton, 1961.

Snead, James. *Figures of Division: William Faulkner's Major Novels*. New York: Methuen, 1986.

Stokes, Mason. *The Color of Sex*. Durham, N.C.: Duke UP, 2001.

Sundquist, Eric J. *Faulkner: The House Divided*. Baltimore, Md.: Johns Hopkins UP, 1983.

Watson, Jay. "Writing Blood: The Art of the Literal in *Light in August*." *Faulkner and the Natural World*. Ed. Donald M. Kartiganer and Ann Abadie. Jackson: UP of Mississippi, 1999. 66–97.

Weinstein, Philip M. *Faulkner's Subject: A Cosmos No One Owns*. New York: Cambridge UP, 1992.

——. *What Else But Love? The Ordeal of Race in Faulkner and Morrison*. New York: Columbia UP, 1996.

Williamson, Joel. *A Rage for Order: Black-White Relations in the American South since Emancipation*. New York: Oxford UP, 1986.

Wittenberg, Judith. "Race in *Light in August*: Wordsymbols and Obverse Reflections."

    The Cambridge Companion to Faulkner. Ed. Philip Weinstein. New York: Cambridge UP, 1995. 146–67.

Wittig, Monique. *The Straight Mind and Other Essays.* Boston: Beacon Press, 1992.

Wright, Gavin. *Old South, New South: Revolutions in the Southern Economy since the Civil War.* New York: Basic Books, 1986.

Yaeger, Patricia. *Dirt and Desire: Reconstructing Southern Women's Writing, 1930–1990.* Chicago: U of Chicago P, 2000.

I'm black. I'm a man of the West.

—RICHARD WRIGHT, *White Man, Listen!*

RICHARD KING

Richard Wright: From the

South to Africa—and Beyond

In recent years Richard Wright's late career has been subject to new scrutiny. The most interesting rereading of Wright is found in Paul Gilroy's *The Black Atlantic* (1993). According to Gilroy, Wright's career between 1947 and 1960 is by no means one of decline, as most critics have claimed it to be. Besides the long novel *The Outsider* (1953), his books of cultural and political reportage, *Black Power* (1954) and *The Color Curtain* (1956), along with the essays in *White Man, Listen!* (1957), build on Wright's experience of growing up in Mississippi and coming to maturity in Chicago and New York, and they relate that experience to the wider world of the black diaspora, including Africa and the West Indies. In this context, Wright's coverage of the Bandung Conference in April 1955 and his active participation in the First International Conference of Negro Writers and Artists in September 1956 in Paris underscore his position as a key figure in the black diasporic community, encompassing Africa, the West Indies, the United States, Britain, and France.

Wright's vision of the modern world can be understood in terms of the problematic relationship between race and culture and between tradition and modernization. In fact, there is a striking continuity between Wright's pre- and post-exile writings precisely in how they relate to the history of modernization and modernity, as is evident through an elaboration on Gilroy's claim that Wright's work was "simultaneously an affirmation and a negation of the western civilisation that formed him" (186).[1] Furthermore, although Wright was an advocate of *political* decolonization—that is, national liberation and self-determination in the former colonial world—he insisted that third-world elites should embrace something like modern western secular humanism. Like his younger, Martinican colleague, Frantz Fanon, Wright rejected the negritude model of cultural revitalization. But while Fanon advocated what might be termed a revolutionary humanism, Wright chose a more reformist alternative to Negritude.

INTELLECTUAL FORMATION

Two things stand out about Wright's literary and intellectual itinerary. First, the trajectory of his life was a kind of repetition-in-reverse, an attempt to undo, as it were, the historical fate of people of African descent who were forcibly transported to the New World. Second, Wright's was clearly a restless, questing mind, driven by uncertainty rather than certainty. As Cedric Robinson has noted, Wright found Marxism useful not only as an analytical tool, despite its limitations as a means of understanding the proletariat of the capitalist world, but also as a way, in Wright's own words, "to find a home, a functioning value and role" for himself and for African Americans (Robinson 423). Besides Marxism, Wright was engaged in an ongoing dialogue, not to say confrontation, with both existentialism and various forms of racially inflected nationalism. While he never entirely settled into a stable philosophical perspective, Wright's were not the reactions of a fickle, proteanlike quick study. He thoroughly investigated and sought to master the most serious intellectual positions of his time.

Indeed, Wright's fiction might well be called a fiction of ideas, an exploration of the ideologies of his time through the novel and short story. There is much truth to the claim that Wright's first literary loyalties were to the naturalist tradition of Theodore Dreiser. But even in *Native Son*, despite later claims from critics such as James Baldwin and Ralph Ellison, Bigger Thomas is more than the sum of his circumstances, more than what his environment has made him. The omnipresence of violence in Wright's fictional world might be interpreted in many ways, including at times as a failure of Wright's fictional imagination. But it can also be understood as emblematic not of the animal-like brute or of the barely human but of a character coming to full awareness of his humanity and revolting against the restrictions placed on the development of self-consciousness. It is this, as several critics have noted, that places Wright's fictional world as close to Dostoevsky as it is to Dreiser, James T. Farrell, or Mike Gold (Fabre, *World* 73; Dickstein 185).

If Marxism gave Wright a more expansive view of historical—and geographical—possibility, it also re-enforced his deep distaste for religion. As revealed in *Black Boy*, Wright's childhood was immersed in black Protestant religiosity, and he came to rebel against its tyrannical hold on his own and his family's life. Not surprisingly, one of the chief objects of Wright's animus in *Black Power* was the figure of the European missionary, whose work he felt had been crucial in shredding the fabric of African societies and preparing the way for the economic, political, and cultural penetration of Africa by the western European powers. Organized religion, whether found in the U.S. South or in Africa, was largely in the service of reaction and the stifling effects of tradition.

During the 1930s, Wright fully absorbed the lessons of contemporary sociology, which he learned from Robert Park and the Chicago School and their students such as St. Clair Drake, Horace Cayton, and E. Franklin Frazier. He was intellectually well equipped to reject claims of white racial/biological superiority and readily endorsed the main conclusions of Gunnar Myrdal's *An American Dilemma* (1944), later becoming good friends of Gunnar and Alva Myrdal (Wright, Introduction). Wright—like Franklin Frazier—shied away from romantic racialist claims to deep spiritual or cultural affinities among people of color. And like Frazier he became convinced quite early that the folk culture of black southerners, both in itself and as it was disrupted by the Great Migration northward, was an inadequate vehicle for black progress in the United States. Thus, Wright was a confirmed member of the party of enlightenment. With Myrdal and Frazier, he was an advocate of modernization for African Americans and for former colonies around the globe.

FROM FOLK TO MODERN

In many ways, Wright was Frazier's novelistic counterpart (Watts 59). Even when his nationalist tendencies were relatively strong, Wright asserted in "Blueprint for Negro Writing" (1937) that "Negro writers must accept the nationalist implications of their lives, not in order to encourage them, but in order to change and transcend them" (42). If for "nationalist implications" one substitutes "the black folk culture of the rural

South," one can capture something of Wright's lack of confidence in the existing institutions and values of premodern, black southern culture. Both as a member of the Communist Party from the early 1930s to the early 1940s and as an analyst of third-world affairs in the 1950s, Wright maintained that modern history was the history of modernity. The central theme of that history was the all but inevitable triumph of the modern over the "feudal" or "folk" or "traditional" past.

A large master narrative informs all of Wright's writing. The modern world was created, he wrote in *12 Million Black Voices* (1941), by the ruthlessly heroic "higher human consciousness" of the "god-like men" who imposed the modern European world on the indigenous societies of Africa and of the western hemisphere (147, 151). Writing in 1945 to a friend, George Davis, Wright set forth his version of the story of modernity as exemplified in the experience of African Americans:

> But I want to take the Negro, starting with his oneness with his African tribe, and trace his capture, his being brought over in the Middle Passage, his introduction to the plantation system, his gradual dehumanization to the level of random impulse and hunger and fear and sex. I want then to trace his embracing of the religion of Protestantism, his gradual trek to the cities of the nation, both North and South; and his gradual urbanization UNDER JIM CROW CONDITIONS and finally his ability to create a new world for himself in the new land in which he finds himself. (qtd. in Fabre, *Unfinished* 273)

Tracing this historical odyssey was not, however, another way of asserting a specifically African American exceptionalism. Rather, it was the paradigmatic case of what modern history had in store for all traditional societies and folk cultures. From this perspective, the once enslaved African Americans were the representative people, on whom the depredations of modernity had been visited. Their future, and the future of all other formerly subjugated people, lay precisely in the future rather than in the past, in joining the historical process rather than seeking refuge in past traditions. To retreat to, or to try to hold onto, the older ways of life was a counsel of despair and a guarantee of failure. Wright's own career in the South and the North foreshadowed and paralleled the fate of "the tragic elite" of the emerging colonial nations of Africa and Asia (Gayle 242).

And yet, much of Wright's fiction, particularly *Native Son*, was concerned with the social and personal costs incurred along this historical trajectory. In his essay "How Bigger Was Born" (1940), Wright claims that, though the fictional Bigger is an individual, he is also a social-historical type: "There was not just one Bigger, but many of them, more than I could count and more than you suspect" (viii). Wright intended Bigger to be emblematic of a life lived in proximity to but excluded from not just white society but the modern world in general. People like him were "so close to the very civilization which sought to keep them out" (xi). Further, the historical contradiction he personified meant that "he had become estranged from the religion and folk culture of his race," that is, from the black southern folk culture. At the same time, he "was trying to react to and answer the call of the dominant civilization whose glitter came to him through the newspapers, magazines, radios, movies, and the mere imposing sight and sound of daily American life" (xiii). The destructive effects of Bigger's racial exclusion were compounded by the social and cultural contradictions of modern capitalism and the exigencies of modern urban existence: "he was hovering unwanted between the two worlds" (xxiv).

In contrast with the often idealized notions of the proletariat circulating in the 1930s, Wright also suggested that types such as Bigger, whatever their race, were perfect material for any political movement that acknowledged their marginality and promised inclusion in some larger movement or entity: "I felt that Bigger, an American product, a native son of this land, carried within him the potentialities of either Communism or Fascism" (xx). At the end of World War II, Wright was still gripped by the idea that the failures of industrial and urban society, particularly the inability to counter the black man's view that "his hopes are hopeless," created a breeding ground for totalitarian movements of the left and right (Introduction xxv). Thus the historical antinomies tearing Bigger apart were symptoms of a spiritual crisis in modern capitalist society. As long as the Communist Party failed to recognize the appeal of fascism to the proletariat or to realize that men such as Bigger could not be written off as mere *lumpen*, then it would never be able to gain the full support of the working class. All this was analysis in the dissident Freudian-Marxist tradition of Wilhelm Reich and Erich Fromm; it was *Native Son* as a fictional rendition of *Escape from Freedom*, Southside Chicago-style.

Yet Bigger was clearly not just a blackface version of modern man in search of a soul. He brought to the North a folk culture rooted in the southern black experience. But being a black southerner rarely meant anything unambiguously positive for Wright, even though he was deeply grounded in that culture. Besides his experience with black Christianity and his distaste for the subservience required of black figures of authority, such as educators, to much more powerful white authorities, the protagonist of *Black Boy* does evoke, at times lyrically and sometimes in a wry comic spirit, the daily pleasures of black life in the South, including playing "The Dozens" with his friends. In fact, Wright later wrote several blues lyrics for black musicians.

Still, Wright was the least nostalgic and sentimental of men. In "Blueprint for Negro Writing," he identified the two most important resources of the Negro as "1) the Negro church; and 2) the folklore of the Negro people" (45). As a quick cultural diagnosis, this was undoubtedly correct, but *Native Son* probably comes closer to Wright's own less-detached feelings about religion when Bigger thinks to himself, "The white folks like for us to be religious, then they can do what they want to with us" (329). Though the church and southern black folk culture were vitally important in the life of African Americans, one would scarcely know it from Wright's own fiction. Even *12 Million Black Voices*, which was subtitled "A Folk History of the Negro in the U.S." and was the closest Wright ever came to a kind of Popular Front evocation of black folk culture, celebrates the power of the church and its music, but concludes, "there are times when we doubt our songs; they are not enough to unify our fragile folk lives in this competitive world" (194). The message was clear. The black folk culture forged in the South equipped black migrants poorly for northern cities such as Chicago: "Perhaps never in history has a more utterly unprepared folk wanted to go to the city" (204; Moore).

Indeed, Wright's own background suggests that the term *folk culture* itself has only the loosest of meanings when applied to African American life in this century. He grew up in small and medium-sized Deep South towns in the decades flanking World War I. Having barely survived the archetypal broken home with his mother and her relatives, Wright looked back on his early years in the South and could see little but "the absence of fixed and nourishing forms of culture" ("Blueprint" 41). It wasn't just the racism and discrimination, along with the omnipresent threat of white violence that drove Wright from the South, though that was bad enough. Black southern life itself stifled his intellectual and emotional development and seemed to promise only dead-ends. Nothing in either white or black southern cultural traditions offered much guidance through the mazes of modern life.

All this is the context for Wright's powerful indictment of southern black life in *Black Boy*. Though a careful reader might remember that *12 Million Black Voices* had hinted as much, Wright's was a devastating indictment, both of the culture he had grown up in and of the way white—and black—observers romanticized it. "I saw what had been taken for our emotional strength was our negative confusions, our flights, our fears, our frenzy under pressure" (45). The passage's extra emotional pathos and its edge of bitterness derive from the fact that Wright's reflections were occasioned by meeting his father, now an old "black peasant," for the first time in a quarter century. On the surface, there is a kind of evocation of the pastoral: "As a creature of the earth, he endured, hearty, whole, seemingly indestructible, with no regrets and no hopes" (43). But Wright has already stated, "We were forever strangers" (42). Like Frazier, Wright insisted that the weaknesses of black southern culture were not traceable to inherent racial inadequacy; rather, exclusion from the dominant culture was at the heart of the problem: "Negroes had never been allowed to catch the full spirit of Western civilization, that they lived somehow in it but not of it" (45). The results led Wright to wonder if the "cultural barrenness of black life" did not suggest that "clean positive tenderness, love, honor, loyalty and the capacity to remember" were not "native to man" but had to be "fostered, won, struggled and suffered for, preserved in ritual from one generation to another" (45). Culture was no automatic endowment of human existence but a hard-won achievement.

Only with this powerful passage in mind can one begin to understand, for instance, Wright's hostility to the work of Zora Neale Hurston, whom he had accused in his 1937 review of *Their Eyes Were Watching God* of "facile sensuality" and of writing not for "the Negro" but "to a white audience whose chauvinistic tastes she knows how to satisfy" ("Between"; Fabre, *Unfinished* 278–82). By allegedly imparting to her readers a stage version of black vitality and sensuality, Wright suggested, Hurston was traducing the pain of black life. Nor, it should be added, was Wright really very much impressed by movements such as the Harlem Renaissance. By the end of the 1930s, he had still read little of the work of its major writers; and in "Blueprint for Negro Writing," he passed the phenomenon off as "a liaison between inferiority-complexed Negro 'geniuses' and burnt-out white Bohemians with money" (37).

Nor, as the passage from *Black Boy* indicates, did the effect of exclusion from white society remain external to the "souls" of the black folk. Wright was pointing to deep-seated, psychic scars that arose from the long history of oppression that began with slavery. Already in *12 Million Black Voices*, Wright speculated quite prophetically about the effects of slavery on black Americans: "our personalities are still numb from its [slavery's] long shocks; and as the numbness leaves our souls, we shall yet have to feel and give utterance to the full pain we shall inherit" (161–62). Thus the sequence of numbing and then release of pain, internal states translated into externalized actions, held the key to understanding the psychology of African Americans as they made the move from the southern homeland to the strange cities of the North.

CLOSING THE CIRCLE: TO AFRICA—AND BEYOND

Readers who expect Wright's *Black Power* to foreshadow the late 1960s Black Power movement in the United States will be severely disappointed. In the self-questioning attitude Wright adopted toward himself—and in his querulous attitude toward the west African society of the Gold Coast (later Ghana) circa 1953, he often sounded more like V. S. Naipaul than he did like Stokely Carmichael or Amiri Baraka.[2] Nor is it entirely clear just what kind of book *Black Power* was intended to be. It contains a good bit of political reportage and analysis, particularly of Kwame Nkrumah's efforts to forge a national political culture in the face of the reactionary pull of tribal loyalties and the resistance of British colonial occupiers. This is linked with, though separate from, Wright's anthropological-sociological analysis of African society and culture, which stresses the centrality of religious tradition in the formation of the African personality. And, finally, *Black Power* is a personal narrative of Wright's own efforts to come to terms with Africa, to figure out just what *attitude* he should adopt toward it and toward the claims of race and culture. Undoubtedly, *Black Power* was shaped by numerous contradictory impulses; yet, like most personal narratives, it gained as much as it lost from the tensions among them.

The theme informing *Black Power* is one that dominated Wright's American writings—the necessity for a people, caught between the traditional and the modern, to choose the modern. Only by doing this could they overcome the loss of the structures of meaning, which had left them bereft of purpose or the capacity for action. From Wright's point of view, the Africans in *Black Power* seem caught in much the same historical and existential dilemma as that which held captive the black Americans in *12 Million Black Voices*, with Wright as the often troubled, sometimes dispassionate, and occasionally critical analyst. Above all, he portrays himself as the knowing voice of rational development

But there were differences, too, between Wright's attitude toward the U.S. South and toward west Africa. Wright was a kind of participant observer, visiting the Gold Coast on the invitation of Kwame Nkrumah. He was clearly a stranger to African culture and just as clearly an emissary of Western culture. By way of contrast, though he was much more intimately acquainted with black southern culture, he was far more alienated from the structures of power in the United States. Throughout the early part of the book in particular, Wright regularly reports on his state of mind. On arrival, he is "excited" yet feels "disquiet" (6–7). More expansively, he notes in himself "an unsettled feeling engendered by the strangeness of a completely different order of life" (42). He experiences an "absolute otherness and inaccessibility" and a "vague sense of mild panic" (44). Some of this panic seems to be erotic in origin. Wright is obsessed with the naked bodies of Africans, particularly with the bare breasts of the women. He is also startled by the sight of two men dancing together, though he is also honest enough to include this reaction in the text. Kwame Anthony Appiah suggests, with some plausibility, that the dominant impression Wright conveys is one of "disgust" (Appiah 187). Yet this negative reaction might also have represented a reaction formation against the attraction Wright felt to what he saw. Africa, where self-consciousness about the body seemed largely absent unless under Western eyes, seems to have unsettled him considerably.

Precisely because African culture seemed so "other," it played a more prominent role in Wright's nonfictional account of Africa than the folk culture of southern blacks played in his representations, fictional and nonfictional, of black southern life. Where Wright recognized himself in the figure of his father in *Black Boy,* even as he rejected him, in Africa Wright had to deal with a "completely different order of life." It is this absence of any sort of identification that helps explain why there are no Bigger Thomases in *Black Power.* In *Native Son* Wright suggested that Bigger's fate was one possibility for all African Americans, at least for all African American males. But in *Black Power, The Color Curtain* and the essays collected in *White Man, Listen!* Wright identified not with the uprooted and dispossessed poor but with the "tragic elite" of African society. Perhaps because of his linguistic and cultural alienation from the masses of Africans, it was only with the Westernized elites that he could make some sort of meaningful contact in his visits.

It is also easy to overlook the importance of the Cold War as a shadowing influence on all of Wright's nonfiction of the 1950s. Throughout Wright's post–World War II career, he had to pick his way through a minefield of political and ideological claims. Having broken with the Communists in the early 1940s, Wright was opposed to the expansion of communism in the newly independent nations. As he noted in the introduction to *Black Power,* he found "Marxist instrumentalities of thought" useful, though this did not mean that he supported Soviet "programs or policies" (xxxviii). Yet Wright never wavered in his belief that the political defeat of European colonialism was the central historical imperative in

Africa; nor was Wright ever guilty of downplaying its destructive impact or emphasizing the beneficence of its intentions. "Hitler's clumsy dreams," he wrote bitingly early in the book, "were picayune when compared with the sanguine vision of these early English Christian gentlemen" who had incorporated themselves in 1663 to carry on the slave trade for "a thousand years" (12). Besides, it was undeniable that "only from Russia—not from the churches or the universities of the Western world—that a moral condemnation of colonial exploitation had come" (33).

In sum, Wright sought to thread his way through the field of contending Cold War forces by adopting a "third way"—*for* political independence in Africa and Asia and *against* Soviet or Chinese political domination of those countries in the wake of the departure of the Western colonial powers. In this respect, both *Black Power* and *The Color Curtain* were consistently anticommunist *and* anticolonial. In fact, Wright's identification with the West betokened a split that had already taken place among African Americans after 1945. For Popular Front radicals such as W. E. B. Du Bois and Paul Robeson, the Soviet Union represented the best hope for postwar anticolonial forces, since the West was hopelessly compromised by its colonial legacy and by the willingness of the United States to embrace that legacy as France and Britain departed the colonial scene. Du Bois, then pretty firmly in the camp of the Soviet Union, had a hard time swallowing Wright's position. As Du Bois wrote to George Padmore, the Pan-African leader and good friend of Wright, Wright's "logic is lousy. He starts out to save Africa from Communism and then makes an attack on British capitalism which is devastating. How he reconciles these two attitudes I cannot see" (qtd. in Horne 260; Von Eschen). One way was that he emphasized cultural rather than economic modernization. Indeed, Wright talked remarkably little of economic development in his nonfictional explorations of life in the third world. His focus instead fell on the psychological and cultural effects of colonialism and the need for political independence.

Wright's position also implied two considerations of considerable subtlety. First, was the (Weberian) insight that both capitalism and socialism were modernizing visions driven by Enlightenment values of secular reason and modern technology and hostile to the forces of tradition and religion. Africa could become socialist and hence modern without becoming communist. Second, Wright seemed to assume that Western colonialism itself had been a force for creative destruction in the third world, despite his forthright desire to see its demise. Indeed, here, Wright was echoing Marx's analysis of the situation in India where British political and economic penetration had helped destroy the feudal, premodern institutions that hindered development. On this issue, Wright was as good a Marxist as Du Bois. For Marx communism was meant to be the successor to, not the historical agent of, economic, political and cultural modernization. Thus, a moral condemnation of capitalism should not, from Wright's vantage point, blind observers to some of its historically progressive effects in bringing modern values to traditional societies.

Wright also had to confront the doctrine of African spiritual unity as developed in the Negritude movement of Léopold Sédar Senghor and Aimé Césaire. According to Senghor, for instance, "In simple terms, Negritude is the African personality. It is the sum total of the values which characterize black civilization"; not a species of racism, it is "open to world influence" ("Impact" 71–72). Its implications were, as Wright rehearsed them, that

> we have a *special* gift for music, dancing, rhythm and movement. . . .
> We have a genius of our own. We were civilized in Africa when white men were still living in caves in Europe. (*Black Power* 6)

If this African essentialism were true, Wright notes, "there ought to be something of 'me' down there in Africa. . . . But I could not feel anything African about myself" (45). This failure to experience the mystic chords linking race and culture in Africa was to lead him to confront Senghor and Césaire at the Paris Conference in September 1956.

But though Wright left Africa with his allegiance to nonracial explanations of culture largely intact, it was not without a certain amount of soul-searching. In Africa he could not ignore the "strange but familiar" (73) group movements, obviously "ring shouts," which he remembered from his youth in the Delta. Confronted with this phenomenon, he first questions his belief that racial explanations fail to explain anything and, then, tentatively takes up Melville Herskovits's controversial view that New World ring shouts were "African survivals," the product not of genetics but historical-cultural transmission. At this point in *Black Power*, Wright's thinking circles around, rather than resolves, the issue. Black Americans often deny any links with Africa, in part because of a normal desire to assimilate into American culture but also, he admits, because for "so long had Africa been described as something shameful" (73). Wright's readers are left in doubt as to his exact position until later in the book.

In *Black Power* Wright offers an intriguing discussion of the "African personality" and the importance of religion in its construction. When analyzing the situation in urban areas, Wright tends to blame Christianity for having created in Africans an endemic suspiciousness, a lack of self-confidence and a certain "childlike" (118) overestimation of their ability to conceal their true feelings. Wright attributes such characteristics to the fact that Africans inhabit a "half-way world" (167). British colonialism, in league with Christian missionaries, had created "millions of detribalized Africans living uneasily and frustrated in two worlds and really believing in neither of them" (72). The results were "eroded personalities" and "psychological damage," the products of a Christianity that had "rendered them numb to their own dearly bought vision of life" (169). Not only was the message of Christianity destructive as such, the missionaries themselves were "prodded by their own neurotic drives" (168). Significant here is Wright's use of the word *numb*, the same word he used in 12 *Million Black Voices* to describe the effects of slavery on black Americans. Not only was Wright developing an African variation on Du Bois's "double consciousness," but his notion of a "half-way world" also anticipated V. S. Naipaul's analysis of former colonial societies as "half-made."

Yet this line of analysis stands in a certain tense relationship with the impressions Wright gathered in less densely populated parts of Accra. There, he observes, Africans seem to merge with the earth as a kind of autochthonous force. This leads him to the "intuitive impression that these people were old, old, maybe the oldest people on earth, and I felt a sense of melancholy knowing that their customs, laboriously created and posited for thousands of years, had been condemned as inferior, and shattered by a strong and predatory nation . . . but surrounded by a new order of life, they didn't and couldn't believe in them as they once had" (*Black Power* 76).

It is crucial, however, to emphasize that Wright looks to a *political* solution for this massive psychological and cultural deracination. Once again, he applies a mass-society model drawn from Western industrial societies to the new African historical reality. Nkrumah's "mass nationalist movement" is founded on the intimate relationship, sealed with an oath, between the leader and the masses and marked by large chanting crowds. It is "a new kind of religion. They were politics *plus!*" (61). Nkrumah had "fused tribalism with modern politics" to fill "the vacuum" left when the tribal culture and religion was destroyed by the British (65).

But, it was not always clear how much the African political culture was the product of colonial penetration and what was indigenous to the place itself. When Wright journeys to the upland interior of the country, a trip that echoes Conrad's *Heart of Darkness* with its intimations of cannibalism and reveries of violence, he finds not only much that is strange but much that is the same as in the cities. The fact that "they [Africans] cannot really conceive of a political party except in the form of a glorious leader" (294) clearly derives from the intense personal loyalty to the tribal chief. And it is while in the backcountry that Wright arrives at his solution to the race versus culture problem. What he comes to see is that the African way of seeing the world is "a natural and poetic grasp of existence" and thus a "basic and primal attitude(s) toward life" (295). Remnants of such a worldview will survive, even when one-time inhabitants of a traditional society land in a modern environment. It is not specifically racial, Wright seems to be saying, but shared by all indigenous, premodern traditional cultures.

The problem still remains: this primordial cultural vision, however fascinating or appealing, produces a people ill-prepared to deal with the modern world. It is not a matter really of simplicity or complexity, though at times Wright does characterize traditional Gold Coast society as simple. But he also suggests at one point that the African in the backcountry is, if anything, "too civilized" (282), too weighed down by the cultural baggage of inherited rituals, beliefs, and forces. All of this testifies to "the omnipotence of thought" in traditional African society (248). What is needed, then, is not a more complex culture but one in which a reorientation—from concreteness to abstraction, from immersion to detachment, and from the past to the future—has taken place. Wherever tradition was, whether in the U.S. South or in Africa, there the modern mentality should be.

Specifically, Wright's analysis rests on the conviction that "jungle life" had failed to "develop a hard and durable ego" in the African (293). The African self is dominated by what psychoanalytic theory identifies as primary process thinking in which the boundary between "reality" and "dream" is effaced and confused (216). The African self is "sensuous, loving images not concepts; personalities, not abstractions; movement, not form; dreams, not reality. . . . System is the enemy of the tribal mind; action proceeds on the basis of association of images" (294). Notably, Wright's characterization of the African personality bears a distinct family resemblance to the one offered by Senghor and the advocates of what might be called "pastoral" Negritude. Wright's disagreement with the advocates of Negritude is not about the nature of African culture but whether that culture was viable in the modern world. His answer is that it is not viable. Wright concludes *Black Power* with an ominous plea to Nkrumah to impose "firm social discipline" (388). In more drastic terms, Wright insists, "AFRICAN LIFE MUST BE MILITARIZED!" (389), not, he hastens to add, for purposes of war-making but to supply the "form, organization, direction, meaning, and a sense of justification to those lives" (389). In order for Africa to become modern, it has to become disciplined.

In retrospect, Wright's failure to suggest what specific forms of self-government might be adopted, how the power of the leader and his retinue might be curbed, and how political participation, beyond the mass meetings, could be encouraged was most disturbing. Also missing was any sense of urgency about developing independent institutions of civil society to replace the older tribal structures, which would, if effective, reduce dependence on strong leaders and inculcate in the population the "habit" of self-government. Instead, Wright stressed the critical role of political elites, and especially the political leader, in mobilizing the population for independence, a standard recommendation in theories of political development during the Cold War. The message to Kwame Nkrumah was straightforward: "It's a secular religion that you [Nkrumah] must slowly create" (392). *Osagyefo* Nkrumah got the message.

THE POLITICS OF CULTURE

The mid-1950s was a time of great political ferment and high optimism in the third world. In April 1955 Wright journeyed to Indonesia to cover the conference of leaders from the nonaligned nations of Africa and Asia. Though Bandung represented a major effort to transcend the Manichaean Cold War atmosphere, Wright's trip was, ironically, funded by the Congress for Cultural Freedom, later revealed to be subsidized by the CIA. Wright got assurances that he would be free to express his opinions, and this demand was apparently respected. Wright's report from Bandung in *The Color Curtain* focused on the public rhetoric of political leaders rather than pursuing the self- and cultural analysis he had offered in *Black Power.* This "tragic and lonely" elite was to be a main focus of Wright's writings from the mid-1950s to his death in 1960 ("Tradition," in *White Man* 63). At Bandung most of Wright's attention fell on Asian societies and Asian leaders, particularly China's Chou En-Lai, who performed very skillfully at Bandung. There, according to Wright, he presented the Chinese position in a nondogmatic manner and showed willingness to cooperate in a new vision of neutrality that was beholden neither to the West nor to the Soviet Union.

For Wright Bandung seemed to reveal three important things. First, he was struck by the irrelevance of the older ideologies of left and right for third-world dreams and realities. Second, he was impressed by the overwhelming importance of race and religion at the Bandung Conference.

About this, Wright was far from happy, since it implied a rejection of the secular universalism at the heart of his modernizing vision. Paradoxically, it was not the West that was now appealing to race and religion but the leaders of the Asian countries themselves; they seemed to detest the West and then mimic its worst features.

Wright's third theme concerned an alternative vision to these racial and religious appeals. Here, Wright was much more conciliatory to the West than he had been in *Black Power*. With regard to the question "Is this secular rational base and thought-feeling in the Western world broad and secure enough to warrant the West's assuming the moral right to interfere without narrow, selfish political motives?" his answer was basically affirmative (*Color Curtain* 299). Such a Western-derived commitment to modernity, he thought, would encourage "rapid industrialization" and the "shaking loose of the Asian-African masses from a static past" (220). The alternatives were unacceptable. The Japanese effort in World War II, what Wright referred to as "Japanese Fascism," had combined modern science and technology with particularist racial and religious ends (218). Communism in power, whether in Stalin's Russia or in Mao's China, had proved to be "secular religiosity of horror and blood" (221).

Though never as interesting as the more complexly rendered and introspective *Black Power*, *The Color Curtain* offered a clear version of the central concerns of Wright's thought until his death—the contest between the secular humanism-universalism of the West and the particularist ideologies of religion, race, and culture for the loyalty of third-world political and intellectual elites. The First International Congress of Black Writers and Artists, held at the Sorbonne in September 1956, provided the forum where debate about these matters could be carried on directly among black writers and intellectuals.[3]

The congress was the brainchild of the Paris-based journal *Présence Africaine*. Wright had been associated with it since its founding in 1947 and was a member of the planning committee for the congress. As Michel Fabre has noted, however, Wright was always closer to Jean-Paul Sartre's *Les Temps Modernes* than to *Présence Africaine*, since the latter was primarily an outlet for francophone Africanists. Moreover, its orientation— one reflected at the congress—was toward cultural rather than political nationalism and was congenial to Negritude rather than to Western humanism. Wright's own interests, insofar as they were directed toward the non-European world, clearly privileged political over cultural self-determination. After all, the central point of both *Black Power* and *The*

Color Curtain was that the values most suited for the emerging African nations were Western and not indigenous African or Asian cultural values.

At the congress—which included sixty-eight participants from eight African and five Caribbean countries, India, and the United States—Wright also had the unenviable task of mediating between the rather moderate U.S. delegation, which was haunted, as he told the non-Europeans, by the threat of McCarthyism, and the more radical voices of the French-speaking Africans and their francophone allies. (Martinique's Aimé Césaire resigned from the Communist Party less than a month after the congress ended.) Many of the clichés about the differences between Anglo-American and francophone cultures proved all-too-true among men of color. (As Wright pointed out, there was a woeful lack of women at the congress.) Those trained in France tended to be more culturally radical and given to grand abstractions and sweeping generalizations, while the contributions of the English-speaking delegates maintained a closer empirical or historical focus, were reformist in tone and substance—and often pretty uninspiring. In fact, except for Wright, the U.S. delegation barely addressed cultural or literary issues at all.

That W. E. B. Du Bois had been denied a visa by the State Department and thus could not attend the congress didn't help; nor did the fact that a somewhat more radical delegation envisaged by Wright—one that might have included poet Melvin Tolson, E. Franklin Frazier, and historian J. A. Rogers—failed to pan out. There was even talk that Josephine Baker would make an appearance (as a speaker not a dancer) and that Langston Hughes might also participate. But, again, things didn't work out, though Hughes and James Baldwin attended as observers. All this may have explained the absence of a certain political and cultural sophistication among the eventual black U.S. delegation of John A. Davis, Horace Mann Bond, James W. Ivy, William Fontaine, and Mercer Cook. In addition, Wright constantly operated under the implicit threat of expulsion by the French government if he spoke out too loudly on Algeria. Not only that, Wright had been under surveillance since the early 1940s by the FBI and other agencies of the U.S. government and feared that his passport would be lifted if he were too vocal in his criticisms of U.S. foreign policy or domestic practices, particularly in the area of race relations. Indeed, there is some evidence that Wright reported to the embassy on possible communist influences at the congress, not exactly a difficult task since Césaire among others was an open member of the French Communist Party (see Gayle 265–70; Rowley 474). Besides delivering a shorter version of the essay "Tradition and Industrialization," later included in modified form in *White Man, Listen!* (1957), Wright posed two crucial questions from the floor after the speakers at the first session of the congress had finished, but not before replying quite sharply to Du Bois's controversial telegram, which impugned the motives of the U.S. delegation. Because the State Department had granted passports to its members and had refused one to him, Du Bois suggested that the members of the U.S. delegation were the stooges of the U.S. government.

The immediate provocation for Wright's questions was Léopold Senghor's address "The Spirit of Civilisation, or the Laws of African Negro Culture." As he closed his speech outlining the classic Negritude position, Senghor insisted, "The spirit of African Negro civilisation . . . animates the best Negro artists and writers of to-day, whether they come from Africa or America" (64). But much as he admired the speech, Wright admitted in the ensuing discussion that he felt "a sense of uneasiness" as he listened to it, since "I wonder where do I, an American Negro . . . where do I stand in relation to that culture?" "I cannot," he continued, "accept Africa because of mere blackness or on trust. . . . Is it possible for me to find a working and organic relationship with it?" (66–67). Senghor's brief response merely reiterated his claim that Negro American writing and culture were in essence part of "the African heritage" and that, specifically, *Black Boy* was "an African American recital" (73–74). Such a response was hardly surprising, since Senghor's African essentialism presupposed what it set out to show—the underlying spiritual affinities among all peoples of African descent.

Césaire's brief intervention in this exchange stressed that just as there were French, German, and Italian cultures within Western culture, so there was also a general African culture in which various national cultures participated (72–73). Césaire's own full presentation, "Culture and Colonisation," delivered on 20 September, included American Negroes within the African world, not because they shared some mystical African essence à la Senghor but because they "occupy . . . an artificial position that can only be understood within the context of a colonialism that has certainly been abolished but whose after-effects still persist down to the present day" (93).

Thus, Césaire's Negritude of protest, one that stressed the importance of Africa as a counter-example to alienated existence under colonialism, had the virtue of taking into account the forces of history and economics in shaping diasporic consciousness rather than simply positing a transhistorical pan-African spiritual unity (Jules-Rosette). In turn, John Davis of the U.S. delegation responded sharply to Césaire's analysis, insisting that American Negroes wanted "complete equal status as citizens" not "self-determination in the belt" (217).[4] In shorthand terms, they wanted "in" not "out." That none of the U.S. delegation, including Wright, raised the possibility of combining political inclusion with cultural nationalism graphically illustrated the point Harold Cruse later made in *The Crisis of the Negro Intellectual* (1967)—that black American intellectuals never developed a nationalist cultural vision or philosophy.[5]

Wright's "Tradition and Industrialization," the last formal presentation of the congress, was a more forceful, if compressed, reiteration of the message of *Black Power* and *The Color Curtain.* Wright insisted that there were specifically Western values and modes of thought, deriving from the Reformation and the Enlightenment, which had created individual consciousness and conscience in the Westerner. This tradition of thought and feeling provided, by implication, an antidote to the lack of definition that characterized the African personality as Wright had depicted it in *Black Power.* He also emphasized the paradox that the protests of the Westernized elite against Western colonial hegemony were themselves derived from Western values. Thus, dialectically, the dominant culture generated the tools for self-criticism and self-examination. Though Wright's prefatory two-page comment to his paper at the congress was not included in the version printed in *White Man, Listen!* it contained Wright's disavowal of the black nationalism that he advocated in his "Blueprint for Black Writing." According to Wright, that position had been appropriate in a time of great hostility against "American Negroes." It "was a reluctant nationalism, a proud and defensive one," but with changes in the racial climate in America, Wright hoped "that nationalism of itself will be liquidated" (355). He assured his audience, however, that nationalism was still valid in places where white rule had yet to be thrown off.

The other large question Wright posed at the end of the first day of the congress barely concealed a scathing view of the African culture that Senghor and others so celebrated. Behind it lay not only Wright's own experience but also French psychoanalyst Octave Mannoni's *Prospero and Caliban: The Psychology of Colonization*, which had appeared in French in 1950 and was based on his experience in Madagascar. It is highly likely that Wright had written his review of Mannoni's study, which had just been published in English, before the congress began. Whatever the case, that review appeared in *Nation* on 20 October, just a month after the congress had adjourned, and was incorporated into his "The Psychological Reactions of Oppressed Peoples," which Wright first gave as a paper in Germany shortly after the congress.

Wright's second question reflected the way his position had been shaped by Mannoni's analysis of the native's "dependency complex," which was referred to several times during the congress.

> Might not the vivid and beautiful culture that Senghor has described not [sic] been—I speak carefully, choosing my words with utmost caution, speaking to my colleagues, hoping that you will understand my intentions—might not that beautiful culture have been a fifth column a corps of saboteurs and spies of Europe? . . . Did that religion help the people to resist fiercely and hardily and hurl the Europeans out? I question the value of that culture in relationship of our future. I do not condemn it. But how can we use it. . . . I have the feeling, uneasy, almost bordering upon dread, that there was a fateful historic complement between a militant white Christian Europe and an ancestral cult religion in Africa. (Debats 67)

Wright's question was clearly triggered by the implications of Mannoni's suggestion that the traditional cultures of Africa, Asia, and the Western Hemisphere were primed to develop cultures of dependency under the pressures of European colonialism, though admittedly Mannoni himself only applied the dependency thesis to Madagascar where he had lived and worked. Like Hannah Arendt's *Origins of Totalitarianism* (1951), to which Wright alluded in his review, Mannoni also emphasized the European rage to dominate African societies and to discover some larger purpose in that collective activity. Rather than the heroic figures he had once suggested they were, Wright, following Mannoni, wrote scathingly of "neurotic, restless Europeans" who created a world that "would permit free play for their repressed instincts" ("Neuroses" 328). Significantly, Senghor did not respond directly to this question concerning the complicity of African culture in its own destruction while Césaire did so only to the extent of insisting that there should be no either/or choice between African and Western culture.

What is striking in retrospect was the failure of anyone to offer an alternative scenario of how Europe was able to establish the slave trade and eventually to bring west Africa, indeed all of Africa, under Western control. One possible response would have been to distinguish between an active "fifth column" role that African culture might have played in encouraging the acceptance of European domination and a more plausible failure to provide the resources for resistance. If the latter rather than former had been emphasized, there would have been room for historical and economic factors then also to be considered. (African leaders along the west coast of Africa saw nothing particularly unusual in selling other Africans into slavery. They did it all the time, as did most slave societies.) Such a response perhaps makes Wright and Mannoni's general point about the lack of adequate resistance, but the assumption that traditional west-African cultures were marked by some *unusual* degree of dependency need not have played a role at all.[6]

One participant at the congress might have responded to Wright but chose not to do so—the thirty-one-year-old, Martinique-born psychiatrist Frantz Fanon. Fanon's thought was clearly in the process of evolution in the mid-1950s. He was just three months away from leaving his post as a psychiatrist in Algeria to take up full-time political work for the Front de Libération Nationale (FLN) against the French. Fanon's speech "Racism and Culture" failed to address the question of the possible complicity of African culture in its own defeat, except to reject both blind assimilation of Western values and unthinking celebration of the African past. (It also apparently caused a stir because Fanon refused to see the French as less racist than other European peoples, that is, than Anglo-Saxons.) Perhaps the situation simply wasn't appropriate or perhaps Fanon was somewhat in awe of Wright, whom he (Fanon) had not met before the congress but from whom he confessed to have learned much. Fanon wrote Wright a letter of homage in 1953; but Wright, according to Michel Fabre, never read entire books in French, so he probably wouldn't have read *Black Skin, White Masks* ("Wright Wronged" 436).

This is an important point, since Fanon's *Black Skin, White Masks* (1952) devotes a whole chapter to a critique of Mannoni's work in terms of both logic and history. First, Fanon asks why, if the "colonial situation" is Mannoni's point of departure, "does he [Mannoni] try to make the inferiority complex something that antedates colonization?" (85). The effect of such a claim, Fanon continues, is to place most of the responsibility for the native's supposed "inferiority complex" on the preexisting, indigenous, dependency culture rather than on the invading French (85). Fanon also notes that of the four million inhabitants of Madagascar, the source of Mannoni's data and observations, the French killed one in fifty (80,000) in a notorious war between 1947 and 1949. The dreams of natives there, which Fanon had analyzed, represented not their sexual fantasies but their torturers. Fanon concluded with a variation on Sartre's analysis of anti-Semitism: "It is the racist who creates his inferior" (93).

Still, Wright's review of Mannoni left no doubt that the Europeans were the aggressors in the colonies. Though Mannoni did not have to be read as "blaming the victims," his work lends itself to such a reading, as does, arguably, Wright's *Black Power*, which also stresses the strong streak of dependency in west-African culture. Significantly, Wright appears never to have directly suggested that black southern folk culture encouraged dependency, though he did think it inadequate to the tasks modernity had set it.

CONCLUSION

There remains a larger question about Wright's vision of the complex relationship between history and cultural change. On the one hand, Wright always stated his position as though Westernized elites had a choice about the choices they were called on to make. Otherwise, he would have hardly spent the last years of his life urging those elites to choose the West culturally but to reject colonial political control in the name of self-determination. In that sense the elites were free, as were the advocates of Negritude, to adopt an alternative understanding of what cultural values were best for Africans to adopt. Beyond that, it is difficult to decide whether Wright thought that modern Western values were better in themselves or whether they merely had the most adaptive value for the survival (and flourishing) of the newly emergent nations. Perhaps such a question made no sense to Wright, since those values were best in themselves that also allowed the people of Africa to survive and flourish.

It is hard to escape the conclusion that Wright had little feeling for African or any non-Western culture (Margolies 409–14). Concern with traditional cultures, much less the glorification of the African past or a return to the black southern folk culture, were luxuries that could be ill afforded. It is significant that Fanon eventually arrived at a similar conclusion but considered revolutionary values, not those of Western humanism, the most viable alternative. Against both the advocates of Negritude and Fanon's revolutionary humanism, Wright contended that there was no virtue in recommending the impossible or undesirable. He might even have agreed with the spirit of the remarks offered by an African father to his son in V. S. Naipaul's *Finding the Center* (1984): "I am not sending you to school to be a white man or a Frenchman. I am sending you to enter the new world. That's all" (160). Whether that *is* all is another matter.

NOTES

1. I will be using *modernization* and *westernization* as rough synonyms for what Wright and his generation referred to as "development" and/or "industrialization and urbanization." Though generally assumed to imply capitalism, modernization, for Wright, could also imply development along socialist or mixed-economy lines. Wright was less

interested in the forms of economic development than the cultural values both pre-supposed and inculcated by that process.

2. In his "A Long Way from Home: Wright in the Gold Coast" Kwame Anthony Appiah, a native of Ghana, gives Wright as good as he gave by suggesting that Wright's condescension and paranoia about Africa and Africans arose from his unrequited affection for the place. Jack Moore, in his "*Black Power* Revisited: In Search of Richard Wright," reports on interviews with several people who talked with Wright during his three month stay in 1953. They were about equally divided between thinking Wright captured something essential about the place and feeling that he was out of his depth. For an analysis of Wright's nonfiction of the 1950s in terms of various generic conventions, see Smith.

3. Here I should emphasize just how indispensable Michel Fabre's work is to the topic under consideration. His *Unfinished Quest* includes seven pages on the congress, but most authoritative is his "Wright, Negritude, and African Writing." James Baldwin wrote a well-known English-language account of the congress, "Princes and Powers," while V. Y. Mudimbe's collection of essays on the congress is a more recent, invaluable compendium.

4. This was clearly a thinly veiled reference to the Communist Party position in the early 1930s, which called for the establishment of a black nation in the Deep South.

5. Ironically, in *The Crisis of the Negro Intellectual,* Cruse also criticized Wright's "Blueprint for Negro Writing" for being more interested in developing a cultural message for the black masses than for the new black intelligentsia. It was more compli-cated than that in general. Wright's work of the 1950s aimed to influence Westernized elites at a global level, yet he specifically warned those elites away from the cultural nationalism that Cruse favored, though Cruse had little interest in Negritude or Africa as such (Cruse 181–89).

6. The Wright-Senghor debate anticipates both the debate over Stanley Elkins's "Sambo" thesis in his *Slavery* (1959), which was based on the paucity of slave revolts in North America, and the controversy aroused by Hannah Arendt's *Eichmann in Jeru-salem* (1963), in which she charged that the Jewish authorities helped facilitate the process of delivery of European Jewry to the death camps in the East.

WORKS CITED

Appiah, Kwame Anthony. "A Long Way from Home: Wright in the Gold Coast." *Richard Wright.* Ed. Harold Bloom. New York: Chelsea House, 1987. 173–90.

Baldwin, James. "Princes and Powers." *Collected Essays.* New York: Library of America, 1998. 143–69.

Césaire, Aimé. "Culture and Colonisation." *Présence Africaine* 18–19 (June–Nov. 1956): 193–207.

Cruse, Harold. *The Crisis of the Negro Intellectual.* New York: William Morrow/Apollo Editions, 1968. 181–89.

Davis, John. Debats. *Présence Africaine* 18–19 (June–Nov. 1956): 216–18.

Dickstein, Morris. "Wright, Baldwin, Cleaver." *Richard Wright: Impressions and Per-*

spectives. Ed. David Ray and Robert M. Farnsworth. Ann Arbor: U of Michigan P, 1973. 183–90.

Fabre, Michel. "Beyond Naturalism." *The World of Richard Wright.* Jackson: UP of Mississippi, 1985. 57–76.

——. "Margaret Walker's Richard Wright: A Wrong Righted or a Wright Wronged?" *Mississippi Quarterly* 42 (fall 1989): 429–50.

——. *The Unfinished Quest of Richard Wright.* 2d ed. Urbana: U of Illinois P, 1993.

——. "Wright, Negritude, and African Writing." *The World of Richard Wright.* Jackson: UP of Mississippi, 1985. 192–213.

Fanon, Frantz. *Black Skin, White Masks.* New York: Grove, 1967.

Gayle, Addison, Jr. *Richard Wright: Ordeal of a Native Son.* Garden City, N.Y. : Anchor, 1980.

Gilroy, Paul. *The Black Atlantic: Modernity and Double-Consciousness.* London: Verso, 1993.

Horne, Gerald. *Black and Red: W. E. B. Du Bois and the Afro-American Response to the Cold War, 1944–1963.* Albany, N.Y.: State U of New York P, 1986.

Jules-Rosette, Bennetta. "Conjugating Cultural Realities: *Présence Africaine.*" *The Surreptitious Speech:* Présence Africaine *and the Politics of Otherness, 1947–1987.* Ed. V. Y. Mudimbe. Chicago: U of Chicago P, 1992. 14–44.

Margolies, Edward. "Richard Wright's Opposing Freedoms." *Mississippi Quarterly* 42 (fall 1989): 409–14.

Moore, Jack B. "*Black Power* Revisited." *Mississippi Quarterly* 41 (spring 1988): 161–86.

——. "The Voice in *12 Million Black Voices.*" *Mississippi Quarterly* 42 (fall 1989): 415–24.

Mudimbe, V. Y., ed. *The Surreptitious Speech:* Présence Africaine *and the Politics of Otherness, 1947–1987.* Chicago: U of Chicago P, 1992.

Naipaul, V. S. *Finding the Center.* Harmondsworth, England: Penguin, 1985.

Robinson, Cedric. *Black Marxism: The Making of the Black Radical Tradition.* Chapel Hill: U of North Carolina P, 2000.

Rowley, Hazel. *Richard Wright: The Life and Times.* New York: Henry Holt, 2001.

Senghor, Léopold Sédar. "The Literary Impact of Negritude." *Negro Digest* 14.7 (May 1965): 71–72.

——. "The Spirit of Civilisation or the Laws of African Negro Culture." *Présence Africaine* 18–19 (June–Nov. 1956): 51–64.

Smith, Virginia Whatley, ed. *Richard Wright's Travel Writings: New Reflections.* Jackson: UP of Mississippi, 2001.

Von Eschen, Penny M. *Race against Empire: Black Americans and Anticolonialism, 1937–1957.* Ithaca, N.Y.: Cornell UP, 1997.

Watts, Jerry G. *Heroism and the Black Intellectual: Ralph Ellison, Politics, and Afro-American Intellectual Life.* Chapel Hill: U of North Carolina P, 1994.

Wright, Richard. "Between Laughter and Tears." *New Masses* 25 (5 Oct. 1937): 22–25.

——. *Black Power: A Record of Reactions in a Land of Pathos.* New York: Harper Perennial, 1995.

——. "Blueprint for Negro Writing." *The Richard Wright Reader.* Ed. Ellen Wright and Michel Fabre. New York: DaCapo, 1997. 36–49.

——. *The Color Curtain: A Report on the Bandung Conference.* Cleveland: World, 1956.

——. Debats. *Présence Africaine* 18–19 (June–Nov. 1956): 66–68.

——. "How Bigger Was Born." *Native Son.* New York: Harper, 1940. vii–xxxiv.

——. Introduction. *Black Metropolis: A Study of Negro Life in a Northern City.* By St. Clair Drake and Horace Cayton. Rev. ed. New York: Harcourt, Brace, 1962. xvii–xxxiv.

——. *Native Son.* New York: Signet, 1961.

——. "The Neuroses of Conflict." *Nation* 20 Oct. 1956: 328–29.

——. "The Psychological Reactions of Oppressed Peoples." *White Man, Listen!* Garden City, N.Y.: Anchor, 1964. 1–43.

——. "Tradition and Industrialization." *Présence Africaine* 18–19 (June–Nov. 1956): 355–69. Rpt. in *White Man, Listen!* Garden City, N.Y.: Anchor, 1964. 44–68.

——. *12 Million Black Voices. The Richard Wright Reader.* Ed. Ellen Wright and Michel Fabre. New York: De Capo. 1997. 144–241.

——. *White Man, Listen!* Garden City, N.Y.: Anchor, 1964. 44–68.

ROBERT H. BRINKMEYER JR.

AND DEBRA RAE COHEN

Forward into the Past: California and the

Contemporary White Southern Imagination

Rather than the East-West axis by which America has characteristically defined itself (America, as Richard Rodriguez has observed, has from its beginnings configured itself longitudinally [44]), southern culture has traditionally employed a North-South axis to set itself off from the rest of America, almost always defined simply as "the North." The cultural oppositions are by now commonplace: cavalier and Yankee, agrarian and industrial, rural and urban, slow and fast, and so on. Since the 1920s, however, as shown in Bob's recent book, *Remapping Southern Literature*, white southern writers have increasingly looked west rather than north in terms of cultural opposition and mythic construction. This emergence of the West as the new source of tension, challenge, and redefinition for the South has only been heightened by the symbolic importance of California as the iconic center of postmodernity, the Ground Zero of a globalism that implicitly derides the southern obsession with regional history and stable location. As we'll explore in this essay, it's exactly that promise of freedom from southern history that contemporary southern writers find so dangerously alluring, mining the postmodern promise of Los Angeles only to find it, ultimately, insufficient.

In turning West rather than North, one could argue, southerners have merely been catching up with the American mainstream in their representation of national ideology. If the Northeast has long been the cultural and economic center of America (with money, power, and influence historically located there), the ideological underpinnings of U.S. nationalism have primarily been located in the West, and particularly in the frontier. The title of an exhibition of western art organized by the Smithsonian Institution, *The West as America*, points to the fact that the United States has all along invented its fundamental national ideology out of the frontier experience and westward movement. As Richard Slotkin and many others have shown, configurations of the West, both real and imagined, underlie American myths of individualism and progress (not to mention those of capitalism and consumption).[1]

There is nothing new here regarding American identity and mythology. What is new is that contemporary southern writers have been responding to the appeal of the West, something that writers of previous generations for the most part avoided. Writers of the Southern Literary Renaissance, for instance, characteristically represented the West as a dangerous space embodying the illusory dream of unchecked freedom. To go west was to step free from history and responsibility, and southern fiction almost always revealed the naïveté of that dream, charting paths west as paths to self-destruction. "Freedom from what? From work? Canaan?" (286), Ike McCaslin in Faulkner's *Go Down, Moses* disdainfully challenges Sophonsiba's husband, who has moved the couple west to Arkansas and spoken to Ike about his dream of starting anew. It's no coincidence that in Welty's *The Golden Apples* the townsfolk of Morgana imaginatively associate King McClain, the wanderer whose restless movement threatens community stability, with the West. "I believe he's been to California," Fate Rainey says of King. "Don't ask me why. But I picture him there. I see King in the West, out where it's gold and all that" (11). Later characterizing the town's efforts to protect King's wife from the dangers of her wandering husband, Fate says simply, "We shut the West out of Snowdie's eyes of course" (14).

Compared with the generation before them, contemporary southern writers have been much more open and adventurous in exploring the dream of the West, even if they frequently in the end find the freedom touted by western mythology to be problematic, if not downright illusory. Writers who have looked west represent a wide spectrum, including Cormac McCarthy, Barbara Kingsolver, Barry Hannah, Doris Betts, Richard Ford, Dorothy Allison, Madison Smartt Bell, Frederick Barthelme, Darcey Steinke, Chris Offutt, and Rick Bass. What binds these diverse writers together, aside from some sort of abiding southernness, is their interest in interrogating the American myths of freedom and progress, myths that have long stood opposed to those of the South.

What these writers also have in common, of course, is their whiteness, and indeed the new westward remapping seems limited almost exclusively to white writers, with African Americans continuing to work primarily along a North-South geocultural axis. While it's possible to over-theorize this disjunction, it seems likely that the "myth of progress" and the dream of unchecked freedom that the West has embodied for the dominant American culture is articulated for African Americans in the northward journey that has played such a large part in their historical experience—from the geographies of slavery to the Great Migration and beyond—and that continues to be interrogated in American writings to this day.

Within the spectrum of responses to the West, California, and Los Angeles in particular, occupy an extreme and particularized position. If the West represents the continuing imaginative presence of American opportunity (including capitalist exploitation), Los Angeles represents that opportunity at its extreme, eroticized limit. Los Angeles is American success at its most lustrous and superficial, a city of glitz, glamour, and commodification that epitomizes Fredric Jameson's image of postmodernism as a "waning of our historicity" ("Cultural Logic" 21). Indeed, the centrality of Los Angeles to theoretical models of postmodernism is unrivalled, from Baudrillard's adoption of Disneyland as template for the postmodern imaginary to Jameson's designation of the Bonaventure Hotel as exemplar of postmodernist space to the popular anointing of Ridley Scott's futuristic Los Angeles in *Blade Runner* as the paradigmatic postmodern tomorrow.

The notion of Los Angeles as a postmodern prototype, the "paradigm of the future," is itself already, as Mike Davis points out, a predigested myth, with both eutopian and dystopian theorists engaging the received notion of Los Angeles as "a place where everything is possible, nothing is safe and durable enough to believe in, where constant synchronicity prevails, and the automatic ingenuity of capital ceaselessly throws up new forms and spectacles" (85).[2] Yet it's exactly that distilled image of the postmodern—the postmodern as itself mediated through representation—with which southern novelists engage, in what it's tempting to call a preemptive negotiation. Theirs is a head-on encounter with a postmodernism that claims to render irrelevant the very regionalism they seek to reinvent, dismissing it as self-delusional "sentimentalization" (Jameson, *Seeds* 148). The comments of Jesse, the protagonist of Darcey Steinke's

Suicide Blonde, on arriving in Beverly Hills recapitulate Baudrillard's evocation of Los Angeles as "nothing more than an immense script and a perpetual motion picture" (353): "I found my way back into Beverly Hills, Mercedes and Porsche dealerships stood on every corner surrounded by palm trees and flowers. Tan people in pastels were radiant in the dark. Was it the soft light? The modernistic architecture? The air itself, heavily scented with smog? What made L.A. look like a touched-up photograph, like a set of actors waiting for the director to yell *Cut?*" (Steinke 177–78). This very superficiality is what Bud, in Frederick Barthelme's *The Brothers*, finds so invigorating; on the way to Los Angeles he says that he has "the California rash. Big lips, bad actresses, sex all over everybody, galactic ideas, top money—it's a wonderland" (11). For Bud, contemporary Los Angeles is a giddy celebration of the already imagined, what Umberto Eco calls "travels in hyperreality."

In terms of contemporary southern fiction, "travels in hyperreality" characterizes well the experiences of almost all of the protagonists in Los Angeles, experiences that are not always happy. Indeed, most southern fiction about California follows a basic narrative pattern of flight and return: faced with all the traditional confinements and constraints found in southern life, characters turn their eyes west to Los Angeles and the freedom and possibility that the city represents. Moving into the heart of postmodern America, these characters typically first revel in the cultural pastiche that is so alien to the southern culture of their upbringing. Freed from family, community, and history, they find the depthlessness and the immediacy of life in Los Angeles invigorating and liberating. Such liberation, however, characteristically gives way to dissatisfaction if not despair; freedom becomes isolation, liberation emptiness, immediacy meaninglessness. Eventually, the wanderers begin to look east, toward the South and home. This turning back typically represents their desire to reground themselves in place and history—what the characters had originally fled from and what is almost entirely absent in the postmodern experience. The return home, however, represents not failure but maturation. Rather than falling back into their old ways, the characters eventually remake themselves and their communities according to the newfound knowledge and strength they have gained through their journeys. Their efforts involve a merging of the postmodern spirit with the traditions of the South, a balancing of the pull toward individual freedom and liberation (to live free from history, as if an amnesiac, starting each day anew) with the demands of community and history (to have a place within a social order and to be responsible to that order).

Of course, not all contemporary southern novels about Los Angeles follow precisely the narrative pattern sketched above. There are any number of variations; some novels, for instance, start with the characters already in Los Angeles; others follow characters journeying to and settling in the city; while others show characters journeying west, driven by a vision of California, but never making it there, their dreams altered by experiences along the road. Despite these significant plot variations, almost all the works nonetheless exhibit a centripetal force toward home and community, the line heading west to the postmodern future drawing back into a circle centered, if not literally then figuratively, in the South— that is, into a configuration of community based in large part, but no longer completely, on family and history. As we have already suggested, this recentering involves the celebration not of unregenerated traditional southern culture but of a remade, transformed southern community, one more open to change, challenge, and transformation, one, in other words, that draws from rather than stonewalls postmodernity.

Of all the contemporary southern novels about Los Angeles, Tim Gautreaux's *The Next Step in the Dance* probably conforms most closely to the basic narrative pattern we've identified. The novel concerns the lives of a couple from a small Louisiana town where economic turmoil has further foreclosed already limited choices. As the marriage falls apart, Colette seeks a new life by moving to Los Angeles, saying of her dream, "I want to know people who sparkle" (23). Paul soon follows Colette out to Los Angeles, though they live apart and fashion quite different lives. Colette dives into the glamorous life of glitz and consumption; Paul gets a good-paying job but remains his down-home working man self, for the most part observing rather than participating in the world Colette covets. She goes into hock to buy a Mercedes; he drives what she calls a "brontosaurus" (85), a used Crown Victoria.

Eventually, Paul and Colette each become dissatisfied with life in Los Angeles. Paul, who has remained more grounded to his connections in Louisiana, is the better observer of the shallowness of Los Angeles's spectacle, and he comes to see life there as too perfectly crafted, too manicured. His thoughts about Los Angeles come into clear focus when he visits Forest Lawn and contrasts it to the cemetery back home in Tiger Island. He sees Forest Lawn as "a tourist attraction, the ultimate amusement park, a Disneyland of the dead" that, like the rest of Hollywood, denies ultimate realities (in this case, of the grave) by celebrating superficial glamour and celebrity. In contrast, the cemetery at Tiger Island *is* the ultimate reality, the place "where all the bullshit of life was put away in the face of a final fact, and a name of one's bloodline on a cross formed not celebrity, but a remembrance of either love or nothing, heaven or hell" (82). Colette's eventual disenchantment stems primarily from her realization that the sparkle of the people she meets is literally skin deep. She sees that the same people who "were good to look at, healthy and smart" are "restless, never satisfied. Most people she had met and spoken with seemed to be waiting for something to happen to them" (79). Before long it's the unhappiness she notices more than the glitter, so that "instead of a glamorous place full of friendly, sparkling people, she found that much of L.A. was as plain as Birmingham" (75).

Similar disenchantment about Los Angeles's promise haunts much southern fiction about California. Jesse's observation in Darcey Steinke's *Suicide Blonde* that Los Angeles appears like a touched-up photograph reflects a common premise: that Los Angeles's surface beauty masks and denies a world as dark as the noir tradition for which the city is also known. Jesse's criticism is mild compared to the comments of Delia in Dorothy Allison's *Cavedweller*. Having fled to Los Angeles to escape her abusive husband, Delia for years played with a rock-and-roll band. But the stardust in her eyes has quickly given way to grit and grime; isolated, lonely, and tired, she seeks the oblivion of drunkenness, and rarely leaves her house. When she finally decides to leave L.A. and head back to Georgia to rebuild her life, she says to a friend, "It's what I should have done years ago. I don't belong here. I never have. Whatever I loved in the music an't got nothing to do with living here. I hate Los Angeles. It's the outer goddamn circle of hell" (6). Los Angeles, she says elsewhere, is the "twilight zone" (98)—that is, a fantasy world, a place cut off from the here-and-now, a place where weird things happen. And even darker: L.A. is the end of things, the twilight of civilization.

It's actually Los Angeles as the embodiment of the apocalypse that propels Del and Jen, the protagonists of Frederick Barthelme's *Painted Desert*, to head there. They're on a screwball vigilante mission to clean up the streets of violence and mayhem and to right the wrong of a particularly disturbing assault that took place during the riots after the Rodney King trial. Before seeing a video of the L.A. riots, Del and Jen had been living fairly contentedly in their Biloxi condominium (their story begins in the companion novel, *The Brothers*), quietly getting along with their lives and spending most of their time and energy in front of the computer and television. But the riot sequences jar both of them from their complacency; once happy as consumers, they now see themselves as being consumed by an authoritarian system controlled by what they can only imagine is a vast conspiracy of the media industry and the government. Del describes their victimization as one encompassing "the tyranny of class, of gender, of sexual preference, of unrehabilitated language. If it's not one thing, it's another, for us. We're in trouble every which way we turn. We can't move. We're sealed in. We're locked out" (80).

Their trip to Los Angeles, to the heart of the beast, will change all that. It's their declaration of independence, their way of taking a stand against the system and freeing themselves from the nets of control. "We've got to do something," Jen explains. "You've got to do something or else you're just part of the shit, part of the fucking landscape. I don't want that anymore" (47–48). Neither does Del, and they set off on a road trip to L.A. They never make it there. On their trip through the desert, the vigilantes become more like tourists, enjoying the landscape. But they're not merely enjoying the landscape: they're *responding* to it. Unlike anything else they've ever seen, the landscape strikes them as completely unmediated—dazzling, stupendous, mystifying. On their trip through Dallas, Dealey Plaza looks unreal to them because it only seems real on television; the western landscape, in contrast, seems somehow so utterly real as to be beyond the scope of representation and comprehension. "There was nothing to compare it with," Del observes about Canyon de Muerto, "so nothing prepared you for what it was like to stand on the edge of the canyon and see sunlight playing on rocks jutting out of the cliff faces" (208). Looking out on Canyon de Chelly, Del says later, "redefined the world, made it more wonderful than we thought—it was like seeing the sky for the first time. Standing on the ridge overlooking the canyon, I had that sense of wonder at the color, of the space, the scale, the farmland on the canyon floor, the great power of the sheered rock—the Red Sea parted in stone" (209).

Moments like these eventually move Del and Jen to give up on their quest and begin a completely different one: a quest to return home and reconfigure their lives according to the magic and beauty they've experienced in the desert. When asked why she has changed her mind about wreaking vengeance on Los Angeles, Jen says that the world is too gorgeous to fixate on vengeance, adding that "putting one foot in the Painted Desert is more satisfying, more fulfilling, more rich and human and decent, than all the vengeance in the world. The country is making us into saints, making us feel like saints, and that's worth everything" (226). At the end of the novel, Del and Jen have decided to get married and settle down in Biloxi; if they are returning to the Sunbelt South, to a postmodern culture marked by mediation and commodification, at least they no longer feel like commodities. Ablaze with imaginative wonder, they will strive to keep that wonder alive in marriage and family and community rather than rage and anger. Los Angeles is far from their minds.

Painted Desert ends before Del and Jen get back to Biloxi, but there's nothing to suggest that they won't find the means to integrate themselves meaningfully and happily into their lives there. But this ease of reintegration is almost unique among the novels we examined, and it's tempting to see it as a by-product of the shared, even conjugal, nature of Del and Jen's quest. For most of the other travelers, the struggle to assimilate the lessons of California to the South—the reinvention of tradition, as it were—is both complicated and mediated by the highly gendered pressures and promises that sent them fleeing the South for L.A. in the first place. Del's brother, for instance, takes off for Los Angeles (in *The Brothers*) on a mid-life impulse; a former "hip young thing with loads of talent" (31), he's now constrained by what he calls "normal shrinkage . . . the law of diminished pleasures" (12). His California escapade has the air of a manic episode (Del thinks he sounds "a little too excited" [13] on the telephone), and his return, too, is characterized by mood swings: long nights glumly watching himself on videotape, frenzied afternoons of unchecked spending. Later, in *Painted Desert,* Bud recalls that in Los Angeles "everybody's gorgeous. They're all dolls. You want to do stuff to them, put parts of your body in parts of their bodies. That's what California is, right?" And he adds, "My own experience is that you begin to ejaculate when you enter the state and you don't finish until you leave" (43). The dysfunctional torpor that marks Bud's marriage when he returns is simply the flip side of this (perhaps only imagined) sexual adventurism. Only eventually, by the time *Painted Desert* takes place, do he and his wife establish a new, idiosyncratic balance, one that acknowledges and acquiesces in his aging, the fact that, as he says glumly in *The Brothers*, he is no longer a sexual "player" (257). California has been a symbolic mechanism through which he tortuously negotiates his own diminished potency.

For female southerners (particularly those drawn by female writers) the eroticized promise of California proves particularly illusory, and reintegration often protracted and arduous. These female characters tend to flee not only specific and individualized frustrations but the structural limitations placed on them by traditional southern constructions of femininity. Women like Colette in *The Next Step in the Dance*, Delia in *Cavedweller,* and Jesse in *Suicide Blonde* all seek in California an alternative to bleak and narrow futures as wife, mother, daughter, futures that promise only to replay what they see as southern women's bleak and narrow past. But for each the sexual empowerment she hoped for from California proves cruelly and ironically double-edged, and for each the return east will involve a reintegration and renegotiation of the very roles she fled.

Perhaps the most emblematic figure here, not although but because she never reaches California, is Luna, the heroine of Doris Betts's *The Sharp Teeth of Love*, who heads west with her self-centered boyfriend, trying to convince herself that "in California she would be tanned, gleeful" (52). As it becomes clear that the ideal marriage to unfold in California is exclusively a masculine ideal ("With a wife like you I'll probably go up the ranks faster," her boyfriend says [30]), Luna flees up into the Sierra Nevada. Guiding her is the minatory presence of Tamsen Donner of the doomed Donner party—the last to be eaten, a woman who could have escaped her fate but stayed behind with her sick husband ("for love? Self-sacrifice? Stupidity?" Luna muses [74]). An illusion to dispel the illusion of California, Tamsen serves as a signpost to deflect Luna from a place where she, too, will be cannibalized for her devotion. At novel's end, Luna is headed back east with a patchwork, self-assembled family, preparing to invent domesticity with new rules.

For most of the heroines of these novels, however, the glitter of California takes time to dissipate, and the illusion of liberation and empowerment is only gradually withdrawn. Delia's journey is the stuff of dreams, at least at first: leaving her abusive husband, she impulsively hops on a rock-and-roll tour bus, takes up with the group's leader, and joins the band as a singer. But we've already noted how unhappy she becomes. Life on the road with the band and in Los Angeles is less liberating than directionless; and when her relationship fades after she bears the rock star's daughter, her lot isn't much better than that of the average cast-off groupie. She endures the boring days and nights with the help of alcohol. "Delia got drunk on the road the same way she did on whiskey," the narrator observes, "a gentle drunk, an easy binge, smiling and loose and careless as death on two legs" (Allison 16). Delia sums up her years away with the simple statement, "I was drunk almost all the time I was in California" (97). While Colette does not sink as low as Delia, never quite feeling like "death on two legs," she's certainly uncomfortable socially and sexually in Los Angeles, even as she tries to maintain her dream of "sparkle." For one thing, her pursuit of sexual adventure is never as wholehearted as Delia's; although she has come to Los Angeles in part to free herself from the constraints of marriage and start anew, Colette feels no desire to romp with her friends in the bedroom. It's just not her way of life. Yet she comes to see that most of the people she knows regard sex, in terms of emotional and psychological import, on the same level as exercise or hobbies—and like those activities, sex is harnessed and subordinated to the drive for success. Significantly, the crisis in California that sends her packing comes when she is propositioned by her boss, who makes it clear that her future with the company depends on her lying down with him. So much for empowerment.

As in *The Brothers*, Colette's and Paul's return from Los Angeles seems to signal at first a deepening of heterosexual dysfunction, as if the lessons of California have to be digested, with queasy difficulty, over time. Paul describes himself as "a broken-down pioneer who couldn't take the frontier anymore" (Gautreaux 133); and broken, too, is the town to which they return, as if it reflects the state of their relationship. Despite her treatment in California's corporate world, Colette brings its practices and attitudes home, first involving herself with the flashy entrepreneur Bucky Tyler, then driving herself with an almost obsessive ambition to succeed as a businesswoman. Both of these phases diminish and emasculate Paul—the first physically (Bucky leaves him critically injured), the second psychically. The pendulum of power in their relationship oscillates wildly, unsettlingly, seeking some sort of balance, which is achieved at last when Colette weds her business acumen to the traditional Tiger Island structures of family loyalty, reintegrating both her relationship with Paul and the broader community. At the end of the novel, just as the whistle of a train heading west—which, for Colette, once symbolized escape—has become an integral part of the sounds of the Tiger Island night, so, too, have her ambitions become part of a reinvented partnership, a reinvented community.

If part of Colette's challenge is, in a sense, to rewrite the rules for marriage by bringing something of California home, Delia's challenge is far more daunting: to reinvent herself as mother. To do this she needs to merge her California daughter, Cissy, and the two girls she left behind into a new and vital community. But she faces an uphill battle; no one is in a forgiving mood when she shows up back in Cayro, Georgia. The first words she hears come from a waitress who welcomes her with "You that bitch ran off and left her babies" (Allison 39); and the town at large considers her "the fallen woman, the whore of Babylon, the bitch-whelp who had abandoned her young" (76). Her family is just about as unforgiving. Her grandfather tells her flat out, "You can't just waltz back into Cayro and think you gonna get what you want" (51). Eventually Delia does get what she wants—forgiveness and acceptance by the town, custody of her children, and a place within a supportive and nurturing family and community—but only after years of effort, including working hard, staying put, and raising her daughters as part of a varied and supportive network of women. Indeed, it's not until people realize that by returning to her children Delia is facing up to rather than downplaying her past that they can accept her. The town is better for this acceptance, as Delia in many ways represents Cayro's future, both in terms of the strength and energy she brings to it, and in terms of the change she has ushered in through her reintegration, a reintegration that has broken down the town's closed-mindedness and resistance to adaptation.

For Jesse, in Darcey Steinke's *Suicide Blonde*, motherhood—engulfing motherhood—is the essence of the Virginia she's trying to escape. Although Jesse has, on the surface, simply fled a dull suburban life for what she perceives as California's bohemian freedom, the novel makes it clear that both the impetus for her escape and the mechanisms of her disillusionment involve her need to resist being her mother's daughter. Indeed, early in the novel, Jesse remembers her mother's body while staring into the mirror at her own, just as her mother's voice chimes incessantly in her head a litany of the humiliations a woman can expect (marriage, betrayal, bitterness). These ongoing intrusions into her consciousness mock her intention to reinvent herself, and it's obvious that her dreams have already soured: "I felt as suspicious about bohemians as I did about professionals in upscale restaurants or suburbanites who catatonically roamed the malls of Palo Alto. I had come here to be different with all the others, but it wasn't working. Maybe it had to do with sheer numbers. It was easy to convince myself in Virginia that I was an interesting person, but here I was no different than other women. I couldn't help thinking that thirty years earlier we'd be married, cooking, knitting, arranging furniture—raising a family. Don't misunderstand me, there are obsessed and brilliant women artists in San Francisco. It was just that coming here made me realize I wasn't one of them" (80).

Oscillating between romantic illusion and self-abasement, Jesse is struggling to keep hold of her boyfriend, Bell, a bisexual man who has sunk into despair over the pending marriage of one of his former male lovers. In the brief time span of the novel, she moves through a sordid world of sexual manipulation, betrayal, and abuse; she is sexually assaulted by a stranger, experiments with prostitution, and discovers Bell's body in the bathtub, dead by his own hand. The relentless sexual drive of the novel becomes self-cancelling, reflecting the nihilism that Jesse comes to see underlying California's easy tolerance and sexual freedom. "I knew adultery was O.K., as was homosexuality and prostitution, but what about incest and older people taking advantage of younger ones?" she asks at one point. "What about murder and cannibalism? It all made me uneasy because I could foresee being able to understand almost anything" (129).

Crucial to Jesse's questionings is her attraction to a domineering prostitute named Madison who flaunts overwhelming sexual power. For Jesse,

Madison stands at the opposite extreme from the sexual propriety preached by her mother, and thus she is transfixed by Madison's manipulation of sex and power. "I liked how she treated her sexuality—like a long distance runner," Jesse comments at one point. "Love wasn't important, endurance was all. What could it be like to live with those stretched and skewed standards?" (107). Jesse's fascination with Madison, who knows "a million ways to kill off the soft parts of yourself" (82), is tied to her unacknowledged quest for self-mutilation as a means of differentiating herself, her own pain, her own body, from her mother's. Just as Madison tries to forget herself and bond with her own murdered mother by "forcing [her] body into extreme situations" (135), Jesse tries to punish the body that is never entirely her own, echoing Madison's dictum that "to devastate yourself is somehow life-affirming" (121).

Eventually, however, Jesse realizes that coldness and cruelty lie at the heart of Madison; she's driven more by hate than anything else, and she relishes inflicting pain and humiliation. In one particularly terrifying scene, Jesse witnesses her fisting a john, sex quickly giving way to torture. Jesse watches the john writhe in agony as Madison digs deeper into him, observing that Madison "was concentrating now, reaching her fingers up toward his heart. *She wants his heart,* I thought, *because she doesn't have one of her own*" (142). Once thinking Madison the opposite of her mother, she comes to see them as cut from the same cloth. Madison "was similar to my mother, both believed that hate was sustaining," Jesse concludes. "They each had a well-developed sense of doom and were convinced it was unresolvable, convinced the only way to lessen their pain was to pass it on to others" (137).

Jesse's reconfiguration of Madison mirrors her eventual reconfiguration of California and what she had once thought of as its bohemian glamour. In a significant passage, she tries to digest her feelings of confusion.

> San Francisco confounded me. First it seemed utopian, with the blue skies, pervasive Mediterranean light, palm trees, organic vegetable stores that sold strawberry juice, the children in funky handmade sweaters. But all that was an overlay—misleading and cosmetic. Underneath was a history of decadence: the opium dens in Chinatown, the thousand whores who worked the gold rush, the voodoo and witchcraft shops. Even the fast-moving fog was nightmarish. There were leather monsters fucking dogs and each other in the alleyways of SoMa and the living dead haunting the Castro cafes. Sure, there were hippies gentle and peace-loving, but there was also the

Manson family, the SLA and the Jim Jones Kool-Aid test. And California is the outpost of rigid conservatism . . . the home of Nixon and Reagan. Satanists are in the hills, chanting Latin, drinking urine, forcing candles into the tops of rotten deer heads. And, of course, there was Hollywood, the mimetic desire capital of the world. (118–19)

Jesse's awareness of the secret history of California, as her words here suggest, leads her to larger understanding also of her own secret history, the desires that drove her to California searching for a separate self and a way to live.

Yet the end of *Suicide Blonde*, like those of so many other contemporary southern novels about California, suggests that those desires may be best achieved by a return home, a suggestion that's given imaginative resonance in one stunning final image. Confronted by Bell's dead body, Jesse embraces his death as a sacrifice that mitigates her own need for self-abasement. Her life stretches out before her in an arc of possibility: "My life fans out like a string of paper dolls. I am malleable, chameleonlike. Each life eats the last until I'm a Russian doll, containing ten women of decreasing size" (191). The image reverses the claustrophobic spectre of the maternal body that has dominated the book; now, Jesse bears her own lives within herself, as if also containing her mother and her female ancestors down through the generations. Bearing the past within herself, she can return to a Virginia reconfigured as a place of sexual temptation (like California) but also of fecundity, "where you can feel the water in the pages of a book and the light rain makes the leaves as tender as skin" (191). "I will plant a rose garden," she says, "and I will wait in that garden for the flick of the snake's tongue that will change me again" (191). She will reinvent her destiny as daughter, this image suggests, by becoming a mother herself.

All of these women use California to reinvent themselves, their particular versions of the South, and the gendered roles they play within them. But there is also some suggestion in these novels that a reciprocal movement may exist, that the lessons of a reintegrated community may come full circle to offer renewed possibility and purpose within even Los Angeles itself. Dorothy Allison's *Cavedweller*, for example, ends with Delia's daughter Cissy poised to return to Los Angeles with Rosemary, an African American woman whose friendship has been essential in helping the family reconfigure itself. As Delia's best friend, Rosemary represents a link to Cissy's heritage, to the South, and to the newly revivified community she leaves behind. Rather than abjuring traditional bonds in her journey west, Cissy will carry with her connections newly reforged not by destiny but by choice, her sense of possibility emboldened not by illusions alone but by a vital link with the past.

A similar sense of promise marks Ann Patchett's *The Magician's Assistant*, certainly the most affirming of the novels under discussion here, which also underscores the tendency of these novels to locate possible fulfillment within the realm of the homosocial. The novel opens after the death from AIDS of two members of an unconventional household: Parsifal, Sabine's gay husband; and Phan, his male lover. Sabine looks back with deep, reverent nostalgia at her unconsummated love for Parsifal and the profound love all three of them shared—yet it's clear that she is repressing the extent to which she remained, and still remains, unawakened and unfulfilled. The novel follows Sabine's deepening relationship with Parsifal's estranged family, whom she goes to visit in Nebraska after she befriends his mother and sister, when they travel to Los Angeles upon hearing of his death. Sabine's visit to Nebraska and her uncovering of Parsifal's troubled past, which he has kept hidden through both silence and deception, lead her to a deeper understanding of the man she loved and the reasons behind his willful effort to erase his history. Parsifal's childhood, Sabine eventually learns, was treacherous and painful: he suffered under an abusive father (whom he eventually killed, defending his mother), and he was homosexual in a small, unforgiving town. If he were to survive, that is, survive as the person he was, he needed to escape Nebraska. Parsifal's mother explains to Sabine the fishbowl dynamics of the town, saying that because the town is small and everyone knows each other, to be different means to be an outsider; moreover, a person's identity is established early on and everyone knows it. One can never start over again; to do that means leaving Nebraska behind.

Sabine's imaginative reconstruction of Parsifal's youth sparks her to see how Los Angeles beckoned to him. "Why wouldn't Los Angeles be the promised land?" she asks herself. "Suddenly to have the privilege of wearing your own skin, the headlong rush of love, the loss of the knife-point of loneliness. That was the true life, the one you would admit to. Why even mention the past? It was not his past. He was a changeling, separated at birth from his own identity" (39). And she also comes to understand, as Parsifal's mother does, why Parsifal buried his past once he got to Los Angeles and started anew: "Parsifal, her friend, her husband, had made himself a happy life like someone else would make a seaworthy boat, following step by careful step. The past was no longer his past and it slid away from him like an anchor, unattached, to the mossy darkness of the ocean floor. She had watched him sleep for years, seen his face the first moment he opened his eyes, and she knew he was not troubled by dreams. This was Sabine's comfort, her joy: Parsifal had gotten away. He was in the boat that saved his life, the boat that was Los Angeles" (175).

There are suggestions sprinkled throughout the novel that as wondrous as Parsifal's transformation in Los Angeles was, he perhaps took forgetting too far, that in burying the past so deeply he could never achieve the forgiveness and reconciliation that are the final fruits of pain and suffering. To a question about how much she thinks about her painful past in pre–World War II Poland, Sabine's mother says, "Only enough not to forget it completely. The trick is to almost forget it, but not completely" (281). That may be the mean that Patchett endorses, a mean that allows people to remake themselves, with eyes on the future, without completely losing themselves and their pasts in the remaking. This appears to be the path that Sabine and Kitty, Parsifal's sister, are taking at the end of the novel. The two have become deeply and physically attached, and when Sabine leaves for home, Kitty will join her. As Los Angeles did for Parsifal years before, the city beckons, offering the two a place. "In Southern California there was very little that went unsaid," Sabine observes. "People lived their lives, heads up, in the bright sun. Take it or leave it" (193).

Unlike Parsifal, Sabine redeems rather than obliterates the past in her return west. Like Cissy in *Cavedweller*, she carries the connection with her in the person of Kitty, who is not just Parsifal's sister but his look-alike. In forging a bond with her, Sabine redeems not only the lost promise of her own past but the breaks and ruptures of Parsifal's. Moreover, as does *Cavedweller*, the novel lets us glimpse a vision of Los Angeles itself redeemed, rescued from superficiality and atomism by local infusions of community. The polarities of journey and return in novels like *The Next Step in the Dance* are here both reinforced and reversed; using the California experience to revivify one's childhood community (as Sabine does for Parsifal's family and as Delia does for Cayro) allows one to reground Los Angeles in history. If Los Angeles attracts discontented southerners because of its postmodern waning of historicity, then, these novels all finally suggest that to cast off one's past and to start anew cannot serve as an end in itself. Eventually the wanderers west must reinvent themselves through the process of rerooting themselves—whether back in the South, or in Los Angeles itself, rewriting tradition through the salutary filter of a destabilizing postmodernity. At a time when globalization threatens to render southernness itself obsolete—when, in Michael Kreyling's words, "for better or worse, there is . . . no recourse to the totalizing and totally authoritative referent: capitalism, patriarchy, the novel, the South" (155)—

these southern writers engage in a dialectic with postmodernism, seeking to reconfigure regionalism as more than "a compensatory ideology" (Jameson, *Seeds* 148). They escape the trap of regionalist self-parody to which postmodern theorists would consign them by interrogating postmodernism on its own symbolic turf—Los Angeles.

NOTES

1. See most particularly Richard Slotkin's trilogy of the mythology of the frontier: *Regeneration through Violence: The Mythology of the American Frontier, 1600–1860*; *The Fatal Environment: The Myth of the Frontier in the Age of Industrialism, 1800–1890*; and *Gunfighter Nation: The Myth of the Frontier in Twentieth-Century America*.

2. Paul Patton describes the cities of postmodernist discourse as "imaginary cities," "complex objects which include both realities and their descriptions: cities confused with the words used to describe them" (112). That both these urban realities and, as Mike Davis points out, their paradigmatic "retranslations" (87) have starkly different references and resonances for African Americans may also help to explain why this remapping through Los Angeles remains primarily a white phenomenon among southern writers. Although two significant southern African American writers, Alice Walker and Ernest Gaines, now live in California (at least for half a year), their most important work remains embedded in the South and the southern experience. In terms of literary inspiration, a number of contemporary African American writers appear to be looking not west but south—to the Spanish Americas—particularly in their use of magical realism, as seen in the work of Toni Morrison and Randall Kenan.

WORKS CITED

Allison, Dorothy. *Cavedweller.* New York: Dutton, 1998.

Barthelme, Frederick. *The Brothers.* New York: Viking, 1993.

——. *Painted Desert.* New York: Viking, 1995.

Baudrillard, Jean. "The Precession of Simulacra." *A Postmodern Reader.* Ed. Joseph Natoli and Linda Hutcheon. Albany: State U of New York P, 1993. 342–75.

Betts, Doris. *The Sharp Teeth of Love.* New York: Simon, 1997.

Brinkmeyer, Robert H., Jr. *Remapping Southern Literature: Contemporary Southern Writers and the West.* Athens: U of Georgia P, 2000.

Davis, Mike. *City of Quartz: Excavating the Future in Los Angeles.* New York: Random, 1992.

Eco, Umberto. *Travels in Hyperreality.* New York: Harcourt, Brace, 1986.

Faulkner, William. *Go Down, Moses.* 1942. New York: Vintage, 1990.

Gautreaux, Tim. *The Next Step in the Dance.* New York: Picador, 1998.

Jameson, Fredric. "The Cultural Logic of Late Capitalism." *Postmodernism, or, The Cultural Logic of Late Capitalism.* Durham, N.C.: Duke UP, 1991. 1–54.

——. *The Seeds of Time.* New York: Columbia UP, 1994.

Kreyling, Michael. *Inventing Southern Literature.* Jackson: UP of Mississippi, 1998.

Patchett, Ann. *The Magician's Assistant.* New York: Harcourt, Brace, 1997.

Patton, Paul. "Imaginary Cities of Postmodernity." *Postmodern Cities and Spaces.* Ed. Sophie Watson and Katherine Gibson. Cambridge, Mass.: Blackwell, 1995. 112–21.

Rodriguez, Richard. "True West: Relocating the Horizon of the American Frontier." *Harper's* September 1996: 37–46.

Steinke, Darcey. *Suicide Blonde.* New York: Atlantic Monthly, 1992.

Welty, Eudora. *The Golden Apples.* New York: Harcourt, Brace, 1949.

In modern life the movies are what
most other forms of art have ceased to
be, not an adornment but a necessity.

—ERWIN PANOFSKY, "Style and
Medium in the Motion Pictures"

LOIS PARKINSON ZAMORA

American Films/American Fantasies:

Moviegoing and Regional Identity

in Literature of the Americas

Michael Wood, English critic and cultural
commentator, has remarked that "movies matter a lot to contemporary Latin
American writers" (43–44). He cites the involvement in filmmaking or
film criticism, and/or the fictive uses of cinematic material of Jorge Luis
Borges, Guillermo Cabrera Infante, Carlos Fuentes, Gabriel García Márquez, and Manuel Puig. For these and other Latin American writers,
continues Wood, the movies "combine the fan's pleasure with the technician's interest, and suggest an ideal apprenticeship in fantasy—or more
precisely in the art of connecting fantasy to the world. Hollywood, and
the French and German film industries, were dream factories for Latin
America" (44). Such an assertion compels agreement, and it remains as
relevant now as it was in 1980, when Wood first made it.

Nonetheless, the comparatist may hesitate for a moment to wonder
whether the movies have mattered any less to U.S. writers and, more
specifically, whether Hollywood has fueled the fantasies of writers of the
U.S. South. I will approach this question in the first section of my essay by
comparing the intertextual use of movies in *The Moviegoer* (1960), by the

Louisiana writer Walker Percy, and *La traición de Rita Hayworth* (*Betrayed by Rita Hayworth*) (1968), by the Argentine writer Manuel Puig. Central to each novel are accounts of stylized or fantastical or otherwise counterrealistic movies that are removed from the characters' worlds in a million different ways, and yet also reflect the very image of their desires. The disjunction between reality and fantasy drives plot and characterization, and it allows the authors to measure the capacity of the novel to encompass disparate modes of imagining. For, despite the great differences between the provincial Argentina of the 1930s portrayed by Puig and the New Orleans of the 1950s created by Percy, the problem of correlating incompatible cultural languages—or, as Michael Wood puts it, "of connecting fantasy to the world," is the principal thematic and structural concern of both novels. In my first section, I will pay close attention to the narrative mechanisms that facilitate the connection.

In my second section, I will propose some comparative generalizations about the social function of films in the U.S. South and in Latin America. If Wood can assert that movies "matter a lot" to Latin American writers, and I can wonder whether movies matter any less to U.S. writers, then surely one could also wonder how the movies matter to their audiences and to the communities in which those audiences live and work and dream. There is voluminous published discussion of the contents of particular Latin American films, the artistry of particular Latin American directors and cinematographers, the life stories of this actor or that actress, and so on. There is, however, surprisingly little research on the social function of film in Latin America, whether on the political and cultural purposes for which movies are created or the audiences for which they are intended or the ways in which they are imported, marketed, distributed, and consumed by their audiences.[1]

More research on these questions has been done in the United States than in Latin America, often in the service of better marketing but also because film courses are now standard aspects of university curricula. A textbook such as John Belton's *American Cinema/American Culture* does offer a historical and cultural overview of themes, trends, audiences, and artists throughout U.S. film history. However, southern regional culture is not listed in the index or treated as a separate category in this otherwise comprehensive study, for despite its unique history and culture, the South is not distinguished from other regions in the United States in terms of its moviegoing patterns, much less in terms of southern writers' investment in the cinematic medium. "The South" is not indexed in *American Cinema/American Culture*, but "race," "class," and "civil rights" are. Given the South's particular relationship to the history of oppression in the United States, we can expect to find relevant information under these topics, as we might (were they listed, which they are not) under such topics as "slavery," "confederacy," or "civil war." But the aim of my essay is larger than these historical categories, even as it also includes them.

For information on the comparative structures of American regional cultures, literature by writers who write *in* and *about* these regions serves as a rich resource, in particular that produced by Latin American and U.S. southern writers who concern themselves with the relations of film and literature in the context of cultural self-definition. And in my third section, I will expand the definition of Southern literature from a geographical category to a conceptual one. If, as we will see, Walker Percy can propose that a "moviegoer" does not necessarily go to the movies, I will propose, in parallel fashion, that a "southern" writer does not necessarily come from the South. The South is a state of mind, and writers who write insightfully *about* the South belong to this region as surely as writers who write from *within* it.[2] Harlem-born writer James Baldwin and Oklahoman Ralph Ellison are prime examples, and are among the best literary observers I know of films about Southern regional identity. My conceptual expansion of the South will allow me to be more inclusive than I could otherwise be, and it will also allow me to speculate on *how* movies matter, and matter differently, in these various American spaces.

In my conclusion, I will continue to breach geographical parameters and wonder why movies have mattered (to use Michael Wood's term once more) in *many* regions of the world where communities are engaged in defining themselves culturally, politically, and socially. My final speculations on postcolonial literature will lead me to consider the *function* assigned by communities to their various art forms, particularly literature and film. These final comments are intended to mitigate the imbalance of my comparisons between writers from a single region of the United States and writers from countries and cultures across Latin America, Central America, and the Caribbean. Asymmetry is not unusual in comparative studies of American literature, given the diversity of cultural communities in the hemisphere, but it would be an oversight not to acknowledge the geographical and cultural imbalance of my essay. I will do so by wondering more broadly what film offers to writers, communities, and individual moviegoers everywhere who find themselves engaged in the processes of self-definition I describe below.

The Moviegoer, Walker Percy's first novel, takes place during one week in the life of John Bickerson Bolling, alias Binx, who lives in a suburb of

New Orleans, works as a stockbroker, and is generally alienated from the society in which he lives and from values or a sense of purpose that might give his life meaning. He often goes to the movies, for only there does he perceive the significance that escapes him in his own experience. The epigraph of the novel is a statement by Søren Kierkegaard from *The Sickness Unto Death* (1849): "The specific character of despair is precisely this: it is unaware of being despair." Binx does, in fact, become progressively self-aware as the third-person linear narrative proceeds according to the conventions of the nineteenth-century European bildungsroman. Binx's developing relationship to the movies structures his sentimental education.

Manuel Puig's first novel, *Betrayed by Rita Hayworth*, also focuses on a young moviegoer. Like Percy's character, Puig's character Toto senses acutely his alienation from the prevailing values of his society and looks to the movies for answers that are not apparent to him elsewhere in his culture. Toto is portrayed from infancy to fifteen years of age in sixteen discontinuous chapters, rendered by many different narrators in widely divergent styles. Only three chapters are narrated directly by Toto (or rather two: one is a school essay, "La película que más me gustó" ["My Favorite Movie"]), but the other narrators know Toto, and they provide information about him from their various points of view. Unlike Binx, Toto ends as he began: a consumer of contradictory cultural languages that he is incapable of reconciling.[3] Only in a much later (and better-known) novel, *El beso de la mujer araña* (1976; *Kiss of the Spider Woman*), does Puig concede the possibility that moviegoing may create meaningful communities, no matter what the actual content of the movies may be.

In *Betrayed by Rita Hayworth* and *The Moviegoer* the structural tensions created by contradictory cultural languages generate their meaning. The dialectical play between these languages can be usefully approached by means of semiotic analysis.[4] Semiotics is generally concerned with systems of signification and communication, and with the relation between languages of description and that which is described; sign systems, whether verbal or articulated via other cultural "texts"—movies, sports, fashion, food—are the proper subject of semiotics. Verbal language, termed a "natural" system by semioticians, is interconnected with most other sign systems on which the "artificial" or secondary sign systems of culture are built. Secondary sign systems model reality "linguistically," but also in other ways. The concept of secondary modeling systems has been developed most notably by Juri M. Lotman, who argues in *The Structure of the Artistic Text* that such secondary systems transpose the level of content of the primary system, thereby creating a new level of content, which is the meaning of the text as a whole.[5]

The first system in any work of literature is, of course, the verbal narrative. In *The Moviegoer* and *Betrayed by Rita Hayworth* this first system points relentlessly to a secondary system of visual signs—the movies that Binx and Toto absorb insatiably, albeit beyond the view of the reader. In the relationship between reader and printed word inheres another (invisible) relation between moviegoer and movie outside the primary system of signs.[6] Not only must this secondary system exist for the characters of the novels but for the reader as well: the circle of representation must be closed by the reader's act of supplying the absent cinematic sign system. (Whether the reader has seen the specific movies to which the characters in both novels refer does not matter to Percy or Puig; it is the act of conjuring and assigning significance that is important.) Both novels oscillate, then, between the interior of the printed text and a world exterior to that text, between the "real" worlds of Vallejos and New Orleans and "fictional" worlds peopled by Rita Hayworth, William Holden, et al. Of course, the opposition of these systems occurs within the single system of the novel itself, so that the conflicting codes may be said to be integrated by the novelist's own narrative efforts; it may further be said that the novel, like the movies and in fact all art, translates the phenomena of life into an aesthetic idiom that is necessarily removed in its own way from Vallejos or New Orleans or whatever other world it should choose to depict. Within each novel, it is this very disjunction between the experiential reality encoded in the verbal text and the worlds projected by the conventional images of the silver screen that results in the betrayal, not only of Toto, as the title of Puig's novel suggests, but, at least temporarily, of Binx Bolling in *The Moviegoer* as well.

This tension between signifying systems is the primary structuring device of both novels and is essential to the portrayal of the main characters and their search for self-definition. Binx emphatically separates his own world of tedious "everydayness" from the heightened reality of the movies, and Toto, while considerably younger and unable to distinguish between the two as Binx does, nonetheless intuitively opposes the sordid reality of Vallejos to the celluloid visions of Ginger Rogers and Fred Astaire dancing on air or of Shirley Temple who, Toto thinks with longing, is always good and always loved by everyone. The films to which Binx and Toto refer are in fact attractive to them (and selected by the novelists) precisely because of their distance from life, their formulaic romanticism. Binx prefers such bland screen icons as Jane Powell, William Holden, and Rory Calhoun, ignoring more individualized actors and actresses from the same period such as James Dean or Marilyn Monroe. Toto has similar tastes, though his choices are less self-conscious and less freely made than Binx's: Toto specifically rejects Myrna Loy in favor of Olivia de Haviland and Luise Rainer; the more realistic 1930s films of, say, James Cagney or Bette Davis, which might in fact create characters and situations not altogether removed from experience, are never mentioned.[7]

The relationship between the verbal sign system in each of these novels and the world that it signifies is based on *similarity*: both Percy and Puig create verbal descriptions that are understood by readers to resemble their referent—Vallejos, New Orleans. In contrast, the relationship between the cinematographic sign systems and the worlds they represent are described by the authors (and understood by the reader) to be based on counterrealistic stereotypes. The separation of the two signifying systems within the novels is important because Binx and Toto attempt to use one system to transform the other, or as is more often the case, to use one system to escape from the other, and it is precisely the disparity between codes that allows this. Binx, when most overwhelmed by a society that is "dead, dead, dead," must lose himself in the "resplendent reality" of a movie, because only a movie can "certify" reality, that is, give it authenticity and meaning. Toto, for his part, perpetually casts himself and his acquaintances in movie roles: that his whole life is a fabric of film clichés only attests to the gulf separating his own experience from cinematic reality. This gulf between image and actuality presupposes a cinematic reality that is impenetrable to the naked eye but quite accessible to the camera. Of course, reality is always "defamiliarized" by art, to use Viktor Shklovsky's word, but art does *not* always imply an alienation from or devaluation of reality, as do the movies in these novels. For Binx and Toto, artistic and extra-artistic space are separated by an insuperable barrier that consoles, even anesthetizes, while it betrays.

That historical meaning should somehow inhere in the space between the two systems, in the very incongruity between the movie's text and the character's context, suggests a paradoxical process that may be described as the "sanctification" of unintelligible texts. The unintelligibility of texts from which an elevated degree of truth is expected is familiar in religious ceremonial language, prophetic utterance, fortunetellers' dicta, doctors' discourse to their patients, legal documents, literary criticism (at times), and other disciplinary discourses. Often, textual significance grows as the text's common linguistic meaning is suppressed, as the text comes to require translation or interpretation for the uninitiated. Particularly for the young Toto, the movies' distance from everyday utterance—their very inaccessibility—facilitates his brilliant textual interpretations (and imag-

inative elaborations) of certain films: nothing in his own world of Vallejos so inspires him. Beyond the obvious cultural distance between Hollywood and Vallejos is the fact that many of the films Toto sees are musicals
in which the songs would not have been translated into Spanish, even if
the rest of the movie were dubbed. Thus the unintelligible melodic language of these films is that much more distanced from the monotony—
both literal and figurative—of Vallejos.

There are two possible directions in which this process of sanctification may move: such unintelligible texts may be repeated endlessly, ac-
cruing meaning as they circulate in the collective, or they may be repeated
until all possibility of meaning has been obviated, until meaning has been
superseded by function. Toto clearly seeks to participate in the former
process, to enliven the cinematic texts as he discusses them over and over
with family and playmates and reruns them repeatedly in his own mind.
The reader sees, however, that it is in fact the second tendency that
operates in Vallejos: with repeated abuse, archetypes become clichés,
unintelligible texts merely meaningless.

Of the characters' self-delusions based on the incessant outpourings of
the Hollywood dream machine, none are more obvious than those that
betray them in their search for sexual definition. Binx invokes movie
stars almost exclusively when he is with women, with his "Marcias and
Lindas," over whom he seeks the same easy mastery that is always available to Rock or Gregory or Rory. He uses his repertoire of film icons to
screen himself off from experience, for when he finds himself coming
close to real emotion, it is movie stars and their experiences rather than
his own that occupy his thoughts. In fact, it is when he cannot avoid
acknowledging the failure of his icons in his one serious sexual relationship that he manages to transcend his delusions and deal directly with his
own individual experience in specific terms.[8]

Toto's betrayal is more serious. His unrecognized homosexuality is
radically at odds with Hollywood's version of romance (although it is the
reader rather than the character who sees the conflict as such). Toto's
sensibility and his preference for activities considered feminine have totally alienated him from his father, who is as deluded by his cultural code
of machismo as Toto is by the sentimentality of the movies. It is a great
irony that Toto's father is considered to be a dead ringer for Carlos Palau,
an Argentine movie star, when he marries Toto's mother. Toto never sees
the resemblance and in fact specifically substitutes other men for his
father in his cinema-inspired fantasies. Symbolic of the incomprehension
between Toto and his father is Toto's preference for Luise Rainer "que
hace siempre de buena que todos la embroman" (*Traición* 81) ["because

she's always playing the good one who everybody's always cheating" (*Betrayed* 64)], whereas Toto's father likes Rita Hayworth best because "hace traiciones" (88) ["she's always betraying somebody" (69)].[9] When his father refuses to answer Toto's questions about why he prefers a star who uses love as a tool of power, Toto cries bitterly.

Puig's suggestion that one must choose between Luise Rainer and Rita Hayworth—that love is necessarily a question of domination and submission, of victim and victimizer—seems to be one of the few points where the movies and life in Vallejos coincide. Unfortunately for Toto, his choice of Luise Rainer in the movies does not eliminate Rita Hayworth from the world in which he lives. Unlike Binx, Toto does not mature into an understanding that the movies can only alienate him further from his own sexual identity. In his essay, written at the age of fourteen, about a movie entitled *The Great Waltz* (a romanticized version of the life of Johann Strauss), Toto identifies with the hero of the movie, casting himself as the adored macho man with powerful chest, strong shoulders, and muscular arms, ready to defend the "weaker sex" whenever necessary. Toto's contempt for his own "femininity"—which Puig conveys as sublimated self-hatred—provides an ironic subtext to his school essay and to his moviegoing generally.

Clearly, both Binx and Toto are romantics in the sense that they are alienated from their societies and long for an unattainable realm that life cannot provide but that the movies can. Both are described in these terms. A friend of Toto's writes of him that he is "always asking the impossible," and Binx, in describing a man on a bus who is reading Stendhal's *The Charterhouse of Parma*, describes himself as well: "He has just begun to suffer from it, this miserable trick the romantic plays upon himself: of setting just beyond his reach the very thing he prizes. . . . He is a moviegoer, though of course he does not go to the movies" (Percy, *Moviegoer* 171). The moviegoer, then, is one for whom life must imitate an imagined ideal, and it follows, in Percy's formulation, that the moviegoer can only suffer the loss of this imagined ideal. In their dependence on cinematic images of desire, Binx and Toto resemble Don Quixote, Madame Bovary, and the governess in Henry James's "The Turn of the Screw," characters who use codes chosen because they are distinct from their own experience (chivalric romance, sentimental and gothic novels) to transcend, however temporarily and unsuccessfully, the worlds described realistically in the novels. More recent fictional predecessors are the characters in Nathanael West's *The Day of the Locust*, who live lives of celluloid fantasy in the midst of the appalling artificiality of Hollywood itself during the 1930s; that West sensed as acutely as Puig and Percy the danger of betrayal inherent in such fantasy is suggested by the original title of his novel, *The Cheated*.[10]

A moviegoer, in Percy's terms, cannot distinguish among realms of experience. Because of the characters' romanticism as I have described it, the cinematic illusions that seem so patently factitious to the reader, especially at some decades' remove, offer the promise of fulfillment to Binx and Toto. The reader understands the self-delusion of the characters: the deceptions of the movies are perceived by the reader even while the characters find them wholly desirable. The circle of representation is closed by visual icons external to the verbal text, but the icons seen in the reader's mind signify very different things from those seen by the characters in the theaters of Vallejos and New Orleans; thus, semiotic strata are themselves stratified as their various "consumers" invest them with meaning. That the same cultural texts are made to contain such different information simultaneously is the primary source of the irony that pervades both novels.

Useful to our thinking about the differences between verbal and visual sign systems is Juri M. Lotman's essay entitled "The Structure of the Narrative Text," in which Lotman contrasts the two systems: "The first means of constructing the narrative text is well known and consists of basing it on natural language: [discrete] wordsigns are united in a chain according to a specific language's rules and the message's content. The second method has the so-called iconic signs as its most prevalent manifestation, and yet it cannot be reduced to the question of mimesis" (193). Like words, iconic signs may serve as the basis of narration, but Lotman distinguishes between the narrative structures of the two in this way: verbal narrative is *spatial* in structure whereas visual narrative is *temporal*—an illustration or series of illustrations over time. A novel is constructed by adding new elements (words, phrases, paragraphs, chapters), that is, by expanding the space of the text, whereas a movie consists in a transformation of one image, a successive combination of elements in time. Lotman summarizes his description of cinematic narrative structure: "For the internally nondiscrete textmessage of iconic type, narration is a transformation, an internal transposition of elements" (195). Lotman insists on this distinction: the basis of novelistic structure is the syntagmatics of elements in space, whereas the semantic basis of the iconic text is the combination, transformation, and movement of an image in time.

While Lotman's assertion reverses traditional notions about the novel and film (it is far more usual for critics to speak of the *spatial* nature of the visual arts and the *temporal* nature of the novel), this reversal nonetheless usefully calls attention to the complex temporality of the cinematic medium as presented in these novels. Toto's film icons are in fact transformations of a single image, "an internal transposition of elements," whether it be Norma Shearer, Robert Taylor, or Alicita's uncle, who has a movie actor's face and works in a bank, where "el piso brilla de mármol, la cara brilla de afeitada" (80) ["the floor shines cause it's marble and the face shines cause it's shaved" (63)]. It is not the syntagmatic elements of plot but the semantic elements of visual icons that matter to Toto, and Binx too envisions images that seem to have little to do with plot: Rock and Rory and Will and Gregory are all interchangeable iconic archetypes of the lady-killer, whether they happen to sleep chastely on the sofa after having tucked Debbie into bed or treat the maids who come to their beds to "as merry a time as [they] could wish for" (159).

This notion of film as an internal transformation of a single image over time appears early on in Latin American film criticism. The Argentine writer Jorge Luis Borges, a great film critic in the pages of *Sur* during the 1930s and 1940s and after, had already commented on this cinematic structure by 1932. In his now famous essay "El arte narrativo y la magia" ("Narrative Art and Magic") he comments on "la infinita novela espectacular que compone Hollywood con los plateados *ídola* de Joan Crawford y que las ciudades releen. Un orden muy diverso los rige, lúcido y atávico. La primitiva claridad de la magia" ("El arte narrativo" 230) ["the endless spectacular fictions made up in Hollywood, with the silvery images of Joan Crawford, that are read and reread the whole world over. A quite different sort of order rules them, one based not on reason but on association and suggestion—the ancient light of magic" ("Narrative" 37)]. Borges's early fascination with the archetypalizing potential of film is dramatized in the first story of his first volume of fiction, "El asesino desinteresado Bill Harrigan" ("The Casual Killer Bill Harrigan") in *Historia universal de la infamia* (1935; *A Universal History of Infamy*), in which Borges retells the story of Billy the Kid and plays with an array of film archetypes—the cowboy, the gunslinger, the local drunk—all of which are integrated into that most archetypal of all film genres, the Western, and its mythic territory, the Wild West.

In the passage that I have just quoted from "Narrative Art and Magic," Borges uses the Latin word *ídola* in conjunction with the plural Spanish adjective *plateados* to underline the irony of the singular yet repeating filmic image. His formulation also amplifies the meaning of the word *idol*, for it recalls the etymological relation of the Latin *ídola* to the

Greek *eídolon*, and by extension to *eîdos* (idea) and *eikon* (image)—all derived from the Greek verb *to see*. The relation between image and idea—between sight and insight—has compelled speculation since Plato established the distinction between an invisible realm of forms and a visible realm of mere likenesses. It is a kind of Platonic duality between "ideal" archetype and endless "real" repetition that Borges encodes in his reference to the divine Joan Crawford as *ídola*. Among Borges's U.S. contemporaries, only Gertrude Stein was equally aware of cinematic structure and its potential to unsettle the structure of narrative realism. Stein used cinematic structures as the basis of her stylistic experiments, as did some of the Cubist painters with whom she associated in France during her residence there in the twenties and thirties. Stein, like Borges, was interested in the repetitive nature of filmic images, but unlike Borges, she translated filmic structure literally into prose narration: her language and syntax reproduce the repetitiveness of film's visual structure to highly idiosyncratic effect. Her narrative and generic experiments remain largely that, experiments, for unlike Borges, Stein is a writer with neither precursors nor followers. Her intertextuality suggests that film structure is better engaged metaphorically than literally, better thematically than formally.

More recent fictional embodiments of Borges's kind of moving "magic" are Julio Cortázar's short story "Queremos tanto a Glenda" (1980; "We Love Glenda So Much") and Carlos Fuentes's short novel *Zona sagrada* (1967; *Holy Place*), Cortázar and Fuentes also describe the moving yet immutable image of a film idol. Cortázar describes a group of fans of movie star Glenda Garson who are so fanatical in their devotion that when she retires, they quietly expurgate from her movies the scenes that they feel to be less than perfect. They succeed in editing all of the copies of her films, thus achieving what they consider to be perfection on film. However, says the rueful first-person narrator, one of her most devout fans, "un poeta había dicho bajo los mismos cielos de Glenda que la eternidad está enamorada de las obras del tiempo" ("Queremos" 23) ["a poet had said under Glenda's same skies that eternity is in love with the works of time" ("We Love Glenda" 15)]: Glenda announces that she will come out of retirement to make more films. Although it is not stated, the reader understands that her disciples will not tolerate such a disruption of the immutable image that they have created: "Queríamos tanto a Glenda que le ofreceríamos una última perfección inviolable" (24) ["We loved Glenda so much that we would offer her one last inviolable perfection" (16)]. We are left to imagine Glenda's murder.

The protagonist in Fuentes's *Holy Place* also hopes to triumph over time and contingency by editing films, in this case films featuring movie star Claudia Nervo, who is his mother. Her son Guillermo is neglected by her, and he longs for her acceptance and love; he creates a montage of wildly disparate variations of her idealized image, as if to possess her at once in all of her forms.

Terrible y bella y lejana, siguen las disolvencias que mandé hacer. Claudia, tú eres la enamorada del general y por él abandonas tu hogar y caminas descalza hacia el crepúsculo con la tropa, hacia el fade out. . . . tú eres, en mi montage, la cantante de cabaret de un falso y humeante Macao, la soldadera de un campo de batalla de rocas acartonadas, la monja castrense de una Lima de utilería virreinal y la reina de la Belle Epoque envuelta en plumas de avestruz; eres la joven increíblemente bella, muerta sobre un caballo, eres la madrota de un burdel de los veintes y la maestra de escuela en un pueblo perdido y triste, eres la princesa maya sentada a los pies de la pirámide del Tajín y tus rostros se suceden en mi pantalla y allí te tengo para siempre. . . . La cámara no te robó tu rostro: lo conservó para mí, tu hijo, el robaestrellas. (*Zona sagrada* 155–56)

Terrible and beautiful and faraway, the dissolves I ordered follow. Claudia, you are the general's mistress and for him you leave your home and walk barefoot toward the twilight with the troops, toward the fade-out. . . . [Y]ou are, in my editing, the cabaret singer in a false and smoking Macao, the camp follower in a battleground of cardboard rocks, the army nun in a Lima of viceregal stage props and the queen of the Belle Epoque in ostrich feathers; you are the incredibly beautiful young woman, dead on a horse, you are the madam of a brothel of the twenties and the school teacher in a lost, sad village, you are the Mayan princess sitting at the foot of the Tajín pyramid and your faces follow one after the other on my screen and there I have you forever. . . . The camera didn't rob you of your face: it preserved it for me, your son, the star napper. (*Holy Place* 121–22)

Guillermo's editing conforms precisely to Lotman's (and Borges's) description of film as an internal transformation of a single image, that is, a successive combination of elements over time. But Fuentes invests this process with irony, for even as Guillermo edits the variations of his mother's image, he rejects those variations, seeking an immutable image behind the variations. Guillermo, like Glenda's fans, is lured by the illusory promise of cinematic perfection, by the promise of a changeless, and hence controllable, ideal. But even if Guillermo thinks he has "captured" his mother on film, he is unable to do so in life. When the movie

projector malfunctions in the final scene of the novel, chewing the celluloid and spewing it on the floor, we realize that he has not even managed to capture her on film.

In *Betrayed by Rita Hayworth* and *The Moviegoer*, it is precisely when
Toto and Binx attempt to change the visual into the verbal, to recount the
plot of a movie, that the reader becomes most aware of the disjunction
between words and images. They project images of themselves into their
verbal accounts of the movies, consciously making themselves into signs,
detachable and discrete "I's" whose identities are simplified and whose
relationships to the particular realities of New Orleans and Vallejos can
thus be the more freely manipulated. They don iconic masks at various
points in their narrations, each character signifying (or hoping to signify)
the particular mode of behavior inherent in the mask of the moment. It is
as if their whole being were nothing but language, text, cinematic image,
created for the purpose of proving that reality does indeed reiterate the
movies. Thus, Toto *becomes* the almost Christlike savior of Shirley Temple as he verbalizes the movie's meaning, or Fred Astaire as he describes
himself dancing with Ginger Rogers on top of the clouds; Binx *becomes* a
glorious composite Tony/Will/Rory when he narrates the car accident
that he had while "spinning along the Gulf Coast" with Sharon, or an
iconic Dick Rover, "the serious-minded Rover boy" (long since divorced
from his literary origins), when he's with his brother Lonnie. The danger
of conceiving of the self as sign is most forcefully rendered in another of
Percy's novels, *Lancelot*, where the protagonist almost casually murders
his wife and several others after having made a videotape of them (and
because of having made a videotape of them) in which electronic distor-
tion causes them to appear as "ciphers," as X's, Y's, triangles, rather than
as human beings. It is Toto who most succinctly captures the contradictory simultaneity of semiotic strata in his world (and this one) when he
describes the maid's reaction to his verbal account of his visual fantasy:
"Felisa se cree todo y es mentira" (*Traición* 38) ["Felisa believes every bit
of it and it's a lie" (*Betrayed* 30)]. The conjunction is *and*, not *but*.

Thus far I have emphasized similarities, but there are also marked
differences between these characters and their respective cultures. Both
don iconic masks in order to disguise themselves, but Toto is obliged to
do so in order to integrate himself into an authoritarian society, whereas
Binx chooses to do so in order to separate himself temporarily from his
staid society, rejecting the role of model citizen even as he mimics it.
Binx is comfortably upper middle class in a comfortably insouciant U.S.
southern city before the civil-rights movement, the women's movement,
Vietnam, Watergate, or any of the other disruptions that were soon to

come. Repressive social structures certainly exist in Binx's culture, but they are not given as problematic because Binx will not be constrained by them. Nothing could be farther from Toto's presumed future. Vallejos is a small town in comparison to New Orleans, especially given the quarter century separating their fictional settings. It is less open to individual idiosyncrasy, less comfortable in its traditionalism, less permissive of departures from established patterns of behavior. Authoritarian cultural mechanisms operate everywhere in Toto's experience; that he finds such power in Hollywood only confirms how little of it he has in Vallejos.

In *The Moviegoer* and *Betrayed by Rita Hayworth*, it is not the imagination of their characters that Puig and Percy impugn but the dead areas of their characters' cultures—the idealized, the sentimental, the euphemistic structures of New Orleans and Vallejos that distance Binx and Toto from their own experience. Their indictment of inauthentic experience and their intertextual strategies for doing so place Percy and Puig in the tradition of John Dos Passos, James Joyce, Virginia Woolf, F. Scott Fitzgerald, Albert Camus. Their creation of texts that contain subtexts submerged but visible within them facilitates their ironic cultural perspective and adds to their ostensible subject a larger concern with the nature and limitations of literary expression. Their intertextuality displays—and questions—the means and media provided by a given culture through which to express human experience. More specifically, it tests the capacity of the novel to confront inauthentic modes of expression by making its own critical distinctness palpable in the experience of the reader (as the movies in question do not, cannot). By invoking the movies, these writers direct the reader's attention to their novels' organizing principles and cultural conditions, reminding us of their status as one more signifying system, among many, within their own cultural context. If Binx and Toto are "moviegoers" in Percy's sense—inferring their reality from their uncritical consumption of cinematic texts—so the novels themselves exist and signify by virtue of their complex relationship to other signifying structures. This multiplicity of semiotic systems within the novels points to the constraints that operate not only in the characters' worlds but in the authors' and the readers' as well.

It is on the severity of these constraints that Percy and Puig differ dramatically. While both share the conviction that human beings can be characterized by the ways in which they use signs and that the aggregate of sign systems within a culture defines that culture, they differ entirely in their relation to the Hollywood film industry. For Puig, as for many Latin American writers, "Hollywood" is a metaphor for U.S. cultural imposi-

tion and, by extension, for social and economic inequities in their regions. Latin American writers use the content of particular movies and
the medium as such to raise issues of communal identity. If Percy can
imagine his character eventually reconciling his values against those of
Hollywood and walking away unscathed, it is because Hollywood does
not have the negative connotations for him that it does for Latin American writers. In any case, the issues raised in *The Moviegoer* are ultimately
existential, not political or social. Percy's novel is about redemption in a
Catholic mode, and though it is critical of the vapidity of the movies in
Binx's New Orleans, its concerns remain largely philosophical. On the
contrary, Puig cannot imagine Toto's eventual accommodation to the
disjunctions created by Hollywood in Vallejos, any more than Fuentes
can in *Zona sagrada* or Cortázar in "Queremos tanto a Glenda." In *Betrayed by Rita Hayworth* Puig indicts Hollywood's cultural imperialism,
and he also indicts Argentina's willingness to be colonized. Communal
identity, Puig shows, cannot be established by imitation.

Before writing his first novel, Puig studied film at the Centro Speri-
mentale di Cinematografia in Rome.[11] During the 1960s, the New Latin
American Cinema movement had all but completed a process begun in
the 1940s, a process of defining itself *against* Hollywood. Fernando Birri,
the noted Argentine documentary film director, preceded Puig at the
Centro, then returned to Argentina to establish the first Latin American
documentary film center at the National University of the Littoral in
Santa Fe, Argentina. Birri notes that "postwar Italian Neorealism was
taking movie houses around the world by storm. *Bicycle Thief, Rome,
Open City*, and *La terra trema* had all appeared in the late forties. For me,
the great revelation of the Neorealist movement was that, contrary to
Hollywood's tenets and example, it was possible to make movies on the
same artistic level as a play, a novel, or a poem" (qtd. in Burton 3–4).[12]
The illusionist Hollywood model gave way to a more socially and politically committed cinema, and the adjective *hollywoodista* (and its flexible
variants *hollywoodesco* and *hollywoodense*) entered the Spanish lexicon,
meaning sentimental, superficial, seductive. Julianne Burton, in the introduction to her interviews with a number of Latin American filmmakers, asserts that this was a period "when talented young people,
acutely conscious of social and economic inequities and anxious to remedy them, began redefining the role of the film medium in the Latin
American context. The nature of their project was shaped by the fierce
rejection of one model of filmmaking and the equally passionate emula-
tion of another" (x). Commercial films were "condemned as alienated
and alienating imitations of the Hollywood model" (xi). As Puig studied

filmmaking before beginning to write fiction, he would have been well aware of Latin America's rejection of Hollywood. Indeed, his first novel now seems an instance of that process on the local level.

I offer one more Latin American literary example before moving northward. Gabriel García Márquez is clearly a writer to whom the "movies matter a lot," a writer who, like Puig, Fuentes, and Cortázar, uses the medium as a mode of cultural critique. Consider the following passage from *Cien años de soledad* (1967; *One Hundred Years of Solitude*). The events described occur late in the novel, long after the gypsies have come and gone with their marvelous gadgets, long after the banana company has built its marvelous town on the outskirts of Macondo—that is, long after the residents of Macondo can be so easily deceived by bearers of cultural marvels from elsewhere. The scene takes place in the new outdoor movie theater of Macondo.

> Deslumbrada por tantas y tan maravillosas invenciones, la gente de Macondo no sabía por dónde empezar a asombrarse. Se trasnochaban contemplando las pálidas bombillas eléctricas, alimentadas por la planta que llevó Aureliano Triste en el segundo viaje del tren, y a cuyo obsesionante tumtum costó tiempo y trabajo acostumbrarse. Se indignaron con las imágenes vivas que el próspero comerciante don Bruno Crespi proyectaba en el teatro con taquillas de bocas de león, porque un personaje muerto y sepultado en una película, y por cuya desgracia se derramaron lágrimas de aflicción, reapareció vivo y convertido en árabe en la película siguiente. El público que pagaba dos centavos para compartir las vicisitudes de los personajes, no pudo soportar aquella burla inaudita y rompió la silletería. El alcalde, a instancias de don Bruno Crespi, explicó mediante un bando, que el cine era una máquina de ilusión que no merecía los desbordamientos pasionales del público. Ante la desalentadora explicación, muchos estimaron que habían sido víctimas de un nuevo y aparatoso asunto de gitanos, de modo que optaron por no volver al cine, considerando que ya tenían bastante con sus propias penas para llorar por fingidas desventuras de seres imaginarios. (*Cien años* 194)

> Dazzled by so many marvelous inventions, the people of Macondo did not know where their amazement began. They stayed up all night looking at the pale electric bulbs fed by the plant that Aureliano Triste had brought back when the train made its second trip, and it took time and effort for them to grow accustomed to its obsessive *toom-toom*. They became indignant over the living images that the prosperous merchant Bruno Crespi projected in the theater with the lion-

head ticket windows, for the character who had died and was buried in one film and for whose misfortune tears of affliction had been shed would reappear alive and transformed into an Arab in the next one. The audience, who paid two cents apiece to share the difficulties of the actors, would not tolerate that outlandish fraud and broke up the seats. The mayor, at the urging of Bruno Crespi, explained in a proclamation that the cinema was a machine of illusion that did not merit the emotional outbursts of the audience. With that discouraging explanation many felt that they had been the victims of some new and showy gypsy business and they decided not to return to the movies, considering that they already had too many troubles of their own to weep over the acted-out misfortunes of imaginary beings. (*One Hundred* 211)

One might at first think this scene a sly self-parody. After all, García Márquez's narrator, Melquíades, also returns from the dead, as do Prudencio Aguilar and several other characters, not to mention the virtual return of Arcadio and Aureliano in each successive generation. But the scene goes beyond self-parody. Unlike Binx and Toto, the apparent problem for Macondo's moviegoers is not too much illusion but too little, for they recognize the actors *as actors*, not as the changeless idols of their romantic dreams. Toto and Binx buy those illusions, whereas the residents of Macondo do not, but in both cases Hollywood is presented as belying their experience. Here, García Márquez engages the same issue of communal identity as Puig, impugning sources of cultural self-definition that are imposed from outside and thus removed from the community's own experience of itself. Their critique does not imply that cultures should be closed entities (impossible, in any case) but that collective judgments must be exercised, as the residents of Macondo appear to be doing, at long last.

García Márquez has written for films, directed, produced, and inspired the production of films in Colombia, Cuba, Mexico, and France, among other countries, and commented extensively on the medium. In an interview in the *Times Literary Supplement* he notes that as a young man he wanted to be a film director and a scriptwriter because he thought that film offered "greater possibilities" than literature. But, he continues, "I was wrong. Film and television have a limitation of an industrial kind that literature doesn't have" ("Of Love" 1152). That *One Hundred Years of Solitude* has not been made into a movie corresponds to García Márquez's sense that visualization in fiction is very different from seeing an image in a movie. He elaborates: "In a novel there is a creative margin for the reader which film doesn't have. In film the image is too imposing, it is a total definition" (1152). He cites his readers' experience of his novel, especially their accounts of identifying with his characters. According to García Márquez, "Film doesn't allow that. In the film [characters] have the face of Anthony Quinn, they have the face of Sophia Loren, they have the face of Robert Redford, and it's very unlikely that any grandfather of ours looks like Robert Redford" (1152). For García Márquez, movies are "too imposing" when they betray the experience of his readers or, in the scene from *One Hundred Years of Solitude*, the residents of Macondo.

García Márquez is emphatic on this point because he, like Puig, understands the magnitude of Hollywood's presence in Latin America. For decades, Hollywood was at the very center of the cultural life of small towns throughout Latin America. I can attest to this fact, having lived for two years in Quimbaya, a village in the state of Quindío, Colombia, during the late 1960s—at the time, in fact, when *One Hundred Years of Solitude* was published. Reading the novel then, it seemed to me that García Márquez had described Quimbaya and its inhabitants, and had simply renamed the town Macondo. The only thing he changed, I thought, was the scene in which Macondo's moviegoers tear up the seats in the movie theater. Quimbayans would never have dreamed of such a thing. This was an era when TVs were still a rarity and cars could not easily reach the town (the rutted roads required jeeps, which were used primarily for hauling produce, not people). The only cultural news regularly entering Quimbaya arrived in canisters. Every morning at seven o'clock, a steam engine pulling two or three freight cars brought the canisters containing the movie to be shown that evening, taking in exchange the canisters from the night before. Thus, the cycle of anticipation was rekindled each morning, with waiting and release to follow each evening. The communal ritual included an early evening stroll around the plaza (boys clockwise, girls counterclockwise), a *pintado* in the Café Brasilia on the plaza, and then, at 8:00, the movie! For Quimbayans, life without Hollywood would have been unthinkable. In this respect, the Italian film *Cinema paradiso* depicts the sociology of Quimbaya more closely than the scene I've cited from *One Hundred Years of Solitude*. García Márquez's fictional treatment of the movies in Macondo, like Puig's in Vallejo, stems from his desire to project a critical self-awareness onto imaginatively engaged spectators. If García Márquez's Macondo had achieved such self-awareness, no such thing had yet happened in Quimbaya.

I began by wondering whether U.S. movies have mattered as much to southern writers as to Latin American writers, and the answer appears to be no. Whereas Latin American writers share a skeptical view of the medium and use it for purposes of cultural critique and communal self-definition, southern writers by and large do not. Though Percy's *The Moviegoer* indicts the superficiality of Hollywood movies, the movies in question are not seen as reinforcing barriers of class or race or gender or sexual preference that prevent Binx from embracing other, presumably better, cultural models whenever he should decide to do so. William Faulkner went to Hollywood to write screenplays, and he used the power of the movies to confront racial and regional stereotypes, but his fiction remains untouched by any consideration of film as a medium of individual or communal identity.[13] Tennessee Williams's plays have been made into great movies, but they are not even remotely *about* the movies. Flannery O'Connor is also unmoved by the medium.[14] In her voluminous correspondence, published as *The Habit of Being*, there is no reference to film (though she does refer approvingly to Percy's novel *The Moviegoer*). And in O'Connor's fiction there appears to be only one reference to a film: in "A Late Encounter with the Enemy," in *A Good Man Is Hard to Find*, the narrator mentions the premiere of an unnamed movie in Atlanta. O'Connor's character in this story, now aged 104, had participated in the "preemy," as he calls it, when he was fourteen, and he remembers it long after he has forgotten his wife and children and everything else. But this story is about the narcissism of youth and extreme old age and the human need for recognition—not about the movies. And Albert Murray, an Arkansan and a brilliant analyst of modes of cultural expression, has little to say about film. In *The Blue Devils of Nada*, with its seemingly inclusive subtitle "A Contemporary American Approach to Aesthetic Statement," film is not to be found; rather, it is music (the blues, jazz, Armstrong, Ellington) and painting (Impressionism, Cubism) that occupy Murray's attention.

If one counts west Texas as part of the South (a geographical stretch, admittedly), there is Larry McMurtry's *The Last Picture Show*, which is framed by opening and closing scenes in the desolate movie theater of the windswept town of Thalia near Wichita Falls. The title of the novel announces its investment in the movies, and though a number of movies and stars are named, their effect on identity, whether communal or individual, is never explored. Nonetheless, movies do provide a source of irony in this novel. By naming particular movies, McMurtry dramatizes the geographical isolation of his characters and indicts the superficiality of their culture. Since we are momentarily considering *The Last Picture Show* as a southern novel, it is worth mentioning one example. One movie he mentions is *Storm Warning*, and the novel's narrator lists its stars: Doris Day, Ronald Reagan, Steve Cochran, and Ginger Rogers. Early in the novel, one of the principal characters, a hapless but well-meaning adolescent stuck in Thalia, enters the movie theater late, where he meets his girlfriend, who wants to make out: "Sonny returned the kiss, but with somewhat muted interest. He wanted to keep at least one eye on the screen, so if Ginger Rogers decided to take her clothes off he wouldn't miss it. The posters outside indicated she at least got down to her slip at one point" (18). There is no further elaboration of Sonny's response to this film, except that he keeps "trying to concentrate on the screen" in spite of his girlfriend's attentions. If the reader happens to know the film, he or she will know that Sonny has completely missed its racial and political message. That he "keeps trying to concentrate on the screen" for the only reason he knows, increases the pathos of his isolation.

The writer James Baldwin recounts *his* experience when he goes to see *Storm Warning*, and not surprisingly, he sees a very different film from that seen by McMurtry's character. In Baldwin's brilliant discussion of films about the South, to which I'll refer in detail below, he notes that *Storm Warning* is about the Ku Klux Klan and that it has been unfairly neglected, "possibly because Ginger Rogers speaks courageously for the Union, and against the Confederacy" (43). How far this Ginger Rogers is from the one whom Sonny has in mind; how far, too, from the Ginger Rogers of Toto's romantic illusions in Puig's novel.

There is something more to say about Larry McMurtry's treatment of picture shows. The term *picture show*, in McMurtry's usage, refers to movie theaters as well as to the movies shown inside them. The picture show—the place itself—is as essential to Thalia's social fabric as the pool hall. Several scenes occur inside the theater that have nothing to do with the movie flickering in front of the characters; indeed, the wonderful movie made of this novel, directed by Peter Bogdanovich, chooses to show bits of films quite different from those mentioned in the novel itself. Bogdanovich's version of the scene I described above shows snippets not of *Storm Warning* but of Elizabeth Taylor and Spencer Tracy in *Father of the Bride*. As people leave the depressed town, or die, the theater is forced to close. Billy, a character who doesn't speak and is considered by everyone to be "dim-witted," cannot understand that the picture show is over and done. "Of all the people in Thalia, Billy missed the picture show most" (McMurtry 273). He sits on the curb outside the picture show night after night, sure that it will open eventually; the television that Sonny buys him does not assuage his longing for this departed "person." In this crucial detail Billy is the author's surrogate, for McMurtry has expressed the hope that "some present-day Walker Evans" will document abandoned "picture shows" such as the one in Thalia where Billy holds his vigil.[15]

In fact, McMurtry's hope has apparently been realized in a recent volume of photographs by Michael Putnam entitled *Silent Screens*. In his images of boarded-up, single-screen movie houses in varying degrees of decay, Putnam presents a photographic essay on the history of movie-going in the United States. The brief notice of this collection in the *New Yorker* refers to Putnam's use of black and white as elegiac in tone, and it describes some of the images as follows: "One series of photographs documents the 1987 demolition of the Pekin Theatre, a bit of architectural Chinoiserie in Pekin, Illinois; another portrays theatres that have been converted into bookstores, restaurants, a shooting gallery, an indoor swimming pool, and, most commonly (and appropriately), churches."[16] Perhaps, too, some present-day Manuel Alvarez Bravo or Guillermo Kahlo will decide to document Latin America's rapidly vanishing single-screen picture shows such as those in Quimbaya and Vallejos. If such photos are ever taken, they will contain an essential piece of the social fabric of Latin American towns of a certain size from the 1930s through the 1970s, and in some cases, up to the present day.

And what about Carson McCullers, Eudora Welty, Robert Penn Warren, Katherine Anne Porter, Peter Taylor? None of these southern writers engages the movies substantially in his or her fiction or essays. This virtually unanimous indifference seems odd. Perhaps, one thinks, their silence on the subject is due to their rural settings, their shared commitment to history and myth, and their remove in time from the more recent Latin American writers I've mentioned. But Vallejos and Macondo are hardly urban centers, and the historical remove of Vallejos and Macondo from the fictional worlds of these southern writers is not sufficient to account for the difference either. In fact, African American writers are closer to Latin American writers in their literary engagement of film than the southern writers I have just named. If film, like literature, is a medium through which a society can ask itself questions *about* itself—that is, a medium for communal self-questioning and critique—then we may begin to suspect that the differences I have noted between Latin American and U.S. southern writers reflect these writers' different understanding of literature as a mode of social commentary. These differences may be usefully gathered under the term *postcolonial*. If communal identity can be taken for granted by writers in the dominant culture, it cannot be by postcolonial writers, that is, writers in communities still in the process of defining themselves *against* the dominant culture. If, as I will argue, writers engage film intertextually as a means of doing just this, then white southern writers are not postcolonial in the sense I intend. They do not consider literature to be part of a process of communal self-creation that necessarily assesses desired values against existing values, as do the Latin American and African American writers I discuss here. While the category of "postcolonial writer" has been widely applied and risks oversimplification, it is nonetheless worth pursuing its characteristics in the work of two African American writers.

New York writer James Baldwin provides brilliant insights into the relations of films, literature, and southern culture as no geographically defined southern writer has done. Oklahoman Ralph Ellison also uses film to address racial questions that are tied inextricably to the South. Baldwin and Ellison are brilliant moviegoers, but not in Percy's sense of *moviegoer* as a metaphor for romantic projection, or in any other ironic sense, for that matter: they go to movies, experience their psychological impact, assess their relation to regional and national American cultures, and locate themselves accordingly as writers and as African Americans. Both are aware of the influence of geography on personality, but their indictment of southern racism and the role of the movies in perpetuating it goes well beyond the influence of a particular place on them as individuals or as writers. Rather, they see a whole class of selves, and they understand the oppression of that group as a function of southern cultural practice.

As James Baldwin grew up in Harlem, he found in the movies' depiction of the Deep South (as he repeatedly calls the region) the image of his own cultural identity as an African American. In his autobiographical essay *The Devil Finds Work*, published in 1976, Baldwin describes this process. Even as a child and quite unlike Percy's and Puig's fictional characters, Baldwin understands the power of the cinematic medium: "That the movie star is an 'escape' personality indicates one of the irreducible dangers to which the moviegoer is exposed: the danger of surrendering to the corroboration of one's fantasies as they are thrown back from the screen" (29). Elaborating on this "irreducible danger," he writes, "The distance between oneself—the audience—and a screen performer is an absolute: a paradoxical absolute, masquerading as intimacy" (29). For Baldwin as for García Márquez, the distinction between filmic illusion and the audience's own experience is essential, for it is the distinction between imposed cultural models and authentic self-definition. The distinction may seem oversimplified, but for Baldwin, to make it is to begin to establish one's own identity, as a self and as a member of society.

Baldwin describes his experience of the movies during the 1940s, at about the same time that Toto would have been watching Ginger Rogers and Rita Hayworth, and a decade or so before Binx would watch Debbie Reynolds and Rock Hudson. Baldwin was twelve, and the film was not about Hollywood or Harlem or the South—it was *A Tale of Two Cities*. Baldwin writes, "My first conscious calculation as to how to go about defeating the world's intentions for me and mine began on that Saturday afternoon in what we called *the movies*, but which was actually my first entrance into the cinema of my mind" (8). This film, so removed in time and space from his own experience, reflects his experience back to him not as fantasy but as social fact. He links his experience of *A Tale of Two Cities* to that of *Uncle Tom's Cabin*: "I had no idea what *Two Cities* was really about, any more than I knew what *Uncle Tom's Cabin* was about, which was why I had read them both so obsessively: they had something to tell me. It was this particular child's way of circling around the question of what it meant to be a nigger" (10–11). The power of make-believe has something to tell him about his own identity as an African American and about the identity imposed on him by American culture at large. Given his awareness of the "irreducible danger" of the medium, films do not betray but inspire and instruct.

Baldwin returns constantly to the doubleness of his experience of moviegoing. He is aware of the movies' power to delude him at the same time that he knows they may be his most important source of cultural information. This duality is confirmed by his reaction to the live theater. He remembers a performance on Broadway of *Native Son* when he was seventeen years old, and he contrasts his experience of the stage to that of the screen: "Canada Lee was Bigger Thomas, but he was also Canada Lee: his physical presence, like the physical presence of Paul Robeson, gave me the right to live. He was not at the mercy of my imagination, as he would have been, on the screen: he was on the stage, in flesh and blood, and I was, therefore, at the mercy of *his* imagination" (33). And referring to a performance of *Macbeth* acted by an all-black company, which he saw at about the same age, he reiterates his point: "Here, nothing corroborated any of my fantasies: flesh and blood was being challenged by flesh and blood. It is said that the camera cannot lie, but rarely do we allow it to do anything else, since the camera sees what you point it at: the camera sees what you want it to see. The language of the camera is the language of our dreams" (34).

Baldwin's relation to film is nowhere more culturally charged than when the film is about the Deep South and thus about African American identity as a collective matter. He mentions *The Birth of a Nation; In the Heat of the Night; In This Our Life*, based on Ellen Glasgow's novel; and

They Won't Forget, based on Ward Greene's novel *Death in the Deep South*, among others. Baldwin discusses the racial stereotypes in these movies, tying his discussion to southern political and cultural institutions. While we might say that any writer whose subject is race is a "southern" writer in the extended sense I have proposed, Baldwin is very specific about the location of these films. He notes that *The Birth of a Nation* (1915), like *Storm Warning*, is about the Ku Klux Klan (it is here that he finds unjustified the renown of the former film as compared to the obscurity of the latter), describes its setting as "the gallant South, on the edge of the great betrayal by the Northern brethren" (45), and dwells bitterly on the film's central image of the mulatto. Bette Davis in *In This Our Life* plays a "spoiled Southern girl" who, in Baldwin's plot summary, has killed someone in a hit-and-run automobile accident and blamed her black chauffeur. The chauffeur goes to jail and the girl attempts to persuade him to confess to the crime with the promise of her eventual sexual favors. Baldwin describes his refusal, noting that the man is "far too proud . . . to strike such a bargain. But the offer has been made, and the truth about the woman revealed" (59). Fifty years later, *In the Heat of the Night*, with Sydney Poitier, is set in the post-civil-rights South, but Baldwin finds little changed to bridge racial and class divisions.

In the Heat of the Night both attracts and repels Baldwin. He describes it in detail because he understands his own identity as an African American to be southern in its source and substance. The film is about a black policeman (Poitier) who goes to a small southern town to investigate a case and about his developing relationship with the town's white sheriff (Rod Steiger). Baldwin's comments go quickly to the structural capacity of the medium to fix and hold the image—not, in this case, the image of romantic desire but rather the image of racial hatred. Baldwin's tone conveys his frustration at an utterly un-self-critical film that nonetheless dramatizes the outrage of racial stereotypes: "The film helplessly conveys—without confronting—the anguish of people trapped in a legend. They cannot live within this legend; neither can they step out of it. The film gave me the impression, according to my notes the day I saw it, of 'something strangling, alive, struggling to get out' " (55–56). The "legend" is not Bogart or Bacall but racism: "It is a terrible thing, simply, to be trapped in one's history, and attempt, in the same motion . . . to accept, deny, reject, and redeem it" (56). Baldwin finds that the effect of the film is "to increase and not lessen white confusion and complacency, and black rage and despair" (55). But about this film, in which "white Americans have been encouraged to continue dreaming," Baldwin concludes that "black Americans have been alerted to the necessity of waking up" (56–57). The distinction between the film's fixed images and the individual moviegoer's experience of them is everything.

Baldwin is the closest of our "southern" writers to contemporary Latin American writers in his understanding of the role of film and literature in defining individual and collective American identities. His self-awareness as an African American writer approximates that of Latin American writers who require of art that it operate in the service of cultural self-definition. Like the Latin American writers previously discussed, Baldwin knows that moviegoing exists in many forms. In addition to his recognition of its "irreducible danger"—"the danger of surrendering to the corroboration of one's fantasies as they are thrown back from the screen"—he also knows that this danger is the basis of film's capacity to enable self-recognition and, by extension, cultural critique, as it did for him, growing up in Harlem. Baldwin is aware of these conjoining dangers, and he inspires his readers to be so as well. This is moviegoing of the most literary kind.

While Baldwin was going to the movies as a boy in Harlem, Ralph Ellison was already beginning to write about them. Born in Oklahoma City in 1914 (a decade before Baldwin), Ellison studied music at Tuskegee Institute from 1933 to 1936, then settled for a time in Dayton, Ohio, where his mother had moved. He had been to New York, met Richard Wright (another writer forged by southern racism), and a year later moved to New York permanently. Geography is important in any account of a writer whose most famous work is about race and is set in the South. Ellison's biographer, John F. Callahan, writes, "Seeking his way home, [Ellison] came to realize that home's true geography lay within. New York was the future he aimed at, Oklahoma the country of memory, and Dayton the strangely familiar spot of his life's crossroads" (xiv–xv). Like Albert Murray, his fellow student at Tuskegee Institute, Ellison uses music as a metaphor for his central aesthetic concerns. He rarely refers to film in his fiction, but in the title essay of *Shadow and Act* (1953), Ellison shows himself to be Baldwin's precursor in his understanding of the power of films to affect communal identity.

Written in 1949 as a film review/article for *The Reporter*, Ellison's "Shadow and Act" describes the racial stereotypes purveyed by Hollywood in *Home of the Brave*, *Lost Boundaries*, and *Pinky*. To these films he opposes Faulkner's screen version of *Intruder in the Dust*, it being "the only film that could be shown in Harlem without arousing unintended laughter. For it is the only one of the four in which Negroes can make complete identification with their screen image" (281). In Faulkner's story the "young Southerner" Chick and his "Southern conception of

Negroes" have evolved so that "the role of Negroes in American life has been given what, for the movies, is a startling new definition" (274–75).

While registering this advance, Ellison's discussion of current films nonetheless draws him, as if by sheer magnetic force, back to D. W. Griffith's *The Birth of a Nation* (1915). Like Baldwin, Ellison notes that this film is based on *The Clansman*, a 1905 novel by the southern writer Thomas Dixon Jr., and he adds that the novel inspired Joseph Simmons to found the Ku Klux Klan. He also claims that the film is responsible for creating the stereotypes of violence and servility with which African Americans have been obliged to live ever since. Referring to film as "the main manipulator of the American dream," Ellison indicts Hollywood for its dehumanizing portrayal of African Americans. After *The Birth of a Nation*, "the propagation of subhuman images of Negroes becomes financially and dramatically profitable. The Negro as scapegoat could be sold as entertainment, could even be exported" (276). The gulf between the film's stereotypes and the viewer's reality is measured by Ellison's rage.

Hollywood is repeatedly described as a conservative cultural force whose "enormous myth-making potential" perpetuates unjust social structures: "In the struggle against Negro freedom, motion pictures have been one of the strongest instruments for justifying some white Americans' anti-Negro attitudes and practices" (276). In his discussion of *Lost Boundaries*, Ellison personifies "Hollywood" as an imperious judge of a mulatto character's desire to pass as white: "Hollywood is uncertain about his right to do this" (278). But Ellison ultimately refuses to arrogate to Hollywood the right to decide this question or any other with respect to race. In his metaphor of shadow and act, he denies that the movies have so much power and American individuals so little: "To direct an attack upon Hollywood would indeed be to confuse portrayal with action, image with reality. In the beginning was not the shadow, but the act, and the province of Hollywood is not action, but illusion. Actually the anti-Negro images of the films were (and are) acceptable because of the existence throughout the United States of an audience obsessed with an inner psychological need to view Negroes as less than men" (276). Ellison charges that Hollywood plays to the largest group of potential consumers, no matter how debased their attitudes and values. Exceptions exist, of course—*Intruder in the Dust* and *Storm Warning* are acknowledged as such—but neither Ellison nor Baldwin is optimistic. For these writers, as for many Latin Americans, Hollywood is at once a metaphor for the imposition of corrupt cultural values and an institution for propagating and maintaining them.

The movies, then, clearly matter most to those who understand their literature to have a social and communal function, and who are disappointed (or outraged) that films have, by and large, refused this function. They understand the mythmaking potential of the medium in a positive sense, but they see this potential being used in negative ways—ways that undermine their own communal project, rather than enhancing it as they know it could. Thus, they begin to engage their literary art as a corrective to film, as a call for something more and better than the stereotypes it purveys. This is true of Baldwin and Ellison, Puig and Fuentes and García Márquez, who correctly perceive mainstream U.S. films to be produced by those already comfortably in possession of cultural identity and social capital—whites, U.S. citizens, males, heterosexuals, depending on the writer's oppositional perspective. This perception, particularly when it takes into account Hollywood's historical dominance of film production in the hemisphere, leads these writers to indict U.S. filmmakers for distributing social, racial, and gender stereotypes that support established structures of power.

Is this generalization true today, given the growth of independent filmmaking in the United States and the development of film industries in Mexico, Cuba, Brazil, Venezuela, and Argentina? Certainly this diversification has expanded the communal consciousness of American films, depending on the country and the filmmaker, but the vast majority of moviegoers in the hemisphere still prefer "mainstream" U.S. films. Any quick check of the *cartelera* in the newspapers of Mexico City, Buenos Aires, or Bogotá will confirm this assertion. Then there are the mainstream preferences of Houston, Baltimore, St. Louis, and the rest of the United States. In the Latin American cities mentioned above, reviews in newspapers and magazines often deride the vapidity and violence of mainstream U.S. films as *hollywoodistas, hollywoodescos, hollywoodenses*, even as the public lines up to see them. Meanwhile, American writers are not in any hurry to celebrate the liberation of the medium from its historical stereotyping of blacks and women, or from its more recent devotion to violence. There may be no contemporary American writer—southern, Latin American or otherwise—who finds in current films a ready basis for the construction of community or conscience.

Are these generalizations true everywhere? Must film, because of its primary function as mass entertainment, gravitate toward what is accepted, familiar, stereotypical? And are writers in all parts of the world bound to find themselves depreciating and/or deploring film as a medium of social exchange?

Apparently not. In *Cinema and the Urban Poor in South India*, a regional study of the social role played by film, Sara Dickey argues that films made in India by Indians about Indian realities have operated within (and on) cultural norms, with social conscience and consequence. The film industry in India appears to be less driven by the theory that moviegoers wish only to have their belief systems reinforced and that movies are likely to sell only if they reflect existing cultural attitudes and values. Recent films by Iranian and Arab filmmakers would also seem to confront the supposition that the medium is necessarily culturally conservative. The Iranian films *The Color of Paradise* and *Divorce Iranian Style* take local events and place them in a broader cultural framework so as to question basic political and social attitudes. Whether literature takes up the theme of film as such is a question for comparatists specializing in the literature of these regions, and the question is worth asking. Its various answers will lead to new comparative connections among writers in the Americas and other postcolonial contexts, and allow comparisons of their understandings of the function of literature in their respective cultures.

My hypothesis is, then, that the creative use of cinematic material in a work of fiction may well serve as a social and political indicator. To answer Michael Wood's question as generally as possible: the movies matter to those writers who understand literature as a social instrument with a communal function. This is so in the Americas, as we have seen, and it appears to be the case in other postcolonial contexts as well. Whether the writer uses the movies to reveal racial and gender stereotyping (Puig, Baldwin, Ellison), cultural isolation (McMurtry), romantic escapism (Percy), personal and communal violence (Fuentes, Cortázar), and/or U.S. cultural imperialism (García Márquez, Puig), their common aim is to suggest alternative social structures, and better ones.

How does reference to the movies lend itself to these ameliorative purposes? Why do these writers indict the movies, when they are largely silent on other visual media? After all, photography, painting, television, or even advertising might also be expected to construct community. Obviously, the movies command vast audiences, many of whom are not in the habit of reading, in part because books are expensive as compared to the cost of a movie in Latin America and most of the postcolonial world. Quimbaya had a thriving movie theater, but it did not have a bookstore, nor does Puig's fictional Vallejos have one; the fact that García Márquez's Macondo *does* have a bookstore is as unrealistic as it is that the residents should protest the unreality of the movies. In towns like Quimbaya movies clearly speak to entire communities as books rarely do. Writers know this, of course, but there are further considerations.

Beyond questions of supply, demand, and distribution, film has the capacity to present contradictory voices and versions simultaneously—a capacity that Mikhail Bakhtin famously refers to as *heteroglossia* and attributes to the novel. Heteroglossia, when achieved in a work of fiction, is, according to Bakhtin, contestatory, critical, subversive: "another's speech in another's language, serving to express authorial intentions but in a refracted way" (324). We know very well that such multivocalism can also be found in the structure of film or, at least, in the perceptions of certain moviegoers. Recall James Baldwin's statement, quoted above, about his experience as a boy: "my first conscious calculation as to how to go about defeating the world's intentions for me and mine began on that Saturday afternoon in what we called *the movies,* but which was actually my first entrance into the cinema of my mind" (8). The movies seen by the young Baldwin do not oppose racism. Indeed, those movies had no other intention than to reinforce racial stereotypes, and yet Baldwin sees in them very different visions and hears different voices. In watching these movies, he is able to understand an oppressive reality and eventually to confront it in his writing. Ellison's metaphor of "shadow and act" is perfectly applicable to Baldwin's experience: "In the beginning was not the shadow, but the act, and the province of Hollywood is not action, but illusion" (276).

The intertextual use of film in fiction raises questions about the media available to a writer in a given culture to represent his or her vision. By referring intertextually to film, postcolonial writers make palpable the critical distinctness of their position, even as they engage Hollywood stereotypes to do so. This multivocal structure is what, according to Bakhtin, "serves authorial intention in a refracted way." The "refraction" of film, when embedded intertextually in literature, lends itself to the ironic (and often idealizing) purposes of postcolonial writers, who must portray reality as it is while at the same time projecting a reality that does not yet (or still) exist. No one knows more about the complex relations of shadow and act than they.

The intertextual uses of film in postcolonial fiction has yet to be fully explored, but Erwin Panofsky, the German art historian, understood early on the nature and appeal of filmic illusion to those concerned with revising reality. Panofsky had migrated to the United States in 1934 after being dismissed as a Jew from his professorship at the University of Hamburg, and he found himself immediately intrigued by the potential of "Hollywood" (a word he uses repeatedly as a synonym for film). In his 1936 essay "Style and Medium in the Motion Pictures," he compares film to an array of other media—mosaic, engraving, music, theater, architecture—though, oddly, he omits the novel from his comparative discussion. He traces the evolution of this new technological medium, which begins as "a product of genuine folk art," into a high art form, and likens the process to the artistic evolution of mosaic and line engraving.

> The evolution from the jerky beginnings [of cinema] to this grand climax [Keaton's *The Navigator* (1924) and Eisenstein's *Battleship Potemkin* (1925)] offers the fascinating spectacle of a new artistic medium gradually becoming conscious of its legitimate, that is, exclusive, possibilities and limitations—a spectacle not unlike the development of the mosaic, which started out with transposing illusionistic genre pictures into a more durable material and culminated in the hieratic supernaturalism of Ravenna; or the development of line engraving, which started out as a cheap and handy substitute for book illumination and culminated in the purely "graphic" style of Dürer. (108)[17]

He also likens the collaborative nature of film production to the construction of medieval cathedrals: "It might be said that a film, called into being by a cooperative effort in which all contributions have the same degree of permanence, is the nearest modern equivalent of a medieval cathedral" (119). He concludes wryly that there are fewer good films than there are good cathedrals.

Panofsky also comments on the commercial status of film. If, for Ellison and the Latin American writers, Hollywood is the very definition of corrupt commercialism, for Panofsky commercialism is a strength. The commercial nature of film requires that it speak to the community, that it be accessible, understandable, "communicable": "It is this requirement of communicability that makes commercial art more vital than noncommercial, and therefore potentially much more effective for better or for worse. The commercial producer can both educate and pervert the general public, and can allow the general public—or rather his idea of the general public—both to educate and to pervert himself" (120). Such is the power of the medium in Panofsky's view that Hollywood should cease to believe that it must produce "what the public wants" and decide to "depart from evil and do good" (120). That is has not, by and large, done so doesn't invalidate Panofsky's proposition.

Also significant for our purposes is Panofsky's discussion of cinematic realism. If he finds film analogous to the development of engraving and the construction of cathedrals, he finds only difference between film and painting. Whereas the painter starts with a blank wall or canvas and organizes it into the likeness of things and persons according to his idea of reality, the process of cinematic realism works the other way around.

Panofsky is emphatic on this point: "It is the movies, and only the movies, that do justice to the materialistic interpretation of the universe which, whether we like it or not, pervades contemporary civilization. . . . [T]he movies organize material things and persons, not a neutral medium, into a composition that receives its style . . . not so much by an interpretation in the artist's mind as by the actual manipulation of physical object and recording machinery" (120, 122). The aesthetic challenge and the essence of the filmic medium is to manipulate and shoot unstylized reality in such a way that the result has style. Panofsky concludes this passage, "The medium of the movies is physical reality as such."

Panofsky's assertion now seems naive, and one may wish to argue that the *camera* and *film* are the filmmaker's media, not the "material things and persons" that he or she films. Nonetheless, I would propose that Panofsky's sense of film's medium as "reality as such" is what impels postcolonial writers to expect social responsibility from film, and it is what inspires them to incorporate film into their fiction and essays. If painting seems to Panofsky to be removed from its object by the painter's intervention, how much more so by the verbal system of the writer. Whereas the medium of film projects the illusion of unmediated reality, fiction can only strive to create that illusion. This is not a value judgment but a semiotic one, and it leads me back to the "requirement of communicability" established by Panofsky. Postcolonial writers are aware of this requirement for their fiction as well, even as they work from the blank page to organize a likeness of the world. In this process, why not appeal to film, with its capacity to create the illusion of reality itself—natural, familiar, transparent? Why not challenge existing power structures and construct communities with "communicability" such as this?

The mass appeal of film translates into enormous social power. In Panofsky's words, more true now than they were when he wrote them almost seventy years ago: "Whether we like it or not, it is the movies that mold, more than any other single force, the opinions, the taste, the language, the dress, the behavior, and even the physical appearance of a public comprising more than 60 percent of the population of the earth. If all the serious lyrical poets, composers, painters, and sculptors were forced by law to stop their activities, a rather small fraction of the general public would become aware of the fact and a still smaller fraction would seriously regret it. If the same thing were to happen with the movies the social consequences would be catastrophic" (94).

Panofsky is right: we may not like it. And yet postcolonial writers can and do aspire to such social consequence as film commands. Indeed, their intertextual engagement of film projects that aspiration, whether the writer critiques an unjust cinematic version of reality or uses film's aesthetic of "communicability" to propose realities of more open and equitable design.

NOTES

1. There are, of course, exceptions. See Burton; Stock; King; Hershfield; Schnitman; and Millán.

2. "The idea of the South" has been examined by social historians at least since the sixties. This trope implies the privileging of intellectual perception against more positivist historical data. For two useful examples of this approach—though neither focuses on writers who are not geographically southern—see O'Brien and Gray.

3. Puig's best-known novel, *Kiss of the Spider Woman*, uses movie plots in related ways. See my discussion of this novel in chapter 6 of my book *The Usable Past*.

4. Percy himself was a semiotician who wrote semiotic analyses of cultural phenomena (see "The Man on the Train" and "Naming and Being"). See also J. P. Telotte's "A Symbolic Structuring of Walker Percy's Fiction," an essay that focuses on the links between Percy's linguistic theories and his novelistic practice.

5. See also Lucid.

6. Puig discusses the significance of that which is absent or outside of his fiction (see Christ 52–61).

7. Furthermore, the plethora of movies made in Hollywood with Latin American stars speaking Spanish are never referred to (see Pintó).

8. Simone Vauthier mentions this point in two very useful essays: "Title as Micro Text" (225) and "Triangle and Triple Alliance" (75). Percy himself comments on the danger of confusing movies with experience (see "Man on the Train" 489; *Message in the Bottle*).

9. Puig has commented on the rigidity of Argentine sexual stereotypes: "In those days, not to fit into the pattern was a great source of anguish. We thought that the pattern was the only one, the pattern of Nature: girls had to be desirable objects and men had to be terribly strong without any hesitation" (Christ 52).

10. See Girard; Lotman, "Problems." Both critics refer specifically to works in which the conflict between cultural and aesthetic norms provides the primary structural principle.

11. Comparing his experiences of writing for films and of writing fiction, Puig comments that he left moviemaking because "the traditional ninety minutes offered by films was simply not enough. The cinema requires synthesis, whereas my themes needed the opposite: they called for analysis, the accumulation of details" ("Cinema" 398).

12. For an overview of the epic comings and goings of actors, directors, and producers between Argentina and Hollywood see Curubeto.

13. The *Faulkner Journal* has recently devoted a double issue to "Faulkner and Film." While I wholly agree that it is worthwhile to study Faulkner's screenplays and the movies based on his novels, this does not change the fact that Faulkner held the

medium in low regard. Edwin T. Arnold, in his introduction to this issue, writes, "Faulkner himself carefully distinguished between his serious writing and his film work and had little interest in the movies made from his books. He was sometimes concerned that his stays in Hollywood compromised his art, and we can find many mordant quotes that show his contempt for the business of films" (3).

14. O'Connor does not write about the movies, but her work has certainly influenced them. Hilton Als concludes his brilliant article on O'Connor: "One can hear her syntax and thoughts in the stories of Raymond Carver, in Robert Duvall's brilliant movie 'The Apostle,' in the Samuel L. Jackson character's final monologue in 'Pulp Fiction.' Her work has moved away from the South as she defined and knew it, all the way to Hollywood, where Americans have embraced it, hearing in O'Connor's voice the uneasy and unavoidable union between black and white, the sacred and profane, the shit and the stars" (88).

15. McMurtry is quoted in an unsigned note on *Silent Screens*, by Michael Putnam, in the *New Yorker* 11 Sept. 2000: 97.

16. *New Yorker* 11 Sept. 2000: 97; no author cited.

17. This essay was first published in 1936, revised the following year, and revised again in 1942.

WORKS CITED

Als, Hilton. "This Lonesome Place: Flannery O'Connor on Race and Religion in the Unreconstructed South." *New Yorker* 29 Jan. 2001: 82–88.

Arnold, Edwin T. "Faulkner Writ Large/Faulkner Ritt Small." *Faulkner Journal* 16 (2000–2001): 3–6.

Bakhtin, Mikhail. "Discourse in the Novel." *The Dialogic Imagination: Four Essays.* Trans. Caryl Emerson and Michael Holquist. Ed. Michael Holquist. Austin: U of Texas P, 1981. 259–422.

Baldwin, James. *The Devil Finds Work.* New York: Dial, 1966.

Belton, John. *American Cinema/American Culture.* New York: McGraw Hill, 1994.

Borges, Jorge Luis. "El arte narrativo y la magia." *Obras completas.* Vol. 1. Buenos Aires: Emecé, 1989. 226–32.

——. "Narrative Art and Magic." *Borges, A Reader: A Selection from the Writings of Jorge Luis Borges.* Ed. Emir Rodríguez Monegal and Alastair Reid. Trans. Norman Thomas di Giovanni. New York: E. P. Dutton, 1981. 34–38.

Burton, Julianne. *Cinema and Social Change in Latin America: Conversations with Filmmakers.* Austin: U of Texas P, 1986.

Callahan, John F. Introduction. *Flying Home and Other Stories.* By Ralph Ellison. Ed. and intro. John F. Callahan. New York: Random, 1996. ix–xxxviii.

Christ, Ronald. "An Interview with Manuel Puig." *Partisan Review* 44 (1977): 52–61.

Cortázar, Julio. "Queremos tanto a Glenda." *Queremos tanto a Glenda.* Mexico City: Nueva Imagen, 1980. 19–28.

——. "We Love Glenda so Much." *We Love Glenda So Much and Other Tales.* Trans. Gregory Rabassa. New York: Knopf, 1983. 8–16.

Curubeto, Diego. *Babilonia Gaucha: Hollywood en Argentina, La Argentina en Hollywood*. Buenos Aires: Planeta, 1993.

Dickey, Sara. *Cinema and the Urban Poor in South India*. Cambridge: Cambridge UP, 1993.

Ellison, Ralph. *Shadow and Act*. New York: Vintage, 1953.

Fuentes, Carlos. *Holy Place. Triple Cross*. Trans. Suzanne Jill Levine. New York: E. P. Dutton, 1972. 11–144.

——. *Zona sagrada*. Mexico City: Siglo Veintiuno, 1967.

García Márquez, Gabriel. *Cien años de soledad*. Buenos Aires: Editorial Sudamericana, 1967.

——. "Of Love and Levitation." *Times Literary Supplement* 20–26 Oct. 1989: 1152, 1165.

——. *One Hundred Years of Solitude*. Trans. Gregory Rabassa. New York: Avon, 1970.

Girard, René. *Mensonge romantique et vérité romanesque*. Paris: Grasset, 1961.

Gray, Richard. *Writing the South: Ideas of an American Region*. Cambridge: Cambridge UP, 1986.

Hershfield, Joanne. *Mexican Cinema/Mexican Woman, 1940–1950*. Tucson: U of Arizona P, 1996.

King, John. *Magical Reels: A History of Cinema in Latin America*. London: Verso, 1990.

Lotman, Juri M. "Problems in the Typology of Culture." *Soviet Semiotics: An Anthology*. Ed., trans., and intro. Daniel P. Lucid. Baltimore, Md.: Johns Hopkins UP, 1977. 213–21.

——. *The Structure of the Artistic Text*. Ed. and trans. D. Barton Johnson. Ann Arbor, Mich.: Ardis, 1976.

——. "The Structure of the Narrative Text." *Soviet Semiotics: An Anthology*. Ed., trans., and intro. Daniel P. Lucid. Baltimore, Md.: Johns Hopkins UP, 1977. 193–97.

Lucid, Daniel P., ed. *Soviet Semiotics: An Anthology*. Trans. and intro. Daniel P. Lucid. Baltimore, Md.: Johns Hopkins UP, 1977.

McMurtry, Larry. *The Last Picture Show*. New York: Dial Press, 1966.

Millán, Márgara. *Derivas de un cine en femenino*. Mexico City: UNAM, 1999.

O'Brien, Michael. *The Idea of the South: 1920–1941*. Baltimore, Md.: Johns Hopkins UP, 1979.

O'Connor, Flannery. "A Late Encounter with the Enemy." *A Good Man Is Hard to Find*. New York: Harcourt Brace, 1983. 155–68.

Panofsky, Erwin. "Style and Medium in the Motion Pictures." *Three Essays on Style*. Ed. and intro. Irving Levin. Cambridge, Mass.: MIT P, 1995. 91–125.

Percy, Walker. "The Loss of the Creature." *Forum* 2 (1958): 6–14.

——. "The Man on the Train: Three Existential Modes." *Partisan Review* 23 (1956): 478–94.

——. *The Message in the Bottle: How Queer Man Is, How Queer Language Is, and What One Has to Do with the Other*. New York: Farrar, 1979. 83–100.

——. *The Moviegoer*. New York: Avon, 1960.

——. "Naming and Being." *Personalist* 41 (1960): 148–57.

Pintó, Alfonso. "When Hollywood Spoke Spanish." *Américas* (Oct. 1980): 3–8.

Puig, Manuel. *Betrayed by Rita Hayworth.* Trans. Suzanne Jill Levine. New York: Avon, 1973.

——. "Cinema and the Novel." *The Oxford Book of Latin American Essays.* Ed. Ilan Stavans. Oxford: Oxford UP, 1997. 395–400.

——. *La traición de Rita Hayworth.* Buenos Aires: Editorial Sudamericana, 1968.

Putnam, Michael. *Silent Screens.* Baltimore, Md.: Johns Hopkins UP, 2000.

Schnitman, Jorge A. *Film Industries in Latin American Dependency and Development.* Norwood, N.J.: Ablex, 1984.

Stock, Anne Marie, ed. *Framing Latin American Cinema: Contemporary Critical Perspectives.* Minneapolis: U of Minnesota P, 1997.

Telotte, J. P. "A Symbolic Structuring of Walker Percy's Fiction." *Modern Fiction Studies* 26 (1980): 227–40.

Vauthier, Simone. "Title as Micro Text: The Example of *The Moviegoer*." *Journal of Narrative Technique* (Sept. 1975): 219–29.

——. "Triangle and Triple Alliance: A Look at the Moviegoer." *Les Americanistes: New French Criticism on Modern American Fiction.* Ed. and intro. Ira D. Johnson and Christian Johnson. Port Washington, N.Y.: Kennikat, 1978. 71–93.

Wood, Michael. "The Claims of Mischief." *New York Review of Books* 24 Jan. 1980: 43–44.

Zamora, Lois Parkinson. *The Usable Past: The Imagination of History in Recent Fiction of the Americas.* Cambridge: Cambridge UP, 1997.

★ ★ ★ **PART THREE**

WILLIAM FAULKNER AND LATIN AMERICA

In the complex dynamic of transference, projection, and introjection that has allowed the U.S. South to seem both Self and Other to both global northerners and tropicopolitans, no literary figure has loomed larger than William Faulkner, who in this psychodynamic often represents a version of the Great White Father. In 1998 and 2000 Michael Kreyling and Patricia Yaeger were still contemplating "dynamiting the rails" of what Flannery O'Connor had called the "Dixie Limited." In this tellingly oedipal bit of transferential offing, Faulkner stands in for all the Great White Fathers of southern literary criticism from the Agrarians through Louis Rubin and, for Yaeger, Richard King and perhaps Kreyling himself. More broadly, as a white North American, Faulkner falls in the line of Thomas Jefferson (the Great White Father spoofed in *Invisible Man*) for some African American critics, while for some Latin American writers he more closely resembles Jefferson's friend and Virginia neighbor James Monroe, whose doctrine continues to shape the political and economic history of the New World.

Yet—and this is a point with which North American critics have had difficulty, being with good reason not kindly disposed to white southern apologias—as a resident of a dirt-poor region colonized by an industrial and imperial north, Faulkner has also, to New World creoles further south, seemed more a postcolonialist writer, the kind of "good" father who shows the way for his intellectual descendants, the writer who, more than any other, deployed and developed modernist techniques precisely to show the plight of a figuratively sterile region stalled on the tracks of modernity's post-Reconstruction, post-1898 New World order. Thus, to read Faulkner simply as "white" or "hegemonic" and thereby to question his importance to Latin American and Caribbean writers (one of the early readers of this collection asked us to explain why Faulkner instead of Booker T. Washington, for example, was so important to writers further south) is to project a largely North American black/white binary onto cultures that have, for much of the twentieth century, though not always in good faith, prized their *mestizaje*. It makes little sense to say that because Faulkner is a white North American, Latin American and Caribbean writers' transferential adoption of him as a kind of father or model necessarily represents pathology or denial. Nor does it make much sense to claim that progressive North American writers' and critics' Othering of him as hegemonic white male represents pathology or denial because Faulkner, though "white" (as the United States fetishizes that property), came from a culture that had experienced defeat under colonialism. Like the "real" South, the "real" Faulkner always dissolves under the transferential pressures of personal and cultural fantasies about power. One can and must study those fantasies, but if one purports to critique them from some objective or normative foundation, one ignores the quicksand of transference on which that foundation is built.

Here, then, is what might be called the standard Latin American account of William Faulkner. Faulkner became a focal author for writers of the region as a result of those writers' (transferential) perception of historical and cultural affinities between the South and Latin America (most frequently defeat in war, racial conflict, underdevelopment, and a generally difficult entrance into modernity), as well as a model for the writers' positioning of themselves vis-à-vis the cultural metropolis. This relationship was one of influence—what Gustavo Pérez Firmat, in the introduction to *Do the Americas Have a Common Literature?*, characterizes as "genetic," the result of direct textual and authorial contact—but was also (again, in Pérez Firmat's terms) one of "apposition": texts by Faulkner and Latin American authors deploy similar features and strategies to portray analogous sociopolitical and historical circumstances (3). Works such as *Absalom, Absalom!* and *As I Lay Dying*, and characters such as Quentin

Compson, Gail Hightower, and Emily Grierson who, unable to extricate themselves from a personal past that is in some way bound up with their region's history, embody the theme of historical paralysis, left a tremendous genetic impact on the development of Latin American narrative from the 1940s on, culminating most noticeably in the works of authors such as Jorge Luis Borges, Carlos Fuentes, Gabriel García Márquez, Juan Carlos Onetti, and Mario Vargas Llosa, who brought Spanish-American literature into an international arena in the 1960s.[1] So, too, did the paradigm of the deathbed or posthumous narration, as well as the perspectivism that marks texts with multiple possibilities of interpretation.

The essays in this section address similarities and differences in the appropriation of Faulkner and his works by authors writing within a postcolonial context. The first four essays are concerned with the creation of a nonrealist aesthetic that is at once endogenous and positioned in relation to a North that has exercised both political and cultural hegemony over the regions from whence the authors hail. Faulkner is as much a participant in this endeavor in his own right as he is, at times, a model and mediator for the work of the Latin American authors. Stephanie Merrim traces the trajectory of wonder from classical formulations to Faulkner and Borges's reworkings thereof—reworkings that render wonder part of a language (and history) of crisis in both regions—and, ultimately, to the underpinnings of the grotesque and of magical realism, excentric, self-exoticizing discursive positions that have come to be seen as coextensive with the South and Latin America, respectively. Wendy B. Faris, in turn, explores how Faulkner's tragic view of history and of a regrettable modernity is shared by Fuentes. Additionally, she shows how both writers render their vision stylistically through recourse to a baroque poetics, an excessive, nonproductive verbal expenditure that she views as a stylistic correlative to Bataille's positing of excess as a critique of capitalist efficiency—a critique that stems, in this case, from the inability of either the South or Spanish America to be successful in the prevailing U.S. economic climate. Philip Weinstein's analyses reveal that the perceived bankruptcy of the Western "plot of progress" underlies not just Faulkner's tragic fiction but also García Márquez's and Toni Morrison's reconfigurations of Western realism within a postcolonial setting. For Faulkner, as for modernists in general, Western culture's generic norms and behavioral models no longer produce narratives of fulfillment. Nevertheless, Faulkner's characters are incapable of reshaping realism's progressive-acquisitive plot but, rather, seem doomed to live it out, only to fail. The fiction of García Márquez and Morrison, in contrast, draws on non-Western and folk cultural resources to reject not just realism's individualizing plots of achievement but modernism's drama of failure as well. Dane Johnson explores another dimension of García Márquez, identifying a noncosmopolitan aesthetic in both the Colombian's work and that of Faulkner. Johnson shows the writers to be mediators between their own regions and the "metropolis" (broadly speaking): both represent their homelands and cultures to more powerful Others who do not understand them, in order to dispel stereotypes about them (e.g., the South and Spanish America as aberrant, backwaters, wastelands). Thus they resist exogenous constructions of their regional identity, even as they strive for success in the metropolitan mainstream.

Where Johnson looks northward, examining Faulkner's and García Márquez's challenges to the cultural marketing of the South and Spanish America to and in the metropolis, Helen Oakley's gaze is directed south in her study of the marketing of Faulkner himself by the U.S. State Department from 1950 until his death in 1962. During these years, the State Department sent him to Europe and Asia, and twice to Latin America, where recent interventions had generated tremendous hostility toward the United States. Faulkner represented U.S. cultural achievement and, due to his popularity among Latin American writers and intellectuals (as attested to by the preceding essays), became a cultural ambassador whose warm welcome brought much positive publicity to the United States during a time of strained political relations. Earl Fitz returns to the question of Faulkner's influence—or rather, to the relative lack thereof—in Brazil, where the work of Joaquim Maria Machado de Assis in the 1880s steered Brazilian literature away from realism and toward an experimental style at an extremely early date. Nevertheless, Fitz affirms that the commonalities shared by the South and Spanish America also extend to Brazil, demonstrating this in a comparative analysis of works by James Agee and Euclides da Cunha.

NOTE

1. There is an extensive bibliography available on this subject. For general studies of Faulkner's influence on Latin American literature, consult works by Cohn, Fayen, Irby, and Pothier. For studies of his influence on specific authors (both Latin American and Caribbean), consult works by Bessière, Christie, Corvalán, Davis, Delay and de Labriolle, Faris, Handley, Kristal, Levine, Ludmer, Mac Adam, O'Bryan-Knight, Oberhelman, Oliveira, Ramos Escobar, Shapiro, Simas, Snell, Tobin, Valente, Vargas Saavedra, and Zamora. The authors themselves have often commented on Faulkner's foundational influence on their work and their relationship to the South that he depicted; see, for example, works by Borges, Donoso, Edwards, Fuentes, García Márquez, Glissant, and Vargas Llosa, as well as the essays in Guibert's *Seven Voices* and

Harss and Dohmann's *Into the Mainstream.* For full bibliographical references, see list of works cited.

WORKS CITED

Bessière, Jean. "Carlos Fuentes Vis-à-Vis William Faulkner: Novel, Tragedy, History." *Faulkner Journal* 11.1–2 (fall–spring 1995–1996): 33–42.

Borges, Jorge Luis. Review of *The Unvanquished,* by William Faulkner. *El hogar* 22 Jan. 1937. Rpt. in *Ficcionario.* Ed. Emir Rodríguez Monegal. Mexico City: Fondo de Cultura Económica, 1985. 123–24.

Christie, John. "Fathers and Virgins: García Márquez's Faulknerian *Chronicle of a Death Foretold.*" *Latin American Literary Review* 21.41 (1993): 21–29.

Cohn, Deborah. "Faulkner and Spanish America: Then and Now." *Faulkner and the Twenty-First Century. Faulkner and Yoknapatawpha, 2000.* Ed. Robert Hamblin and Ann Abadie. Jackson: UP of Mississippi, 2003.

——. *History and Memory in the Two Souths: Recent Southern and Spanish American Fiction.* Nashville, Tenn.: Vanderbilt UP, 1999.

——. "Teaching Faulkner and the Spanish American Novel." *Teaching Faulkner Newsletter* 19 (fall 2001): 1–4.

Corvalán, Octavio. "Faulkner y García Márquez: Una aproximación." *Sur* 349 (July–Dec. 1981): 71–88.

Davis, Mary E. "The Haunted Voice: Echoes of William Faulkner in García Márquez, Fuentes, and Vargas Llosa." *World Literature Today* (autumn 1985): 531–35.

——. "William Faulkner and Mario Vargas Llosa: The Election of Failure." *Comparative Literature Studies* 16 (1979): 332–43.

Delay, Florence, and Jacqueline de Labriolle. "Márquez: Est-il le Faulkner colombien?" *Revue de Littérature Comparée* 47 (1973): 88–123.

Donoso, José. *Historia personal del "boom."* Barcelona: Seix Barral, 1983.

Edwards, Jorge. "Yoknapatawpha in Santiago de Chile." *Faulkner: International Perspectives. Faulkner and Yoknapatawpha, 1982.* Ed. Doreen Fowler and Ann Abadie. Jackson: UP of Mississippi, 1984. 60–71.

Faris, Wendy. "Marking Space, Charting Time: Text and Territory in Faulkner's 'The Bear' and Carpentier's *Los pasos perdidos.*" *Do the Americas Have a Common Literature?* Ed. Gustavo Pérez Firmat. Durham, N.C.: Duke UP, 1990. 243–65.

Fayen, Tanya T. *In Search of the Latin American Faulkner.* Lanham, Md.: UP of America, 1995.

Fuentes, Carlos. *Casa con dos puertas.* Mexico City: Joaquín Mortiz, 1970.

——. *La nueva novela hispanoamericana.* Mexico City: Joaquín Mortiz, 1969.

García Márquez, Gabriel. "Los problemas de la novela." *El Heraldo* (Barranquilla) 24 Apr. 1950. Rpt. in *Obra periodística,* vol. 1: *Textos costeños.* Ed. Jacques Gilard. Barcelona: Bruguera, 1980.

García Márquez, Gabriel, and Mario Vargas Llosa. *La novela en América Latina: Diálogo.* Lima: Carlos Millá Batres/Universidad Nacional de Ingeniería, 1968.

Glissant, Edouard. *Faulkner, Mississippi.* Trans. Barbara Lewis and Thomas C. Spear. New York: Farrar, 1999.

Guibert, Rita. *Seven Voices.* Trans. Frances Partridge. New York: Knopf, 1973.

Handley, George. *Postslavery Literatures in the Americas: Family Portraits in Black and White.* Charlottesville: UP of Virginia, 2000.

Harss, Luis, and Barbara Dohmann. *Into the Mainstream: Conversations with Latin-American Writers.* New York: Harper, 1967.

Irby, James East. "La influencia de William Faulkner en cuatro narradores hispano-americanos." M.A. thesis. Universidad Nacional Autónoma de México, 1956.

Kristal, Efraín. *Temptation of the Word: The Novels of Mario Vargas Llosa.* Nashville, Tenn.: Vanderbilt UP, 1998.

Levine, Suzanne Jill. *El espejo hablado: Un estudio de "Cien años de soledad."* Caracas: Monte Avila Editores, 1975.

Ludmer, Josefina. "Onetti: 'La novia (carta) robada (a Faulkner).'" *Hispamérica* 9 (1975): 3–19.

Mac Adam, Alfred. "Carlos Fuentes: The Burden of History." *World Literature Today* 57.4 (1983): 558–63.

Oberhelman, Harley. "Faulknerian Techniques in Gabriel García Márquez's Portrait of a Dictator." *Proceedings of the Comparative Literature Symposium*, vol. 10: *Ibero-American Letters in a Comparative Perspective.* Ed. Wolodymyr T. Zyla and Wendell M. Aycock. Lubbock: Texas Tech UP, 1978. 171–81.

——. "García Márquez and the American South." *Chasqui* 5.1 (Nov. 1975): 29–38.

——. *The Presence of Faulkner in the Writings of García Márquez.* Graduate Studies No. 22. Lubbock: Texas Tech UP, 1980.

——. "William Faulkner and Gabriel García Márquez: Two Nobel Laureates." *Critical Essays on Gabriel García Márquez.* Ed. George McMurray. Boston: G. K. Hall, 1987. 67–79.

——. "William Faulkner's Reception in Spanish America." *American Hispanist* 3.26 (1978): 13–17.

O'Bryan-Knight, Jean. "From Spinster to Eunuch: William Faulkner's 'A Rose for Emily' and Mario Vargas Llosa's *Los cachorros.*" *Comparative Literature Studies* 34.4 (1997): 328–47.

Oliveira, Celso de. *Faulkner and Graciliano Ramos.* Tübingen: Francke, 1993.

Pérez Firmat, Gustavo, ed. *Do the Americas Have a Common Literature?* Durham, N.C.: Duke UP, 1990.

Pothier, Jacques. "Voices from the South, Voices of the Souths: Faulkner, García Márquez, Vargas Llosa, Borges." *Faulkner Journal* 11.1–2 (fall–spring 1995–1996): 101–18.

Ramos Escobar, J. L. "Desde Yoknapatawpha a Macondo." *En el punto de mira: Gabriel García Márquez.* Ed. A. M. Hernández de López. Madrid: Editorial Pliegos, 1985. 287–311.

Shapiro, J. P. "'Une histoire contée par un idiot . . .': W. Faulkner et J. Rulfo." *Revue de Littérature Comparée* 53 (1979): 338–47.

Simas, Rosa. "'Ripples,' a 'Gyrating Wheel,' and a 'Spiral on a Square': Circularity in Three Twentieth-Century Novels of the Americas." Diss. U of California, Davis, 1990.

——. " 'Ripples,' *'Una rueda giratoria,'* and *'A Espiral e o quadrado'*: Circularity in Three Twentieth-Century Novels of the Americas." *Translation Perspectives* 6 (1991): 87–98.

Snell, Susan. "William Faulkner, un guía sureño a la ficción de García Márquez." *En el punto de mira: Gabriel García Márquez.* Ed. A. M. Hernández de López. Madrid: Editorial Pliegos, 1985. 315–26.

Tobin, Patricia Drechsel. *Time and the Novel: The Genealogical Imperative.* Princeton, N.J.: Princeton UP, 1978.

Valente, Luiz. "Marriages of Speaking and Hearing: Mediation and Response in *Absalom, Absalom!* and *Grande Sertão: Veredas.*" *Faulkner Journal* 11.1–2 (fall–spring 1995–1996): 149–63.

——. "The Reader in the Work: Fabulation and Affective Response in João Guimarães Rosa and William Faulkner." Diss. Brown University, 1983.

Vargas Llosa, Mario. "Faulkner en Laberinto." 1981. *Contra Viento y Marea II (1972–83).* Barcelona: Seix Barral, 1986. 299–302.

——. *A Writer's Reality.* Ed. M. Lichtblau. Syracuse, N.Y.: Syracuse UP, 1991.

Vargas Saavedra, Luis. "La afinidad de Onetti a Faulkner." *Cuadernos hispanoamericanos* 98.292–4 (1974): 257–65.

Zamora, Lois Parkinson. "The End of Innocence: Myth and Narrative Structure in Faulkner's *Absalom, Absalom!* and García Márquez's *Cien años de soledad.*" *Hispanic Journal* 4.1 (fall 1982): 23–40.

——. *Writing the Apocalypse: Historical Vision in Contemporary U.S. and Latin American Fiction.* Cambridge: Cambridge UP, 1989.

STEPHANIE MERRIM

Wonder and the Wounds of

"Southern" Histories

Wonder, an *intellectual* emotion, is inherently plural. As a rare and almost oxymoronic hybrid of cognition and passion, it holds boundless appeal. Wonder radiates into a broad semantic field (in the languages of concern here, English and Spanish: wonder, awe, astonish / *maravillar, asombrar, admirar*) and has inspired a host of enduring foundational constructions.[1] To establish a baseline over and against which to measure the work of wonder in the U.S. South and in South America, one can consider the following bedrock genealogy of these constructions.

Plato's dialogue *Theaetetus* posits wonder as the intellectual energy that comprises the starting point of all philosophical inquiry (21, 155 c–d). Similarly, centuries later, Descartes writes in *Les Passions de l'Âme* (The Passions of the Soul), "Wonder is a sudden surprise of the soul which causes it to apply itself to consider with attention the objects which seem to it rare and extraordinary" (362). For Descartes, wonder is a "first encounter" and is prior to moral judgment (358–59; Greenblatt 20). Aristotle both shares Plato's view of wonder as the impetus for philosophical inquiry and conditions Descartes's discomfort with the onrush of "surprise" generated by ignorance, since the Greek philosopher sees wonder as an initial passion that intellectual investigation should ultimately dispel (*Metaphysics* 1554, 1.2 982b 10–18; see Daston and Park chap. 3).

In his *Poetics*, on the other hand, Aristotle invests literature with the basic function of producing a salutary wonder. Broaching the thorny question of verisimilitude, Aristotle argues that to incite wonder, the poet may present things as they are said or thought or ought to be rather than as they were (133, 1460 a–b). Over the course of the Renaissance and beyond, Aristotle's loophole in mimesis was inflated into the generative locus of literary production and criticism. Those who sought to escape the constraints of imitation weaned poesis from mimesis. The wonderful or marvelous, *admiratio*, thus came to be identified with the full play of the imagination, *inventio*, in its all-embracing manifestations as textual subject, stylistics, and effect on the reader (see Hathaway chap. 2).

Despite their capacious and paradigmatic natures, none of the preceding formulations fully comprehends the wonder that emanates from texts of the U.S. South and from South America. I begin my account of the ways in which wonder is implicated in the wounds of history with two writers who, in the eyes of many, epitomize "southern" writing: William Faulkner and Jorge Luis Borges. As do the other writers whom this essay will treat, Faulkner and Borges kidnap the energies of wonder for an alien use.[2] They lace wonder with the fearful edge inherent in amazement, *asombro*. They wrench wonder from epistemology and mimesis and insert it in history, refunctioning and overloading it. Their catachrestic deployment of wonder, the wounding of its meaning(s), is the language of crisis. Stephen Greenblatt, of course, has examined in his *Marvelous Possessions* (1991) the poisoning of the marvelous in the colonialist discourse configured during the crises of the age of Spanish conquest and expansion. For my part, I will carry the crisis of the marvelous up to the twentieth century as well as into the post- or neocolonial "Souths." After examining the overdetermining of wonder in texts of the U.S. South and South America, I conclude with a critique of the magical realism that evolves from the southern position and from history itself to constitute yet another hemispheric literary tie. The ever-expanding, troubled, and ultimately troubling story of wonder that I outline herein will begin by taking its cue and in the end derive its hope from the two visionary southern writers, Faulkner and Borges.

A dark, Gothic wonder marks both the inception and the terminus of the storytelling, history-making project of Faulkner's *Absalom, Absalom!* (1936). Speaking in a "grim haggard amazed voice" (3), with an "unbearable amazement" that might have "even been a cry aloud once" (9), Rosa begins the incredible tale of the fraternity between Bon and Henry that had ended in fratricide. All these years later still amazed, confounded, and conflicted by the convolutions of the southern saga, Rosa insinuates her listener, Quentin Compson, into the "long unamaze" (4). It then falls to Quentin to experience and parse out the heterotopia packed into that phrase. Quentin will become ghosted and a-mazed as he enters and negotiates the labyrinth of history. He will cede to the paralysis of amazement, his inability to pass through the door of the past (142), yet go on to confront the Minotaur(s) at its center. Quentin and his Ariadne, the cupidlike Shreve, will together manufacture the thread that pulls Quentin to the center and out of the maze, first into catharsis (he jerks violently and then feels fine [288]) and finally into a jagged paroxysm (*"I dont! I dont hate it! I dont hate it!"* [303]) that, as one knows from *The Sound and the Fury*, is in the final instance not unakin to Rosa's initial haggard amazement.

Only by means of slowly gathering acts of the imagination can Quentin and Shreve make sense of the labyrinth. At the culminating point, just as the clock strikes midnight, they fabricate characters who, although they "perhaps had never existed at all anywhere" (243), nevertheless center the fratricide on the racial issues of Bon's black heritage and potential miscegenation and thus shape the history of Henry and Bon into a meaning-full as well as wonder-full story of the South per se. That is to say, by means of their fabulations, Quentin and Shreve conceive not *a* but *the* story of the South. "In the hearing and sifting and discarding the false and conserving what seemed true or fit the preconceived" (253), the two youths arrive at "that true wisdom which can comprehend that there is a might-have-been which is more true than true" (115).

As these unmistakable evocations of inventio and verisimilitude signal, Faulkner inscribes *Absalom* in an Aristotelian framework. Amazement proves to be an avatar of admiratio and shades into inventio. By its end, the novel has activated an Aristotelian sense of history versus poetry (that is, a fragmented, local sense of events versus a panoptic view that extracts general principles), of catharsis, and of allegory (which, in classical poetics, justifies departures from mimesis). Faulkner here spins out Aristotelian amazement together with other of the philosopher's consecrated literary premises into their ultimate, tragic, and peculiarly southern consequences. Even as he subscribes to the letter of the *Poetics*, Faulkner freights amazement with the burdens of southern history.

Moreover, Faulkner establishes an intimate connection between wonder and the very act of wounding history. The second chapter of the novel takes readers into the breach, the era in which Thomas Sutpen "abrupted" onto the scene and began to institute the design that would (in Quentin and Shreve's contrivances) convert Jefferson, Mississippi, into an emblem of the South. Emphatically, at each step, Sutpen's actions inspire amazement. The French architect lurks on the construction scene of Sutpen's Hundred with an "expression of grim and embittered amazement . . . his air something between a casual and bitterly disinterested spectator and condemned and conscientious ghost—amazement" (28). The townspeople watch "in shocked amazement" (32) as Sutpen lays siege to Mr. Coldfield and marries Ellen (31). The crux of the townspeople's amazement lies in their "realization that he [Sutpen] was getting it involved with himself" (33). Yet the townspeople, the main players of the novel, and the French architect alike are all in essence reacting to the wounding or violation of their former way of life, to the alienation from self and loss of volition that derives from their having been precipitously and uncomprehendingly interpellated into a perhaps fated and certainly ill-fated design. Faulkner delivers a Cartesian "first encounter" grounded in awe, but amazement is never happy in *Absalom*. As in Plato, amazement does indeed compel inquiry. However, not philosophy but *history* begins in wonder here.

Borges read, reviewed, and translated Faulkner toward the end of the 1930s, perhaps glimpsing some special import in *Absalom*'s amazement.[3] For asombro makes an insistent (if sparing) appearance only in Borges's very first collection of outright stories, *El jardín de senderos que se bifurcan* (1941; *The Garden of Forking Paths*), where it consistently enters the narrative scene at crucial, over-viewing moments. Nevertheless, the Argentine author's renditions of amazement and its etiology are neither as classical in origin nor as classically neat as Faulkner's. Like much else in the volume, they are baroque: multiple and twisting like the labyrinth to which the work's title alludes, and turning on sophism and oxymoron as well as catachresis. The prologue that Borges appended in 1954 to his previous work of imaginative prose, a pastiche of other authors' works overlaid with Borgesian moves and entitled *Historia universal de la infamia* (1935; *A Universal History of Infamy*), lays out the theory of the baroque that drives *Historia* as well as the *ficciones* of *Jardín*: "Yo diría que barroco es aquel estilo que deliberadamente agota (o quiere agotar) sus posibilidades y que linda con su propia caricatura" (9) ["I would define the baroque as that style that deliberately exhausts (or tries to exhaust) its own possibilities, and that borders on self-caricature" (*Collected Fictions* 4)]. He goes on to state that "*Barroco* (*Baroco*) es el nombre de uno de los modos de silogismo; el siglo XVIII lo aplicó a determinados abusos de la arquitectura y de la pintura del XVII; yo diría que es barroca la etapa final de todo arte, cuando éste exhibe y dilapida sus medios" (*Historia* 9) ["'*Baroco*' was a term used for one of the modes of syllogistic reasoning; the eighteenth century applied it to certain abuses in seventeenth-century architecture and painting. I would venture to say that the baroque is the final stage in all art, when art flaunts and squanders its resources" (*Collected Fictions* 4)]. Entranced with its decadence and abuses, like Pierre Menard (in the story found in *Jardín*), Borges will conflate the seventeenth with the twentieth century.

Pierre Menard's "amazing" (50) and heroic anachronism necessarily implicates the affinities between Cervantes and Borges's crisis-ridden times, both struggling with hegemony. Borges invokes the seventeenth century much in the way that Walter Benjamin calls on history, that is, "to seize hold of a memory as it flashes up at a point of danger" (255). Although Borges chooses not to articulate the political implications of "Pierre Menard," he does engage in political commentary elsewhere. Indeed, the Argentine author associated with fantastic literature took strong stands against fascism and totalitarianism in the magazine *Sur* (South) and in other works. Fascism had already impacted Argentina itself (for example, in a burgeoning of anti-Semitism [see Aizenberg chap. 5]) and would eventually lead to the rise of Perón. In keeping with the pro-Allied stance of *Sur* and against the grain of Argentina's official support of the Axis, Borges wrote a series of articles that, while maintaining their author's characteristic subtlety and refinement, blasted totalitarianism.[4]

Such worldly and global inclinations make their way into Borges's earliest *ficciones*, where they are conjugated with his quasi-Berkeleyan idealist philosophy, "going transcendental" (McGuirk 186). Stories in *Jardín* with an antitotalitarian thrust include some of Borges's most famous and occupy more than half the volume: "Tlön, Uqbar, Orbis Tertius," "La lotería en Babilonia" ("The Lottery in Babylon")—he states in the foreword that the story "no es del todo inocente de simbolismo" (*Ficciones* 11) ["is not wholly innocent of symbolism" (*Collected Fictions* 67)], "La Biblioteca de Babel" ("The Library of Babel"), and, of course, "El jardín de los senderos que se bifurcan" ("The Garden of Forking Paths"). They implicate *asombro*, drawing it into the oxymoronic web that makes political commentary a branch of fantastic literature. In *Jardín*, Borges's transition volume from poetry and essay into the hybrid and fantastic *ficciones*, *asombro* oscillates between a sense of empty artifice, such as that which for Borges characterized Góngora's ultrabaroque poetic contrivances,[5] and the Aristotelian "admiración" with which *Don Quijote* abounds. Throughout the *Quijote*, admiración marks the flash point where fiction jostles reality, erupts into life. Both senses of asombro appear in the political stories and perhaps most pointedly, as do other of Borges's baroque impulses, in a story of the contamination of so many things: "Tlön, Uqbar, Orbis Tertius."

Disarmingly, disingenuously, the narrator "Borges" associates his first reading of the encyclopedia that contains the keys to the purportedly mythical Tlön with asombro—"Me puse a hojearlo y sentí un vértigo asombrado" (*Jardín* 18) ["I began to leaf through it and experienced an astonished and airy feeling of vertigo" (*Labyrinths* 6–7)]—and with the divine revelation of the Islamic "Night of Nights." Fiction has overspilled into reality, inciting a cosmic awe. The narrator then explains at length the nature of the planet Tlön, a reification of Borgesian/Berkeleyan idealism. Not the least of Tlön's apparent attractions, certainly a sly characterization of Borges's own incipient ficciones, is the fact that the "metafísicos de Tlön no buscan la verdad ni siquiera la verosimilitud: buscan el asombro. Juzgan que la metafísica es una rama de la literatura fantástica" (*Jardín* 23) ["metaphysicians of Tlön do not seek for the truth or even verisimilitude, but rather for the astounding. They judge that metaphysics is a branch of fantastic literature" (*Labyrinths* 10)]. That first vertigo, and then the disregard of truth or even of verisimilitude accompany asombro signify its degeneration from a revelation. The two descriptors of asombro also augur an unfastening from referentiality that quickly assumes a parodic and eventually a dire political cast. In a baroque expansion *ad absurdum*, Borges's explanation of Tlön deliberately plays out an idealism laden with asombro to the point where it exhausts its possibilities and implodes, becoming a caricature of itself. The impossibility of materialism and causality, the denial of history, the Platonic nightmare of copies (*hrönir, ür*) indistinguishable from the original: all these features of the idealist Tlön careen toward total incoherence and instability. Oxymoronically, the utopia has proved to harbor a dystopia.[6] Borges has inserted an eighteenth-century philosophy into a baroque machine that has whirled idealism into a cruel dissolution.

He has also, one must note, sacrificed his own most cherished philosophical notions. Or, more aptly, scapegoated them. In the substantial "Postscript," purportedly of 1947 ("Tlön" was first published in 1940), to the story, Borges lays bare the political substance and sophistry that underwrote the none-too-ironic description of Tlön. The philosophy and even objects of the supposedly mythical Tlön have entered the world.

> Casi inmediatamente, la realidad cedió en más de un punto. Lo cierto es que anhelaba ceder. Hace diez años bastaba cualquier sime-

tría con apariencia de orden—el materialismo dialéctico, el antisemi-
tismo, el nazismo—para embelesar a los hombres. ¿Cómo no some-
terse a Tlön, a la minuciosa y vasta evidencia de un planeta ordenado?
(*Jardín* 33)

Almost immediately, reality yielded on more than one account.
The truth is that it longed to yield. Ten years ago any symmetry with a
semblance of order—dialectical materialism, anti-Semitism, Nazism—
was sufficient to entrance the minds of men. How could one do other
than submit to Tlön, to the minute and vast evidence of an orderly
planet? (*Labyrinths* 17)

Borges has already surreptitiously deconstructed the seeming "order"
of Tlön. Now he equates its sham appeal with the hubris of appropriating
a divine function: "Inútil responder que la realidad también está or-
denada. Quizá lo esté, pero de acuerdo con leyes divinas—traduzco: con
leyes inhumanas—que no acabamos nunca de percibir" (*Jardín* 33–34)
["It is useless to answer that reality is also orderly. Perhaps it is, but in
accordance with divine laws—I translate: inhuman laws—which we can
never quite grasp" (*Labyrinths* 17)]. Alarmed and disgusted, the narrator
retreats from the world to devote himself to a "Quevedian" translation of
Sir Thomas Browne's baroque "Urne Burial." As in another text revered
by Borges at this stage, G. K. Chesterton's *The* Amazing *Adventures of
Father Brown* (my emphasis), what began in metaphysics or philosophy
has ended in a strange but formidably real iniquity.

Borges concluded a later work, his essay "La esfera de Pascal" ("Pascal's Sphere"), with the statement that "quizá la historia universal es la
historia de la diversa entonación de algunas metáforas" (*Otras inquisiciones* 16) ["perhaps universal history is the history of the diverse intonation of a few metaphors" (*Other Inquisitions* 9)]. We have just traversed
one set of intonations of wonder, its association with history in two
southern texts. This opening act sets the stage for the big picture and for
the larger contentions of my essay. I maintain that *the commonality between the literatures and discursive strategies of the "Souths" is to a significant degree a history of the intonation of wonder.*[7] Like Borges and
Faulkner, southern discourse repositions wonder, demanding that it enter the fray of a troubled reality. Moreover, the southern discourse to
which we now turn materializes wonder into a pivotal feature of regional
identity politics. As Sutpen enthralled the unwitting townspeople of Jefferson, Mississippi, it interpellates wonder into an imbricated design. Yet
"Southern" discourse directly counters Sutpen's design, for it charges
wonder with *salving the wounds of history.* An emollient force, even a

patent myth in some of its incarnations, wonder provides a platform for diverse moves against the dominant cultures.

Why wonder and history in the "Souths"? The outlines of one response to the necessary question can be found in history. Greenblatt's *Marvelous Possessions* tells the tale of the colonizing of wonder in the fifteenth and sixteenth centuries. According to Greenblatt, Europeans channeled their anxious, imperialist impressions of the Other by means of wonder. Wonder had the ability to mediate between the known and the unknown, subject and object, inside and outside, imagination and observation (see Greenblatt's introduction). Particularly in the sixteenth century the Other or the new found ready expression in the exoticizing that had characterized previous treatments of wonder. Spanish observers of the New World hastened to manage the shock of the new by writing it into Pliny's and medieval paradoxography, that is, by presenting the new not in the throes of wonder but *as* wonders, as odd and delightful exotica. Columbus, Ramón Pané, Gonzalo Fernández de Oviedo, Pedro Mártir, Cortés, and Juan de la Cueva to varying degrees and in a panoply of ways defused wonder and the new into exhibits in a museum, rendering them epistemologically palatable and available to easy consumption as mere curiosities.

Marvelous Possessions and the sixteenth century close down before the New World reaction to colonialist discourse sets in. That reaction, which one can understand as a decolonizing of wonder, emerged in seventeenth-century Latin American Creole writers. The decolonizing of wonder draws its ammunition from the insatiable baroque proclivity for strangeness and exoticism that afforded Cervantes, and thus Borges, the hypertrophic admiratio of the *Quijote*.[8] As Octavio Paz writes, "The goal of the baroque was to astonish and astound; that is why it sought out and collected all extremes, especially hybrids and monsters" (58). Paz further notes that to "the baroque sensibility the American world was marvelous. . . . Among all these American marvels there is one that from the beginning, from the writings of Terrazas and Balbuena, was glorified by the criollo: his own being. In the seventeenth century the aesthetic of the strange expressed with rapture the strangeness of the criollo" (58; also see González Echevarría chap. 6). In literature and historiography, seventeenth-century Creole writers such as Sor Juana Inés de la Cruz, Juan de Espinosa Medrano ("Lunarejo"), Juan Rodríguez Freyle, and Bartolomé de Arzáns de Orsúa y Vela appropriated the tropes of strangeness employed in Spanish Renaissance historiography and later privileged by the hispanic baroque. Sor Juana's poetic representations of herself as a "*rara avis*," a sideshow freak, the "Tenth Muse," in short as a one woman spectacle, constitute only the most famous manifestations of the iconography of anomaly enacted by many of her contemporaries. Creole writers flaunted their own and their regions' oddity, their composite nature as a wondrous artifact (González Echevarría 157), parlaying the exotic into a badge of New World identity. Creole *self*-exoticizing contests and mimics the colonizers' discourse.

Though literarily and culturally conditioned, and as far as I know or can imagine not a phenomenon present in coeval North America, the contestatory self-exoticizing of Creole writers is nevertheless a transhistorical and transnational phenomenon. Marginalized nations, social or ethnic groups, and individuals tend notably—though certainly not inevitably—to take up exotic, eccentric, excentric discursive positions. Though small entities, as it were, they project a large image by means of their radical and extreme literary games (see Paré's suggestive *Exiguity: Reflections on the Margins of Literature*). I must leave it to my readers to fill in the blanks from their own experience, because here I only have space to go "South." There, as South American and U.S. southern writers position themselves vis-à-vis their respective norths, the preceding assertions come into unmistakable focus. And the notion of excentricity that I have begun to sketch will shed light on the much-celebrated alignment of South American literature with the fantastic and U.S. southern literature with the grotesque.

The crisis of modernity—the influx of technology, capitalism, and resulting sense of southern underdevelopment—imputed to their respective norths, reached a boiling point that warranted a defining discursive response in Spanish America in 1899 and in the U.S. South in 1925–1930. The Spanish-American War sharpened extant awareness of U.S. imperialism in the southern continent, shifted the adversary from Spain to the United States, and prompted the crystallization of the emerging anti-U.S. discourse into the polemical lines of José Enrique Rodó's *Ariel* (1900), which retain their authority to this day (see Alonso chap. 1; Jrade 15; Ramos part 2, "Introducción"). In the U.S. South, the Scopes trial of 1925, which occasioned the vituperation of the South by the northern press, galvanized the Fugitive poets of Nashville to formulate the Agrarian position that attained its brief apex in the Twelve Southerners' *I'll Take My Stand* (1930) (see Stewart part 1, chap. 3). Faced with the menace of the North, both texts express a desire for and institute a sustaining myth of their region. Rodó elects Shakespeare's Ariel: "Ariel, genio del aire, representa, en el simbolismo de la obra de Shakespeare, la parte noble y alada del espíritu. . . . el término ideal a que asciende la selección humana, rectificando en el hombre superior las tenaces vestigios de Calibán, sím-

bolo de sensualidad y de torpeza, con el cincel perseverante de la vida"
(*Ariel* [1967] 24) ["Shakespeare's ethereal Ariel symbolizes the noble,
soaring aspect of the human spirit. . . . the ideal toward which the human
select ascends, the force that wields life's eternal chisel, effacing from
aspiring mankind the clinging vestiges of Caliban" (*Ariel* [1988] 31)]. The
Agrarians, who had previously scorned antebellum nostalgia, seek to
restore a "commanding image of the South's past in those forms, fictional, poetical or dramatic, that have the character of myth" (Donald
Davidson qtd. in Young 2).

Despite the momentous differences in time and place and history (as
well as ignorance of *Ariel* by the Twelve Southerners), both texts frame
their myths in remarkably similar terms. *Ariel* and *I'll Take My Stand*
both establish a force field in which the North represents the materialism,
industrialism, utilitarianism, capitalism, and progress to which the South
opposes its own superior humanism, classicism, spirituality, leisure, idealism, and conservatism. Their myth-making engages in egregious self-
idealization, in exactly the same directions. They furnish, for example,
the following defenses of leisure. Rodó writes, "El ocio noble [the classical notion of *otium*] era la inversión del tiempo que oponían, como
expresión de la vida superior, a la actividad económica" (*Ariel* [1967] 62)
["Noble leisure was the investment of time that they expressed as a superior mode of life opposed to the commercial enterprise" (*Ariel* [1988]
47)]. John Crowe Ransom writes, "It is my thesis that all [in the antebellum South] were committed to a form of leisure, and that their labor
itself was leisurely" (*I'll Take My Stand* 14). This mutual glorification of a
feudal past rankles but perhaps does not surprise as much as the essentialist feminine paradigm that both texts similarly exploit in characterizing their regions. Rodó valorizes a Spanish America allied with nature
that is "hospitalaria para las cosas del espíritu" ["hospitable to the world
of the spirit"], "serena y firme" ["serene and firm"], "resplandeciente con
el encanto de una seriedad temprana y suave" ["resplendent with a calm
purpose"] that resembles "un rostro infantil" ["a child's face"] (*Ariel*
[1967] 173; *Ariel* [1988] 94), thus recalling the natural slave that Aristotle
identifies with women and children. Rodó opposes, deplores, and rejects
the overtly "masculine" tendencies of North America: their "arrebato de
una actividad viril" (133) ["paroxysms of vigorous activity" (77)], their
"culto pagano de la salud, de la destreza, de la fuerza" (132) ["pagan cult
of health, of skill, of strength"] their "aspiración insaciable de dominar"
(132) ["insatiable appetite for dominance" (76–77)]. For his part, Ransom characterizes industrialism as a rape of nature (*I'll Take My Stand* 7),
identifies Progress with the masculine (10), and tropes the loss of south-

ern identity as a kind of rape: "how far shall the South surrender its moral, social, and economic autonomy to the victorious principle of Union?" (ix). Both Souths are carrying on a conservative romance with an idealized and feminized past.

By now there should remain no doubt, to continue the romantic figurations, that the two texts have also wholeheartedly *embraced* self-exoticizing. In the pressing and acute effort (so acute as to impel a resort to feminizing) to define themselves over/against northern titans, they have not effaced but capitalized on their ancillary and marginalized position by constructing themselves as otherly to the North. They have staged their own marginality (see Huggan chap. 3) in choosing a profile that is eccentric, odd and off-center, by virtue of its rejection of the phallogocentric. What the center represses has been brought to the fore as the center of the margin's resistance. In more than one sense, the southerners have framed "structures of feeling."

For although the U.S. South and Spanish America had long since left behind a *strictu sensu* colonialism, we are witnessing in their discursive reactions to the encroachments of the North a textbook enactment of the anticolonialist nationalism theorized by Partha Chatterjee in terms of then colonial India. Chatterjee writes, "By my reading, anticolonial nationalism creates its own domain of sovereignty within colonial society well before it begins the political battle with imperial power. It does this by dividing the world of social institutions and practices into two domains— the material and the spiritual" (6; also see Alonso 35). Anticolonial nationalism relegates to the outer domain of the material those aspects of modernity, such as technological, economic, and political superiority, that it cannot afford not to replicate (Rodó famously remarks that he does not love but does admire the United States [*Ariel* (1967) 133; *Ariel* (1988) 77]). At the same time it sanctifies an inner preserve of autochthonous values, the realm of the so-called spiritual, as impervious to the colonizer. "The more nationalism engaged in its contest with the colonial power in the outer domain of politics, the more it insisted on displaying the marks of 'essential' cultural difference so as to keep the colonizer from that inner domain of national life and to proclaim its sovereignty over it" (Chatterjee 26). In the case of the Souths the inner realm houses, among other things, a humanism that is concomitant with aesthetics and literature. *Ariel* and *I'll Take My Stand* both enshrine literature as a way of knowing superior to science (Jrade 15). Applying the words of Julio Ramos to both "Souths," I would say that they "ontologize aesthetic authority" (150), claiming it as a matrix of regional identity over/against their more technologically advanced adversaries to the North.

As the twentieth century progresses, the lines of the polemic propagated by *Ariel* and *I'll Take My Stand* reverberate, fittingly enough, into literature per se. Self-exoticizing and ex-centricity make their way into literatures that claim the freest flights of the imagination as their trademark. Admiratio finessed by Aristotle into inventio comes to characterize southern literatures that eschew traditional realism—the logical, the logos, the norm—in favor of those more imaginative and oblique forms of representation, the grotesque and the fantastic. Further, more elementary forms of wonder, the marvelous and the mysterious, protagonize southern literatures. They implicitly project the North/South dichotomy that has so affected their regions' history onto an (again, essentialized) West/East axis that opposes reason to magic. Two milestone essays on literature written at midcentury, as uncannily akin to each other as the works of Rodó and the Twelve Southerners and just as far-reaching in their impact, confirm the centrality to southern literatures of the ex-centric marvelous. Cuban writer Alejo Carpentier, in his 1967 essay "De lo real maravilloso americano" ("On the Marvel of the Real in America"; originally the prologue to his 1949 novel on Haiti, *El reino de este mundo* [*The Kingdom of This World*], and then expanded into the essay of this title published in *Tientos y diferencias,* 1967), and the Georgian Flannery O'Connor, in "The Grotesque in Southern Fiction" (published in *Mystery and Manners,* 1957), defend and define their regions' literatures.[9]

In their programmatic pieces, the two novelists confront not the crisis of modernity but the crisis of representation or realism that, in accordance with the tenets of my essay, can be construed as ensuing from the previous state of siege. O'Connor indicts the prevalent tendency of American letters to esteem novels "concerned with the social or economic or psychological forces that they necessarily exhibit" (38) and the consequent devaluation of southern literature that adheres to the grotesque. She views the comic-grotesque tendencies of southern literature as a deeper kind of realism, whose "fictional qualities lean away from typical social patterns, toward mystery and the unexpected" (40), and that is "wild," "violent," and "comic," peopled by "freaks," and "the concern of prophets and poets" (43–45). Carpentier disavows the "regreso a lo real" ("Maravilloso" 117) ["return to the real" ("Marvel" 30)] found in socialist realism and existential literature. More important, he pits *le merveilleux,* lionized by the surrealists, against "lo real maravilloso *americano*" (emphasis added), to expose the bankruptcy and fraudulence of the former. Carpentier argues that the surrealists conjure up this marvel at all costs, invoking it from a state of disbelief and as a mere literary ploy. Latin American literature, in contrast, can capitalize on the style of its own history ("Maravilloso" 113; "Marvel" 28) as well as on other autochthonous features, to effect an authentically marvelous literature—for what, he queries in the last lines of the essay, "es la historia de América toda sino una crónica de lo real maravilloso?" (120) ["is the history of America if not a chronicle of the Marvel of the real?" (30)].

Mystery and the Marvel: both rest on the same premises outside the prison house of reason. In legitimating their regions' literatures, O'Connor and Carpentier appeal to faith, to miracles. Carpentier declares that "lo maravilloso comienza a serlo de manera inequívoca" ["the Marvel only emerges unmistakably as such"] when it arises from an "inesperada alteración de la realidad (el milagro), de una revelación privilegiada de la realidad, de una iluminación inhabitual o singularmente favorecedora de las inadvertidas riquezas de la realidad" ("Maravilloso" 116) ["unexpected alteration of reality (a miracle), a privileged revelation of reality, an unaccustomed or singularly enhancing illumination of the riches of reality that had passed unnoticed" ("Marvel" 29)]. In order for Latin American literature to be true to its origins, it must believe in the miracle: "Para empezar, la sensación de lo maravilloso presupone una fe" (116) ["To begin with, the experiencing of the Marvel presupposes an act of faith" (29)]. Somewhat less apocalyptically but still as if in tandem with the Cuban author, O'Connor writes, "In these grotesque works, we find that the writer has made alive some experience which we are not accustomed to observe every day, or which the ordinary man may never experience in his ordinary life" (40). O'Connor's writer of grotesque fiction looks for the image that connects what is concrete with what is invisible "but believed in by him firmly, just as real to him, really, as the one that everybody sees" (42). O'Connor's "Christ-haunted" U.S. South (44) here merges with Carpentier's "caudal de mitologías" ("Maravilloso" 120) ["wealth of mythologies" ("Marvel" 30)] of Latin America to predicate southern literature on the miracle that stands at the etymological root of the marvel (ad*mir*are) (Fisher 11).

The tale of an equivocal miracle, Borges's aptly titled "El Sur" ["The South"] affords an example and an allegory of precisely the excentric dynamics of the "Souths" that the foregoing pages of my essay have advanced. Like the Twelve Southerners and their South, the story's protagonist Juan Dahlmann has mythologized Argentina's recent past into a heroic era. Dahlmann locates the glorious past in the South of Argentina, in his military ancestors, and more specifically, in the family ranch that allegedly awaits him there. At the same time, he suffers from a clash within his own genealogy between his bookish and his soldierly forebears. Literally and figuratively felled by blood poisoning, the protagonist finds himself trapped in a Buenos Aires hospital that incarnates the odious scientific sterility of the modern age. At this point, either in his mind or in actuality, Dahlmann dissociates himself from modernity and from his fetters to undertake a journey to the yearned-for South.

Traveling south in fact or in a dream, Dahlmann enters a magical, palliative, truly inalienable and unseizable zone. The story's *Turn of the Screw*-like, irreducibly double-edged narration suspends Dahlmann's South in a limbo between reality and fiction. Remarkably akin to Chatterjee's spiritual and material realms, Borges's ambiguous textualization of the South endows Dahlmann's perhaps private and immaterial South with an imposing textual reality that dominates the second half of the story. Moreover, the southern space that assumes so palpable a presence in the text clearly gains force from the imagination, being forged from literature: "su directo conocimiento de la campaña era harto inferior a su conocimiento nostálgico y literario" (*Ficciones* 191) ["his direct knowledge of the country was considerably inferior to his nostalgic, literary knowledge" (*Collected Fictions* 177)]. The South defies time: "viajaba al pasado y no sólo al Sur" (192) ["he was traveling not only into the South but into the past" (177)]. Simultaneously, it ascends to the realm of Plato's archetypes entirely beyond time and space as Dahlmann enters the "tierra elemental" (192) ["elemental earth" (177)]: in Borges's iconography *lo elemental* signifies the archetypal. The old gaucho of the South who "estaba como fuera del tiempo, en una eternidad" ["seemed to be outside time, situated in eternity"] and in whom Dahlmann saw a "cifra del Sur (del Sur que era suyo)" (195) ["a symbol of the South (his South)" (179)] throws down the gauntlet to Dahlmann to defend himself against an unmotivated attack. Only in the miraculous, hypostatic territory of the South can Dahlmann realize the heroic self-defense and death that resolve his history and salvage his existence.[10]

Equally weighty, if less romantic, benefits accrue to the southern literatures that have shared the ethereal territory mapped out in "El Sur." In fulfilling the dictates of the regions' manifestoes both southern literatures have attained international prominence, a high profile. Southern works exploiting the full potential of the imaginative act have effected a certain revenge on their northern counterparts by achieving a literary and commercial success that has, by turns, eclipsed their neighbors' achievements. So powerful has the excentric stance become that the reading public tends to identify *all* southern literature with it, disregarding specificities and blocking access to commercial viability for authors who do not conform to the stereotype (witness O'Connor's lament that "anything that comes out of the South is going to be called grotesque by the Northern reader,

unless it is grotesque, in which case it is going to be called realistic" [40]).
Paraphrasing and extending Carpentier's query, one might ask: what, in
the public eye, is the history of southern literatures if not a chronicle of
the marvel of the real?

The triumph of the wonderful, we begin to see, can backfire. In so
doing, it can also detract from the wounds of history that over the course
of its development southern wonder has sought to salve. Each of the dual
bases on which Carpentier premises his construction of the American
marvelous in fact harbors a different volatility. On the one hand, Carpentier makes an ontological argument for marvelous realism. He maintains
that the very nature of Latin America, and particularly its history, so rife
with incredible events, render it the native territory of the marvel. Latin
America's style, he writes, progressively affirms itself in its fabulous history ("Maravilloso" 113; "Marvel" 28). In his 1954 revisiting of the earlier
essay, Carpentier confirmed the equation of *lo real maravilloso* with the
"strange occurrences" that happen every day in Latin America ("Baroque" 107).

Subsequent literary incarnations of Carpentier's ontological stance
have confirmed its productivity as well as its potential for corrosion. One
can think of García Márquez's wildly successful *Cien años de soledad* (*One
Hundred Years of Solitude*) and its many spin-offs, with their whimsical
accounts of history into which are woven supernatural or bizarre events
presented matter-of-factly. One can also think of the way in which U.S.
southern literature has institutionalized the grotesque and Faulkner's
Gothic as intrinsic to its region's modus operandi and inhabitants. The
aftermath of the ontological perspective heralded by Carpentier has often
naturalized the problematic, shocking aspects of their regions and their
histories, folding them into latter-day fairy tales. García Márquez himself
eventually bemoaned this turn of literary events in his important Nobel
Prize acceptance speech of 1982. In it the Colombian author impressed on
his audience that Latin America, though an endless stimulus for the
imagination, also has serious problems that need to be acknowledged.
The "strange occurrences" to which Carpentier referred, the wonders of
Latin America, have their down side, their dark side. García Márquez, in
sum, appears to recognize that the phenomenon he captained has so
projected the image of a world intrinsically bizarre that it runs the risk of
domesticating, de-ideologizing, and thereby neutralizing in the public
eye the urgent issues of his continent.

Carpentier's second construction of the marvel returns us to the notion of faith and will ultimately attempt to regenerate the absolute core of
a troubled history. Though it invokes O'Connor, this last argument of my

essay involves the marvelous realism that has permeated not U.S. Southern but Latino/a literature, creating yet another hemispheric literary bond (a prime example is Rudolfo Anaya's superb *Bless Me, Ultima*; also see Zamora and Faris, and Saldívar chap. 5). The matters to which I now turn, however, do place a new spin on and play out some final implications of the concerns that my essay has treated throughout.

The importance that both Carpentier and O'Connor ascribe to faith grounds their deeper realism in epistemology. That is to say, the efficacy of marvelous or mysterious fiction depends on the belief—of those in the narrated world and hopefully of the reader—in the miraculous events that the text purveys. For O'Connor, mystery entails receiving grace, the descent of the Holy Spirit into ordinary lives. Carpentier, in *El reino de este mundo*, has in mind the fact that "millares de hombres ansiosos de libertad creyeron en los poderes licantrópicos de Mackandal [the powers of this Haitian revolutionary to assume animal forms], a punto de que esa fe colectiva produjera un milagro el día de su ejecución" ("Maravilloso" 118) ["thousands of men, avid for their freedom, believed in the lycanthropic powers of Mackandal to the point where their collective faith produced a miracle on the day of his execution" ("Marvel" 30)]. The Cuban author has displaced the surrealist notion of the marvel, which gives access to the unconscious, onto the collective unconscious or imaginary. Carpentier's epistemological justification of the marvel harks back to Aristotle's amplification of verisimilitude into doxa, which provides a platform for things as they are said or perceived to be.

In the wake of Carpentier's essay and novel, the epistemological claim has taken on a new and plethoric life in marvelous realism (or, as it has come to be known, magical realism). Critics and novelists of both hemispheres construe marvelous realism as presenting a seemingly magical indigenous perspective as real, from within. José David Saldívar's influential *The Dialectics of Our America* (1991) reads Carpentier as posing the ideological question of "how to write in a European language—about realities and thought structures never before seen in Europe" (92). Fernando Alegría goes to the heart of the issue, saying, "Magical realism represents an acceptance of the surrounding reality and of the interior world on a prelogical plane to which a rationalist order of causality is not applied" (312, my translation). Walter Mignolo characterizes the quasi-anthropological problematics of marvelous realism, noting that the narrative artifice "that strives to resolve the confrontation of these two realities [Western vs. traditional and folkloric] must renounce . . . narration by an external observer who, installed in the myth of reason, *informs* us about mythical reasoning. On the contrary, it must textually create the effect of their coexistence" (40, my translation). As distinct from more properly "fantastic" literature such as Borges's "El Sur," which obliges the reader to hesitate between a "real" and an "unreal" solution, marvelous realism refuses to problematize the supernatural event (see Chanady chap. 1). Marvelous realism thus approaches, albeit with an undeniable ideological mission, what Tzvetan Todorov terms the marvelous in its pure state, which accepts the supernatural rather than calling it into question.

That marvelous realism is a myth of and for our times has been amply borne out by the most recent phase in its reception, itself rather wonderful. The epistemological claim reified in the literature of marvelous realism has catapulted it into the quintessential postmodern, postcolonial mode. Multiculturalism, identity politics, speaking from the margins, contestation, subversion, transgression, border-crossing: the center stage constructs of the present politicized critical climate are seen to inhere in marvelous realism. The monumental 580-page collection edited by Lois Parkinson Zamora and Wendy B. Faris in 1995, *Magical Realism: Theory, History, Community*, makes clear marvelous realism's currency, in both senses of the word. The editors' introduction states that marvelous realism is "especially alive and well in postcolonial contexts" and that it "creates space for the interactions of diversity. In magical realist texts, ontological disruption serves the purpose of political and cultural disruption: magic is often given as a cultural corrective" (2). They consider marvelous realism to be "a mode suited to exploring—and transgressing—boundaries, whether the boundaries are ontological, political, geographical, or generic" (5). It undertakes an "assault on [the] basic structures of rationalism and realism" (6) that destabilizes normative oppositions, displacing them onto alternative structures. Theo D'Haen's essay in the volume, "Magical Realism and Postmodernism: Decentering Privileged Centers," concludes that marvelous realism and postmodernism "now seem almost the only shorthand available to categorize contemporary developments in Western fiction" (193). Even Marxist critic Fredric Jameson has written two articles on the subject, contending that "magic realism depends on a content which betrays the overlap or the coexistence of precapitalist with nascent capitalist or technological features" (311).

Rightful and laudable as well as righteous, the varied pronouncements of such critics all make clear one simple and poignant point: marvelous realism speaks not just *to* the present but *of* the past. With its foregrounding and valorizing of the indigenous point of view, the marvelous replays and reverses the colonial past, that is, the forcible encounter between Western and non-Western cultures with grave consequences for the latter. Marvelous realist literature emerges as the postcolonial residue of colonial tensions and transactions. The marvelous realism generated by Carpentier thus, once again, aims to redress the wounds of history. It literally conjures the indigenous worldview into a usable past or a pseudo-past, the idealized, pure past of the disenfranchised. It dramatizes a more "innocent" worldview that heals the past by staging it largely in terms of magic vs. reason. As a distillation, both metaphorical and metonymical, of the past, as well as of the southern history of wonder that my essay has traced, marvelous realism's privileging of non-Western logic contests colonialism and its ever-present legacy.

"*And yet, and yet,*" as Borges writes in the coda to his "Nueva refutación del tiempo" ("New Refutation of Time"), "el mundo, desgraciadamente, es real" (*Otras inquisiciones* 220) ["the world, unfortunately is real" (*Other Inquisitions* 186)]. While, as we have seen, the ontologizing of the marvelous both salves wounds and creates them afresh, marvelous realism's epistemological claim gives rise to utopian projections that can occlude or betray the cultural and political clashes—among them, ongoing strife between Norths and Souths—that endure to the present day. In its erasure of binaries, marvelous realism provides a sweet and easy resolution of persisting conflicts. It presents the wounds of history as *always already resolved.* The emollient myth that presses the marvelous into its service twists into a reductive panacea. Wonder has shed its thrilled Platonic perplexity to embrace, for better and for worse, its two Aristotelian edges. Marvelous realism resolves history into a palatable, crisis-palliating story diametrically opposed to Faulkner's classically inflected yet unregenerate tragic story of the South. Paradoxically and perhaps to their detriment, both faces of Carpentier's project for the marvelous have, in their later ramifications, in fact induced a *nihil admirare,* the abrogation of an attitude of wonder.

For solace, one may look in conclusion to Faulkner and to the southern conjunction of Faulkner and Borges. In contrast to the static, atemporal resolutions of the wounds of history and to the erasure of binaries in marvelous realism, *Absalom* propounds a dynamic imminence in which differences and shibboleths are *always about to* surrender and coalesce into a harmonious unity. *Absalom*'s epicene characters live in their difference (black/white, master/slave, masculine/feminine, North/South) but are pregnant with the potential for a desired indifferentiation: "But let flesh touch with flesh, and watch the fall of all the eggshell shibboleth of caste and color too" (112). The "triumvirate" or trinity of Clytie, Judith, and Rosa achieve that utopian state during the war—"with no distinction among the three of us of age or color"; "It was as though we were one being, interchangeable and indiscriminate" (125)—only to have it break down, as ever due to Sutpen's intervention. *Absalom* lays out a plan for redemption but chooses to occupy the space of imminence pulsating with potential, of "the jigsaw puzzle integers . . . waiting, almost lurking, just beyond his reach, inextricable, jumbled, and unrecognisable yet on the point of falling into pattern" (250).

In Borges's idealist works, a synonymous space of possibility ripe with the potential to explode monolithic thinking and structures hovers over the present. Typical of other works, the title story of *Jardín* reveals to the narrator Yu Tsun, a collaborator with Germany, "infinitas series de tiempo, . . . una red creciente y vertiginosa de tiempos divergentes, convergentes y paralelos. Esa trama de tiempos que se aproximan, se bifurcan, se cortan o que secularmente se ignoran, abarca *todas* las posibilidades" (*Ficciones* 109–10) ["an infinite series of times, in a growing, dizzying net of divergent, convergent and parallel times. This network of times which approach one another, fork, break off, or are unaware of one another for centuries, embraces *all* possibilities of time" (*Labyrinths* 28)]. In the pluralized future toward which the story "Jardín" gestures, Yu Tsun will be the man he is about to kill and the man he is about to kill will be Yu Tsun. Moreover, using words almost identical to Faulkner's, Borges consecrates precisely the same space of imminence embraced by *Absalom* as the essence of literature itself: "esta inminencia de una revelación que no se produce, es, quizá, el hecho estético" (*Otras inquisiciones* 12) ["the imminence of a revelation that is not yet produced is, perhaps, the aesthetic fact" (*Other Inquisitions* 5)]. Perhaps in that future New World— where painfully felt, longstanding differences cease to obtain—wonder will recover its Platonic mission and no longer be obliged to shoulder the burdens of history.

NOTES

This essay is dedicated to Meera S. Viswanathan, who many years ago was the first to encourage my "Southern" project.

1. *Webster's Unabridged Dictionary* defines the noun *wonder* as follows: "[a portent. The original sense is *awe,* lit. *that from which one turns aside*]. 1. a person, thing, event that excites surprise; a strange thing, a cause of astonishment or admiration; a prodigy or miracle. 2. the feeling of surprise, admiration, and awe which is excited by something new, unusual, strange, great, extraordinary or not well understood. 3. a miracle. Synonyms: admiration, appreciation, astonishment, reverence, surprise, amazement, prodigy."

2. I borrow the final phrase of the sentence from Fisher 41.

3. Borges reviewed *Absalom* in 1937, *The Unvanquished* (which he translated) in 1938, and *Wild Palms* in 1939. In his review of *Wild Palms* Borges deems Faulkner the fore-

most novelist of the times. The review of *The Unvanquished* contains Borges's important characterization of Faulkner as a Latin American author: "Rivers of brown water, crumbling mansions, black slaves, battles on horseback, idle and cruel: the strange world of *The Unvanquished* is a blood relation of this America, here, and its history; it, too, is *criollo*" (*Selected Non-Fictions* 186). English versions of the reviews appear in Borges, *Selected Non-Fictions*; the originals are reprinted in Borges, *Textos cautivos*.

4. Borges's political writings have been collected in *Borges en* Sur and *Selected Non-Fictions*. On the political context in Argentina and its reverberations in *Sur*, see Aizenberg (chap. 5) and King.

5. Borges repeatedly develops this theme in his little-read early essays from the 1920s and 1930s that treat *Ultraísmo* and his backlash against it: *Inquisiciones* (1925), *El idioma de los argentinos* (1928), *Historia de la eternidad* (1936).

6. Beatriz Sarlo, in her *Jorge Luis Borges: A Writer on the Edge,* and John King, in his introduction to Sarlo's work, note the dystopic aspects of "Tlön" and the other politically inclined stories of *Jardín* (xiii, 75–76, 81).

7. For a synthetic discussion of the historical, political, social, and economic parallels between the two Souths on which my essay is predicated, see Cohn.

8. I do not mean to imply that Borges wittingly engages in the exoticizing of Latin America. Much as his fantastic fictions may have contributed to the exotic profile of his continent, the gist of Borges's important 1932 essay, "El escritor argentino y la tradición" (*Discusión*)—that Argentine and South American writers in general "have a right" to European tradition and can handle "all European themes," albeit with an irreverence that derives from their marginal position—runs counter to self-exoticizing ("The Argentine Writer and Tradition," *Labyrinths* 184).

9. Carpentier's 1949 novel treats the same Haitian rebellions that play a large part in *Absalom, Absalom!*; *El reino de este mundo* and its prologue also date from the same year for which Faulkner received the Nobel Prize.

10. *La invención de Morel* (*The Invention of Morel and Other Stories*), published in 1940 by Borges's close friend and collaborator, Adolfo Bioy Casares, can be seen as a gloss and expansion of "El Sur." The novel abounds in asombro and adds to the components of politically suggestive elements in "El Sur."

WORKS CITED

Aizenberg, Edna. *The Aleph Weaver: Biblical, Kabbalistic, and Judaic Elements in Borges.* Potomac, Md.: Scripta Humanistica, 1984.

Alegría, Fernando. *Nueva historia de la novela hispanoamericana.* Hanover: Ediciones del Norte, 1986.

Alonso, Carlos J. *The Burden of Modernity: The Rhetoric of Cultural Discourse in Spanish America.* New York: Oxford UP, 1998.

Aristotle. *Aristotle's Poetics.* Trans. and with commentary by George Whalley. Ed. John Baxter and Patrick Atherton. Montreal: McGill-Queen's UP, 1997.

——. *Metaphysics.* Trans. W. D. Ross. *The Complete Works of Aristotle: Revised Oxford Translation.* Vol. 2. Ed. Jonathan Barnes. Princeton, N.J.: Princeton UP, 1984.

Benjamin, Walter. *Illuminations*. Ed. Hannah Arendt. Trans. Harry Zohn. New York: Schocken, 1968.

Bioy Casares, Adolfo. *The Invention of Morel and Other Stories*. Austin: U of Texas P, 1985.

Borges, Jorge Luis. *Borges en Sur: 1931–1980*. Ed. Sara Luisa del Carril and Mercedes Rubio de Socchi. Buenos Aires: Emecé, 1999.

——. *Collected Fictions*. Trans. Andrew Hurley. New York: Viking, 1998. (Contains *A Universal History of Infamy*, Prologue to *The Garden of Forking Paths*, "The South.")

——. *Discusión*. Buenos Aires: Emecé, 1964.

——. *Ficciones*. Buenos Aires: Emecé, 1956. (Contains all of *El jardín de senderos que se bifurcan*.)

——. *Historia universal de la infamia*. Madrid: Alianza, 1971.

——. *Labyrinths: Selected Stories and Other Writings*. Trans. Donald A. Yates and James E. Irby. New York: New Directions, 1964. (Contains "Tlön, Uqbar, Orbis Tertius," "The Garden of Forking Paths.")

——. *Other Inquisitions*. Trans. Ruth L. C. Simms. Austin: U of Texas P, 1975.

——. *Otras inquisiciones*. Buenos Aires: Sur, 1952.

——. *Selected Non-Fictions, Jorge Luis Borges*. Ed. Eliot Weinberger. New York: Viking, 1999.

——. *Textos cautivos*. Ed. Enrique Sacerio-Garí and Emir Rodríguez Monegal. Barcelona: Tusquets, 1986.

Carpentier, Alejo. "The Baroque and the Marvelous Real." *Magical Realism: Theory, History, Community*. Ed. Lois Parkinson Zamora and Wendy B. Faris. Durham, N.C.: Duke UP, 1995. 101–7.

——. "De lo real maravilloso americano." *Tientos y diferencias*. Montevideo: Arca, 1967.

——. "On the Marvel of the Real in America." Trans. Stephanie Merrim. *Review* 28 (1981): 28–30.

——. *El reino de este mundo*. Barcelona: Seix Barral, 1984.

Chanady, Amaryll Beatrice. *Magical Realism and the Fantastic: Resolved Versus Unresolved Antinomy*. New York: Garland, 1985.

Chatterjee, Partha. *The Nation and Its Fragments*. Princeton, N.J.: Princeton UP, 1993.

Cohn, Deborah N. *History and Memory in the Two Souths: Recent Southern and Spanish American Fiction*. Nashville, Tenn.: Vanderbilt UP, 1999.

Daston, Lorraine, and Katherine Park. *Wonder and the Order of Nature 1150–1750*. New York: Zone, 1998.

Descartes, René. *The Philosophical Works of Descartes*. 1911. Vol. 1. Trans. Elizabeth S. Haldane and G. R. T. Ross. Cambridge: Cambridge UP, 1978.

D'Haen, Theo. "Magical Realism and Postmodernism: Decentering Privileged Centers." *Magical Realism: Theory, History, Community*. Ed. Lois Parkinson Zamora and Wendy B. Faris. Durham, N.C.: Duke UP, 1995. 191–208.

Faulkner, William. *Absalom, Absalom!* New York: Vintage, 1972.

Fisher, Philip. *Wonder, the Rainbow, and the Aesthetics of Rare Experiences*. Cambridge, Mass.: Harvard UP, 1998.

García Márquez, Gabriel. "The Solitude of America." Nobel Prize Acceptance Speech, Dec. 1982. Trans. Marina Castañeda. *Gabriel García Márquez and the Powers of Fiction.* Ed. Julio Ortega. Austin: U of Texas P, 1988. 87–91.

González Echevarría, Roberto. *Celestina's Brood: Continuities of the Baroque in Spanish and Latin American Literature.* Durham, N.C.: Duke UP, 1993.

Greenblatt, Stephen. *Marvelous Possessions: The Wonder of the New World.* Chicago: U of Chicago P, 1991.

Hathaway, Baxter. *Marvels and Commonplaces: Renaissance Literary Criticism.* New York: Random, 1986.

Huggan, Graham. *The Postcolonial Exotic: Marketing the Margins.* London: Routledge, 2001.

Jameson, Fredric. "On Magic Realism in Film." *Critical Inquiry* 12.2 (winter 1986): 301–25.

Jrade, Cathy L. *Modernismo, Modernity, and the Development of Spanish American Literature.* Austin: U of Texas P, 1998.

King, John. Sur: *A Study of the Argentine Literary Journal and Its Role in the Development of a Culture, 1931–1970.* Cambridge: Cambridge UP, 1986.

McGuirk, Bernard. *Latin American Literature: Symptoms, Risks, and Strategies of Post-Structuralist Criticism.* London: Routledge, 1997.

Mignolo, Walter. *Literatura fantástica y realismo maravilloso.* Madrid: La Muralla, 1983.

O'Connor, Flannery. "The Grotesque in Southern Fiction." *Mystery and Manners.* Ed. Sally and Robert Fitzgerald. New York: Farrar, 1961. 36–50.

Paré, François. *Exiguity: Reflections on the Margins of Literature.* Trans. Lin Burman. Waterloo, Ontario: Wilfried Laurier UP, 1997.

Paz, Octavio. *Sor Juana.* Trans. Margaret Sayers Peden. Cambridge, Mass.: Harvard UP, 1988.

Plato. *Theaetetus.* Trans. John McDowell. Oxford: Clarendon, 1973.

Ramos, Julio. *Desencuentros de la modernidad en América Latina.* Mexico City: Fondo de Cultura Económica, 1989.

Rodó, José Enrique. *Ariel.* New York: Las Américas, 1967.

——. *Ariel.* Trans. Margaret Sayers Peden. Austin: U of Texas P, 1988.

Saldívar, José David. *The Dialectics of Our America: Genealogy, Cultural Critique, and Literary History.* Durham, N.C.: Duke UP, 1991.

Sarlo, Beatriz. *Jorge Luis Borges: A Writer on the Edge.* Ed. John King. London: Verso, 1993.

Stewart, John L. *The Burden of Time: The Fugitives and Agrarians.* Princeton, N.J.: Princeton UP, 1965.

Todorov, Tzvetan. *The Fantastic: A Structural Approach to a Literary Genre.* Trans. Richard Howard. Ithaca, N.Y.: Cornell UP, 1975.

Twelve Southerners. *I'll Take My Stand: The South and the Agrarian Tradition.* Ed. Louis D. Rubin Jr. New York: Harper, 1962.

Young, Thomas Daniel. *The Past in the Present: A Thematic Study of Modern Southern Fiction.* Baton Rouge: Louisiana State UP, 1981.

Zamora, Lois Parkinson, and Wendy B. Faris, eds. *Magical Realism: Theory, History, Community.* Durham, N.C.: Duke UP, 1995.

WENDY B. FARIS

Southern Economies of Excess:

Narrative Expenditure in William

Faulkner and Carlos Fuentes

When in his essay on the notion of expenditure Georges Bataille maintains that in some respects modern "humanity recognizes the right to acquire, to conserve, and consume rationally, but it excludes in principle *nonproductive expenditure*" (117), he suggests a fruitful avenue along which to explore certain developments in modernist narrative as it articulates an economy of excessive verbal expenditure that runs contrary to this trend. The ways in which U.S. southern and Spanish American fiction share a common ground, based on particular histories and narrative strategies, can be better understood by triangulating them with Bataille's ideas about primitive economies of excess.[1] A juxtaposition of *The Death of Artemio Cruz* and *As I Lay Dying*, and in particular of the "appositional" connections between them, highlights similarities between Spanish American and U.S. southern literature.[2] But such meaningful appositions also imply genetic relations, such that these two texts can be read fruitfully through Fuentes's early essay on Faulkner, "La novela como tragedia," which he wrote contemporaneously with *The Death of Artemio Cruz*.

As it studies Spanish American and U.S. southern texts, this discussion fits between Fuentes's much-cited remark about his affinity with Faulkner's literature of defeat in a nation of success as conjoined to his stylistic "Dixie Gongorism," and Deborah Cohn's recent book, *History and Memory in the Two Souths*, especially her discussion of modernist techniques as they allowed for the exploitation of memory.[3] According to Cohn, "For both southern and Spanish American authors, memory, the point at which notions of time and individual perspective intersect, came to be a particularly powerful correlative to explorations of historical consciousness. In this respect, Faulkner's depiction of his characters' immersion in and obsessive reliving of the south's history was an especially potent model for the Spanish Americans" (26–27). Similarly, according to Antonio Márquez, Fuentes is inspired by Faulkner in his "novelistic stratagem . . . to make the past part of the present, the present expressive of the past, and to bring into this scheme a 'collective voice' representative of a greater historical reality" (91). Furthermore, continuing in an even more specifically postcolonial direction of inquiry, the specific "southernness" of the narrative projects of "Faulkner and cross-cultural authors like Rushdie," according to Jacques Pothier, is that "their peripheral southern homelands must accommodate their own outcasts" (368). Referring to Eliot's idea that Joyce's mythical method makes the chaos of the modern world into an artistic order, Pothier argues that "the southern brand of the 'mythical method' consists in upsetting this 'shape' by translating the religious or historical myths into the language of the oppressed, the poor or the colonized, so that metropolitan readers can hear the voice of the defeated instead of fooling themselves into believing that man now masters his history" (368).

Taking off from this focus on the historical consciousness of southern American narrative, the idea of narrative excess, the expenditure of more narrative time and descriptive detail than is strictly necessary for the recording of an event or a scene, provides a guiding metaphor. In these particular fictions, such excess operates in two registers: narrative structure and semantics. In narratological terms, it appears in the abundant use of repeating narrative (something that happens only once but is recounted several times) and in the infrequent use of iterative narrative (something that happened several times but which is recounted only once).[4] This repeating narrative is a kind of narrative potlatch.[5] In semantic terms, the choice of words and the way they are placed endows parts of the text with poetic and ritual overtones.

From a broad historical perspective, both Faulkner's and Fuentes's fictions bear the burden of what Louis D. Rubin defined some time ago as a characteristic of U.S. southern literature: "the impossible load of the past," both in the sense that "the image of the heroic past renders the distraught present doubly distasteful just as it is the guilt and falseness of this same heroic past that has caused the present" ("Southern Literature" 42).[6] In the South this past concerns the gentility of the Old South, the courage of Confederate heroes, and the legacy of slavery; in contemporary Mexico the past-time frame is doubled, as it were: the present looks back both on the glory of the Aztec empire with its subsequent destruction and also on the much more dubious glory and subsequent betrayal of the ideals of the revolution, a second chance for a new beginning not yet fully realized. These two texts do not compare smoothly, however. Unlike the strong presence of the revolution in *The Death of Artemio Cruz*, history in *As I Lay Dying* is private history, the burden of the past is generalized and focused through the Bundren family, so that for the most part it eludes the specifically racial and historical questions that pervade much of the rest of Faulkner's fiction. One might even argue that because of its present-time orientation, *As I Lay Dying* represents a respite from the relentless historicity of the other texts, which are in that respect closer to *The Death of Artemio Cruz*. But the past looms in Addie's still-present will; as Dewey Dell reminds Anse, "You promised her. . . . If you don't do it, it will be a curse on you" (109). Hence Addie's hold over her family even after her death can also be seen to suggest the burden of the past in the South.

In any case, it is in the company of Faulkner that Fuentes defines the novel as tragic (qtd. in van Delden 142). And that tragedy involves history. Fuentes relates that past orientation to writing by maintaining that "el ser, en el mundo de Faulkner, es lo que se *lega:* sólo lo legado será *legible*" ["being, in Faulkner's world, is inherited: only what is inherited is readable"] ("La novela" 54). In this same essay, Fuentes first compares Faulkner's world to Balzac's because of its vastness and its internal correspondences; however, because of its future orientation, Balzac's *Human Comedy* eliminates tragedy. Thus, Fuentes goes on to contrast King Lear and Old Goriot, presumably aligning Faulknerian tragedy with the former: "No hay nada después de Lear. Después de Goriot, la sociedad sigue adelante, en su carrera febril hacia el porvenir. Lear cumple su destino. El destino de Goriot lo cumple la sociedad. En Shakespeare, la historia es para Lear. En Balzac, Goriot es para la historia. La memoria, el pasado, no cuentan" ["There is nothing after Lear. After Goriot, society goes forward, in its feverish dash toward the future. Lear achieves his destiny. Goriot's destiny is achieved by society. In Shakespeare, history is for Lear. In Balzac, Goriot is for history. Memory, the past, don't count"] ("La novela" 56). Note Fuentes's use in both these formulations of a kind of modified double chiasmus, an excessive rhetorical trope that arrests narrative time and displays verbal wealth.

One reason why Faulkner's historical vision inspired Fuentes and other Spanish Americans was that while his vision was tragic, it was a tragedy that left room for hope because it ultimately affirmed man's freedom; it was also "una búsqueda, a través de la fatalidad, de la libertad final de las criaturas" ["a search, through fate, of the final freedom of beings"] ("La novela" 73). That element of hope appears in another similar formulation in the same essay: "En Proust el tiempo, por definición, se ha perdido; el tiempo es realmente pasado, al perderse y aun al recobrarse como tal pasado. En Balzac, el tiempo está por ganarse: es futuro siempre, aun en su presente, pues el presente es sólo actividad—ambición, transacción comercial, intriga—designada para el futuro. En Faulkner, el tiempo ni se pierde ni se gana: es siempre presente, obsesión de la memoria carnal incandescente" ["In Proust time, by definition, is lost; time is really past, in being lost and even in being found as that past. In Balzac, time is to be won; it is always future, even in its present, because the present is only activity—ambition, commercial transaction, plotting—aimed at the future. In Faulkner, time is neither lost nor won; it is always present, an obsession of carnal incandescent memory"] ("La novela" 68–69). That Fuentes repeats again the contrast of Faulkner and Balzac, associating the latter with ambition, commercialism, and plotting, is worth noting, because in it he seems to be struggling against the forward-looking impetus of modern culture as he articulates his own style. (And the triple entendre of *tiempo ganado*, which can mean time won, time saved, or time earned, allows Fuentes to play on the commercial implications of Balzacian temporal dynamics.) The notion of incandescence at the end of this passage is particularly striking. It sums up Fuentes's attraction to Faulkner, expressing the appeal of texts that shine and beckon with a powerful and inspiring light, but a light that glows in the aftermath of a past conflagration.

Faulkner's fiction thus presented a sense of historical tragedy embodied in a bleak and yet verbally inspired vision at a time when Spanish American writers were confronting the burdens of continuing colonialism, now largely from the North, but wishing to develop a distinctive continental style. Thus the combination of this tragic view of history with an inventive and baroque poetics was especially enabling for Spanish American writers. In discussing Faulkner and García Márquez, François Pithavy maintains that although in Faulkner's fiction history "does not so much end up in final extinction and oblivion as it remains static, doomed from the start by the presence of evil," nevertheless man's "histories remain open" (342–43). In García Márquez, on the other hand, according to Pithavy, there is no such transcendence. Faulkner, however, is probably located closer to both García Márquez and Fuentes than Pithavy suggests. While it is true that *As I Lay Dying* is open-ended, the members of Addie's family all comically achieving their separate goals in Addie's last journey to Jefferson, the bitterness of Addie's life, which lingers through her voice, and Darl's inspired but tortured insanity, seriously compromise that comedy. And any transcendence is achieved as much through language as through event. As Pithavy formulates it with regard to *One Hundred Years of Solitude*, "Macondo had been ultimately a city of words" (342). Similarly, what one might see as Artemio's liberative poetics exists alongside but does not triumph over his actions and his mortality.[7]

In this temporally burdened tragic world, constraints on freedom are overcome by various methods of excessive narrative expenditure. The regrettable modernity these novels chronicle—in Fuentes's words, "el pueblo nuevo de Jefferson, chato, vulgar, brillantón" ["the new town of Jefferson, low, vulgar, flashy"] ("La novela" 52)—finds its narrative compensation, as it were, in the overdetermined repetitions of the narrative. Faulkner's statement that *As I Lay Dying* was his tour de force might also be said of *The Death of Artemio Cruz*, both embodying excessive efforts to encode the past in the present of their narrative instances.[8] Since neither South conforms to or succeeds in the prevailing North American economic climate, these texts adopt an alternative economy, a textual poetics of extravagant expenditure.[9] However, the historical tragedy at the base of these fictions, coupled with their narrative strategies—which, as Donald Kartiganer says of Faulkner's works, describe distinct voices in fragments of a "design that never denies its dubious status, its origins in contingency" (xvii)—confers on them a certain fragility.

To understand the textual expenditure these novels enact, it is helpful to consult Bataille, much of whose work could be characterized as an apologia of excess and hence as an explicit critique of capitalist efficiency. Bataille upholds as fundamental to human activity "the principle of loss," a loss that results from expenditure on "unproductive forms," such as "luxury, mourning, war, cults, the construction of sumptuary monuments, games, spectacles, arts, perverse sexual activity" (118). This principle of loss through expenditure has disappeared, he maintains, because "as the class that possesses the wealth—having received with wealth the obligation of functional expenditure—the modern bourgeoisie is characterized by the refusal in principle of this obligation" (124). Now "the hatred of expenditure is the *raison d'être* and the justification for the bourgeoisie" (124–25).

Considered in this context, both *As I Lay Dying* and *The Death of Artemio Cruz* can be seen as implicitly taking their distance from what Bataille considers the bourgeois refusal of unproductive expenditure. If one regards the Flaubertian idea of the mot juste, the economically efficient use of verbal signs to designate their referents, as the embodiment of this bourgeois tendency toward "the strictly economic representation of the world—economic in the vulgar sense, the bourgeois sense, of the word" (124), they move in the opposite direction, embodying what one might term a narrative economy of excess, of unproductive expenditure. One hears events told a number of different times, from several different perspectives. Many more words are spent than are needed to convey the information one receives about the Bundren family's and Artemio's movements and thoughts, for example. In both cases, it is not only that one hears repeated accounts but that excess is underscored by a principle of inefficiency; because the interior perspective with its attendant confusion of pronouns means that even though one hears an event more times than in a traditional omniscient or a first-person narrative, the retellings do not clarify it substantially.[10]

Like their equivalents in society, these expenditures of narrative energy are gifts that impose obligations on their readers to respond in kind, cocreating readerly rather than writerly texts.[11] As Bataille, basing himself on Marcel Mauss, explains, it is the aim of the potlatch, with its lavish gift-giving, to obligate gift recipients to return the favors and also to put them in the giver's debt, an obligation that is later redeemed by even more extravagant gifts. "*Potlatch* excludes all bargaining and, in general, it is constituted by a considerable gift of riches, offered openly and with the goal of humiliating, defying, and *obligating* a rival" (121). The difficult question in regard to narrative is the aspect of obligation. Perhaps one might resolve it by proposing that these narrative potlatches may take place in and portray regions of comparative material failure but that their excessive expenditures of narrative time obligate their readers to "pay" attention over and over again. It is a payment that symbolically offsets the poverty of their environments. Such an excessive expenditure allows them to participate in the experience of potlatch with its attendant assertion of power, from which they would otherwise be excluded.[12]

In adopting this type of "primitive" textual economy of excess, Fuentes in *The Death of Artemio Cruz*, like Faulkner before him, remains a modernist primitivist, if a disillusioned one, no longer in search of an originary truth but unwilling to abandon entirely the dream of cultural knowledge that it represents. Furthermore, the tone of lament that often inheres in Bataille's opinion of modern life also matches that of Faulkner and Fuentes in these two texts. According to Bataille, today, "the representatives of the bourgeoisie have adopted an effaced manner," with the result that "wealth is now displayed behind closed doors," and "everything that was generous, orgiastic, and excessive has disappeared" (124). They collectively anticipate Fuentes's prophetic statement in *Terra Nostra*, in which he proposes that "la vida del Nuevo milenio debe expulsar las nociones del sacrificio, trabajo y propiedad, para instaurar un solo principio, el del placer" ([1975] 33) ["life in the new millennium must eradicate all notions of sacrifice, work and property in order to instill one single principle: that of pleasure" ([1976] 29)]. By "sacrifice," he does not mean Bataille's notion of ritual expenditure but rather that of restraint, the curbing of excessive instincts in favor of the kind of hoarding of investments that Bataille describes, a restraint that he proposes to replace with an excess of pleasure.

Besides the phenomenon of repetition, other narrative techniques contribute to these verbal economies of excess. In examining them more closely, Dorothy Hale's discussion of Faulkner's heterogeneous discourse helps to track how Fuentes builds on Faulkner's potlatches. Hale points out that the interior monologues in *As I Lay Dying* deviate from the colloquial into the poetic, lending a character a language not consonant with her realistic representation (6–7). Listen to Dewey Dell: "He could fix it all right, if he just would. And he don't even know it. He could do everything for me if he just knowed it. The cow breathes upon my hips and back, her breath warm, sweet, stertorous, moaning" (63). Hale's point is that the marginally literate Dewey Dell would hardly use a word like *stertorous*. Even more frequently, Darl's visions, such as this spare and elegant description of Jewel and his horse, lift his discourse out of his colloquial milieu: "then Jewel is enclosed by a glittering maze of hooves as by an illusion of wings; among them, beneath the upreared chest, he moves with the flashing limberness of a snake. . . . [He] sees his whole body earth-free, horizontal, snake-limber. . . . They stand in rigid terrific hiatus" (12). A similar discordant diction characterizes Artemio's paeans to Mexico, which appear in the second-person sections and which expand his poetic repertoire beyond realistic plausibility.

> ¿Recordarás el país? Lo recordarás y no es uno; son mil países con un solo nombre. Eso lo sabrás. Traerás los desiertos rojos, las estepas de tuna y maguey, el mundo del nopal, el cinturón de lava y

cráteres helados, las murallas de cúpulas doradas y troneras de piedra, las ciudades de cal y canto, las ciudades de tezontle, los pueblos de adobe . . . las peinetas jarochas, las trenzas mixtecas, los cinturones tzotziles . . . heredarás la tierra. (*Muerte* 274–76)

Remember this country? You remember it. It is not one; there are a thousand countries, with a single name. You know that. You will carry with you the red deserts, the hills of prickly pear and maguey, the world of dry cactus, the lava belt of frozen craters, the walls of golden domes and rock thrones, the limestone and sandstone cities, the tezontle-stone cities, the adobe pueblos . . . the Veracruz combs, the Mixtec braids, Tsotil belts. . . . [Y]ou will inherit the land. (*Death* 266–68)

Thus both Darl's and the second-person Artemio's narrations, different as they are, dismantle the individually coherent self, with its coordinates of identity, and partially replace them with fragments of a cosmic poetry. In another example from *The Death of Artemio Cruz*, the narrative expenditure seems even more extravagant, so ritualistically repetitive is the language:

Un día cualquiera, que sin embargo será un día excepcional, hace tres, cuatro años; no recordarás; recordarás por recordar; no, recordarás porque lo primero que recuerdas, cuando tratas de recordar, es un día separado, un día de ceremonia, un día separado de los demás por los números rojos; y éste será el día—tú mismo lo pensarás entonces—en que todos los nombres, personas, palabras, hechos de un ciclo fermentan y hacen crujir la costra de la tierra. (*Muerte* 249–50)

On an ordinary day, that nevertheless will be an exceptional day, three or four years ago; you will not remember it, you will remember by remembering; no, you will remember because the first thing that you remember, when you try to remember, is a day set apart, a day of ceremony, a day marked in red: and this will be the day—you yourself will think then—when all the names, people, words, and deeds of a full cycle will ferment and break the crust of the earth. (*Death* 241)

In this particular instance, of course, the ritualistic language reinforces the virtually explicit references to the cyclical time of the Aztecs, an example of the coincidence of private voice and ancient communal time. (Switching Faulknerian texts for a moment, another example of that coincidence is that—something like Melquíades's room, where it is always March and always Monday, and which is in some senses the origin of the narration of *One Hundred Years of Solitude*—both Miss Rosa's "dim hot airless room all closed and fastened for forty-three summers" on the first page of *Absalom, Absalom!* and Ludivinia Menchaca's "nido de olores apretados" that was "mustia, encalada" and that "olía a trópico encerrado" (*Muerte* 290) ["nest of closed-in smells . . . hot and musty . . . smelled of the tropics" (*Death* 281)] stand at the origins of the strongly individual and yet temporally indeterminate narrations in *Absalom, Absalom!* and *The Death of Artemio Cruz.*) In terms of narrative economy, the lyrical interludes in *The Death of Artemio Cruz*, like the repetitions of time that the multivocal structures achieve, are excessive. In some sense, of course, all literary narrative belongs in this category, but these texts increase the quotient of narrative excess and inefficiency. One way Fuentes achieves such an increase is to include poetry in the novel, a form that Bataille characterizes as "creation by means of loss," considering it "close to *sacrifice*" because "it can be considered synonymous with expenditure" (120). That extravagant presence of typographic poems is reinforced by the second-person address, which Fuentes considers both a poetic and a collective form.[13]

This initial similarity regarding disconsonant diction leads to another even more striking one: in distinguishing several levels of language in *As I Lay Dying*, Hale illustrates how it prefigures Fuentes's division of Artemio's discourse into tripartite form. Hale posits four levels in Faulkner's text, all of which are present in *The Death of Artemio Cruz*, though with some variation. Hale's first level is "quoted dialogue," which "represents the most extreme public expression; it stands as an objective record of a character's public language" (12). Quoted dialogue corresponds to the third-person narration in *The Death of Artemio Cruz* that recounts public, external events and includes dialogue. The second of Hale's levels is "first-person narration that is composed and mimetic [and] shows the integration of the private and public self; the self represents its experience to itself in public language" (12). This kind of narration corresponds in spirit to Artemio's third-person account of the past, because it is "composed" and constitutes the self representing its experience to itself in public language; however, because of the first-person form it also seems present in the sections that narrate in the first person Artemio's bodily suffering. Those sections embody Hale's idea of an integration of public and private selves—more private than the third person, less intimate than the second, but existing at the epidermal level, as it were, admitting the bodily realities of the actual approach of death but guarding the self's right to record them in its own hesitating language.

Hale's third level is "mimetic stream-of-consciousness[, which] represents what a character might say if he could compose his thoughts" (12). This level is also evident in Artemio's first-person sections because one hears what he is thinking to himself. Toward the end, however, with the disintegration of his mind approaching death, the thoughts become increasingly less composed. The fourth level, "private language, wholly unsayable language, is figured by nonmimetic vocabulary and tone" (12). It corresponds to Artemio's second-person narration, in which he imagines a different life for himself as well as a kind of "uncreated conscience" for himself and his race. Like Faulkner's "stylized representation of consciousness," Fuentes's stylization of Artemio's discourse, including his use of the second person, "rejects th[e] method of mimetic representation because . . . the true self is glimpsed only in its struggle against the normative power of social language" (12), a power that Artemio has also been in a position to exploit, but at the cost of actualizing the hopes and dreams of this private, lyrical self. In both cases, then, "to the degree that his interior language resembles his dialogue, a character has sacrificed his private self to the public norm" (12). Artemio Cruz, like the Bundrens, "represent[s] various versions of the struggle between the private and public self" (12), a strength of Fuentes's writing signaled by Octavio Paz in characterizing it as fascinated by public and private spaces, revealing "the bedroom and the public square, the couple and the crowd, the young girl in love in her room, and the tyrant caught in his den," demonstrating a concern with "desire and power, love and revolution" (Paz 225).

Because of this heightened dialogism, together with the lyricism, one might consider these texts as Warwick Wadlington views Faulkner's, as inscriptions of communal tragic performances, an interpretation that accords both with Bataille's idea of excess as encoding loss and with Fuentes's idea about Faulkner, whose "obras ocupan el tiempo circular y el espacio vacío de la tragedia" ["works occupy the circular time and the empty space of tragedy"] ("La novela" 61).[14] However, taking into account Hale's idea about their encoding of the private self, they are tragic monologues; they modify the classical dramatic form in a modernist direction, foregrounding the individual and the cosmic as against the social and the historical. They provisionally celebrate the death of the actual historical past and propose the possibility of its rebirth reconstructed in the text. At the same time, however, and paradoxically, the persistence of that past simultaneously subverts this imaginary death and resurrection.

Because the voices in these texts, being internal, are at least partially disembodied, the reader is induced to take them on, and thus to perform a (truncated and incomplete) mortuary ritual.[15] The dignity of such narrative rites counteracts the actual misuse of personal power that connects Sutpen and Artemio Cruz, and that Fuentes terms "fate." He explains, "La libertad faulkneriana es la suma afirmativa de la violación-culpa-redención-amor. La fatalidad es esa misma libertad sirviéndose de los demás hombres como instrumentos: negándolos" ["Faulknerian freedom is the affirmative accumulation of violation-guilt-redemption-love. Fate is that same freedom using other men like tools: denying them"] ("La novela" 73–74). In other words, man achieves freedom if he redeems his violation of nature through love, but he succumbs to fate if he achieves the goal of dominating the world through using other people. In the way that it incorporates people with their emotions and intimate relations into an opportunistic plan, Sutpen's "design" to establish and ensure the continuity of his legacy, which involves repudiating his octoroon wife and firstborn son because they contaminate his racially pure dynastic landowning project, corresponds to the way in which Artemio proceeds with his plan: he alters the facts of Bernal's death and his role in it in order to propose to Catalina, inherit the family's lands, and incorporate them into his financial empire by selling them in exchange for real estate in Puebla and by making deals to ensure that highways and railways cross this land to his profit. Catalina, subliminally aware of his "design," tells herself that she was "sin voz ni actitud, comprada, testigo mudo de él" (*Muerte* 97) ["bought. Without voice, will, bought, a mute witness to his stone purposes" (*Death* 91)]. In these narrative rites, by contrast, the timbre of individual voices combines with the broader ranging discourses of poetry and myth. Such a combination in that ritual discourse pulls it toward the past and belief rather than toward the future and material progress, again embodying economies of "unproductive" verbal expenditure.

Absalom, Absalom! is more comparable to *The Death of Artemio Cruz* as a serious tragedy than is *As I Lay Dying*, which possesses a larger comic component. In spite of that difference, however, both *The Death of Artemio Cruz* and *As I Lay Dying* can be experienced as formal rites, including but surpassing colloquial language. Thus the monologues present a curious mixture of earthiness and elevation, roughness and ritual. The voices within the characters in both texts perform their tragedies in the lyric language of ritual. In *As I Lay Dying* it is Darl's monologues that sound this ritual note most emphatically because much of the rest of the family are comically undignified in their enactment of the funeral rites. At one point, Darl describes the scene of the fire that nearly destroys Addie's coffin in terms (like the fire-flowers blooming out of his undershirt) that, even within the comic confusion, elevate it to the level of a ritual incineration that the actual body never achieves. Jewel and Gillespie are struggling

> like two figures in a Greek frieze, isolated out of all reality by the red glare.... We watch through the dissolving proscenium of the doorway as Jewel runs crouching to the far end of the coffin and stoops to it.... [The coffin] looms unbelievably tall. ... Then it topples forward, gaining momentum, revealing Jewel and the sparks raining on him too in engendering gusts, so that he appears to be enclosed in a thin nimbus of fire. Without stopping it overends and rears again, pauses, then crashes slowly forward and through the curtain. This time Jewel is riding upon it, clinging to it, until it crashes down and flings him forward and clear and Mack leaps forward into a thin smell of scorching meat and slaps at the widening crimson-edged holes that bloom like flowers in his undershirt. (211–12)

This makes of Jewel, perhaps, a living, burning, suffering, floral offering for his mother's coffin?

The Death of Artemio Cruz evokes mortuary ritual even more explicitly in a long lyrical chapter near the end, when Artemio envisions what might be seen as the soul's final journey to an eternal land (which is also the beginning of a new Aztec temporal cycle), in which he will be

> liberado de la fatalidad de un sitio y un nacimiento.... Todo parecerá marchar, en ese instante de ojos cerrados, a un tiempo, hacia adelante, hacia atrás y hacia el suelo que lo sostiene.... Contemplarás la tierra dormida.... Toda la tierra.... Serás ese nuevo elemento del paisaje que pronto desaparecerá para buscar, del otro lado de la montaña, el futuro incierto de su vida.... Y te sentirás en la noche, en el ángulo perdido del sol: en el tiempo.... Eres, serás, fuiste el universo encarnado, ... Para ti se encenderán las galaxias y se incendiará el sol. (*Muerte* 309–13)

> freed from the destiny of birth and birthplace.... In that instant when your eyelids are down, everything will seem to move forward and backward and toward the supporting earth.... You will contemplate the sleeping earth.... You will be that new element in the landscape which will go away to seek, on the other side of the mountain, your life's uncertain future.... [You will feel yourself to be in] darkness, the sun's lost angle, and in time.... You are, you will be, you have been the universe incarnate. For you galaxies will flame and the sun will burn. (*Death* 299–304)

In moments like these, the secret self's narrative expenditure, its anachronistic resistance to ordinary language and the defeats of history and the body, reveals a tentative hope for the survival of that self. In other words, the private self as the repository of ritual lyric connects with both a collective past and an immortal soul and thereby partially lightens its temporal burdens.[16] (Note the similarity of "Bundren" to *burden*.) In performing these rites, by animating the voices of the participants, the reader repays the obligations incurred by the narrative potlatch she has been offered. In a sense, it is true that the dead cannot be repaid by actual gifts in life as potlatch tradition requires, but since their voices are ceremonial, textual voices, perhaps in a textual sense they can; one repays them by reading more words in these narrative expenditures than humans are normally accorded in recounting events. Similarly, although one might argue that death is a final end with no remainder or excess and hence no possibility of engaging in a potlatch, these texts seem to revise that pragmatic perspective, implicitly proposing instead, through their willfully anachronistic and excessive modes, that such rules do not always apply.

The ritual mourning in these texts suggests that they are not entirely trapped in a narrative fetishism as described by Eric Santner, which defers the act of mourning by expunging traces of past traumas. Even if all of the Bundrens except Darl and Vardaman, whose mother "is a fish," seem to do just that by making Addie's funeral serve their own purposes, the comedy of that appropriation and its inadequacy in the face of death, together with Darl's enactment of his own trauma, means that readers do not. Even if most of the family enacts "a strategy of undoing, in fantasy, the need for mourning by simulating a condition of intactness," the text does not (Santner 144). Similarly, the textual division of Artemio into three forestalls any such simulation of intactness, causing the process of mourning to proceed.

As Carlos Alonso claims that García Márquez's *The General in his Labyrinth* does in more complete fashion, these ritual narratives of mourning achieve a partial conversion of melancholy—in which, according to Freud, the ego is unconsciously and irretrievably identified with the lost love object—into the therapeutic process of mourning, in which the ties to the lost object become progressively looser, and the mourner's libido is liberated. The lost object in the cases of *As I Lay Dying* and *The Death of Artemio Cruz* is the past and its idealized and failed projects—the gentility of southern plantation culture and the democratic ideals of the Mexican Revolution, respectively. The texts, in acknowledging and mourning these deaths, contribute to a cultural healing of sorts. Yet, unlike Fuentes's *La campaña*, which according to Alonso is "emblematic of the successful passing from melancholy to mourning and beyond, that is, to the final awareness that loss must somehow be turned into memory if life is to abide and prevail" (262), this process remains incomplete in *As I Lay Dying* and *The Death of Artemio Cruz*, the losses of history still leaving melancholy scars, since the dissociation from modernity that the more jocularly heterotopic spirit of postmodernism arranges had only just begun when they were written.

For one thing, these portraits of figures who embody the recent past retain traces of the "self-reproaches and self-revilings" that Freud considered characteristic of melancholia (153). Freud's discussion of "how in this condition one part of the ego sets itself over against the other, judges it critically, and, as it were, looks upon it as an object" (157) seems especially relevant to Artemio's division into acting (in the third person) and judging (in the second person) selves. Because of the lack in the South and in Spanish America of present material success to which the mourning ego could otherwise reattach itself, the burden of the lost past remains very heavy and "the free libido [is] . . . withdrawn into the ego and not directed to another object" (159). Furthermore, in the cases of both Souths, the reason for the pull toward melancholia is illuminated by Freud's explanation of this condition as stemming from a "narcissistic type of object choice" (160)—in this case, the investment and identification of the cultural self with past institutions and ideals.[17]

Even though it does not prevent the psychic process of mourning, the repetitive presence of the past in *As I Lay Dying* and *The Death of Artemio Cruz* perhaps slows down its process and may recreate the past as a more anthropologically oriented fetish—dangerous but powerful and in need of propitiation. As Apter has pointed out, fetishism both harks back to an unrepeatable first form and compulsively repeats it.[18] Events seen from the various perspectives of Artemio and Catalina, of Artemio in the third person, of Artemio in the second person, and of Vardaman, Darl, Cash, and so on fix the past both as past and as ever present. According to Fuentes, this is the temporal irony of Faulkner: "todo es recuerdo, pero todo se recuerda en el presente. Todo lo que fue está siendo. El círculo se cierra para abrirse. El hombre sin pasado, todo futuro, de Balzac, ha cedido el lugar al hombre que es puro pasado de Proust; y éste ha conducido al hombre de Faulkner, que sólo es pasado en el presente y por ello, otra vez, inminencia de futuro" ["everything is memory, but everything is remembered in the present. All that was exists now. The circle closes in order to open. Balzac's man without a past has given way to

Proust's man who is pure past, who in turn has led to Faulkner's man who is the past in the present and therefore once again impending future"] ("La novela" 68). Similarly, such differing perspectives on the past both clarify and confuse the reader about its meanings, creating both narrative and epistemological excess, positing both irretrievability and reordering, and resulting in texts in which chaos and order face off.

That face-off suggests that a meaningful connection between Faulkner and Fuentes stems from the "fragmentary structure" that, according to Kartiganer, is "the core of Faulkner's novelistic vision" (xiii), in which he describes a world of broken orders, a world in which the meetings of men and words need to be imagined again. That necessity to reimagine characterizes the particular connection between history and narrative investigated here, the simultaneous presence of fragmentation and the positing of an alternate albeit fragile order. If Joyce's mythical method in *Ulysses* made the modern world possible for art, then Fuentes learns from Faulkner's method of narrative fragmentation that the modern southern world is often made impossible by the past. Lest one merge Fuentes and Faulkner too closely, however, a distinction needs to be made. Perhaps because of Fuentes's interest in the indigenous—and Joycean—mythical substructure, *The Death of Artemio Cruz* is more formally ordered than *As I Lay Dying*. Artemio's life falls apart but his text falls together, as it were. The ending in which the three voices coincide at his death, that death as it coincides with the renewal of the Aztec calendrical cycle, together with the tripartite divisions of the story, achieve a more highly structured, if similar, design than Faulkner articulates in the diverse monologues that compose *As I Lay Dying*.[19]

As is the case with stream-of-consciousness narration generally, these texts not only document the wounds of division within family and society by isolating characters within their own interior monologues, but they also, paradoxically, heal them by connecting those isolated monologues. They thus enact the sociotextual dynamics of Paz's labyrinth of solitude— the masks of Mexican solitude momentarily removed in the fiesta of poetry itself. While Deborah Cohn's position that extratextual factors have played a role in the relationship between Faulkner and Spanish American writers, including Fuentes, is not inaccurate, such realities seem secondary to the fact that, as Tanya Fayen articulates, the very nature of modernist stream-of-consciousness writing also means that such a style serves as something of an escape from regional concerns to international Joycean realms of silence, exile, and cunning narrative invention.

Another paradox that resembles the communion achieved by the textual amalgamation of individual monologues in these novels is the presence of death as a narrative enabler. If the living are haunted almost out of existence by the historical past, then the nearness of death also partially— and once again, paradoxically—frees their voices. It belongs to a kind of narrative return of the repressed, something like the process of mourning. The difficulty of such a fictional task is interpreted by Fuentes at the end of his essay on Faulkner as Faulkner's having chosen pain rather than nothingness, a choice that is presumably his own as well. In *As I Lay Dying* the matriarch near death in some sense frees the voices of her children. Similarly, in *The Death of Artemio Cruz* the near-death of the patriarch frees the voices within himself that represent forces within the Mexican social fabric that have been silent as he has built his empire. Thus, this intransigence of the past and its traumas is present, not in the form of ghosts, as is often the case in magical realist fictions, but in a more strongly present voice in the process of becoming a ghost. It is an especially compelling presence in the reader's universe because it retains the living person's power to act, to which it adds the otherworldly and frightening authority and finality of the pronouncements of the dead.

But this is not an easily assimilated presence. The presence of the deaths also means that the past is engaged with traumatically. The returning repressed surges forth urgently. That presence of death may be responsible for what André Bleikasten defines as the potency of the narrative present in Faulkner's novel, in which "narrative and fictional time tend to coincide": "whatever the point reached in the course of reading, it coincides most often with the 'now' of a vision and an action: we are in the present, we share it with the hero-narrators of the story, associated with both an action and a narrative in progress" (50–51). It is perhaps the narrative equivalent of the land in the South that Fuentes characterizes as not aging because it doesn't forget (" 'no envejece . . . porque no olvida' " ["La novela" 53]) and that corresponds to the Mexican land as Fuentes portrays it in *The Death of Artemio Cruz*: "esta naturaleza que se niega a ser compartida o dominada, que quiere seguir existiendo en soledad abrupta y sólo ha regalado a los hombres unos cuantos valles, unos cuantos ríos, para que en ellos o a su vera se entretengan; ella sigue siendo la dueña arisca de los picachos lisos e inalcanzables, del desierto plano, de las selvas y de la costa abandonada" (*Muerte* 275–76) ["nature that refuses to be compared or controlled, that wants to live on in harsh loneliness and has granted men only a few outlying valleys and rivers for them to cling to her skirts; nature that goes on ruling the smooth unattainable peaks, the flat burned deserts, the forests and the deserted coast" (*Death* 267)].[20]

Narrative excess clearly belongs to the New American baroque as a narrative economy of expenditure. There is also, perhaps, another connection between the two Souths, one less historical and more stylistic or generic than those that are usually made between Faulkner and his Spanish American descendents.[21] And that is a line of development that would connect Faulkner with magical realism. The precursors of magical realism are usually understood to be more European than American, in part because Spanish American writers frequently looked across the Atlantic; one generally thinks of Cervantes, Gogol, Kafka, and Woolf, among others, rather than of Faulkner. However, an inter American perspective might reveal a more hybrid genetic profile.

Viewed from that perspective, the narrative excesses engendered out of the burdens of the past might lead toward magical realism, toward the creation of alternative worlds. In his discussion of the turn from modernism to postmodernism, a moment inhabited by magical realism, McHale locates a point in *Absalom, Absalom!* in which Quentin and Shreve abandon their attempts to remember and begin to reconstruct, to self-consciously (re)invent the past. That moment signals a switch, according to McHale, from the epistemological mode of modernism, in which one asks how we know something, to the ontological dominant of postmodernism, in which one inquires what it is and wonders which of our selves will interact with it (10). Might one connect such a particularly southern moment of narrative excess engendered by historical devastation and desire to the early magical realist inventions of Faulkner's Spanish American descendents, to Fuentes's idea that Faulkner is one of the novelists who "invents a second reality, a parallel reality" "through language and structure" rather than through the earlier realist resources of plot and psychology (*La nueva novela* 19)? The Spanish American magical realists enlarge that narrative inventiveness toward, but not all the way to, the fantastic, delicately suggesting the existence of second realities within the habitual one. If a first—historical—reality is a nightmare from which one is trying to awake, perhaps Spanish American magical realism, taking one of its cues from Faulkner's reconstructions of the past in the U.S. South, achieves the beginning of a narrative reawakening.[22] It is a reawakening that takes the form of a narrative excess that, as Bataille might formulate it, counteracts a world in which "everything that was generous, orgiastic, and excessive has disappeared" (124).

NOTES

1. Though she is discussing southern women's writing, and in an almost entirely thematic (rather than a stylistic) register, several of the points that Patricia Yaeger takes up in her study *Dirt and Desire* provide a complement to the literary economy of

excess described herein. This is especially true of the way in which Yaeger wants to replace the cliché of miniature in accounts of southern women's writing with that of giant, citing the gargantuan woman Eudora Welty describes in her story "A Memory" as an initial and convincing example and continuing to analyze a number of excessively large bodies, including the swelling of Miss Eckhart's as she gives her piano recital in Welty's "June Recital," all of which question the "demure alcoves of white southern women's fiction" (Yaeger 122). And it is also true of her sense of place as trash heap—a kind of excess—in these writers' texts. Yaeger additionally illustrates a particular kind of excess in southern women's writing that she associates with its treatment of whiteness, not as Toni Morrison has characterized it in the writings of white male canonical authors, as "'mute, meaningless, unfathomable, pointless, frozen, veiled, curtained, dreaded, senseless, implacable,' [but rather] in the landscapes imagined by these women writers, whiteness speaks in water moccasin tongues; it erupts with too much meaning; it is terrifyingly dynamic, vulnerable, agitated, tortured, vertiginous. Or, it is partial, fragmented, an intensive source of labor, a site of confusion that gums up the works" (qtd. in Yaeger 21). In other cases, however, Yaeger's refiguration of southern women's writing as "reverse autochthony," in which bodies are not animated out of the ground but rather are put with their words back into it—buried—seems to constitute a kind of obverse or flip side, a verbal poverty, that contrasts with what I describe herein as a verbal excess that compensates for the historical atrocities it chronicles. This is the case for the "landscapes loaded with trauma unspoken, with bodies unhealed or uncared for" that she discovers in southern women's writing (17–18). But in both cases there still remains a kind of excess—the landscapes are "loaded"—that figures "a world encumbered with endless melancholy" (20).

2. I am adopting the term from Gustavo Pérez Firmat's characterization of the juxtaposition of texts that reveal formal and thematic continuities (Pérez Firmat 4).

3. The "Dixie Gongorism" statement appears in Fuentes, "La novela" (66).

4. I am using these terms as they are formulated by Gérard Genette in his *Narrative Discourse* (121).

5. Elsewhere I have connected this impulse more specifically to the erotic in Fuentes's fiction. Now, I wish to extend it more specifically to narrative poetics; see my "'Without Sin, and with Pleasure.'" As I noted there, Fuentes is familiar with Bataille's work, citing it in the list of books he used while writing *Terra Nostra*, so that, again, as with Faulkner, while I am not primarily concerned with genetic relations, they do exist.

6. Lois Parkinson Zamora makes this tendency a connection between the South and Latin America: "a sense of history as both compelling and oppressive links Southern U.S. fiction to Latin American fiction" (121); so, more recently, does Cohn (2, 31).

7. Jean Bessière sees a similar duality with regard to history in Faulkner's work as it is absorbed by Fuentes: "Faulkner's world is perhaps a finished world; however, in terms of temporal representation, of historical representation, it is a never-ending world. In other words, it is also the paradoxical alliance of fatality and freedom. To use a term that belongs neither to Faulkner nor to Fuentes, Fuentes places the Faulknerian tragedy under the sign of a possible consciousness" (36).

8. Deborah Cohn has pointed out that novels like *Ulysses* and *Mrs. Dalloway* (and, I would like to add, *As I Lay Dying*) may be seen as the paradigm for several Latin American novels, including *The Death of Artemio Cruz*, that compress national history into the frame of a single day (23). This compression is an especially effective technique for dealing with the past, one that provides a kind of temporal frame that can accommodate the narrative excesses discussed herein.

9. In a similar vein, Yaeger points to the prevalence of an economy of scarcity in the South and to creative strategies for overcoming it, such as Sethe's "wonderful bricolage" in putting together her wedding dress in Morrison's *Beloved* (Yaeger 196).

10. Cohn makes these same points with regard to modernism's general influence on Latin American narrative. In comparing Faulkner's texts to García Márquez's *One Hundred Years of Solitude*, "a polyphonic style . . . describes the same event from different perspectives" (30), and "the temporal confusion, conflations, and manipulations of both authors are complemented by the use of pronouns without clarification of their referents" (28).

11. For an application of some of these same notions to Emerson, see Grusin, who maintains that for Emerson it is not the reader but God whom he wants to put in debt.

12. Because of her focus on women's writing, Yaeger understandably focuses even more on the sense of loss and exclusion than does my analysis of male writing. For example, she notices how the "rag bundle"—a kind of excess, or throwaway—that Clytie in *Absalom, Absalom!* has become elides the trauma of her race's loss and grief that Faulkner doesn't explore (80–81).

13. Speaking of *The Death of Artemio Cruz*, Fuentes states, "El *tú* se ha estado usando desde que la poesía es poesía" ["The *tu* has been being used since poetry was poetry"] ("Memoria" 26). He has also said, "In fact, I think that all of Faulkner's novels are narrated by a collective voice. So for me the '*tu*' was totally important as a recognition of the other, as a stylistic means to recognize the other; it is perhaps the Mexican people—the collective voice—that speaks to Artemio Cruz saying '*tú, tú, tú*'" (qtd. in Márquez 91–92).

14. For a discussion of the ways in which *As I Lay Dying* functions as ritual drama, see Wadlington (101–30).

15. Louis D. Rubin writes that, in regard to *As I Lay Dying*, "we are forced into our own participation as the central consciousness of the novel, so that events happen around us" (*Writers* 62).

16. Hale writes, "By making a character's speaking voice mimetically appropriate and by rendering his internal voice in a stylized, non-mimetic manner, Faulkner distinguishes the private self from the public criterion of plausible language use" (9).

17. The way I am interpreting these novels as textual economies of excess would presumably locate them in a moment just previous to the postmodernism that scrutinizes modernity and that Alonso describes as "a commodity" that "claims to satisfy the desire to be free from consumption" (253). That sense of historical difference is confirmed when Alonso cites García Márquez's postface to *The General in his Labyrinth*, which he claims requests the reader to "conceptualize the novel as a collage of multiple

transmissions of information" and continues to define "the simulacrum of the author that is described by *El general en su laberinto*" as "perhaps a metaphor for the radical transformation undergone by the figure of the Spanish-American author during the last twenty years. The former conjurer of totalizing fictions that purported to encompass and incorporate in his works the essence of Spanish America disperses himself, disseminates himself in those recent Spanish-American texts that appeal to the dialogic multiplicity of the fragment, to eroticism, humor, local circumstance and personal idiosyncracy" (Alonso 262). In *As I Lay Dying* and *The Death of Artemio Cruz* perhaps Faulkner and Fuentes signal the demise of that totalizing impulse while still participating in it. Even though the chronologies and degrees of passage from melancholia to mourning differ in the novels he analyzes and those I am treating here, Alonso's delineation of how even as Garcia Marquez's narrative depicts Bolivar's historical twilight, it also attempts to portray the beginnings of modern Spanish American history is a similar example of what one might term a narrative expenditure that confronts history in order to mourn it excessively and therapeutically.

18. "Fetishism records the trajectory of an idée fixe or *noumen* in search of its materialist twin (god to idol, alienated labor to luxury item, phallus to shoe fetish and so on)" (Apter 4).

19. As Deborah Cohn has helpfully pointed out to me, Artemio's death—and the writing of Fuentes's novel—also coincide with the Cuban Revolution (to which it points by its envoi from both Mexico and Havana), suggesting the possibility of a new order emerging from the old. Because it belongs to the cycles of history, however, rather than to those of a mythic understanding of history, it seems to me that that connection points to a less orderly design than the Aztec resonance does.

20. Fuentes cites Faulkner to characterize the South in this way ("La novela" 53).

21. Zamora's excellent discussion of *Absalom, Absalom!* and *One Hundred Years of Solitude* exemplifies the tendency to focus on temporal issues in the two novels (33–45). Cohn's discussion of *Absalom, Absalom!* and Vargas Llosa's *The Real Life of Alejandro Mayta* as cases of "fabricated facts" focuses on the same scene McHale highlights, and illustrates well this quality of narrative excess I have been discussing, but she does not connect it specifically with magical realism as such.

22. After having formulated this idea, I reread the ending of McHale's *Postmodernist Fiction*, in which he proposes virtually the same idea in regard to Joyce's texts (though not grounding it in Bataille's notion of excess), moving from the deaths that figure modernism in "The Dead" and *Ulysses* to the one that figures postmodernism in *Finnegans Wake*: "As modernist texts 'The Dead' and *Ulysses* project unified ontological planes, no more nor less than one world each. Death here, even death displaced into sleep, constitutes an absolute limit beyond which these texts do not venture. . . . Anna Livia breaks off in mid-sentence . . . but of course this sentence is resumed elsewhere—on the first page of *Finnegans Wake*. . . . Dead on the last page, this discourse is resurrected, 'by a commodius vicus of recirculation' on the first. Postmodernist writing in *Finnegans Wake* models not only the ontological limit of death, but also the dream of a return" (234–35).

WORKS CITED

Alonso, Carlos. "The Mourning After: García Márquez, Fuentes, and the Meaning of Postmodernity in Spanish America." *MLN* 109 (1994): 252–67.

Apter, Emily. Introduction. *Fetishism as Cultural Discourse*. Ed. Emily Apter and William Pietz. Ithaca, N.Y.: Cornell UP, 1993. 1–9.

Bataille, Georges. *Visions of Excess: Selected Writings 1927–1939*. Trans. and ed. Allan Stoeckl, with Carl R. Lovitt and Donald M. Leslie Jr. Minneapolis: U of Minnesota P, 1985.

Bessière, Jean. "Carlos Fuentes Vis-à-vis William Faulkner: Novel, Tragedy, History." *Faulkner Journal* 11.1–2 (1995–1996): 33–42.

Bleikasten, André. *Faulkner's* As I Lay Dying. Trans. Roger Little. Bloomington: Indiana UP, 1973.

Cohn, Deborah. *History and Memory in the Two Souths*. Nashville, Tenn.: Vanderbilt UP, 1999.

Faris, Wendy B. " 'Without Sin, and with Pleasure': The Erotic Dimensions of Fuentes's Fiction." *Novel* 21.1 (1986): 62–77.

Faulkner, William. *Absalom, Absalom!* 1936. New York: Penguin, 1971.

——. *As I Lay Dying*. 1930. New York: Random, 1969.

Fayen, Tanya. *In Search of the Latin American Faulkner*. Lanham, Md.: UP of America, 1995.

Freud, Sigmund. "Mourning and Melancholia." *Collected Papers*. Vol. 4. Trans. by Joan Riviere. New York: Basic, 1957. 152–70.

Fuentes, Carlos. *The Death of Artemio Cruz*. 1964. Trans. Sam Hileman. New York: Farrar, 1976.

——. "Memoria y deseo." Interview with Carlos Fuentes by Miguel Angel Quemain. *Quimera* 120 (1993): 24–32.

——. *La muerte de Artemio Cruz*. 1962. Mexico City: Fondo de Cultura Económica, 1965.

——. "La novela como tragedia." *Casa con dos puertas*. Mexico City: Joaquín Mortiz, 1970. 52–78.

——. *La nueva novela hispanoamericana*. Mexico City: Joaquín Mortiz, 1969.

——. *Terra Nostra*. 1975. Barcelona: Seix Barral, 1985.

——. *Terra Nostra*. Trans. Margaret Sayers Peden. New York: Farrar, 1976.

Genette, Gérard. *Narrative Discourse: An Essay in Method*. Trans. Jane E. Lewin. Ithaca, N.Y.: Cornell UP, 1980.

Grusin, Richard A. "Put God in Your Debt: Emerson's Economy of Expenditure." *PMLA* 103.1 (1998): 35–44.

Hale, Dorothy. "*As I Lay Dying*'s Heterogeneous Discourse." *Novel* 23.1 (1989): 5–23.

Kartiganer, Donald. *The Fragile Thread: The Meaning of Form in Faulkner's Novels*. Amherst: U of Massachusetts P, 1979.

Márquez, Antonio C. "Faulkner in Latin America." *Faulkner Journal* 11.1–2 (1995–1996): 83–100.

McHale, Brian. *Postmodernist Fiction*. New York: Methuen, 1987.

Paz, Octavio. "Presentación de Carlos Fuentes, en su conferencia inaugural en el Colegio Nacional el martes 17 de octubre de 1972." *Memoria del Colegio Nacional* 7.3 (1972): 223–26.

Pérez Firmat, Gustavo. Introduction. *Do the Americas Have a Common Literature?* Durham, N.C.: Duke UP, 1990. 1–5.

Pithavy, François. "William Faulkner and Gabriel García Márquez: A Fictional Conversation." *Faulkner, His Contemporaries, and His Posterity*. Ed. Waldemar Zacharasiewicz. Tübingen, Germany: A. Franke, 1993. 336–48.

Pothier, Jacques. "Southern Modes of Commitment: Faulkner and Rushdie." *Faulkner, His Contemporaries, and His Posterity*. Ed. Waldemar Zacharasiewicz. Tübingen, Germany: A. Franke, 1993. 361–71.

Rubin, Louis D., Jr. "Southern Literature: The Historical Image." *South: Modern Southern Literature in Its Cultural Setting*. Ed. Louis D. Rubin Jr. and Robert D. Jacobs. New York: Doubleday, 1961. 29–47.

——. *Writers of the Modern South: The Faraway Country*. Seattle: U of Washington P, 1966.

Santner, Eric. "History Beyond the Pleasure Principle: Some Thoughts on the Representation of Trauma." *Probing the Limits of Representation: Nazism and the "Final Solution."* Ed. Saul Friedlander. Cambridge, Mass.: Harvard UP, 1992. 143–54.

Van Delden, Maarten. *Carlos Fuentes, Mexico, and Modernity*. Nashville, Tenn.: Vanderbilt UP, 1998.

Wadlington, Warwick. *Reading Faulknerian Tragedy*. Ithaca, N.Y.: Cornell UP, 1987.

Yaeger, Patricia. *Dirt and Desire: Reconstructing Southern Women's Writing 1930–1990*. Chicago: U of Chicago P, 2000.

Zamora, Lois Parkinson. *Writing the Apocalypse: Historical Vision in Contemporary U.S. and Latin American Fiction*. Cambridge: Cambridge UP, 1989.

PHILIP WEINSTEIN

Cant Matter/Must Matter:

Setting Up the Loom in Faulknerian

and Postcolonial Fiction

The moment in *Absalom, Absalom!* is unforgettable: Judith Sutpen—an "unwived widow"—approaching Grandmother Compson in the middle of Jefferson and offering her the murdered Charles Bon's love letter, telling her to keep it or destroy it, as she wishes, saying, "it cant matter, you know that, or the Ones that set up the loom would have arranged things a little better, and yet it must matter because you keep on trying" (101). This Faulknerian vignette crystallizes the Old South's incapacity to acknowledge its subjects' endeavors: it "cant matter" because of how the "Ones" in control have set up the loom. The larger dilemma common to Faulkner and modernism more generally is that the loom—Western patriarchal culture's array of models for individual endeavor—no longer functions. Whether the writer be Joyce or Proust or Kafka or Faulkner, the subjects being centrally imagined fail to negotiate the cultural loom and thus cease to progress. This loom is functional in realism, becomes dysfunctional in modernism, and is set up in other (non-Western) ways in postcolonialism.

Judith offers the figure of the loom as a metaphor for describing how social arrangements sabotage her attempts at meaning-making. The loom, read literally, represents the warp and woof of social space and time.[1] As *social* indicates, space and time are never encountered immediately, as brutely physical conditions of nature. Rather, cultures *design* the space and time their subjects experience, proposing normative pathways through them. Judith's metaphysical indictment of "the Ones that set [it] up" reads more tellingly, then, as cultural critique. Inasmuch as individuals take on identity by negotiating normative pathways, Judith's subjectivity here encounters its culturally generated impasse. *Subject*, *space*, and *time*, in fact, function as radically interdependent terms: space and time operate as an ideologically configured staging upon which all subjectivity is performed. It is the stance toward this "looming"—this aligning of subjects within socially charted space and time—that alters dramatically in modernism, and then alters again in postcolonialism. Faulkner's way of inserting the subject into a space and time whose designed pathways have dead-ended serves as a representative modernist instance, an instance that allows one to see what is at stake in prior realist management of these matters as well as in later postcolonial management of them—the latter embodied in the work of García Márquez and Toni Morrison. Put starkly, time in the Western Enlightenment model is continuous and linear; space is orientational and open to acquisition; and the subject is the Lockean individual entitled to life, liberty, and the pursuit of happiness. It goes well in realism, but produces disaster in modernism.[2] I begin with the Faulknerian moment.

Judith's way of being "arrested"—her temporal project annihilated—resonates throughout the Faulknerian fiction. Donald Mahan paralyzed, Bayard Sartoris traumatized, Quentin Compson moving without progress on 2 June 1910—these figures are followed in *Absalom, Absalom!* by Henry and Rosa and Wash and Sutpen himself, all of them stopped in their tracks, assaulted by something incomprehensible, thinking "I kaint have heard what I know I heard" (231). The list could be extended, and it goes beyond Faulkner. "History is what hurts," Fredric Jameson has written (102); the form of that hurting in modernism is arrest, a paralyzing moment in which the culturally furnished subject becomes unfurnished, caught up in orientations suddenly revealed as incoherent.[3] This is a crisis of patriarchal ideology, for a culture's furnishings are, precisely, its ideological resources. Inasmuch as ideology enables subjects to move purposefully through space and time (in sync with an authorized frame of "looming") by furnishing them with models of subjectivity that align them with other subjects sharing those models, much Western modernist fiction—in savaging these procedures—enacts the assault of history on ideology. Where but in a modernist novel could the concluding words so purely confound the patriarchal pact as "*I dont. I dont! I dont hate it! I dont hate it!*" (Faulkner, *Absalom* 303)?

An examination of a single "career" in *Absalom*, that of Charles Bon's son, opens up the spatial-temporal dimensions of such arrest. Born in a New Orleans in which he "could neither have heard nor yet recognised the term 'nigger,' who even had no word for it in the tongue he knew who had been born and grown up in a padded silken vacuum . . . where pigmentation had no more moral value than the silk walls and the scent and the rose-colored candle shades" (161), this child is seized by Clytie and transported—without explanation or even a shared language—to a northern Mississippi where the literal space he inhabits has altered seismically, beyond assimilation.

> The few garments (the rags of the silk and broadcloth in which he had arrived, the harsh jeans and homespun which the two women bought and made for him, he accepting them with no thanks, no comment, accepting his garret room with no thanks, no comment, asking for and making no alteration in its spartan arrangements that they knew of until that second year when he was fourteen and one of them, Clytie or Judith, found hidden beneath his mattress the shard of broken mirror: and who to know what hours of amazed and tearless grief he might have spent before it, examining himself in the delicate and outgrown tatters in which he perhaps could not even remember himself, with quiet and incredulous incomprehension) hanging behind a curtain contrived of a piece of old carpet nailed across a corner. (162)

Recognizing oneself in a mirror: Lacan, with his essay "The Mirror Stage," has bewitched a generation of critics into seeing, there and in miniature, the founding institution of (Western) culture within the not-yet-subject. The infant sees in the mirror a radiant image, sutured and mobile, of who he is-to-be. The image proposes an unattainable imaginary wholeness that spurs the infant into the social framework he would make his own. The mother's eyes confirm the infant's desire and launch the forward-moving progress through time that, for Lacan, is simultaneously alienation and "maturity." Either way, the physics of the scene organizes space as a mirroring frame in which the infant projects his desire-fueled image of himself-to-be. The drama is essentially projective, its telos patriarchal.[4]

Bon's son's mirror operates in reverse. It shows him the chasm between what he was and what he is. Each present item of clothing reads as the despoliation of a former item of clothing. His New Orleans-furnished body has been intolerably displaced by his Mississippi-furnished body, none of this his own choice. As in Lacan, this is an identity-launching moment, but it inaugurates not a centering but an implosion. Charles Etienne St. Valery Bon materializes as a culturally impossible being, torn between here and there, now and then. He lacks, utterly, the ideological resources that might resolve this tearing. Puritan northern Mississippi and Catholic New Orleans, the jagged racist present and the harmonious race-neutral past share him equally and incoherently. His solution to these incompatible cultural markings is to combine them as crucifixion. Identity, as always in Faulkner, operates as social coding registering on the body; and Bon's son's body is worse than a palimpsest—it is a contra-dictory social scripting that permits no erasures.[5] One needs an infrared light to read the black man in this white man, but he makes it easy by guaranteeing, through premeditated acts of violence, that he be rec-ognized as both at once. Performing white and black codes to fiendishly intelligible effects, a cultural semiotician before the term existed, he chooses for a wife exactly the kind of black woman that white and black alike will decode (for opposed reasons) as scandalous. Stunningly abreast of the nuances of every cultural code that entraps him, he naturalizes nothing, learns nothing, projects nothing except trouble on black and white alike. Viewed from the pedagogic stance that guides realist matura-tion, he is—like Joe Christmas—a figure of nightmarish negativity.

Faulkner "says" Charles Etienne's torment by jamming his motion in the socially configured time and space available to him. Unwilling to suture a factitious self in northern Mississippi's cohesive time (to get on with things as either white or black), the young man fractures in scandal time, transforms any event where he appears into a spectacle of violence. No time can further him, no space can accommodate him, no mores fit him; his clothes are irreparably wrong long before they become bloodied as well. He does not so much communicate through language as strike through gesture. Time, space, mores, clothes, and language function as social resources for subject-development only so long as there is a mini-mal ideological consensus. If one asks why Charles Etienne seems to epitomize modernist crisis, one could say that he exposes cultural narra-tives as no more than warring ideologies: which he experiences as a lurid unfurnishing.

When Walter Benjamin spoke of wisdom as "the epic side of truth" (87), he meant that the older narratives of the West (unlike novels both realist and modernist) served to furnish wisdom to their audience by drawing on a consensual (ideologically ordered) sense of experience that gave value to subjects' movement through time and space.[6] By contrast, Benjamin claimed, one finds in post-Enlightenment narratives less the sharing of experiential wisdom than the stimulus of new information (the "novel" in the novel). Time segments into ever-smaller and instrumental units, ceasing to be an ideologically secured medium for intersubjective, developmental lives. By the advent of late-nineteenth-century Western modernism, this temporal dilemma, further exacerbated, finally splits apart into the brittle extremes of inauthentic habit, on the one hand, and unassimilable shock, on the other. Disappeared is the wisdom that once lay between them and bound the events of a moment into a larger viable order. What is *Absalom, Absalom!*—and especially the career of Charles Bon's son—but the abruption of shock on convention, of history on ideology?[7]

Charles Etienne St. Valery Bon's dilemma—his impasse, at once traumatic and traumatizing, within space and time—torpedoes the masterplot of Western realism. That genre's representational "contract" for coordinating the notions of subject, space, and time prohibits Bon's appearance from two centuries of Western fiction. If one asks where realism's laws governing the subject's normative trajectory come from, one might start perhaps by citing the fundamental architect of Western Enlightenment scientific norms, Newton.

> 1. Every body continues in its state of rest, or of uniform rectilinear motion in a right line, unless it is compelled to change its state by forces impressed upon it.
>
> 2. The change of motion is proportional to the motive force impressed; and is made in the direction of the right line in which that force is impressed.
>
> 3. To every action there is always opposed an equal reaction: or, the mutual actions of two bodies upon each other are always equal, and directed to contrary parts. (*Mathematical Principles* 14)

Drawing on Galileo's experimentation a century earlier with falling bodies, Newton arrives at both the laws of gravity and the calculus of differential equations for plotting the motion of bodies in time and space. Newton's formulae for scientific plotting not only stabilize and make knowable the surrounding world, they also undergird the norms of subsequent realist plotting: an affair of substantial bodies in motion within uniform space and time, headed toward encounter with other substantial bodies and responsive to that encounter in lawful, satisfying ways. (*Res/realia*, the Latin root of *thing*—thinginess—already indicates where realism's responsibility lies: to take the measure, assess the weight, and plot the course of things-in-motion.) Mimesis emerges as the core tenet of realism's representational logic; coming to know better "the mutual actions of . . . bodies upon each other" drives its plot. Like Newton, realist writers keep their eye sharply fixed on moving objects, know how to chart the fallout that occurs on collision, and finally share this knowledge with their protagonist(s). The entire scene is moralized. "To every action . . . an equal reaction" sounds like a biblical warning (as you sow, so shall you reap), a categorical imperative a century before Kant, in which one's encounters with others in space produce, so to speak, exactly what each deserves, for good and ill. It takes uniform space and lots of time for these encounters to generate all their consequences—Pip must wait for years before Magwitch stands fully revealed to him—and the realist novel takes exactly the time and space it needs to unfold its spectrum of causes and effects, to produce in protagonist and reader that gravity known as Bildung. The time-space loom it works with is assumed to be rational, objective, impartial.

It is not difficult to identify the ideological consensus nourishing the subject who moves through this scenario of calculability. Realism's respect for continuous time and manageable space harbors an Enlightenment premise of the subject as (potentially) rational mapper, shaper, and owner. The drama of "projective" protagonists supplies the material of the genre from *Robinson Crusoe* to *Jude the Obscure*. However doomed this latter figure is, he has his place within a repertory of epistemological projects that unfold in lawful time and space.[8] Desiring to move upward through class and education, Jude would know the world more fully, and to that end he maps and remaps it. The institutions that control entry into Christminster, however, reject artisan applications. The social barriers blocking Jude are familiar to Hardy's readers; this text records a lifelong projective failure, not, as in Faulkner, a series of incandescent "abruptions." Projective: insofar as the realist novel insists on this investment in tomorrow as a showcasing of individual will, it models time and space as lawful frames permitting rational subjective achievement. Jude fails at this, but realism did not die with Hardy or the nineteenth century. Indeed, its blandishments (its privileging of subjective project, of the exploitation of calculable space and time) are durably with us. Mitchell's *Gone With the Wind* differs from *Absalom, Absalom!* in precisely the ways that realism does from modernism. Whereas Mitchell's Civil War is a temporal-spatial entity domesticated, mapped, identifiable in its accommodation or frustration of individual projects, Faulkner's Civil War remains unnarratable, monstrous, possessed of a half-life still disorienting its twentieth-century narrators in 1909 and 1910, even its twentieth-century author in 1936. Sutpen's Hundred burns and Quentin hates/does not hate the South. Tara remains and Scarlett knows that tomorrow is another day. The modernist text shows the damaged subject careening outside the furnished paths of space and time: ideology shattered. The realist text shows the subject bloody but unbowed, wiser for her travails, her will redirected rather than undone: project revised and thus intact.

It is one thing to grant *Absalom*'s difference from realist fictions that precede it, and another to insist on its difference from postcolonial ones that follow it. In fact, one of the vibrant strands of current cultural studies—amply represented in this larger volume—is bent on enlarging perspectives on narratives of the U.S. South by pursuing their hemispheric kinship with narratives of that other South, Latin America.[9] A growing number of scholars have sought to pair Faulkner with his Latin American counterparts, not least because those counterparts have recognized his kinship and enabling influence. More, Faulkner's *modernism* is crucial in this recognition, for his experimental modes invited—through their reconfiguring the relations of subject, time, and space—a Latin American rethinking of problem and possibility outside the norms of progressive Western realism.[10] These connections, however, reveal differences as least as telling as the resemblances, as becomes evident through a comparison of Faulkner with the postcolonial writer most often linked with him: García Márquez.[11]

The major similarities are already well established, and they revolve around a broadly shared "history that hurts": imaginative chroniclers of two cultures minoritized and dominated by larger ones (the South by the North, Latin America by the United States); writers who have experienced and conveyed the bitter taste of economic and cultural defeat (as opposed to the seemingly resistless material progress of the nonsouthern United States); novelists creatively suspicious of the ideology lurking in authorized versions of history (Benjamin's position that history is written by the victors, not the vanquished); writers with firsthand and troubling familiarity with the colonial dimensions of their own culture (Faulkner's polarized whites and blacks, Latin America's subtler array of white, blacks, Indians, and mixed-race figures); and therefore artists aware that southern subjects may live out a relation to space and time quite different from the instrumental models proposed by Enlightenment-spawned realism. More than any of his modernist peers, Faulkner "spoke" to García Márquez as one whose work revealed how much reality was omitted (or brutalized) by such linear-progressive narratives.

Yet Faulkner's representational forms differ crucially from García Márquez's in their ways of engaging the subject-space-time loom. However fiercely Faulkner jams the progressive-acquisitive plot, he cannot jettison it. The centuries-old Newtonian epistemological premise—of mapping objects in lawful space and time, of seeking to discern the real from within the welter of appearances—lodges in his practice at a level deeper than choice. Consensus about the objectively real begins notoriously to dissolve in modernism, yet modernist fictions obsess over the quandary this slippage brings, the ordeal of getting the object right, of producing a mimetic canvas that achieves adequation between representation and the real.[12] These conflicting givens propel Faulkner's fictions of tragic encounter, motivating the arrest, vertigo, and subjective anguish that is their hallmark. The negativing shadow of Flaubert, Hardy, and Conrad (all prototragic writers, all alienated from the bourgeois subject-pact, even as they share realist norms for representing subject motion through space/time) lies heavy on Faulkner, intimating the futility of desire within a scene arranged according to the logic of the patriarchal loom, a scene in which the anxious subject either fails to know or cannot bear what is finally known. García Márquez is culturally positioned otherwise in relation to both this Western history and its hegemonic fictional forms. To be sure, his work cannot avoid the colonizing history abetted by Enlightenment rationalism, but it *can* savage (in ways Faulkner could never permit himself) the representational form most authorized by that history: realism.

This point can be briefly illustrated by seeing what misprisions occur when one thinks of both writers as simply subscribing to a realist mode of character and plot. On the kinship of *Absalom, Absalom!* and *One Hundred Years of Solitude*, Lois Parkinson Zamora writes, "Each [Sutpen and José Arcadio Buendía] is hoping to forget his past and begin history again, for both are convinced that in a world without a past, the future can be molded to their historical design. As stubborn and strong as they are in holding to their visions of historical renewal, they learn that the moral burdens of the past are not so easily sloughed off" (35). All true for Faulkner's novel, but while each detail may be plausible for García Márquez's novel, the ensemble is profoundly misleading, virtually a misrecognition of the latter text's *genre*. José Arcadio Buendía is not broodingly psychologized as Sutpen is, nor does *One Hundred Years of Solitude* unfold as a heavily moralized rebuke of the first Buendía's sinful design. There is no doubt that Charles Bon embodies the "moral burdens of the past" that Faulkner's narrative weave forces Sutpen to reencounter, but Prudencio Aguilar? He's more a colorful (and minor) piece of a many-generational history than the all-revealing index of a failed design. Zamora's terms for assessment—"hoping to forget," "visions of historical renewal," and most concisely that verb "learn"—draw on a vocabulary appropriate to Bildung (realism) or to Bildung collapsed (modernism) but misapplied to the steamroller energy of unfolding character-and-event—the subject, time, space "contract"—that flourishes in *One Hundred Years of Solitude*. Her model of time and space as lawfully charged domains in which the singular subjective drama comes inevitably to moral resolution or collapse—a model as old as Sophocles' oedipal trilogy—is simply blind to the utopian swerves, the muscular renewals that characterize each Buendía's unique self-enactment upon the familial/historical stage.[13]

It is not surprising, then, that Charles Etienne and his entourage are unthinkable in this supreme text of García Márquez. No one in *One Hundred Years of Solitude* (until the final Buendía) anguishes over who, when, and where he is.[14] No existential crises, no epistemological quandary (no what happened? we know exactly what happened), no vertigo within time and space: plenty of solitude, but no alienation. Macondo is a culture increasingly invaded from without, but it *furnishes* those within. To be, for the Buendías, is to move securely within time, space, and identity. What other family in twentieth-century literature is so surely in possession of themselves as the Buendías? And to be, for this novel, is to be emphatically narrated. There is not a single *perhaps* in the telling of *One Hundred Years of Solitude*. (Think how that epistemologically laden word modulates the narratives of Mr. Compson and Quentin and Shreve.) As García Márquez is in possession of his materials, so his characters are in possession of their cultural roles, playing them out unhesitatingly until their death. José Arcadio Buendía, his two sons, Ursula, Amaranta and Rebeca, Arcadio and his two sons, Aureliano Segundo's offspring (José Arcadio and Meme and Amaranta Ursula), then the last Aureliano: does anyone really have difficulty telling them apart? They share and repeat family traits, of course, but each with his or her own memorable (unique yet culturally understandable) accents. They thus elude the central agon of Faulknerian tragedy: that, as Judith knew so well, *others are in the way*. From Locke's pursuit of individual happiness to Tolstoy's stewing over the laws that undermine free will to Faulkner's unworkable loom to Sartre's "l'enfer, c'est les autres," Western narrative has been fixated on the crucial encounter between individual project and external constraint. By contrast, García Márquez's Buendías wear their communal history as orientation, not obstruction. Their omnipresent culture—their "Macondan-ness": unthinking self-acceptance, relatedness to other Buendías present and past, membership in a shared community, spontaneous desire to defend this—is the nourishing ground of resources they draw on to be distinctively themselves. Knowing unthinkingly who they are (read: where, when, and with whom they are), they elude self-doubt, and this accounts for the sheer authority of their moves: José Arcadio Buendía's search for the philosopher's stone, José Arcadio's earth-shattering intercourse, Colonel Aureliano's thirty-two uprisings, Rebeca's dirt eating, Amaranta's weaving of her shroud, Meme's courtship and silent suffering . . .

Their being at ease in their setting allows them to perform, in full, what is in them to perform—figuring for us what we might perform if he were wholly present within culturally coherent space and time. Unlike the pathos of García Márquez's earlier negatived Colonel, none of these characters' interior resources is hoarded or wasted or stymied. To demonstrate this on a minor note, the "Elephant" is a sublime eater not for Western competitive reasons ("be the best eater you can be") but because "a person who had all matters of conscience in perfect shape should be able to eat until overcome by fatigue" (*One Hundred* 275). Why not? Ideally aligned body becomes spirit through effortless expansion, not by soul-driven, punitive correction. That same note of unconstrained being sounds in Remedios the Beauty's rising into the air when it is time for her to depart. Read in numerous ingeniously allegorical ways, this event may yield more as a physical enactment of what can occur when the embodied human being is perfectly oriented in space and time. Why not? The opposite of Charles Etienne, Remedios performs, completely, what is in her to perform: this is a performing that releases her. "I am fire and air, my other elements I give to baser life," Shakespeare's Cleopatra proclaims (5.2.289–90), but her final performance is hard-won, loss-driven, tragically self-destroying because self-transcending—a performance constrained by warring ideologies. Remedios rises into the air *as* Remedios, not as a transcending of Remedios, not as an escape from Remedios's conditions. The book thus joins its realistic and its fabulous doings by aligning its people within a folklore-provided weave of personally appropriate trajectories that become (in the doing) memorable realities.[15] Through such doings these characters appear to be virtually hardwired with identity—identity as plenitude rather than lack. There is, of course, no ignoring the bitterness that can suffuse them: Amaranta and her shroud, Rebeca in her solitude, Colonel Aureliano and his fishes. Indeed, Rey Chow has properly warned against idealizing the Other as if it were "essentially . . . beyond the contradictions that constitute our own historical place" (xx).[16] But the point is that García Márquez is deploying a representational technique that expresses not the idealized but the possible. It is not that the setting of Macondo rewards the Buendías but that it accommodates their moves.

"Can a person marry his own aunt?" a startled Aureliano José asks a passing soldier, and he receives the following answer: "He not only can do that, but we're fighting this war against the priests so that a person can marry his own mother" (163). Why not? *One Hundred Years of Solitude* recognizes that children want to mate with their mothers—that plenitude is the full embrace of the mother, the ultimate providing of space/time (of *home*) to the desiring subject, that everything else is substitute—and it delineates a native culture that releases this desire by half-screening it. It's not hard to see that Pilar and Petra and Amaranta are all mother-substitutes. Not that the book lacks a sense of taboo—its hundred years of doings will come to term through the breaking of a taboo—but unlike *Absalom, Absalom!* (and Faulkner's father-haunted fictions more generally), the No of the father governs the conclusion but not everything that happens in between. A cornucopia of happenings occurs in between—all of them crystalline—and this is possible only because a cultural imaginary that envisages the desiring subject moving through a space and time configured as cooperative is operating here. No Cartesian instrumentality, no bourgeois rationalizing of means and ends, no patriarchal design: no Western plotting.[17] This generosity toward what can happen extends beyond incest and into miscegenation. It is the Western patriarchal edict of racial purity that confounds, makes schizoid Faulkner's dual-cultured Charles Etienne; in a racist culture where he must be this or that but not conceivably both he has only two options: passing (never a temptation for Faulkner's figures) or self-crucifixion. By contrast, as Alejo Carpentier saw decades ago, "America, a continent of symbiosis, mutations, vibrations, *mestizaje,* has always been baroque [and has thereby generated in its subjects] the awareness of being Other, of being new . . . of being a *criollo*" ("Baroque" 98–100). "The awareness of being other": no less a reality than the desire to marry your aunt, both realities as understandable in García Márquez's capacious Macondo as they are scandalous in Faulkner's boundary-obsessive South.

The butterflies orchestrate Meme's lovemaking not because García Márquez is sentimental enough to pretend things happen like this but because, within his folklore-nourished representational schema, the natural world is in sync with Buendían energies—"in sync" not in the saccharine sense of "support" but in the neutral sense of "aligned with." The deaths in this novel—José Arcadio Buendía's, Arcadio's, Colonel Aureliano Buendía's, Amaranta's, José Arcadio's—are unforgettable because, accented personally, they rise from within the being who is to die. "In the course of modern times," Benjamin writes, "dying has been pushed further and further out of the perceptual world of the living" (93–94). In the modern bourgeois world, he goes on to say, one dies a standard death issued by sanatoria and hospitals. Not so in García Márquez's novel, in which one dies as oneself, eventually going elsewhere, but capable of returning if need be. Death is here a dimension of ineffaceable identity, not—as the Enlightenment/scientific tradition has insisted for 400 years—its permanent extinction. Put otherwise, folk cultures around the globe encountered and found terms for death millennia before Western science took on the task. Recurrently in their view, death is a "chapter" in the human drama, not the end of the book.

The genre enacted in *One Hundred Years of Solitude* is of course magical realism. At the heart of the aesthetic moves that constitute that genre, moreover, there is a pervasive political resonance. Magical realism's swerves from realism operate, as Kumkum Sangari and others have argued, as a critical revision *of* realism.[18] This is reseeing, not escape from seeing. "Metaphor is turned into *event*," Sangari writes, "precisely so that it will *not* be read *as* event, but folded back into metaphor as disturbing, resonant image" (164). Metaphor shows what is missing. In Chanady's terms, magic realism "challenges realistic representation in order to introduce *poeisis* into *mimesis*" (130).[19] In Faulkner, by contrast, poetic metaphor cannot be granted precedence over mimetic event; the event retains narrative priority. (If it cannot be known authoritatively, it must be delivered perspectivally, speculatively.) Given the Newton-descended commitment to mimesis that he inherits from realism (its "adequation" aesthetics), given realism's patriarchal plot of male-to-male inheritances, acquisitions, and progressive mastery over one's place in space and time—given such a plot and the disastrous history to which it corresponds, Faulkner's only available swerve is not to write another plot but to *jam* the inherited one. His creative response to a 200-year-old narrative tradition of traffic in goods across uniform space and time is arrest, vertigo, the collapse of project-fueled motion. In all of this, the loom set up earlier for enabling subjects to move acquisitively through space and time cannot be set up otherwise. Thomas Sutpen's patriarchal design is doomed before he even conceives of it, but there are no other available moves. Rather than reshape his culture's arrangements, Faulkner shows, with ceaseless repercussion, how and why they must collapse. Mocking the poignant energies of "must matter," "cant matter" guarantees the tragic thrust of his fiction, registering the inescapable "hurt" that is history's assault on the subject's endeavors. The "might-have-been" his wounded people dream of may be "more true than truth," but it remains—within a representational field governed by the traditional loom—all but unwritable.

García Márquez does not jam the loom; he *reconfigures* it. Sangari writes, "The power of Márquez's narratives lies in the insistent pressure of freedom as the absent horizon—which is neither predictable or inevitable. . . . This may be an absent freedom, but it is not an abstract freedom: it is precisely that which is made present and possible by its absence—the lives people have never lived *because* of the lives they are forced to live or have chosen to live. That which is desired and that which exists, the sense of abundance and the sense of waste, are dialectically related" (176). Free of Newton's legacy, enriched by a folk-culture's capacious vision of collective human beings, García Márquez recovers images of human possibility. The Buendía lives he portrays do not escape the pressures of colonial history, but his prose is oriented—as no prose of realism can afford to be—toward the graphing of human desire in its actual grandeur. Desire as intensity rather than lack, and sufficient unto itself because beyond teleological project. In such a fiction of sufficiency—liberated from Western realism's tortured "but was it really like that?"—García Márquez rewrites Faulkner's "might-have-been" as "what might be," on a canvas wherein the human figure is once again furnished with self-enacting moves within cooperative time and space. Fiction written according to the logic of this other loom allows us to recognize, by positive rather than negative silhouette, the cost of all our waste, and the need to become what we potentially are.[20]

I have discussed Faulkner and García Márquez as instances of how the representational practices of modernism and postcolonialism respond to a defective Western loom. Broadly speaking, the patriarchal arrangements that underwrite this loom—proposing the subject's acquisitive/ orientational moves through uniform time and space, licensing the narrative of individual mastery (or deserved failure)—seemed adequate for two centuries of Enlightenment-based realism. However disastrous it becomes by the end of the nineteenth century, this loom remains impervious to dismantling in Faulkner's work. By contrast, García Márquez's vertiginous Latin American history and variegated folkloric culture position him sufficiently outside realist norms—and suspicious of their claim to monovocal, noncontradictory mimetic authority—to refuse the patriarchal premises that "set up" that loom in the first place. More, he has an array of modernist practices before him to help him on his way, representational procedures that jam the loom prior to his (and other postcolonialists') reconfiguring of it.

Toni Morrison enters the discussion as a postcolonial writer whose ways of narrating the damage her people suffer from that patriarchal paradigm are enabled, suggestively, by the prior practice of both Faulkner and García Márquez. There is hardly a single-line influence from Faulkner to García Márquez, then from García Márquez to Morrison. Rather, she *joins* García Márquez, even as she comes after him, as a writer intent on escaping some of the Enlightenment-based aesthetic/ideological constraints that still bind the modernist, Faulknerian text. This analysis attends to the figuring of arrest in both Faulkner and Morrison's careers, before turning to Morrison's increasingly nonrealistic strategies for representing release. The guiding citation is no longer "the ones who set up the loom"—the ideological contract for the subject's moves through space and time—but Morrison's provocative phrase from *Beloved*: "the grace they could imagine." How, given the paralyzing injury done to American blacks by whites for more than 300 years, might grace and release—an emancipatory remobilizing of the subject in space and time—be responsibly imagined? What untapped plotlines outside the linear mandate of a realism that has been blind to black resource are open to narrative deployment? As Morrison puts it in *Paradise*, looking at her endangered women from the perspective of weapons trained on them and about to fire, "In that holy hollow between sighting and following through could grace slip through at all?" (73).

Faulkner's first indelible portrait of arrest—of incapacity to negotiate the progressive loom—is the unfurnished idiot Benjy Compson.[21] Here is the opening of *The Sound and the Fury*:

> Through the fence, between the curling flower spaces, I could see them hitting. They were coming to where the flag was and I went along the fence. Luster was hunting in the grass by the flower tree. They took the flag out, and they were hitting. . . . Then they went on, and I went along the fence. Luster came away from the flower tree and we went along the fence and they stopped and we stopped and I looked through the fence while Luster was hunting in the grass.
>
> "Here, caddie." He hit. They went away across the pasture. I held to the fence and watched them going away.
>
> "Listen at you, now." Luster said. "Aint you something, thirty three years old, going on that way. After I done went all the way to town to buy you that cake. Hush up that moaning. Aint you going to help me find that quarter so I can go to the show tonight?" (3)

Through the fence: Benjy on the other side of that fence, hemmed in, defective, speechless; a game of golf described by one who has no idea what it means and who thinks it is taking place on a pasture; a golfer's casual command ("Here, caddie") that inexplicably triggers an outburst of tears in Benjy. This passage stages an idiot's unceasing disorientation: he cannot know why people do what they do, lacks any sense for his culture's projects, learns nothing, makes nothing happen. He is dysfunctional—ideology-deprived—as no realist protagonist can be. Since he cannot master language, he thinks a golf caddie refers to his sister, Caddy, and he weeps because she is not there. Since he has no understanding of time, he thinks what was once his pasture is still his pasture (though golfers play on it). Incapable of negotiating space and time, plotless, he is still waiting by the fence for Caddy (gone these past eighteen years) to come home.

This passage, like the larger text, registers and produces spatial-temporal disorientation on a scale inconceivable in realism. Faulkner's narrative refuses to "see past" the sound and fury of such uncomprehending, though the Reverend Shegog does provide, in the novel's closing Easter sermon, a figure for Benjy's arrest—in the image and aftermath of the crucified Christ: "O blind sinner! Breddren, I tells you; sistuhn, I says to you, when de Lawd did turn His mighty face, say, Aint gwine overload heaven! I can see de widowed God shet His do" (184–85). "Aint gwine overload heaven": Benjy emerges as heaven's orphan, his innocence unaccommodated, his plight incurable. All paths in this novel circulate about this unfurnished child. In his lack one reads the larger incapacity of an inbred, incompetent, disoriented southern white culture at the end of its belief system. The progress Faulkner knows of is unendorsable; the progress he could endorse is unimaginable. The widowed God has shut his door; Faulkner is not about to try to open it.[22]

As he continues his career, Faulkner's gaze widens, and he begins to find the cultural coordinates for such dysfunction. In the turmoil of *Light in August*'s Joe Christmas and of *Absalom, Absalom!*'s Thomas Sutpen he presents a stunning diagnosis of southern self-wounding. These are canvases in which white and black share the most intimate spaces (even as white cannot bear to know this sharing), in which male and female, landed and sharecropper, Mississippi puritan and New Orleans sensualist live each other's lives, breathe each other's breaths. However spacious, Faulkner's world is suffocating—lacking racial, gender, and class norms in which these opposed figures can fruitfully imagine or encounter each other, and thus issuing into cries of outrage and disbelief. The patriarchal loom mangles rather than orients, "the strings are all in one another's way" (*Absalom* 101); none of this can be righted. Hightower in *Light in August*, Quentin and Shreve in *Absalom, Absalom!*, though helpless to alter the outcome, take the measure of their culture's monstrous insistence on crucifying rather than accommodating its others: Hightower glimpses "a more inextricable compositeness" amalgamating the opposed "faces" in his story, all striving "in turn to free themselves one from the other" (*Absalom* 491), yet (in a figure related to that of the death-dealing loom) inseparably bound on the same wheel of torture. His southern culture cannot imagine its own grace—an incapacity silhouetted against his most perspicacious narrators' capacity to imagine it but not to bring it into being. The pathos of the might-have-been beats continuously, but Heaven's door remains shut.

Toni Morrison's career opens, as Faulkner's did, on the crucifixion of an unfurnished child. *The Bluest Eye* begins by acknowledging the abused and sacrificed Pecola Breedlove—dead before the narrative gets under way. Like her parents, Pecola lacked the homegrown resources of a native black culture, yearning instead for the commodified white icons of Shirley Temple dolls and impossible blue eyes. All three Breedloves are culturally dysfunctional, focused on a meretricious grace imagined by and for whites, thus "always wrong to the light," as Robert Frost would say, "so never seeing / Deeper down in the well" (208). Morrison's later novels could be seen as a range of attempts to see "deeper down in the well," to refuse the disorientation and madness to which a preoccupation with the patriarchal loom leads. It is not that the widowed God has shut his door but that the Breedlove family is looking for it in the wrong place, fantasizing others' grace rather than working out the possibilities of their own. The creative turn—the black cultural refurnishing—occurs in *Sula*.

Sula records simultaneously Morrison's exit from the realist fiction of black victimization and her taking possession (in her own inimitable way) of some of the resources of Latin American magical realism. Not García Márquez's non-Newtonian events—in which the "scientificity" of the represented world is suspended—but rather a deployment of events that are possible yet simultaneously fabulous: the appearance of the indistinguishable Deweys, the drowning of Chicken Little, the burnings of Plum and Hannah. Her practice here departs from realist norms in ways that Faulknerian modernism never does (his characters' weirdest behavior, like that of the Bundrens throughout *As I Lay Dying*, is always, so to speak, statistically credible, if only because they pass through a human landscape of normal and scandalized others).[23] Morrison's departures lead cleanly somewhere else, past individual or family eccentricity. That elsewhere is a vividly delineated, nonbourgeois black folk-culture whose narratives she draws on with increasing power: "We are very practical people, very down-to-earth, even shrewd people. But within that practicality we also accepted what I suppose could be called superstition and magic, which is another way of knowing things" ("Rootedness" 342).[24] Such black folklore quietly harbors a refusal of Newtonian givens, an interest in textualizing the non-Western world's ways of understanding life outside the teleological register of subjects mapping and mastering objects in lawful space and time.

In different ways all of her texts after *Sula* testify to the postcolonial task that Morrison calls "the reclamation of the history of black people in this country" ("Interview" 418). She writes, "There is a confrontation between old values of the tribe and new urban values. It's confusing. There has to be a mode to do what the music did for blacks, what we used to be able to do with each other in private and in that civilization that existed underneath the white civilizations" ("The Language" 371). Spoken nine years before the publication of *Jazz*, these words are prescient. Tribe, enchantment, music, a civilization beneath a civilization—the traditions she would make contact with are black: the staying power of the matriarchal black family and the tissue of shared beliefs and behaviors that make up a community; the dignity-enabling roots of black families as these go back to nineteenth-century records and then further back to folk myths of flying men and swamp women; the survival of black people even during the depredations of slavery, thanks to their mutual dependencies and inventiveness, their fragmented yet still viable grasp on an African heritage that predated the Middle Passage; and finally the irresistible music with which they colonized the New York of the 1920s into a series of interlocking neighborhoods at once intimate and dangerous.

If *Sula* is Morrison's breakthrough novel—her exit from realist victimization—*Beloved* reveals where this departure can take her, perhaps most suggestively in the figure of Beloved herself. Perfectly clear, perfectly mysterious, this character embodies a prodigious undertaking: a crazed and abused black girl who believes Sethe to be her mother, Sethe's murdered daughter come back from the dead and seeking both the maternal embrace and the infant's revenge, and finally the symbolic embodiment of all those shipwrecked and injured slaves whose voices were never recorded, whose silenced cries began with the nightmare of the Middle Passage. How radiantly different this overdetermined figure is from either Charles Etienne or Pecola. Equally damaged (and by the same murderous racism), Beloved is yet not alienated—arrested—but instead a carrier of precious, otherwise irretrievable racial memories, an umbilical connection to an unspeakable past that will continue to inflict damage until, somehow, it gets spoken. And this is a speaking that neither the bright logic of realism nor the dark logic of modernism can deliver; both logics are Western and remain attached to Newton.[25] Stamp Paid, listening to the sounds outside the door of 124, hears more—folklorically—than realism concedes can be heard between heaven and earth: "he believed he knew who spoke them. The people of the broken necks, of fire-cooked blood and black girls who had lost their ribbons. What a roaring" (181). "This is not a story to pass on" (275), for it retrieves, through the returned figure of Beloved, too much to acknowledge and keep on living. "So they forgot her. . . . Sometimes the photograph of a close friend or relative— looked at too long—shifts, and something more familiar than the dear face itself moves there. They can touch it if they like, but don't, because they know things will never be the same if they do" (275).

The drowned girl who had lost her ribbon, the suicidal Pecola who wanted blue eyes, Sethe's undone infant, the murdered Dorcas in *Jazz*: all figures for the unfurnished orphan child, all figures of dysfunction within a patriarchal frame, yet becoming something other than figures of mere dispossession. Morrison is learning how to say their significance outside an achievement model. The loss is turning into gain, the dispossession into richness, within a racial/folkloric schema steeped in non-Western values. The returned Beloved is priceless even as she is heartbreaking, and Joe Trace muses in *Jazz* that "when [Adam] left Eden, he left a rich man. Not only did he have Eve, but he had the taste of the first apple in his mouth for the rest of his life. . . . To bite it down, bite it down. Hear the crunch and let the red peeling break his heart" (133). The broken heart figures in *Jazz* as a kind of wealth wholly unrelated to ideological integrity or attainment, one that you cannot "project" but must experience instead, one that neither realism nor modernism is prepared to articulate.[26] This novel signals Morrison's return to damaged lives as uniquely capacious—lives that must be narrated in new ways that do not merely report the damage. "Something is missing there [in that negative register]," *Jazz*'s narrator muses, "Something rogue. Something else you have to figure in before you can figure it out" (228).[27] Figuring it in— letting her readers see the resource that accompanies the deprivation (the Grace in Gigi, the Consolata in Connie)—accounts for Morrison's setting up in *Paradise* a new loom where metaphor reconfigures event and where fatal damage yields to the grace she can imagine.

Morrison begins by granting the full damage done to her thrown-away women gathered together in the Convent. In responsible realism or modernism they would be out for the count. But she has other plans for them, choosing, like García Márquez, to delineate not the constraining details of the given but rather the yeasty ones of desire, beginning with the magic of a maternal care embodied first in "mother," then in Connie, and finally in the generative capacity that flourishes anew in each of the orphan girls secure in her retreat. So generative, in fact, that Mavis's dead children come back to life within the Convent's womblike walls—not seeking revenge like Beloved but chirping with newfound life. As though the difference between life and death were a permeable membrane and not an uncrossable barrier, the Convent bestows on its women an elasticity beyond the appearance/reality epistemology that confines realism and haunts modernism. Readers do not know whether the women are killed or wounded by the attack of Ruby men, whether their final reappearance in their old haunts is imagined by others or a real event, whether the last locale in the novel is or is not Paradise. The authority of the prose is not invested in such mastery of *knowing*. Morrison places her reader, at novel's end, deep within what in Faulkner's mimetic world would be a might-have-been, yet one presented here as real.

"Don't you want the world to be something more than what it is?" (208), Violet asks Felice at the end of *Jazz*. Morrison's genius in these later novels is to intimate to the reader that the world is always more than what fidelity to the materially given claims it to be. Breaking with such authority, she supplies that dimension beyond the statistically real, figuring in that "something rogue," as when Connie is visited by a mysterious friend: "Suddenly he was next to her without having moved. . . . Not six inches from her face, he removed his tall hat. Fresh tea-colored hair came tumbling down, cascading over his shoulders and down his back. He took off his glasses then and winked, a slow seductive movement of a lid. His eyes, she saw, were as round and green as new apples" (252). Is he real? Fictive? Does it matter? Epistemological questions are as beside the point here as in the magical realism of *One Hundred Years of Solitude*. All one knows is that this "friend" supplements the real, shows what is missing, completes the scenario of human desire. At Connie's supreme final moment— " 'You're back,' she says, and smiles" (289) at her former lover Deacon, even as his brother, Steward, shoots her between the eyes—does one know whether she is addressing the flesh-and-blood Deacon or her mysterious spirit-Friend? Whether she is actually dead or not? Does it matter?

"Don't separate God from His elements. He created it all" (244), Lone advised Connie. Opposing realms cohabit; as in other postcolonial texts, the dead come back to life. "Stepping in," Lone calls this gift of resuscitation, as she urges Connie to draw on her native/God-given resources to breathe life back into the dead body of Soane's child; and Connie does, and his life returns. "Stepping in": this is Morrison's rogue move, the making of the world more than what it is, the figuring in of what is uncannily necessary if one would figure it out, seeing the world as it might look according to another loom. That move is steeped in mystery, yet utterly quotidian. Richard and Anna glimpse, at the end of *Paradise*, a closed door (or is it an open window?), and they think: "what would happen if you entered? What would be on the other side? What on earth would it be? What on earth?" (305). As with that shimmering photograph at the end of *Beloved*, if one dares to enter, if one "steps in" and sees more than Newton's optics allow to be there, all will be changed—though no one can say in advance how. What can be said is that the change will be here and now, both given and imagined—partially wrought out there and wholly to be sustained in here. The transfigured space will be the home one thought one knew, not an exotic elsewhere, for the afterlife is but an ever-present dimension of the present one—what the present one looks like in visionary mode, when all the lights are on. In *Paradise*, as in *One Hundred Years of Solitude*, all the lights are on.[28] "Now they will rest," Morrison writes as the last line of her latest novel, "before shouldering the endless work they were created to do down here in Paradise" (318).

However the modernist Faulkner longs for Paradise, his deepest conviction is that it is not here, not now, not ours. The pathos of his history-haunted fiction is that the grace it luminously imagines is unavailable to any of his white characters in this dispensation, but is rather the mark and measure of their loss. No vision of a might-have-been can undo damage that is done, refurbish an ideological fabric tattered beyond repair. The widowed God has shut his door: aint gwine overload Heaven. For reasons that have been gathering for centuries, the loom of Western patriarchy—its sanctioned designs for white males moving through space and time—begets not fulfillment but, in a culture filled with others who are both disowned and one's own, disaster. No one knows better than Faulkner how intricately the resultant "cant matter" trumps human desire's unceasing "must matter."

How might one see beyond such collapse, into the not-yet-realized yet realizable territory of a non-Newtonian world where human beings might once again flourish in culturally refurnished space and time, outside the patriarchal mandate? How might one forge a representational model in which "must matter" would trump "cant matter" without pretending that "cant matter" does not intrude with all the weight of the Western colonial legacy? These are the unsentimental utopian questions of much postcolonial fiction, and I have sought to show their reach in the practice of García Márquez and Morrison, as well as why Faulkner the Western modernist cannot find his way into this territory. Refusing the progressive individualizing projects of realism, going beyond the arrest and alienation of modernism, drawing on non-Western tropes of folkloric wisdom, their work must, and does, envisage new ways of setting up the loom. In this representational schema, the arrest of the real goes hand-in-hand with the release of desire. For both García Márquez and Morrison, yet in such different ways, the world is always more, potentially other, than what it is. Of course History remains what hurts, its alienating force undeniable; the gorgeous cosmos of Macondo ends by being "wiped out by the wind and exiled from the memory of men" (*One Hundred* 422). But history in *One Hundred Years of Solitude*, however damaging, shares the scene with desire, such that the novel stubbornly refuses to succumb to its own final sentence, instead staying in the mind as a luminous reservoir of images of what we might be like if we were both free and at home. As for Morrison, the grace she can imagine is that Paradise has never been overloaded, never been shut off from us, never been easy, never been anywhere but here.

NOTES

1. This piece is part of a larger study (to be entitled *Unknowing: The Work of Modernist Fiction*) of the reconfiguring of modernist subjects within a postrealist frame of time and space.

2. That the subject is conceived as "committed to life, liberty, and the pursuit of happiness" hardly means that these goals are represented as achievable. The late-nineteenth-century European fiction designated "naturalism" attends even more darkly than modernism to the failure of subject quests. It envisages these quests, however, within the same narrative conventions as the realism it follows: it tells the same stories, but they finish disastrously. Modernist fiction tells its stories differently—plots the subject trajectory through space/time differently—without, however, dismantling the loom of assumptions it had inherited from its Enlightenment origins. The freshness of much postcolonial fiction will lie in its reconceiving of the loom itself.

3. The phrase, cited so frequently as to have taken on a life of its own, appears at the end of the stunning first chapter of Jameson's *The Political Unconscious*. I do not quote Jameson elsewhere in this piece, but his larger argument about ideology as a selective textualizing of a process—History—that exceeds textuality underlies my own claims about ideology's necessity and limitation as a repertory of sanctioned pathways through social time and space.

4. One of the most provocative readings of Lacan's argument is that proposed by Jane Gallop in *The Daughter's Seduction*.

5. For further discussion of this moment of body coding in *Absalom, Absalom!*, see my *Faulkner's Subject* (131–35). It is worth noting that such subjective vertigo registers precisely in Bon's son's incoherent passage through space and time: from New Orleans to Jefferson, from Jefferson to "frowsy stinking rooms in places—towns and cities—which likewise had no names . . . broken by other periods, intervals, of furious and incomprehensible and apparently reasonless moving" (Faulkner, *Absalom* 167). In him "existence" ceases to be "experience" and appears—spatially and temporally unfurnished—as absurd.

6. Benjamin makes this remark in "The Storyteller," the essay on Leskov in which,

drawing on Lukacs's *Theory of the Novel*, he speculates most directly on the kinds of alienation wrought into the very institution of the novel as an Enlightenment print-genre. Benjamin analyzes the notion of "experience" within two distinct categories: *Erfahrung*, a coherent subject-trajectory through space/time, as opposed to *Erlebnis*, events that have been brutely lived but not turned into subjective value. He sees this polarizing of experience as an inevitable byproduct of increasing Western rationalization, reaching its alienating extremes in the habit/shock opposition characteristic of modernist narratives. Benjamin's essays on Proust, Kafka, and above all Baudelaire (all three in *Illuminations*) explore this phenomenon more fully.

7. Benjamin's "habit" and "shock" are necessary but insufficient concepts for understanding Faulknerian trauma. A third notion—the clash of local and incompatible ideologies—is required for understanding the explosive class and race drama that Faulkner's greatest fictions explore.

8. Hardy serves in some ways as a limit case of realist fiction. Time and space remain available to protagonistic mastery in his novels as they do in earlier realism, but in *Jude the Obscure* (as in *Tess* and *The Return of the Native*) no protagonist can rise to this challenge and turn experience into insight. Hardy's people don't get wiser, and the fruitless trekking across Wessex landscapes—like Jude's hopeless departures and returns to Christminster—seems unintentionally to parody realism's generic epistemological promise. Yet the *form* of masterable experience remains intact in Hardy: space and time *seem* open to subjective investment. My point might be clarified by juxtaposing the Bundren need to cross the flooded river in *As I Lay Dying* with Hardy's figures' need to traverse the countryside: in Faulkner's novel it is patently clear (to everyone except the Bundrens) that the landscape has suddenly metamorphosed into territory simply unamenable to human mapping and control.

9. The archive for exploring Faulkner's relation to the Boom writers is considerable; salient texts include Patricia Drechsel Tobin's *Time and the Novel*, José Saldívar's *The Dialectics of Our America*, Lois Parkinson Zamora's *Writing the Apocalypse*, and Deborah Cohn's *History and Memory in the Two Souths*.

10. As Amaryll Chanady claims, "It is against this complex background of the colonized subject's rebellion against imposed models [among these, read: realism], the resistance of the newly independent Latin American countries to neocolonial domination and the European philosophical delegitimation of metaphysical and epistemological paradigms that we must situate certain twentieth-century literary practices" (136). A key dimension of these imposed models is the hegemonic authority of a linear/mimetic vision of things—such as realism (and its philosophical counterpart, positivism) so adroitly puts in place. The contestatory "practices" Chanady speaks of share, of course, an investment in magical realism.

11. Fuentes and Vargas Llosa have been equally laudatory in their tribute to Faulkner's germinal practice, but since García Márquez is my figure for comparison, his words are most pertinent. Faulkner, he says, is "a writer from the Caribbean," for the Caribbean "extends from northern Brazil to the U.S. South. Including, of course, Yoknapatawpha County" (qtd. in Cohn 44).

12. For useful analyses of the crisis in epistemology (and, relatedly, in representation)

that characterizes so much modernist work, see Everdell, Eysteinsson, Kern, Rorty, and Williams, among others.

13. Only in the last two pages of the text do "sighs of disappointment" (García Márquez, *One Hundred* 447) briefly take over the narrative voice, impose a retrospective judgment laden with disapproval, and—for a moment—make this book look like a gathered Faulknerian indictment. While it would be a mistake to overlook this unexpected souring of narrative tone, it would be a greater mistake to generalize it as the disillusioned keynote of the entire novel's structure of feeling—a greater mistake because an imposition of teleological means/end thinking on a text whose way of inserting the subject in space/time has so magnanimously operated otherwise during the previous 445 pages.

14. *One Hundred Years of Solitude* is, of all of García Márquez's works, the one that aligns best with my reading. Indeed, I would claim that this breakthrough text rivals Faulkner—precisely by escaping from Faulknerian procedures. *As I Lay Dying* hovers too closely over *Leaf Storm*, and the brooding paralysis of *Sartoris* suffocatingly recurs in *No One Writes to the Colonel*. These early texts are modernist-inspired: portentous, immobile, heavy with a lurid atmosphere of stifled aspirations, ghosts waiting in the wings. The scene they set is one of dysfunction, intolerable stasis. In the terms of my argument, they are still attached to the realist loom of performance, yet they access it in modernist terms, as purely disabling. It may follow, then, that—compelling as these early fictions are—García Márquez comes into his own only when he conceives that other way of setting up the loom that is magical realism. For it is magical realism that frees his work from oppressive mimesis and gives it, for the first time, *motion and scope*—the freedom to move everywhere in space and time. (As Wendy B. Faris puts it, "These fictions [of magical realism] question received ideas about time, space, and identity" [173].) The immobilized psychological Colonel transforms into the released archetypal Colonel of thirty-two uprisings; the latter figure, equally tragic in his implications, has become available to a new kind of narration. In other words, his very emptiness attains gigantic resonance: the writer has figured out how to *activate* his cast of characters, how to choreograph their being rather than intimate their failed-being.

15. It is widely acknowledged that, from early days with his grandparents through his cub-reporting and into his own mature research, García Márquez has remained fascinated with Colombian folk materials. The artistic use of such materials allows him to escape "the limitations that rationalists and Stalinists from all eras have attempted to impose" on a reality bursing with difference, as he put it in *The Fragrance of Guava* (59–60). The freshness such materials bring to *One Hundred Years of Solitude* is attested to by such vignettes as the rising from the earth of Remedios the Beauty and Father Nicanor (in such different yet appropriate ways); Petra Cotes's feeding her last mule on her remaining sheets, rugs, and velvet drapes; the poor girl who—to recompense her grandmother for accidentally allowing her house to burn down—must sleep with customers every night for the next ten years (at a rate of seventy men per night). For related commentary on the folkloric dimension of García Márquez's work, see Griffin, Kutzinski, and Bell-Villada.

16. J. Michael Dash's *The Other America* is likewise devoted to the importance of this

argument. Recognizing that postcolonial and postmodern discourses are repeatedly tempted by "the current intellectual zeitgeist of the romance of otherness" (x), Dash seeks to offer a flexible and still-developing regional paradigm for Caribbean literature that might avoid both the myopia of nationalist thinking and the systematization of global thinking. Dash effectively exposes the limitation of binary structures by speculating on Hong Kong, a city at present situated uneasily between two colonial powers. See his "Between Colonizers" (in *The Other America*) for the problematic of Hong Kong's culture as not accurately mappable onto either British or Chinese models.

17. By "no Western plotting" I do not mean that Western plotting is absent from *One Hundred Years of Solitude*. I mean, rather, that such plotting is figured as colonial incursion (indeed, the plot of the West) rather than as *subjectified* within Buendía trajectories. A host of Western myths (as opposed to a structure of Western plot) is generously deployed in the novel, along with the array of folk materials already discussed.

18. Lest my remarks about magical realism sound naively laudatory, I acknowledge that no artistic form, however emancipatory, is free from becoming commodified and, so to speak, mass-produced by later writers. The signature moves of magical realism, like those of experimental modernism and surrealism earlier, are no exception to this point. As early as 1949 Carpentier saw that "the result of willing the marvelous or any other trance is that the dream technicians become bureaucrats. . . . Poverty of the imagination, Unamuno said, is learning codes by heart" ("America" 85).

19. Cortázar makes a kindred point when he speaks of *Hopscotch* as a narrative "where everything has value as a sign and not as a theme of description" (qtd. in Chanady 139). Put this extremely, magical realism becomes indistinguishable from an aesthetics of postmodernism, both of them in flight from an arid and played out aesthetics of mimesis. Ever since Carpentier's earliest comments about magical realism, however, many critics have mounted a vigorous counterargument, claiming a *cultural* resonance for these nonmimetic procedures that realism itself could never deliver. For my purposes, this is both a precious distinction and a necessary undertaking, given the degree to which realism has systemically denatured non-Western history by representing it within hegemonic (linear-progressive-centered) forms of narrative. Postmodernism, I argue in my forthcoming *Unknowing: The Work of Modernist Fiction*, the larger study of which this is a piece, differs significantly from postcolonialism on just this issue: the former's verbal texture (as in the descriptions in Calvino's *Invisible Cities*) is composed of purely nonrepresentational, "unremembering" signs, whereas García Márquez's "Elephant" (not to mention Morrison's *Beloved*) comes to the reader inexhaustibly saturated in folk-custom and racial/ethnic memory.

20. I cannot leave *One Hundred Years of Solitude* without speculating (somewhat along the lines of Chow's and Dash's critiques) on the complex non-innocence of García Márquez's representational strategies. As Dash might say, this novel insinuates in its own manner a story of "between colonizers": the Buendías as both descendants of Hispanic colonizers and victims of U.S.-capitalist incursions. Superior to indigenous Indians, they suffer at the hands of foreigners. The text's center-periphery imaginary (Macondo as authenticity, elsewhere—the highlands, the United States—as colorless

bureaucracy and power) seems oddly colonial in its own right. Finally, how better to endorse "native" Buendía vitality than to silhouette it against the impossible Fernanda of the highlands, a character that the text keeps extensively available for narrative abuse? This text so suspicious of "othering" does its own share of just this activity, and perhaps García Márquez's shrewdest move is to conclude his novel in a way that intimates interior malaise even as it shows the full destructive measure of external Western incursions.

21. It took Faulkner four years (and three prior novels) to find his way into the speechless dispossession that is Benjy. Donald Mahon and Bayard Sartoris are trial figures en route to Benjy. Their wounds are as decisive as his, but Faulkner has not yet learned how to make his own language "speak the wound." Once he achieves this in Benjy, he brilliantly redeploys it in several of his most memorably afflicted characters (Darl and Vardaman in *As I Lay Dying*, Joe Christmas in *Light in August*).

22. The best study of Faulkner's will to tragedy is Wadlington's. See also Bleikasten, as well as my *Faulkner's Subject*.

23. This general schema for the creative arc of Morrison's career was first developed (with less reference to modernism and postcolonialism) in my *What Else But Love?*

24. Morrison returns in her essays to the folkloric dimension of her practice: "If my work is to confront a reality unlike that received reality of the West, it must centralize and animate information discredited by the West—discredited not because it is not true or useful or even of some racial value, but because it is information described as 'lore' or 'gossip' or 'sentiment'" ("Memory, Creation, and Writing," qtd. in Otten 2).

25. Beloved's African origin takes that text—geographically and generically—beyond the familiar territory and procedures of Western realism. Crossing the death-barrier is linked, in Morrison's work, to crossing the Newtonian gravity-barrier: in both instances the human figure is launched onto a spatial-temporal trajectory incompatible with the limits and powers of individualism. Sula's strange moment of postdeath consciousness leads to *Song of Solomon*'s "flying Africans"—Morrison is seeking ways to figure life even in the midst of death—and these non-Newtonian tropes coalesce memorably in Beloved. For a suggestive meditation on the use of African American motifs in García Márquez's work (more specifically, the motif of the "flying Africans" implicitly lodging in his story "A Very Old Man with Enormous Wings"), see Kutzinski. The Caribbean/slave trade nexus plays a crucial role in Morrison's most recent novel, *Paradise*, as well, surfacing in the Convent women's death-eluding practice of the African-Brazilian religion of Candomblé. See Bouson (238–41) for discussion of how Morrison draws on such folk religion to access ways of thinking and feeling outside the range of instrumental reason.

26. One is tempted to compare Joe Trace's fallen Adam with Derek Walcott's "second Eden": "The myth of the noble savage could not be revived, for that myth . . . has all along been the nostalgia of the old world, its longing for innocence. The great poetry of the New World does not pretend to such innocence, its vision is not naïve. Rather, like its fruits, its savor is a mixture of the acid and the sweet, the apples of its second Eden have the tartness of experience. In such poetry there is a bitter memory and it is the bitterness that dies last on the tongue. It is the acidulous that supplies its energy"

(372). It would be hard to better these sentences from Walcott's "The Muse of History" in their capacity to gesture toward the post-tragic territory shared by García Márquez and Morrison. For telling differences between Faulkner's and Morrison's critiques of innocence, see my *What Else But Love?* (115–20).

27. The "rogue" element in *Jazz*—its refusal to proceed "lawfully"—has been noted by Eusebio Rodrigues: "The text, vibrant with sound and rhythm, invites us, we slowly realize, to set aside Cartesian logic in order to enter a magic world that cries out for deeper modes of knowing" (734).

28. Western readers sufficiently inured to realism may fail to note how many lights must be turned off for it to function. Meditation on its procedures allows one to glimpse how remarkably cautious and conservative realism is, how taut with epistemological worries—is this real? is it merely appearance?—its mandated vigilance requires it to be. Writing about magical realism, Rawdon Wilson speculates on the innate propensity of narrative to exceed the austerity of realist discipline: "The magicalness of magic realism lies in the way it makes explicit (that is, unfolds) what seems always to have been present. Thus the world interpenetration, the dual worldhood [acknowledging both the real and the fabulous] . . . of magic realism . . . are an explicit foregrounding of a kind of fictional space that is perhaps more difficult to suppress than to express. . . . Realism's typical limpidity arises from the muscular suppression of narrative potential" (226).

WORKS CITED

Bell-Villada, Gene H. *García Márquez: The Man and His Work*. Chapel Hill: U of North Carolina P, 1990.

Benjamin, Walter. "The Storyteller." *Illuminations*. Ed. Hannah Arendt. Trans. Harry Zohn. New York: Schocken, 1969. 83–109.

Bleikasten, André. *The Ink of Melancholy: Faulkner's Novels from "The Sound and the Fury" to "Light in August."* Bloomington: Indiana UP, 1990.

Bouson, J. Brooks. *Quiet as It's Kept: Shame, Trauma, and Race in the Novels of Toni Morrison*. Albany: State U of New York P, 2000.

Carpentier, Alejo. "On the Marvelous Real in America." *Magical Realism: Theory, History, Community*. Ed. Lois Parkinson Zamora and Wendy B. Faris. Durham, N.C.: Duke UP, 1995. 76–88.

——. "The Baroque and the Marvelous Real." *Magical Realism: Theory, History, Community*. Ed. Lois Parkinson Zamora and Wendy B. Faris. Durham, N.C.: Duke UP, 1995. 89–108.

Chanady, Amaryll. "The Territorialization of the Imaginary in Latin American Self-Affirmation and Resistance to Metropolitan Paradigms." *Magical Realism: Theory, History, Community*. Ed. Lois Parkinson Zamora and Wendy B. Faris. Durham, N.C.: Duke UP, 1995.125–44.

Chow, Rey. *Ethics after Idealism: Theory–Culture–Ethnicity–Reading*. Bloomington: Indiana UP, 1998.

Cohn, Deborah N. *History and Memory in the Two Souths: Recent Southern and Spanish American Fiction*. Nashville, Tenn.: Vanderbilt UP, 1999.

Dash, J. Michael. *The Other America: Caribbean Literature in a New World Context*. Charlottesville: UP of Virginia, 1998.

Everdell, William R. *The First Moderns: Profiles in the Origins of Twentieth-Century Thought*. Chicago: U of Chicago P, 1997.

Eysteinsson, Astradur. *The Concept of Modernism*. Ithaca, N.Y.: Cornell UP, 1992.

Faris, Wendy B. "Scheherezade's Children: Magic Realism and Postmodern Fiction." *Magical Realism: Theory, History, Community*. Ed. Lois Parkinson Zamora and Wendy B. Faris. Durham, N.C.: Duke UP, 1995. 165–90.

Faulkner, William. *Absalom, Absalom!* New York: Vintage, 1990.

——. *As I Lay Dying*. In *Faulkner: Novels, 1930–1935*. New York: Library of America, 1985.

——. *Light in August*. New York: Vintage, 1990.

——. *The Sound and the Fury*. Ed. David Minter. 2nd ed. New York: Norton, 1994.

Freud, Sigmund. "The Uncanny." 1919. *The Standard Edition of the Complete Psychological Works of Sigmund Freud*. Ed. and trans. James Strachey. Vol. 17. London: Hogarth Press, 1953–74. 217–52. 24 vols.

Frost, Robert. "For Once, Then, Something." *Robert Frost: Collected Poems, Prose, and Plays*. Ed. Richard Poirier and Mark Richardson. New York: Library of America, 1995. 208.

Gallop, Jane. *The Daughter's Seduction: Feminism and Psychoanalysis*. Ithaca, N.Y.: Cornell UP, 1982.

García Márquez, Gabriel. *One Hundred Years of Solitude*. Trans. Gregory Rabassa. New York: Harper Perennial, 1998.

——. *The Fragrance of Guava*. Trans. Ann Wright. London: Verso, 1983.

Griffin, Clive. "The Humour of *One Hundred Years of Solitude*." *Gabriel García Márquez: New Readings*. Ed. Bernard McGuirk and Richard Cardwell. Cambridge: Cambridge UP, 1987. 81–94.

Hardy, Thomas. *Jude the Obscure*. Ed. Norman Page. 2nd ed. New York: Norton, 1999.

Jameson, Fredric. *The Political Unconscious: Narrative as a Socially Symbolic Act*. Ithaca, N.Y.: Cornell UP, 1981.

Kern, Stephen. *The Culture of Time and Space, 1880–1918*. Cambridge, Mass.: Harvard UP, 1983.

Kutzinski, Vera M. "The Logic of Wings: Gabriel García Márquez and Afro-American Literature." *Modern Critical Views: Gabriel García Márquez*. Ed. Harold Bloom. New York: Chelsea House, 1989. 169–82.

Lacan, Jacques. "The Mirror Stage." *Ecrits: A Selection*. Trans. Alan Sheridan. New York: Norton, 1977. 1–7.

LeClair, Thomas. "'The Language Must Not Sweat': A Conversation with Toni Morrison." *Toni Morrison: Critical Perspectives Past and Present*. Ed. Henry Louis Gates Jr. and K. A. Appiah. New York: Amistad, 1993. 369–77.

Mitchell, Margaret. *Gone with the Wind*. New York: Macmillan, 1936.

Morrison, Toni. *Beloved*. New York: New American Library, 1987.

——. *The Bluest Eye*. New York: Plume, 1994.

——. "Interview with Toni Morrison." By Christina Davis. *Toni Morrison: Critical Perspectives Past and Present*. Ed. Henry Louis Gates Jr. and K. A. Appiah. New York: Amistad, 1993. 412–20.

——. *Jazz*. New York: Penguin, 1992.

——. *Paradise*. New York: Knopf, 1998.

——. *Playing in the Dark: Whiteness and the Literary Imagination*. New York: Random, 1993.

——. "Rootedness: The Ancestor as Foundation." *Black Women Writers (1950–1980)*. Ed. Mari Evans. Garden City, N.Y.: Anchor/Doubleday, 1984. 339–45.

——. *Song of Solomon*. New York: New American Library, 1977.

——. *Sula*. New York: New American Library, 1973.

Newton, Isaac. *Mathematical Principles*. *Great Books of the Western World*. Vol. 34. Chicago: Encyclopedia Britannica, 1952.

Otten, Terry. *The Crime of Innocence in the Fiction of Toni Morrison*. Columbia: U of Missouri P, 1989.

Rodrigues, Eusebio L. "Experiencing *Jazz*." *Modern Fiction Studies* 39 (1993): 733–54.

Rorty, Richard. *Philosophy and the Mirror of Nature*. Princeton, N.J.: Princeton UP, 1980.

Saldívar, José David. *The Dialectics of Our America: Genealogy, Cultural Critique, and Literary History*. Durham, N.C.: Duke UP, 1991.

Sangari, Kumkum. "The Politics of the Possible." *Cultural Critique* 7 (fall 1987): 157–86.

Spillers, Hortense. "Mama's Baby, Papa's Maybe: An American Grammar Book." *diacritics* 17 (1987): 65–81.

Tobin, Patricia Drechsel. *Time and the Novel: The Genealogical Imperative*. Princeton, N.J.: Princeton UP, 1978.

Wadlington, Warwick. *Reading Faulknerian Tragedy*. Ithaca, N.Y.: Cornell UP, 1987.

Walcott, Derek. "The Muse of History." *The Post-Colonial Studies Reader*. Ed. Bill Ashcroft, Gareth Griffiths, and Helen Tiffin. London: Routledge, 1995.

Weinstein, Philip M. *Faulkner's Subject: A Cosmos No One Owns*. New York: Cambridge UP, 1992.

——. *What Else But Love? The Ordeal of Race in Faulkner and Morrison*. New York: Columbia UP, 1996.

Williams, Raymond. *The Politics of Modernism*. Ed. Tony Pinckney. London: Verso, 1989.

Wilson, Rawdon. "The Metamorphosis of Fictional Space: Magic Realism." *Magical Realism: Theory, History, Community*. Ed. Lois Parkinson Zamora and Wendy B. Faris. Durham, N.C.: Duke UP, 1995. 209–33.

Zamora, Lois Parkinson. *Writing the Apocalypse: Historical Vision in Contemporary U.S. and Latin American Fiction*. New York: Cambridge UP, 1989.

There must have been a time when an artist could be genuinely representative *of* the tribe and *in* it; when an artist could have a tribal or racial sensibility and an individual expression of it.

—TONI MORRISON, "Rootedness"

North and south expected, what is expected north and south expect, expect north and south. . . . Here and there a name North a name. Here and there Mary a name. Here and there Mary a name South a name. Here and there a name North a name. Here and there a name south a name. Here and there a name.

—GERTRUDE STEIN, "Wherein the South Differs from the North"

DANE JOHNSON

"Wherein the South Differs from the North": Tracing the Noncosmopolitan Aesthetic in William Faulkner's *Absalom, Absalom!* and Gabriel García Márquez's *One Hundred Years of Solitude*

In William Faulkner's *Absalom, Absalom!* Quentin's Canadian roommate at Harvard, Shreve, insists on calling Rosa Coldfield—a participant in and narrator of the Sutpen saga that is being retold throughout the novel—"Aunt Rosa" or "this Aunt Rosa" and then "the Aunt Rosa" (218, 221, 370, and elsewhere). All of these denominations irritate the southerner Quentin: he corrects, he glares, he falls obstinately silent. When he narrates, Quentin consistently refers to her in the traditional southern form as "Miss Rosa," and he points out repeatedly to Shreve that she is no family relation. Shreve's slip is perhaps unconscious, a linguistic tic, but this slight misnaming is fraught with tension during the highly charged cocreation of Quentin's southern heritage, his southern self, through the reconstruction of Thomas Sutpen's rise and fall. Shreve is mythologizing Rosa Coldfield with syntax, forging the South into one big family tragedy and blurring meaningful distinctions among history, story, and genealogy, while Quentin is struggling with his relation to such (his)stories in a time (1910) and place (the North) where a white southerner's identity is perversely overdetermined.

In the whirlwind conclusion to the history of Macondo in Gabriel García Márquez's *One Hundred Years of Solitude*, the last Aureliano, last of the wondrous Buendía clan, deciphers Melquíades's manuscripts and learns, among many things, "that Sir Francis Drake had attacked Riohacha only so that they [Aureliano and his aunt Amaranta Úrsula] could seek each other through the most intricate labyrinths of blood until they would engender the mythological animal [a child with a pig's tail] that was to bring the line to an end" (382–83).[1] While tying up threads begun in the opening chapter—and being tied to a series of allusions to conquest and neoconquest in Spanish America—this line playfully flips historical notions of margin and center. It also disrupts foundational fictions that have so often repressed the horrors behind the founding while tapping into teleological notions of the inevitability of "progress."[2] Attention to the innocently aggressive confusion of such scenes and other deceptively complicated exchanges in these two novels is a first step in tracing the noncosmopolitan aesthetic in the works of William Faulkner and Gabriel García Márquez.

In *Absalom, Absalom!* and *One Hundred Years of Solitude* these authors engage strategies of representation that open their texts to a wide range of readings while also figuring resistance to a dominant culture. Through an array of forms, which can be grouped under the rubric of the noncosmopolitan aesthetic, Faulkner and García Márquez position themselves as mediators between the place from which they come and the culture of the metropolis. The noncosmopolitan aesthetic does not necessarily have *fixed* attributes, properties, or even characteristics beyond an individual author's search for forms that engage and contest the homogenizing force of the supposedly universal. Thus, the terms *metropolis*, *cosmopolitan*, and *universal* represent relational rather than essential categories. In this essay, *Universal*, for example, signifies an obliquely marked set of discourses generated and controlled by the metropolis, the dominant culture of a particular place and time, that is, "cosmopolitan culture." *Metropolis* implies a complicated combination of the socioeconomic (major city, mother city of an overseas colony), with suggestions of the urbane, and, hidden in earlier usage, a past as an ecclesiastical designation. While *universal* and *cosmopolitan* feign worldly neutrality, those who define—and exclude—remain in the metropolis. While the specifics of cosmopolitan culture are different, albeit closely overlapping, for these two writers, their sense of being in relation to an area with more capital of all kinds is functionally similar. Thus, *noncosmopolitan* suggests both opposition and inextricable relation, and these authors' positioning both begets and can be read by aesthetic choices.

While *One Hundred Years of Solitude* and *Absalom, Absalom!* are in some ways exemplars of "regional" literature, they are also narratives of contact and contestation, whereby protagonists are compelled to represent not only themselves but also the "tribe" from which they come to some other group that does not understand them.[3] As a result, their characters formulate identity through attempts to explain themselves and their culture to another, specifically a more powerful Other. Therefore, in addition to standing for particular regions, these two novels develop forms, possibilities, and conditions for representational exchange.[4] As savvy border negotiators who know the metropolis but retain their critical difference and distance, Faulkner and García Márquez trade on both their urbanity and their presumed authenticity as exotic Others. There seems to be no other option for breaking into cosmopolitan discourse.

In his discussion of Salman Rushdie and other "Third World Cosmopolitans" Timothy Brennan explains that the celebration of these novelists allows for a sense of change that ensures some kinds of continuity. Likewise, in reading Faulkner and García Márquez vis-à-vis the metropolis (bearing in mind that the U.S. South has often been figured as a kind of third world of "our" own), it becomes clear that the nonsouthern, non-Latin American, "mainstream" public's embrace and even adoration of these authors contributes to a new mythology of "world" inclusion. As Brennan puts it, "Alien to the public that read them because they were black, spoke with accents or were not citizens, they were also like that public in tastes, training, repertoire of anecdotes, current habitation" (ix). While Brennan's focus is reception, the emphasis herein is production. To describe Faulkner's and García Márquez's positioning and aesthetic choices as noncosmopolitan highlights the ways in which their writing contests, or at least addresses, the appropriation described by Brennan.[5]

OF THE TRIBE AND IN IT

How do Faulkner and García Márquez conceptualize their role as Artist and negotiate with notions of tradition? What are their strategies for coping with the burdens of representation, that is, the tension between the universal and the particular, between the desire for recognition and the fear of being mis-taken?[6] Despite their differences in cultural background and era, Faulkner and García Márquez share a remarkably similar sensibility: their goals and their vision of writing's possibilities are congruent with a humanist, Romantic version of the literary and the literary artist. Nevertheless, both self-consciously position themselves in dialogue with a perceived metropolitan tradition, expressing the anxiety of the author from the provinces: the desire to reach a wider audience and to be part of the grand narrative of art coupled with the awareness of the exclusion their region has met.[7]

With regard to the ramifications of exclusion, Toni Morrison posits, with evident nostalgia, "There must have been a time when an artist could be genuinely representative *of* the tribe and *in* it" (339). This statement pithily suggests one side of the noncosmopolitan aesthetic: the loss of a unified community—that might never have existed—and the anxiety of separation from the community leading to the representation of processes of cultural transformation. It also resonates with what might be called the "tragic nostalgia" of Faulkner and García Márquez. For both writers a sense of the tragic history of their region or nation is constitutive for their writing; at the same time, part of this tragic past is the sense of lost wholeness from another time—even if that time is sometimes represented as difficult or even barbaric. While Faulkner and García Márquez long to write of and remain in their respective tribes, they are conscious of being marked as coming from a defeated "tribe." They know that, as they compose, they must contend with the outside world's negative perception of their people.

As has been twice-told and probably thrice-forgotten, William Faulkner had to contend with an outsized reality, or at least the reality of overblown perceptions about the South. How could Faulkner outdo or contest, for example, H. L. Mencken's infamous and roughly contemporary description of the South as a "stupendous region of worn-out farms, shoddy cities and paralyzed cerebrums. . . . [I]t is almost as sterile, artistically, intellectually, culturally, as the Sahara Desert" (136)?[8] Faulkner's approach, in self-fashioning and in authorship, was to both deploy and deconstruct these stereotypes.

Between the Scylla and Charybdis of Mencken's wasteland and popular nostalgia for the white columns of the Big House, Faulkner insisted on representing a South in opposition to but also in complex interrelation with the South of the popular imagination.[9] While eschewing the romantic visions of "historical" novels—"to keep the hoop skirts and plug hats out, you might say" (*Selected Letters* 78–79)—Faulkner marks his distance from the South, to the point of, at times, matching even the most outrageous versions of the region coming from a provocateur like Mencken. In the mid-1930s, for example, Faulkner wrote, "Art is no part of Southern life. In the North it seems to be different" ("Introduction" 410). Terming it a "dream," he also understood the "South" to be constructed: "I speak in the sense of the indigenous dream of any given collection of men having something in common, be it only geography and climate, which shape their economic and spiritual aspirations into cities, into a pattern of houses or behavior" (411).

Faulkner's complex mix of aspiration and exasperation comes out nicely if not concisely in his now famous 1944 letter to Malcolm Cowley, wherein Faulkner tries to summarize his craft and his vision.

> I am telling the same story over and over, which is myself and the world. . . . Tom Wolfe was trying to say everything, the world plus "I" or filtered through "I" or the effort of "I" to embrace the world in which he was born and walked a little while and then lay down again, into one volume. I am trying to go a step further. This I think accounts for what people call the obscurity, the involved formless "style," endless sentences. I'm trying to say it all in one sentence, between one Cap and one period. . . . I'm inclined to think that my material, the South, is not very important to me. I just happen to know it. . . . Though the one I know is probably as good as another, life is a phenomenon but not a novelty, the same frantic steeplechase toward nothing everywhere and man stinks the same stink no matter where in time. (Cowley 14–15)

Read in tandem with other forms of noncosmopolitan positioning, this lengthy passage evokes the separation between Faulkner and the South, his effort to mediate between *the* world and his world—the North and the South. Even the direct denial of the South's importance speaks to the ties, for Faulkner is forever of and creating the South in the popular imagination. This passage also suggests his aspiration as a universal writer who, aware of his cosmopolitan critics, feels compelled to explain himself and the South—an explanation that is linked to form in Faulkner's anxiety to "say it all in one sentence."

García Márquez also explicitly presents himself as responding to cosmopolitan culture while representing his own. He often plays with metropolitan ignorance of Latin America, noting in accepting the 1972 *Books Abroad*/Neustadt International Prize for Literature, for instance, that he hails "from a remote and mysterious country" (Ivask 440). In his Nobel Prize acceptance speech in 1982, García Márquez made the question of Latin American representation even more complex. He noted that, "Europeans of good will—and sometimes those of bad, as well—have been struck, with ever greater force, by the unearthly tidings of Latin America, that boundless realm of haunted men and historic women, whose unending obstinacy blurs into legend" ("Solitude" 231). "Unearthly," "boundless," "haunted"—these are the words of legend. But do they represent the European vision of the New World, García Márquez's version, or Latin American reality itself?

García Márquez laments his separation from his people, his Colombia, talking about homesickness and "losing contact with . . . [his] myths" (Harss and Dohmann 318). This sense of possible loss leads him to write, to preserve. Nevertheless, only separation of some kind could lead one to see Latin American reality as "fantastic," "unbelievable," "incredible" (García Márquez, "Impossible Reality" 13–15), for it takes the normative reference point of an Other to see and represent your "own" reality as exceeding the norm.[10] This multiple yet all-encompassing perspective on Latin American reality is then built into the representational strategies of *One Hundred Years of Solitude.*

Attention to noncosmopolitan positioning and its aesthetic ripples opens up new perspectives on Faulkner's mediating role between North and South and García Márquez's attempt to write a Latin American subject that can withstand incursions from Europe and the United States. Faulkner's commitment to this oppositional aesthetic stems in part from the fact that he had to confront an image of U.S. literature and culture that included the South only as aberration. Embedded within the multiple narratives of *Absalom, Absalom!* is the story of a southerner gone North trying to explain his culture. García Márquez acknowledges drinking from the fount of Faulkner (while eliding influence from much of the Latin American literature with which he was familiar), a line of rigid descent that U.S. critics have contributed to by designating García Márquez's imagined community of Macondo "a Latin American Yoknapatawpha" (Sheppard 87).[11] At the same time, *One Hundred Years of Solitude* is the writing of a homogenized Latin American cultural space—a kind of representational defense against the colossus from the North—even if the unified, *criollo* subjectivity García Márquez presents nearly erases the Native American and African presence throughout the region. But noncosmopolitan positioning creates a dual movement: separation from a community, with subsequent personal and artistic repercussions, and defense of that community from a more powerful Other.[12] Bluntly put, conceptualizing literatures and cultures as southern, Latin American, and so on is part of creating a sense of unified consciousness that might have not been there before. The novels themselves—manifestations of the noncosmopolitan aesthetic—interrogate the boundaries of culture and stereotypes of the exotic Other through a vast array of representational strategies.

Gertrude Stein's 1928 poem "Wherein the South Differs from the North" ends with a playful paean to the arbitrariness of naming: "Here and there a name North a name. Here and there a name south a name. Here and there a name" (37). And the poem is littered with the typical Steinian word- and syntactic-play that call attention to how conventions of reading and writing not only describe but also do things. But this close attention to the formulaic ways in which language works is not in opposition to discussion of thematic issues. Language is both arbitrary (North and South a name) and not (these names carry resonances that cannot be denied). This "not" is abruptly and forcefully brought up earlier in the poem:

> North and south negroes.
> No one means that.
> South and north settle.
> No one means that.
> No one means that south and north settle, South and north
> settle no one means that.
> Furthermore. (20)

That "furthermore" represents aesthetic choices that keep in play "North" and "South" as both arbitrary and resonant.

Staging semiotic confrontations between North and South is a part of the noncosmopolitan aesthetic in *Absalom, Absalom!* and *One Hundred Years of Solitude*.[13] During the symbolic exchanges in these two texts, stereotypes are deployed, turned upside down, and twisted, with readers likely to be taken in a variety of ways. Faulkner's attention to this sort of confrontation in *Absalom, Absalom!* is most explicit when one focuses on the Quentin and Shreve interchange, although it is evident in all parts of the novel. García Márquez plays with many of the typical North-South stereotypes in part by turning center-periphery models inside out, with Macondo becoming the center of the universe around which the rest of the world—even Sir Francis Drake—revolves. García Márquez's "North" comes in many disguises, from the magical gypsies to the bullying U.S. banana company to the snotty highlanders, one of whom, Fernanda del Carpio, manages to infiltrate—but not to be integrated into—the Buendía clan.

Absalom, Absalom! is framed by the conflicted consciousness of Quentin Compson, and Faulkner's depiction of Quentin's sense of self displays many traits typical of double-consciousness or hybrid subjectivity. There is a sense of having no place for Quentin to just be, for he is always being determined by others. The emphasis on such a liminal figure foregrounds cultures in vigorous contact and transformation. From the opening, Quentin is split in trying to reconcile the stories, listening to "two separate Quentins"—or a barracks full of ghosts—"still too young to deserve yet to be a ghost but nevertheless having to be one for all that, since he was born and bred in the deep South." It is identity through negation, through having a story that can neither be told nor heard adequately: "the two separate Quentins now talking to one another in the long silence of notpeople in not-language" (5).

Part of Rosa Coldfield's impulse to tell Quentin is in knowing that he will be leaving, going north with his story. She, too, is keenly aware of the split between North and South, for "Northern people have already seen to it that there is little left in the South for a young man" (6). Miss Rosa surmises that Quentin may enter the literary profession, "as so many Southern gentlemen and gentlewomen too are doing now" (9), perhaps putting his or her oral tale into print. Miss Rosa sees stories—at least *her* version of this story—as acts of cultural and material survival. But it is the stories themselves that challenge Quentin's self: "Quentin had grown up with that; the mere names were interchangeable and almost myriad. His childhood was full of them; his very body was an empty hall echoing with sonorous defeated names; he was not a being, an entity, he was a commonwealth" (9). Here, even the body as the last sign of an inviolable self is questioned, with Quentin's self-assertion impossible until he both pieces together the story and challenges the gaze of the Other (as he does later).

It is about halfway into the novel when Quentin arrives at Harvard, and the reader has already marched back across much of Sutpen's past via several layered forms of knowing, several reflections on enigmas that may never be known, many forms of both telling stories that cannot be adequately told and listening to things that are always already known. These formal dodges around telling "it" straight—choices typical of the noncosmopolitan aesthetic—come out of Faulkner's mediating position. In commenting on Faulkner's *supposedly* "oral" style, Hortense Spillers outlines one of the formal results of Faulkner's narrators speaking from a less powerful—the noncosmopolitan—subject position: "[Faulkner's] syntactical protocol seems dominated by the anxieties of revision and a severe oppositional movement to the uncertainties of 'improvised' speech. More exactly, Faulkner's narrative device appears to generate speaking-as-repentance, in which case whatever one might speak at one moment becomes, on second thought, inadequate, as the latter is not effaced so much as 'improved' upon and 'essayed' over and over again. This seems the dominant semiotic burden of *Absalom, Absalom!* as characters 'listen' to themselves talk and appear to revise and correct, aggrandize and elaborate in the moment" (24, n. 23).

The formal give and take suggested above is part of how Faulkner evinces the contested exchange of stories. And, while the Quentin-Shreve relationship epitomizes this, most of Faulkner's characters have their sense of self formed and informed by "wherein the south differs from the north": their subjectivity is shaped through contact even if their sense of self is strongly regional—with that regional self based on the power of collective memory. This contact, however, need not always be direct.

In some ways Mr. Compson is even more paradigmatic; though there is no mention of his traveling, no mention of actual encounters with the metropolis, his entire manner of processing the Sutpen saga is replete with the tension of contact, for he transforms this southern story into a universal epic through the lens of classic Western (especially Greek, but also British Renaissance and Romantic) literature. Mr. Compson is a product of a European-accented education but feels profoundly alienated from that heritage, profoundly cynical about the present of the South, profoundly bombastic about its past. Sutpen himself represents a tale of contact that in some way makes him more southern; it is a sort of reenactment of the luck-and-pluck story, as he leaves one part of the South for the South's south of the Caribbean, returning to a different part of the South only to build a stereotypical southern dynasty that may be as far from his direct heritage as that of any other character.

To turn back to Quentin specifically, Quentin has just received a letter from his father telling of the death of Rosa Coldfield. At this point, Quentin's repressed anxiety at being the representative of the strange South for inquisitive northerners is for the first time introduced directly.[14] He begins to read his father's letter, "and he soon needing, required, to say 'No, neither aunt cousin nor uncle Rosa. Miss Rosa. Miss Rosa Coldfield' . . . and then Shreve, 'You mean she was no kin to you, no kin to you at all, that there was actually one Southern Bayard or Guinevere who was no kin to you? then what did she die for?' and that not Shreve's first time, nobody's first time in Cambridge since September: *Tell about the South. What's it like there. What do they do there. Why do they live there. Why do they live at all*" (218).

In the wake of the questions and the mocking names and the incessant need to know, the formation and assertion of Quentin's sense of self, which is certainly *one* of the stories running through this complicated novel, occurs in part through a defense of the South against the received stereotypes. While one learns much of the possible Sutpen—and the probable Quentin and Shreve and so many more—from listening to the "happy marriage of speaking and hearing" (395) between these two, the unequal exchange of stories comes out just as forcefully in what is described between the lines: an ongoing narration of slowly changing physical reactions; habitual "no's" turning to loud but unheard silences; Shreve's percussive "Wait" so that he can hear more shifting to Quentin's "Wait" so that he need hear never again. After having heard much of the Sutpen saga, for example, Shreve is incredulous: " 'So he just wanted a grandson,' he said. 'That was all he was after. Jesus, the South is fine, isn't it. It's better than the theatre, isn't it. It's better than Ben Hur, isn't it. No wonder you have to come away now and then, isn't it' " (271). This time, Quentin does not answer as he did before.

In the climactic scene of their co-creation, Shreve's jocularity—one small indication of the casual power of the "normal"—is tied to Quentin's final blow-up of ambivalent and ambiguous self-revelation.[15] First, Shreve mocks the supposed "Southern diction" that he seems to have learned from listening to Quentin read his father's letters: " 'out of the wilderness proud honor semesterial regurgitant.' " Shreve then adds, " 'I didn't know there were ten in Mississippi that went to school at one time.' " Of course, "Quentin didn't answer . . . and now, although he was warm and though while he had sat in the cold room he merely shook faintly and steadily, now he began to jerk all over, violently and uncontrollably until he could even hear the bed, until even Shreve felt it and turned . . . to look at Quentin" (449–50). In a broad sense, the narration from Harvard is structured like a stock scene of "racial discovery," with Quentin seeing his "difference" only through the looks of horror and humor from the others around him. The South is assumed to be abnormal, and Quentin, separated from his heritage yet not able to pass into the northern world, has a tortured double-consciousness, his difference both curse and benefit. Shreve continues, " 'Wait. Listen. I'm not trying to be funny, smart. I just want to understand it if I can and I dont know how to say it better. Because it's something my people haven't got' " (450–51). Quentin replies, " 'You cant understand it. You would have to be born there' " (451). And this confrontation between the desire of others to know and the impossibility of explaining generates Quentin's self and much of Faulkner's discourse. The novel ends with Quentin anxiously answering Shreve's "Why do you hate the South?" with an insistent, repeated "*I dont hate it*" (471), the signifier and signified of this phrase as painfully crisscrossed as Quentin's—or any reader's—certainty about Sutpen, South, or self.[16]

Although the ultimate goal in the exchange of stories is to replace stereotypes with a more nuanced cross-cultural understanding, in situations of unequal power, the humorous deployment of stereotypes is often used to undermine the force of metropolitan othering. While engagement with Quentin's painful self-assertion in *Absalom, Absalom!* might lead to a reader's self-examination of their own stereotypes, García Márquez is more likely to turn the tables with humor.[17] In *One Hundred Years of Solitude*, for example, the characters Fernanda del Carpio and Petra Cotes set up a duel between "North" and "South," and the South wins. Fernanda's cosmopolitan culture (begat by more direct colonial heritage than most characters) is useless in the new Latin America of Macondo, the noncosmopolitan world. The narrator drolly suggests this by filling in the back-story of her fine but failed education (in pointed contrast to the natural education of Remedios the Beauty): "At the end of eight years, after having learned to write Latin poetry, play the clavichord, talk about falconry with gentlemen and apologetics with archbishops, discuss affairs of state with foreign rulers and affairs of God with the Pope, she returned to her parents' home [in frigid, cosmopolitan Bogotá] to weave funeral wreaths. She found it despoiled. . . . [S]he had never heard mention of the wars that were bleeding the country" (195–96).

Here, knowledge of "the best that has been thought and said"—the vaunted arts and letters from the West—means being cut off from family and nation, and living in a dream world; such "northern" learned irrationality is echoed many times over in her character. Petra, by contrast, is simply the best of the Americas: "a clean young mulatto woman" with "a generous heart and a magnificent vocation for love" (180). The quicksilver shifts and the bawdy vulgarities that make up the many attacks on Fernanda's snobbery can be taken as the provincials' smiling middle finger to a Colombia seen to be controlled by Bogotá, but they also serve notice to all educated readers: you better wonder who is mocking whom.

As a counterweight to a metropolis that presumes to have knowledge of the Other, these authors deploy challenging forms, depict the exchange of stories, and proceed with subversive humor. Tied in to stories that remain and revolve but do not resolve is the fact that the noncosmopolitan is associated with circular or cyclic time (or at least a tension between the cyclic and the linear) while the cosmopolitan North runs on linear time. "Progress" is linear, and within the noncosmopolitan aesthetic, it is not unconsciously accepted but explicitly questioned, in part through a critique of capitalism. Both novels contain stories of living under the false God of free-market economics; there is a strong suggestion that the focus on money is coming from the metropolis and that it destroys other forms of value from within. Sutpen's ruthless rise, for example—all within the unbending logic of the capitalism of his day—is associated in the novel with a pact with the devil.

The critique of capitalism in *One Hundred Years of Solitude* overturns northern assumptions of the possibility of a perpetually expanding economy for all who participate in so-called free trade. On one level, the basic rationality of the system is questioned. In a series of scenes, Aureliano Segundo becomes the most prodigious capitalist of Macondo due to his wildly multiplying animals: "he barely had time to enlarge his overflowing barns and pigpens. It was a delirious prosperity that even made him laugh" (183).[18] This ironic twisting of the traditional tale of luck and pluck is twisted further in Colonel Buendía's business of "selling little gold fishes" (189). His mother Úrsula, however, is confused: "With her terrible practical sense she could not understand the colonel's business as he exchanged little fishes for gold coins and then converted the coins into little fishes, and so on, with the result that he had to work all the harder with the more he sold in order to satisfy an exasperating vicious circle. Actually, what interested him was not the business but the work" (190).

In scenes that deliciously fragment so many people's expectations, the Colonel participates in the market economy but subverts it by taking no profit, plowing nothing but gold coins back into fishes in a circle of industrious escape that is as opposed to the upward sloping linear logic of the business world as his thirty-two armed uprisings were to politics as usual. More devastating than any of this, of course, is Aureliano Triste's unfortunate train, which brought with it the hurricane force of the gringo banana company—the embodiment of multinational, neocolonial capitalism—that would take over the town like an enraged God, leaving a lost massacre and a few inconsolable memories.[19]

The North-South confrontations enacted in these texts illustrate unequal economic and political exchange as well as the differential exchange of stories. Within the play of stereotypes and overdetermined expectations is a resistance to those who might misread stories from southern lands.[20] While the complicating of assumptions does not in itself ensure a large readership, it does suggest that Faulkner and García Márquez understood the diverse audiences by which their stories might be received. While one can imagine readers who enjoy these tales for their representation of a place that they feel has been mis-taken or for their depiction of an exotic alternative land, one can almost as easily see how these texts would push cosmopolitan readers to interrogate their desire for and creation of such exotic others.

Given the multiple possibilities for being misread, it is not surprising that marginalized groups often find that getting their story straight and protecting their heritage is difficult. An obsession with past defeats is one common result, which often takes the form of genealogy or family history. Such a story then stands in opposition to the official story, even if sometimes felt as burden: Miss Rosa's "tedious repercussive anti-climax of it" (187); Quentin's "I have heard too much" (259); so many Buendías poring over the magical parchments of Melquíades. As is well-known, *Absalom, Absalom!* and *One Hundred Years of Solitude* are both epic genealogies and texts that question the ways in which we "know" history, story, or genealogy.

For *Absalom, Absalom!*'s Mr. Compson, "It's just incredible. It just does not explain. Or perhaps that's it: they dont explain and we are not supposed to know" (124–25). The narrators of *Absalom, Absalom!* struggle mostly together to tell a story that they admit cannot be told adequately. The narrators cannot bracket off this or that: people get in the way of the picture; feelings get in the ways of their faces; ghosts intrude on the present; truth is always a matter of contradictions. It is a world where an idea about something can carry the force of a scythe to the neck.[21] The questionable veracity of the competing visions of Sutpen is constantly foregrounded. This suggests the historicity of myth, the myth of history (these stories were really passed down and really believed to be true), and the layering of identity (one's investment in stories that cannot possibly all be true when one hears multiple versions still changes the way one sees and lives oneself). Insistently, the narration is punctuated by "perhaps," "maybe," and that wonderfully hedgy word "doubtless," which always throws the statement into doubt. But a world of action has been represented as following from these almost mystical beliefs. This is generally true and can be boiled down to pithy truisms; however, when the world being depicted is one that is more assumed than known—as so often happens with the noncosmopolitan—the stakes in foregrounding unknowability are considerably higher.

It is in *One Hundred Years of Solitude* where the clash between the official story and what is known to be true by a select few is most directly laid out. Bear in mind that the turning point in the history of Macondo is the transformation of the town that occurred as a result of the incursion of the North American banana company and its ruinous departure amid a massacre—the latter action having been completely erased from the history books.[22] This episode and its aftermath represent a particularly direct form of questioning the value of literacy—the written, official history—for if such words can eliminate horrendous actions, then words have very little value but much potential power.[23] When the banana company's workers consider going on strike, words drive them out of existence after the lawyers for the banana company do their work: "by a decision of the court it was established and set down in solemn decrees that the workers did not exist" (280). The real elimination of the workers and their families comes in the form of a massacre in which only José Arcadio Segundo Buendía survives. Not even his twin brother will believe his story: "The official version, repeated a thousand times and mangled out all over the country by every means of communication the government found at hand, was finally accepted: there were no dead, the satisfied workers had gone back to their families, and the banana company was suspending all activity until the rains stopped" (287).

Unable to be heard—the discordant play of "official" and "mangled" suggests but cannot tell of the brutal event—José Arcadio Segundo dedicates himself to the perusal of the manuscripts of Melquíades, turning to private reading of magical prophecy when truthful talk and witnessed history was found to be futile in countering the official story. Reading and writing, being both interpretive and representative acts, are potentially negative, even destructive, each additional letter from the Catalan bookseller, for example, killing off the possibility of another lived moment. The Buendía quest to read and interpret the manuscripts—their self—leads directly to the final destruction of the town. In *Absalom, Absalom!* Quentin's reading of the old tales and letters in the quest for self-understanding leads to self-loathing and, perhaps, self-destruction.

Despite such apocalyptic endings, the act of tracing the noncosmopolitan aesthetic is potentially ameliorative.[24] Taken as a whole, the noncosmopolitan aesthetic offers possibilities for accepting, understanding, and preserving cultural difference without homogenization, for it dramatizes how messy culture is—even the culture of Others under the metropolitan gaze. And, taken as a whole, I have only traced a few aspects of representational strategies in these two novels—and the work of these two authors more generally—that can be better understood as part of a noncosmopolitan aesthetic. In *One Hundred Years of Solitude*, for example, the Western tradition is invoked both in broad terms and with minute details (see, for example, Samuel García), creating an illusion of instant communicability with non-Colombian readers; however, the linking of writing, reading, and interpretation with destruction in the denouement of the plot (not unlike Faulkner's *Absalom, Absalom!*) suggests a questioning in the final instance of traditional notions of cultural transmission. The deployment of biblical rhetoric and topoi in Faulkner and García Márquez has a similar effect: the noncosmopolitan effect of distancing oneself both from the city—the godless city—and the god-fearing, bible-as-the-undisputed-word-of-god communities with which these writers are familiar.[25] Stepping back to the broader perspective, in both texts there are multiple dramatizations of the relation between culture and subculture. As an effect of cultural reclamation, a tradition of another order emerges from these novels. It is a tradition in which one always says more than one means, whether this is called "ambiguity," "double-voicedness," "signifyin(g)," or "heteroglossia." The question remains, however, exactly where this tradition is located. Suggested in both the examined texts and their reception is the idea that, for all their complications and vexations, fictions matter, and also that the metropolis needs voices from outside to heal and reveal itself, even if these voices are usually mediators between the city and the country and not "authentic." While fulfilling this desire for the voice of the Other in their noncosmopolitan way, Faulkner and García Márquez embody the paradoxical nature of representation: the person who represents a group is already separated from it. If one takes Faulkner and García Márquez only as the best that has been thought and said, as universal writers, as august Nobel prize winners, one may forget some of their most important lessons: a "the" can make all the difference; the direction of history is unknown; there are other voices out there.

NOTES

1. To include those who only read English as well as those who are bilingual in English and Spanish, quotations from works originally in Spanish are taken from the published English translations; when these are not available, the translations are my own.

2. I allude here to Doris Sommer's *Foundational Fictions*, a work in which she explores the twinning of literary and political fictions in Latin America. See her introduction for elaboration on García Márquez's relation to this tradition.

3. I am intentionally deploying the term *region* ambiguously when speaking of Faulkner and García Márquez and their texts, for their sense of region—and they both address this sense in nonfictional utterances—pulls in different directions: Faulkner and a sense of a coherent subculture within a national culture; García Márquez and a sense of a supranational Latin American culture. In this indeterminate usage, *region* is thus useful as another relational keyword, leaving open other categories as relevant at different points. It is beyond the scope of this essay to detail what is at stake in using one among many possible designations such as *community, subculture, region, nation*. For a useful discussion of these stakes specific to white U.S. southern culture, see Michael Kreyling's *Inventing Southern Literature*.

4. Hortense Spillers suggests ways in which *Absalom, Absalom!* reaches far beyond the confines of Yoknapatawpha County, a reach that aggressively crosses the North-South divide and challenges any simplified notion of region: "The historical triangular trade interlarded a third of the known world in a fabric of commercial intimacy so tightly interwoven that the politics of the New World cannot always be so easily disentangled as locally discrete moments." Spillers adds that *Absalom, Absalom!* "choreographs

Canada, the Caribbean, Africa, Europe, and the United States as geographical and/or figurative points of contact in this fictive discourse" (9). The same could almost be said of *One Hundred Years of Solitude*, even though it is usually read in terms of a unified "Latin American" region.

5. I discuss this subject much more fully in my forthcoming book, *William Faulkner, Gabriel García Márquez, Toni Morrison, and the Creation of Literary Value*. A shorter discussion of change and continuity with the canonization of García Márquez can be found in my article "The Rise of Gabriel García Márquez and Toni Morrison." My focus on these authors comes out of an attempt to understand the processes by which single authors have become iconic representatives of complex cultures. This focus in no way belies the literary context—the Southern Renaissance and the Latin American Boom—within which these authors wrote or certain parallels in historical moment. See, for example, Deborah N. Cohn's introduction to *History and Memory in the Two Souths* for a useful discussion of the shared sense of defeat that links the U.S. South and Latin America.

6. Here and throughout this essay, I play off of the dual sense of representation as "speaking for" in the political sense and as "re-presentation" in the artistic sense. Internationally successful novelists from "other" places are valued in part for their "native" accounts of exotic lands. For further explication of this duality, see Gayatri Spivak's "Can the Subaltern Speak?" especially 275–76.

7. It may be surprising at first glance that I dwell on what might be called the aesthetic politics of personality, but it is implicit in my argument that these authors' self-fashioning is at least partially an aesthetic proposition. There are obvious limitations to the use of an author's own pronouncements if employed as the key to hermeneutic truth. Nevertheless, the way authors present and position themselves affects how they are read and evaluated while also providing a glimpse into their creative process.

8. Although, to my knowledge, Faulkner never made a formal response to Mencken's various articles skewering the South, it is most certain that he was aware of this work. Faulkner probably discussed it while in New Orleans during the early and mid-1920s through his association with the *Double Dealer*, one of the little magazines that sprouted up in that purported cultural desert, fertilized by anger at Mencken. Fred Hobson's *Serpent in Eden* provides a full discussion of the southern response to Mencken; Joseph Blotner's biography of Faulkner scrupulously details Faulkner's New Orleans peregrinations (see especially 329–30).

9. One indicator of national desires for the plantation myth was the fact that *Gone with the Wind* sold more than 50,000 copies in 1936, its initial year of publication, also garnering the 1937 Pulitzer Prize in literature. Furthermore, the now forgotten Century Publishers had its own little Southern Gothic industry, putting out such fare as Marie Conway Oemler's *Flower of Thorn* (1931): "A Romantic novel of the sectional pride and prejudice of the old South . . . undoubtedly the most haunting love story ever written" (advertisement in the *New York Times Book Review* 27 Sept. 1931: 18).

10. This is one aspect of what I call "*criollo* consciousness," which in some ways could also be ascribed retroactively to Faulkner, too. For the Latin American criollo, the unstated, perhaps unconscious, assumption is that "we" can represent all of Latin

America because only we know and understand all parts of Latin America. The term *criollo* means, in the first instance, a person born in Spanish America but of Spanish descent, that is, neither mestizo, mulatto, nor indigenous (acknowledging that the Portuguese roots of the word suggest even more complicated crossings). In the twentieth century, *criollo* is more generally used to designate educated middle- and upper-class males, who happen to be, for the most part, those of lighter skin (although there is significant regional variation in the deployment of this term). Thus, "criollo" is a shifting cultural category, not a strictly racial one. It is under these terms that I would label García Márquez a creole writer.

Taking a wider look at criollo writing, Mary Louise Pratt notes that the foundational texts of the Latin American independence period contain a common trope: "a panorama of the vast and empty American wilderness, the future national territory onto which the writer goes on to inscribe the march of human history." This description fits *One Hundred Years of Solitude*. But not just anyone is likely to coopt such a trope: "The potential master is the creole [*criollo*] speaking subject, the new American citizen who is the seer in these panoramas and who himself remains unseen" (95). García Márquez both toys with this trope and is called on to play this role.

11. While García Márquez openly acknowledges Faulkner's position as a lodestar for his own writing, I see the multiple and intertwining connections as more than just influence. Faulkner's road to the Nobel, for example, parallels in some ways the cultural shifts necessary for acceptance of Latin American writing, with Faulkner as the rescued genius from a languid land that time and art forgot. Ironically, the success of García Márquez has contributed to a re-situation of Faulkner, allowing him to be read now as simultaneously "classic" and "postcolonial," as southern, black, Caribbean, and even as "our most Latin American writer" (Chevigny 355; see also Spillers). I analyze these complex relations in my forthcoming book, *William Faulkner, Gabriel García Márquez, Toni Morrison, and the Creation of Literary Value*. For a thorough overview of Faulkner's legacy in Latin America, see Deborah N. Cohn's *History and Memory in the Two Souths*, especially 8–16.

12. Theories of minority and postcolonial writing, culture, and subjectivity have contributed to my reading of Faulkner's and García Márquez's noncosmopolitan positioning and aesthetic. From W. E. B. Du Bois's pithy "How does it feel to be a problem?" (9), to Homi Bhabha's rapping "almost the same, but not quite" (86), to Wlad Godzich's distinction between "casual" and "noncasual" racial being (29–30), I have learned much about modes for overdetermining consciousness and forms of representing oneself to a more powerful Other. However, I am in no way equating the histories of oppression behind the theories above with the backgrounds of Faulkner and García Márquez. While they share a sense of defeat, Faulkner and García Márquez, as Euro-American males, enjoyed considerable advantages in ascending to the role of revered and respected artists. They tapped into that part of the metropolitan cultural system that receives the young man from the provinces. Thus, the notion of criollo consciousness is a necessary additional distinction, even if there are functional similarities in the positioning of ethnic minority cultures with respect to the dominant culture that lead to linked aesthetic strategies.

13. As with my deployment of *cosmopolitan* and *metropolis*, I do not use the terms *North* and *South* in an essential manner but rather as semifluid terms of division employed in different ways by different groups. Despite this ambiguity and the ease with which such homogenizing notions can be deconstructed (as well as the subtlety with which these two authors undercut strict divisions of North and South), the terms both carry weight and continue to have power. In 1785, while in Paris, Thomas Jefferson wrote up a list of traits for the northerner and the southerner. The first items on the list for the North were "cool," "sober," and "laborious"; the South was juxtaposed with the adjectives "fiery," "voluptuary," and "indolent" (qtd. in Dekker 275). One could easily generate broader terms along these lines: rational/emotional; mind/body; rich/poor; dominant/dominated. When I have asked groups of students for associations they had with the two words—prior to any discussion of these types of stereotypes—they have consistently produced a list remarkably like that of Jefferson.

14. I echo here Jon Smith's formulation of the Quentin-Shreve exchange as one of patient and analyst, although my reading of the novel follows different, albeit not contradictory, lines of inquiry (4). I should also make explicit the obvious in that I am following a long line of Faulkner critics both in seeing the form as part of the story and in considering the Quentin and Shreve exchange to be particularly important (see, for example, McPherson and Millgate, among many others). I differ primarily in trying to isolate forms of the noncosmopolitan aesthetic.

15. I should add that Shreve's positioning is equally complex even if not depicted in the same detail as Quentin's. While I have lumped him together with the cosmopolitan North—and his insistent queries are a detailed version of Harvard's more general "tell about the South"—Shreve is not only Canadian but from Alberta, another New World margin. This analogous positioning may explain their meeting of minds (and is in fact directly invoked with Faulkner's suggestion of the Mississippi as a shared umbilical cord), but the never-resolved tension suggests a defiant insistence on difference.

16. Attention to the complexities of racial division also undermines any southern certainties, a point that has been well covered in Faulkner scholarship. Thadious Davis's reflections on "Race and Region," for example, complements my broader notion of the noncosmopolitan aesthetic. On Faulkner, see especially 426–29, where she notes that Faulkner "moved away from the existing discourses on race in the South by extracting an alternative vision of life offered by Southern African Americans, in particular, as a major part of the tensions about being, existence, and place that characterized the dialectic of much of his work as a modernist and fictionist" (427). With regard to regional and racial interconnections, she concludes that Faulkner "attended to the problems and dynamics of race relations, caste privilege, and agrarian reform with the contexts of industrialization and urbanization in a region reluctant and resistant to change. Race, then, was one of the facets of regional continuity and regional transformation that he could not deny and would not ignore" (429). See also James Snead's *Figures of Division*.

17. In no way, however, do I intend to imply that *Absalom, Absalom!* is humorless— certainly not whenever Mr. Compson takes over the narration!

18. The outsized proliferation of animals can be seen as one minor example of García

Márquez's much discussed "magical realism," a critical category that fits within my notion of the noncosmopolitan aesthetic. The magical happenings that are accepted as normal *within* Macondo wondrously resist the homogenizing gaze of accepted Western knowledge, suggesting that there are worlds that will always be unknown to the outsider. At the same time, the narrative point of view—what makes them "magical" and not merely "real"—requires separation. Lois Parkinson Zamora and Wendy B. Faris's anthology is the best place to start in following up the copious criticism on magical realism; see especially their introduction and the bibliography.

19. For a fuller discussion of this scene, see José David Saldívar's " 'Squeezed by the Banana Company.' "

20. The relationship between Sutpen's legitimate and illegitimate sons, Henry and Bon (as narrated by Mr. Compson), provides another form for displaying and splaying myths of North and South, cosmopolitan and provincial, a division complicated by the fact that Bon is both the sophisticate, as a city-dweller who has traveled, and the "savage," for he has that drop of black blood, the mystery of Catholicism, and lives in New Orleans (pre-twentieth-century America's contact zone par excellence). Bon's "seduction" of both Henry and Judith sets up a contrast between Henry the provincial versus Bon the urban/cosmopolitan replete with humorous regional crossings that are usually erased in the overdetermined divisions of North and South.

21. The dramatization of history as problematic (and the fact that that view is dramatized at all linguistic levels and not only in direct exposition) in *Absalom, Absalom!* has surely contributed to its continuing critical acclaim in a period when most of our grand narratives, historical and otherwise, have been deconstructed.

22. The malleability of history is established early on in the aftermath of Colonel Aureliano Buendía's unsuccessful suicide attempt: "The failure of his death brought back his lost prestige in a few hours. The same people who invented the story that he had sold the war for a room with walls made of gold bricks defined the attempt at suicide as an act of honor and proclaimed him a martyr" (172).

23. Writing and literacy as problematic comes out in myriad forms in *One Hundred Years of Solitude*. Writing—traditionally tied to the North, the rational, the dominant culture—is highly valued among the studious members of the Buendía clan. Examples range from the poems of Colonel Aureliano Buendía to the letters of misrepresentation between Fernanda del Carpio and her children. Yet writing is often associated with sickness or problem, an imperfect solution for the troubled. When the insomnia plague hits, soon after the founding of Macondo, for example, writing is believed to be the cure, but it eventually fails: "Thus they went on living in a reality that was slipping away, momentarily captured by words, but which would escape irremediably when they forgot the values of the written letters" (53). In the end, even the Catalan bookseller repudiates the life of the mind, suggesting to his acolytes that they "shit on Horace" (370).

24. Counterintuitively, perhaps, I believe my "noncosmopolitanism" also dovetails with recent, positive rewritings of "cosmopolitanism"; broadly speaking, see Pheng Cheah and Bruce Robbins's anthology *Cosmopolitics*; more specifically, see Robbins's "Introduction" and his "Comparative Cosmopolitanisms." Speaking of a hoped-for

cosmopolitanism of the left in the latter, Robbins questions the too-easy assumption of a connection between agency and the particular (252), concluding with a call for "cosmopolitanism as the provocatively impure but irreducible combination of a certain privilege at home, as part of a real belonging in institutional places, with a no less real but much less common . . . extension of democratic, anti-imperial principles abroad" (261). Whereas Robbins takes to task left academics—and I include myself among the general target group—for not recognizing their cosmopolitanism, my emphasis is on recognizing the noncosmopolitanism that is part of the work of Faulkner and García Márquez. The seeming opposition of these two positions dissolves when one notes that Robbins focuses on the work of academics and looks to the future while my essay focuses on the earlier work of novelists and leafs through the past. My reading of these novels through the lens of the noncosmopolitan aesthetic makes no claims to the "authentically" local, for I see these texts as engaged and engaging, and I see the noncosmopolitan aesthetic as both a writing and reading strategy that connects with Robbins's call for a "cosmopolitanism" of "multiple attachment" ("Introduction" 3). But the "non-" seems necessary for the analysis of these texts in order to highlight oppositions that have been erased, opposition to an *earlier* cosmopolitanism that, in Robbins's words, "has often seemed to claim universality by virtue of its independence, its detachment from the bonds, commitments, and affiliations that constrain ordinary nation-bound lives. It has seemed to be a luxuriously free-floating view from above" ("Introduction" 1). And it is this cosmopolitanism that has masked the cultural politics of exclusion.

25. Or, in another direction, one could say that in some sense both novels share something with detective novels (oft a refuge for marginal individuals), without arguing that they belong in that genre. The morality in these often amoral detective stories is in getting to the Truth in whatever way possible. A driving force in these novels is a desire for clarification, of a world often obfuscated by more-powerful others. They evoke, just like mysteries, the problem of locating the authoritative voice, for there is always a risk of confusing revelation with imagination. A key distinction, however, between these novels of detection and detective fiction is that in the former there is some sense of group representation that does not exist in paradigmatic detective novels. Whereas the detective ultimately compensates for the absence of truly omniscient narrators by concluding with clarification, these two novels resolve with the sense of still further stories to be told and learned.

WORKS CITED

Bhabha, Homi K. *The Location of Culture.* Routledge: London, 1994.
Blotner, Joseph. *Faulkner: A Biography.* 2 vols. New York: Random, 1974.
Brennan, Timothy. *Salman Rushdie and the Third World.* New York: St. Martin's, 1989.
Chevigny, Bell Gale. "Teaching Comparative Literature of the United States and Spanish America." *American Literature* 65 (1993): 354–58.
Cohn, Deborah N. *History and Memory in the Two Souths: Recent Southern and Spanish American Fiction.* Nashville, Tenn.: Vanderbilt UP, 1999.

Cowley, Malcolm. *The Faulkner-Cowley File: Letters and Memories, 1944–1962.* New York: Viking, 1966.

Davis, Thadious M. "Race and Region." *The Columbia History of the American Novel.* Ed. Emory Elliott. New York: Columbia UP, 1991. 407–36.

Dekker, George. *The American Historical Romance.* Cambridge: Cambridge UP, 1987.

Du Bois, W. E. B. *The Souls of Black Folk.* Ed. Henry Louis Gates Jr. and Terri Hume Oliver. New York: Norton, 1999.

Faulkner, William. *Absalom, Absalom!* 1936. New York: Vintage, 1987.

——. "An Introduction to *The Sound and the Fury.*" Ed. James B. Meriwether. *Mississippi Quarterly* 26 (summer 1973): 410–15.

——. *Selected Letters of William Faulkner.* Ed. Joseph Blotner. New York: Random, 1977.

García, Samuel. *Tres mil años de literatura en "Cien años de soledad": Intertextualidad en la obra de García Márquez.* Medellín: Ediciones Paragrama, 1977.

García Márquez, Gabriel. "Latin America's Impossible Reality." Trans. Elena Brunet. *Harper's* (Jan. 1985): 13–15.

——. *One Hundred Years of Solitude.* 1967. Trans. Gregory Rabassa. New York: Avon, 1971.

——. "The Solitude of Latin America." Trans. Marina Castañeda. *Lives on the Line.* Ed. Doris Meyer. Berkeley: U of California P, 1988. 230–34.

Godzich, Wlad. "Emergent Literature and the Field of Comparative Literature." *The Comparative Perspective on Literature.* Ed. Clayton Koelb and Susan Noakes. Ithaca, N.Y.: Cornell UP, 1988. 18–36.

Harss, Luis, and Barbara Dohmann. "Gabriel García Márquez, or the Lost Chord." *Into the Mainstream.* New York: Harper, 1967. 310–41.

Hobson, Fred. *Serpent in Eden: H. L. Mencken and the South.* Chapel Hill: U of North Carolina P, 1974.

Ivask, Ivar. "Allegro Barbaro, or Gabriel García Márquez in Oklahoma." *Books Abroad* 47 (1975): 419–40.

Johnson, Dane. "The Rise of Gabriel García Márquez and Toni Morrison." *Cultural Institutions of the Novel.* Ed. Deidre Lynch and William B. Warner. Durham, N.C.: Duke UP, 1996. 129–56.

Kreyling, Michael. *Inventing Southern Literature.* Jackson: UP of Mississippi, 1998.

McPherson, Karen. "*Absalom, Absalom!* Telling Scratches." *Modern Fiction Studies* 33 (1987): 431–50.

Mencken, H. L. "The Sahara of the Bozart." *Prejudices: Second Series.* New York: Knopf, 1920. 136–54.

Millgate, Michael. "*Absalom, Absalom!*" *The Achievement of William Faulkner.* New York: Random, 1966. 150–164.

Morrison, Toni. "Rootedness: The Ancestor as Foundation." *Black Women Writers (1950–1980).* Ed. Mari Evans. New York: Anchor, 1984. 339–45.

Pratt, Mary Louise. "Criticism in the Contact Zone: Decentering Community and Nation." *Critical Theory, Cultural Politics, and Latin American Narrative.* Ed. Steven M. Bell, Albert H. Le May, and Leonard Orr. Notre Dame, Ind.: U of Notre Dame P, 1993. 83–102.

Robbins, Bruce. "Comparative Cosmopolitanisms." *Cosmopolitics: Thinking and Feeling beyond the Nation.* Ed. Pheng Cheah and Bruce Robbins. Minneapolis: U of Minnesota P, 1998. 247–64.

——. "Introduction Part I: Actually Existing Cosmopolitanism." *Cosmopolitics: Thinking and Feeling beyond the Nation.* Ed. Pheng Cheah and Bruce Robbins. Minneapolis: U of Minnesota P, 1998. 1–19.

Saldívar, José David. " 'Squeezed by the Banana Company': Dependency and Ideology in Macondo." *The Dialectics of Our America.* Durham, N.C.: Duke UP, 1991. 23–48.

Sheppard, R. Z. "Numero Uno." Review of *The Autumn of the Patriarch* by Gabriel García Márquez. *Time* 1 Nov. 1976: 87.

Smith, Jon. "Southern Culture on the Skids: Punk, Retro, Narcissism, and the Burden of Southern History." *South to a New Place: Region, Literature, Culture.* Ed. Suzanne W. Jones and Sharon Monteith. Baton Rouge: Louisiana State UP, 2002. 76–95.

Snead, James A. *Figures of Division: William Faulkner's Major Novels.* New York: Methuen, 1986.

Sommer, Doris. *Foundational Fictions.* Berkeley: U of California P, 1991.

Spillers, Hortense J. "Introduction: Who Cuts the Border? Some Readings on 'America.' " *Comparative American Identities: Race, Sex, and Nationality in the Modern Text.* Ed. Hortense Spillers. New York: Routledge, 1991. 1–25.

Spivak, Gayatri. "Can the Subaltern Speak?" *Marxism and the Interpretation of Culture.* Ed. Cary Nelson and Lawrence Grossberg. Urbana: U of Illinois P, 1988. 271–313.

Stein, Gertrude. "Wherein the South Differs from the North." *Useful Knowledge.* 1928. Barrytown, N.Y.: Station Hill, 1988. 19–37.

Zamora, Lois Parkinson, and Wendy B. Faris, eds. *Magical Realism: Theory, History and Community.* Durham, N.C.: Duke UP, 1995.

HELEN OAKLEY

William Faulkner and the Cold War:

The Politics of Cultural Marketing

Over the past few decades, an increasing amount of scholarship has been devoted to the impact of William Faulkner's work on Latin American fiction. This growing trend is part of a wider shift within the discipline of American studies, which is continually expanding its parameters in order to study U.S. culture from a variety of contrasting cultural perspectives. Critics have argued persuasively that Faulkner's modernist narrative techniques helped Latin American writers to break away from constricting Spanish models and that his Southern context reflected their own shared sense of historical defeat and racial conflict.[1] But what about the cultural construction and marketing of Faulkner himself within the Cold War period? An examination of the upsurge in Faulkner's profile in the United States in the late 1940s, in conjunction with the role played by the William Faulkner Foundation and Faulkner's trips to Latin America in the 1950s and 1960s, reveals how seemingly positive cultural interchanges obscure deeper power-related tensions between the United States and Latin America.

At first glimpse it would seem that Faulkner's contact with and reception by Latin American writers produced an opportunity to exchange knowledge that was beneficial to both parties. Faulkner had his first direct contact with Latin America in 1954, when he attended an international writers' conference at São Paulo as part of the celebrations for the city's quadricentennial. Faulkner stayed in Brazil for five days and afterward announced that he intended to study Hispanic literature and make a return visit.

In 1961 he returned to Latin America, this time to Venezuela. As Harley D. Oberhelman notes, "The visit to Venezuela was an effort by the United States government working in concert with the North American Association of Venezuela to cement relations between the two countries" (15). In a letter written in May 1961, Muna Lee, Office of Public Affairs adviser in Washington at the time, quotes C. Allan Stewart, a member of the embassy who had witnessed Faulkner's visit and testified to the warm welcome that he received: "William Faulkner's trip is one of the greatest boons to U.S.-Venezuelan relations that has happened for a long time. He was decorated by the Minister of Education this morning with the order of Andrés Bello, First Class, reserved only for the highest intellectual figures. He responded to the Minister's award speech by reading a statement in excellent Spanish."[2]

In the first substantial critical work on the subject of Faulkner's relationship with Latin American fiction James East Irby argues that Faulkner was a member of a "lost generation" whose work makes use of experimental techniques in order to react against the sense of disillusionment and fragmentation in American life that had been created by the advent of World War I. According to Irby, Faulkner and his contemporaries in the United States influenced a subsequent generation of Latin American writers of the 1930s and 1940s, who were undergoing "la crisis del realismo" [the crisis of realism], which meant that they were rejecting constraining Spanish models and searching for new artistic inspiration from other countries such as the United States (36).

Contemporary critics have assessed Faulkner's impact on more recent Latin American fiction dating from the so-called "Boom" in Latin American writing in the 1960s and 1970s. Issues that have been explored include the ways in which the legacy of the Civil War, racial turmoil, and economic underdevelopment—which form the context to Faulkner's fiction—strike resonances in the work of later writers such as the Mexican Carlos Fuentes and the Colombian Gabriel García Márquez. For example, Mark Frisch examines how both the U.S. South and Latin America have been subject to shared processes of social change: "El desarrollo tecnológico veloz, las migraciones desde las áreas rurales, el crecimiento de las grandes ciudades y la transición de una cultura agraria a una cultura industrializada han alterado la relación del hombre con la tierra" ["The rapid technological development, the migrations from the rural areas, the growth of the big cities, and the transition from an agrarian culture to an industrial culture have altered the relationship of man with the earth"] (17).

Many contemporary Latin American writers have openly admitted their debt to Faulkner. One author who has been particularly forthcoming about his admiration for Faulkner is the Uruguayan Juan Carlos Onetti. In his *Réquiem* he seems to eulogize Faulkner almost as a personal God. The subtitle itself, "Padre y maestro mágico" ("Father and Magical Teacher") implies a parental and submissive relationship (164). Onetti states that "Era, literariamente, uno de los más grandes artistas del siglo" ["He was, literally, one of the greatest writers of the century"] (166). Onetti then equates Faulkner's importance to American literature with Shakespeare's to English literature.

However, although Faulkner was certainly warmly received by Latin America in general, and by Onetti in particular, his role was not necessarily entirely liberating. Although Onetti seems to be accepting a patriarchal model, he has also expressed his views about the constricting power of Spanish influence on Latin American writing, which implies a more universal point that the concept of influence can be equated with the invasion of indigenous creativity. Onetti writes, "Pero no hay aún una literatura nuestra, no tenemos un libro donde podamos encontrarnos . . . Se trata del lenguaje del escritor; cuando aquél no nace de su tierra, espontáneo e inconfundible, como un fruto del árbol, no es instrumento apto para la expresión total" ["But we still do not have our own literature, we do not have a book where we can find ourselves. . . . It's a question of the writer's language; when it is not born of the land, spontaneously, unmistakably, like the fruit of the tree, it is not a suitable tool for total expression"] (18, qtd. in Tavarelli 146).

Onetti does not claim that Faulkner represents the voice of U.S. cultural imperialism nor that he actively tried to impose cultural control over Latin American fiction. However, the manner in which Faulkner was promoted abroad by intellectual elites as well as by the U.S. government inevitably caused his legacy to be assimilated into cultural battles waged by the United States during the Cold War.

Contemporary Latin American writer Gabriel García Márquez has publicly stated that he has experienced Faulkner's influence as inhibiting. Although paradoxically acknowledging Faulkner's importance to Latin American fiction, he has nevertheless portrayed himself as locked in a struggle with an annoying pest who will not leave him alone: "That's why I have said that my problem was not how to imitate Faulkner, but how to destroy him. His influence had screwed me up" (qtd. in Márquez 93). García Márquez's comment can be interpreted not as an outright rejection of Faulkner himself but rather as an acknowledgment of the ways in which the critical construction of Faulkner's reputation can throw a daunting shadow over contemporary writers who are trying to establish their own individual identity.

In order to understand why Faulkner came to have such a powerful effect on Latin American fiction it is necessary to trace how he was culturally constructed by U.S. critics and subsequently marketed abroad. Although reviews and translations of Faulkner's work started trickling into the Latin American literary scene in the 1930s and 1940s, it was in the 1950s that promotion of his works in Latin America increased dramatically. The resurrection of Faulkner's reputation within the United States in the late 1940s and early 1950s caused a radical domino effect that precipitated his rise to international fame. That in turn caused the concept of "Faulkner" to be exported to Latin America as a cultural commodity.

In a persuasive argument, Lawrence H. Schwartz examines the political reasons for Faulkner's rapid rise to fame in the postwar period. Schwartz's line of reasoning is unusual in that it situates Faulkner within the cultural context of the Cold War rather than seeing him as a "self-conscious modernist" (2) who helped to activate the Southern Renaissance. Schwartz concentrates on how critics such as Malcolm Cowley played an active role in rerouting the direction of Faulkner criticism in the late 1940s, whereas in the 1930s and early 1940s some Faulkner critics tended to regard his work as primarily lurid and melodramatic (see Lewis).

Cowley's publication of *The Portable Faulkner* in 1946 marked a turning point, as the very elements of Faulkner's work that had been disparaged were now considered to be among its strongest assets. Faulkner was interpreted not so much as a southern regionalist but more as a spokesman for the exploration of universal moral themes. His propensity for portraying violent scenes in his fiction, far from being assessed as sleazy sensationalism, was transmuted into a drama that stressed "the individual struggle against an irrational world" (Schwartz 36).

Cowley's introduction to *The Portable Faulkner* bears out some of the points that Schwartz makes, although it does not reveal an attitude entirely uncritical of Faulkner. For example, Cowley is skeptical about Faulkner's stylistic experiments: "Two or three of his books as a whole and many of them in part are awkward experiments" (4). However, overall, Cowley does take an assenting view of Faulkner, interpreting the sensational elements of Faulkner's novels as important symbols that effectively dramatize problems of universal import. For example, Cowley argues that Popeye's commission of the corn-cob rape in *Sanctuary* is analogous to the rape of America by "mechanical civilization" (15).

Schwartz focuses on the way in which the New York intellectuals and New Critics who contributed to *Partisan Review* championed the avant-garde as part of the universal struggle for the assertion of man's freedom and right for democracy. Although the ideological outlooks of the intellectual groups who contributed to this journal were various, they shared "the underlying ideology" that implied that aesthetic pronouncements on literature were "to be judged by 'men of letters' and with political disinterest" (157).

Nevertheless, the seemingly apolitical abstraction of Faulkner from his southern context was in fact a supremely political statement, inextricably linked to the demands of Cold War ideology: "In the arts, so the argument went, the United States encouraged individual expression and experimentation, while the Soviet Union accepted only the monolithic, the banal, and the propagandistic" (201). The awarding of the Nobel Prize to Faulkner in this context was not only a rewarding of his intrinsic merits but also, equally, an acknowledgment of the ideological power of the United States.

By the 1950s, Faulkner's reputation had soared considerably. For example, in a 1951 article in *Partisan Review*, Harvey Breit argues that Faulkner "typifies the main line of the American creative impulse" and that his work reveals the distinctively American characteristics of "isolation, introspection, moralism" (89). Notably, Breit suggests that Faulkner's work explores the individual struggle against mechanization and mass production: "He believes the present is a machine age which, though it has not destroyed the writers, is destroying their material" (93). Breit does not overtly push a particular political cause, yet the strong emphasis he places on Faulkner's American democratic values suggests that they symbolize a valiant struggle against global instability caused by a variety of threatening elements such as communism.[3]

In a provocative study of the CIA's manipulation of cultural warfare during the Cold War, Frances Stonor Saunders argues that intellectuals connected with *Partisan Review* were closely involved with cultural organizations funded by the CIA, organizations designed to promote U.S. artistic achievement with a clear anticommunist purpose. For example, Sidney Hook was an important driving force behind the foundation of the American Committee for Cultural Freedom in 1951 (Saunders 157).

This organization was affiliated with the European Congress for Cultural Freedom, which from 1950 to 1967 played a vital role in disseminating U.S. ideology in western Europe. In 1952 *Partisan Review* published a symposium entitled "Our Country and Our Culture," which "confirmed a new and positive relationship between intellectuals and the nation state" (159). In fact, Saunders claims, in 1953 *Partisan Review* received a grant of $2,500 from the "festival account" of the Committee for Cultural Freedom, which put up the money from CIA funds. When later questioned as to whether *Partisan Review* had ever received CIA backing, coeditor William Phillips denied it.

The expansion of the book market and the role of the mass media also need to be taken into account in understanding the various ways in which a strongly nationalistic version of U.S. cultural identity was promoted. Critical interest in Faulkner could not be sustained without some corresponding degree of success in the commercial marketplace. Although in the war economy certain goods were rationed, books were readily obtainable. The anxieties generated by the war itself meant an increased demand for news, which in turn generated profits for the book industry itself. Schwartz points out that it was not until after Faulkner won the Nobel Prize in the 1950s that his marketability soared, and so the beginnings of the expansion in the postwar book market preceded Faulkner's meteoric rise to fame by a few years.

Another significant factor was the growing internationalization of the book market during this period. One of the first enterprises of this nature was "Overseas Editions," which comprised "a series in English or translation that would be distributed in the liberated areas of Western Europe" (Schwartz 49). The explosion in the book market coincided with an expansionist U.S. foreign policy. Schwartz's argument can therefore be appropriated into a discussion of Faulkner's impact in Latin America. He was not simply discovered by the earnest readership of Latin American writers but was actively propelled onto the international scene by U.S. market forces that identified his work as a valuable cultural commodity. U.S. foreign policy was therefore interlinked with a process of artistic colonization: "With the absence of British, French, German, and Japanese competition, American publishers moved aggressively, under a series of postwar government support and propaganda programs, to create, for the first time, an export market" (50).

The celebration of writers such as Faulkner by elite intellectual circles in the late 1940s occurred alongside the mass media's promotion of "the American way of life," which also played an important role in the cultural Cold War. Magazines such as *Life*, which was directed at a middle-class audience, and *Daily News*, which was aimed more at a working-class readership, tended to advocate Truman's increasingly interventionist and anticommunist international stance. African American magazines such as *Ebony* were critical about the government's attitude toward civil rights, but they still supported intervention in Korea in 1950.

Also, visual images of U.S. global power became prevalent in magazine advertising during this period: "These messages were most conspicuously embodied in representations of world-wide air travel as a defining feature of American consumer culture in the new 'Air-Age World' " (Fousek 73). The mass media's emphasis on the capacity of the United States to reach all areas of the world contributed to the depiction of its role as moral "redeemer" and "exemplar": "As redeemer, the United States actively brings its values to the world. As exemplar it sets a model for the world to follow" (83).

Parallels can therefore be drawn between the emphasis that the mass media placed on the ethical guiding role of the United States and the way in which journals such as *Partisan Review* presented Faulkner's work as to some extent morally redeeming. The CIA was well aware of the ideological power of the media in shaping international public opinion, and it funded magazines in Europe and Latin America. These journals acted as cultural filters for U.S. propaganda without being overtly linked to the CIA. For example, as Saunders documents, the 1950s saw the founding of *Encounter* in England, *Quadrant* in Australia, *Quest* in India, and *Jiyu* in Japan. *Cuadernos* was aimed at Latin American intellectuals, and it was founded in 1953 from Paris by Julian Gorkin. *Mundo Nuevo*, another journal directed at Latin Americans, was also based in Paris. These magazines published a diverse range of articles that helped introduce major icons of U.S. culture, such as Faulkner, to a wider audience.

Another method employed by the U.S. government to disseminate U.S. ideology was to sponsor conferences and major cultural events overseas. The American Committee for Cultural Freedom was instrumental in financing the "Masterpieces of the Twentieth Century" festival, which was staged in Paris in April 1952. The Boston Symphony orchestra was presented "as a billboard for America's symphonic virtuosity" (Saunders 125). The literary dimension of the festival featured debates on topics prescribed by the committee. Faulkner was asked to contribute to the literary discussions, which focused on universal issues such as isolation, communication, and revolt.

Faulkner had participated in several successful trips to Europe, so it is not surprising that he was approached in order to extend the influence of U.S. artistic supremacy in Latin America. On a closer reading, Faulkner's trips to Latin America, which were sponsored by the U.S. government, appear to be politically motivated visits that partly covered up troubled U.S. foreign policy toward Latin America. The following letter from Philip Raine reveals that the United States was having problems creating a good cultural relationship with Brazil, and it was not keen on letting in potential dissident elements. Raine sends the letter on behalf of the U.S. government in reply to a dispatch sent in May by the consulate general of São Paulo regarding Faulkner's proposed visit to Brazil in 1954.

> U.S. participation in the Writer's Congress, with at least such limited official support as this travel grant to William Faulkner would represent, is particularly desirable because of the flood of adverse publicity which the Department received because of alleged indifference and non-support of the U.S. exhibits in the International Exhibition of Modern Art which was a pre-Quadricentennial event inaugurating the series of festivities. . . . A further reason for officially sponsoring our Nobel winner is the bitter criticism made of us in the Brazilian press when the Brazilian writer, Joao Lins de Rago [José Lins do Rego], was temporarily denied a U.S. visa because of alleged connections with political fellow travelers and favorable reviews of his work in some leftist papers. Although he was later given his visa, the incident clouded our cultural relations with Brazil to some extent. It is ARA/R's urgent recommendation that IES make every effort to secure William Faulkner's participation in the International Writer's Congress at São Paulo. (BP 9–11)

It is worth pausing here to consider the general state of U.S.-Latin American relations contemporary to Faulkner's 1954 trip. Eisenhower's policy toward Latin America in the mid-1950s was very much geared to the Cold War. As Stephen G. Rabe has observed, the struggle against communism tended to take precedence over attempts to improve human rights or economic conditions in Latin America: "In pursuit of hemispheric solidarity, the Eisenhower administration would, in 1953 and 1954, offer money, medals, and military support to Latin American leaders who were anti-Communists, including those who were dictators" (26).

The drive to eliminate what was perceived as the infiltration of communism from Latin America resulted in the imposition by the United States of its own anticommunist propaganda. The Eisenhower Administration believed that President Truman's Latin American foreign policies had lacked direction and had been too lenient toward the communist threat. In contrast, Eisenhower's government was determined to "turn the tide against the red menace" (Rabe 29). Anticommunist propaganda produced in the United States was widely distributed in Latin America. Rabe notes that the U.S. Information Agency spent approximately $5.2 million a year in the distribution of 90,000 anticommunist cartoon books, which were sent to Central America, as well as anticommunist comic books for Latin American newspapers and scripts for radio shows in Cuba.

Although there is no hard evidence to suggest that Faulkner's trip formed part of an anticommunist plot staged by the U.S. government, it is surely not coincidental that the visit to Brazil took place in 1954, the year in which the CIA offensive to wipe out the threat of communism in Guatemala had reached its most intense stage. In this sensitive climate, the promotion of good relations with other Latin American countries would have been paramount to the U.S. government, and the use of culture as an ideological tool was an indirect way of doing so. Additionally, U.S.-Brazilian relations had also been strained because the United States nearly reneged on a loan that had been promised to Brazil by the previous administration. Eisenhower wished to halve the loan that Truman had agreed to, but he gave in to pressure to fulfill the original promise, particularly as in 1950 the United States had loaned $125 million to Argentina. The U.S. government's intensive drive to root out communism in Latin America had the effect of risking economic neglect and subsequent alienation of many countries.

A report on Faulkner's trip to Venezuela written in 1962 by a government official called Hugh Jencks also presents his visit in the cultural context of the Cold War: "The cultural leaders of Venezuela, many of whom are predisposed to take an anti-U.S. attitude on all international issues, include writers, artists, newspaper commentators (particularly those connected with *El Nacional*), educators and people in government. The group also includes many on-the-fencers. Its members tend to agree with the Communist tenet that the United States is grossly materialistic, with no cultural achievements. To bring a literary figure of the stature of Faulkner to Venezuela was an effective refutation of this view."[4]

The state of U.S.-Latin American relations in the late 1950s, in the years leading up to Faulkner's Venezuelan trip, were approaching a new crisis point. On Vice President Nixon's tour of Latin America in 1958, he was harassed by angry protestors in Montevideo, Lima, and Caracas. U.S.-Venezuelan relations were particularly rocky at this stage: "Venezuelans, for example, denounced the administration for its past connivance with the deposed Marcos Pérez Jiménez and its present harboring of the fugitive dictator and his chief of secret police, the notorious Pedro Estrada. They also correctly feared that, in order to protect domestic oil producers, the United States was about to limit imports of Venezuelan fuel oil" (Rabe 102).

It is also significant that Faulkner's trip to Venezuela coincided with the crisis in the relationship between the United States and Cuba and the Dominican Republic, just as, rather similarly, the previous decade's trip to Brazil had been organized at the same time as the Guatemalan intervention. In 1960 the Eisenhower Administration became extremely worried about the potential communist threat posed by the right-wing Dominican dictatorship and the increasing links between Cuba and the Soviet Union. This intense anxiety on the part of the United States precipitated campaigns to overthrow Fidel Castro and Rafael Trujillo. In this paranoid climate it was particularly difficult for certain Latin American writers who were thought to be critical of the imperialist nature of U.S. foreign policy to obtain entry into the United States. For example, Carlos Fuentes was denied a visa to appear on an NBC talk show in 1962, and in May 1964 he was again blocked from giving a lecture, although he subsequently obtained a temporary five-day visa, presumably as a result of public pressure.

Ironically, at the same time that some Latin American writers were finding it a struggle to enter the United States, the CIA was actively attempting to gain a stronger degree of cultural control within Latin America. Saunders points out that in 1962, in a manner similar to Faulkner, Robert Lowell was sent as a kind of cultural ambassador to Latin America. In 1964 the CIA intervened to prevent Pablo Neruda from winning the Nobel Prize because of concerns about his supposed communist sympathies. From 1961 to 1963 the Institute of International Labor Research, based in New York, "focused on CIA projects in Latin America, including a seed-bed for democratic political leaders called the Institute of Political Education, which was run by Norman Thomas and Jose Figueres in Costa Rica" (Saunders 355).

Another organization that played a vital ideological role in the unfolding drama of Faulkner's relationship with Latin America was the William Faulkner Foundation, established in 1960 in Charlottesville, Virginia, where Faulkner lived as writer-in-residence in the final years of his life. The foundation used Faulkner's prestige as a means of promoting educational programs within the United States and to further cement good relations with Latin America. The mission statement of the foundation was publicized in June 1961: "Many novels of the highest literary quality written by Ibero-American authors in their native languages are failing to reach appreciative readers in English-speaking North America; accordingly, the William Faulkner Foundation, at the suggestion of William

Faulkner himself, is undertaking a modest corrective program in the hope of contributing to a better cultural exchange between the two Americas, with an attendant improvement in human relations and understanding" (MSS 10677).

The foundation established a competition in which the best Latin American postwar novel from each of fourteen Latin American countries was to be chosen by judges from each of the respective countries. The judges had to be young enough to be aware of the latest literary currents, preferably twenty-five years of age or younger. The award winners from each country, announced in February 1963, included *El astillero* by Juan Carlos Onetti and *Cumboto* by Venezuelan novelist Ramón Díaz Sánchez. All winning entries from the first stage of the competition were then judged against each other in order to obtain one winner. In the event it was *Cumboto*. The grand prize was supposed to be the translation of the winner's novel into English. However, despite the expansion in the publishing market that Schwartz identifies at this point, some U.S. publishers were still resistant to imports from Latin America. The William Faulkner Foundation wrote numerous letters to all kinds of publishers in an attempt to get *Cumboto* translated and published, but it received many rejection letters. The following extract from a letter sent to the foundation in July 1966 by W. W. Norton and Company sums up the general attitude of publishers toward the book: "We have had a reading now of *Cumboto*, the Faulkner award novel, and I am sorry to say we are not going to make an offer of publication. It is most certainly a worthy book, but I am afraid it would elicit very little response from a broadly-based North American audience, which I suppose is another way of saying it does not seem to us to be important enough to be worth the time and effort of translation and publication" (MSS 10677).

This placed the foundation in a very embarrassing position. It had set up the competition in order to promote appreciation of Latin American writing within the United States, but it was blocked by market forces beyond its control. While it is clear that the foundation itself was obviously not part of a conspiracy designed to defraud Latin American writers, a bitter letter from the prize-winner himself, Ramón Díaz Sánchez, sent to the foundation in July 1965, reveals how he came to view his award as a hollow mockery. It is worth quoting him at length.

The resistance of North American publishers to publish Latin American literary works is well known to me, which is more than sufficiently explained by the contempt with which the people of North America look down on our Southern countries, on their institutions, their history, and their language. I had thought that the prize for a novel granted by the William Faulkner Foundation was actually aiming to help break down this barrier of contempt and inexorable utilitarianism which the North Americans have created between the two racial zones of the New World and to lend a bit of ethical and aesthetic dignity to the relationship between the greatest power of modern history and our small and under-developed countries.

The only satisfaction and the only positive value that such a tournament could give us, the writers of Latin America, would be the publication in the U.S. of the books produced in our countries and which carry a message of good faith, because besides this there is nothing very attractive about the giving away of a metal disk not any more important or honoring than those distributed for propaganda purposes for international industrial products. By this I do not mean to say that I consider the Faulkner prize to be a mere artifice invented for advertising one of these products, but the truth is that up to this moment, it looks quite a bit like it. (MSS 10677)

Eventually, in March 1967, the foundation did receive an acceptance letter, from the University of Texas Press, which offered to publish *Cumboto* using a different English translation, but unfortunately this occurred after the novelist's death.

The study of the cultural construction and marketing of Faulkner in Latin America exposes how he was inevitably drawn into the power struggles played out in the wider political arena. It is important not to dismiss the undoubted benefits received by Latin American writers through means of direct contact with Faulkner's fiction itself nor to deny that Faulkner himself believed there was a positive point behind his trips to Latin America. However, Faulkner's visits to Brazil and Venezuela cannot be bracketed off from the political context of the U.S. government's increasingly imperialist anticommunist foreign policy during the 1950s and 1960s. The CIA was closely involved with many seemingly independent magazines, and it certainly made efforts to export cultural products in Europe and Latin America in the name of freedom and democracy. The effect of this discussion is to reveal how comparative analysis can defamiliarize the way that major icons of U.S. culture are perceived.

NOTES

1. See Irby; Frisch; Fayen; and Cohn. Hereafter, all quotations in Spanish will be accompanied by a translation in English. Unless otherwise stated, all translations are my own.

2. Quoted from a letter by Muna Lee, contained in the Blotner Papers, University of South East Missouri, Cape Girardeau, Missouri, box 9-28. Hereafter, all quotations from the Blotner Papers will be indicated by the initials BP, followed by the box number.

3. See Guilbaut. Guilbaut argues that commentators who wrote in *Partisan Review* deployed the same kind of ironic apolitical politicism to their criticism of art, just as Schwartz states was the case with articles written about Faulkner. Guilbaut illustrates how abstract art's formlessness and seeming neutrality seemed to offer a liberal alternative to left- or right-wing extremism, and governmental agencies soon appropriated it as a cultural weapon in the Cold War. Although Guilbaut and Schwartz's approaches are similar, Guilbaut attributes greater self-consciousness of ideological orientation to the abstract artists themselves than Schwartz does to Faulkner.

4. Quote in a report by Hugh Jencks, contained in the Special Collections, University of Virginia, MSS 7258F. Hereafter, all quotations from the collection at the University of Virginia will be indicated by the prefix MSS followed by the box number.

WORKS CITED

Breit, Harvey. "A Sense of Faulkner." *Partisan Review* 18 (1951): 88–94.

Cohn, Deborah N. *History and Memory in the Two Souths: Recent Southern and Spanish American Fiction.* Nashville, Tenn.: Vanderbilt UP, 1999.

Faulkner, William. *The Portable Faulkner.* Ed. Malcolm Cowley. New York: Viking, 1946.

Fayen, Tanya T. *In Search of the Latin American Faulkner.* Lanham, Md.: UP of America, 1995.

Fousek, John. *To Lead the Free World: American Nationalism and the Cultural Roots of the Cold War.* Chapel Hill: U of North Carolina P, 2000.

Frisch, Mark F. *William Faulkner: Su influencia en la literatura hispanoamericana: Mallea, Rojas, Yáñez y García Márquez.* Trans. Rolando Costa Picazo. Buenos Aires: Corregidor, 1993.

Guilbaut, Serge. *How New York Stole the Idea of Modern Art: Abstract Expressionism, Freedom, and the Cold War.* Trans. Arthur Goldhammer. Chicago: U of Chicago P, 1983.

Irby, James East. "La influencia de William Faulkner en cuatro narradores latinoamericanos: Lino Novás Calvo, Juan Carlos Onetti, José Revueltas, Juan Rulfo." M.A. thesis. Universidad Nacional Autónoma de México, 1956.

Lewis, Wyndham. "William Faulkner (The Moralist with a Corn Cob)." *Men Without Art.* London: Cassell, 1934. 42–64.

Márquez, Antonio C. "Faulkner in Latin America." *Faulkner Journal* 11.1–2 (1995–1996): 83–100.

Oberhelman, Harley D. *The Presence of Faulkner in the Writings of Gabriel García Márquez.* Lubbock: Texas Tech UP, 1980.

Onetti, Juan Carlos. *Réquiem por Faulkner y otros artículos.* Montevideo: Arca Editorial, 1975.

Rabe, Stephen G. *Eisenhower and Latin America: The Foreign Policy of Anticommunism.* Chapel Hill: U of North Carolina P, 1988.

Saunders, Frances Stonor. *Who Paid the Piper? The CIA and the Cultural Cold War.* London: Granta, 1999.

Schwartz, Lawrence H. *Creating Faulkner's Reputation: The Politics of Modern Literary Criticism.* Knoxville: U of Tennessee P, 1988.

Tavarelli, Evelyn. "Juan Carlos Onetti: A Voice that Has Not Yet Sounded." *Faulkner Journal* 11.1–2 (1995–1996): 146–47.

EARL FITZ

William Faulkner, James Agee, and Brazil:

The American South in Latin American

Literature's "Other" Tradition

The U.S. South has long been linked to Brazilian literature and culture. For many years, scholars have in particular noted the numerous parallels between Brazil's Northeast and the U.S. South. The noted anthropologist, Charles Wagley, for example, speaks of how the northeast sugar coast became "the Virginia of Brazil" (32), dominating the colonial economy and producing many of Brazil's early statesmen and writers, while the historian Marshall Eakin observes that the Brazilian Northeast is "the rough equivalent of the U. S. South" (71), with its arid, poverty-ridden *sertão* (backlands) like a Brazilian Appalachia. The eminent Brazilian sociologist Gilberto Freyre underscores this argument, noting, "In the South of the United States, there evolved, from the seventeenth to the eighteenth century, an aristocratic type of rural family that bore a greater resemblance to the type of family in northern Brazil before abolition than it did to the Puritan bourgeoisie . . . of North America" (401). Literary scholar Fred P. Ellison also finds this comparison valid, commenting, with regard to the social, economic, and cultural parallels between the Brazilian Northeast and the Deep South of the United States, that "there is a strong resemblance. Like the South, the Northeast was during the colonial era the center of a rich agricultural economy based not on cotton so much as on sugar cane, and its society was an aristocracy of large landholders marshaling armies of slaves. . . . The parallel of our Old South with the Northeast of Brazil is striking indeed" (*Novel* 3, 7). Finally, as if in summation, literary historian Samuel Putnam finds that "there exists a peculiar affinity between our South and the Brazilian northeast where slave-owning, sugar-planting patriarchs held sway" (9).[1]

But there are other parallels as well. As in the Brazilian Northeast, the U.S. South did not develop a diversified colonial economy; it did not begin to encourage a comprehensive system of public education until 1865 (New England had done so by the middle of the sixteenth century); and it did not erect a social structure in which socioeconomic mobility was easily attained or in which sociopolitical change was easily accommodated. Finally, the U.S. South suffered a terrible civil war, one larger and more protracted than the conflict that afflicted the Brazilian Northeast between 1896 and 1897 but not more wrenching in its immediate effects or in its long term aftermath. In both Brazil and the United States, the specter of this civil war (including the regional differences that spawned it) has continued to haunt all aspects of their societies, becoming, finally, a defining point of reference for both cultures.

It comes as no surprise, then, that the literature of the U.S. South, particularly William Faulkner's, has also figured prominently in the development of letters in Brazil, though it would seem (certain specific cases notwithstanding) to be less a matter of traditional influence and reception than of the Brazilian intelligentsia's recognition of a great writer and of the numerous cultural and thematic affinities that exist between his work and the Brazilian social, political, and aesthetic experience. In essence, Brazilian writers, readers, and critics of the 1930s saw in Faulkner's stories and novels a great many things that were of keen interest and that they felt they understood, but at least three issues would have resonated deeply—and restively—with them: race, class, and history (more specifically, the weight of the past on the present and future). In many ways, but perhaps most pointedly in the area of race relations, educated Brazilians of the time would have felt as if they knew Faulkner's world very well. However, the nature of Faulkner's influence in Brazil is very different from the importance Faulkner and his work have in Spanish America, where, surprising as it may be, the American master may be regarded as a legitimate progenitor of the justly famous *nueva novela* (new novel) of the 1960s.[2] Brazil's literary history is quite distinct from that of Spanish America, and this difference is critical in evaluating Faulkner's impact on

Brazilian letters. While Faulkner was rightly regarded as an important and innovative writer in Brazil (a literary culture traditionally very open to and knowledgeable about other literatures and cultures), and while his technical brilliance was widely acknowledged and applauded, he did not fundamentally alter the way fiction would be written in Brazil, as he did in Spanish America. Why this is so has to do with the unique development of creative writing in Brazil and especially with the evolution of its rich, inventive, and cohesive narrative fiction tradition, one that, as Roberto González Echevarría notes, was, by the second half of the nineteenth century, "unequaled in the rest of Latin America in terms of production and quality" (15).

Critics have, for many years, linked Faulkner to a variety of Brazilian writers: Graciliano Ramos (Cerqueira; Oliveira), Guimarães Rosa (Valente; Lowe; Vizzioli; Rodman), Autran Dourado (McClendon; Merquior; Gledson; Patai), Lúcio Cardoso (Putnam); Adonias Filho (Sayers; Ellison; Merquior; Gledson), José Lins do Rego (Daniel; Standley), and Machado de Assis (Shimura). Another prominent Brazilian author, Maria Alice Barroso, long associated with the Brazilian nueva novela of the 1960s, is also thought to have been influenced by Faulkner, especially in works like *História de um casamento* (1960) and *Um simples afeto recíproco* (1963), texts that, as John M. Parker believes, cultivate "the long, clause-ridden Faulknerian sentences" and "the multiple vision achieved through the statements supplied to the questioning narrator by a series of witnesses" (15; see also Patai 46–47). Faulkner was being written about in Brazil already in the late 1930s and early 1940s and had seen "A Rose for Emily" and *Sanctuary* (1931) translated into Portuguese in 1945 and 1948, respectively (Englekirk 88, 95).[3] From 9 August to 14 August 1954, moreover, Faulkner made a State Department-sponsored visit to São Paulo to participate in an International Writers' Congress hosted by the Brazilians, who were eagerly awaiting his visit. During this trip, he learned that *Sanctuary* and *Light in August* (the latter being deeply concerned with miscegenation, an issue of longstanding interest to Brazilians, who often view themselves as a mixed-race people) were his two best-known novels in Brazil and that the writer and critic, Oscar Pimentel, had been an influential advocate of him and his work since the 1930s, when he had come across some Sartre pieces on Faulkner (Monteiro 96, 104).[4] It is clear, then, that by the 1950s, Faulkner was both widely known and greatly admired in Brazil. What is not so clear, however, is the exact nature of this relationship; specifically, what was Faulkner's impact, if any, on the development of narrative fiction in Brazil?

The question is critical because, in answering it, one is naturally led to compare Faulkner's importance to the history of narrative in Brazil with his importance to the evolution of modern narrative in Spanish America, where his influence was crucial to the emergence of the nueva novela. Faulkner's importance to the development of the new narrative in Spanish America has been well studied. The late Emir Rodríguez Monegal, for example, has suggested that Borges's superb 1940 Spanish translation of Faulkner's *The Wild Palms* (*Las palmeras salvajes*) was instrumental in the rise of the "new narrative" in Spanish America, because it so successfully reproduced Faulkner's stylistic nuances and structural innovations as well as his thematic breakthroughs that it in effect showed an entire generation of fledgling Spanish American writers how a new and essentially antirealistic novel might be written (Monegal, *Jorge Luis Borges* 372–73).[5] The Borges translation, observes Monegal, "was not only faithful to the original but created in Spanish a writing style that was the equivalent of the original's English. For many young Latin American novelists who did not know enough English to read the dense original, Borges's tight version meant the discovery of a new kind of narrative writing. They had, in Borges, the best possible guide to Faulkner's dark and intense world" (373).

An equally key point is that Borges would likely have seen in Faulkner's unconventional and largely antimimetic texts a vivid demonstration of the kind of writing he himself was seeking to achieve, also in the 1930s, in his famous *ficciones* (fictions).[6] Borges, in other words, must have recognized in Faulkner a kindred spirit, another writer who was seeking to break free from the confining bonds of realistic fiction. This is undoubtedly why, as Monegal puts it, Borges "praised Faulkner for being as concerned with the verbal artifices of narrative as with the 'passions and works of men' " and why he was so impressed with "Faulkner's ability to play with time," style, and structure (*Jorge Luis Borges* 372–73). Because of the revolutionary nature of Faulkner's novels themselves and because of the extraordinary quality of Borges's translation of *The Wild Palms*—it has been considered "as good or even better than the original" (Monegal 373)—one can easily see how Faulkner's genius directly influenced an entire generation of Spanish American novelists and the nature of the novels they would write.[7] Deborah Cohn is quite right when, summing up his enormous importance to twentieth-century Spanish American narrative, she writes that Faulkner's work, "in conjunction with that of other modern writers, represents a turning point in Spanish American literature" (15), a point after which García Márquez, thinking of the region's history, culture, and literature, will find it possible to speak of the southern United States as constituting the northernmost reaches of Latin America.

Brazil's literary history, however, is different in several important ways from that of Spanish America, a term that refers, rather problematically, not to some monolithic and homogeneous entity but to a highly diverse clutch of nations and regions linked together by a more or less common language (Spanish) but separated by vastly different cultural, political, economic, and historical experiences. The linguistic and historical differences between, say, Honduras, Argentina, and Mexico are so great as to make meaningful comparisons a tricky proposition, even for trained Latin Americanists. So while Portuguese-speaking Brazil is most certainly a part of Latin America (it is, in fact, the largest and wealthiest nation in Latin America and, arguably, the possessor of its most stable and internally coherent literary traditions), the relationship between its narrative tradition and the work of William Faulkner is quite distinct from that of its hemispheric neighbors.

The decisive point, comparatively speaking, has to do with the relative state of the novel form in Brazil and Spanish America during the second half of the nineteenth century, a period dominated, in Latin America, by the techniques and outlooks of European realism and naturalism. The Spanish American novel in particular was suffering from an overly slavish imitation of prevailing European aesthetics, a tendency that, with very few exceptions, had resulted in a novel form that was, as many critics have pointed out, weak and unoriginal. When viewed from a historical perspective the essential problem, according to Alfred Mac Adam, may well have been that "the devices of Realism and Naturalism were not suited to the recreation of Spanish American reality" (21), but it is also imperative that one not underestimate the roles that innovation and originality play in the evolution of a particular literary genre, in this case, Brazilian narrative.

In Brazil, then, the situation was quite distinct, and had been since 1881, the year Machado de Assis saw his *The Posthumous Memoirs of Brás Cubas* appear as a book (it had appeared the year before in serialized form). "A radically different kind of prose fiction" (Mac Adam 21), Machado's landmark novel rejected realism by championing an antirealistic, ironic, and self-referential metafiction, a kind of narrative that had never before been seen in Latin America. As D. P. Gallagher notes, for example, "With the exception of the Brazilian novelist Machado de Assis (1839–1908), Latin American writers in the nineteenth century were usually too immature and too derivative to merit the serious consideration of anyone not specifically interested in the Latin American context as such" (1). Focusing on the revolutionary features of *The Posthumous Memoirs of Brás Cubas*, Mac Adam avers, "Flying in the face of Realism, Machado chose fantasy: His novel is narrated by a dead man. Machado's use of the fantastic, together with his decision to reduce character to stereotype and to present society as a madhouse set him apart from his Latin American contemporaries" (21). Cultivating the complexities and ambiguities of human reality by dismissing the strictures and confines of literary realism (Rabassa 448–49), "Machado invents modern Latin American narrative" (Mac Adam 22), becoming a true innovator in the process, a master whose extensive corpus of novels and short stories is "unrivaled in Latin American letters" (Monegal, *Anthology* 299). In the larger inter-American context, it is also worth noting that Machado (as he is known in Brazil), along with Henry James and Mark Twain (though going, perhaps, even further than his U.S. counterparts), must be credited with elevating the New World novel to the level of a technically sophisticated and intellectually serious art form (Fitz 95–120; Brakel).

In 1881, then, with the appearance of *The Posthumous Memoirs of Brás Cubas*, the Brazilian novel emancipates itself, technically and thematically speaking, from the realistic tradition, something that does not occur in Spanish American narrative until the efforts of Borges and his ficciones in the 1930s (republished together under the title of *Ficciones* in 1944). With Machado's quite spectacular effort (in addition to his subsequent works), the Brazilian novel breaks free from the imitative stance that had long plagued Latin American literature and begins to create its own tradition, one influenced by foreign texts, to be sure, and one hinted at by earlier Brazilian authors (principally, José de Alencar, whose efforts really legitimized the novel form in Brazilian literature), but one that would now begin to develop according to its own principles, designs, and purposes. One can thus conclude that Brazilian narrative tradition, which was characterized after 1881 by an open and deliberate cultivation of revolutionary and essentially antirealistic tendencies and which by the 1930s had entered into its "golden period" (Coutinho 245), did not require the liberating influence that Faulkner brought to Spanish America in the 1930s.

Faulkner, then, was more essential to the development of Spanish America's "new narrative" than he was to Brazil's "new narrative" tradition, which, dating from 1880–1881, had begun some fifty years earlier with Machado de Assis. Although Faulkner was known and admired in Brazil from the 1930s on, and although he can be profitably studied in connection with a host of important Brazilian writers, his overall influence on the evolution of Brazilian narrative is simply not as dramatic or as profound as it is on modern Spanish American narrative. Indeed, four of Brazilian literature's most radical and inventive narratives—Mário de Andrade's ironically mythopoetic *Macunaíma* (1928); Oswald de Andrade's two darkly satiric and deeply subversive antinovels, *The Sentimental Memoirs of John Seaborne* (1924) and *Seraphim Grosse Pointe* (1933); and Patrícia Galvão's cinematic and feminist *Industrial Park* (1933)—show the clear mark of Machado's earlier experiments in style, structure, and point of view, and in so doing amply demonstrate why the Brazilian narrative that was being written at this time was considerably more avant-garde and iconoclastic than the narrative being written in Spanish America during the same period. In sum, Machado did for Brazilian narrative in 1880 what Faulkner and Borges would do in the 1930s for Spanish American narrative.

But Faulkner is not the only writer from the U.S. South to have been linked to Brazilian literature.[8] James Agee, born 27 November 1909 in Knoxville, Tennessee, is an American author whose best work is deeply rooted in his southern heritage. When Agee died in 1955, he was recognized in the United States as a writer who had spent a lifetime struggling with the question of how one perceives and records experience as well as a writer deeply concerned about the ability of art to treat with integrity the moral crises of the twentieth century, one of which, for Agee, was the Great Depression. Although he later gained fame as a film critic and novelist, Agee is perhaps most widely remembered today for the Pulitzer Prize-winning *Let Us Now Praise Famous Men* (1941), an egregiously underappreciated classic of American literature.[9] Deeply idiosyncratic and eclectic in its blending of often very different styles, forms, and tones, and prefaced by several pages of stunning black-and-white photographs by Walker Evans, *Let Us Now Praise Famous Men* chronicles the lives of three Alabama tenant-farmer families—the Gudgers, the Woods, and the Ricketts—in the mid-1930s. Originally a journalistic assignment given to Evans and Agee by *Fortune*, the text that finally emerges is utterly unique, a volatile admixture of impressionistic prose, vivid and powerful poetry, meticulous catalogues and inventories of the houses and possessions of these desperately poor people, and impassioned disquisitions on a variety of social, political, and cultural issues.[10] What ties *Let Us Now Praise Famous Men* together, however (and what really animates it), is its angry, caustic tone, its sense of moral outrage that in a nation as materially rich as the United States people like these have been abandoned, left behind to live out their miserable existences in squalor and hopelessness—a theme that most Brazilians, though most particularly those depicted in Euclides da Cunha's seminal 1902 treatise, *Rebellion in the Backlands*, would immediately recognize and respond to.

In order to contextualize this yoking of Agee and da Cunha (who had published his linguistically very difficult magnum opus nearly forty years before Agee published his), one is well advised to consider for a moment the complex issues of literary history that inform this comparison. In Brazil, naturalism, which developed as a clearly delineated movement and produced several outstanding novels, begins in 1881 (the same year that Machado brought out *The Posthumous Memoirs of Brás Cubas*) and runs until 1902 and the appearance of Graça Aranha's *Canaan* and da Cunha's *Rebellion in the Backlands*. Although Machado, the great emancipator of Brazilian narrative, disparaged naturalism (like Henry James, Machado found it superficial and, finally, boring), he did not hesitate to avail himself of certain of its methods when it suited his purposes to do so. Machado's iconoclastic but canny brilliance was thus coming into its own at precisely the time (the 1880s and 1890s) that naturalism was flourishing in Brazilian letters. But while naturalism lasted approximately twenty years as a coherent movement (one deriving largely from the principles outlined by Émile Zola in *Le Roman experimental* [1880]), its impact was still being felt in Brazilian narrative through the 1930s in works like Graciliano Ramos's *Barren Lives*, Jorge Amado's *The Violent Land*, and Rachel de Queiroz's *The Three Marias*, among many others. By understanding the importance of naturalism to the development of Brazilian narrative, one is better able to understand how it is that a generically hybrid work like *Rebellion in the Backlands* remains so profoundly deterministic—and, for some, pessimistic—even as it breaks new ground in terms of narrative technique.

In the United States, naturalism is, of course, associated with such writers as Steven Crane, Frank Norris, and Theodore Dreiser, their best work becoming synonymous with the so-called proletarian literature of the early twentieth century, a literature that, as in Brazil, increasingly concerned itself with political, social, and economic problems, class conflict, Freudian psychology, unrestricted capitalism, Spencerian "survival of the fittest," biological determinism (an issue widely debated in Brazil and one that da Cunha tried to come to terms with), and Marxism. After 1900, Dreiser gradually became the chief exponent of this movement, his monumental *An American Tragedy*, in many ways the paradigmatic expression of this type of literature, appearing in 1925. Although naturalism would continue to be a powerful force in both Brazil and in the United States (perhaps because of its potency as a force for justice and social change), the new techniques of such European masters as Joyce, Proust, and Kafka were steadily eroding its position and prominence as a literary movement even as they enhanced its moral efficacy in the hands of socially conscious writers. The result was that for da Cunha as well as for

Agee the sharp sense of social pathology that characterizes naturalistic writing at its best was still very much a vital, living tradition, even in a time of artistic change and renewal.

In contrast to Faulkner, however, the connection of Agee and *Let Us Now Praise Famous Men* to Brazilian literature is not a direct one; rather, it is a matter of comparative literary history and rapprochement, a recognition that what it deals with and how it does so have a surprising parallel in a classic work of Brazilian literature, Euclides da Cunha's epic masterpiece *Os Sertões* (1902), known in Samuel Putnam's excellent (if somewhat dramatically enhanced) English translation as *Rebellion in the Backlands.* Like Agee's text, *Rebellion in the Backlands* also deals with a particular subculture, a small group of forgotten people caught in the throes of poverty and despair and left to fend for themselves as the rest of their nation marches forward. And, again like Agee, da Cunha deliberately mixes styles, forms, and tones in order to challenge his readers to face up to some very unpalatable truths about their nation and the codes of conduct by which it purports to live and progress. Finally, both Agee and da Cunha come eventually to defend their miserable subjects, to impart to them a sense of dignity and worth that they felt had been denied them by their respective societies.

To fully understand the importance of these key similarities, however, it is essential that one grasp the larger significance of three other decisive commonalities, ties that continue to bind the U.S. South and the Brazilian Northeast together: history, socioeconomic upheaval, and the presence of a still-strong regionalist tradition.[11] The U.S. South and Brazil's Northeast have long been discussed in a comparative context. The historical prevalence of slavery in both places, of lucrative, if precarious, one-crop agricultural economies (cotton and sugar cane), and of flourishing plantation systems replete with a landed gentry and slavery, all conspired to make these two regions the colonial centers of learning and culture. In time, however, the influence of both cultures would be greatly diminished by tremendous social, political, and economic disruption (in the United States by the Civil War and in Brazil by the abolition of slavery, which was achieved in 1888 but without compensation for the slaveholders). Because economic recovery was so slow in coming to the South and the Northeast, both regions suffered tremendously during the Great Depression of the 1930s, a period that, interestingly enough, produced some brilliant and very comparable literature in both locales. Yet however much the U.S. South and the Brazilian Northeast saw their respective hegemonies undercut by the mid- to late nineteenth century, they never lost their uniqueness as regions, as distinctive areas within a larger national fabric, even retaining identifiable dialects. Indeed, it is no exaggeration to say that in both Brazil and the United States regionalism has always been a powerful and not infrequently fractious force, one that strongly marks both political and literary activity to this day.

Although *Let Us Now Praise Famous Men* is undoubtedly the more lyrical and personal of the two works, the one in which the author's voice is the most assertive and distinctive, *Rebellion in the Backlands*, dealing as it does with a brief but shockingly violent civil war in Brazil's Northeast (again, the region most often associated with the U.S. South), is by far the more dramatic, becoming in part 2 much more like a novel than mere reportage, which it originally was intended to be.[12] Selden Rodman, however, who notes a "rough-hewn resemblance" between the two works, also observes that *Let Us Now Praise Famous Men* and *Rebellion in the Backlands* begin in much the same way: "Like Agee, who begins by expiating his guilt with a description of every nail and knothole in the Alabama shanty town on which he is spying, Cunha starts off by detailing the geology of the backlands with exhaustive objectivity" (126). The essential difference here is that da Cunha seeks, especially in part 1, to explain the bloody rebellion at Canudos by showing that it was predestined, that, given the historical and geopolitical factors involved, the tragic events at Canudos were inevitable. This is why, always moving from the general to the specific and from the cosmically abstract to the culturally and historically concrete, da Cunha takes pains to show, in the long sections "The Land" and "The Man," how the leader of the rebellion, Antonio Conselheiro, was himself a product of powerful forces beyond his control. As da Cunha, relying both on geological and scientific metaphors and on a pungent sense of irony (which, since the time of Machado de Assis, has also been a characteristic feature of Brazilian fiction), expresses it,

> É natural que estas camadas profundas da nossa estratificação étnica se sublevassem numa anticlinal extraordinária—Antônio Conselheiro. . . .
> A imagem é corretíssima. Da mesma forma que o geólogo interpretando a inclinação e a orientação dos estratos truncados de antigas formações esboça o perfil de uma montanha extinta, o historiador só pode avaliar a altitude daquele homem, que por si nada valeu, considerando a psicologia da sociedade que o criou. . . . Por isto o infeliz destinado à solicitude dos médicos, veio, impelido por uma potência superior, bater de encontro a uma civilização, indo para a história como poderia ter ido para o hospício. (*Os Sertões* 80)

It was natural that the deep-lying layers of our ethnic stratification should have cast up so extraordinary an anticlinal as Antonio Conselheiro.

The metaphor is quite correct. Just as the geologist, by estimating the inclination and orientation of the truncated strata of very old formations, is enabled to reconstruct the outlines of a vanquished mountain, so the historian, in taking the stature of this man, who in himself is of no worth, will find it of value solely in considering the psychology of the society which produced him. . . . As the upshot of it all, this unfortunate individual, a fit subject for medical attention, was impelled by a power stronger than himself to enter into conflict with a civilization and to go down in history when he should have gone to a hospital. (*Rebellion* 117–18)

Although in *Let Us Now Praise Famous Men* the land gets a great deal of attention, primarily in the form of richly textured poetic description, it is not so resolutely presented, as it is in *Rebellion in the Backlands*, as the primeval force that produces the people who reside upon it and that determines the nature of the existences they will lead. As Agee writes, "The land, pale fields, black cloudy woodlands, and the late lamps in the central streets of the rare and inexpiable cities: New Orleans; Birmingham; whose façades stand naked in the metal light of their fear: the land, in its largeness: stretches: is stretched: it is stretched like that hollow and quietness of water that is formed at the root of a making wave, and it waits . . . and waits" (85).

Yet Agee, too, is occasionally capable of casting his beleaguered subjects in a more fatalistic universe, as being powerless to control their own destinies. Because "they do not own themselves," he writes, and because they are "without hope or interest, that which they cannot eat and get no money of but which is at the center of their duty and greatest expense of strength and spirit, the cultivation and harvesting of cotton: and all this takes place between a sterile earth and an uncontrollable sky in whose propitiation is centered their chief reverence and fear, and the deepest earnestness of their prayers, who read in these machinations of their heaven all signs of a fate which the hardest work cannot much help, and, not otherwise than as the most ancient peoples of the earth, make their plantations in the unpitying pieties of the moon" (325).

But whether its source is the natural environment or the human culture that seeks to coexist with it, a powerful sense of fatalism pervades both texts. In *Let Us Now Praise Famous Men* it stems not from its immediate chronological context (that is, the Depression era) but from the harsh "reconstruction" treatment the South was forced to endure after the Civil War, a cataclysmic event in the American psyche and one that, as both Faulkner and Agee show, left the white South with a sense of humiliation and inferiority, of being a defeated and unworthy people, of being strangers in their own land. For da Cunha, however, the source of this same fatalism is less specific, though the Brazilian author is much more systematic in arguing for its importance—to the "backlanders" who began the rebellion and to the government soldiers who fought them and who ultimately emerged victorious, though not until implementing a ruthless scorched-earth policy that, in ways analogous to the South's experience, devastated the region. It is interesting to note, moreover, that both authors (da Cunha more so than Agee) present the basic conflicts of their narratives in terms of the inevitability one associates with Greek tragedy, the literary form that, as Mary Chesnut is said to have once observed, best characterized the South's role in the war. Short of both men and supplies, neither the *sertanejos* nor the Confederates ever really had a chance of emerging victorious in their respective struggles; defeat was unavoidable, yet their dramas, once set in motion, would have to be played out to their bloody and dehumanizing conclusions.

At the same time, one must note that although both writers make extensive use of land imagery, of the physical environment generally, for Agee, a published poet, the land is, obviously enough, a central and wholly natural feature of the tenant-farmer's existence. In the case of da Cunha, a military engineer steeped in the theories of positivism, the hostile geography of the sertão, "a land of calamity" (Ellison, *Novel* 5), emerges as one of the primary forces that determine the nature of the life-forms that, including the human, survive there. For da Cunha, then, the land is a much more deterministic factor than it is for Agee, who sees it (particularly in its ravaged condition) as both a cruel legacy of the Civil War and as a beautiful albeit tragically scarred part of the larger Depression-era picture.

At the heart of both books, however, is the deeply conflicted human creature who resides there. For Agee, "a Communist by sympathy and conviction" (249) who declares openly that his narrative is intended to be "an insult, and a corrective" (ix)—presumably to the complacency with which the rest of wealthy and moralistic America could so easily accept "the unpleasant situation down South" (14)—it is clear that he is painfully aware that he will be prying intimately "into the lives of an undefended and appallingly damaged group of human beings," a trio of "ignorant and helpless" rural families (7). These people, Agee writes, "live in a steady shame and insult of discomforts, insecurities, and inferiorities, piecing these together into whatever semblance of comfortable living they can, and the whole of it is a stark nakedness of makeshifts and the lack of means: yet they are also, of course, profoundly anesthetized" (210). Acutely aware of the stark and "outlandish beauty" of the people whose story he was seeking to tell, Agee nevertheless sees "in their eyes so quiet and ultimate a quality of hatred, and contempt, and anger, toward every creature in existence beyond themselves, and toward the damages they sustained, as shone scarcely short of a state of beatitude" (33).

Agee thus suffers from the same ambivalent feelings toward his subjects that da Cunha eventually demonstrates toward his sertanejos, the similarly disadvantaged and abandoned inhabitants of the Brazilian sertão. In contrast to Agee, however, whose outrage at the ways the tenant-farmers are forced to live subtly generates the basic ethos of the book, da Cunha comes, late in his text, to state, almost clinically, one of his purposes in writing it:

> Decididamente era indispensável que a campanha de Canudos tivesse um objetivo superior à função estúpida e bem pouco gloriosa de destruir um povoado dos sertões. Havia um inimigo mais sério a combater, em guerra mais demorada e digna. Toda aquela campanha seria um crime inútil e bárbaro, se não se aproveitassem os caminhos abertos à artilharia para uma propaganda tenaz, contínua e persistente, visando trazer para o nosso tempo e incorporar à nossa existência aqueles rudes compatriotas retardatários. (*Os Sertões* 250)

> It was plain that the Canudos Campaign must have a higher objective than the stupid and inglorious one of merely wiping out a backlands settlement. There was a more serious enemy to be combatted, in a warfare of a slower and more worthy kind. This entire campaign would be a crime, a futile and barbarous one, if we were not to take advantage of the paths opened by the artillery, by following up our cannon with a constant, stubborn, and persistent campaign of education, with the object of drawing these rude and backward fellow-countrymen of ours into the current of our times and our own national life. (*Rebellion* 408)

Agee, too, eventually comes to make a plea for a better, more just society, one that, as with da Cunha, will depend on an improved educational system.[13] "What I have tried to suggest," Agee writes, is that,

> not only within present reach of human intelligence, but even within reach of mine as it stands today, it would be possible that young human beings should rise onto their feet a great deal less dreadfully

crippled than they are, a great deal more nearly capable of living well, a great deal more nearly aware, each of them, of their own dignity in existence, a great deal more qualified, each within his limits, to live and to take part toward the creation of a world in which good living will be possible without guilt toward every neighbor: and that teaching at present, such as it is, is almost entirely either irrelevant to these possibilities or destructive of them, and is, indeed, all but entirely unsuccessful even within its own "scales" of "value." (294)

Yet, the reader feels, like da Cunha's backlanders, Agee's tenant-farmers "are about as poorly equipped for self-education as human beings can be. Their whole environment is such that the use of intelligence, of the intellect, and of the emotions is atrophied" (Agee 294). Neither group, moreover, possesses any "recourse against being cheated" (Agee 294–95), exploited, or marginalized by the smug and condescending society that surrounds them. Nevertheless, by the end of his book, Agee, reflecting on the future and echoing da Cunha's pronouncement about what needs to come out of the debacle at Canudos, leaves the reader with a sense of hope: "let us know, let us *know* there is cure, there is to be an end to it, whose beginnings are long begun, and in slow agonies and all deceptions clearing; and in the teeth of all hope of cure which shall pretend its denial and hope of good use to men, let us most quietly and in most reverent fierceness say, not by its captive but by its upmost meanings" (439).

Although da Cunha argues that the subject of his treatise, "O homem dos sertões . . . mais do que qualquer outro está em função imediata da terra" (*Os Sertões* 77) ["The man of the backlands . . . , more than any other, stands in a functional relation to the earth" (*Rebellion* 112)] and that he "É uma variável dependente no jogar dos elementos" (*Os Sertões* 77) ["is a variable, dependent upon the play of the elements" (*Rebellion* 112)], the Brazilian author is also concerned with an issue—miscegenation—that does not figure into Agee's text.[14] Indeed, for da Cunha the issue of racial mixing, so central to Brazilian society generally (modern Brazilian Portuguese has at its disposal more than three hundred terms with which to describe different shades of skin color), turns out to be an explosive topic, a problem that, for reasons both public and private, gradually emerges as the great undeclared—and unresolved—conflict in *Rebellion in the Backlands*. Broaching the issue openly, da Cunha, in a famous passage, makes the following statement.

Abramos um parêntese. . . .

A mistura de raças mui diversas é, na maioria dos casos, prejudicial. Ante as conclusões do evolucionismo, ainda quando reaja sobre o produto o influxo de uma raça superior, despontam vivíssimos estigmas da inferior. A mestiçagem extremada é um retrocesso. (*Os Sertões* 61)

Here we must make a few parenthetical remarks. . . .

An intermingling of races highly diverse is, in the majority of cases, prejudicial. According to the conclusions of the evolutionist, even when the influence of a superior race has reacted upon the offspring, the latter shows vivid traces of the inferior one. Miscegenation carried to an extreme means retrogression. (*Rebellion* 84–85)

Many scholars have commented on the implications of this passage, noting that in making it da Cunha seems to accept the concept, widely accepted at the time (in the United States—*The Great Gatsby*, for example— as well as in Brazil), of "superior" and "inferior" races. The Brazilian social scientist Gilberto Freyre, for example, has studied da Cunha's "racial pessimism," his "racial fatalism," his "rigid biologic determinism," and his "ethnocentric exaggerations" and finds that "he was 'the victim of scientific preconceptions with the appearance of anthropologic truths' such as were common at the turn of the century. . . . In other words, these views, according to Freyre, were inspired by too great a reliance on his sources" (Samuel Putnam, in da Cunha, *Rebellion* 84–85 n.64). Commentators throughout the twentieth century have generally come to the same conclusion, that da Cunha, trained to believe in science and to trust its findings, was simply misled on this issue by what are now known to have been incorrect assumptions; the best scientific minds of the time were wrong about miscegenation but da Cunha (along with many others, in Brazil and elsewhere) accepted their erroneous conclusions, with the result that, in studying the backlanders and the tragic events at Canudos, he became deeply troubled, on biologic grounds, about the future of his racially mixed country. Thus he writes, in reference to the sertanejos, that

E o mestiço—mulato, mamaluco ou cafuz—menos que um intermediário, é um decaído, sem a energia física dos ascendentes selvagens, sem a altitude intelectual dos ancestrais superiores. . . . [E]spíritos fulgurantes, às vezes, mas frágeis, irrequietos, inconstantes, deslumbrando um momento e extinguindo-se prestes, feridos pela fatalidade das leis biológicas, chumbados ao plano inferior da raça menos favorecida. (*Os Sertões* 62)

The mestizo—mulatto, mameluco, or cafuso—rather than an intermediary type, is a degenerate one, lacking the physical energy of his savage ancestors and without the intellectual elevation of his ancestors on the other side. . . . A brilliant mind at times, but unstable, restless, inconstant, flaring one moment and the next moment extinguished, victim of the fatality of biologic laws, weighted down to the lower plane of the less favored race. (*Rebellion* 85)

Agee, too, deals with the question of race, but in a very different context. As it emerges in the pages of *Let Us Now Praise Famous Men*, the racial issue shows itself to be one of the pernicious effects of segregation and of the radically unequal treatment of blacks and whites in the county being studied by Agee and Evans. Although miscegenation certainly has existed in the South, it has never been as widespread or as culturally defining as it has been in Brazil, even the Brazil of da Cunha's time, and it does not figure into the racial issue as it is developed by Agee in his text (though, of course, it does with Faulkner, this being one of the primary links between Faulkner and Brazil). The problem, as Agee presents it, lies in relations between the races, the hatreds and sociopolitical inequalities that so bitterly divide them. In speaking of the superior educational system available to white children, for example, Agee writes, "The schoolhouse itself is in Cookstown; a recently built, windowy, 'healthful' red brick and white-trimmed structure which perfectly exemplifies the American genius for sterility, unimagination, and general gutlessness in meeting any opportunity for 'reform' or 'improvement'" (297). Noting, however, that in 1935 (the year of Agee's sojourn in Alabama) the school population of Hale County "is five black to one white" and that in spite of this "not a cent" of the county tax money "has gone into negro schools," Agee then observes, "The negro children, meanwhile, continue to sardine themselves, a hundred and a hundred and twenty strong, into stove-heated one-room pine shacks which might comfortably accommodate a fifth of their number if the walls, roof, and windows were tight" (297). Nowhere, however, does the question of racial mixing come up, making this issue a major point of distinction between the two texts.

A final basic difference between *Let Us Now Praise Famous Men* and *Rebellion in the Backlands* has to do with each author's view of his subjects, the ways Agee and da Cunha relate to the people they are describing. Da Cunha, whose respect and sympathy for the ragged, outnumbered and out-gunned sertanejos deepens as the narrative develops, eventually comes to see them as "heróico" (*Os Sertões* 268) ["heroes" (*Rebellion* 435)] and "um titã" (*Os Sertões* 64) ["Titans" (*Rebellion* 90)], as nothing less than the essence of Brazilian national identity. It has been said, in fact, that "the central dynamic of Euclides da Cunha's book is the tension between the Eurocentrism inherent in the science or pseudo-science he attempts to apply to his subject and the visceral nationalism that compels him to identify with landscapes, societies, and individuals defined by Eurocentrism as negative factors in Brazil's development as a modern nation" (González Echevarría, Pupo-Walker, and Haberly 6). The impoverished but indomitable sertanejos whose insurrection was being quelled by the federal troops were, for da Cunha, "o cerne de uma nacionalidade. Atacava-se a fundo a rocha viva da nossa raça. Vinha de molde a dinamite" (*Os Sertões* 285) ["the very core of our nationality, the bedrock of our race . . . and dynamite was the means precisely suited" (*Rebellion* 464)]. The civil war engendered by the revolt at Canudos was, therefore, "uma consagração" (*Os Sertões* 285) ["at once a recognition and a consecration" (*Rebellion* 464)], for "aquela rude sociedade, incompreendida e olvidada, era o cerne vigoroso da nossa nacionalidade" (*Os Sertões* 57) ["this society, misunderstood and forgotten, was the vigorous core of our national life" (*Rebellion* 78)].

While Agee is never this explicit about the ideological importance of the people whose lives he is detailing, he too is capable of reading a larger significance into his commentary. "All it had brought me," he writes, pondering, late in the text, his own involvement in this project, "was this terrible frustration, which had in its turn drawn me along these roads and to this place scarce knowing why I came, to the heart and heart's blood of my business and my need" (391), "for there it was proved me in the meeting of the extremes of the race" (392) our "scarcely controlled outrage" (393).[15] So while, for Agee, the tenant-families do not necessarily represent the "bedrock" of their "race" (the concept of race, again, playing a more decisive role in da Cunha's work), they can be viewed, through Agee's aggrieved eyes, if not exactly as the "core of our nationality" then certainly as the living proof of all that has gone wrong, politically, economically and morally, in America. Just as *Rebellion in the Backlands* develops the metaphor, famous among Brazilianists, of the "two Brazils"—the rich, urban and progressive South, and the poor, rural and backward North (the Northeast in particular)—so too does Agee imply that there are two Americas, one being rich, sanctimonious, and very self-satisfied, while the other, epitomized by the plight of these Alabama families, is desperately poor, cruelly marginalized, and without recourse. The result is that, in both works, a palpable sense of moral outrage permeates the commentary, a sense of outrage so acute that such injustice is allowed to continue that both texts come, finally, to be ringing indictments of the abandonment and exploitation of the disadvantaged by the advantaged, of the poor by the rich, and of the weak by the strong.

Overall, then, one can say that, in spite of their several differences *Let*

Us Now Praise Famous Men and *Rebellion in the Backlands* have many points in common: both freely make use of a wide variety of forms, styles, and tones; both celebrate not the victors but the vanquished; both decry the hypocrisy and sham moralizing of their respective societies. It might also be argued that, in their separate and distinctive ways, both authors struggle with the question of how best to capture in prose the over-whelming sense of shame and national disgrace that they both feel per-tains to the plight of their subjects. In reading these two works together, and in trying to keep in mind their importance to their respective Ameri-can, or New World, societies, one gets the feeling that both da Cunha and Agee are first incensed, then stupefied at their discovery of the appalling conditions faced by the hitherto faceless people they had been sent to write about: the poorly armed sertanejos who battled, literally to the last man, against hopeless odds at Canudos; the hardscrabble, barely subsistence-level farm families struggling to survive in rural, Depression-era Alabama. The problem for each writer is how to deal with the all-consuming outrage that confronts them, how to capture in words the truth of what has happened to these people and why, what it all means, to them and to the rest of us. In surprisingly parallel fashion, both authors grapple with this larger, more complex question throughout their narra-tives (albeit in ways that are quite distinctive and unique), and at various points it leads them to reflect metafictively not only on the tenuous relationship of narrative to life (and on any moral claims that apologists of narrative might make about its ability to affect human conduct) but also on language's ability to accurately represent (re-present) reality at all. It is not unreasonable to conclude, then, that the unexpected socio-aesthetic connection between these two extraordinary works—the con-frontation with a human reality so grotesquely unjust and so shamefully shunted aside that the writer is, momentarily at least, rendered speech-less, unable to find the words necessary to complete his task—is, finally, the bond that most profoundly ties them together.

Yet for all this, they remain vastly different books. Whereas Agee's text tends to be intense and viscerally personal (and, in a sense, as much about him and his feelings about the value system of Depression-era America as it is about his Alabama tenant-farmers), da Cunha's often has the cool detachment one associates with scientific analysis—except for the many sardonic asides that constantly remind the reader of the author's own doubts about the veracity of the "official" report he is ostensibly writing. Also, Agee's struggle with his text and his subject is much more open, public, and angry than da Cunha's, which is much more private, con-flicted, and anguished, a possible sign of da Cunha's anxiety about his and his nation's mixed racial heritage. Da Cunha's narrative, moreover, reads like a novel (especially in part 2, which describes in riveting detail both the military struggle itself and the larger social and political drama that was engulfing the entire country), which, contrary to what many think, it is not.[16] In observing the stylistic changes that distinguish part 1 from part 2, it is clear that da Cunha, a military engineer, must have come to realize that, in order to tell his story honestly, he would have to resort to the devices of fiction, that objective reportage alone could not express the full truth of what had happened at Canudos. In formal, stylistic terms, the singularity of *Rebellion in the Backlands* thus rests on its author's extraordinary success in harnessing the techniques of fiction to do the work of nonfiction. Viewed as a novel per se (as it often is), *Rebellion in the Backlands* relentlessly calls into question (as a postmodern novel might) the ability of narrative to tell the complete truth even about events one witnesses with one's own eyes (a quality Vargas Llosa would make much of in *The War of the End of the World*, an overtly "fictionalized" rewriting of the nonfictional da Cunha text). Their differences notwithstanding, *Rebellion in the Backlands* and *Let Us Now Praise Famous Men* remain two of the most unique and compelling texts ever produced in the Americas, coming, finally, to occupy very special places in their respective literary histories.

To understand why this is so requires some careful thinking not only about literary history as an intellectual activity but as a crucial aspect of the fast-developing field of inter-American studies generally. As difficult as it is to practice well in terms of a single national literature, comparative literary history is even more challenging, demanding, as it does, serious expertise in multiple languages and cultures. Perhaps most important of all, however, the scholar who undertakes comparative literary history must possess the analytical ability to discern the similarities (theme, style, genre, and so on) that bind together works from different cultures and languages but to do so without minimizing the all-important differences that separate them and that make them unique works of art. Just as the United States and Latin America are separated by different literary and cultural histories (to say nothing of their very divergent political and economic histories and their historically acrimonious relationships), so, too, are Brazil and Spanish America separated by a wide range of differences, from the linguistic and literary to the racial and political. Unless scholars understand these essential differences and keep them in mind as they proceed (as this volume attempts) with discussions of inter-American topics, they run the very real risk of arriving at some ill-advised conclusions. To prevent this from happening, scholars need to learn more about each other, although, to speak candidly, most Latin Americanists would argue that, by dint of necessity, professional training, and personal experience, they tend to know more about the United States than students of U.S. literature and culture know about Latin America.[17] As it currently exists, the relationship is far too one-sided, and this does not bode well for either party. To correct this problem and to facilitate a more balanced and mutually respectful approach to inter-American relations in the future, scholars need to free themselves from the prejudices of religion, language, history, and cultural "worth" that have plagued them for so long and cultivate new ways of looking at things "American." And while one might quibble with the applicability of the term *postcolonialism* to Latin American literature (writers from Brazil and Spanish America have been dealing with the staples of postcolonialism since the early 1800s, after all), one must nevertheless seriously consider Cathy Davidson's assertion (regarding the future of American studies as a discipline) that "postcolonialism is the theory; inter-American studies is the practice" (130). Janice Radway comes to a similar conclusion, arguing that inter-American studies "would have the advantage of comparatively connecting the study of U.S. history and cultures to those of North, Central, and South America and to the countries and cultures of the Caribbean as well" (62), a point amply borne out in the already extensive bibliography that marks this emergent field. In order to have long-term success with this daunting venture, however, it is also clear that scholars need to breech the institutional walls that separate them and talk more, to engage their departments of English, French, Spanish, Portuguese, and Comparative Literature in constructive dialogue about the vast common ground and the tremendous opportunities that the inter-American project affords them. From such a dialogue, new team-taught courses involving the various New World literatures could emerge, as could other joint projects involving faculty research projects, dissertations, and even degree programs. It is precisely in this inter-American context—wherein cultures long thought to be hopelessly segregated from each other are now discovering all that they have in common—that the sort of innovative comparative literary history advocated here will play its most valuable role.

Rebellion in the Backlands and Let Us Now Praise Famous Men are far from being the only connections between the literature of the U.S. South and that of Brazil, its giant hemispheric neighbor.[18] Brazilian artists and intellectuals have long been aware of the numerous parallels that exist between the U.S. South and Brazil's Northeast, and they have not failed to develop these ties in their work. In the realm of literature, William Faulkner occupies a special place in the development of twentieth-century Brazilian narrative. However, it is equally clear that strong and revealing comparisons can be made between Euclides da Cunha and both Faulkner and James Agee. As formally experimental as Machado (though in distinctive ways), Faulkner is like da Cunha in that he can be both harshly critical of his region and passionate in his defense of it (as in *Intruder in the Dust*). And, like both Machado and da Cunha, Faulkner exudes a deep-seated admiration for those who, regardless of class or race, exhibit the qualities of selflessness, love, courage, fortitude, and endurance. Traditionally associated with a very particular time and place—Machado with the "Cariocas," the people in and around Rio de Janeiro during the second half of the nineteenth century; da Cunha with the impoverished but fanatical backlanders of the Brazilian Northeast in the final decade of the nineteenth century; and Faulkner with the denizens of the mythical Yoknapatawpha County, Mississippi—all three writers rely heavily on the language, themes, histories, and cultural types of their respective regions to construct their stories. At the same time, however, Machado, da Cunha, and Faulkner distance themselves from lesser talents by using this localism, or provincialism, as a springboard, as a mechanism to explore the timeless themes of the greater human condition, which, it is clear, is where the real power of each writer is generated. Faulkner's genius at using the local, in all its complexity, to come to grips with the eternal, with the fundamental themes of human existence, for example, would have been obvious and deeply attractive to Brazilian readers, who would have recognized it as the same strategy used by three of their greatest writers: Machado de Assis, Euclides da Cunha, and Guimarães Rosa, the latter a writer much of whose work (also set in the early-twentieth-century Brazilian Northeast) continues to elicit comparisons with that of Faulkner. Brazilians would have also not failed to note how, as in *Absalom, Absalom!* and *Light in August*, Faulkner was concerned with the relationship between individual men and women and the often too-rigid, violence inducing, and hypocritical social codes and mores that guided and informed their existences. Often couched in terms of race relations, cronyism, narrow-mindedness, conformity, fanaticism, religious bigotry, and a class-conscious obsequiousness, such concerns permeate modern Brazilian literature, as they do Faulkner's greatest works, and they would have served as catnip for Brazilians anxious to create a modern, progressive society for themselves.

Nevertheless, it is imperative to remember that, in seeking to assess Faulkner's overall influence in Latin America, one need always to understand Brazil as having a significantly different social, political, and cultural history than Spanish America, and that this has had a direct bearing on the particular nature of Faulkner's reception in Brazil. Largely a function of Machado's groundbreaking work in the late nineteenth and early twentieth centuries, Brazil's narrative tradition was by the 1930s already more self-consciously experimental and innovative, in contrast to that of Spanish America; indeed, these qualities were its defining characteristics. One can conclude, therefore, that although Faulkner is unquestionably important to both Spanish American and Brazilian narrative, he is much more crucial for the Spanish American tradition than for the Brazilian, where a continuous and quite deliberate cultivation of new narrative techniques has been in existence since 1880 and the publication of *The Posthumous Memoirs of Brás Cubas*. Though less obvious and less celebrated, the relevance of James Agee and *Let Us Now Praise Famous Men* to Brazilian literature is perhaps even more striking, since this too-often-neglected classic of New World literature affords an unusually compelling connection with one of the most seminal Brazilian texts of the twentieth century. In reading *Rebellion in the Backlands* and *Let Us Now Praise Famous Men* comparatively, even as parts of very different literary and cultural histories, one feels certain that Agee's tenant families and da Cunha's sertanejos would have understood each other very, very well. From the larger perspective of inter-American literature, what Faulkner and Agee show, finally, is that the U.S. South and the Brazilian Northeast do, indeed, have a great many features in common. Taking into account José de Alencar, Machado de Assis, Mário de Andrade, Oswald de Andrade, and Patrícia Galvão, this view tends to underscore González Echevarría's deliciously provocative contention that "Brazil's is, with that of the United States, the richest national literature in the New World" (xii). From history to politics and from economics to literary and cultural studies, these two hugely influential New World regions offer the scholar prepared to accept a new and hemispherically expanded sense of "American" literary history a multitude of fascinating teaching and research possibilities.

NOTES

1. The great difference, however, centers on the issue of racial mixing. As many scholars have pointed out (see Freyre; Wagley; Eakin; and Burns), Brazilian society was early on characterized by active and extensive sexual relationships between its three founding "races": the Europeans, the black Africans, and the Amerindians. Putnam, for example, noting the "Anglo-Saxon attitude of racial superiority" (8) that would poison race relations in the United States for generations to come, argues that "in Brazil," by way of contrast, "miscegenation has come to be viewed as the means of racial assimilation in

the achievement of national unity, and this will account for the prominent part that the Indian and the Negro play in literature" (9).

2. Faulkner can, for example, be directly linked to such Spanish American masters as Carlos Fuentes, Mario Vargas Llosa, and, above all, Gabriel García Márquez.

3. For a more detailed study of the importance of "A Rose for Emily" to Brazilian literature (and specifically its importance to a novel by Autran Dourado), see McClendon.

4. Monteiro also asserts that the very influential *O Estado de São Paulo* "was one of the first newspapers outside the United States to call attention to William Faulkner's work" and that "at a time when in his own country—that is, around fifteen years ago [ca. 1968]—Faulkner was not yet sufficiently known and appreciated, this newspaper was already publishing articles calling attention to the extraordinary importance of this author" (98).

5. Monegal notes, interestingly, that "although Faulkner's novel *Sanctuary* had already been translated into Spanish by the Cuban novelist Lino Novás Calvo and had been published in Spain in 1934, the translation was mediocre and had been tampered with by the publisher, who was afraid to be too specific about the way Popeye manages to rape Temple Drake" (*Jorge Luis Borges* 373).

6. Two articles written by Borges, "La postulación de la realidad" ("The Postulation of Reality") and "El arte narrativo y la magia" ("Narrative Art and Magic"), both of which appeared in *Discusión* in 1932, clearly present Borges's theory about what a new, antirealistic narrative would be like. While the first essay deals with the question of verisimilitude, the second focuses on the nature of magic, understood in its epistemological and anthropological function, as a basic structuring force for this new narrative. When taken together, these two famous articles expound a theory of "magical" or "fantastic" literature that Borges would later seek to demonstrate in his fiction writing. Given the nature of the new narrative theory that Borges is developing in these two essays, it is easy to understand why he would have been so taken with the Faulkner narratives that he was reading and writing about.

7. Although Faulkner had generally good Portuguese-language translators at this time, he did not enjoy a translator of Borges's consummate skill, and this could have had a detrimental effect on his reception in Brazil. A study that is yet to be done would seek answers to the following questions: who, in Brazil, was reading Faulkner? Were they reading him in the original English or in Portuguese (or perhaps, thinking of the Novás Calvo and Borges translations, in Spanish)? And, finally, what was the quality of the translations that did exist, and how faithfully did they reproduce Faulkner's famous style?

8. Jorge Amado, Brazil's most widely translated novelist, for example, has indicated a special fondness for the work of Erskine Caldwell and Mark Twain, in addition to that of such U.S. writers as Hemingway, Sinclair Lewis, Upton Sinclair, Richard Wright, and the young John Steinbeck (Rodman 122).

9. Published posthumously in 1957, Agee's novel *A Death in the Family* won immediate critical acclaim, while his film criticism has come to be regarded as the foundational development of this field in English.

10. The editorial staff of *Fortune* rejected the manuscript, however, finding its style, tone, and content to be unsuitable for the magazine's readership.

11. It is worth noting that regionalism has been very influential in the literary history of both Brazil and the United States.

12. Perhaps the single most striking difference between *Let Us Now Praise Famous Men* and *Rebellion in the Backlands* is that the second half of the Brazilian work chronicles an actual war. Beginning with part 2, "The Rebellion," the narrative shifts its focus from "The Land" and "Man" to concentrate on the ebb and flow of the war itself, which lasted from December 1896 to October 1897. The result is a riveting narrative that, cultivating such fictional techniques as dramatic structuring, irony, dialogue, and changing perspectives, comes to read much more like a novel than nonfiction.

13. One key difference between Agee's and da Cunha's perspectives on the role that education can, or should, play in the lives of the tenant-farmers and sertanejos is that Agee, an avowed communist writing in 1935, is much more skeptical about the effects "education" will have on these people than does da Cunha, a turn-of-the-century engineer trained under the star of positivism. As Agee writes, for example, " 'Education' as it stands is tied in with every bondage I can conceive of, and is the chief cause of these bondages, including acceptance and respect, which are the worst bondages of all. 'Education,' if it is anything short of crime, is a recognition of these bondages and a discovery of more and a deadly enemy of all of them" (308).

14. This is in contrast to Faulkner, for whom miscegenation is, of course, of paramount importance, playing a key role in many of his greatest works, including *Absalom, Absalom!* and *Light in August*. Given the popularity of *Light in August* in Brazil, in fact, one is led to wonder whether the Brazilians weren't drawn to Faulkner's handling of this issue.

15. It is interesting to note that, in telling their stories, both Agee and da Cunha come to feel like strangers in their own land. Agee, for example, writes that he is so alien to the tenant families he is seeking to understand that he might as well say, "I am from Mars, and let it go at that" (405), while da Cunha, an eyewitness to the terrible events at Canudos, says with regard to how he and the federal troops felt as they penetrated ever further into the sertanejos' stronghold: "Descordância absoluta e radical entre as cidades da costa e as malocas de talha do interior, que desequilibra tanto o ritmo de nosso desenvolvimento evolutivo e perturba deploravelmente a unidade nacional. Viam-se em terra estranha. Outros hábitos. Outros quadros. Outra gente. Outra língua mesmo, articulada em gíria original e pinturesca. Invadia-os o sentimento exato de seguirem para uma guerra externa. Sentiam-se fora do Brasil" (*Os Sertões* 249) ["Here was an absolute and radical break between the coastal cities and the clay huts of the interior, one that so disturbed the rhythm of our evolutionary development and which was so deplorable a stumbling-block to national unity. They were in a strange country now, with other customs, other scenes, a different kind of people. Another language, even, spoken with an original and picturesque drawl. They had, precisely, the feeling of going to war in another land. They felt that they were outside Brazil" (*Rebellion* 405)].

16. So powerful are the novelistic qualities of *Rebellion in the Backlands* (and especially

of part 2) that Peruvian writer Mario Vargas Llosa based his 1981 novel, *La guerra del fin del mundo* (*The War of the End of the World*, 1984), on it.

17. To avoid confusion and to maximize clarity and precision, the term "Latin America" should not be used unless one intends to refer to *both* Spanish America and Brazil. It is misleading, therefore, to speak of the Brazilian and Latin American literary traditions.

18. In terms of total land mass and square miles, Brazil is actually slightly larger than the continental United States.

WORKS CITED

Agee, James, and Walker Evans. *Let Us Now Praise Famous Men*. Boston: Houghton, 1941.

Brakel, Arthur. "Ambiguity and Enigma in Art: The Case of Henry James and Machado de Assis." *Comparative Literature Studies* 19.4 (winter 1982): 442–49.

Burns, E. Bradford. *A History of Brazil*. 3rd ed. New York: Columbia UP, 1993.

Cerqueira, Nelson. "Hermeneutics and Literature: A Study of William Faulkner's *As I Lay Dying* and Graciliano Ramos's *Vidas Secas*." *Dissertation Abstracts International* 47.5 (Nov. 1986): 1719A.

Cohn, Deborah N. *History and Memory in the Two Souths: Recent Southern and Spanish American Fiction*. Nashville, Tenn.: Vanderbilt UP, 1999.

Coutinho, Afrânio. *An Introduction to Literature in Brazil*. Trans. Gregory Rabassa. New York: Columbia UP, 1969.

da Cunha, Euclides. *Os Sertões*. Rio de Janeiro: Editorial Ediouro, 1992.

——. *Rebellion in the Backlands*. Trans. Samuel Putnam. Chicago: U of Chicago P, 1944.

Daniel, Mary L. "Brazilian Fiction from 1900 to 1945." *The Cambridge History of Latin American Literature*. Vol. 3. Ed. Roberto González Echevarría and Enrique Pupo-Walker. Cambridge: Cambridge UP, 1996. 157–87.

Davidson, Cathy. "Loose Change." *American Quarterly* 46.2 (1996): 123–38.

Eakin, Marshall C. *Brazil: The Once and Future Country*. New York: St. Martin's, 1997.

Ellison, Fred P. *Brazil's New Novel*. Berkeley: U of California P, 1954.

——. Introduction. *Memories of Lazarus*. By Adonias Filho. Trans. Fred P. Ellison. Austin: U of Texas P, 1969. ix–xiv.

Englekirk, John E. *A Literatura Norteamericana no Brasil*. Mexico: 1950.

Fitz, Earl E. *Rediscovering the New World: Inter-American Literature in a Comparative Context*. Iowa City: U of Iowa P, 1991.

——. *Brazilian Narrative Traditions in a Comparative Context*. New York: MLA Publications, 2004 (forthcoming).

Freyre, Gilberto. *The Masters and the Slaves: A Study in the Development of Brazilian Civilization*. 2d ed. Trans. Samuel Putnam. New York: Knopf, 1971.

Gallagher, D. P. *Modern Latin American Literature*. Oxford: Oxford UP, 1973.

Gledson, John. "Brazilian Prose from 1940 to 1980." *The Cambridge History of Latin*

American Literature. Vol. 3. Ed. Roberto González Echevarría and Enrique Pupo-Walker. Cambridge: Cambridge UP, 1996. 189–206.

González Echevarría, Roberto, ed. *The Oxford Book of Latin American Short Stories*. New York: Oxford UP, 1997.

González Echevarría, Roberto, and Enrique Pupo-Walker, eds. *The Cambridge History of Latin American Literature*. Vol. 3. Cambridge: Cambridge UP, 1996.

González Echevarría, Roberto, Enrique Pupo-Walker, and David Haberly. "Introduction to Volume 3." *The Cambridge History of Latin American Literature*. Vol. 3. Cambridge: Cambridge UP, 1996. 1–10.

Lowe, Elizabeth. "Visions of Violence: From Faulkner to the Contemporary City Fiction of Brazil and Colombia." *Proceedings of the Xth Congress of the International Comparative Literature Association* (New York, 1982). Ed. Anna Balakian and James J. Wilherlm. *Inter-American Literary Relations*. Vol. 3. Ed. Mario J. Valdés. New York: Garland, 1985. 13–19.

Mac Adam, Alfred. *Textual Confrontations: Comparative Readings in Latin American Literature*. Chicago: U of Chicago P, 1987.

McClendon, Carmen Chaves. "A Rose for Rosalina: From Yoknapatawpha to *Ópera dos Mortos*." *Comparative Literature Studies* 19.4 (winter 1982): 450–58.

Merquior, J. G. "The Brazilian and the Spanish American Literary Traditions: A Contrastive View." *The Cambridge History of Latin American Literature*. Vol. 3. Ed. Roberto González Echevarría and Enrique Pupo-Walker. Cambridge: Cambridge UP, 1996. 368–82.

Monteiro, George. "Faulkner in Brazil." *Southern Literary Journal* 16.1 (fall 1983): 96–104.

Oliveira, Celso de. "Faulkner and Graciliano Ramos." *Faulkner, His Contemporaries and His Posterity*. Ed. Waldemar Zacharasiewicz. Tübingen: Francke, 1993. 52–67.

Parker, John M. "Maria Alice Barroso." *Dictionary of Contemporary Brazilian Authors*. Comp. David William Foster and Roberto Reis. Tempe: Center for Latin American Studies, Arizona State U, 1981. 14–15.

Patai, Daphne. *Myth and Ideology in Contemporary Brazilian Fiction*. Rutherford: Fairleigh Dickinson, 1983.

Putnam, Samuel. *Marvelous Journey: Four Centuries of Brazilian Literature*. New York: Knopf, 1948.

Rabassa, Gregory. "Beyond Magic Realism: Thoughts on the Art of Gabriel García Márquez." *Books Abroad* 47.3 (summer 1973): 444–50.

Radway, Janice. "What's in a Name?" *The Futures of American Studies*. Ed. Donald E. Pease and Robyn Wiegman. Durham, N.C.: Duke UP, 2002. 45–75.

Rodman, Selden. *South America of the Poets*. New York: Hawthorn, 1970.

Rodríguez Monegal, Emir. *The Borzoi Anthology of Latin American Literature*. Vol. 1. New York: Knopf, 1984.

——. *Jorge Luis Borges: A Literary Biography*. New York: Dutton, 1978.

Sayers, Raymond. "Brazilian Literature." *Latin American Literature in the Twentieth Century*. Ed. Leonard S. Klein. New York: Ungar, 1986. 47–55.

Shimura, Masao. "Faulkner, de Assis, Barth: Resemblances and Differences." *Faulkner*

Studies in Japan. Comp. Ohashi Kenzaburo and Ono Kiyoyuki. Ed. Thomas L. McHaney. Athens: U of Georgia P, 1985. 76–87.

——. "Faulkner, De Assis, Barth: Resemblances and Differences." *William Faulkner: Materials, Studies, and Criticism* [Tokyo: *Shinjuku-ky*] 2.2 (1979): 67–79.

Simas, Rosa. " 'Ripples,' a 'Gyrating Wheel,' and a 'Spiral on a Square': Circularity in Three Twentieth-Century Novels of the Americas." Diss. University of California, Davis, 1990.

——. " 'Ripples,' 'Una rueda giratoria,' and 'A Espiral e o quadrado': Circularity in Three Twentieth-Century Novels of the Americas." *Translation Perspectives* 6 (1991): 87–98.

Standley, Arline. "Here and There: Now and Then." *Luso-Brazilian Review* 23.1 (summer 1986): 61–75.

Valente, Luiz. "Marriages of Speaking and Hearing: Mediation and Response in *Absalom, Absalom!* and *Grande Sertão: Veredas.*" *Faulkner Journal* 11.1–2 (fall–spring 1995–1996): 149–64.

——. "The Reader in the Work: Fabulation and Affective Response in João Guimarães Rosa and William Faulkner." Diss. Brown University, 1983.

Vizzioli, Paulo. "Guimarães Rosa e William Faulkner." *O Estado de São Paulo, Suplemento Literário* 11 Apr. 1970: 1.

Wagley, Charles. *An Introduction to Brazil.* Rev. ed. New York: Columbia UP, 1971.

★ ★ ★ **PART FOUR**

FROM PLANTATION TO HACIENDA:

GREATER MEXICO AND THE U.S. SOUTH

The questioning of cultural, political, and ethnic boundaries between the United States and Mexico following the U.S.-Mexican War and the attendant reconfiguration of notions of citizenship are at the heart of the issues explored in part 4. Commonalities bridging the South and (Greater) Mexico are, of course, not coincidental; nor are they attributable to geographical overlap alone. Both regions' socioeconomic systems were predicated on similar structures—the plantation and the hacienda—whose presence left the regions facing parallel race, class, and economic issues. The presence of plantation structures in both regions, in turn, has underlain relationships of literary influence, for the southern plantation novel became a model for a narrative of Mexican-American cultural memory and nostalgia in the twentieth century. Moreover, as José Limón details, the white South and the needs of its political economy had an active role in bringing about the U.S.-Mexican War and in determining the course of development of Greater Mexico—and its development *as* a racially stratified economy—following 1848 (8–9). The great irony of this is, of course, that, in this manner, "the [white] South—with its own sense of itself as a culturally distinct and beleaguered weaker region relative to the Yankee North—[was] party to an imposition of U.S. federal authority on a culturally and structurally similar Greater Mexico" (13).[1] Ultimately, marginalized groups in both regions paid the highest price, for they were not only subordinated to the dominant local white elite but also "experienced the worst effects of Northern capitalist domination, a domination always deeply inflected with and complicated by racism" (18).

Barbara Ladd has argued that the incorporation of the Louisiana Territory, which had followed an assimilationist policy under French rule, into the increasingly segregationist United States begged the question of the color line—and, by extension, of who could be(come) an "American"—in the early nineteenth century (and, again, during Reconstruction).[2] John-Michael Rivera and Vincent Pérez similarly explore the constructions of U.S. nationalism that arose in response to the need to ascertain the material rights and racial status of Mexicans and to evaluate their claim to U.S. citizenship in the years following the U.S.-Mexican War. The question of Mexicans' racial status is further used by the authors as a springboard for exploring the position, rights, and treatment of African Americans and Native Americans in the South and throughout the United States.

Extending Américo Paredes's "Greater Mexican" formulation of the Americas, John-Michael Rivera argues that the American "South" in cultural and literary studies should not be solely viewed as a domestic inquiry into the Civil War, slavery, and African American rights, but rather as a (trans)national study into the southern geopolitical relationship that the United States has with Mexico and its inhabitants. Reading María Amparo Ruiz de Burton's Reconstruction narrative *Who Would Have Thought It?* (1872), Rivera argues that she anticipates Paredes's hemispheric understanding of the emergence of U.S. nationalism and capitalism by locating the "Mexican Question" at the heart of the Reconstruction-era public. In the end, her work demonstrates that the development of the United States's domestic understanding of itself as a nation is ironically informed by geopolitical discourses that crystallized during the U.S.-Mexican War of 1846–1848—the "war between the republics"—and the questions concerning the material rights and racial status of Mexican "foreigners" after the war.

Vincent Pérez starts by noting how a number of early Mexican-American literary works set out to revise hegemonic histories of the Southwest by restoring the region's Hispanic heritage. Many of these writings have depicted the nineteenth-century hacienda or rancho as a site of Mexican-American origins and ethnicity. Just as the antebellum plantation social economy was from the late nineteenth century to the modern era the subject of many U.S. southern historical romances, the hacienda during the same era formed the cornerstone of many nostalgic literary projects by Mexican-American writers. In some parts of the Southwest, the feudalistic and patriarchal hacienda system lasted until after 1900, shaping all levels of early Mexican-American culture and society. In Pérez's analysis of a recently recovered hacienda text, *Caballero* (written in the late 1930s and published in 1996), by Texas writers Jovita González and Eve Raleigh, he argues that the project of recuperating a colonial "old world" institution as a means of restoring the Hispanic history of the Southwest raises many of the same ideological and cultural contradictions examined in criticism on plantation literature. Most noticeably, he explores how *Caballero* dramatizes the convergences and divergences of history and fiction in a manner reminiscent of Margaret Mitchell's sentimental romance *Gone with the Wind* (1936), a novel that may have served as a model for González and Raleigh's pastoral hacienda novel.

NOTES

1. Chapter 1 of Limón's *American Encounters*, "The Other American South: Southern Culture and Greater Mexico," develops these and other links between the two regions in greater detail.
2. See especially "Race and National Identity in the Work of White Writers" in Ladd's *Nationalism and the Color Line*.

WORKS CITED

Ladd, Barbara. *Nationalism and the Color Line in George W. Cable, Mark Twain, and William Faulkner.* Baton Rouge: Louisiana State UP, 1996.
Limón, José E. *American Encounters: Greater Mexico, the United States, and the Erotics of Culture.* Boston: Beacon, 1998.

And finally, impelled by that liking, the doctor betook himself to California, which is full of "*natives.*" And as a just retribution for such perverse liking, the doctor was well-nigh "roasted by the natives," said the old lady. Whereupon, in behalf of truth, I said, "Not by the natives, madam. The people called '*the natives*' are mostly of Spanish descent, and are not cannibals. The wild Indians of the Colorado River were doubtless the ones who captured the doctor and tried to make a meal of him." "Perhaps so," said the old lady, visibly disappointed. "To me they are all alike,—Indians, Mexicans or Californians,—they are all horrid."

—MARÍA AMPARO RUIZ DE BURTON,
Who Would Have Thought It?

JOHN-MICHAEL RIVERA

Embodying Greater Mexico:
María Amparo Ruiz de Burton and the
Reconstruction of the Mexican Question

The opening scene of María Amparo Ruiz de Burton's *Who Would Have Thought It?* (1872) reveals the novel's central theme: the problems of locating what was in the nineteenth century referred to as the "Mexican Question" in an antebellum American culture that based its racial and geographic imaginary primarily on black/white and South/North binaries.[1] That the scene depicted in the epigraph centers on the eating of white northern bodies—"the roasting" of the New Englander Dr. Norval—by racial others imagined as cannibals announces that the novel's questions concerning the politics of defining the Mexican race are inextricable from attendant discourses of the human body. Indeed, it is this opening scene that introduces the reader to the protagonist, an orphan named Lola Medina, whose metamorphic body represents the novel's inquest into the Mexican Question's geopolitical and racial discourses.[2]

Born in Baja California in 1832, María Amparo Ruiz de Burton came from the landed Mexican classes. In 1850, two years after the signing of the Treaty of Guadalupe Hidalgo, which ended the U.S.-Mexican War (1846–1848), she married Col. Henry S. Burton, who was sent to Baja

California to quell a Mexican uprising. After their nuptials, Ruiz de Burton went with Colonel Burton to the Northeast, where she began her literary career as a novelist. The Northeast would affect her tremendously, and in 1869 she began writing *Who Would Have Thought It?*, a novel that captures her experiences of New England well.[3] Taking place against the backdrop of the Civil War, Western expansionism, and industrialization, the plot of *Who Would Have Thought It?* unfolds when Dr. Norval "saves" Lola from Indian captivity and brings her back to his New England home. Because Lola's Indian captors have dyed her body, her racial and cultural identities in New England are entirely ambiguous. As the story progresses, the reader learns not only her true identity but that she has inherited gold and diamonds, which her mother acquired while they were in captivity. The remainder of the novel traces her life and focuses on how she becomes a part of New England culture and the Anglo middle class.

The trajectory of Lola's assimilation into Anglo-American culture and her "worth" in New England corresponds precisely to the fading of her dyed body; as it fades, she undergoes numerous changes in racial status, which overlap and effectively generate her simultaneous acquisition of material wealth and cultural capital.[4] As Lola changes racially, so too does the economic position that the Norvals hold in New England culture, metaphorically representing how Anglo America and the northern United States prospered economically from their acquisition of Mexican lands following the U.S.-Mexican War. This essay explores the ways in which Lola's metamorphosis presents an alternative reading of U.S. racial and material culture during Reconstruction. I want to suggest that her embodied metamorphosis complicates the geopolitical binaries associated with the Civil War (black/white, southern/northern) and reveals the extent to which the geographic and racial identities of the inhabitants of Greater Mexico were important to the capitalist expansion and national identity of the United States.

This represents a historical and cultural departure from Karen Sánchez-Eppler's foundational study of nineteenth-century culture, *Touching Liberty*, wherein she argues that two discourses of social protest affected the body's political significance: "the abolitionist concern with claiming personhood for the racially distinct and physically owned slave body, and the feminist concern with claiming personhood for the sexually distinct and domestically circumscribed female body (1). Sánchez-Eppler, however, does not consider the important role that expansion and Mexicans would play in the United States's political understanding of the body. To extend Sánchez-Eppler's domestic analysis of the politics of black/white female bodies: the corporeal location of Mexicans in the United States following the Treaty of Guadalupe Hidalgo—the document that both defined the racial status of Mexicans and annexed millions of acres of Mexican lands to the United States—revealed that the Mexican body was an equally complicated site of not only domestic but also geopolitical contestation in the United States, a public inquest known as the Mexican Question.

It is of no small importance that John O'Sullivan introduced the term "Mexican Question" to the public spheres in 1845 in *Democratic Review* just one month after he coined the term "Manifest Destiny" in his essay "Annexation." O'Sullivan considered his essay "The Mexican Question" to be a racial inquiry into the United States's "natural rights" to expand west into Mexican lands. The Mexican Question both revealed the geopolitical rights-based language that fueled America's expansion into the "foreign" territories of Mexico and the anxiety that racial others and their lands created for U.S. democratic culture. In the end, O'Sullivan's notion of Manifest Destiny granted the United States the "natural right" to expand democracy into Mexico's northern territories. Consequently, as historian Nancy Isenberg argues, expansionism "promoted a distinct perspective, that the sovereign [white] people were a corporate body unified by 'one flesh,' a virtually homogeneous population with a common heritage and shared manifest destiny" (134). O'Sullivan and his colleagues in the *North American Review* secured this notion of a homogeneous white body politic in the public spheres by arguing that Mexicans' racial bodies were not bestowed with the same abstract "natural rights" as those of Americans. Indeed, shortly after O'Sullivan's essay appeared, expansionist statesman Caleb Cushing wrote in the *Democratic Review* that the Mexican population are "Indian and half-breeds" and that Americans will look in "vain" for an "enlightened population" (438).

The Mexican Question that emerged in the public spheres in the mid-nineteenth century would set a foundational precedent for American and Mexican contact in the decades that followed. The inquest of the Mexican Question melded the democratic ideals of natural rights, land expansion, and the racialization of Mexicans that would set the rhetorical dimensions of the Mexican Question for more than a century and a half. For the immediate manifest designs of O'Sullivan and the nation, the Mexican Question would fuel the justification for a "rightful" and "just" war against Mexico. Indeed, one year after O'Sullivan wrote "The Mexican Question," the United States declared war against Mexico and began its "rightful expansion" into the west through force. Rights-based arguments of expansion gave the United States the moral justification to limit the freedoms of the Mexican republic and, in the years that followed, the Mexican inhabitants of Greater Mexico.

When using the phrase "Greater Mexico," I am following the lead of Américo Paredes, who defined it as "all areas inhabited by people of Mexican American culture—not only within the present limits of the Republic of Mexico but in the United States as well—in a cultural rather than political sense" (xiv). This formulation of Greater Mexico, then, connotes a geopolitical understanding of the Americas according to a hemispheric logic, whereby the study of the "south" (Mexico) and the "north" (United States) becomes a transnational exploration into the economic and cultural underpinnings that destabilize the boundaries between the two republics. In a Greater Mexican formulation of the Americas, the investigation of the U.S. "South" in cultural and literary studies is not only a domestic inquiry into the Civil War, slavery, white women's suffrage, and African American rights, but also a transnational study of the often overlooked but entirely related geopolitical relationship that the United States has with Mexico and its inhabitants. In this way, the U.S.-Mexican War—the "war between the republics"—and the inquest into the material rights and racial status of Mexicans during and after that war are among the first pivotal geopolitical indicators of U.S. democratic culture during the nineteenth century. Ruiz de Burton anticipates Paredes's Greater Mexican understanding of the emergence of U.S. democratic culture and capitalism by (re)positioning the inquest into the material rights and racial status of Mexicans within the embodied discourses that Sánchez-Eppler locates in her study. In doing so, she not only challenges the masculinist geopolitical and racial questions that O'Sullivan's Mexican Question presents to the eastern public but is also able to create a counter-public space for Spanish-Mexican women's bodies within the geographic boundaries of the United States.[5]

BLACKNESS OF ANOTHER KIND

In her book *RaceChanges* Susan Gubar locates an American cultural trope she defines as "racechange," which she argues "is meant to suggest the traversing of race boundaries, racial imitation or impersonation, cross racial mimicry or mutability, white posing as black or black passing as white, panracial mutability" (5). Though Gubar focuses on African and Anglo-American racial performance, her ideas help explain how *Who Would Have Thought It?* subverts this binary through the racechanges of Lola Medina. What is so intriguing about Lola is that her metamorphic body represents a racial chain of being, one that mutates from African American to Native American and diseased to Mexican to white sexualized Spanish-Mexican woman. And though the reader slowly learns that Lola's racechanges occur because Indians dyed her skin, the Anglo characters in the novel do not fully understand her embodied identity. Much of the novel, then, centers on defining Lola's racial status and what her place should be in the domestic and public spheres. In this way, the varying racechanges that occur in the story and the national race questions that they represent complicate Gubar's white/black binary.

The second chapter of *Who Would Have Thought It?*—entitled "The Little Black Girl"—begins to reveal some of the complicated racechanges that occur in the novel. Returning from an anthropological study of the newly conquered southwestern territories—now defined in New England as America's "public domain"—Dr. Norval encounters the novel's central protagonist, the orphaned Lola Medina.[6] Lola enters New England culture as a specimen, "A nigger girl! . . . who was very black" (Ruiz de Burton, *Who Would* 16). Questioning her racial identity through reference to her body composition, the New England Anglos undertake a crude form of phrenology and begin to study Lola as if she were one of the rocks that Dr. Norval brought back from his trip.

Never giving Lola the ability to speak for herself about her racial identity, Mattie, Mrs. Norval, and Ruth—figuring as three New England images of the young and old white Republican Mother—begin to question what type of "nigger" she is, for she doesn't fit into the category of black they have seen in their abolitionist causes. "Look what magnificent eyes she has, and what red and prettily cut lips," states Mattie. Mrs. Norval asks, "How could she have such lips?—Negroes' lips are not like those." Mattie then comments, "I do not think she is so black, see the palm of her hand is as white as mine—and a prettier white for it has such a pretty pink shade to it" (18).

Lola's ambiguous racial body presents the women with a problem of identity, one that begins to affect their own ideas of their whiteness. Disturbed by the inference that a "nigger specimen" could have prettier features and even a prettier hue of white, Mrs. Norval tells Mattie not to touch the specimen, for she may have a disease that could infect them all—thus introducing the biopolitical discourse of disease that figures throughout the novel. When Lola's body cannot be defined according to one racial type, the Anglos view her as diseased, and her embodied identity comes into question. After Lola's body is depicted as diseased, Ruth, the young daughter of Mrs. Norval, suggests that perhaps Lola is both an Indian and an African.

This scene reveals much about the phenotypical body's importance in defining race. The "look" of another person is the prima facie ground of our knowledge of him or her (O'Neill 23). In this way, one takes another's appearance at face value, never questioning if the body is deceiving; culture treats physical characteristics as a "racial" reality (24). Therefore, as John O'Neill astutely argues in *Five Bodies*, one seeks out other bodies in society as mirrors of oneself; one understands who one is and who one isn't according to other bodies. Indeed, this ideology helped define whiteness in nineteenth-century America (Dyer 8–11). Because of the expansion of U.S. slavery into Mexican and Native American territories, however, newly constituted racial bodies of the frontier began to rupture this dialectic. African, Native American, and Mexican bodies did not mirror the white body; they were its antithesis. But this antithesis, as Frantz Fanon has suggested, is what in fact helps normalize whiteness as abstract and thus leads to the racial subordination of nonwhite bodies (38).

Yet, at this point in the novel, Lola's ambiguous racial body and its more pronounced but still only partial hue of white challenge the embodied identity of New Englanders. She appears as African, Indian, Mexican, and diseased in the first two pages alone, yet she also has European features and a different hue of white when they look carefully. At first sight, Lola's body calls attention to white as a racial category, but it does so by showing that there are different hues of white. In *Who Would Have Thought It?* whiteness becomes a trope of economic and sexual power debated not by the bourgeois eastern Anglos alone, for as the novel progresses whiteness becomes a desired universal marker of political and cultural power for both Anglos and newly constituted Mexicans. What constitutes the "white race" and who can claim a white body is one of the complicated racial questions the novel explores.

Lola's disruption of whiteness and her metamorphic racial body symbolically represent the historical questions of what U.S. whites will do with their own racial minorities after slavery, the extermination of Native Americans, and the U.S.-Mexican War. Indeed, when Lola is first misread as an African American, her body is commodified like an African slave's body. After questioning the position that Lola will have in the family, Mrs. Norval, who is an activist for the abolitionist cause, hypocritically refuses to accept Lola into her household or to educate her as she has her white daughters. She states, "She will work—I'll see to that—and a good worker is sure of a home in New England. Mrs. Hammerhard will want such a girl as this, I hope, to mind the baby, and she will give her some of her cast off clothes and her victuals. . . . [S]he can't expect to grow up in idleness and be a burden to us" (23–24). Lola's position as a worker for Anglos and as an enslaved captive will serve as a subplot throughout *Who*

Would Have Thought It? When Lola first enters as a racial object, her body enables the Norvals to advance economically. This plot line metaphorically situates Lola's body as a "stand in" for the historical reality of African slavery and the position that African Americans, whose black bodies are commodified, hold after the Civil War (Reid-Pharr 3–46).

Mrs. Norval does not want Lola, who is assumed at this point to be a "little black girl," to have an education and control her own wealth. She does not want to give Lola the ability to reason and hold a similar subject position as other "civilized" New Englanders who are able to enter the public sphere as reasoned and abstracted bourgeois citizens. Based on Lola's body, which Mrs. Norval believes renders her part of the "Negroid race," Mrs. Norval feels that Lola should remain a docile subject within the private sphere. As Mrs. Norval's actions suggest, the body of the black is what defines his or her role as a domestic laborer for the white elites (Sánchez-Eppler 18). This racist sentiment is further demonstrated when Mrs. Norval argues that she must condition Lola to do what is "natural" for black bodies: that is, they should work and not become idle or citizen-subjects.

Mrs. Norval's sentiments about Lola's body represent a racial and economic "unconscious" discourse in the United States. Indeed, the novel calls attention to the United States's democratic hypocrisy by revealing that this "free" country was built on a slavocracy and on the backs of Africans. The question of Lola's position in Mrs. Norval's domestic space, then, is a symbolic question regarding what space African bodies will occupy after the Civil War and during Reconstruction: the private or public spheres? This reading contradicts Sánchez and Pita's introductory argument that *Who Would Have Thought It?* does not fully deal with slavery, abolitionism, African Americans or the Reconstruction era.[7] As this and later scenes will demonstrate, slavery, the South, and blackness are in fact important tropes in Ruiz de Burton's novel. That the novel begins with such African American racial questions is significant, eventually informing the novel's relocation of the Mexican Question.

Who Would Have Thought It? represents African Americans, strategically, with a guarded sympathy. It calls attention, for instance, to a purportedly inherent racism that whites have against black-skinned peoples and the problems that the United States believes it has with its African population, a population just entering the public sphere following Reconstruction. This phenomenon was commonly known as the "Negro Problem" (Foner 43–58). In the last page of *Who Would Have Thought It?* Beau, a power-driven politician who is against the corrupt Grant Administration emphatically argues that "I never cared about the color of the skin or about the character of my followers. . . . My blood curdles with horror! My brain reels with indignation! I can hardly articulate, but it must be told. He [President Grant] has dared to slight a colored gentleman! No less distinguished a citizen of African descent than Mr. Fred Douglass" (298).

Unlike other muckraking and roman à clef novels written during Reconstruction—Henry Adams's *Democracy*, for example—*Who Would Have Thought It?* addresses President Grant's failure to invite Frederick Douglass to the White House and refers to Grant's weak policies in helping African Americans after the Civil War. This concluding scene demonstrates that the (black) politics of the body are present up to the last page. Moreover, Ruiz de Burton's use of Douglass and her implicit allusion to the Negro Problem is important because it reveals yet another complicated subplot in the novel: the historical and cultural interweaving of African Americans, the South, and the Civil War with the U.S.-Mexican War and the Mexican Question in the United States.

To further understand the novel's use of Douglass to create a connection between the politics of blackness and of Mexicanness, it is important to contextualize Douglass's relationship to the U.S.-Mexican War and the Mexican Question. In *A Negro View of the Mexican War* Douglass argues against U.S. expansion into Mexico and against entering the war. He felt that the United States was plundering Mexico for lands and was creating a "hypocritical pretense of a regard for peace and that they were partaking in the most barbarous outrages committed upon an unoffending people" (422). He continued to argue that the war with Mexico was an act of wholesale murder.[8]

Although it will never be known if Ruiz de Burton read Douglass's article, one can speculate that she did, since the article was published widely while she lived in New England. Either way, by addressing Anglo-Americans' problems with African Americans and blackness, *Who Would Have Thought It?* is able to create a sustained critique of how the United States constructs race in binary terms, white vs. black, which, during the antebellum period, were created out of the geographic polarities between the domestic South and North and between white and black bodies. Hence the novel complicates what many cultural historians have argued: that African Americans made Anglos aware of their own race and whiteness in the public spheres, as well as making them consider the implications of blood and the body in distinguishing racial categories in the United States (Gordon 103–8). Indeed, as the novel continues, Ruiz de Burton shows that Mexican bodies represent an equally ambivalent location in U.S. public culture.

This does not mean that *Who Would Have Thought It?* is an abolitionist text primarily interested in the biopolitics of African American bodies and the "Negro Question" during Reconstruction. Indeed, elite Mexican-American relations with African Americans during the nineteenth century were strained at best. Many landed-class Mexican Americans, such as Ruiz de Burton, distinguished themselves from southern blacks in order to create their own bailiwick of political power and maintain land rights in a U.S. culture that privileged whiteness and disdained blackness. And as Neil Foley has argued, how Mexican Americans were racially defined in the United States had to do not only with Anglo distinctions from the African American black body and blood but also with middle-class Mexicans' own racial distinctions from blackness (23–37).[9] Debates over the racial constitution of Mexicans in Ruiz de Burton's native California would reveal a similar construction. When the California constitution was being written, for example, the citizenship status of Mexicans came down to an embodied discourse that classified Mexicans as "semi-civilized" whites in order to exclude the African races of the south from full participation in California laws (Almaguer 56). In these debates, both elite Mexicans and Anglos had much to gain by defining Mexicans as semicivilized whites and not black.

Within this complicated historical matrix, *Who Would Have Thought It?* uses blackness as a backdrop in order to problematize how racial constructs have affected race consciousness in the United States. Blackness, abolitionism, and the Civil War, then, are used as historical and cultural tropes to expose the text's central provocation: the Mexican Question. The novel is therefore not an abolitionist text that fights for the equality of African Americans but rather an abolitionist text that fights for the rights and status of what Ruiz de Burton would define in her second novel, *The Squatter and the Don*, as "the white slaves of the Southwest" (234), that is, the newly constituted Mexican Americans.

"PLAYING INDIAN"

Ruiz de Burton's focus on African American blackness in *Who Would Have Thought It?* should be seen as one part of her strategy to set up the most compelling racial effort in the book, defining the limits of the Mexican Question. However, one cannot consider the Mexican Question in the novel without understanding its relationship to the "Indian Question." Although the first metamorphosis of Lola's body helps bring about the novel's exploration of African blackness and its role in American culture, the dialectic that occurs when Lola's embodied identity borders on the Native American and the Mexican American invokes a complicated view of Mexican racial identity that affects Chicanos to this day.[10] Once again, to explore the complicated dynamics of racechanges in the novel, we need to return to the first chapters of the novel.

After listening to his wife's racist comments about Lola and her position as a worker, Dr. Norval explains to his wife that Lola is not African American, despite her "looking" like she is part of that race. He explains to her that Indians dyed Lola's body, that her blood is of pure Spanish descent, and that she comes from an elite family with a rich heritage (24–25). The dye, he argues, will wear off in time. What is presented through Lola's body is a debate about defining race and subjectivity through the visible body or its underlying genetic code: blood. On one narrative level, the novel represents the body as a vital tool in identifying any differences pertaining to race. And race, of course, is crucial in the process of distinguishing differences among bodies or, in this case, of interpreting Lola's body.

The novel complicates and exposes this discourse of race by bringing forth the element of blood and its defining of corporeal subjectivity. Dr. Norval, for example, insists that Lola's blood and ancestry give her the ability to enter the Norval household as an equal and not as a servant. If her body is seen as white, then she has the ability to enter the private sphere as an equal. Dr. Norval goes on to argue that when Lola is able to acquire the wealth that her mother left her, she will not be seen as an Indian or a "nigger," for her money will give her the appearance of equality (27). Class, he hopes, will inscribe her racial body.

What becomes apparent in the novel, however, is that the tension between Lola's blood and her potential economic wealth lies behind a body that "deceives" Anglo perceptions, a body that renders her as racialized. The novel's question, then, is if blood or the body defines the rights and status of Mexicans in the United States. Blood, as Foucault suggests, may be a historical reality, but what *Who Would Have Thought It?* explores are nineteenth-century scientific discourses that posited blood or the body as defining racial subjects (Foucault 23–45). In the late nineteenth century, the idea of blood became an important "scientific" discourse that helped define race in America, just as genetics has in the twentieth (Dyer 24).[11] But the body, too, was a central discourse in defining race in the nineteenth century. In this way, what constitutes Mexican racial identity—the skin or the blood—becomes central to the Mexican Question. But in this novel the skin is a false (and falsified) signifier; it is surface, the "phenomenal" in Kantian terms, while the blood represents depth, the "noumenal."[12]

This issue is particularly evident when Lola's body begins its last metamorphosis. As this occurs, she begins to develop dark spots. With dark spots, she is no longer "seen" by the New England public as African, for the spots phenotypically define her as part of the Pinto Indian tribe. The Pinto Indians, Mr. Hackwell reminds the Norvals, have spots all over their bodies. Thus, Lola's body finally has a racial match. And although Lola's "Spanish" bloodline and her dyed skin have become public knowledge, the eastern public still assumes that since her body *looks* spotted, she must be a Pinto Indian; and if she isn't, she must be diseased (78–80).

The allusion to Pinto Indians is historically important and reveals how the novel "plays Indian" in order to expose the racial distinctions between Mexicans and Anglos that develop in the nineteenth century.[13] An editorial written after the U.S.-Mexican War in the *San Diego Herald*, for example, describes the racial distinction that occurs between Pinto Indians and Mexicans in the Southwest: "The Population of the State of Guerrero is nearly Aztec, and the descendents of the tribes who fought desperately against the Spaniards. The Pintos, i.e. they are covered with blotches upon the skin, blue, white, and chocolate color—that give them an aspect of ferocity, which has been fearfully verified on all occasions— they have no sympathy or feeling in common with any people who boast of Castillian extraction" (1 April 1854, 23). Although the article and *Who Would Have Thought It?* demonstrate the ignorance of Anglos, Ruiz de Burton's novel (and the article, albeit implicitly) creates a racial distinction between Indians and Mexican Americans by Lola "playing Indian." This distinction exists, in part, because landed Mexicans desired such a racial distinction before and after the war with the United States. Indeed, much as the article depicts Pintos and Indians as savages, so too does *Who Would Have Thought It?* maintain this racist discourse. Moreover, the racialization of Indians in the book by both Anglos and Mexican Americans occurs because of the racial consciousness that was developing among landed Mexican Americans about their own mestizo blood, an embodied ideology called the "Spanish fantasy heritage."

The racial distinction between Mexicans and Indians is particularly evident in the novel's use of Indian captivity and the attendant sympathy it evokes with the demise of Lola's captive mother, Doña Medina. Lola's mother, a "civilized" Mexican woman, is held captive by Indians, whom the narrator, the Mexican, and the Anglo characters describe as a "savage" race. And because Doña Medina has become the wife of the Indian chief, the novel implicitly acknowledging that she is his sexual partner, she cannot return with Dr. Norval; her body has been tainted and violated by the "savage race." The narrator sardonically concludes that although he/she is "not a political philosopher," this tragedy of Indian captivity and savagery has occurred because the Mexican government allows Indian savages to "devastate Mexican lands."

The racial antagonism toward Native Americans that the novel endorses is not surprising, especially considering that bourgeois Mexican Americans have racialized Indians for centuries. Defining themselves as *gente de razón* (people with reason) and white, landed Mexican Americans held racist views of Indians and constructed a peonage, a hacienda-based economic system that was similar to the plantation economy of the U.S. South. Though they did not create a genocidal frontier like Anglos after the war with Mexico, Mexicans were nonetheless racist in their views. This is ironic, however, since elite Mexican Americans of nineteenth-century California were mestizos, half-Indian and half-Spanish, which is why Anglos racially defined Mexicans as "semi-civilized" and "mongrels."[14] However, despite the end of the Spanish-Mexican casta system and the ideology of gente de razón after the war, the newly constituted Mexican Americans conflated their discourses of gente de razón with Anglo-American discourse of whiteness to create the Spanish fantasy heritage.

New Anglo ideologies of racial classification and whiteness began to center around blood as well as the skin, creating a tension that the novel explores but never resolves in its depiction of Lola's metamorphic body. Under the pressure of this emergent obsession with blood and skin, manifested in the racial images of Mexicans in the Anglo public sphere, landed Californios endorsed a mythical bloodline that created a racial distinction from their "true" Native American and African ancestry. What *Who Would Have Thought It?* explores through Lola's blood and body, then, is the intersection of the elite Mexican-American and Anglo-American "scientific" ideas of race and whiteness, an intersection created out of competing colonial discourses. Elite Mexicans denied their Indian and African bodies, their "true" heritage, not only because of the mythic Spanish colonial ideology distinguishing gente de razón from racial others, but also, in equal measure, in response to how the conquering Anglos perceived the newly colonized Mexican population who resided in the southwestern lands after the war. How Mexicans created distinctions between themselves and the other races of the Americas reveals the contradictory nature of the Mexican Question, which Ruiz de Burton's novel captures well. Her novel problematizes the black/white racial ideologies structuring the Civil War only by effectively endorsing a bourgeois, conservative Spanish fantasy heritage, thus normalizing Mexicans as whiter and therefore more classed than Native Americans, African Americans, and Anglo-Americans in the public sphere (232).

This race and class dynamic culminates when Lola explains to Julian—an Anglo-American in whom she develops a romantic interest—that her body should not classify her as an African or an Indian, for her blood comes from a wealthy Mexican family and therefore she is "white." In this scene, Lola is first able to articulate her own identity and obtains agency. "I was an object of aversion because my skin was black. And yet I was too proud to tell you that the blackness of my skin would wear off, that it was only stained by Indians to prevent our being rescued. My mother also was made to stain her lovely white skin all black. . . . I wanted to tell you this many times. . . . I didn't care whether I was thought white or black by others, I hated to think that you might suppose I was Indian or black. But I did not want to say anything to you because I thought you might laugh at me, and not believe me" (101). Julian replies that he knew otherwise, for his father had told him that Lola's blood was pure Spanish. Lola, however, is aware of the tensions between skin and blood in New England racial ideology: "But I often heard your mother say things by which I could plainly see she did not believe that I was white. And when the dye began to wear off, and my skin got all spotted, she sent me away, because she thought I had a contagious disease, and she said that Mr. Hackwell said that perhaps I belonged to the Pintos and my skin was naturally spotted" (101).

This scene marks the turning point in the novel, for at this midpoint, Lola's final metamorphosis begins and thus her body reveals the interrelated complexities of Mexican and Anglo ideologies of whiteness that the novel explores.[15] After this scene, Lola's "white" blood begins to match her now fully faded white body. And Spanish blood, according to Julian and Lola, affords her the status of other white Europeans, defining part of the ideology that landed Mexicans endorsed in California. Yet, once the Anglo characters perceive Lola's body and her blood as white, Lola's (Mexican) white body becomes sexualized and thereby symbolically represents the reconstitution of the Anglo Mexican Question.

The novel's opening allusion to Mexicans, Californios, and Indians as equally horrid races, then, is in fact the novel's central provocation. Mexicans, Indians, and Californios are not, of course, cultural equivalents, although Anglo-Americans constructed them as such in the public sphere. *Who Would Have Thought It?* offers the Reconstruction-era public a particular education, namely, that Mexican Californios are a distinct race, one that is different from America's other dark races, one that is also Euro-American and, in fact, a "prettier" hue of white. As the novel ends, the Anglo characters begin to comprehend Lola's embodied identity and are thus able to understand the central lesson of Californio racial ideology: that Indians and landed Mexicans are not the same. Mattie, for example, who began the novel by comparing Lola to Africans and Indians, eventually asserts, "Talk of Spanish Women being dark! Can anything be whiter than Lola's neck and shoulders?" Ruth and Emma respond by confirming that Lola is "a Mexican" and infer that, as such, she comes from a race that is whiter than their own (232).[16]

AN ECONOMIC ROMANCE OF REUNION

As a white Mexican who is now in control of her body, Lola is able to romantically unite with Julian, a turn of plot symbolically representing the complex reunion between the Mexican south and Anglo north after the U.S.-Mexican War. As the role of Lola's inheritance suggests, the courtship and concluding romantic betrothal between Lola and Julian reveals that this symbolic union is ultimately interested in resolving the racial discourse surrounding the Mexican Question according to a capitalist relation. Thus the concluding betrothal should be read as a union of two distinct elite "white" bodies, a union that will enable economically landed Mexican-American women to take control of their raced and sexed bodies through a "proper" or "chosen" heterosexual union with a white, northern man. The romantic ending between Lola and Julian, then, represents a desire for not only racial but also economic uplift through a geographic union between the members of the bourgeois Mexican south and Anglo north. This geoeconomic union between landed Mexican white and Anglo-Saxon white blood is not a new trope for Ruiz de Burton. Her novel *The Squatter and the Don* would also end with a similar union between a Mexican-American "white" woman and an Anglo male. Nor is this literary trope unique to Ruiz de Burton's novels. Many landed and middle-class Mexican-American women writers well into the early twentieth century would explore heterosexual relations between Anglo men and Mexican-American women through an equally interesting exploration of relations between Greater Mexico and the United States. Jovita González's *Dew on the Thorn* and *Caballero* would also explore race and sexuality in similar unions. Moreover, historians of this period have found that this literary trope reflected a historical reality for many landed Mexican-American women after the U.S.-Mexican War.[17] In the wake of that war, Mexican women became trophies much like the land itself, and white men were the heroic conquerors and bearers of civilization. Indeed, Ruiz de Burton herself married an Anglo officer.

The ending of this novel resembles the Reconstruction-era novels that

Nina Silber defines as "Romance to Reunion" (39–66). Silber argues that the reconciliation of North and South following the Civil War depended as much on cultural imagination as on the politics of Reconstruction. Therefore, between the years 1865 and 1900, novels as diverse as Lydia Maria Child's *Romance of the Republic* (1867), John de Forest's *Miss Ravenal's Conversion From Secession to Loyalty* (1867), and Henry James's *The Bostonians* (1892) created southern and northern protagonists who would symbolically unite at the end of the novel, thus resolving the "real" sectional tension that existed between the U.S. South and North after the Civil War. In *Who Would Have Thought It?*, the concluding romance-to-reunion trope extended far beyond the sectional opposition between the domestic south and north. Indeed, what the conclusion reveals is that Ruiz de Burton subverts this popular trope into a transnational configuration between the Mexican south and the U.S. north, thus describing the Greater Mexican understanding of U.S. culture that the opening scene of the novel brings to the foreground. Hence, the trope of romance to reunion—so popular in the southern discourses about the Civil War and Reconstruction that have firmly taken hold in U.S. public culture—serve Ruiz de Burton as a metaphor for the unresolved, misunderstood, and forgotten conflict between the Mexican south and the U.S. north after the U.S.-Mexican War of 1848. By inserting Spanish-Mexicans into the center of Reconstruction-era embodied politics and literary discourses, Ruiz de Burton hoped to introduce the U.S. public to the question that had affected her and her fellow Mexicans since the Treaty of Guadalupe: what place do we have in the United States?

Although the novel's concluding "reunion" attempts to normalize the rights and status of newly constituted Mexican Americans with and against the other races in the United States and endorses a classed and racial uplift, it should not be seen as an act of resistance or blatant assimilation. Rather, for Ruiz de Burton, the concluding union was an attempt to demonstrate that the complex national and racial questions that were shaping New England culture during Reconstruction were not centered solely on domestic northern-southern relations or on the place that African Americans would hold in the white northern public spheres. Ruiz de Burton believed that the Mexican Question, and its Greater Mexican implications, should also be a focus of inquiry. Such a geopolitical configuration in the novel also serves as a reminder that the nineteenth-century domestic South was a transnational space, one that overlapped with and helped shape both Anglo America and Greater Mexico.

Nevertheless, her novel was not as successful as Anglo-American romance-to-reunion novels. Indeed, cultural productions that dealt with the Mexican Question were never as successful as novels about the domestic South, African Americans, or Native Americans. And as history and popular culture demonstrates, the Civil War, not the U.S.-Mexican War, has been the most important cultural marker for U.S. cultural production and race relations (Young 1–23; Cullen 8–28; Streeby 1–24).

This is not surprising, however. Since John O'Sullivan's utterance of the term in 1845, America has never truly dealt with the Mexican Question, and it has remained an ambivalent discourse precisely because it makes visible the imperialist geopolitical designs of U.S. democracy. Perhaps due to their semicivilized status in the nineteenth-century public sphere—part Spanish and thus European, part Native American and thus a mongrel race—Mexicans in the United States have shaped U.S. culture through a democratic contradiction that results from the relationship between their designated racial status and universal ideals of citizenship. They are in theory U.S. citizens because of the Treaty of Guadalupe, and yet they are racialized as second-class "mongrel" citizens because they are not fully white Americans.

Indeed, at the same time that the treaty granted the semblance of legal citizenship to Mexicans, literary and political spheres racialized and undermined them as U.S. citizens. After the war, southern Senator John C. Calhoun, for example, stated to Congress, as later printed in the *Congressional Record*, that Mexicans represented "a motley amalgamation of impure races, not [even] as good as Cherokees and Choctaws" (29 July 1849, 17). He continued to ask the American public if they could "incorporate a people so dissimilar in every respect—so little qualified for free and popular government—without certain destruction to our political institutions. We do not want the people of Mexico, either as citizens or subjects." Senator Calhoun's anxiety that the inclusion of Mexican mongrels would destroy the fabric of U.S. democracy was not historically isolated to the years of the treaty. What was so important about Ruiz de Burton's novel, then, was that it offered the first Mexican-American response in English to Anglo-American inquiries into the democratic rights and racial status of Mexicans in Greater Mexico. Ruiz de Burton does this by inserting landed Californios/as into the rhetoric of U.S. (white) reunification and thus disrupting the corporeal body-politic unified by "one flesh."[18] She thus creates a compelling and contradictory model for shifting the focus of domestic investigations of U.S. nationalism and racial imaginary to a more transnational and inclusive view of American cultural production, a view that takes into account the effects that the Mexican Question had in shaping the U.S. South and New World studies.

1. I have located hundreds of instances of the term "Mexican Question" in nineteenth- and early-twentieth-century cultural forms, the first of which was published in the *United States Magazine and Democratic Review* in 1845. The term itself is an expansionist inquest into the democratic rights and racial status of Mexicans in the United States and, as such, reveals the contradiction between nineteenth-century racial ideologies, territorial expansion, and the universal norms and ideals of U.S. democracy. Antonia Castañeda's work on Mexican women and the land has been invaluable for my understanding of the gendered dimensions of the Mexican Question. See "Que Se Pudieran Defender." I thank her and all of the Chicana feminists who have done groundbreaking work in this area, such as Emma Pérez, Deena González, Alicia Gaspar De Alba, Katheryn Ríos, Mary Pat Brady, and Sandy Soto. I also had the privilege of reading an essay Castañeda is working on entitled "Malinche, Califia y Toypurina: Of Myths, Monsters, and Embodied History." Without it and her assistance, this essay would have never been fully realized.

2. My use of the term *geopolitical* is meant to confront and analyze the geographical imagination of the state, its foundational myths, and the political norms and ideals that develop from U.S. territoriality. I explore the interrelationship between *geo-* and *political* in order to analyze the mutually constitutive relationship between the construction of political cultures, racial ideologies, and geographic discourses. What is of interest to me, then, is how geography and politics became so important in the project of democratic culture and the racialization of Mexicans. Equally important, though, is how this relationship was normalized in order to elide the racial inquests that mediate its contradictory logic. See the introduction to Tauthail and Dalby for a recent example of the relationship between the geographic imagination and the formation of political cultures. See also Jacobson.

3. I owe much of this biographical information to José Aranda. He has been an invaluable reader and colleague. See his *When We Arrive.*

4. It is important to note that this trope was also seen in Latin American literature of the nineteenth century and was called *blanqueamiento.* I thank distinguished professor of Spanish Nicolás Kanellos for his help on this draft and ideas of racechanges.

5. I use "Spanish-Mexican" because Ruiz de Burton's novel uses both terms, "Mexican" and "Spanish," to define Lola's racial status. This is not to say, however, that María Amparo Ruiz de Burton was a Mexican American. Her obfuscation of "Mexican" with "Spanish-Mexican" occurs because of the contradictory racial inquest that *both* Anglos and the newly constituted "Mexican American" created when attempting to define the race and status of Mexicans in the United States. In the nineteenth century, some landed Mexicans in the United States fashioned themselves as white Spanish Americans in order to normalize their racialized bodies for U.S. public spheres. Nevertheless, since the Treaty of Guadalupe Hidalgo all Mexicans in U.S. political and literary spheres have been, at one time or another, constituted as a racial minority. Indeed, under the disembodied and universal ideals and norms of democratic inclusion, *all* Mexicans in the United States have been racialized as Others, and their status

and rights have therefore always been suspect in public culture. Although María Amparo Ruiz de Burton may fashion her character as a Spanish American, in the public sphere Spanish-Mexican women were nevertheless objects of racial, territorial, and sexual conquest. For an excellent examination of the complicated ways in which Mexican women fashioned themselves in the public sphere in the age of U.S. expansion, see González.

6. By the 1870s the Southwest was considered public domain, and Anglo-Americans were free to take anything from these lands. A number of maps depicted this public space at the time and were widely circulated throughout New England; one important example was Thompson's "National Map of Public Domain, 1873," created one year after the novel was published. This map was used to help define the boundaries of the U.S. Census maps in 1880.

7. Although I do not agree with Sánchez and Pita's points about the novel's representation of the Civil War and African Americans, I find their introduction to *Who Would Have Thought It?* a brilliant analysis of the novel (xviii).

8. Douglass was perhaps aware that the lands ceded to the United States after the war would become slave states.

9. This may also have to do with the fact that Mexicans were racialized as having African American blood and "Negroid features." See De León 45. Also see Menchaca's excellent study of Mexican racial classification, *Recovering History, Constructing Race.*

10. The denial of the Native American body by "landed" Mexican Americans is much different from the working-class ideology that embraced the mestizo body after El Movimiento. That both of these discourses were framed through race, class, and the body is a subject I will discuss in my book.

11. For a detailed discussion of the rise of scientific racism, see Wade.

12. I thank Jon Smith for pointing this out. I would also like to thank him for reading this essay so carefully. Extending the Kantian duality between the phenomenal and noumenal, *Who Would Have Thought It?* can be said to represent the phenomenal body as the false signifier of racial and political ontology and thus to challenge the white, disembodied, and metaphysical norms and ideals of public-sphere inclusion. In contrast, the noumenal "blood" of the body is the realm of the thinkable, a metonym for the political and racial ontology of the Spanish-Mexican citizen and thus enables the possibility of Mexican-American political inclusion through a similar metaphysical abstraction as white Americans. The noumenal body is cognizable and only its possibility is thinkable (Kant 255).

13. Pat Hilden pointed this out when I gave a talk at the University of Oregon. Also see Deloria's *Playing Indian.*

14. See, for example, William R. Lighton's "The Greaser" in *The Atlantic,* 1899.

15. Note that, after this scene, the novel defines Lola as Mexican and Spanish interchangeably.

16. Here is a prime example of the Spanish-Mexican terminology used in the novel.

17. For an excellent analysis of relations between Mexican women and Anglo men in the nineteenth century, see González.

18. This biblical metaphor of "one flesh" was a common phrase used by southern and

northern politicians in the age of expansion. The Whig Alexander H. Stephens of Georgia, for example, employed it to describe Texans as Anglo-Saxons: "They are from us; bone of our bone, and flesh of our flesh" (qtd. in Isenberg 250). What is important to point out is that embodied discourses constitute political solidarity.

WORKS CITED

Almaguer, Tomas. *Racial Fault Lines: The Historical Origins of White Supremacy in California.* Berkeley: U of California P, 1994.

Aranda, José, Jr. *When We Arrive: A New Literary History of Mexican America.* Tucson: Arizona UP, 2002.

Castañeda, Antonia. "Que Se Pudieran Defender [So You Could Defend Yourselves]: Chicanas, Regional History, and National Discourses." *Frontiers* 32.3 (2001): 84–115.

Cullen, Jim. *The Civil War in Popular Culture: A Reusable Past.* Washington, D.C.: Smithsonian Institution P, 1995.

Cushing, Caleb. "Mexico." *Democratic Review* 18 (1846): 838–44.

De León, Arnoldo. *They Call Them Greasers: Anglo Attitudes toward Mexicans in Texas, 1821–1900.* Austin: U of Texas P, 1983.

Deloria, Philip. *Playing Indian.* New Haven, Conn.: Yale UP, 1998.

Douglass, Frederick. *Frederick Douglass: A Critical Reader.* Ed. Bill E. Lawson and Frank M. Kirkland. Malden: Blackwell, 1999.

Dyer, Richard. *White.* New York: Routledge, 1997.

Fanon, Frantz. *Black Skin, White Masks.* New York: Grove, 1991.

Foley, Neil. *White Scourge: Mexicans, Blacks, and Poor Whites in Texas Cotton Culture.* Berkeley: U of California P, 1999.

Foner, Eric. *Reconstruction: America's Unfinished Revolution, 1863–1877.* New York: Norton, 2002.

Foucault, Michel. *Technologies of the Self.* Amherst: U of Massachusetts P, 1988.

González, Deena J. *Refusing the Favor: The Spanish-Mexican Women of Santa Fe 1820–1880.* Oxford: Oxford UP, 1999.

Gordon, Linda. *The Great Arizona Orphan Abduction.* Cambridge, Mass.: Harvard UP, 1999.

Gubar, Susan. *RaceChanges: White Skin, Black Face in American Culture.* New York: Oxford UP, 1997.

Gutiérrez, David. *Walls and Mirrors: Mexican Americans, Mexican Immigrants, and the Politics of Ethnicity.* Berkeley: U of California P, 1995.

Isenberg, Nancy. *Sex and Citizenship in Antebellum America.* Chapel Hill: U of North Carolina P, 1998.

Jacobson, David. *Place and Belonging in America.* Baltimore, Md.: Johns Hopkins UP, 2002.

Kant, Immanuel. *Critique of Pure Reason.* Trans. N. Kemp Smith. New York: Palgrave Macmillan, 1965.

Lighton, William. "The Greaser." *The Atlantic* July 1899: 986–1021.

Menchaca, Martha. *Recovering History, Constructing Race: The Indian, Black, and White Roots of Mexican Americans*. Austin: U of Texas P, 2001.

O'Neill, John. *Five Bodies: The Human Shape in Modern Society*. Ithaca, N.Y.: Cornell UP, 1985.

O'Sullivan, John L. "The Mexican Question." *Democratic Review* 16 (1845): 422–28.

Paredes, Américo. *A Texas-Mexican Cancionero*. Austin: U of Texas P, 1995.

Reid-Pharr, Robert. *Conjugal Union: The Body, the House, and the Black American*. Oxford: Oxford UP, 1999.

Ruiz de Burton, María Amparo. *The Squatter and the Don*. Ed. and intro. Rosaura Sánchez and Beatrice Pita. Houston: Arte Público, 1997.

——. *Who Would Have Thought It?* Philadelphia: Lippincott, 1874. Ed. and intro. Rosaura Sánchez and Beatrice Pita. Houston: Arte Público, 1995.

Sánchez-Eppler, Karen. *Touching Liberty: Abolition, Feminism, and the Politics of the Body*. Berkeley: U of California P, 1993.

Silber, Nina. *The Romance of Reunion: Northerners and the South, 1865–1900*. Chapel Hill: U of North Carolina P, 1997.

Streeby, Shelley. *American Sensations: Class, Empire, and the Production of Popular Culture*. Berkeley: U of California P, 2002.

Tauthail, Gearóid, and Simon Dalby, eds. *Rethinking Geopolitics*. New York: Routledge, 1998.

Wade, Maurice. "From Eighteenth- to Nineteenth-Century Racial Science: Continuity and Change." *Race and Racism in Theory and Practice*. Ed. Berel Lang. Lanham, Md.: Rowman and Littlefield, 2000. 27–44.

Young, Elizabeth. *Disarming the Nation: Women's Writing and the American Civil War*. Chicago: U of Chicago P, 1999.

The Americans are strong, powerful, fearless, and
seem to have unlimited wealth. . . . But most of them
lack what we have: dignity, self-respect, pride, nobility,
traditions, and an old and sound religion.

—JOVITA GONZÁLEZ AND EVE RALEIGH, *Caballero*

VINCENT PÉREZ

Remembering the Hacienda:

History and Memory in Jovita González

and Eve Raleigh's *Caballero: A Historical Novel*

n the past decade a group of scholars associated
with the Recovering the U.S. Hispanic Literary
Heritage project has been engaged in the on-
going endeavor to recuperate literary texts by early Latino and Latina
writers. An interdisciplinary venture directed by Nicolás Kanellos and
located at the University of Houston, the Recovery Project's mission is to
identify, recover, interpret, and preserve Hispanic writings from the colonial period to 1960. As noted by one of its distinguished scholars, José F.
Aranda Jr., the project's related objective "is the narration of the lives
of people of Hispanic descent since the sixteenth century, using such
sources as histories, diaries, memoirs, prose, poetry, fiction, and newspapers" (563). In its first decade the Recovery Project has uncovered a
wealth of formerly unknown writings, works that would otherwise have
remained silenced by racialized disciplinary practices that consigned
some of them for more than a century to discursive oblivion. One of
those works is the Recovery Project's recently recovered text *Caballero: A
Historical Novel*, by the Mexican-American educator and folklorist Jovita
González and her Anglo-American coauthor, Eve Raleigh.[1] A historical

romance about Mexican-Anglo conflict and conciliation, *Caballero* is set on a south Texas livestock hacienda during the U.S.-Mexican War (1846–1848). Though written in the 1930s and early 1940s, it was first published in 1996.

As a hacienda narrative, *Caballero*'s striking similarities to U.S. southern plantation fiction serve to illustrate the complexities and contradictions of the Recovery Project's reconstruction of literary history.[2] In its cultural and historical convergences with plantation narrative, *Caballero* explodes Chicano/a studies categorizations that would define such early Mexican-American literature as uniformly subaltern, an assumption embraced by numerous Recovery Project scholars in readings of newly recovered early texts.[3] Critical reception to one such text, María Amparo Ruiz de Burton's formerly unknown 1885 novel *The Squatter and the Don* (republished in 1992) provides a case in point. Though Recovery Project scholars such as Aranda and Manuel Martín-Rodríguez have identified ideological contradictions in this novel's ostensibly progressive critique of U.S. (capitalist) practices, other critics continue to place *The Squatter and the Don* in the tradition of counterhegemonic Mexican-American literary production.[4] As Aranda notes, "in the growing critical industry being built around the reemergence" of Ruiz de Burton, "many have followed the lead of her recoverers, Rosaura Sánchez and Beatrice Pita, in locating a 'resistance' narrative in her life and writings and historicizing her biography as 'subaltern'" (554).

Just as Aranda and Martín-Rodríguez reject a simplistic reading of *The Squatter and the Don* as "resistant," I propose that *Caballero* similarly demonstrates the need for rigorously historicized and comparatist studies of early Mexican-American literary texts. *Caballero*'s intersection with plantation narrative presents a compelling model for carrying out this interpretive project. Contradicting ethnic nationalism through its depiction of unions between Mexicans and Anglo-Americans, *Caballero* simultaneously upsets a narrowly defined Chicano/a literary recovery model through its aesthetic affiliation with the southern (white) literary tradition. Ambiguously affirming a common historic identification based on a shared sense of ethnicity while displacing much of what the semifeudal hacienda came to symbolize for its authors, *Caballero*, like Ruiz de Burton's novel, speaks to the heterogeneity of Mexican-American culture and history and the multiplicity of current and past (Mexican-American) identities as shaped by this myriad experience. One means by which a Mexican-American (literary) history can be recovered without being romanticized as always already ethnically defined resistance can be found by exploring the dual postcolonial origins of the Chicano/a population—Spanish and U.S.—as captured in the space of the hacienda in González and Raleigh's novel.

The southern analogy for *Caballero* draws on several recent literary models. The plantation novel's political strategies parallel the nation-building project of nineteenth-century romantic fiction in Latin America as these have been explicated in Doris Sommer's *Foundational Fictions*. Sommer views the Latin American romance as a novelistic projection of, and device for, national political consolidation in a period of internal intersectional conflict in the newly ascendant nineteenth-century republics. It is in this interpretive context that José E. Limón, who with María Cotera recovered and edited *Caballero*, observes that marriages between representatives of opposed groups in the novel symbolically resolve inter-ethnic and regional conflict, projecting a consolidated U.S. nation into which Mexican Texans have been fully integrated. Though Limón does not repeat the subaltern argument, he does point to the possible influence of the Latin American, and particularly the Mexican, historical romance on *Caballero*. However, plantation narrative was just as likely a source, a possibility that would overturn a Chicano/a recovery model by placing González at the center of discourses typically associated with Anglo America.[5] This comparatist interpretation would account more fully for the novel's focus on nineteenth-century hacienda history as well as the work's foregrounding of (modern) Anglo America over (semi-feudal) Mexico. That the Missouri-born Raleigh "had some large role probably in crafting the overall romantic narrative development of the plot" makes the argument for a southern influence even more compelling (Limón, Introduction xx). Limón emphasizes Raleigh's role in "crafting González's contribution into the form of the romance novel" (xix–xx). Correspondence between the authors also makes clear to Limón, however, that this creative process occurred "with the active participation of González" (xxi), whose "family-ancestral background" provided the source of the novel's historical context and setting (xx). Finally, although a strict Chicano/a recovery model perhaps cannot be expected to imagine her as such, as a native-born Texan González was also a southerner by birth.

My analysis of *Caballero* differs from Limón's reading of the novel in another fundamental way. Mexican integration into U.S. society, as depicted in *Caballero*, is itself bifurcated along North and South lines, and is therefore more complicated than Limón's criticism suggests. Reflecting a not-always-repressed identification with Mexican Texas as a conquered region, the novel presents the conjugal union of two central characters—María de los Angeles Mendoza (Angela) and Alfred "Red" McLane—who represent opposing sides in the war, as a marriage of convenience even as this romance metonymically acknowledges benefits to the Mexican population in an imagined future U.S. Texas.[6] In a parallel interethnic union, however, the idealized "true" love between Angela's sister, Susanita Mendoza, and the southern planter Robert Davis Warrener contrasts markedly with the pragmatic union of Angela and Red. Whereas Limón uses Angela and Red's marriage of convenience as a primary frame of reference, both of these parallel romances must be examined in order to understand how the novel defines a path for Mexican-Anglo relations during the period in which the novel was written in the 1930s and 1940s.

Just as one cannot remove Margaret Mitchell's 1936 historical romance *Gone with the Wind*—a work that may well have served as the inspiration for *Caballero*—from the plantation tradition, one cannot understand González and Raleigh's novel without "remembering" the nineteenth-century history that it recovers.[7] Although, like Mitchell's novel, *Caballero* employs nineteenth-century history to explore social and cultural dilemmas of the modern (i.e., post-1900) era, as in *Gone with the Wind* this early history does not serve merely as an empty canvas devoid of cultural and ideological meaning. Much like plantation narratives that remember the Old South, *Caballero* recovers the Southwest's own "premodern" agrarian socioeconomic institution—the semifeudal hacienda—to negotiate a cultural and political path in the modern era for a population that, like the Old South, had been conquered in the mid-nineteenth century by the United States. Even if the novel diverges in important ways from plantation writings, *Caballero* evinces cultural, ideological, and political preoccupations strikingly similar to those of plantation works produced by white southerners—and particularly Mitchell's crowning text. And yet, unlike the plantation myth in much southern fiction, *Caballero*'s criticism of (Mexican) patriarchy and paternalism asserts the benefits of Mexican integration within the modern U.S. social order. Interethnic romance in the novel thus projects Mexican-American inclusion within a liberal "New South(west)," an imagined biracial society in which the "premodern" agrarian culture of its Mexican (i.e., southern) minority has not been lost but has served instead to enrich and transform a modern Anglo-American society driven by individualism and capitalism.

History and memory interplay in the hacienda as a site of memory in many early Mexican-American novels and autobiographies. Sites of memory, in Pierre Nora's formulation, are symbolic representations of the past that embody the interaction between history and memory. Forms of national or group affiliation, they include geographical places, monuments, historical figures, literary and artistic objects, emblems, commemorations, and other such "sites" of remembrance. Vestiges of a recovered history constructed in response to a modern world that no longer values memory or tradition, sites of memory, as Nora writes, are the ultimate "embodiment of a commemorative consciousness that survives in a [present] history which, having renounced memory, cries out for it" (Nora 6). Just as plantation narratives obscure the roles that race, class, and gender played in traditional southern society, in many early Mexican-American narratives the hacienda as memory-place cements layers of history and memory together into an iconic monument to the past, burying contrary memories in their project to buttress Mexican-American ethnic identity.

In *Caballero* the hacienda as memory-place operates in a more complex fashion, incorporating the countermemories of disenfranchised groups such as women and the lower classes. But much as in other early Mexican-American narratives, in *Caballero* the hacienda as memory-place also functions broadly as an ethnic cultural icon, one that emerges amid the socioeconomic transformation that occurred with the arrival of modern capitalism in the Mexican southwest. In Texas this change took place between 1880 and 1920, an era Richard Flores, in his recent study of the Alamo, calls the Texas Modern. During this period "local" Mexican agricultural and cattle-related practices in the region were replaced by commercial farming, a change that was made possible by the economic and social displacement of the Mexican worker (Flores 5). It was also during this period that the "construction of Mexican subjectivity as 'subjugated Otherness' [was] codified" (11). The cultural memory of the Alamo contributed to this codification, providing "semantic justification for slotting Mexicans and Anglos into an emerging social order brought forth by the material and ideological forces that gripped Texas between 1880 and 1920" (xvii). The significance of the cultural memory of the Alamo after the turn of the century, according to Flores, "makes interpretive sense only when read as both emerging from and constitutive of the changing material conditions of this period" (10). These conditions were formalized into "segregated, prejudicial, and devalued social relations between Anglos and Mexicans" (10). It was within this highly charged sociohistorical and cultural context that González and Raleigh, seeking to give voice to the silenced historical memory of Mexican Texans, wrote *Caballero*.

Caballero accomplishes its project by drawing on the centuries-long cultural memory of hacienda and ranching society in the U.S. Southwest and Mexico. If the plantation forms the historical foundation of U.S. southern society and culture, the hacienda may be said to dominate the pre-1900 history of Greater Mexico, that other southern region of North America encompassing present-day Mexico and the Mexican-American southwest. Feudalistic, paternalistic, and patriarchal, the hacienda's agrarian economic and cultural order shaped the character of all levels of Spanish and Mexican society throughout much of this region from the seventeenth through nineteenth centuries. Although the hacienda may appear more remote for contemporary Chicanos and Chicanas than the plantation has been for both white and black southerners, *Caballero* recalls this colonial institution's historical proximity, illustrating its cultural role as a site of memory and identity for early Mexican-American writers. The hacienda's conflicted meaning in *Caballero* also illustrates the heterogeneous historical experience of Mexican Americans—descendants of Spanish and U.S. colonialisms—a history that *Caballero*, more than other early Mexican-American narrative, succeeds in capturing.

Set on a livestock hacienda in south Texas, the border region between the Nueces River and the Rio Grande, *Caballero* opens in 1846 with news of the 1845 U.S. annexation of the Republic of Texas. Reflecting both Mexico's refusal to recognize the seizure of its northern territory and regional *Tejano* (Mexican Texan) resistance to Anglo-American aggression, Don Santiago de Mendoza y Soría, the patriarch of Rancho la Palma de Cristo, expresses shock at the news of the arrival of U.S. troops: "We laughed at their Republic of Texas," he tells his neighbor, "and at the flag they made and turned our backs to it and said 'We are in Mexico'" (11). "We do not choose to be dirty *Americanos*. We are Mexicans, our mother land was Spain. Not all of their laws can change us" (9). The novel is set during the two-year war that followed and ends in 1848. But the foreword harkens back to the colonial era of the previous century, establishing both the Mendoza family's genteel Hispanic/Creole pedigree and its almost mystical identification with the family hacienda, established in the 1740s by the Mendozas' pioneer ancestor, Don José Ramón. The hacienda buildings, it seems, were an obsession with Don José: "he loved every bit of mortar and every wooden pin that bound it" (xxxviii). Decades later, as a young man, Santiago is told by his dying grandmother that he will some day inherit the hacienda property and cultural legacy. The hacienda, she says, was "your grandfather's dream, which he built into reality. It was my entire life. . . . [B]e worthy of Rancho La Palma, and the things for which it stands . . . religion, traditions, [and] gentility" (xxxix).

Just as its semifeudal agrarian setting recalls the plantation landscape, *Caballero*'s sentimental plot, set amid the backdrop of war, mirrors the storytelling style of the historical romance as it developed in the U.S.

South. The novel abounds in the melodrama of romantic unions between star-crossed young lovers of opposed backgrounds as it depicts the tragedies of war and intrigues of genteel agrarian society. The themes of conflict and conciliation between Anglo-American and Mexican develop through a central romantic union between Lieutenant Robert Warrener, a soldier in the U.S. army—and a Virginia planter and slaveholder—and Susanita, Don Santiago's youngest child. Though the military conflict threatens to end this romance, the narrator throughout identifies the cause of Don Santiago's opposition to this relationship as Mexican patriarchy thinly disguised as patriotism. In keeping with Mexican cultural tradition, the Don simply wishes to maintain his unquestioned authority in the domestic sphere. Whereas, for example, Don Santiago and his son Alvaro uphold arranged marriages, Mexican women oppose such unions as an archaic custom of the premodern (hacienda) era. In *Caballero* Mexican nationalism and patriotism in this manner go hand-in-hand with patriarchal privilege. It is in this important regard that the hacienda world of *Caballero* is neither the Eden of the romantic colonizer nor the pastoral idyll of plantation lore. As María Cotera comments, in its "unflinching depiction of patriarchal values . . . [and] its deconstruction of the idealized male hero" *Caballero* "forecasts the cultural production of women of color" that emerged in response to "nationalistic male-centered discourses" (340).

Two other romances between Mexican women and American men complete the work's strategy to project Mexican integration within U.S. Texas while displacing Mexican patriarchy. Susanita's sister, Angela, also against their father's wishes, marries Red McLane, a transplanted Yankee entrepreneur who hopes to enhance his political career through marriage to an established Mexican family. Rejecting Alvaro's marriage proposal, Susanita's friend Inez Sánchez elopes with Johnny White, a member of the Texas Rangers, a paramilitary unit that fought against Mexican guerrillas during and after the war. Other pairings drive home the theme of interethnic union. Befriending an American military physician, the Don's other son, Luis Gonzaga, leaves the hacienda for the East to study art. For these perceived transgressions of Mexican custom and nationhood, the Don unhesitatingly disowns both Susanita and Luis. As the United States takes control of Mexican south Texas, even the Don's trusted peons, who are portrayed as exploited victims of the hacienda social order, leave Rancho la Palma to pursue the American Way. One peon, Manuel, whose family had worked on the Mendoza hacienda for several generations, joins Warrener, with whom, as he later writes, he is "very content" (205). Cotera points out that Don Santiago's peons "reject the slave-like system of the hacienda in order to explore their identities as labor in a world of capital" (341). In this way, "the power base that Don Santiago has been consummately unaware of, yet which has held his hacienda together, begins to erode beneath him" (341).

The novel traces Don Santiago's growing isolation from family and community and concomitant decline as patriarch, a process that symbolizes the eclipse of Mexican (hacienda) ranching society in the region and the emergent consolidation of U.S. rule in the late nineteenth and early twentieth centuries. Portrayed early in the novel as the personification of his community's genteel culture and history, as the primary obstacle to Mexican-Anglo union, Don Santiago becomes the narrative's unexpected antagonist. The novel's other antagonist, Alvaro, carries out his father's beliefs through his guerrilla activities against the U.S. army and misogynistic relations with his sisters and other women. The novel's title is therefore ironic in every conceivable sense, suggesting that, although the Don is, in the eyes of his community, an honorable gentleman-rancher— the literal translation of "caballero"—he is also a patriarchal relic of the semifeudal Mexican colonial era. He embodies both the genteel Mexican/Hispanic past but more crucially its social contradictions and iniquities. As a prisoner to cultural tradition, the Don continues to uphold a patriarchal code even as his hacienda world collapses under the influence of what the novel portrays as a more progressive and egalitarian (U.S.) society. The last "caballero" in the Texas border tradition, Don Santiago becomes a tragically enervated figure, an anachronistic patriarch in a conquered and occupied homeland. After Alvaro is killed by the Texas Rangers, Don Santiago dies alone, an image symbolic of the Don's loss of family, community, culture, and nation. This, the narrative warns, represents the likely fate of Mexicans who, rather than pragmatically looking to the (modern capitalist) U.S. future, stubbornly cling to the (semifeudal) Mexican past. At the end of the novel, Warrener discovers the Don's body at the foot of a cliff overlooking Rancho la Palma, where he had often retreated. He dies on the same day that Robert and Susanita, seeking to reconcile with him, have returned with his first grandchild.

Veiling a political message in romantic unions set in a semifeudal agrarian landscape, *Caballero* recalls nineteenth-century southern domestic (plantation) fiction as practiced by such writers as Caroline Gilman, Augusta Evans, and Maria McIntosh, as well as works in the same tradition by such twentieth-century writers as Margaret Mitchell.[8] Although the nineteenth-century southern domestic novel espoused the inherent superiority of the (white) South over the North, it imagined a desired resolution, through metonymic romantic union, to regional faction. In the typical domestic novel northern men who became romantically attached to southern women were invariably converted to the southern cause in the process—a scenario that, interestingly, *Caballero* inverts, with the United States now *favored* over the (Mexican) "south" (Moss 27). The projection of sectional rivalries into sexual politics also occurred through the marriage of a northern woman to a southern man, with the virile or southern position dominant.[9] Once again, *Caballero* reverses this strategy in order to assert the benefits of the modern "north" over the semifeudal Mexican "south." But regardless of the outcome of such unions, in southern domestic fiction, as in *Caballero*, these romantic pairings were consummately political. As Moss notes, in them "intersectional rivalries initiated by interfering Northerners eventually separate lovers, split families, and destroy lives. Imported Northern values (temporarily) debase the moral currency of southern society and throw the community into disarray" (13). But in the end romance resolves regional rivalry to the inevitable advantage of the southern (plantation) community. This reflects the conservative political and cultural perspective of southern domestic novelists and their mostly native-born audience, an agrarian-based politics that *Caballero* clearly rejects. "Distressed by the spread of individualism and materialism," southern domestic novelists associated these so-called evils of modernization with the North and "sought to protect their region from infection through their fiction" (28) If placed in this comparative context, *Caballero* appears less a novel of conciliation with the new social order than a politically progressive attack not only on the premodern traditions embodied by the hacienda but their modern cultural and political legacy. Unlike the plantation texts from which it draws, *Caballero* does not wax nostalgic about the premodern era and in fact serves as an extended eulogy for its passing.

Although *Caballero* symbolically resolves interethnic conflict through integration rather than a retreat to a pastoral hacienda past, it portrays the elite Mexican families of the border region in a manner that mirrors the portrait of southern culture found in plantation narrative. Whereas the "Americans are strong, powerful, fearless, and seem to have unlimited wealth," declares Don Santiago early in the novel, they lack what (landed) Mexicans have: "dignity, self-respect, pride, nobility, traditions, and an old and sound religion" (21). Given that González counted some of these landowning families among her ancestors, such a passage cannot be regarded as ironic, despite the Don's later role as antagonist. Of the many American characters in *Caballero*, only Warrener, a southerner, will prove to be an exception to the Don's rule distinguishing Mexicans from Americans. Despite the novel's strategy to promote a resolution to this interethnic conflict, it makes clear that the premodern "organic" community of the Mexican hacienda rests on a "doctrine of traditionalism" according to which "religion, gentility, family rank, and patriarchalism" take precedence over modern (U.S.) values such as individualism and the quest for money (21). This recalls the description of traditional southern culture as "nonaggressive [and] noncommercial . . . one in which people were not grasping, always in a hurry, greedy to make more and more money" (Conkin 86). *Caballero* repeats other supposed U.S. southern traits to such an extent that the following summary of the Agrarian view of southerners applies just as well to the Mexican gentry of *Caballero*. Southerners, as Paul K. Conkin comments, "have a special relationship to the land, to local space, to roots. They are closely tied to immediate family or to networks of kin. They love leisure . . . [and] finally, southerners [are] more religious than people in other sections of the country" (86).

It therefore does not seem coincidental that González and Raleigh chose to include the scion of a southern planter family as a countervailing romantic protagonist. As a southern gentleman, Warrener embraces a traditional "southern" doctrine not unlike that of the Mexican elite. In contrast to Red, Warrener, as a southern planter-aristocrat, possesses the "dignity, self-respect, pride, nobility, [and] traditions" that early in the novel are associated with the hacienda oligarchy. Luis Gonzaga at one point describes him as "an hidalgo [nobleman] in his country as [the Mendozas] are in Texas" (108). When Angela informs her sister Susanita about her plan to marry Red, the latter immediately draws a distinction between the two Americans. Unlike the honorable southerner, Red, who is originally from New York, "bribes" Mexicans with "nonsense like helping [our] people. . . . [He] can't be anything but repugnant" (213). When Red tells "Roberto" Warrener that they'll soon be "brothers," "Warrener's answer was a grunt. Brothers, he and McLane!" (244). On the last page of the novel, Warrener even sympathizes with Don Santiago's plight as a fallen patriarch, seeing the Don's lifeless body as a symbol of the socio-historical status of border Mexicans. He recalls that his wife had told him that Mexicans had "been in Texas close to a hundred years" and that "the men piling into [Texas] were asserting their rights as 'Americans' . . . wearing the rainbow of the pioneer as if it were new and theirs alone. Already talking loudly about running all Mexicans across the Rio Grande from this 'our' land" (336). These sympathetic words could never have come from the Don's other future son-in-law, Red, who is portrayed as a southwestern version of a carpetbagger.[10]

Caballero also incorporates numerous overtly "anti-Yankee" passages, recalling the southern plantation romance's political premise, from references to atrocities committed against Mexicans by the Texas Rangers to passages that depict the usurpation of Mexican land by American squatters. At times, the pastoral motif facilitates this commentary, as when, for example, the narrator counterposes the green space of the border (haciendas) to the invading Americans who have violated Mexican territory: "Americans roamed over the land in groups, looked for places where the grass was the greenest. . . . Coveting. Visioning homes. Building dreams of empire. Not caring—too many of them not caring that homes had stood here for a hundred years" (301). At one point, the narrator denounces the arrival of Americans in south Texas as an invasion. As she states, " 'Remember the Alamo!' [the Americans] shouted and visited the sins of Santa Anna upon all his countrymen, and considered themselves justified in stealing the lands of the Mexicans. . . . They pillaged and stole, and insulted, and called themselves a sword of the avenging God, and shouted their hymns to drown their consciences" (195). This scene was "repeated in variation for many years to come, until an empire of state would rise on land that had scarcely a square yard of it that had not been wet with blood" (195). As a result, native-born "Mexicans formed wagon trains and fled [the region] dominated by the invading peoples they considered inferior" (301).

Throughout *Caballero* the hacienda subject and setting in this manner work to establish the historical and cultural primacy of Mexican over Anglo Texas, countering the discourse of U.S. colonialism by recovering a minority community history that in the 1930s and 1940s and earlier had received little public or official recognition. In the "Authors' Notes" that serves as an introduction to the novel González and Raleigh indicate the importance of recovering this forgotten regional history. "Seeing the need to cover a phase of history and customs heretofore unrecorded," they first sent *Caballero* to publishers in 1939, the year the release of the movie version of *Gone with the Wind* reflected the southern romance genre's mass cultural appeal.

After being conquered by the United States, southern whites and Mexican Texans separately resisted "Yankee" intervention, in part, by remembering their preconquest society, (re)defining themselves in the aftermath of defeat by imagining their agrarian origins as fundamentally distinct from the new socioeconomic order. Although this process has more commonly been associated with the South, Genaro Padilla's research on the role of nostalgia in early Mexican-American literature demonstrates that in the aftermath of the U.S. conquest in the Mexican southwest a similar form of cultural remembrance emerged. Yet the post-Reconstruction plantation myth developed from the need to justify white supremacist

Jovita González, San Antonio, Texas, 1934. Courtesy of E. E. Mireles and Jovita González de Mireles Papers, Special Collections and Archives, Bell Library, Texas A&M University, Corpus Christi.

support for Jim Crow segregation in the 1880s and 1890s, not simply from white southern desire to recover the social world of the Lost Cause to resist Yankee intervention. It was because the freedmen represented a substantial political and social threat to the privileges of whiteness that a concerted cultural and political movement developed to disenfranchise them. As a text that draws on plantation narrative, *Caballero* similarly emerged from the racially charged context of the Jim Crow South. But in stark contrast to southern literature's use of the plantation myth to justify the entrenched racial hierarchy, in *Caballero* the hacienda theme and particularly the unions between Anglos and Mexicans instead would have functioned—had the novel been published in the era in which it was written—as an argument *against* Jim Crow segregation. Quite unlike southern plantation and domestic fiction, a literary genre that Mark Twain satirizes in *Huckleberry Finn* and that González and Raleigh also seek to turn on its head, *Caballero* would have appeared within a racial setting inimical to the very community whose early history formed the subject of its sentimental story.[11]

After the U.S. South and Mexico were defeated by the United States, "the subaltern sectors of north Greater Mexico and the South . . . experienced the worst effects of Northern capitalist domination, a domination always deeply inflected with and complicated by racism" (Limón, *American Encounters* 18). Although the late-nineteenth-century decline of the Mexican ranching system in south Texas ideally should have led to greater freedom for its population of laborers, by the turn of the twentieth century Mexicans were instead relegated to a subordinate status that closely resembled the African American experience in the South. In racial and socioeconomic terms, Mexicans in Texas and elsewhere in the territory annexed by the United States became the southwest equivalent of freed slaves who despite being released from the plantation had not yet achieved real freedom and equality. "The most striking aspect about the new social arrangement [in Texas]," as David Montejano explains, "was its obvious racial character" (160). He continues, "The modern order framed Mexican-Anglo relations in stark 'Jim Crow' segregation. Separate quarters for Mexican and Anglo were to be found in the farm towns of South Texas" (160). Born in 1899, González spent her childhood in one such community, Roma, located on the present-day border, the heart of the old Mexican ranching society of South Texas.[12] In that era, within the south Texas farm order, "specific rules defined the proper place of Mexicans and regulated interracial contact. . . . The separation was so complete and seemingly absolute that several historians have described the farm society as 'castelike.' " Although, as Montejano points out, the notion of caste applies poorly to Jim Crow segregation in the United States, "it suggests, nonetheless, the degree to which race consciousness and privileges permeated social life in the [south Texas] farm order" (160).

By 1910, the Mexican Texan gentry whose culture and history González and Raleigh had meticulously documented in *Caballero* had been displaced by Anglo-American ranchers and farmers and a new socio-economic hierarchy had been established. The process by which Mexican rancheros in Texas were dispossessed was complex and varied. As Montejano explains, "Mexicans in Texas, especially above the Nueces [i.e., outside of south Texas], lost considerable land through outright confiscation and fraud" (52). Below the Nueces, "the experience of displacement was more complex. While fraud and coercion played an important part, the more systematic, more efficient mechanism of market competition also operated there. The accommodation between American mercantile groups and the Mexican upper class was, from a financial standpoint, inherently unequal" (50). The "peace structure" between the two elites— as *Caballero*'s interethnic romantic unions suggest—saved some upper-class Mexicans, but it did not forestall the outcome of the competition between the two (52). After the turn of the century, the landed upper class to which González traced her ancestry and with which she closely identified was extinct except in a few border enclaves.[13] "Not only did the new American law fail to protect the Mexicans but it also was used as the major instrument of their dispossession" (52). Perhaps as a result of this socioeconomic upheaval in the region, in 1910 the González family's "fortunes had changed for the worse, and they moved to San Antonio, drawn by better opportunities, including a good education in English, and by the gradual emergence there of a small but stable Mexican middle class" (Limón, "Mexicans" 242).

The former Mexican ranching industry had its origin in the Nueces-Rio Grande area, where *Caballero* is set, with the livestock establishments of the Rio Grande rancheros. Armando C. Alonzo traces this industry to a group of founding hacienda estates established by colonists from New Spain in the mid-1700s, precisely the lineage traced in *Caballero*'s foreword. As Alonzo notes, "Under Spanish and Mexican rule, ranching and commerce became the principal economic activities of the settlers, especially in the Lower Rio Grande Valley. . . . While the towns served as centers of local government and trade, stock-raising developed in the surrounding territory, especially in the north bank area" (67). Of the two key enterprises, "stock-raising easily became the more popular occupation of the Hispanic settlers, who not only took advantage of the benefits provided by the virgin plains but also utilized a long history of ranching to develop stock-raising" (67). As Limón notes, *Caballero*'s "historical material, the plot of ethnic conflict, and the characters . . . [were] based on González's professional research and cultural background" ("Mexicans" 243). Her family history, as stated earlier, was apparently a key source. The González family "were in part descended from [the] landed Spanish elites who had come to southern Texas in the eighteenth century" (242).

As Flores's study of the Alamo demonstrates, during the Texas Modern, as the Mexican ranching industry crumbled, the increasingly subordinate status of Mexicans was "naturalized" through a selective remembrance of regional history. Cultural memory of the official and unofficial wars fought against Mexicans in the nineteenth century played a social role analogous to southern memory of Reconstruction and the Civil War during the Jim Crow era (Montejano 223–24). The Texas Wars of Independence (1835–1836) and the U.S.-Mexican War functioned in Texan memory in much the same way as did military and political conflict with the North in post-Reconstruction southern memory.[14] Commenting on this point in his study of border *corridos* (ballads), "*With His Pistol in His Hand,*" Américo Paredes identifies the comparable roles played by Mexicans and blacks in these mirror-image romantic narratives of southern history. In Texas in the late nineteenth century, "The 'cattle barons' built up their fortunes at the expense of the Border Mexican by means which were far from ethical. One notes that the white Southerner took his slave women as concubines and then created an image of the Negro male as a sex fiend. In the same way he appears to have taken the Mexican's property [i.e., land] and then made him out a thief" (20). The memory of the Alamo and of later military conflicts with Mexicans, as Paredes explains, "provided a convenient justification for outrages committed on the Border by Texans of certain types, so convenient an excuse that it was artificially prolonged for almost a century" (19).

By the mid-1930s, anti-Mexican sentiment in Texas and elsewhere in the Southwest had become institutionalized in states' segregation discourses and laws regulating relations between whites and nonwhites, particularly Mexican Americans and African Americans (Montejano 78). Although this certainly suggests their shared historical condition under Jim Crow, in other ways these two groups' histories diverge, particularly in the striking patterns of affiliation between Mexican Texas and the *white* South, as illustrated in *Caballero*. Quite distinct from the war against the United States in which Texas participated, the region's semifeudal agrarian origins as a Spanish colonial territory and its nominal solidarity, as a part of Texas, with the Confederacy during the Civil War make the analogy perhaps more obvious than it might first appear. Cultural identifi-cation with a semifeudal agrarian social order—the hacienda and the plantation—which was eroded as a result of military defeat at the hands of "northerners," further binds these two regions, as *Caballero*'s southern affinities again demonstrate. In the late eighteenth century and for much of the nineteenth century this premodern agrarian order dominated its region's cultural and socioeconomic landscape. Although the analogy can be extended to include much of the Mexican southwest—and perhaps all of Greater Mexico—south Texas best illustrates the historical irony that to this day "unites" white southerners and Mexican Americans.[15]

This historical irony not only accounts for *Caballero*'s use of southern (plantation) literary and historical motifs but also helps explain how the novel semi-allegorically resolves interethnic and regional rivalry. White southerners, of course, were the earliest and most populous group of U.S. settlers in Mexican Texas, arriving in large numbers in the 1820s. In *Caballero* a countervailing "southern" critique of Yankee values and mo-tives identifies the marriage between Red and Angela as one based not on love but rather on a mutually beneficial convenience.[16] The narrator contrasts this marriage to the "true" love of the "southerners" Robert and Susanita, an idealized romantic union embedded symbolically in the pastoral agrarian imagery that later reappears even as the novel works to displace the Mendoza family's hacienda world. Through the juxtaposi-tion of these two marriages the novel makes a case for Mexican, masked as southern, culture as it acknowledges the inevitability and benefits of integration under U.S. (Yankee) rule.

In the interest of imagining this national consolidation, in chapter 19 the narrator reproves Don Santiago for refusing to cooperate with Red McLane in his proposition to influence postwar south Texas politics. Had Don Santiago been shrewder, states the narrator, "He might have taken his visitor for an example of these *Americanos* swarming into Texas, and profited thereby; and seen the impotence of a handful of people who measured greatness by old traditions and old blood, and the camouflage of pomp and ceremony and dress which only money can obtain" (182). Had the Don been more like his daughter, Susanita, he might have fore-seen a future U.S. Texas in which Mexicans participated in a potentially beneficial relationship with arriving Anglo-Americans like McLane. He also might have recognized that Mexicans could accept foreigners like Red without necessarily choosing to embrace them culturally.

Through other characters *Caballero* makes a similar statement for in-tegration and conciliation based on pragmatism rather than love. When Don Santiago asks his friend Don Gabriel whether he too "loves" the

Americans, Gabriel's response invokes the novel's central political premise: "Love them, Santiago? If I had the gift of prophesy I would say that there would never be love between us as a people. Yet a repulsing of those who would bring us at least understanding, like this Señor McLane, will bring us nothing of advantage" (327). The priest, Padre Pierre, echoes this view when he advises his parishioners, who have gathered to discuss their options in the face of the U.S. occupation, to "seek the *Americano* officials who have influence and invite them to your homes and entertainments. Show them that we have much to give them in culture, that we are not the ignorant people they take us to be, that to remain as we are will neither harm them nor be a disgrace to their union of states" (58). Through passages such as these *Caballero* appears to place its hope in McLane's promise to Don Santiago that "you Mexicans are a conquered race, but what you are as yet unaware of is that the conquering boot of the *Americano* has no heel. . . . [A]s a nation we do not confiscate. . . . What I am trying to tell you . . . is that you are no longer a colony of Mexico, and adjustment will have to be made to make you a part of the new Texas" (180).

Limón suggests that Red and Angela's romance more than Robert and Susanita's symbolizes the projected U.S. social order into which Mexicans shall be incorporated. But if Red's marriage to Angela is any indication, a future U.S. Texas will be marked as much by division and conflict as by mutual respect based on pragmatic self-interest. Without love, the novel intimates, this (national) marriage of convenience may prove to be unstable at best. Many characters who embrace Red do so with knowledge of the risks. Though Don Gabriel believes that "it is men like [Red] who will really build Texas," he also "fears many will be harder than he" (327). Angela, without openly expressing doubt, has no answer to her father's admonition that Red's "concern over the misery his countrymen are visiting upon the poor Mexicans is to further his personal ambitions" (312). He bluntly tells Angela that she is "to be a lady of mercy so that he will have their allegiance for his schemes" (312). It is not simply that Red and Angela's marriage suggests that the "new social formation must, for the foreseeable future, admit the Mexican in a still-subordinate position" (Limón, "Mexicans" 246); through the contrast between its realistic portrait of Red and its idealized image of Robert, *Caballero* makes a case—however repressed this argument may be by the novel's conciliatory premise—for southern (i.e., Mexican) culture in the context of pragmatic recognition that Red represents the future. Despite his power and influence, the novel's southern affinities seem to declare, Red can never possess the qualities that "southerners" like Robert and Don Santiago have imbibed since childhood—the dignity, self-respect, pride, and morality identified with a traditional agrarian society. Although the novel's attack on (Mexican) patriarchy and paternalism throughout counters this southern analogy, *Caballero* does not renounce all aspects of traditional Mexican culture, just as it resists a blanket valorization of Red's modern capitalist perspective. If Anglo-Americans do not respect and learn from their incorporated Mexican (southern) culture, the future may not be as harmonious as the novel's romances otherwise project.

The birth of Susanita and Robert's child, the biracial New South(west) personified, is to be the catalyst for a reunion between Susanita and her father. Susanita returns with her family to her hacienda home in the hope that the Don's first grandchild will soften the patriarch's heart. When he fails to show up as expected, Susanita asks that they visit the bluff where he often went to view his ranch. Warrener discovers Don Santiago's body. The narrator underscores the irony "that an American, and the man who took his most beloved child, should be the one to close the lids over the eyes of Don Santiago de Mendoza y Soría" (336). More ironic, though not unexpected given the novel's intersection with plantation fiction, on the final page Robert—a slaveholder who will return with his new Mexican wife to his antebellum Virginia plantation—stands at the location where Don Santiago's Spanish colonist ancestors first looked out across the land that would become Rancho la Palma de Cristo.

The final paragraph directs the reader back to the Mendoza family's heritage and its hacienda mythology. A ranch hand reminds Warrener, "See, there is the cross on the bluff. Don Santiago's father's father saw Rancho la Palma de Cristo in a dream from there, and when the dream came true he built the cross in thanksgiving to God. The family has been in Texas close to a hundred years, señor, if you did not know" (336). In the final lines Warrener wonders what Don Santiago's last thoughts had been as he stood on the bluff just before his death: "Had he held to the last to the staff of his traditions, speeding his soul with his head held high in the right of his convictions, to stand unafraid before God whom he had worshiped and, he believed, obeyed?" (337). If the U.S. nation, encompassing the border region, must be built, the (genteel) Spanish/Mexican history and culture embodied by Don Santiago, the novel suggests, must not be forgotten.

The novel's socially symbolic project to depose Don Santiago, who is described at one point as the "monarch" of all he surveyed, in this way exists in precarious balance with its efforts at historical recovery and cultural validation. *Caballero* must dethrone the Don in order to pave the way for what it posits as the beneficial integration—during and after the period in which the novel was written—of the Mexican border population into U.S. society. But since cultural assimilation, whether in the nineteenth century or the modern period, was always problematic for Mexican Americans, the genteel history and culture that the Don embodies must be preserved, a particularly important objective for middle-class Mexican Americans like González seeking inclusion in segregated Texas society. This culture may have also had other inherent value and meaning for the authors of *Caballero*. The novel's historical recovery project, which "[works] backward to establish the character of the Spanish Mexicans . . . and forward to record the Texas Ranger-led racist oppression and violence that descended on a seemingly tranquil, unified community," could have also served other political purposes (Limón, "Mexicans" 244). "Such a strategy," Limón believes, "might appeal to the guilt and anxiety of González's Anglo liberal audience and enlist its sympathy while affirming the historical primacy and moral rightness of the new Mexican middle-class elites in their efforts to lead their community" (244–45).

Hacienda texts like *Caballero* demonstrate one means by which nineteenth- and twentieth-century Mexican-American writers remembered the Mexican and Spanish past to recover, (re)construct, and affirm their ethnic cultural identity. Set against the discursive and material threats posed by Anglo-American society, these works recover the hacienda as a cultural symbol of Mexican-American origins and identity even as many depend, like plantation narratives, on the silencing of memories that would undermine nostalgic remembrance. Scholars of the Mexican-American and Latino/a past today must also remember the hacienda, seeing in it a sign of historical differences rather than of unity, and of the multiple identities shaped by disparate historical and cultural experiences. Hacienda narratives such as *Caballero* stand as reminders that, as Stuart Hall writes, "cultural identities . . . have histories . . . [and] undergo constant transformation," that "far from being eternally fixed in some essentialized past, they are subject to the continuous 'play' of history, culture and power" (52). Hall's further explication of identity suggests *Caballero*'s particular relevance to the Recovering the U.S. Hispanic Literary Heritage Project: as he explains, "Far from being grounded in a mere 'recovery' of the past, which is waiting to be found, and which, when found, will secure our sense of ourselves into eternity, identities are the names we give to the different ways we are positioned by, and position ourselves within, the narratives of the past" (52).

1. Eve Raleigh was the pen name of Margaret Eimer, a Missourian who, according to the novel's recoverer and editor, José E. Limón, "had a considerable hand in the writing of *Caballero*" ("Mexicans" 243). Though Raleigh's specific role in the writing of the novel remains unclear, Limón states that "the historical material, the plot of ethnic conflict, and the characters" were based on González's "professional research and cultural background" (243). He refers to González's scholarly research as a folklorist and cultural historian who during the late 1920s and early 1930s recorded "the customs and traditions of her native [South Texas] community" (242). *Dew on the Thorn*, a novel written solely by González during the 1920s and 1930s, was published in 1997.

2. I draw on Aranda's discussion of the politics of Recovery Project scholarship (553). Although it had many regional and historical variations in Greater Mexico, the hacienda was basically a semifeudal agrarian ranching institution, dependent on a labor force controlled through debt peonage, that "produced subsistence goods as well as a market surplus and usually contained a blacksmith's shop and often a pottery and carpentry shop as well. Some of the wealthiest haciendas maintained a chapel, although resident priests were seldom present. The largest units covered many square miles and had outlying corrals, line shacks, and some dispersed housing for [laborers and] tenants" (Burkholder and Johnson 184). Large estates were self-sufficient (i.e., autarkic), with crops, flocks and herds, wooded areas, flour mills, forges, and workshops. Haciendas "provided the physical focus for both social life and production. The owner's large house dominated the hacienda's residential core" (184).

3. *Caballero*'s hacienda theme and setting suggest that González and Raleigh were familiar with southern plantation and domestic narratives, a literary tradition that extends to the early nineteenth century when white southerners first began to shape in writing a distinctive regional identity in opposition to the North. Some of the better-known plantation narratives include John Pendleton Kennedy's *Swallow Barn: Or, a Sojourn in the Old Dominion* (1851), Thomas Nelson Page's *In Ole Virginia* (1887), Thomas Dixon's *The Leopard's Spots* (1902), as well as later narratives of plantation community like Margaret Mitchell's *Gone with the Wind* (1936) and William Faulkner's *Absalom, Absalom!* (1936). As a professionally trained Texas historian and folklorist, and as an aspiring novelist, González would have had at least some familiarity with these seminal literary narratives of southern society. González was educated at the University of Texas under the guidance of the romantic folkloristic ethnographer J. Frank Dobie, whose works apologized for the Anglo-American colonization of south Texas—one carried out primarily by southerners—during an era when Texas historiography was dominated by folkloristic historian Walter Prescott Webb.

4. See Aranda and Martín-Rodríguez's early article. For criticism that places Ruiz de Burton in the tradition of counterhegemonic Mexican-American and Latino literary production, see, for example, Sánchez and Pita's Introduction or the comparatist essay by each on Ruiz de Burton and José Martí in *José Martí's "Our America."* See also José David Saldívar's remarks on Ruiz de Burton's novel in *Border Matters*.

5. I draw from Aranda's comments on Ruiz de Burton (554). Limón writes that "it seems impossible that [González] would not have known Mexico's most famous romance novel and its revered author—Ignacio Altamirano's *El Zarco: Episodes of Mexican Life in 1861–1863*—published in 1901 and extremely popular in Mexico in [the] formative years of González's literary life. . . . [L]ike *Caballero* Altamirano's work has as its theme the overcoming of deep social divisions through romance and it foregrounds war, guerrillas, and young lovers of opposed racial backgrounds" (Introduction xx).

6. Repressed in the sense that the novel's romances generally do not provide a space for the validation of the Don's resistant nationalist consciousness. I draw on Limón's observation that González's folklore writings "at times [appear] to be repressing a certain admiration for . . . [the Mexican lower] classes and an acknowledgment of the state of war" between the Mexican border community and Anglo-Americans. "From the beginning," states Limón, "this contradiction is evident in her work" (*Dancing* 62).

7. I base my view that Mitchell's novel may have served as the inspiration for *Caballero* not only on the similarities between their respective stories and settings but also on the popularity of *Gone with the Wind* during the era in which *Caballero* was written. In a June 1978 letter to a friend González mentions having "re-read" *Gone with the Wind* and been favorably impressed by it. The letter is stored in the E. E. Mireles and Jovita González Papers, Special Collections and Archives, Texas A&M University–Corpus Christi, Bell Library, where the original handwritten manuscript of *Caballero* was discovered by Limón and Cotera.

8. Though not as well-known as their male counterparts (mentioned in note 3 above), nineteenth-century southern domestic novelists like Gilman, Evans, and McIntosh "left a lasting impression on the American imagination" (Moss 29). "Writing in the language of domesticity," these writers "appealed to the women of America, using the images of home and hearth to make a case for Southern culture" (29). Contrasting the (southern) plantation home to the (northern) market world, they sought to defend the South when it faced threats from its powerful regional rival. In Gilman's geography, for example, "the plantation is Home and the city is the Other—not quite the same thing as a dichotomy between good and evil, but a sharp duality of values nonetheless" (MacKethan 232). While they believed in the fundamental superiority of their native region and its slavery-dependent social order, they placed the southern aristocratic female at the center of the project to define and defend her community. As Moss explains, these women writers believed that "through the development of her physical, intellectual, and moral faculties, the discharge of her feminine responsibilities, and the proper use of her 'influence' . . . the aristocratic Southern female could protect her community from Northern encroachment; conversely, by succumbing to the myriad temptations that [were] associated exclusively with northern society, that same woman could precipitate regional decline" (10). For this reason twentieth-century southern women writers like Ellen Glasgow and Elizabeth Lyle Saxon, who "rebelled against what they perceived as the oppressive bonds of contemporary southern womanhood," invoked "domestic fiction in their literary definition of the South's 'new woman'" (6). *Gone with the Wind* remains the crowning achievement of south-

ern domestic fiction. Mitchell's novel symbolically brought to a climax a series of pastoral and nostalgic southern literary works and historical, cultural, and racial developments that helped create the atmosphere in which a hacienda romance like *Caballero* could be written.

9. Richard Slotkin points out that in the typical plantation novel "the sexual identities of the partners suggest that the reconciliation requires the submission of one to the other, with the virile or southern position dominant. The imagery of the plantation novel assimilates to the planter class an abstraction of those heroic traits which had been associated with various figures (and classes) in the Myth of the Frontier" (144).

10. Red personifies an "industrialist" ethic antithetical to traditional southern doctrine. W. J. Cash has commented that "it was the conflict with the Yankee which really created the concept of the South as something more than a matter of geography, as an object of patriotism, in the minds of Southerners" (66). After the Civil War, in southern plantation and domestic fiction the northern carpetbagger served as metonymic foil to everything constructed as traditionally southern. Despite Red's ostensible sympathy for the plight of border Mexicans and relative immersion in their culture, *Caballero* also portrays him as an amoral opportunist who adopts a foreign (i.e., Mexican and Texan) identity to further his business enterprises and particularly his political aspirations in postwar south Texas. Red's political agenda marks him as an analogue to the southern conception of the northern interloper during Reconstruction who meddled in regional politics without regard for the interests of the southern (white) population. Red's political mantra drives home the parallel. As the narrator notes, "The end, [Red] was certain, justified the means, therefore [deception] was entirely fair" (214).

11. At the end of *Huckleberry Finn*, the boy hero intends to light out for the territories, bringing him in close proximity to Greater Mexico.

12. González's scholarly research during the 1920s and 1930s as a folklorist and historian of her native border community formed the basis of *Caballero*'s historical saga. See González's 1930 master's thesis, "Social Life in Cameron, Starr, and Zapata Counties."

13. As Montejano comments, "Landed Mexicans represented the complicating factor in the Mexican-Anglo relations of the frontier period. Even during the worst times of Mexican banditry, the permanent Mexican residents who were landowners were seen as "good citizens" while the large "floating" population employed on ranches were seen as sympathizers of the raiders who opposed the Americans" (52).

14. As Weber comments, "After their victory, Anglo-American rebels controlled not only Texas, but the writing of its history. They adopted the story line of their propagandists and added an additional twist—they portrayed themselves as heroic, a superior race of men. Heroes needed villains, and Texas's earliest historians found them full-blown, nurtured in the Hispanic past. . . . Painting the Spanish era in dark hues enabled Texas historians to contrast it with the Texas rebellion" (339–40).

15. See Limón's discussion of the historical and cultural parallels between Greater Mexico and the U.S. South in *American Encounters* (7–33).

16. I draw on Limón's comment that "their marriage is to be based not on rapturous

love but on what I shall call convenience with consciousness and conscience and on respect and deep mutual admiration" ("Mexicans" 246).

WORKS CITED

Alonzo, Armando C. *Tejano Legacy: Rancheros and Settlers in South Texas, 1734–1900.* Albuquerque: U of New Mexico P, 1998.

Altamirano, Ignacio. *El Zarco: Episodios de la Vida Mexicana en 1861–63.* 1901. México D.F.: Ediciones Oceano, S.A., 1986.

Aranda, José F. "Contradictory Impulses: María Amparo Ruiz de Burton, Resistance Theory, and the Politics of Chicano/a Studies." *American Literature* 70.3 (Sept. 1998): 551–79.

Burkholder, Mark A., and Lyman L. Johnson. *Colonial Latin America.* New York: Oxford UP, 1990.

Cash, W. J. *The Mind of the South.* 1941. New York: Random, 1991.

Conkin, Paul K. *The Southern Agrarians.* Knoxville: U of Tennessee P, 1988.

Cotera, María. "Hombres Necios: A Critical Epilogue." *Caballero: A Historical Novel.* By Jovita González and Eve Raleigh. College Station: Texas A&M UP, 1996. 339–46.

Dixon, Thomas. *The Leopard's Spots.* 1902. New York: Irvington, 1979.

Faulkner, William. *Absalom, Absalom!* 1936. New York: Vintage, 1972.

Flores, Richard. *Remembering the Alamo: Memory, Modernity, and the Master Symbol.* Austin: U of Texas P, 2002.

González, Jovita. *Dew on the Thorn.* Houston: Arte Público, 1997.

——. "Social Life in Cameron, Starr, and Zapata Counties." Master's thesis. University of Texas, 1930.

González, Jovita, and Eve Raleigh. *Caballero: A Historical Novel.* College Station: Texas A&M UP, 1996.

Hall, Stuart. "Cultural Identity and Diaspora." *Identity and Difference.* Ed. Kathryn Woodward. London: Sage, 1997. 51–59.

Kennedy, John Pendleton. *Swallow Barn: Or, A Sojourn in the Old Dominion.* Rev. ed. New York: Putnam, 1851.

Limón, José E. *American Encounters: Greater Mexico, the United States, and the Erotics of Culture.* Boston: Beacon, 1998.

——. *Dancing with the Devil: Society and Cultural Poetics in Mexican-American South Texas.* Madison: U of Wisconsin P, 1994.

——. Introduction. *Caballero: A Historical Novel.* By Jovita González and Eve Raleigh. College Station: Texas A&M UP, 1996. xii–xxvi.

——. "Mexicans, Foundational Fictions, and the United States: *Caballero,* a Late Border Romance." *The Places of History: Regionalism Revisited in Latin America.* Ed. Doris Sommer. Durham, N.C.: Duke UP, 1999. 236–48.

MacKethan, Lucinda H. "Domesticity in Dixie: The Plantation Novel and *Uncle Tom's Cabin.*" *Haunted Bodies: Gender and Southern Texts.* Ed. Anne Goodwyn Jones and Susan V. Donaldson. Charlottesville: UP of Virginia, 1997. 223–42.

Martín-Rodríguez, Manuel M. "Textual and Land Reclamations: The Critical Reception of Early Chicano/a Literature." *Recovering the U.S. Hispanic Literary Heritage.* Vol. 2. Ed. Erlinda Gonzales-Berry and Chuck Tatum. Houston: Arte Público, 1996. 40–58.

Mitchell, Margaret. *Gone with the Wind.* 1936. New York: Warner, 1993.

Montejano, David. *Anglos and Mexicans in the Making of Texas, 1836–1986.* Austin: U of Texas P, 1987.

Moss, Elizabeth. *Domestic Novelists in the Old South: Defenders of Southern Culture.* Baton Rouge: Louisiana State UP, 1992.

Nora, Pierre. "General Introduction: Between Memory and History." *Realms of Memory: Rethinking the French Past.* Under the direction of Pierre Nora. English-language edition ed. Lawrence D. Kritzman. Trans. Arthur Goldhammer. Vol. 1. New York: Columbia UP, 1996. 2–20.

Padilla, Genaro M. *My History, Not Yours: The Formation of Mexican American Autobiography.* Madison: U of Wisconsin P, 1993.

Page, Thomas Nelson. *In Ole Virginia: Or, Marse Chan and Other Stories.* 1887. Chapel Hill: U of North Carolina P, 1969.

Paredes, Américo. *"With His Pistol in His Hand": A Border Ballad and Its Hero.* 1958. Austin: U of Texas P, 1990.

Pita, Beatrice. "Engendering Critique: Race, Class, and Gender in Ruiz de Burton and Martí." *José Martí's "Our America": From National to Hemispheric Cultural Studies.* Ed. Jeffrey Belnap and Raúl Fernández. Durham, N.C.: Duke UP, 1998. 129–44.

Saldívar, José David. *Border Matters: Remapping American Cultural Studies.* Berkeley: U of California P, 1997.

Sánchez, Rosaura. "Dismantling the Colossus: Martí and Ruiz de Burton on the Formulation of Anglo América." *José Martí's "Our America": From National to Hemispheric Cultural Studies.* Ed. Jeffrey Belnap and Raúl Fernández. Durham, N.C.: Duke UP, 1998. 115–28.

Sánchez, Rosaura, and Beatrice Pita. Introduction. *The Squatter and the Don.* By María Amparo Ruiz de Burton. Houston: Arte Público, 1992. 5–51.

Slotkin, Richard. *The Fatal Environment: The Myth of the Frontier in the Age of Industrialization, 1800–1890.* Norman: U of Oklahoma P, 1985.

Sommer, Doris. *Foundational Fictions: The National Romances of Latin America.* Berkeley: U of California P, 1991.

Weber, David J. *The Spanish Frontier in North America.* New Haven, Conn.: Yale UP, 1992.

POSDATA

ILAN STAVANS

Beyond Translation: Jorge Luis Borges

Revamps William Faulkner

Early 1999 I published in the *Times Literary Supplement* a review of *Collected Fictions*, by Jorge Luis Borges, translated by Andrew Hurley. This volume was part of an orchestrated effort by the publisher Viking, and supported by Andrew Wyle Literary Agency, to repackage the oeuvre of the Argentine master in three easily manageable anthologies of fiction, nonfiction, and poetry, respectively. The editorial effort was made to coincide with Borges's centennial: he was born in 1899 and died in 1986. Hurley's was the first of the three anthologies to appear. My essay praised it, although it also expressed sadness at the realization that Hurley's versions were destined to replace earlier English translations, in particular the admirable ones by Donald A. Yates and James E. Irby in *Labyrinths: Selected Stories and Other Writings*. My review included a statement that, to my surprise, proved to be considerably controversial, to the effect that the best translations of Borges's oeuvre, not only into Shakespeare's tongue but also into the language of Flaubert and Valéry, might have superseded the original in quality. I also suggested that, given his early British education in Buenos Aires, to read the Argentine in English is, in a way, "to bring him back home." I invoked the famous fact that he read *Don Quixote* in English first and, years later, when stumbling on Cervantes's original, he felt it was a lousy translation.

My comment was greeted with immediate and far-reaching clamor. An exchange in the *Times Literary Supplement* correspondence section lasted several weeks, probing these and other aspects of the review and of the editorial effort. The commotion reverberated in other periodicals as well. Several of Borges's translators, editors, and biographers entered the debate, which was less about the value of Hurley's translations than about the status of the Argentine in twentieth-century literature. In the Spanish-speaking world, on the other hand, the controversy revolved around "losing" the author of "El Aleph" and *Other Inquisitions: 1937– 1952* to an "abductor": the English language. It is this aspect of the polemic that interests me. In Argentina, in the pages of *La Nación*, a deliberation ensued on the value of reading Borges in a foreign language. Other reactions appeared in Spain and the Americas, in monthlies such as *Cuadernos Hispanoamericanos*. I apparently offended people for whom Borges is "a milestone of Hispanic culture." To have said that he tastes equally good or better in translation than in Spanish amounted to heresy, in effect denying a civilization rights to one of its coveted treasures.

I'm not the first to endorse such an apostasy: Martin Amis, J. M. Coetzee, and Salman Rushdie, among others, have expressed similar opinions; but since none of them is fully versed in Quevedo's tongue, their views might be considered fanciful. I, however, come from *lo español*, at least partially, and translation, the art and act of it, are for me essential, as constitutive as breathing. I have reflected on this aspect of my life in *On Borrowed Words: A Memoir of Language*. My education in Mexico was in three languages—Yiddish, Spanish, and Hebrew—and eventually I embraced a fourth one: English. It is almost impossible for me, at this stage, to establish which is closest to my heart. Translation is therefore my daily routine; it is everywhere I go and in everything I do. And so is literature, which, as far as I'm concerned, has no owner: once it is out and about, it is less the property of the author than of any and all readers. It is said in "Borges and I" (in Irby's translation): "what is good belongs to no one . . . but rather to the language and to tradition." Is this sentence better than its Spanish counterpart: "lo bueno ya no es de nadie, ni siquiera del otro, sino del lenguaje o la tradición"? Does it really matter which of these universes is better than any other of equal caliber? To translate is to make the particular universal, to enter a Leibnitzian reality in which simultaneous universes coexist.

Borges's syntax is revolutionary because, among other things, it cleansed Spanish of excesses that even the *Modernistas* (Rubén Darío, José Martí, et al.) indulged in, let alone the symbolists and Parnassianists. He made the Spanish language more precise, succinct, almost mathematical—he made it sound like English. Or else, he made English more accessible, less remote to readers in Buenos Aires and hence to the rest of the Hispanic orbit. I want to address his obsession with translation, though; it will allow me to explore the tension between original and "replica" in a way that, I hope, is a response to my critics. His preoccupation with translation dates back to his adolescence: at the age of seven Borges drafted in English a summary of Greek mythology, and a couple of years later he rendered into Spanish "El príncipe feliz," a story by Oscar Wilde, which, with the help of his relative Alvaro Melián Lafinur, he published; readers thought the translation was by his father, Jorge *Guillermo* Borges. This passion persisted throughout his life: translators are protagonists in myriad stories of his, from "Pierre Menard, Author of the *Quixote*" to "Averroes's Search" to "The Secret Miracle." In essays such as "The Translator of the *1001 Nights*," "The Homeric Versions," and "The Enigma of Edward Fitzgerald," he ponders the role translators play in the *rezeptionsgeschichte* of a book or in the buildup of its heritage.

All this is part of the Argentine's readily available oeuvre, but there are less-accessible aspects, too. Not long ago, I acquired in Manhattan a copy of *Borges: Obras, reseñas y traducciones inéditas: Diario "Crítica," 1933–34,* which contains many early efforts by Borges to translate international figures into Spanish: G. K. Chesterton, Lafcadio Hearn, Kipling, Dickens, Jack London, George Bernard Shaw, Swift, Wilde, Carl Sandburg, Eugene O'Neill, and T. E. Lawrence, as well as French and German figures like Marcel Schwob and Gustav Meyrink. Borges was in his mid-thirties at the time and the literary pages of *Crítica* were his to experiment with. The results are decidedly mixed, but this, to me, is less important than the fact that these experiments occurred in the first place; the Argentine was clearly in search of a voice and a viewpoint, and through these translations he found, or at least solidified them. In due time, several nonfiction pieces from *Crítica*, especially from *Revista Multicolor de los Sábados*, made it into his collection *Universal History of Infamy*, and one or two of them into *Discusión* and *El hacedor* also. This, of course, doesn't necessarily reveal anything significant about Borges's views on translation. Scores of litterateurs translate in their free time: for money, most often, but also for posterity.

So what were his views? He didn't prepare an Ars Poetica on translation; it would be preposterous to produce one that might only simplify and pervert. Instead, I consider four pertinent examples, the first being Pierre Menard, who both is and isn't a translator of Cervantes. He is indeed described as the author of "a manuscript translation," into French, of Quevedo's *Aguja de navegar cultos*, entitled *La boussole des précieux*; he is also credited with a translation, including a prologue and notes, of *Libro de la invención liberal y arte del juego del axedrez*. But his version of *Don Quixote* isn't a translation in the strict sense of the term; instead, it is a "rewriting." Might it be implied similarly that, in Borges's view, a translation might also be another original work? Second is a sentence in "On Vatek, by William Beckford," one of my favorite lines: "the original might be unfaithful to the translation." This, I think, is a forceful statement: Borges didn't see translation as a substitute, a replacement, a hand-me-down; instead, he perceived it—especially the translations of classics such as *The Iliad* and Dante's *Divine Comedy*—to result in equal, if not more valuable originals. This desire to experiment with language and to give birth to a text in a particular linguistic realm is evident in his two so-called English poems, drafted in 1934 and dedicated to the improbable Beatriz Babiloni Webster de Bullrich. They are part of *El otro, el mismo*. I quote from the second.

> I offer you my ancestors, my dead men, the ghosts that living men have honoured in marble: my father's father killed in the frontier in Buenos Aires, two bullets through his lungs, bearded and dead, wrapped by his soldiers in the hide of a cow; my mother's grandfather —just twenty-four—heading a charge of three hundred men in Peru, now ghosts on vanished horses.
>
> I offer you whatever insights my books may hold, whatever manliness or humour my life.

While echoes of Borges's Spanish poetry abound, these two poems are in English: they were not translated, but delivered in Browning's tongue; and they still inhabit it. (The Argentine included them in his *Obras Completas*.) Appearing only in English, too, is his "Autobiographical Essays," produced in collaboration with Norman Thomas Di Giovanni for the *New Yorker*.

Third is "The Translator of *1001 Nights*," published in Spanish in 1935 and collected in *Historia de la eternidad*. In it the Argentine contrasts the four major translators of *Quitab alif laila ua laila*, as it is known in Arabic: Richard Francis Burton, Edward Lane, Antoine Galland, and J. C. Mardrus. Borges wonders, for instance, by which process of misappropriation—for example, mistranslation—the title *Book of the Thousand Nights and One Night* came into being. It is enlightening, in this context, to realize that he did not consider a single one of the three Spanish renditions of the book until the thirties. This is symptomatic: how is it that an erudite, cosmopolitan Spanish-language critic in remote Buenos Aires compares a handful of English, German, and French versions, but never the ones emanating from his milieu? The answer is straightforward: at no time did Borges perceive himself to be trapped in the Spanish language. Language isn't a prison, after all, but a springboard. As a perfect polyglot, Borges realized—and seized on the fact—that his own territory, his milieu was not limited to Argentine letters and Spanish culture in particular but to world literature in its entirety and with every language at his disposal.

This, truly, is his outstanding contribution to the topic of translation: why be imprisoned in one's own environment? In "The Argentine Writer and Tradition"—in my eyes one of his most significant pieces—he announced, "I believe our tradition is all of Western culture, and I also believe we have a right to that tradition, greater than that which the inhabitants of one or another Western nation might have. . . . I believe that we Argentines, we South Americans in general . . . , can handle all European themes, handle them without superstition, with an irreverence which can have, and already does have, fortunate consequences. . . . Anything we Argentine writers can do successfully will become part of our Argentine tradition, in the same way that the treatment of Italian themes belongs to the tradition of England through the efforts of Chaucer and Shakespeare."

I hereby come to my fourth and last example, about which I have a bit more to say. Beyond the almost two-dozen uneven exercises in *Crítica*, Borges's sustained efforts at translation include a cluster of full-fledged books and numerous stories, essays, and aphorisms commissioned for publication by publishers as self-sufficient volumes or as integral parts of anthologies the Argentine edited alone and in collaboration with Adolfo Bioy Casares and others. A decade or so ago, in Madrid, I came across in a bookstore his rendition of Virginia Woolf's *Orlando*, as well as his version of her influential essay "A Room of One's Own," both released in Spanish by Ediciones Sur in 1937, both having been assigned to Borges by his friend and editor-in-chief of the monthly *Sur*, Victoria Ocampo. I've also held in my hands his translation from the French of André Gide's *Persephone* and Henri Michaux's *A Barbarian in Asia*. And I have in my library his translation of *The Wild Palms*, William Faulkner's novel of 1939.

I have a handful of impressions to offer on the latter. The edition I have of it—*Las palmeras salvajes* (Buenos Aires: Editorial Sudamericana, 1970), with a prologue by Juan Benet—has a copyright of 1962, twenty-three years after Faulkner originally published it in English. But the Uruguayan critic and Yale professor Emir Rodríguez Monegal, in his 1978 biography of the Argentine and in an anthology called *Borges: A Reader*, dates the translation to 1941, a period of intense creativity: many of the stories in *Ficciones* and "El Aleph," as well as the essays collected in *Other Inquisitions*, date from that time. Monegal argues that as a result of this translation, Faulkner's literature, "intense and baroque," became "naturalized" in Spanish, thus easing "its assimilation and adaptation in the pens of young narrators such as Juan Carlos Onetti (*Para esta noche*, 1943), Juan Rulfo (*Pedro Páramo*, 1955) and Gabriel García Márquez (*La mala hora* [*Evil Hour*], 1963)." Hence, it is implied that Borges's rendition of *The Wild Palms* opened the door to Faulkner's mammoth influence on south-of-the-border literature at midcentury. This is true only in part: the Argentine's version did have a considerable impact, but Faulkner was already a well-known figure in the Spanish-speaking world by 1940; among others, Lino Novás Calvo, the Cuban poet, had translated him into Quevedo's tongue (Calvo rendered *Sanctuary* in 1934). But this translation was barely passable, as were several other attempts; Borges, on the other hand, mimicked the American's style elegantly, making it fluid, electrifying, breathtaking in Spanish. Monegal argues, "[His] translation was not only faithful to the original but created in Spanish a writing style that was the equivalent of the original's English. For many young Latin American novelists who did not know enough English to read the dense original, Borges's tight version meant the discovery of a new kind of narrative writing. They had [in it] the best possible guide to Faulkner's dark and intense world." A set of questions arise: why did Borges, at the time a tetragenarian of national prominence—not until 1961 was he awarded, along with Samuel Beckett, the International Publisher's Prize—decide to translate the author of *As I Lay Dying*? And why embark specifically on *The Wild Palms*, a fairly mediocre title in Faulkner's corpus (the original title, changed by the U.S. publisher, was *If I Forget Thee, Jerusalem* [Psalms 137:5])?

James Woodall, another of Borges's biographers, suggests that, in addition to the novel, the Argentine translated for Emecé Editores one or more stories by Faulkner, although I've not seen them. What I have not only seen but scrutinized in detail are the Argentine's opinions on Faulkner. For the most part, he delivered them in the second half of the 1930s, in three reviews he wrote for the Argentine magazine *El Hogar*: in order of appearance, on *The Unvanquished* (22 January 1937); on *Absalom, Absalom!* (21 January 1938); and on *The Wild Palms* (5 May 1939). In these commentaries he articulated his wholehearted admiration for the American: in a nutshell, he describes Faulkner as an author that doesn't attempt to explain his characters but simply portrays what they feel, how they act.

I quote (in Spanish): "El mundo que imagina es tan real, que también abarca lo inverosímil." *Absalom, Absalom!*, the Argentine announces, possesses "an almost intolerable intensity," and he equates it, in quality, to *The Sound and the Fury.* "I don't know if there's higher praise," he concludes. In contrast, *The Wild Palms* strikes him as a lesser work, its technical novelties less attractive than uncomfortable, less justifiable than exasperating. He concludes (again, in Spanish): "Es verosímil la afirmación de que William Faulkner es el primer novelista de nuestro tiempo. Para trabar conocimiento de él, la menos apta de sus obras me parece *The Wild Palms*, pero incluye (como todos los libros de Faulkner) páginas de una intensidad que notoriamente excede las posibilidades de cualquier otro autor."

Borges, then, was not only familiar with English but had thoroughly internalized it. The style is English, and so is the manner. Notice I wrote *manner*, not *mannerism*: the former denotes measure; the latter denounces excess. Expressions like "Para trabar conocimiento" [To get acquainted with] and "Es verosímil la afirmación" [It is feasible to affirm] are direct imports from expressions in Walt Whitman's tongue. But they are something else too: appropriations, reinventions. And so is the overall style of the sentences. *Verosímil* in particular, a Borgesian adjective, is infrequent in Spanish: its cognates include *accurate, feasible, realistic,* and, at the suggestion of the Oxford Spanish Dictionary, *plausible*.

Monegal is right: from Rulfo to Mario Vargas Llosa (and even to this day, to figures such as Ricardo Piglia), Faulkner remains an enormous literary influence in Latin America. But what inspired the majority of authors—the suffering, devastation, and defeat in the Deep South—did not attract Borges. What he saw in the author of "The Hamlet" was altogether different: a mastery of artifice, that is, a novelist devoted to recreating the inner life of his characters and to experimenting with the elasticity of the novel as a literary genre. It wasn't pain with which the Argentine empathized, but the capability of turning it into the core of a self-contained parallel universe. For him History, with a capital H, was less significant than the effects of literature on the reader. In his eyes, Faulkner was first and foremost a technician; that Yoknapatawpha is to be found in Mississippi is, I think, a sheer accident.

I imagine Borges in the late 1930s, in need of money, sharing with Victoria Ocampo his willingness to translate from the English. She probably asked him who his choices were; he named Wilde, H. G. Wells, Stevenson, Melville, Kipling, Faulkner . . . The list prompted a series of business contacts on her part, and thus the list was reduced to a couple of concrete possibilities. In other words, I think it is less plausible that the

Argentine selected *The Wild Palms* than that it was selected for him. On its publication in the United States, the novel had been welcomed with scant enthusiasm. In *New Masses* (7 February 1939), Edwin Berry Burgum wrote, "In his distinguished career, Mr. Faulkner has not written a more thoroughly satisfying novel than [this one]." But in the *Listener* (30 March 1939), Edwin Muir dissented, "Mr. Faulkner's world of imagination is really a prolonged dream or rather a nightmare, into which civil functionaries from another dream intrude now and then; but the tortured inner eye cannot account for these people, for to it the ordinary is the sharpest surprise of all. Mr. Faulkner has flashes of genius . . . ; but his novel accounts for nothing."

The time has come to compare the originals by Faulkner in English and Borges in Spanish. I've opened at random *Novels 1936–1940*, edited by Joseph Blotner and Noel Polk. My eyes fall on pages 516 and 517.

> He had been in the hospital almost two years now. He lived in the intern's quarters with the others who, like him, had no private means; he smoked once a week now: a package of cigarettes over the week-end and he was paying the note which he had executed to his half sister, the one- and two-dollar money orders in reverse now, returning to source; the one bag would still hold all he owned, including his hospital whites—the twenty-six years, the two thousand dollars, the railroad ticket to New Orleans, the one dollar and thirty-six cents, the one bag in a corner of a barracks-like room furnished with steel army cots; on the morning of his twenty-seventh birthday he walked and looked down his body toward his foreshortened feet and it seemed to him that he saw the twenty-seven irrevocable years diminished and fore-shortened beyond them in turn, as if his life were to lie passively on his back as though he floated effortless and without volition upon an unreturning stream. He seemed to see them: the empty years in which his youth had vanished—the years for wild oats and for daring, for the passionate tragic ephemeral loves of adolescence, the girl- and boy-white, the wild importunate fumbling flesh, which had not been for him; lying so he thought, not exactly with pride and certainty not with the resignation which he believed, but rather with that peace with which a middle-aged eunuch might look back upon the dead time before his alteration, at the fading and (at last) edgeless shapes which now inhabited only the memory and not the flesh: *I have repudiated money and hence love. Not abjured it, repudiated. I do not need it; by next year or two years or five years I will know to be true what I now believe to be true: I will not even need to want it.*

On pages 37 and 38 of *Las palmeras salvajes*:

Hacía casi dos años que estaba en el hospital. Vivía en los pabellones de internos con otros que como él carecían de recursos particulares; fumaba una vez por semana, un atado de cigarrillos para el fin de semana, y estaba pagando la deuda que había reconocido a su propia hermana: los giros de uno o dos pesos que volvían ahora a su fuente de orígen; la única valija contenía aún todo lo que poseía, incluyendo sus uniformes blancos de hospital—sus 26 años, los 2.000 dólares, el billete de tren a Nueva Orleáns, el dólar 36 centavos en esa única valija, en el rincón de un cuarto como un cuartel con camas militares de hierro en la mañana de su vigesimoséptimo cumpleaños. Se despertó y miró su cuerpo tendido hacia el escorzo de los pies y le pareció ver los veintisiete irrevocables años como disminuídos y escorzados detrás, como si su vida flotara sin esfuerzo y sin voluntad por un río que no vuelve. Le parecía verlos: los años vacíos en que había desaparecido su juventud—los años para la osadía y las aventuras, para los apasionados, trágicos, suaves, efímeros amores de la adolescencia, para la blancura de la muchacha y del muchacho, para la torpe, fogosa, importuna carne, que no había sido para él; acostado, pensaba, no exactamente con orgullo y no con la resignación que suponía, sino más bien con una paz de eunuco ya entrado en años que considerara el tiempo muerto que precedió a su alteración, que considerara las formas borrosas y (al fin) desdibujadas que sólo habitan en la memoria y no ya en la carne: He repudiado el dinero y por consiguiente el amor. No abjurado, repudiado. No lo necesito; el año que viene o de aquí a dos años o cinco sabré que es cierto lo que ahora creo que es cierto: ni siquiera querré desearlo.

The resemblance—in syntax, in spirit—is startling: Borges builds his text almost word by word; he compresses Faulkner subtly, but does so while reproducing the cadence of the English version. His translation (in "Los traductores de las *1001 Noches*," perhaps symptomatically, he uses the Spanish term *traslación* for *translation*) takes few tangible liberties; the riskiest intangible liberty it takes is to emulate Faulkner in Spanish by "readapting" Cervantes's language to fit the needs. Indeed, he might have allowed, in Monegal's phrase, "the discovery of a new type of narrative." One might argue that the Argentine failed to give his translation any autonomy. But the autonomy is in it: silent, unobtrusive, unsettling the target tongue.

There are many approaches to translation. They might be reduced to two: the Flaubertian Way, in which the translator disappears without trace, and the Nabokovian Way, in which the translator endlessly stresses the artificiality of his endeavor. In *The Wild Palms* Borges endorses the first approach: he is behind Faulkner, not in front or at his side. His use of italics, a prominent fixture in Faulkner (also, by the way, in the Argentine's own oeuvre), is exactly like the one in the English original; and the translator's footnotes are minimal. On page 27, for instance, he digresses: "Old Man: El Viejo: nombre familiar del río Misisipí"; another footnote explains the name Jesse James: "Léase los Juan Moreira, los Hormiga Negra," and so on. And on page 96, regarding the line "Drink up, ye armourous sons in a sea of hemingwaves," Borges states that it's an example of "Retruécanos más bien intraducibles a la manera de James Joyce. Armourous = armour + amorous; hemingwaves = waves + Hemingway." And yet. . . . For most people, the act of reading a work in a language other than the original is a way into another culture. But when the reader is acquainted with the original tongue, the act procures an altogether different meaning: it becomes an exercise of concordance. In spite of its resourcefulness, the Spanish version by Borges in my view isn't superior to its English counterpart. For a reader unfamiliar with Faulkner, *Las palmeras salvajes* is lucid, startling even; but the fact that the Argentine venerated the author of *The Wild Palms* and not the book itself is in display.

This brings me back to my original queries: Why is it so distressing to suggest that Borges in English feels like "at home"? And why does it infuriate that a translation might supersede its source? Because our approach to literature is filtered through the lens of malleable nationalist feelings. We enjoy claiming that an author, any author, is the sole property of an individual culture, that he could only have sprung from that culture and that his oeuvre holds the keys to understand it. This view, needless to say, promotes the idea of human imagination as a series of loosely interrelated ghettos, each controlled by its own self-righteous inhabitants. But translation as an endeavor presupposes that no man is an island. It also proclaims that the only artist that is handcuffed is the one convinced that he is indeed an island unto his own.

It matters little if the Argentine, who is nobody's property, is read in French, Portuguese, English . . . as long as the translations are enraptured by the same zeitgeist as his own Spanish versions.

CONTRIBUTORS

JESSE ALEMÁN is an assistant professor of English at the University of New Mexico, where he teaches nineteenth-century American and Chicano/a literatures. His articles appear in *MELUS, Recovering the U.S. Hispanic Literary Heritage Project* (vol. 3), *Aztlán*, and several book collections. His introduction to and republished edition of Loreta Janeta Velazquez's 1876 Civil War account, *The Woman in Battle*, was published in 2003. He is currently working on a manuscript on the pulp fiction of the U.S.-Mexican War.

ROBERT H. BRINKMEYER JR. is Professor and Chair of English at the University of Arkansas. He has published widely in twentieth-century southern literature; his most recent book is *Remapping Southern Literature: Contemporary Southern Writers and the West* (2000). He recently received a John Simon Guggenheim Fellowship to work on a book on European totalitarianism and the white southern imagination.

DEBRA RAE COHEN is an assistant professor of English at the University of Arkansas and the author of *Remapping the Home Front: Locating Citizenship in British Women's Great War Fiction* (2002).

DEBORAH COHN is an associate professor of Spanish and Portuguese at Indiana University, Bloomington. She has published articles in *Comparative Literature Studies*, *CR: The New Centennial Review*, *Latin American Literary Review*, and elsewhere. Her book, *History and Memory in the Two Souths: Recent Southern and Spanish American Fiction*, was published in 1999. She is currently working on a book entitled *Creating the Boom's Reputation: The Promotion of the Boom in and by the United States*.

J. MICHAEL DASH is a professor of French and director of African Studies at New York University. He has translated Edouard Glissant's *The Ripening* (1985) and *Caribbean Discourse* (1989) into English. His publications include *Literature and Ideology in Haiti* (1981), *Haiti and the United States* (1988), and *Edouard Glissant* (1995). His most recent books are *The Other America: Caribbean Literature in a New World Context* (1998), *Libete: A Haiti Anthology* (1999) with Charles Arthur, and *Culture and Customs of Haiti* (2001). He is at present working on surrealism in the francophone Caribbean.

LEIGH ANNE DUCK is an assistant professor of English at the University of Memphis. She has published on Zora Neale Hurston, William Faulkner, and Alice Walker in *American Literary History*, *Faulkner in the Twenty-First Century*, and *Mississippi Quarterly*, and her article on Hurston's response to Haitian cultural politics is forthcoming in the *Journal of American Folklore*. She is currently completing a book, *The Nation's Region: Depression-Era Southern Literature and U.S. National Narrative*.

WENDY B. FARIS is a professor of English and comparative literature at the University of Texas, Arlington. Her books include *Carlos Fuentes* (1983); *Labyrinths of Language: Symbolic Landscape and Narrative Design in Modern Fiction* (1988); *Magical Realism: Theory, History, Community* (1995), a critical anthology coedited with Lois Parkinson Zamora; and *Ordinary Enchantments: Magical Realism and the Remystification of Narrative* (2004).

EARL FITZ is a professor of Portuguese, Spanish, and comparative literature at Vanderbilt University, where he also serves as director of the Program in Comparative Literature. He is the author of several books, including *Rediscovering the New World: Inter-American Literature in a Comparative Context* (1991) and *Ambiguity and Gender in the New Novel of Brazil and Spanish America: A Comparative Assessment* (1993) with Dr. Judith Payne. The Modern Language Association will publish his *Brazilian Narrative Traditions in a Comparative Context* in 2004.

KIRSTEN SILVA GRUESZ is an associate professor of literature at the University of California, Santa Cruz, where she teaches inter-American and Latino literatures. Her book *Ambassadors of Culture: The Transamerican Origins of Latino Writing* was published in 2002, and she is currently at work on a book about bilingualism.

GEORGE B. HANDLEY is an associate professor of humanities and comparative literature at Brigham Young University and is the author of *Postslavery Literatures in the Americas* (2000). He is currently coediting a comparative volume of ecocriticism of Caribbean literature and is working on a book-length study, *The Adamic Imagination*, that explores how Walt Whitman, Pablo Neruda, and Derek Walcott conceptualize the natural environment and its relationship to New World history.

STEVEN HUNSAKER teaches Spanish at Brigham Young University, Idaho. He has published in journals such as *Hispania*, *Biography*, and *Canadian Review of Studies in Nationalism*. He is the author of *Autobiography and National Identity in the Americas* (1999).

DANE JOHNSON is an associate professor in the Department of Comparative and World Literature at San Francisco State University. His contribution to this volume forms part of a book that he is currently completing entitled *William Faulkner, Gabriel García Márquez, Toni Morrison, and the Creation of Literary Value.*

RICHARD H. KING teaches in the School of American and Canadian Studies at the University of Nottingham, U.K.; he was a visiting professor of history at Vanderbilt University in 2002–3. His *Race into Culture*, an intellectual history of race, racism, and culture between 1940 and 1970 will appear in 2004. The author of *Southern Renaissance* (1980) and *Civil Rights and the Idea of Freedom* (1992), he has most recently coedited *Dixie Debates* (1996) with Helen Taylor.

JANE LANDERS is an associate professor of history and an associate dean of the College of Arts and Sciences at Vanderbilt University. She is the author of *Black Society in Spanish Florida* (1999), editor of *Colonial Plantations and Economy of Florida* (2000) and *Against the Odds: Free Blacks in the Slave Societies of the Americas* (1996), and coeditor of *The African American Heritage of Florida* (1995).

JOHN T. MATTHEWS is a professor of English at Boston University. He is the author of *The Play of Faulkner's Language* (1982) and *"The Sound and the Fury": Faulkner and the Lost Cause* (1991). He is currently at work on a book, *Raising the South: Plantation, Neocolonialism, and Modern U.S. Fiction*, from which his essay in this collection is drawn.

STEPHANIE MERRIM is a professor of comparative literature and Hispanic studies at Brown University. She has published widely in the fields of colonial and modern Latin American literature. Her most recent book is *Early Modern Women's Writing and Sor Juana Inés de la Cruz* (1999).

HELEN OAKLEY works as an associate lecturer at the Open University in the East Midlands, U.K., and as a special lecturer in American studies at Nottingham University, U.K. She is the author of *The Recontextualization of William Faulkner in Latin American Fiction and Culture* (2002).

VINCENT PÉREZ is an associate professor of American literature at the University of Nevada, Las Vegas, and has published articles on Chicano and African American literature in such journals as *Texas Studies in Literature and Language* and *MELUS*. His book, *Remembering the Hacienda: History and Memory in the Mexican American Southwest*, is forthcoming in 2004.

JOHN-MICHAEL RIVERA is an assistant professor of English and a faculty member at the Center of the American West at the University of Colorado, Boulder. His essay in this volume forms part of his book-length study entitled *The Emergence of Mexican America: Recovering the Cultural Politics of Democracy, 1824–1939,* which explores the relationship between cultural representations and the early formation of Mexican political and racial personhood in the United States.

SCOTT ROMINE is an associate professor of English at the University of North Carolina, Greensboro. He is the author of *The Narrative Forms of Southern Community* (1999). He is currently at work on a project investigating the effects of globalization on contemporary southern narrative.

JON SMITH is an assistant professor of English at the University of Montevallo. His work has appeared in *American Literary History, Contemporary Literature, The Faulkner Journal, The Forum for Modern Language Studies* (for which he edited a special issue on the South), *Modern Fiction Studies, The Southern Literary Journal,* and elsewhere. His book

Southern Culture on the Skids: Narcissism, Civic Branding, and the Burden of Southern History is forthcoming.

ILAN STAVANS is the Lewis-Sebring Professor in Latin American and Latino Culture at Amherst College. His books include *The Hispanic Condition* (1995), *The Oxford Book of Latin American Essays* (editor, 1997), *Mutual Impressions* (editor, 1999), *On Borrowed Words: A Memoir of the Language* (2001), and *Spanglish: The Making of a New American Language* (2003). He is also the editor of *The Poetry of Pablo Neruda* (2003). His work has been translated into half a dozen languages. Routledge published *The Essential Ilan Stavans* in 2000.

PHILIP WEINSTEIN is Alexander Griswold Cummins Professor of English at Swarthmore College. He teaches and publishes on American, British, and comparative fiction. His books include *Henry James and the Requirements of the Imagination* (1971), *The Semantics of Desire: Changing Models of Identity from Dickinson to Joyce* (1984), and *Faulkner's Subject: A Cosmos No One Owns* (1992). More recently, he is the editor of *The Cambridge Companion to William Faulkner* (1995) and author of *What Else But Love? The Ordeal of Race in Faulkner and Morrison* (1996). He is currently completing a book on modernism entitled *Unknowing: The Work of Modernist Fiction*.

LOIS PARKINSON ZAMORA is a professor in the Departments of English, History, and Art at the University of Houston. Her area of specialization is contemporary fiction in the Americas. Her books include *Writing the Apocalypse: Historical Vision in Contemporary U.S. and Latin American Fiction* (1989); *Magical Realism: Theory, History, Community* (1995), co-edited with Wendy B. Faris; *The Usable Past: The Imagination of History in Recent Fiction of the Americas* (1997); and *Image and Memory: Photography from Latin America 1866–1994* (1998). She frequently writes about the visual arts and their relation to Latin American literature, and is preparing a book on that subject to be entitled *The Inordinate Eye: Baroque Designs in Contemporary Latin American Fiction*.

INDEX

Page, Thomas Nelson, 176, 179–85, 186
Panofsky, Erwin, 296–98
Paradise (Morrison), 368, 372–74
Paré, Francois, 319
Paredes, Américo, 485
Parry, Benita, 186
Partisan Review, 409–11
Patchett, Ann, 264–65
Patria, La (newspaper): ambivalence and, 75; bilingualism of, 63–66; loss of, 74; name of, 59; origins of, 58; poetry in, 71; U.S.-Mexican War covered by, 60–61
Patriarchy, Mexican, 476–80, 488
Paz, Octavio, 318
Percy, Walker, 279. *See also Moviegoer, The*
Pérez-Firmat, Gustavo: "Bilingual Blues," 130, 146; *Life on the Hyphen*, 131; "Limen," 134; *Next Year in Cuba*, 130–37, 143–45
Performance, 342
Pintado, Vicente Sebastian, 88–89
Plantation America, 22, 447
Plantation fiction, 472–75, 479, 483, 486–89
Plantation myth, 477, 481–83
Plato, 314, 316, 324; *Theatetus*, 311
Poetics (Aristotle), 312–13
"Political incest," 36–37
Postcolonial(ism): fiction and, 304, 355–56, 361, 367, 374, 472; film and, 295–97; studies of, 3, 6, 9–10, 14, 172–74, 288, 289
Posthumous Memoirs of Brás Cubas, The (de Assis), 423–26, 439–40
Postmodernism, 251–57, 265–66, 346, 349
Potlatch, 334, 338–39, 345
Premodern, 474, 477–79, 486
Prieto, Guillermo, 71
Primitivism, 338
Print communities, 56, 66, 72, 75
Progressivism, 188, 192–94
Prospect Bluff Fort, 88–89

Prospero and Caliban (Mannoni), 244–46
Proto-lesbianism, 115–16
Proust, Marcel, 336
Provincialism, 176, 189
Public sphere, 73–75
Puig, Manuel, 268, 295; *Kiss of the Spider Woman*, 271. See also *Betrayed by Rita Hayworth*

Quintero, José Augustin, 56

Racism, in U.S. South, 150–51, 154, 158–63, 166–67
Ramos, Julio, 321
Ranching, 483–85
Ransom, John Crowe, 320
Ratmar, Fernández, 122, 124
Realism, 322, 325–26, 356–73; crisis of, 406
Rebellion in the Backlands (da Cunha): authorial voice in, 428; background information to, 427; land imagery in, 429–31; miscegenation in, 432–33; shame and national disgrace in, 436. See also *Let Us Now Praise Famous Men*
Reconstruction, Mexicans and, 457, 463–65
Recovering the U.S. Hispanic Literary Heritage, 471, 489
Redneck, as trope, 151, 165–67
Red Rock (Page): as novel of Reconstruction, 176, 186; plot of, 179–85; racism in, 182–85. *See also* Agrarians; Hybridity
"Regreso," 139, 143
Religious Sanctuary policy, 81
Renaissance, Southern, 408
Representation, 388, 397
Repression, 151–52, 168
"Reverse colonization," 192
Rhys, Jean, 38–39
Revolución, La (newspaper), 57
Ripening, The (Glissant), 101

Transference, 151, 156–57, 161–62, 165, 168, 304

Translation, 496–500; Flaubertian, 503; Nabokovian, 504

Transnationalism, 60, 75

Transvestism, as allegory for transnationalism, 111–16, 122–24

Trauma, 176–77, 184, 189, 194–95

Travel writing, 150–52, 155

Treaty of Guadalupe Hidalgo, 451–53, 465–66

Treaty of Paris, 82

Trinidad, 150–52, 156–58

Truman, Harry S., 411–13

Turla, Leopoldo, 56

Turn in the South, A (Naipaul): narratives of, 153–54, 157, 160; racism and elitism in, 150, 157–69; studies of U.S. South and, 151–69; Trinidad and, 150, 155–58

Turner, Bryan S., 131, 136

Twain, Mark, 483

Twelve Million Black Voices (Wright), 230–34

Twelve Southerners, 319–23

Ulysses (Joyce), 347

Uncle Tom's Cabin (Stowe), 189–91

Unión, La (newspaper), 74

United Kingdom, 153, 157

Universal History of Infamy, A (Borges), 277, 314–15

U.S-Mexican War, 57, 60–63, 73, 113, 121, 452–54, 485; Douglass and, 458

Velazquez, Don Diego, 113, 118, 121

Velazques, Don Diego Rodriguez, 118, 124

Velazquez, Loreta Janeta: authenticity of, 112; as character, 111, 116; as Confederate soldier, 112–13, 120; as Confederate spy, 113; cross-dressing and, 112–17, 120–22; as Cuban woman, 111, 117–18, 120; as Harry T. Buford, 112–21, 125; performance of identity and, 112; sexuality of, 113, 116–17; whiteness and, 112. See also *Woman in Battle, The*

Verdad, La (newspaper), 57, 74

Villaverde, Cirilo, 56

Walcott, Derek, 29–32, 42, 46; *The Bounty*, 39; Nobel Prize awarded to, 29

Walker, William, 56, 65–66

Wallerstein, Immanuel, 2, 151

War of 1812, 88

Warren, Robert Penn, 288

"We Love Glenda So Much" (Cortázar), 278, 283

Welty, Eudora, 36, 288; *The Golden Apples*, 252

West Indies, 2, 5–8, 14, 22–25, 33, 152, 155, 159–62; literature of, 304. *See also* Slavery

West, Nathanael, 275

White Man, Listen! (Wright), 227, 235, 243–44

Whiteness, southern identity and, 177, 185–89, 191, 194–95

White supremacy, 176–77, 182, 186–88, 190–91, 195. *See also* Racism

Whitman, Walt, 64–67

Whitten, Prince, 87

Who Would Have Thought It? (Ruiz de Burton): central theme of, 451; racial issues in, 454–66; setting of, 452

Wild Palms, The (Faulkner), 499–504; Borges's translation of, 422, 500–503

With His Pistol in His Hand (Paredes), 485

Woman in Battle, The (Velazquez): authenticity of, 110–12, 125; as Civil War narrative, 112–13, 122–24; as fiction, 111–12, 126

Wonder, 311–14, 316–18, 322, 324, 325

Wood, Michael, 268–70, 295

Wright, Richard, 227–47; *Black Boy*, 229, 232–35, 243; black folk culture and, 229–32; *Black Power*, 227–29, 234–36, 239–41, 244; "Blueprint for Negro

Library of Congress Cataloging-in-Publication Data

Look away! : the U.S. South in New World studies /
edited with an introduction by Jon Smith and Deborah Cohn.

p. cm. — (New Americanists)

Includes bibliographical references and index.

ISBN 0-8223-3304-x (cloth : alk. paper)

ISBN 0-8223-3316-3 (pbk. : alk. paper)

1. Southern States—Study and teaching. 2. Southern
States—Historiography. 3. Latin America—Study and teaching.
4. Latin America—Historiography. 5. Caribbean Area—Study and
teaching. 6. Caribbean Area—Historiography. 7. Regionalism—
Southern States. 8. Regionalism—Latin America. 9. Regionalism—Caribbean
Area. I. Smith, Jon. II. Cohn, Deborah N. III. Series.

F208.5.L66 2004   970'.0071—dc22   2004001303